ARAB SOCIETY AND CULTURE

Arab Society and Culture

An Essential Reader

Edited by

Samir Khalaf
Roseanne Saad Khalaf

SAQI

ISBN: 978-0-86356-616-5

A full CIP record for this book is available from the British Library.
A full CIP record for this book is available from the Library of Congress.
Manufactured in Lebanon

SAQI

26 Westbourne Grove, London W2 5RH
2398 Doswell Avenue, Saint Paul, Minnesota, 55108
Tabet Building, Mneimneh Street, Hamra, Beirut
www.saqibooks.com

Contents

Note from the Editors

Editing a volume of around fifty disparate essays, extracted from multiple sources and inevitably involving complicated publication rights, is a delicate and cumbersome venture. We would like to gratefully acknowledge the arduous labor of Ms. Shikha Sethi of Saqi Books in preparing the final manuscript for publication and assisting in the tedious task of securing copy rights from authors, editors and publishers. We are also indebted to Mr. André Gaspard. His sober counsel, sustained support and accomplished publishing skills provided much helpful guidance throughout.

We would like to thank several colleagues for addressing our editorial requests, particularly those who made efforts to update and polish their original contributions. Altogether this has made the volume more cogent, timely and relevant.

The tedious task of scanning original copies and retyping numerous passages fell on Mrs Leila Jbara. Our volume would not have seen the light of print without her assistance and patience.

Mr. Ghassan Moussawi and Mr. Sleiman Hajj, our resourceful and genial research assistants, were helpful in scouting for sources and offering feedback on certain selections.

Unfortunately, at times the process of compiling our volume was handicapped by unforeseen circumstances. This accounts for the delay in delivering the manuscript to press.

We have decided to leave the spellings, reference styles, etc. as they appear in the original texts. Thus the reader will encounter different spellings and variations of the same word.

PART ONE

Promises of the Sociological and Literary Imagination

Introduction

The first piece of an edited volume, much like the opening passage of an essay or keynote, must be riveting enough, perhaps even somewhat intriguing, if it is to spark the attention of the reader. It must tell a good story and tell it well. It must also be contextually meaningful; in that it should serve to inform and draw together the seemingly disparate issues and problems exposed throughout the volume. As we were about to finalize our selections we came across Orhan's Pamuk's "My Father's Suitcase", the Nobel Lecture he delivered at Stockholm in December 2006. It was a serendipitous windfall. We couldn't have done better.

Pamuk, of course, was narrating the episodes and circumstances in his life which account for his decision to become a writer, how he came to have such literary gifts, particularly in a country which showed little interest in its artists, and the role writing came to play in his life.

It is telling in this regard how Pamuk came to realize, very early in his life, that success in his calling as a writer demanded he isolate himself from the rest of society. He also recognized the writer's secret as being not so much inspiration but stubbornness and endurance. The apt Turkish adage—"to dig a well with a needle"—was invoked by Pamuk to legitimize the tedium of his lonely labor. But in the secluded privacy of his room, he was soon to discover that instead of being alone, he was in the good company of the works of all those who came before him. It is discontent, Pamuk suggests, along with the need to escape that remains the starting point of true literature.

This connection between discontent and the need to escape was discovered when he began to imagine the contents of the suitcase his father had bequeathed to him. His father, a scion of a fairly prosperous Turkish family, had aspired to become a poet of some renown but was, it seems, painfully aware of his responsibilities and/or shortcomings alongside the demands and drawbacks of his culture. Istanbul was "not at the center" and there was a rich world out there that Istanbul had nothing to do with. Consequently, his father found refuge in frequent visits to Paris and in the works of Montaigne, Valery, Balzac, Baudelaire and the like, even in fondly recollecting the times he had seen Sartre on the sidewalks of Paris.

Pamuk soon realized that to "read, to write, was like leaving one world to find consolation in the otherness of another, in the strange and the wondrous." But as an authentic writer, he must have the artistry to tell his own stories as if they were other people's stories, and to tell other people's stories as if they were his own. This, to Pamuk, is the promise of true literature. And as we shall see, it is also the promise of the sociological and anthropological imagination.

Though crediting his father for ushering him into the wondrous world of literature, Pamuk remains disappointed at his father's refusal to "quarrel" enough "with his life." Yet it is precisely such dissonance that prodded Pamuk to eventually ask the more forbidding existential questions:

What is happiness? Is happiness believing that you live a deep life in your lonely room? Or is happiness leading a comfortable life in society, believing in the same things as everyone else, or, at least, acting as if you did? Is it happiness or unhappiness to go through life writing in secret, while seeming to be in harmony with all that surrounds you?

Pamuk's exposure to his father's suitcase leaves a profound impact on him as he starts to realize, with considerable anguish and fear, that he is beset with two universal afflictions: a sense of being marooned in the provinces and the fear that he lacks authenticity. To Pamuk, this is the redemptive and enabling character of literature. The writer uses his wounds, the "darkness within", to connect with others who carry the same wounds. It is then that private anguish is illuminated by being transformed into a universal single humanity.

All true literature rises from this childish, hopeful certainty that we resemble one another. When a writer shuts himself up in a room for years on end, with this gesture he suggests a single humanity, a world without a center.

Pamuk goes on, much like the abstract insights advanced by C. Wright Mills, Clifford Geertz and Charles Taylor, to assert that the "great majority of people on this earth live with the same feeling of inauthenticity and Chekhovian provinciality, and that many suffer from an even deeper sense of insufficiency, insecurity and degradation than I do."

To him, the promise of literature in this regard is more formidable and compelling. Yes, of course, the media and other mundane sources of knowledge can readily expose the dilemmas and predicaments beleaguering humanity: problems of hunger, homelessness, collective violence and political unrest. But literature is much better equipped to expose and explore humanity's basic and most enduring fears:

The fear of being left outside, the fear of counting for nothing, and the feeling of worthlessness that comes with such fears—the collective humiliations, vulnerabilities, slights, grievances, sensitivities and imagined insults, and the nationalist boasts and inflations that are their next of kin ...

This is precisely when the redemptive attributes of literature, according to Pamuk, come to our rescue. The sense of being excluded, marginalized, provincial, or even being deeply melancholic and angry is allayed. One discovers an entire new world beyond these dreaded symptoms and the feeling of being decentered is quelled. The Istanbul which once disenchanted his father becomes, to his son, the "center of the world."

> What I feel now is the opposite of what I felt as a child and a young man: for me, the center of the world is Istanbul. This is not just because I have lived there all my life but because, for the past thirty-three years, I have been narrating its streets, its bridges, its people, its dogs, its houses, its mosques, its fountains, its strange heroes, its shops, its famous characters, its dark spots, its days, and its nights, making them a part of me, embracing them all. A point arrived when this world that I had made with my own hands, this world that existed only in my head, was more real to me than the city in which I actually lived. That was when all these people and streets, objects and buildings seemed to begin to talk among themselves, began to interact in ways that I had not anticipated, as if they lived not just in my imagination or my books but for themselves, This world that I had created, like a man digging a well with a needle, then seemed truer than anything else.

Literary narratives, particularly non-fictional accounts written as autobiographical sketches or memoirs like those of Orhan Pamuk, Amin Maalouf, Edward Said and Nawal El-Saadawi, provide vivid testimonies and grounded commentaries on the changing manners and morals of the socio-cultural setting they are engrossed in. Much like the great classics, they too confront the eternal existential angst which is at the root of the perennial tension between them and their society. This is, after all, what underlies C.W. Mills' promise of the sociological imagination: i.e., the quality of mind essential to grasp the interplay of man and society, of biography and history, of self and the world. Only by doing so, Mills tells us, can we begin to understand the private troubles we endure in terms of the broader historical changes and institutional contradictions. Because we fail to recognize this connection, many of the problems we face today are exacerbated, Mills warns, by widespread feelings of unease and indifference; not yet formulated in such a way as to permit the work of reason and sensibility.

Another seminal essay, Clifford Geertz's, "From the Native's Point of View", also makes a similar plea. In all the three societies Geertz studied—Javanese, Balinese and Moroccan—he attempted to determine how the people define themselves as persons, what determines the idea they have of what a self. And in each case:

> I have tried to get at this most intimate of notions not by imagining myself someone else, a rice peasant or a tribal sheikh, and then seeing what I thought, but by searching out and analyzing the symbolic forms—words, images, institutions, behaviors—in terms of which, in each place, people actually represented themselves to themselves and to one another.

As we have seen, Mills sees modern man as being trapped by a series of private troubles which cannot be transformed into public issues and hence the failure of individual men and women to transcend their immediate locales and address the problems that have to do with historical and societal contradictions. In much the same vein, Charles Taylor sees the decline and sense of loss which beleaguers our failure to understand the broader historical and structural transformations compounding these problems. Indeed, the defining elements of modern society—disenchantment with excessive individualism inherent in a permissive and narcissistic society and the threat of instrumental reason associated with unrestrained technology and the loss of freedom—are all sources of increasing bewilderment and confusion. They run the risk of reducing us to what Max Weber decried as "specialists without spirit and sensualists without heart."

My Father's Suitcase

Two years before his death, my father gave me a small suitcase filled with his writings, manuscripts and notebooks. Assuming his usual joking, mocking air, he told me he wanted me to read them after he was gone, by which he meant after he died.

"Just take a look," he said, looking slightly embarrassed. "See if there's anything inside that you can use. Maybe after I'm gone you can make a selection and publish it."

We were in my study, surrounded by books. My father was searching for a place to set down the suitcase, wandering back and forth like a man who wished to rid himself of a painful burden. In the end, he deposited it quietly in an unobtrusive corner. It was a shaming moment that neither of us ever forgot, but once it had passed and we had gone back into our usual roles, taking life lightly, our joking, mocking personas took over and we relaxed. We talked as we always did, about the trivial things of everyday life, and Turkey's neverending political troubles, and my father's mostly failed business ventures, without feeling too much sorrow.

I remember that after my father left, I spent several days walking back and forth past the suitcase without once touching it. I was already familiar with this small, black, leather suitcase, and its lock, and its rounded corners. My father would take it with him on short trips and sometimes use it to carry documents to work. I remembered that when I was a child, and my father came home from a trip, I would open this little suitcase and rummage through his things, savouring the scent of cologne and foreign countries. This suitcase was a familiar friend, a powerful reminder of my childhood, my past, but now I couldn't even touch it. Why? No doubt it was because of the mysterious weight of its contents.

I am now going to speak of this weight's meaning. It is what a person creates when he shuts himself up in a room, sits down at a table, and retires to a corner to express his thoughts—that is, the meaning of literature.

When I did touch my father's suitcase, I still could not bring myself to open it, but I did know what was inside some of those notebooks. I had seen my father writing things in a few of them. This was not the first time I had heard of the heavy load inside the suitcase.

My father had a large library; in his youth, in the late 1940s, he had wanted to be an Istanbul poet, and had translated Valéry into Turkish, but he had not wanted to live the sort of life that came with writing poetry in a poor country with few readers. My father's father—my grandfather—had been a wealthy businessman; my father had led a comfortable life as a child and a young man, and he had no wish to endure hardship for the sake of literature, for writing. He loved life with all its beauties—this I understood.

The first thing that kept me distant from the contents of my father's suitcase was, of course, the fear that I might not like what I read. Because my father knew this, he had taken the precaution of acting as if he did not take its contents seriously. After working as a writer for 25 years, it pained me to see this. But I did not even want to be angry at my father for failing to take literature seriously enough ... My real fear, the crucial thing that I did not wish to know or discover, was the possibility that my father might be a good writer. I couldn't open my father's suitcase because I feared this. Even worse, I couldn't even admit this myself openly. If true and great literature emerged from my father's suitcase, I would have to acknowledge that inside my father there existed an entirely different man. This was a frightening possibility. Because even at my advanced age I wanted my father to be only my father—not a writer.

A writer is someone who spends years patiently trying to discover the second being inside him, and the world that makes him who he is: when I speak of writing, what comes first to my mind is not a novel, a poem, or literary tradition, it is a person who shuts himself up in a room, sits down at a table, and alone, turns inward; amid its shadows, he builds a new world with words. This man—or this woman—may use a typewriter, profit from the ease of a computer, or write with a pen on paper, as I have done for 30 years. As he writes, he can drink tea or coffee, or smoke cigarettes. From time to time he may rise from his table to look out through the window at the children playing in the street, and, if he is lucky, at trees and a view, or he can gaze out at a black wall. He can write poems, plays, or novels, as I do. All these differences come after the crucial task of sitting down at the table and patiently turning inwards. To write is to turn this inward gaze into words, to study the world into which that person passes when he retires into himself, and to do so with patience, obstinacy, and joy.

As I sit at my table, for days, months, years, slowly adding new words to the empty page, I feel as if I am creating a new world, as if I am bringing into being that other person inside me, in the same way someone might build a bridge or a dome, stone by stone. The stones we writers use are words. As we hold them in our hands, sensing the ways in which each of them is connected to the others, looking at them sometimes from afar, sometimes almost caressing them with our fingers and the tips of our pens, weighing them, moving them around, year in and year out, patiently and hopefully, we create new worlds.

The writer's secret is not inspiration—for it is never clear where it comes from—it is his stubbornness, his patience. That lovely Turkish saying—to dig a well with a needle—seems to me to have been said with writers in mind. In the old stories, I love the patience of Ferhat, who digs through mountains for his love—and I understand it, too. In my novel, *My Name is Red*, when I wrote about the old Persian miniaturists who had drawn the same horse with the same passion for so many years, memorising each stroke, that they could recreate that beautiful horse even with their eyes closed, I knew I was talking about the writing profession, and my own life. If a writer is to tell his own story—tell it slowly, and as if it were a story about other people—if he is to feel the power of the story rise up inside him, if he is to sit down at a table and patiently give himself over to this art—this craft—he must first have been given some hope. The angel of inspiration (who pays regular visits to some and rarely calls on others) favours the hopeful and the confident, and it is when a writer feels most lonely, when he feels most doubtful about his efforts, his dreams, and the value of his writing—when he thinks his story is only his story—it is at such moments that the angel chooses to reveal to him stories, images and dreams that will draw out the world he wishes to build. If I think back on the books to which I have devoted my entire life, I am most surprised by those moments when I have felt as if the sentences, dreams, and pages that have made me so ecstatically happy have not come from my own imagination—that another power has found them and generously presented them to me.

I was afraid of opening my father's suitcase and reading his notebooks because I knew that he would not tolerate the difficulties I had endured, that it was not solitude he loved but mixing with friends, crowds, salons, jokes, company. But later my thoughts took a different turn. These thoughts, these dreams of renunciation and patience, were prejudices I had derived from my own life and my own experience as a writer. There were plenty of brilliant writers who wrote surrounded by crowds and family life, in the glow of company and happy chatter. In addition, my father had, when we were young, tired of the monotony of family life, and left us to go to Paris, where—like so many writers—he'd sat in his hotel room filling notebooks. I knew, too, that some of those very notebooks were in this suitcase, because during the years before he brought it to me, my father had finally begun to talk to me about that period in his life. He spoke about those years even when I was a child, but he would not mention his vulnerabilities, his dreams of becoming a writer, or the questions of identity that had plagued him in his hotel room. He would tell me instead about all the times he'd seen Sartre on the pavements of Paris, about the books he'd read and the films he'd seen, all with the elated sincerity of someone imparting very important news. When I became a writer, I never forgot that it was partly thanks to the fact that I had a father who would talk of world writers so much more than he spoke of pashas or great religious leaders. So perhaps I had to read my father's notebooks with this in mind, and remembering how indebted I was to his large library. I had to bear in mind that when he was living with us, my father, like me, enjoyed being alone with his books and his thoughts—and not pay too much attention to the literary quality of his writing.

But as I gazed so anxiously at the suitcase my father had bequeathed me, I also felt that this was the very thing I would not be able to do. My father would sometimes stretch out on the divan in front of his books, abandon the book in his hand, or the magazine and drift off into a dream, lose himself for the longest time in his thoughts. When I saw on his face an expression so very different from the one he wore amid the joking, teasing, and bickering of family life—when I saw the first signs of an inward gaze—I would, especially during my childhood and my early youth, understand, with trepidation, that he was discontent. Now, so many years later, I know that this discontent is the basic trait that turns a person into a writer. To become a writer, patience and toil are not enough: we must first feel compelled to escape crowds, company, the stuff of ordinary, everyday life, and shut ourselves up in a room. We wish for patience and hope so that we can create a deep world in our writing. But the desire to shut oneself up in a room is what pushes us into action. The precursor of this sort of independent writer—who reads his books to his heart's content, and who, by listening only to the voice of his own conscience, disputes with other's words, who, by entering into conversation with his books develops his own thoughts, and his own world—was most certainly Montaigne, in the earliest days of modern literature. Montaigne was a writer to whom my father returned often, a writer he recommended to me. I would like to see myself as belonging to the tradition of writers who—wherever they are in the world, in the East or in the West—cut themselves off from society, and shut themselves up with their books in their room. The starting point of true literature is the man who shuts himself up in his room with his books.

But once we shut ourselves away, we soon discover that we are not as alone as we thought. We are in the company of the words of those who came before us, of other people's stories, other people's books, other people's words, the thing we call tradition. I believe literature to be the most valuable hoard that humanity has gathered in its quest to understand itself. Societies, tribes, and peoples grow more intelligent, richer, and more advanced as they pay attention to the troubled words of their authors, and, as we all know, the burning of books and the denigration of writers are both signals that dark and improvident times are upon us. But literature is never just a national concern. The writer who shuts himself up in a room and first goes on a journey inside himself will, over the years, discover literature's eternal rule: he must have the artistry to tell his own stories as if they were other people's stories, and to tell other people's stories as if they were his own, for this is what literature is. But we must first travel through other people's stories and books.

My father had a good library—1500 volumes in all—more than enough for a writer. By the age of 22, I had perhaps not read them all, but I was familiar with each book—I knew which were important, which were light but easy to read, which were classics, which an essential part of any education, which were forgettable but amusing accounts of local history, and which French authors my father rated very highly. Sometimes I would look at this library from a distance and imagine that one day, in a different house, I would build my own library, an even better library—build myself a world. When I looked at my father's library from afar, it seemed to me to be a small picture of the real world. But this was a world seen from our own corner, from Istanbul. The library was evidence of this. My father had built his library from his trips abroad, mostly with books from Paris and America, but also with books bought from the shops that sold books in foreign languages in the 40s and 50s and Istanbul's old and new booksellers, whom I also knew. My world is a mixture of the local—the national—and the West. In the 70s, I, too, began, somewhat ambitiously, to build my own library. I had not quite decided to become a writer—as I related in *Istanbul*, I had come to feel that I would not, after all, become a painter, but I was not sure what path my life would take. There was inside me a relentless curiosity, a hope-driven desire to read and learn, but at the same time I felt that my life was in some way lacking, that I would not be able to live like others. Part of this feeling was connected to what I felt when I gazed at my father's library—to be living far from the centre of things, as all of us who lived in Istanbul in those days were made to feel, that feeling of living in the provinces. There was another reason for feeling anxious and somehow lacking, for I knew only too well that I lived in a country that showed little interest in its artists—be they painters or writers—and that gave them no hope. In the 70s, when I would take the money my father gave me and greedily buy faded, dusty, dog-eared books from Istanbul's old booksellers, I would be as affected by the pitiable state of these second-hand bookstores—and by the despairing dishevelment of the poor, bedraggled booksellers who laid out their wares on roadsides, in mosque courtyards, and in the niches of crumbling walls—as I was by their books.

As for my place in the world—in life, as in literature, my basic feeling was that I was "not in the centre". In the centre of the world, there was a life richer and more exciting than our own, and with all of Istanbul, all of Turkey, I was outside it. Today I think that I share this feeling with most people in the world. In the same way, there was a world literature, and its centre, too, was very far away from me. Actually what I had in mind was Western, not world, literature, and we Turks were outside it. My father's library was evidence of this. At one end, there were Istanbul's books—our literature, our local world, in all its beloved detail—and at the other end were the books from this other, Western, world, to which our own bore no resemblance, to which our lack of resemblance gave us both pain and hope. To write, to read, was like leaving one world to find consolation in the other world's otherness, the strange and the wondrous. I felt that my father had read novels to escape his life and flee to the West—just as I would do later. Or it seemed to me that books in those days were things we picked up to escape our own culture, which we found so lacking. It wasn't just by reading that we left our Istanbul lives to travel West—it was by writing, too. To fill those notebooks of his, my father had gone to Paris, shut himself up in his room, and then brought his writings back to Turkey. As I gazed at my father's suitcase, it seemed to me that this was what was causing me disquiet. After working in a room for 25 years to survive as a writer in Turkey, it galled me to see my father hide his deep thoughts inside this suitcase, to act as if writing was work that had to be done in secret, far from the eyes of society, the state, the people. Perhaps this was the main reason why I felt angry at my father for not taking literature as seriously as I did.

Actually I was angry at my father because he had not led a life like mine, because he had never quarrelled with his life, and had spent his life happily laughing with his friends and his loved ones. But part of me knew that I could also say that I was not so much "angry" as "jealous", that the second word was more accurate, and this, too, made me uneasy. That would be when I would ask myself in my usual scornful, angry voice: "What is happiness?" Was happiness thinking that I lived a deep life in that lonely room? Or was happiness leading a comfortable life in society, believing in the same things as everyone else, or acting as if you did? Was it happiness, or unhappiness, to go through life writing in secret, while seeming to be in harmony with all around one? But these were overly ill-tempered questions. Wherever had I got this idea that the measure of a good life was happiness? People, papers, everyone acted as if the most important measure of a life was happiness. Did this alone not suggest that it might be worth trying to find out if the exact opposite was true? After all, my father had run away from his family so many times—how well did I know him, and how well could I say I understood his disquiet?

So this was what was driving me when I first opened my father's suitcase. Did my father have a secret, an unhappiness in his life about which I knew nothing, something he could only endure by pouring it into his writing? As soon as I opened the suitcase, I recalled its scent of travel, recognised several notebooks, and noted that my father had shown them to me years earlier, but without dwelling on them very long. Most of the notebooks I now took into my hands he had filled when he had left us and gone to Paris as a young man. Although I, like so many writers I admired—writers whose biographies I had read—I wished to know what my father had written, and what he had thought, when he was the age I was now, it did not take me long to realise that I would find nothing like that here. What caused me most disquiet was when, here and there in my father's notebooks, I came upon a writerly voice. This was not my father's voice, I told myself; it wasn't authentic, or at least it did not belong to the man I'd known as my father. Underneath my fear that my father might not have been my father when he wrote, was a deeper fear: the fear that deep inside I was not authentic, that I would find nothing good in my father's writing;

this increased my fear of finding my father to have been overly influenced by other writers and plunged me into a despair that had afflicted me so badly when I was young, casting my life, my very being, my desire to write, and my work into question. During my first ten years as a writer, I felt these anxieties more deeply, and even as I fought them off, I would sometimes fear that one day, I would have to admit to defeat—just as I had done with painting—and succumbing to disquiet, give up novel writing, too.

I have already mentioned the two essential feelings that rose up in me as I closed my father's suitcase and put it away: the sense of being marooned in the provinces, and the fear that I lacked authenticity. This was certainly not the first time they had made themselves felt. For years I had, in my reading and my writing, been studying, discovering, deepening these emotions, in all their variety and unintended consequences, their nerve endings, their triggers, and their many colours. Certainly my spirits had been jarred by the confusions, the sensitivities and the fleeting pains that life and books had sprung on me, most often as a young man. But it was only by writing books that I came to a fuller understanding of the problems of authenticity (as in *My Name is Red* and *The Black Book*) and the problems of life on the periphery (as in *Snow* and *Istanbul*). For me, to be a writer is to acknowledge the secret wounds that we carry inside us, the wounds so secret that we ourselves are barely aware of them, and to patiently explore them, know them, illuminate them, to own these pains and wounds, and to make them a conscious part of our spirits and our writing.

A writer talks of things that everyone knows but does not know they know. To explore this knowledge, and to watch it grow, is a pleasurable thing; the reader is visiting a world at once familiar and miraculous. When a writer shuts himself up in a room for years on end to hone his craft—to create a world—if he uses his secret wounds as his starting point, he is, whether he knows it or not, putting a great faith in humanity. My confidence comes from the belief that all human beings resemble each other, that others carry wounds like mine—that they will therefore understand. All true literature rises from this childish, hopeful certainty that all people resemble each other. When a writer shuts himself up in a room for years on end, with this gesture he suggests a single humanity, a world without a centre.

But as can be seen from my father's suitcase and the pale colours of our lives in Istanbul, the world did have a centre, and it was far away from us. In my books I have described in some detail how this basic fact evoked a Chekhovian sense of provinciality, and how, by another route, it led to my questioning my authenticity. I know from experience that the great majority of people on this earth live with these same feelings, and that many suffer from an even deeper sense of insufficiency, lack of security and sense of degradation, than I do. Yes, the greatest dilemmas facing humanity are still landlessness, homelessness, and hunger ... But today our televisions and newspapers tell us about these fundamental problems more quickly and more simply than literature can ever do. What literature needs most to tell and investigate today are humanity's basic fears: the fear of being left outside, and the fear of counting for nothing, and the feelings of worthlessness that come with such fears; the collective humiliations, vulnerabilities, slights, grievances, sensitivities, and imagined insults, and the nationalist boasts and inflations that are their next of kin ... Whenever I am confronted by such sentiments, and by the irrational, overstated language in which they are usually expressed, I know they touch on a darkness inside me. We have often witnessed peoples, societies and nations outside the Western world—and I can identify with them easily—succumbing to fears that sometimes lead them to commit stupidities, all because of their fears of humiliation and their sensitivities. I also know that in the West—a world with which I can identify with the same ease—nations and peoples taking an excessive pride in their wealth, and in their having brought us the Renaissance, the Enlightenment, and Modernism, have, from time to time, succumbed to a self-satisfaction that is almost as stupid.

This means that my father was not the only one, that we all give too much importance to the idea of a world with a centre. Whereas the thing that compels us to shut ourselves up to write in our rooms for years on end is a faith in the opposite; the belief that one day our writings will be read and understood, because people all the world over resemble each other. But this, as I know from my own and my father's writing, is a troubled optimism, scarred by the anger of being consigned to the margins, of being left outside. The love and hate that Dostoyevsky felt towards the West all his life—I have felt this too, on many occasions. But if I have grasped an essential truth, if I have cause for optimism, it is because I have travelled with this great writer through his love-hate relationship with the West, to behold the other world he has built on the other side.

All writers who have devoted their lives to this task know this reality: whatever our original purpose, the world that we create after years and years of hopeful writing, will, in the end, move to other very different places. It will take us far away from the table at which we have worked with sadness or anger, take us to the other side of that sadness and anger, into another world. Could my father have not reached such a world himself? Like the land that slowly begins to take shape, slowly rising from the mist in all its colours like an island after a long sea journey, this other world enchants us. We are as beguiled as the western travellers who voyaged from the south to behold Istanbul rising from the mist. At the end of a journey begun in hope and curiosity, there lies before them a city of mosques and minarets, a medley of houses, streets, hills, bridges, and slopes, an entire world. Seeing it, we wish to enter into this world and lose ourselves inside it, just as we might a book. After sitting down at a table because we felt provincial, excluded, on the margins, angry, or deeply melancholic, we have found an entire world beyond these sentiments.

What I feel now is the opposite of what I felt as a child and a young man: for me the centre of the world is Istanbul. This is not just because I have lived there all my life, but because, for the last 33 years, I have been narrating its streets, its bridges, its people, its dogs, its houses, its mosques, its fountains, its strange heroes, its shops, its famous characters, its dark spots, its days and its nights, making them part of me, embracing them all. A point arrived when this world I had made with my own hands, this world that existed only in my head, was more real to me than the city in which I actually lived. That was when all these people and streets, objects and buildings would seem to begin to talk amongst themselves, and begin to interact in ways I had not anticipated, as if they lived not just in my imagination or my books, but for themselves. This world that I had created like a man digging a well with a needle would then seem truer than all else.

My father might also have discovered this kind of happiness during the years he spent writing, I thought as I gazed at my father's suitcase: I should not prejudge him. I was so grateful to him, after all: he'd never been a commanding, forbidding, overpowering, punishing, ordinary father, but a father who always left me free, always showed me the utmost respect. I had often thought that if I had, from time to time, been able to draw from my imagination, be it in freedom or childishness, it was because, unlike so many of my friends from childhood and youth, I had no fear of my father, and I had sometimes believed very deeply that I had been able to become a writer because my father had, in his youth, wished to be one, too. I had to read him with tolerance—seek to understand what he had written in those hotel rooms.

It was with these hopeful thoughts that I walked over to the suitcase, which was still sitting where my father had left it; using all my willpower, I read through a few manuscripts and notebooks. What had my father written about? I recall a few views from the windows of Parisian hotels, a few poems, paradoxes, analyses ... As I write I feel like someone who has just been in a traffic accident and is struggling to remember how it happened, while at the same time dreading the prospect of remembering too much. When I was a child, and my father and mother were on the brink of a quarrel—when they fell into one of those deadly silences—my father would at once turn on the radio, to change the mood, and the music would help us forget it all faster.

Let me change the mood with a few sweet words that will, I hope, serve as well as that music. As you know, the question we writers are asked most often, the favourite question, is: why do you write? I write because I have an innate need to write! I write because I can't do normal work like other people. I write because I want to read books like the ones I write. I write because I am angry at all of you, angry at everyone. I write because I love sitting in a room all day writing. I write because I can only partake in real life by changing it. I write because I want others, all of us, the whole world, to know what sort of life we lived, and continue to live, in Istanbul, in Turkey. I write because I love the smell of paper, pen, and ink. I write because I believe in literature, in the art of the novel, more than I believe in anything else. I write because it is a habit, a passion. I write because I am afraid of being forgotten. I write because I like the glory and interest that writing brings. I write to be alone. Perhaps I write because I hope to understand why I am so very, very angry at all of you, so very, very angry at everyone. I write because I like to be read. I write because once I have begun a novel, an essay, a page, I want to finish it. I write because everyone expects me to write. I write because I have a childish belief in the immortality of libraries, and in the way my books sit on the shelf. I write because it is exciting to turn all of life's beauties and riches into words. I write not to tell a story, but to compose a story. I write because I wish to escape from the foreboding that there is a place I must go but—just as in a dream—I can't quite get there. I write because I have never managed to be happy. I write to be happy.

A week after he came to my office and left me his suitcase, my father came to pay me another visit; as always, he brought me a bar of chocolate (he had forgotten I was 48 years old). As always, we chatted and laughed about life, politics and family gossip. A moment arrived when my father's eyes went to the corner where he had left his suitcase and saw that I had moved it. We looked each other in the eye. There followed a pressing silence. I did not tell him that I had opened the suitcase and tried to read its contents; instead I looked away. But he understood. Just as I understood that he had understood. Just as he understood that I had understood that he had understood. But all this understanding only went so far as it can go in a few seconds. Because my father was a happy, easygoing man who had faith in himself: he smiled at me the way he always did. And as he left the house, he repeated all the lovely and encouraging things that he always said to me, like a father.

As always, I watched him leave, envying his happiness, his carefree and unflappable temperament. But I remember that on that day there was also a flash of joy inside me that made me ashamed. It was prompted by the thought that maybe I wasn't as comfortable in life as he was, maybe I had not led as happy or footloose a life as he had, but that I had devoted it to writing—you've understood ... I was ashamed to be thinking such things at my father's expense. Of all people, my father, who had never been the source of my pain—who had left me free. All this should remind us that writing and literature are intimately linked to a lack at the centre of our lives, and to our feelings of happiness and guilt.

But my story has a symmetry that immediately reminded me of something else that day, and that brought me an even deeper sense of guilt. Twenty-three years before my father left me his suitcase, and four years after I had decided, aged 22, to become a novelist, and, abandoning all else, shut myself up in a room, I finished my first novel, *Cevdet Bey and Sons*; with trembling hands I had given my father a typescript of the still unpublished novel, so that he could read it and tell me what he thought. This was not simply because I had confidence in his taste and his intellect: his opinion was very important to me because he, unlike my mother, had not opposed my wish to become a writer. At that point, my father was not with us, but far away. I waited impatiently for his return. When he arrived two weeks later, I ran to open the door. My father said nothing, but he at once threw his arms around me in a way that told me he had liked it very much. For a while, we were plunged into the sort of awkward silence that so often accompanies moments of great emotion. Then, when we had calmed down and begun to talk, my father resorted to highly charged and exaggerated language to express his confidence in me or my first novel: he told me that one day I would win the prize that I am here to receive with such great happiness.

He said this not because he was trying to convince me of his good opinion, or to set this prize as a goal; he said it like a Turkish father, giving support to his son, encouraging him by saying, "One day you'll become a pasha!" For years, whenever he saw me, he would encourage me with the same words.

My father died in December 2002.

This is Orhan Pamuk's Nobel Lecture (December 7, 2006) that he delivered in Stockholm. This lecture was originally published in the *New Yorker* (25 December 2006–1 January 2007). It is printed here with the permission of The Nobel Foundation.

The Promise

Nowadays men often feel that their private lives are a series of traps. They sense that within their everyday worlds, they cannot overcome their troubles, and in this feeling, they are often quite correct. What ordinary men are directly aware of and what they try to do are bounded by the private orbits in which they live; their visions and their powers are limited to the close-up scenes of job, family, neighborhood; in other milieux they move vicariously and remain spectators. And the more aware they become, however vaguely, of ambitions and of threats which transcend their immediate locales, the more trapped they seem to feel.

Underlying this sense of being trapped are seemingly impersonal changes in the very structure of continent-wide societies. The facts of contemporary history are also facts about the success and the failure of individual men and women. When a society is industrialized a peasant becomes a worker; a feudal lord is liquidated or becomes a businessman. When classes rise or fall, a man is employed or unemployed; when the rate of investment goes up or down, a man takes new heart or goes broke. When wars happen, an insurance salesman becomes a rocket launcher; a store clerk, a radar man; a wife lives alone; a child grows up without a father. Neither the life of an individual nor the history of a society can be understood without understanding both.

Yet men do not usually define the troubles they endure in terms of historical change and institutional contradiction. The well-being they enjoy, they do not usually impute to the big ups and downs of the societies in which they live. Seldom aware of the intricate connection between the patterns of their own lives and the course of world history, ordinary men do not usually know what this connection means for the kinds of men they are becoming and for the kinds of history-making in which they might take part. They do not possess the quality of mind essential to grasp the interplay of man and society, of biography and history, of self and world. They cannot cope with their personal troubles in such ways as to control the structural transformations that usually lie behind them.

The very shaping of history now outpaces the ability of men to orient themselves in accordance with cherished values. And which values? Even when they do not panic, men often sense that older ways of feeling and thinking have collapsed and that newer beginnings are ambiguous to the point of moral stasis. Is it any wonder that ordinary men feel they cannot cope with the larger worlds with which they are so suddenly confronted? That they cannot understand the meaning of their epoch for their own lives? That—in defense of selfhood—they become morally insensible, trying to remain altogether private men? Is it any wonder that they come to be possessed by a sense of the trap?

It is not only information that they need—in this Age of Fact, information often dominates their attention and overwhelms their capacity to assimilate it. It is not only the skills of reason that they need—although their struggles to acquire these often exhaust their limited moral energy.

What they need, and what they feel they need, is a quality of mind that will help them to use information and to develop reason in order to achieve lucid summations of what is going on in the world and of what may be happening within themselves. It is this quality, I am going to contend, that journalists and scholars, artists and publics, scientists and editors are coming to expect of what may be called the sociological imagination.

The sociological imagination enables its possessor to understand the larger historical scene in terms of its meaning for the inner life and the external career of a variety of individuals. It enables him to take into account how individuals, in the welter of their daily experience, often become falsely conscious of their social positions. Within that welter, the framework of modern society is sought, and within that framework the psychologies of a variety of men and women are formulated. By such means the personal uneasiness of individuals is focused upon explicit troubles and the indifference of publics is transformed into involvement with public issues.

The first fruit of this imagination—and the first lesson of the social science that embodies it—is the idea that the individual can understand his own experience and gauge his own fate only by locating himself within his period, that he can know his own chances in life only by becoming aware of those of all individuals in his circumstances. In many ways it is a terrible lesson; in many ways a magnificent one. We do not know the limits of man's capacities for supreme effort or willing degradation, for agony or glee, for pleasurable brutality or the sweetness of reason. But in our time we have come to know that the limits of 'human nature' are frighteningly broad. We have come to know that every individual lives, from one generation to the next, in some society; that he lives out a biography, and that he lives it out within some historical sequence. By the fact of his living he contributes, how ever minutely, to the shaping of this society and to the course of its history, even as he is made by society and by its historical push and shove.

The sociological imagination enables us to grasp history and biography and the relations between the two within society that is its task and its promise. To recognize this task and this promise is the mark of the classic social analyst.

No social study that does not come back to the problems of biography, of history and of their intersections within a society has completed its intellectual journey. Whatever the specific problems of the classic social analysts, however limited or however broad the features of social reality they have examined, those who have been imaginatively aware of the promise of their work have consistently asked three sorts of questions:

1. What is the structure of this particular society as a whole? What are its essential

components, and how are they related to one another? How does it differ from other varieties of social order? Within it, what is the meaning of any particular feature for its continuance and for its change?

2. Where does this society stand in human history? What are the mechanics by which it is changing? What is its place within and its meaning for the development of humanity as a whole?

    How does any particular feature we are examining affect, and how is it affected by, the historical period in which it moves? And this period—what are its essential features? How does it differ from other periods? What are its characteristic ways of history-making?

3. What varieties of men and women now prevail in this society and in this period? And what varieties are coming to prevail? In what ways are they selected and formed, liberated and repressed, made sensitive and blunted? What kinds of "human nature" are revealed in the conduct and character we observe in this society in this period? And what is the meaning for 'human nature' of each and every feature of the society we are examining?

Whether the point of interest is a great power state or a minor literary mood, a family, a prison, a creed—these are the kinds of questions the best social analysts have asked. They are the intellectual pivots of classic studies of man in society—and they are the questions inevitably raised by any mind possessing the sociological imagination. For that imagination is the capacity to shift from one perspective to another—from the political to the psycho, from examination of a single family to comparative assessment of the national budgets of the world, from the theological school to the military establishment, from considerations of an oil industry to studies of contemporary poetry. It is the capacity to range from the most impersonal and remote transformations to the most intimate features of the human self—and to see the relations between the two. Back of its use there is always the urge to know the social and historical meaning of the individual in the society and in the period in which he has his quality and his being.

That, in brief, is why it is by means of the sociological imagination that men now hope to grasp what is going on in the world, and to understand what is happening in themselves as minute society. In large part, contemporary man's self-conscious view of himself as at least an outsider, if not a permanent stranger, rests upon an absorbed realization of social relativity and of the transformative power of history. The sociological imagination is the most fruitful form of this self-consciousness. By its use men whose mentalities have swept only a series of limited orbits often come to feel as if suddenly awakened in a house with which they had only supposed themselves to be familiar. Correctly or incorrectly, they often come to feel that they can now provide themselves with adequate summations, cohesive assessments, comprehensive orientations.

Perhaps the most fruitful distinction with which the sociological imagination works is between "the personal troubles of milieu" and "the public issues of social structure." This distinction is an essential tool of the sociological imagination and a feature of all classic work in social science.

Troubles occur within the character of the individual and within the range of his immediate relations with others; they have to do with his self and with those limited areas of social life of which he is directly and personally aware. Accordingly, the statement and the resolution of troubles properly lie within the individual as a biographical entity and within the scope of his immediate milieu—the social setting that is directly open to his personal experience and to some extent his willful activity. A trouble is a private matter: values cherished by an individual are felt by him to be threatened.

Issues have to do with matters that transcend these local environments of the individual and the range of his inner life. They have to do with the organization of many such milieux into the institutions of an historical society as a whole, with the ways in which various milieux overlap and interpenetrate to form the larger structure of social and historical life. An issue is a public matter: some value cherished by publics is felt to be threatened. Often there is a debate about what that value really is and about what it is that really threatens it. This debate is often without focus if only because it is the very nature of an issue, unlike even widespread trouble, that it cannot very well be defined in terms of the immediate and everyday environments of ordinary men. An issue, in fact, often involves a crisis in institutional arrangements, and often too it involves what Marxists call "contradictions" or "antagonisms."

In these terms, consider unemployment. When, in a city of 100,000 only one man is unemployed, that is his personal trouble, and for its relief we properly look to the character of the man, his skills, and his immediate opportunities. But when in a nation of 50 million employees, 15 million men are unemployed, that is an issue, and we may not hope to find its solution within the range of opportunities open to any one individual. The very structure of opportunities has collapsed. Both the correct statement of the problem and the range of possible solutions require us to consider the economic and political institutions of the society, and not merely the personal situation and character of a scatter of individuals.

Consider war. The personal problem of war, when it occurs, may be how to survive it or how to die in it with honor; how to make money out of it; how to climb into the higher safety of the military apparatus; or how to contribute to the war's termination. In short, according to one's values, to find a set of milieux and within it to survive the war or make one's death in it meaningful. But the structural issues of war have to do with its causes; with what types of men it throws up into command; with its effects upon economic and political, family and religious institutions, with the unorganized irresponsibility of a world of nation-states.

Consider marriage. Inside a marriage a man and a woman may experience personal troubles, but when the divorce rate during the first four years of marriage is 250 out of every 1,000 attempts, this is an indication of a structural issue with the institutions of marriage and the family and other institutions that bear upon them.

Or consider the metropolis—the horrible, beautiful, ugly, magnificent sprawl of the great city. For many upper-class people, the personal solution to "the problem of the city" is to have an apartment with private garage under it in the heart of the city, and forty miles out, a house on a hundred acres of private land. In these two controlled environments—with a small staff at each end and a private helicopter connection—most people could solve many of the problems of personal milieux caused by the facts of the city. But all this, however splendid, does not solve the public issues that the structural fact of the city poses. What should be done with this wonderful monstrosity? Break it all up into scattered units, combining residence and work? Refurbish it as it stands? Or, after evacuation, dynamite it and build new cities according to new plans in new places? What should those plans be? And who is to decide and to accomplish whatever choice is made? These are structural issues; to confront them and to solve them requires us to consider political and economic issues that affect innumerable milieux.

In so far as an economy is so arranged that slumps occur, the problem of unemployment becomes incapable of personal solution. In so far as war is inherent in the nation-state system and in the uneven industrialization of the world, the ordinary individual in his restricted milieu will be powerless—with or without psychiatric aid—to solve the troubles this system or lack of system imposes upon him. In so far as the family as an institution turns women into darling little slaves and men into their chief providers and unweaned dependants, the problem of a satisfactory marriage remains incapable of purely private solution. In so far as the overdeveloped megalopolis and the overdeveloped automobile are built-in features of the overdeveloped society, the issues of urban living will not be solved by personal ingenuity and private wealth.

What we experience in various and specific milieux, I have noted, is often caused by structural changes. Accordingly, to understand the changes of many personal milieux we are required to look beyond them. And the number and variety of such structural changes increase as the institutions within which we live become more embracing and more intricately connected with one another. To be aware of the idea of social structure and to use it with sensibility is to be capable of tracing such linkages among a great variety of milieux. To be able to do that is to possess the sociological imagination.

What are the major issues for publics and the key troubles of private individuals in our time? To formulate issues and troubles, we must ask what values are cherished yet threatened, and what values are cherished and supported, by the characterizing trends of our period. In the case both of threat and of support we must ask what salient contradictions of structure may be involved.

When people cherish some set of values and do not feel any threat to them, they experience *well-being*. When they cherish values but *do* feel them to be threatened, they experience a *crisis*—either as a personal trouble or as a public issue. And if all their values seem involved, they feel the total threat of *panic*.

But suppose people are neither aware of any cherished values nor experience any threat? That is the experience of *indifference*, which, if it seems to involve all their values, becomes apathy. Suppose, finally, they are unaware of any cherished values, but still are very much aware of a threat? That is the experience of *uneasiness*, of anxiety, which, if it is total enough, becomes a deadly unspecified malaise.

Ours is a time of uneasiness and indifference—not yet formulated in such ways as to permit the work of reason and the play of sensibility. Instead of troubles—defined in terms of values and threats—there is often the misery of vague uneasiness; instead of explicit issues there is often merely the beat feeling that all is somehow not right. Neither the values threatened nor whatever threatens them has been stated; in short, they have not been carried to the point of decision. Much less have they been formulated as problems of social science.

But the values threatened in the world today are often neither widely acknowledged as values nor widely felt to be threatened. Much private uneasiness goes unformulated;

much public malaise and many decisions of enormous structural relevance never become public issues. For those who accept such inherited values as reason and freedom, it is the uneasiness itself that is the trouble; it is the indifference itself that is the issue. And it is this condition, of uneasiness and indifference, that is the signal feature of our period.

It is now the social scientist's foremost political and intellectual task—for here the two coincide—to make clear the elements of contemporary uneasiness and indifference. It is the central demand made upon him by other cultural workmen—by physical scientists and artists, by the intellectual community in general. It is because of this task and these demands, I believe, that the social sciences are becoming the common denominator of our cultural period, and the sociological imagination our most needed quality of mind.

The sociological imagination is becoming, I believe, the major common denominator of our cultural life and its signal feature. This quality of mind is found in the social and psychological sciences, but it goes far beyond these studies as we now know them. Its acquisition by individuals and by the cultural community at large is slow and often fumbling; many social scientists are themselves quite unaware of it. They do not seem to know that the use of this imagination is central to the best work that they might do, that by failing to develop and to use it they are failing to meet the cultural expectations that are coming to be demanded of them and that the classic traditions of their several disciplines make available to them.

An abridged version which originally appeared in *The Sociological Imagination* (Oxford University Press, 1972): 3–24. It is printed here with the permission of the publisher.

CLIFFORD GEERTZ

From the Native's Point of View: On the Nature of Anthropological Understanding

I

Several years ago a minor scandal erupted in anthropology: one of its ancestral figures told the truth in a public place. As befits an ancestor, he did it posthumously, and through his widow's decision rather than his own, with the result that a number of the sort of right-thinking types who are with us always immediately rose to cry that she, an in-marrier anyway, had betrayed clan secrets, profaned an idol, and let down the side. What will the children think, to say nothing of the layman? But the disturbance was not much lessened by such ceremonial wringing of the hands; the damn thing was, after all, already printed. In much the same fashion as James Watson's *The Double Helix* exposed the way in which biophysics in fact gets done, Bronislaw Malinowski's *A Diary in the Strict Sense of the Term* rendered established accounts of how anthropologists work fairly well implausible. The myth of the chameleon fieldworker, perfectly self-tuned to his exotic surroundings, a walking miracle of empathy, tact, patience, and cosmopolitanism, was demolished by the man who had perhaps done most to create it.

The squabble that arose around the publication of the *Diary* concentrated, naturally, on inessentials and missed, as was only to be expected, the point. Most of the shock seems to have arisen from the mere discovery that Malinowski was not, to put it delicately, an unmitigated nice guy. He had rude things to say about the natives he was living with, and rude words to say them in. He spent a great deal of his time wishing he were elsewhere. And he projected an image of a man about as little complaisant as the world has seen. (He also projected an image of a man consecrated to a strange vocation to the point of self-immolation, but that was less noted.) The discussion was made to come down to Malinowski's moral character or lack of it, and the genuinely profound question his book raised was ignored; namely, if it is not, as we had been taught to believe, through some sort of extraordinary sensibility, an almost preternatural capacity to think, feel, and perceive like a native (a word, I should hurry to say, I use here "in the strict sense of the term"), how is anthropological knowledge of the way natives think, feel, and perceive possible? The issue the *Diary* presents, with a force perhaps only a working ethnographer can fully appreciate, is not moral. (The moral idealization of fieldworkers is a mere sentimentality in the first place, when it is not self-congratulation or a guild pretense.) The issue is epistemological. If we are going to cling—as, in my opinion, we must—to the injunction to see things from the native's point of view, where are we when we can no longer claim some unique form of psychological closeness, a sort of transcultural identification, with our subjects? What happens to *verstehen* when *einfühlen* disappears?

As a matter of fact, this general problem has been exercising methodological discussion in anthropology for the last ten or fifteen years; Malinowski's voice from the grave merely dramatizes it as a human dilemma over and above a professional one. The formulations have been various: "inside" versus "outside," or "first person" versus "third person" descriptions; "phenomenological" versus "objectivist," or "cognitive" versus "behavioral" theories; or, perhaps most commonly "emic", versus "etic" analyses, this last deriving from the distinction in linguistics between phonemics and phonetics, phonemics classifying sounds according to their internal function in language, phonetics classifying them according to their acoustic proper ties as such. But perhaps the simplest and most directly appreciable way to put the matter is in terms of a distinction formulated, for his own purposes, by the psychoanalyst Heinz Kohut, between what he calls "experience-near" and "experience-distant" concepts.

An experience-near concept is, roughly, one that someone—a patient, a subject, in our case an informant—might himself naturally and effortlessly use to define what he or his fellows see, feel, think, imagine, and so on, and which he would readily understand when similarly applied by others. An experience-distant concept is one that specialists of one sort or another—an analyst, an experimenter, an ethnographer, even a priest or an ideologist—employ to forward their scientific, philosophical, or practical aims. "Love" is an experience-near concept, "object cathexis" is an experience-distant one. "Social stratification" and perhaps for most peoples in the world even "religion" (and certainly "religious system") are experience-distant; "caste" and "nirvana" are experience-near, at least for Hindus and Buddhists.

Clearly, the matter is one of degree, not polar opposition—"fear" is experience-nearer than "phobia," and "phobia" experience-nearer than "ego dyssyntonic." And the difference is not, at least so far as anthropology is concerned (the matter is otherwise in poetry and physics), a normative one, in the sense that one sort of concept is to be preferred as such over the other. Confinement to experience-near concepts leaves an ethnographer awash in immediacies, as well as entangled in vernacular. Confinement to experience-distant ones leaves him stranded in abstractions and smothered in jargon. The real question, and the one Malinowski raised by demonstrating that, in the case of "natives," you don't have to be one to know one, is what roles the two sorts of concepts play in anthropological analysis. Or, more exactly, how, in each case, ought one to deploy them so as to produce an interpretation of the way a people lives which is neither imprisoned within their mental horizons, an ethnography of witchcraft as written by a witch, nor systematically deaf to the distinctive tonalities of their existence, an ethnography of witchcraft as written by a geometer.

Putting the matter this way—in terms of how anthropological analysis is to be conducted and its results framed, rather than what psychic constitution anthropologists need to have—reduces the mystery of what "seeing things from the native's point of view" means. But it does not make it any easier, nor does it lessen the demand for perceptiveness on the part of the fieldworker. To grasp concepts that, for another people, are experience-near, and to do so well enough to place them in illuminating connection with experience-distant concepts theorists have fashioned to capture the general features of social life, is clearly a task at least as delicate, if a bit less magical, as putting oneself into someone else's skin. The trick is not to get yourself into some inner correspondence of spirit with your informants. Preferring, like the rest of us, to call their souls their own, they are not going to be altogether keen about such an effort anyhow. The trick is to figure out what the devil they think they are up to.

In one sense, of course, no one knows this better than they do themselves; hence the passion to swim in the stream of their experience, and the illusion afterward that one somehow has. But in another sense, that simple truism is simply not true. People use experience-near concepts spontaneously, un-self-consciously, as it were colloquially; they do not, except fleetingly and on occasion, recognize that there are any "concepts" involved at all. That is what experience-near means—that ideas and the realities they inform are naturally and indissolubly bound up together. What else could you call a hippopotamus? Of course the gods are powerful, why else would we fear them? The ethnographer does not, and, in my opinion, largely cannot, perceive what his informants perceive. What he perceives, and that uncertainly enough, is what they perceive "with"—or "by means of," or "through" or whatever the word should be. In the country of the blind, who are not as unobservant as they look, the one-eyed is not king, he is spectator.

Now, to make all this a bit more concrete, I want to turn for a moment to my own work, which, whatever its other faults, has at least the virtue of being mine—in discussions of this sort a distinct advantage. In all three of the societies I have studied intensively, Javanese, Balinese, and Moroccan, I have been concerned, among other things, with attempting to determine how the people who live there define themselves as persons, what goes into the idea they have (but, as I say, only half-realize they have) of what a self, Javanese, Balinese, or Moroccan style, is. And in each case, I have tried to get at this most intimate of notions not by imagining myself someone else, a rice peasant or a tribal sheikh, and then seeing what I thought, but by searching out and analyzing the symbolic forms—words, images, institutions, behaviors—in terms of which, in each place, people actually represented themselves to themselves and to one another.

The concept of person is, in fact, an excellent vehicle by means of which to examine this whole question of how to go about poking into another people's turn of mind. In the first place, some sort of concept of this kind, one feels reasonably safe in saying, exists in recognizable form among all social groups. The notions of what persons are may be, from our point of view, sometimes more than a little odd. They may be conceived to dart about nervously at night shaped like fireflies. Essential elements of their psyches, like hatred, may be thought to be lodged in granular black bodies within their livers, discoverable upon autopsy. They may share their fates with *doppelgänger* beasts, so that when the beast sickens or dies they sicken or die too. But at least some conception of what a human individual is, as opposed to a rock, an animal, a rainstorm, or a god, is, so far as I can see, universal. Yet, at the same time, as these offhand examples suggest, the actual conceptions involved vary from one group to the next, and often quite sharply. The Western conception of the person as a bounded, unique, more or less integrated motivational and cognitive universe, a dynamic center of awareness, emotion, judgment, and action organized into a distinctive whole and set contrastively both against other such wholes and against its social and natural background, is, however incorrigible it may seem to us, a rather peculiar idea within the context of the world's cultures. Rather than attempting to place the experiences of others within the framework of such a conception, which is what the extolled "empathy" in fact usually comes down to, understanding them demands setting that conception aside and seeing their experiences within the framework of their own idea of what selfhood is. And for Java, Bali, and Morocco, at least, that idea differs markedly not only from our own but, no less dramatically and no less instructively, from one to the other.

II

In Java, where I worked in the fifties, I studied a small, shabby inland county-seat sort of place; two shadeless streets of whitewashed wooden shops and offices, and even less substantial bamboo shacks crammed in helter-skelter behind them, the whole surrounded by a great half-circle of densely packed rice-bowl villages. Land was short, jobs were scarce, politics was unstable, health was poor, prices were rising, and life was altogether far from promising, a kind of agitated stagnancy in which, as I once put it, thinking of the curious mixture of borrowed fragments of modernity and exhausted relics of tradition that characterized the place, the future seemed about as remote as the past. Yet in the midst of this depressing scene there was an absolutely astonishing intellectual vitality, a philosophical passion really, and a popular one besides, to track the riddles of existence right down to the ground. Destitute peasants would discuss questions of freedom of the will, illiterate tradesmen discoursed on the properties of God, common laborers had theories about the relations between reason and passion, the nature of time, or the reliability of the senses. And, perhaps most importantly, the problem of the self—its nature, function, and mode of operation—was pursued with the sort of reflective intensity one could find among ourselves in only the most recherché settings indeed.

The central ideas in terms of which this reflection proceeded, and which thus defined its boundaries and the Javanese sense of what a person is, were arranged into two sets of contrasts, at base religious, one between "inside" and "outside," and one between "refined" and "vulgar." These glosses are, of course, crude and imprecise; determining exactly what the terms involved signified, sorting out their shades of meaning, was what all the discussion was about. But together they formed a distinctive conception of the self which, far from being merely theoretical, was the one in terms of which Javanese in fact perceived one another and, of course, themselves.

The "inside"/"outside" words, *batin* and *lair* (terms borrowed, as a matter of fact, from the Sufi tradition of Muslim mysticism, but locally reworked) refer on the one hand to the felt realm of human experience and on the other to the observed realm of human behavior. These have, one hastens to say, nothing to do with "soul" and "body" in our sense, for which there are in fact quite other words with quite other implications. *Batin*, the "inside" word, does not refer to a separate seat of encapsulated spirituality detached or detachable from the body, or indeed to a bounded unit at all, but to the emotional life of human beings taken generally. It consists of the fuzzy, shifting flow of subjective feeling perceived directly in all its phenomenological immediacy but considered to be, at its roots at least, identical across all individuals, whose individuality it thus effaces. And similarly, *lair*, the "outside" word, has nothing to do with the body as an object, even an experienced object. Rather, it refers to that part of human life which, in our culture, strict behaviorists limit themselves to studying—external actions, movements, postures, speech—again conceived as in its essence invariant from one individual to the next. These two sets of phenomena—inward feelings and outward actions—are then regarded not as functions of one another but as independent realms of being to be put in proper order independently.

It is in connection with this "proper ordering" that the contrast between *alus*, the word meaning "pure," "refined," "polished," "exquisite," "ethereal," "subtle," "civilized," "smooth," and *kasar*, the word meaning "impolite," "rough," "uncivilized," "coarse," "insensitive," "vulgar," comes into play. The goal is to be *alus* in both the separated realms of the self. In the inner realm this is to be achieved through religious discipline, much but not all of it mystical. In the outer realm, it is to be achieved through etiquette, the rules of which here are not only extraordinarily elaborate but have something of the force of law. Through meditation the civilized man thins out his emotional life to a kind of constant hum; through etiquette, he both shields that life froth external disruptions and regularizes his outer behavior in such a way that it appears to others as a predictable, undisturbing, elegant, and rather vacant set of choreographed motions and settled forms of speech.

There is much more to all this, because it connects up to both an ontology and an aesthetic. But so far as our problem is concerned, the result is a bifurcate conception of the self, half ungestured feeling and half unfelt gesture. An inner world of stilled emotion and an outer world of shaped behavior confront one another as sharply distinguished realms unto themselves, any particular person being but the momentary locus so to speak, of that confrontation, a passing expression of their permanent existence, their permanent separation, and their permanent need to be kept in their own order. Only when you have seen, as I have a young man whose wife—a woman he had in fact raised from childhood and who had been the center of his life—has suddenly and inexplicably died, greeting everyone with a set smile and formal apologies for his wife's absence and trying, by mystical techniques, to flatten out, as he himself put it, the hills and valleys of his emotion into an even, level plain ("That is what you have to do," he said to me, "be smooth inside and out") can you come, in the fade of our own notions of the intrinsic honesty of deep feeling and the moral importance of personal sincerity, to take the possibility of such a conception of selfhood seriously and appreciate, however inaccessible it is to you, its own sort of force.

III

Bali, where I worked both in another small provincial town, though one rather less drifting and dispirited, and, later, in an upland village of highly skilled musical instruments makers, is of course in many ways similar to Java, with which it shared a common culture to the fifteenth century. But at a deeper level, having continued Hindu while Java was, nominally at least, Islamized, it is quite different. The intricate, obsessive ritual life—Hindu, Buddhist, and Polynesian in about equal proportions—whose development was more or less cut off in Java, leaving its Indic spirit to turn reflective and phenomenological, even quietistic, in the way I have just described, flourished in Bali to reach levels of scale and flamboyance that have startled the world and made the Balinese a much more dramaturgical people with a self to match. What is philosophy in Java is theater in Bali.

As a result, there is in Bali a persistent and systematic attempt to stylize all aspects of personal expression to the point where anything idiosyncratic, anything characteristic of the individual merely because he is who he is physically psychologically, or biographically, is muted in favor of his assigned place in the continuing and, so it is thought, never-changing pageant that is Balinese life It is dramatis personae, not actors, that endure, indeed it is dramatis personae, not actors, that in the proper sense really exist. Physically men come and go, mere incidents in a happenstance history, of no genuine importance even to themselves But the masks they wear, the stage they occupy, the parts they play, and, most important, the spectacle they mount remain and comprise not the façade but the substance of things, not least the self. Shakespeare's old-trouper view of the vanity of action in the face of mortality—all the world's a stage and we but poor players, content to strut our hour, and so on—makes no sense here. There is no make-believe; of course players perish, but the play does not, and it is the latter, the performed rather than the performer, that really matters.

Again, all this is realized not in terms of some general mood the anthropologist in his spiritual versatility somehow captures, but through a set of readily observable symbolic forms: an elaborate repertoire of designations and titles. The Balinese have at least a half-dozen major sorts of labels, ascriptive, fixed, and absolute, which one person can apply to another (or, of course, to himself) to place him among his fellows. There are birth-order markers, kinship terms, caste titles, sex indicators, teknonyms, and so on and so forth, each of which consists not of a mere collection of useful tags but a distinct and bounded, internally very complex, terminological system. When one applies one of these designations or titles (or, as is more common, several at once) to someone, one therefore defines him as a determinate point in a fixed pattern, as the temporary occupant of a particular, quite untemporary, cultural locus. To identify someone, yourself or somebody else, in Bali is thus to locate him within the familiar cast of characters—"king," "grandmother," "third-born," "Brahman"—of which the social drama is, like some stock company roadshow piece—*Charley's Aunt* or *Springtime for Henry*—inevitably composed.

The drama is of course not farce, and especially not transvestite farce, though there are such elements in it. It is an enactment of hierarchy, a theater of status. But that, though critical, is unpursuable here. The immediate point is that, in both their structure and their mode of operation, the terminological systems conduce to a view of the human person as an appropriate representative of a generic type, not a unique creature with a private fate. To see how they do this, how they tend to obscure the mere materialities—biological, psychological, historical—of individual existence in favor of standardized status qualities would involve an extended analysis. But perhaps a single example, the simplest further simplified, will suffice to suggest the pattern.

All Balinese receive what might be called birth-order names. There are four of these, "first-born," "second-born," "third-born," "fourth-born," after which they recycle, so that the fifth-born child is called again "first-born," the sixth "second-born," and so on. Further, these names are bestowed independently of the fates of the children. Dead children, even stillborn ones, count, so that in fact, in this still high-birthrate, high-mortality society, the names do not really tell you anything very reliable about the birth-order relations of concrete individuals. Within a set of living siblings, someone called "first-born" may actually be first, fifth, or ninth-born, or, if somebody is missing, almost anything in between, and someone called "second-born" may in fact be older. The birth-order naming system does not identify individuals as individuals, nor is it intended to; what it does is to suggest that, for all procreating couples, births form a circular succession of "firsts," "seconds," "thirds," and "fourths," an endless four-stage replication of an imperishable form. Physically men appear and disappear as the ephemerae they are, but socially the acting figures remain eternally the same as new "firsts," "seconds," and so on emerge from the timeless world of the gods to replace those who, dying, dissolve once more into it. All the designation and title systems, so I would argue, function in the same way: they represent the most time-saturated aspects of the human condition as but ingredients in an eternal, footlight present.

Nor is this sense the Balinese have of always being on stage a vague and ineffable one either. It is, in fact, exactly summed up in what is surely one of their experience-nearest concepts: *lek*. *Lek* has been variously translated or mistranslated ("shame" is the most common attempt); but what it really means is close to what we call stage fright. Stage fright consists, of course, in the fear that, for want of skill or self-control, or perhaps by mere accident, an aesthetic illusion will not be maintained, that the actor will show through his part. Aesthetic distance collapses, the audience (and the actor) lose sight of Hamlet and gain it, uncomfortably for all concerned, of bumbling John Smith painfully miscast as the Prince of Denmark. In Bali, the case is the same: what is feared is that the public performance to which one's cultural location commits one will be botched and that the personality—as we would call it but the Balinese, of course, not believing in such a thing, would not—of the individual will break through to dissolve his standardized public identity. When this occurs, as it sometimes does, the immediacy of the moment is felt with excruciating intensity and men become suddenly and unwillingly creatural, locked in mutual embarrassment, as though they had happened upon each other's nakedness. It is the fear of faux pas, rendered only that much more probable by the extraordinary ritualization of daily life, that keeps social intercourse on its deliberately narrowed rails and protects the dramatistical sense of self against the disruptive threat implicit in the immediacy and spontaneity even the most passionate ceremoniousness cannot fully eradicate from face-to-face encounters.

IV

Moroccan, Middle Eastern and dry rather than East Asian and wet, extrovert, fluid, activist, masculine, informal to a fault, a Wild West sort of place without the barrooms and the cattle drives, is another kettle of selves altogether. My work there, which began in the mid-sixties, has been centered around a moderately large town or small city in the foothills of the Middle Atlas, about twenty miles south of Fez. It's an old place, probably founded in the tenth century, conceivably even earlier. It has the walls, the gates, the narrow minarets rising to prayer-call platforms of a classical Muslim town, and, from a distance anyway, it is a rather pretty place, an irregular oval of blinding white set in the deep-sea-green of an olive grove oasis, the mountains, bronze and stony here, slanting up immediately behind it. Close up, it is less prepossessing, though more exciting: a labyrinth of passages and alleyways, three quarters of them blind, pressed in by wall-like buildings and curbside shops and filled with a simply astounding variety of very emphatic human beings. Arabs, Berbers, and Jews; tailors, herdsmen, and soldiers, people out of offices, people out of markets, people out of tribes, rich, superrich, poor, superpoor, locals, immigrants, mimic

Frenchmen, unbending medievalists and somewhere according to the official government census for 1960, an unemployed Jewish airplane pilot—the town houses one of the finest collections of rugged individuals I, at least, have ever come up against. Next to Sefrou (the name of the place), Manhattan seems almost monotonous.

Yet no society consists of anonymous eccentrics bouncing off one another like billiard balls, and Moroccans, too, have symbolic means by which to sort people out from one another and form an idea of what it is to be a person. The main such means—not the only one, but I think the most important and the one I want to talk about particularly here—is a peculiar linguistic form called in Arabic the *nisba*. The word derives from the triliteral root, n-s-b, for "ascription," "attribution," "imputation," "relationship," "affinity," "correlation," "connection," "kinship." *Nsib* means "in-law"; *nsab* means "to attribute or impute to"; *munāsaba* means "a relation," "an analogy," "a correspondence"; *mansūb* means "belonging to," "pertaining to"; and so on to at least a dozen derivatives, from *nassāb* ("genealogist") to *nisbīya* ("[physical] relativity").

Nisba itself, then, refers to a combination morphological, grammatical, and semantic process that consists in transforming a noun into what we would call a relative adjective but what for Arabs is just another sort of noun by adding ī (f., *īya*): *Sefrū*/Sefrou—*Sefrūwī*/ native son of Sefrou; *Sūs*/region of southwestern Morocco—*Sūsī*/man coming from that region; *Beni Yazga* /a tribe near Sefrou— *Yazgī*/a member of that tribe; *Yahūd*/ the Jews as a people, Jewry—*Yahūdī* /a Jew; *Adlun* /surname of a prominent Sefrou family— *Adlūnī*/ a member of that family. Nor is the procedure confined to this more or less straightforward "ethnicizing" use, but is employed in a wide range of domains to attribute relational properties to persons. For example, occupation (*hrār*/silk—*hrārī*/ silk merchant); religious sect (*Darqāwā*/a mystical brotherhood—*Darqāwī*/an adept of that brotherhood or spiritual status), (*Ali*/The Prophet's son-in-law—*Alawī*/descendant of the Prophet's son-in-law, and thus of the Prophet).

Now, as once formed, *nisbas* tend to be incorporated into personal names—Umar Al-Buhadiwi/Umar of the Buhadu Tribe; Muhammed Al-Sussi/Muhammed from the Sus Region—this sort of adjectival attributive classification is quite publicly stamped onto an individual's identity. I was unable to find a single case where an individual was generally known, or known about, but his or her *nisba* was not. Indeed, Sefrouis are far more likely to be ignorant of how well-off a man is, how long he has been around, what his personal character is, or where exactly he lives, than they are of what his *nisba* is—Sussi or Sefroui, Buhadiwi or Adluni, Harari or Darqawi. (Of women to whom he is not related that is very likely to be all that he knows—or, more exactly, is permitted to know.) The selves that bump and jostle each other in the alleys of Sefrou gain their definition from associative relations they are imputed to have with the society that surrounds them. They are contextualized persons.

But the situation is even more radical than this; *nisbas* render men relative to their contexts, but as contexts themselves are relative, so too are *nisbas*, and the whole thing rises, so to speak, to the second power: relativism squared. Thus, at one level, everyone in Sefrou has the same *nisba*, or at least the potential of it—namely, Sefroui. However, within Sefrou such a *nisba*, precisely because it does not discriminate, will never be heard as part of an individual designation. It is only outside of Sefrou that the relationship to that particular context becomes identifying. Inside it, he is an Adluni, Alawi, Meghrawi,

Ngadi, or whatever. And similarly within these categories: there are, for example, twelve different *nisbas* (Shakibis, Zuinis, and so forth) by means of which, among themselves, Sefrou Alawis distinguish one another.

The whole matter is far from regular: what level or sort of *nisba* is used and seems relevant and appropriate (to the users, that is) depends heavily on the situation. A man I knew who lived in Sefrou and worked in Fez but came from the Beni Yazgha tribe settled nearby—and from the Hima lineage of the Taghut subfraction of the Wulad Ben Ydir fraction within it—was known as a Sefroui to his work fellows in Fez, a Yazghi to all of us non-Yazghis in Sefrou, an Ydiri to other Beni Yazghas around, except for those who were themselves of the Wulad Ben Ydir fraction, who called him a Taghuti. As for the few other Taghutis, they called him a Himiwi. That is as far as things went here, but not as far as they can go in either direction. Should, by chance, our friend journey to Egypt, he would become a Maghrebi, the *nisba* formed from the Arabic word for North Africa. The social contextualization of persons is pervasive and, in its curiously unmethodical way, systematic. Men do not float as bounded psychic entities, detached from their backgrounds and singularly named. As individualistic, even willful, as the Moroccans in fact are, their identity is an attribute they borrow from their setting.

Now as with the Javanese inside/outside, smooth/rough phenomenological sort of reality dividing, and the absolutizing Buddhist title systems, the *nisba* way of looking at persons—as though they were outlines waiting to be filled in—is not an isolated custom, but part of a total pattern of social life. This pattern is, like the others, difficult to characterize succinctly, but surely one of its outstanding features is a promiscuous tumbling in public settings of varieties of men kept carefully segregated in private ones—all-out cosmopolitanism in the streets, strict communalism (of which the famous secluded woman is only the most striking index) in the home. This is, indeed, the so-called mosaic system of social organization so often held to be characteristic of the Middle East generally: differently shaped and colored chips jammed in irregularly together to generate an intricate overall design within which their individual distinctiveness remains nonetheless intact. Nothing if not diverse, Moroccan society does not cope with its diversity by sealing it into castes, isolating it into tribes, dividing it into ethnic groups, or covering it over with some common-denominator concept of nationality, though, fitfully, all have now and then been tried. It copes with it by distinguishing, with elaborate precision, the contexts—marriage, worship, and to an extent diet, law, and education—within which men are separated by their dissimilitudes, and those—work, friendship, politics, trade—where, however warily and however conditionally, they are connected by them.

To such a social pattern, a concept of selfhood which marks public identity contextually and relativistically, but yet does so in terms—tribal, territorial, linguistic, religious, familial—that grow out of the more private and settled arenas of life and have a deep and permanent resonance there, would seem particularly appropriate. Indeed, the social pattern would seem virtually to create this concept of selfhood, for it produces a situation where people interact with one another in terms of categories whose meaning is almost purely positional, location in the general mosaic, leaving the substantive content of the categories, what they mean subjectively as experienced forms of life, aside as something properly concealed in apartments, temples, and tents. *Nisba* discriminations can be more specific or less, indicate location within the mosaic roughly or finely, and they can be adapted to almost any changes in circumstance. But they cannot carry with them more than the most sketchy, outline implications concerning what men so named as a rule are like. Calling a man a Sefroui is like calling him a San Franciscan: it classifies him, but it does not type him; it places him without portraying him.

It is the *nisba* system's capacity to do this—to create a framework within which persons can be identified in terms of supposedly immanent characteristics (speech, blood, faith, provenance, and the rest)—and yet to minimize the impact of those characteristics in determining the practical relations among such persons in markets, shops, bureaus, fields, cafés, baths, and roadways that makes it so central to the Moroccan idea of the self. *Nisba*-type categorization leads, paradoxically, to a hyperindividualism in public relationships, because by providing only a vacant sketch, and that shifting, of who the actors are—Yazghis, Adlunis, Buhadiwis, or whatever—it leaves the rest, that is, almost everything, to be filled in by the process of interaction itself. What makes the mosaic work is the confidence that one can be as totally pragmatic, adaptive, opportunistic, and generally ad hoc in one's relations with others—a fox among foxes, a crocodile among crocodiles—as one wants without any risk of losing one's sense of who one is. Selfhood is never in danger because, outside the immediacies of procreation and prayer, only its coordinates are asserted.

V

Now, without trying to tie up the dozens of loose ends I have not only left dangling in these rather breathless accounts of the senses of selfhood of nearly ninety million people but have doubtless frazzled even more, let us return to the question of what all this can tell us, or could if it were done adequately, about "the native's point of view" in Java, Bali, and Morocco. Are we, in describing symbol uses, describing perceptions, sentiments, outlooks, experiences? And in what sense? What do we claim when we claim that we understand the semiotic means by which, in this case, persons are defined to one another? That we know words or that we know minds?

In answering this question, it is necessary, I think, first to notice the characteristic intellectual movement, the inward conceptual rhythm, in each of these analyses, and indeed in all similar analyses, including those of Malinowski—namely, a continuous dialectical tacking between the most local of local detail and the most global of global structure in such a way as to bring them into simultaneous view. In seeking to uncover the Javanese, Balinese, or Moroccan sense of self, one oscillates restlessly between the sort of exotic minutiae (lexical antitheses, categorical schemes, morphophonemic transformations) that make even the best ethnographies a trial to read and the sort of sweeping characterizations ("quietism," "dramatism," "contextualism") that make all but the most pedestrian of them somewhat implausible. Hopping back and forth between the whole conceived through the parts that actualize it and the parts conceived through the whole that motivates them, we seek to turn them, by a sort of intellectual perpetual motion, into explications of one another.

All this is, of course, but the now familiar trajectory of what Dilthey called the hermeneutic circle, and my argument here is merely that it is as central to ethnographic interpretation, and thus to the penetration of other people's modes of thought, as it is to literary, historical, philological, psychoanalytic, or biblical interpretation, or for that matter to the informal annotation of everyday experience we call common sense. In order to follow a baseball game one must understand what a bat, a hit, an inning, a left fielder, a squeeze play, a hanging curve, and a tightened infield are, and what the game in which these "things" are elements is all about. When an *explication de texte* critic like Leo Spitzer attempts to interpret Keats's "Ode on a Grecian Urn," he does so by repetitively asking himself the alternating question "What is the whole poem about?" and "What exactly has Keats seen (or chosen to show us) depicted on the urn he is describing?," emerging at the end of an advancing spiral of general observations and specific remarks with a reading of the poem as an assertion of the triumph of the aesthetic mode of perception over the historical. In the same way, when a meanings-and-symbols ethnographer like myself attempts to find out what some pack of natives conceive a person to be, he moves back and forth between asking himself, "What is the general form of their life?" and "What exactly are the vehicles in which that form is embodied?," emerging in the end of a similar sort of spiral with the notion that they see the self as a composite, a persona, or a point in a pattern. You can no more know what *lek* is if you do not know what Balinese dramatism is than you can know what a catcher's mitt is if you do not know what baseball is. And you can no more know what mosaic social organization is if you do not know what a *nisba* is than you can know what Keats's Platonism is if you are unable to grasp, to use Spitzer's own formulation, the "intellectual thread of thought" captured in such fragment phrases as "Attic shape," "silent form," "bride of quietness," "cold pastoral," "silence and slow time," "peaceful citadel," or "ditties of no tone."

In short, accounts of other peoples' subjectivities can be built up without recourse to pretensions to more-than-normal capacities for ego effacement and fellow feeling. Normal capacities in these respects are, of course, essential, as is their cultivation, if we expect people to tolerate our intrusions into their lives at all and accept us as persons worth talking to. I am certainly not arguing for insensitivity here, and hope I have not demonstrated it. But whatever accurate or half-accurate sense one gets of what one's informants are, as the phrase goes, really like does not come from the experience of that acceptance as such, which is part of one's own biography, not of theirs. It comes from the ability to construe their modes of expression, what I would call their symbol systems, which such an acceptance allows one to work toward developing. Understanding the form and pressure of, to use the dangerous word one more time, natives' inner lives is more like grasping a proverb, catching an allusion, seeing a joke—or, as I have suggested, reading a poem—than it is like achieving communion.

Originally published in Richard A. Scweder (eds), *Robert A. Levine, Culture Theory*, (Cambridge University Press, 1984): 123–136. Printed here with the permission of the publisher.

CHARLES TAYLOR

Three Malaises

I want to write here about some of the malaises of modernity. I mean by this features of our contemporary culture and society that people experience as a loss or a decline, even as our civilization "develops." Sometimes people feel that some important decline has occurred during the last years or decades—since the Second World War, or the 1950s, for instance. And sometimes the loss is felt over a much longer historical period: the whole modern era from the seventeenth century is frequently seen as the time frame of decline. Yet although the time scale can vary greatly, there is certain convergence on the themes of decline. They are often variations around a few central malaises. I want to pick out two such central themes here, and then throw in a third that largely derives from these two. These three by no means exhaust the topic, but they do get at a great deal of what troubles and perplexes us about modern society.

The worries I will be talking about are very familiar. No one needs to be reminded of them; they are discussed, bemoaned, challenged, and argued against all the time in all sorts of media. That sounds like a reason not to talk about them further. But I believe that this great familiarity hides bewilderment, that we don't really understand these changes that worry us, that the usual run of debate about them in fact misrepresents them—and thus makes us misconceive what we can do about them. The changes defining modernity are both well-known and very perplexing, and that is why it's worth talking still more about them.

Individualism

The first source of worry is individualism. Of course, individualism also names what many people consider the finest achievement of modem civilization. We live in a world where people have a right to choose for themselves their own pattern of life, to decide in conscience what convictions to espouse, to determine the shape of their lives in a whole host of ways that their ancestors couldn't control. And these rights are generally defended by our legal systems. In principle, people are no longer sacrificed to the demands of supposedly sacred orders that transcend them.

Very few people want to go back on this achievement. Indeed, many think that it is still incomplete, that economic arrangements, or patterns of family life, or traditional notions of hierarchy still restrict too much our freedom to be ourselves. But many of us are also ambivalent. Modem freedom was won by our breaking loose from older moral horizons. People used to see themselves as part of a larger order. In some cases, this was a cosmic order, a "great chain of Being," in which humans figured in their proper place along with angels, heavenly bodies, and our fellow earthly creatures. This hierarchical order in the universe was reflected in the hierarchies of human society. People were often locked into a given place, a role and station that was properly theirs and from which it was almost unthinkable to deviate. Modern freedom came about through the discrediting of such orders.

But at the same time as they restricted us, these orders gave meaning to the world and to the activities of social life. The things that surround us were not just potential raw materials or instruments for our projects, but they had the significance given them by their place in the chain of being. The eagle was not just another bird, but the king of a whole domain of animal life. By the same token, the rituals and norms of society had more than merely instrumental significance. The discrediting of these orders has been called the "disenchantment" of the world. With it, things lost some of their magic.

A vigorous debate has been going on for a couple of centuries as to whether this was an unambiguously good thing. But this is not what I want to focus on here. I want to look rather at what some have seen to be the consequences for human life and meaning.

The worry has been repeatedly expressed that the individual lost something important along with the larger social and cosmic horizons of action. Some have written of this as the loss of a heroic dimension to life. People no longer have a sense of a higher purpose, of something worth dying for. Alexis de Tocqueville sometimes talked like this in the last century referring to the "petits et vulgaires plaisirs" that people tend to seek in the democratic age. In another articulation, we suffer from a lack of passion. Kierkegaard saw "the present age" in these terms. And Nietzsche's "last men" are at the final nadir of this decline; they have no aspiration left in life but to a "pitiable comfort."

This loss of purpose was linked to a narrowing. People lost the broader vision because they focused on their individual lives. Democratic equality, says Tocqueville, draws the individual towards himself. In other words, the dark side of individualism is a centring on the self, which both flattens and narrows our lives, makes them poorer in meaning, and less concerned with others or society.

This worry has recently surfaced again in concern at the fruits of a "permissive society," the doings of the "me generation," or the prevalence of "narcissism," to take just three of the best-known contemporary formulations. The sense that lives have been flattened and narrowed, and that this is connected to an abnormal and regrettable self-absorption, has returned in forms specific to contemporary culture. This defines the first theme I want to deal with.

Instrumental Reason

The disenchantment of the world is connected to another massively important phenomenon of the modern age, which also greatly troubles many people. We might call this the primacy of instrumental reason. By "instrumental reason" I mean the kind of rationality we draw on when we calculate the most economical application of means to a given end. Maximum efficiency, the best cost-output ratio, is its measure of success.

No doubt sweeping away the old orders has immensely widened the scope of instrumental reason. Once society no longer has a sacred structure, once social arrangements and modes of action are no longer grounded in the order of things or the will of God, they are in a sense up for grabs. They can be redesigned with their consequences for the happiness and wellbeing of individuals as our goal. The yardstick that henceforth applies is that of instrumental reason. Similarly, once the creatures that surround us lose the significance that accrued to their place in the chain of being, they are open to being treated as raw materials or instruments for our projects.

In one way this change has been liberating. But there is also a widespread unease that instrumental reason not only has enlarged its scope but also threatens to take over our lives. The fear is that things that ought to be determined by other criteria will be decided in terms of efficiency or "cost-benefit" analysis, that the independent ends that ought to be guiding our lives will be eclipsed by the demand to maximize output. There are lots of things one can point to that give substance to this worry: for instance, the ways the demands of economic growth are used to justify very unequal distributions of wealth and income, or the way these same demands make us insensitive to the needs of the environment, even to the point of potential disaster. Or else, we can think of the way much of our social planning, in crucial areas like risk assessment, is dominated by forms of cost-benefit analysis that involve grotesque calculations, putting dollar assessments on human lives.

The primacy of instrumental reason is also evident in the prestige and aura that surround technology, and makes us believe that we should seek technological solutions even when something very different is called for. We see this often enough in the realm of politics. But it also invades other domains, such as medicine. Patricia Benner has argued in a number of important works that the technological approach in medicine has often sidelined the kind of care that involves treating the patient as a whole person with a life story and not as the locus of a technical problem. Society and the medical establishment frequently undervalue the contribution of nurses, who more often than not provide this humanly sensitive caring, as against that of specialists with high-tech knowledge.

The dominant place of technology is also thought to have contributed to the narrowing and flattening of our lives that I have just been discussing in connection with the first theme. People have spoken of a loss of resonance, depth, or richness in our human surroundings. Almost 150 years ago, Marx, in the Communist Manifesto, remarked that one of the results of capitalist development was that "all that is solid melts in air." The claim is that the solid, lasting, often expressive objects that served us in the past are being set aside for the quick, shoddy, replaceable commodities with which we now surround ourselves. Albert Borgman speaks of the "device paradigm," whereby we withdraw more and more from "manifold engagement" with our environment and instead request and get products designed to deliver some circumscribed benefit. He contrasts what is involved in heating our homes, with the contemporary central heating furnace, with what this same function entailed in pioneer times, when the whole family had to be involved in cutting and stacking the wood and feeding the stove or fireplace. Hannah Arendt focused on the more and more ephemeral quality of modem objects of use and argued that "the reality and reliability of the human world rest primarily on the fact that we are surrounded by things more permanent than the activity by which they are produced." This permanence comes under threat in a world of modern commodities.

This sense of threat is increased by the knowledge that this primacy is not just a matter of a perhaps unconscious orientation, which we are prodded and tempted into by the modern age. As such it would be hard enough to combat, but at least it might yield to persuasion. But it is also clear that powerful mechanisms of social life press us in this direction. A manager in spite of her own orientation may be forced by the conditions of the market to adopt a maximizing strategy she feels is destructive. A bureaucrat, in spite of his personal insight, may be forced by the rules under which he operates to make a decision he knows to be against humanity and good sense.

Marx and Weber and other great theorists have explored these impersonal mechanisms, which Weber has designated by the evocative term of "the iron cage." And some people have wanted to draw from these analyses the conclusion that we are utterly helpless in the face of such forces, or at least helpless unless we totally dismantle the institutional structures under which we have been operating for the last centuries—that is, the market and the state. This aspiration seems so unrealizable today that it amounts to declaring us helpless.

I believe that these strong theories of fatality are abstract and wrong. Our degrees of freedom are not zero. There is a point to deliberating what ought to be our ends, and whether instrumental reason ought to have a lesser role in our lives than it does. But the truth in these analyses is that it is not just a matter of changing the outlook of individuals, it is not just a battle of "hearts and minds," important as this is. Change in this domain will have to be institutional as well, even though it cannot be as sweeping and total as the great theorists of revolution proposed.

Loss of Freedom

This brings us to the political level, and to the feared consequences for political life of individualism and instrumental reason. One I have already introduced. It is that the institutions and structures of industrial-technological society severely restrict our choices, that they force societies as well as individuals to give a weight to instrumental reason that in serious moral deliberation we would never do, and which may even be highly destructive. A case in point is our great difficulties in tackling even vital threats to our lives from environmental disasters, like the thinning ozone layer. The society structured around instrumental reason can be seen as imposing a great loss of freedom, on both individuals and the group—because it is not just our social decisions that are shaped by these forces. An individual life style is also hard to sustain against the grain. For instance, the whole design of some modern cities makes it hard to function without a car, particularly where public transport has been eroded in favour of the private automobile.

But there is another kind of loss of freedom, which has also been widely discussed, most memorably by Alexis de Tocqueville. A society in which people end up as the kind of individuals who are "enclosed in their own hearts" is one where few will want to participate actively in self-government. They will prefer to stay at home and enjoy the satisfactions of private life, as long as the government of the day produces the means to these satisfactions and distributes them widely.

This opens the danger of a new, specifically modern form of despotism, which Tocqueville calls "soft" despotism. It will not be a tyranny of terror and oppression as in the old days. The government will be mild and paternalistic. It may even keep democratic forms, with periodic elections. But in fact, everything will be run by an "immense tutelary power," over which people will have little control. The only defence against this, Tocqueville thinks, is a vigorous political culture in which participation is valued, at several levels of government and in voluntary associations as well. But the atomism of the self-absorbed individual militates against this. Once participation declines, once the lateral associations that were its vehicles wither away, the individual citizen is left alone in the face of the vast bureaucratic state and feels, correctly, powerless. This demotivates the citizen even further, and the vicious cycle of soft despotism is reinforced.

Perhaps something like this alienation from the public sphere and consequent loss of political control is happening in our highly centralized and bureaucratic political world. Many contemporary thinkers have seen Tocqueville's work as prophetic. If this is so, what we are in danger of losing is political control over our destiny, something we could exercise in common as citizens. This is what Tocqueville called "political liberty." What is threatened here is our dignity as citizens. The impersonal mechanisms mentioned above may reduce our degrees of freedom as a society but the loss of political liberty would mean that even the choices left would no longer be made by ourselves as citizens, but by irresponsible tutelary power.

These, then, are the three malaises about modernity. The first fear is about what we might call a loss of meaning, the fading of moral horizons. The second concerns the eclipse of ends, in face of rampant instrumental reason. And the third is about a loss of freedom.

Of course, these are not uncontroversial. I have spoken about worries that are widespread and mentioned influential authors, but nothing here is agreed. Even those who share some form of these worries dispute vigorously how they should be formulated. And there are lots of people who want to dismiss them out of hand. Those who are deeply into what the critics call the "culture of narcissism" think of the objectors as hankering for an earlier, more oppressive age. Adepts of modern technological reason think the critics of the primacy of the instrumental are reactionary and obscurantist, scheming to deny the world the benefits of science. And there are proponents of mere negative freedom who believe that the value of political liberty is overblown, and that a society in which scientific management combines with maximum independence for each individual is what we ought to aim at. Modernity has its boosters as well as its knockers.

An abridged version which originally appeared in *The Ethics of Authenticity* (Cambridge: Mass: Harvard University Press, 1991, © Charles Taylor and the Canadian Broadcasting Company): 1-12. It is printed here with the permission of the publisher.

What I Have Lived For

Three passions, simple but overwhelmingly strong, have governed my life: the longing for love, the search for knowledge, and unbearable pity for the suffering of mankind. These passions, like great winds, have blown me hither and thither, in a wayward course, over a deep ocean of anguish, reaching to the very verge of despair.

I have sought love, first, because it brings ecstasy—ecstasy so great that I would often have sacrificed all the rest of life for a few hours of this joy. I have sought it, next, because it relieves loneliness—that terrible loneliness in which one shivering consciousness looks over the rim of the world into the cold unfathomable lifeless abyss. I have sought it, finally, because in the union of love I have seen, in a mystic miniature, the prefiguring vision of the heaven that saints and poets have imagined. This is what I sought, and though it might seem too good for human life, this is what—at last—I have found.

With equal passion I have sought knowledge. I have wished to understand the hearts of men. I have wished to know why the stars shine. And I have tried to apprehend the Pythagorean power by which number holds sway above the flux. A little of this, but not much, I have achieved.

Love and knowledge, so far as they were possible, led upward toward the heavens. But always pity brought me back to earth. Echoes of cries of pain reverberate in my heart. Children in famine, victims tortured by oppressors, helpless old people a hated burden to their sons, and the whole world of loneliness, poverty, and pain make a mockery of what human life should be. I long to alleviate the evil, but I cannot, and I too suffer.

This has been my life. I have found it worth living, and would gladly live it again if the chance were offered me.

This is the prologue to *In Autobiography* (Routledge, 1998). Printed here with the permission of the Bertrand Russell Peace Foundation and Taylor and Francis.

PART TWO

Cultural Variations in Everyday Life

Introduction

It might be odd to begin our discussion of abiding values and normative expectations by using Orhan Pamuk's treatment of "*Hüzün*," extracted from his recent autobiographical portrait of *Istanbul*. *Hüzün*, etymologically in both Turkish and Arabic, is associated with melancholy and conveys a sense of deep spiritual loss, grief and agony. Yet to Pamuk it is seen as a cherished value and preferential state of mind. He provides a rich and vivid inventory of all the scenes, objects, characters and memories which evoke the sense of *Hüzün* not as the melancholy of a solitary person but as the "black mood shared by millions of people and binds them together... and which they absorb with pride and share as a community." To him this pervasive feeling of pain, conveying worldly failure, is unique to Istanbul and is not at odds with communal purpose.

Interestingly, rather than dwelling on its bleak and despondent features, *Hüzün* is transformed by Pamuk into a positive and enabling collective state of mind; a source of esteem and honor. He traces its emergence in two distinct philosophical traditions, namely worldly pleasures, and sufi and mystical predispositions. In this sense it becomes "ultimately self-affirming as it is negating". Much like Levi-Strauss's treatment of *distress* in tropical cities, *Hüzün* should not be seen in terms of the anguish and suffering which afflicts a solitary being. Though it is associated with pain, it evolves into a communal feeling, a coveted and uplifting spiritual state cultivated and shared by millions... "It is the pain they feel for all that which has been lost, but it is also what compels them to invest new defeats and new ways to express their impoverishment."

In this sense, the *Hüzün* Pamuk is celebrating has little to share with the anguished literary heroes of Balzac and Montaigue whose solitary sorrow "eats away at the mind of a man who lives alone with his books." Rather, he has much in common with the emotional solitude of Thoreau or with how Dostoyevsky struggled to understand the pride Genevans took in their city. "They gaze at even the simplest objects, like street poles, as if they are the most splendid and glorious things on earth."

Pamuk concludes his chapter by reiterating the following parting message:

> The *Hüzün* of Istanbul suggests nothing of an individual standing against society; on the contrary, it suggests an erosion of the will to stand against the values and mores of the community, encourages us to be content with little, honoring the virtues of harmony, uniformity, humility. *Hüzün* teaches endurance in times of poverty and deprivation, it also encourages us to read life and history of the city in reverse. It allows the people of Istanbul to think of defeat and poverty not as a historical endpoint, but as an honorable beginning fixed long before they were born. So the honor we derive from it can be rather misleading. But it does suggest that Istanbul does not bear its *Hüzün* as an incurable illness that has spread throughout the city, as an immutable poverty to be endured like grief, or even as a perplexing failure to be viewed in black and white: it bears its *Hüzün* with honor.

Just like *Hüzün* was transformed by Pamuk into an enabling spiritual force of renewal, Fadwa El Guindi treats veiling in contemporary Egypt as a social movement which incorporates both sacred and ideological considerations. Rather than seeing the veil as a monolithic and fixed cultural entity representing the seclusion and isolation of woman within an austere and prohibitive political culture, she treats it instead as a movement which has gone through several transitional stages, particularly since the 1970s.

She begins by reminding us that the experience of veiling in Egypt is quite different from those in Iran or Turkey. In Iran the *chador* (a black head-to-toe wrap) is a body cover largely worn by rural and urban traditional women before the revolution. To Westernize the country, the *chador* was banned by the Shah. The Khomeini Revolution, by way of preserving the purity and religiosity of Islamic rituals and symbols, imposed the veil. In Turkey, changes in dress codes were also subjected to state legislation. Of course, Kamal Attaturk, the founder of the Turkish Republic, prohibited the fez and other traditional symbols and artifacts. Today Turkey is still trapped between the contested dualism of advocates of Islamism who wish to restore the modesty of the veil and the extreme secularists who want to ban it.

The experience of Egypt differs yet in another sense in that it was primarily a voluntary grass-root, bottom-up movement, introduced by college women and not imposed by the al-Azhar authorities, who normally *prescribe* Islamic behavior by decree. The public mood of religiosity, *mitdayyinin*, was traced by El Guindi to two socio-political events: the 1967 defeat in the Six Day War and 1973 victory in the Ramadan (or October) War. In the aftermath of the swift and humiliating 1967 defeat, a climate of intense religious zeal was a reaction to pervasive feelings of doubt, humiliation, insecurity and diminished national esteem. Disbelief turned to disillusion, anger, discontent and resignation. Sufi and mystical orders became popular. If defeat brought people close to God, so did victory; particularly over the myth of the invincible Israel. The fact that this feat was accomplished during the holy month of Ramadan, becoming a *mitdayyin* was elevated into a state of religious conviction (*Iqtina'*). They also shared the bond of compliance, discipline and commitment (*Iltizam*).

Interestingly, in the early phase of the movement, the core of its informal student membership did not form their own separate organizations. Rather, they continued as assimilated students interacting with the rest. Eventually, they formed as a family (*Osrah*) and started to establish their own Islamic-based ideological groups in opposition to the recreational and mainstream social clubs.

By the mid 1980s, as the movement grew stronger and extended beyond university campuses, the label *mitdayyinin* gave way to *Islamyyin*. It is then that it became a major oppositional political force and *al-Ziyy al Islami* (the Islamic dress) started to assume the image of "privacy, humility, piety and moderation, the cornerstones of the idealized Islamic belief system."

El Guindi devotes the bulk of her paper to a close documentation of the origin and reformulation of this dress code to specific *suras* in the Qura'n and Hadith to account for how it evolved into a distinct social and moral code of conduct. For example, and unlike other religious, "Orthodox Islam accepts sexuality as a normative aspect of both ordinary and religious life and fluidity accommodates both sacred and worldly activity." El Guindi invokes particular suras to show how "concealing and revealing are tied to cultural notions of respectability, sexuality, eroticism and privacy... and that within Islam a women's sexuality does not diminish her respectability."

El Guindi's conclusion in which she asserts that the popularity of the Islamic dress could be seen as manifestation of the renewal of traditional cultural identity deserves to be quoted in full:

> By dressing this way in public these young women translated their version of Islamic ideals by becoming exemplary contemporary models. Encoded in the dress style is a new public appearance and demeanor that reaffirms an Islamic identity and morality and rejects Western materialism, consumerism, commercialism, and values. The vision behind the Islamic dress is rooted in these women's understanding of early Islam and, as earlier presented, in primary and secondary textual sources. But it is a contemporary movement about contemporary issues... Reserve and restraint in behavior, voice and body movement are not restrictions. They mobilize a renewal of traditional cultural identity.

In her study of volunteerism of women in *al-Dahiyya* (the southern suburbs of Beirut), Lara Deeb provides proof that the binary distinctions between the sacred and secular, traditional and modern, or the public/private spheres are inadequate in helping us understand realities on the ground. She tells us that women's motivation for volunteering vary, but no matter how and why a woman initially joins a *jam'iyya*, it soon becomes an integral part of her life and identity, especially her identity as a pious member of her community. In fact, the participation of women in community services is transformed into a religious duty on par with prayer.

Her vivid data and participant observation documents the role of *mu'amalat*, mutual reciprocal social relations, as a venue through which personal piety is brought into the public sphere. Demonstrating a sense of social responsibility becomes a critical aspect of being a moral person for many volunteers, and it is important to fulfill that responsibility before oneself and God.

Deeb does not shy away from asserting that community service in *al-Dahiyya* is gender-specific, holding particular salience for women. Indeed, in her view, women are believed to be inherently suitable for community work due to an understanding of essentialized sex differences that posits women as more nurturing than men. She goes further, to maintain that women's natural empathetic and emotional capacities equip her to handle the emotional stress of dealing with poverty, proper upbringing of orphans and education of the poor.

Interestingly, these essentialized sex differences are not necessarily interpreted as limiting women to domestically oriented roles in society. Many in *al-Dahiyya* believe women have the potential to make excellent doctors, engineers, politicians. The only exception is the battlefield where women are still considered to be innately unsuited to military service. Yet, volunteering for many women is seen as a form of martyrdom paid, as Deeb puts it, in sweat instead of blood.

Finally, Deeb advances the notion that women volunteers in *al-Dahiyya* challenge the conventional assumptions regarding the gendered public/private divide. Clearly, participating in voluntary associations, as part of a public sphere, is not a monopoly of men. Equally important it is also a reflection of the porosity and the blurring of the public/private dichotomous division.

Naturally, it is through socialization that the basic norms and expected patterns of behavior are imparted to children. Although these normative expectations are universal in Man's experience, each local manifestation is unique. The essay of Susan Davis on "Growing up in Morocco" graphically illustrates this. After observing childrearing practices in a Moroccan town in the mid 1970s, Davis noted some striking patterns which departed from common practices observed among American families. As expected, gender and patrilineal considerations were very visible. Males are preferred for social and economic reasons and not necessarily religious reasons. Despite the taxing demands women are beset with, they seem to welcome the added chore of looking after a child without any resentment. It is not considered a burden or a disagreeable nuisance.

Though a child is occasionally cuddled, fondled and briefly admired, it is not the object of too much attention on the focal interest of the group. Indeed, very early a child is introduced to *ghder* (treachery and betrayal) to realize the hardship and setbacks he is destined to face in life. This is why the process of weaning is very abrupt. On the whole Moroccan children are less sheltered and protected and, hence, grow up to become more resilient, durable and independent. Much of their early socialization is devoted to acquisition of pragmatic skills.

Interestingly, the more favored attention infant boys receive, clearly an inveterate gender bias, is also marked in early childhood. Somehow, girls do not seem upset by such discrepant expectations. Indeed, they do not feel upset, neglected or slighted when boys receive much privileged treatment. For example, boys are allowed, and sometimes encouraged, to hit their older sisters. The latter, even if and when it seems legitimate, are not allowed to reciprocate. They are expected to accept such harsh rebuke with resignation.

As in other segments of Arab society, *hushuma* (shame) is the most common form of controlling behavior. Other than this pervasive but elusive normative expectation, there seems to be no concentrated efforts to teach children precisely what is right or wrong. They are also punished and rewarded indiscriminately, depending on the mood or whim of the parent rather than the nature of the particular act.

Hüzün

Hüzün, the Turkish word for melancholy, has an Arabic root; when it appears in the Koran (as "*huzn*" in two verses and "hazen") in three others) it means much the same thing as the contemporary Turkish word. The Prophet Mohammed referred to the year in which he lost both his wife Hatice and his uncle, Ebu Talip, as "*Senettul hüzün*" or the year of melancholy; this confirms that the word is meant to convey a feeling of deep spiritual loss. But if *hüzün* begins its life as a word for loss and the spiritual agony and grief attending it, my own readings indicate a small philosophical faultline developing over the next few centuries of Islamic history; with time we see the emergence of two very different *hüzüns*, each evoking a distinct philosophical tradition.

According to the first tradition, we experience the thing called *hüzün* when we have invested too much in worldly pleasures and material gain: the implication is that "if you hadn't involved yourself so deeply in this transitory world, if you were a good and true Muslim, you wouldn't care so much about your worldly losses." The second tradition, which rises out of Sufi mysticism, offers a more positive and compassionate understanding of the word and of the place of loss and grief in life. To the Sufis, *hüzün* is the spiritual anguish we feel because we cannot be close enough to Allah, because we cannot do enough for Allah in this world. A true Sufi follower would pay no attention to worldly concerns like death, let alone goods or possessions: he suffers from grief, emptiness and inadequacy because he can never be close enough to Allah, because his apprehension of Allah is not deep enough. Moreover, it is the absence, not the presence, of *hüzün* that causes him distress. It is the failure to experience *hüzün* that leads him to feel it; he suffers because he has not suffered enough; and it is by following this logic to its conclusion that Islamic culture has come to hold *hüzün* in high esteem. If *hüzün* has been central to Istanbul culture, poetry and everyday life over the past two centuries, if it dominates our music, it must be at least partly because we see it as an honor. But to understand what *hüzün* has come to mean over the past century, to convey its enduring power, it is not enough to speak of the honor that Sufi tradition has brought to the word. To convey the spiritual importance of *hüzün* in the music of Istanbul over the last hundred years, to understand why *hüzün* dominates not just the mood of modern Turkish poetry but its symbolism, and why, like the great symbols of Divan poetry, it has suffered from overuse and even abuse; to understand the central importance of *hüzün* as a cultural concept conveying worldly failure, listlessness and spiritual suffering, it is not enough to grasp the history of the word and the honor we attach to it. If I am to convey the intensity of the *hüzün* that Istanbul caused me to feel as a child, I must describe the history of the city following the destruction of the Ottoman Empire, and—even more important—the way this history is reflected in the city's "beautiful" landscapes and its people. The *hüzün* of Istanbul is not just the mood evoked by its music and its poetry, it is a way of looking at life that implicates us all, not only a spiritual state, but a state of mind that is ultimately as life affirming as it is negating.

To explore the ambiguities of the word, we must return to the thinkers who see *hüzün* not as a poetic concept or a state of grace but as an illness. According to El Kindi, *hüzün* was associated not just with the loss or death of a loved one, but also with other spiritual afflictions like anger, love, rancor and groundless fear. (The philosopher-doctor Ibn Sina saw *hüzün* in the same broad terms, and this was why he suggested that the proper way of diagnosing a youth in the grip of a helpless passion was to ask the boy for the girl's name while taking his pulse.) The approach outlined by these classic Islamic thinkers is similar to the one proposed in *The Anatomy of Melancholy*, Burton's enigmatic but entertaining tome of the early seventeenth century. Like Ibn Sina, Burton takes an encyclopedic view of the "black pain", listing fear of death, love, defeat, evil deeds and any number of drinks and foods as its possible causes, and his list of cures ranges just as broadly; combining medical science with philosophy, he advises his readers to seek relief in reason, work, resignation, virtue, discipline and fasting—another interesting instance of common ground underlying these two texts that rise out of such very different cultural traditions.

So *hüzün* stems from the same "black passion" as melancholy, whose etymology refers to a basis in humors first conceived in Aristotle's day (*melan khole*—black bile) and gives us the coloration normally associated with this feeling and the all-occluding pain it implies. But here we come to the essential difference between the two words: Burton, who was proud to be afflicted, believed that melancholy paved the way to a happy solitude; because it strengthened his imaginative powers, it was, from time to time, to be joyfully affirmed; it did not matter if melancholy was the result of solitude or the cause; in both instances, Burton saw solitude as the heart, the very essence, of melancholy. But, for El Kindi, who saw *hüzün* both as a mystical state (engendered by the frustration of our common aim to be at one with Allah) and as an illness, the central preoccupation, as with all classic Islamic thinkers, was the *cemaat*, or the community of believers. He judged *hüzün* by the values of the *cemaat* and suggested remedies that return us to it: essentially, he saw *hüzün* as an experience at odds with the communal purpose.

My starting point was the emotion that a child might feel while looking through a steamy window. Now we begin to understand *hüzün* as, not the melancholy of a solitary person, but the black mood shared by millions of people together. What I am trying to explain is the *hüzün* of an entire city, of Istanbul.

But what I am trying to describe now is not the melancholy of Istanbul, but the *hüzün* in which we see ourselves reflected, the *hüzün* we absorb with pride and share as a community. To feel this *hüzün* is to see the scenes, evoke the memories, in which the city itself becomes the very illustration, the very essence, of *hüzün*. I am speaking of the evenings when the sun sets early, of the fathers under the street lamps in the back streets returning home carrying plastic bags. Of the Bosphorus ferries moored to deserted stations in the middle of winter, where sleepy sailors scrub the decks, a pail in their hand and one eye on the black-and-white television in the distance; of the old booksellers who lurch from one financial crisis to the next and then wait shivering all day for a customer to appear; of the barbers who complain that men don't shave as much after an economic crisis; of the children who play ball between the cars on cobblestone streets; of the covered women who stand at remote bus stops clutching plastic shopping bags and speaking to no one as they wait for the bus that never arrives; of the empty boathouses of the old Bosphorus villas; of the teahouses packed to the rafters with unemployed men; of the patient pimps striding up and down the city's greatest square on summer evenings in search of one last drunken tourist; the crowds rushing to catch ferries on winter evenings; of the wooden buildings whose every board creaked even when they were pashas' mansions, and all the more now that they have become municipal headquarters; of the women peeking through the curtains as they wait for husbands who never manage to come home until late at night; of the old men selling thin religious treatises, prayer beads and pilgrimage oils in the court yards of mosques; of the tens of thousands of identical apartment-house entrances, their façades discolored by dirt, rust, soot and dust; of the broken seesaws in empty parks; of ships' horns booming through the fog; of the city walls, ruins since the end of the Byzantine Empire; of the markets that empty in the evenings; of the dervish lodges, the *tekkes*, that have crumbled: of the seagulls perched on rusty barges caked with moss and mussels, unflinching under the pelting rain; of the tiny ribbons of smoke rising from the single chimneys of hundred-year-old mansions on the coldest day of the year; of the crowds of men fishing from the sides of the Galata Bridge; of the cold reading rooms of libraries; of the street photographers; of the smell of exhaled breath in the cinemas, once glittering affairs with gilded ceilings, now porn cinemas frequented by shamefaced men; of the avenues where you never see a woman alone after sunset; of the crowds gathering around the doors of the state-controlled brothels on one of those hot, blustery clays when the wind is coming from the south; of the young girls who queue at the doors of establishments selling cut-rate meat; of the holy messages spelt out in lights between the minarets of mosques on holidays that are missing letters where the bulbs have burned out; of the walls covered with frayed and blackened posters; of the tired old *dolmuşes*, 1950 Chevrolets that would be museum pieces in any Western city but serve here as shared taxis, huffing and puffing up the city's narrow alleys and dirty thoroughfares; of the buses packed with passengers; of the mosques whose lead plates and rain gutters are forever being stolen; of the city cemeteries that seem like gateways to a second world and of their cypress trees; of the little children in the streets who try to sell the same packet of tissues to every passer-by; of the clock towers no one ever notices; of the history books in which children read about the victories of the Ottoman Empire and of the beatings these same children receive at home; of the days when everyone has to stay at home so that the electoral roll can be compiled; of the days when everyone has to stay at home so that the census can be taken; of the days when a sudden curfew is announced to facilitate the search for terrorists, and everyone sits at home fearfully awaiting "the officials"; of the man who has been selling postcards in the same spot for the past forty years; of the beggars who accost you in the least likely places and those who stand in the same spot uttering the same appeal day after day; of the powerful whiffs of urine that hit you on crowded avenues, ships, passageways and underpasses; of the earliest hours of the morning, when everyone is asleep except for the fishermen heading out to sea; of the third-rate singers doing their best to imitate American singers and Turkish pop stars in cheap nightclubs, and of first-rate singers, too; of the bored high-school students in never-ending English classes where after six years no one has learned to say any thing but "yes" and "no"; of everything being broken, worn-out, past its prime; of the storks flying south from the Balkans and north and western Europe as autumn nears, gazing down over the entire city as they waft over the Bosphorus and the islands of the Marmara; of the crowds of men smoking cigarettes after the national football matches, which during my childhood never failed to end in abject defeat: I speak of them all.

It is by seeing *hüzün*, by paying our respects to its manifestations in the city's streets and views and people that we at last come to sense it everywhere: on cold winter mornings, when the sun suddenly falls on the Bosphorus and that faint vapor begins to rise from the surface, the *hüzün* is so dense that you can almost touch it, almost see it spread like a film over its people and its landscapes.

So there is a great metaphysical distance between *hüzün* and the melancholy of Burton's solitary individual; there is, however, an affinity between *hüzün* and another form of melancholy described by Claude Lévi-Strauss in *Tristes Tropiques*. Lévi-Strauss's tropical cities bear little resemblance to Istanbul, which lies on the 41st parallel and where the climate is gentler, the terrain more familiar, the poverty not so harsh; but the fragility of people's lives in Istanbul, the way they treat each other, and the distance they feel from the centres of the West, make Istanbul a city that newly arrived Westerners are at a loss to understand, and out of this loss they attribute to it a "mysterious air", thus identifying *hüzün* with the *tristesse* of Lévi-Strauss. *Tristesse* is not a pain that affects a solitary individual; *hüzün* and *tristesse* both suggest a communal feeling, an atmosphere, and a culture shared by millions.

But the words and the feelings they describe are not identical, and if we are to pinpoint the difference it is not enough to say that Istanbul is much richer than Delhi or São Paolo. (If you go to the poor neighborhoods, the cities and the forms poverty takes are in fact all too similar.) The difference lies in the fact that in Istanbul the remains of a glorious past and civilization are everywhere visible. No matter how ill-kept they are, no matter how neglected or hemmed in they are by concrete monstrosities, the great mosques and other monuments of the city, as well as the lesser detritus of empire in every side street and corner—the little arches, fountains and neighborhood mosques—inflict heartache on all who live amongst them.

These are nothing like the remains of great empires to be seen in Western cities, preserved like museums of history and proudly displayed. The people of Istanbul simply carry on with their lives amongst the ruins. Many Western writers and travelers find this charming. But for the city's more sensitive and attuned residents, these ruins are reminders that the present city is so poor and confused that it can never again dream of rising to the same heights of wealth, power and culture. It is no more possible to take pride in these neglected dwellings, in which dirt, dust and mud have blended into their surroundings, than it is to rejoice in the beautiful old wooden houses that as a child I watched burn down one by one.

While traveling through Switzerland, Dostoyevsky struggled to understand the inordinate pride Genevans took in their city. "They gaze at even the simplest objects, like street poles, as if they were the most splendid and glorious things on earth," wrote the West-hating chauvinist in one letter. So proud were the Genevans of their historic city that even when asked the simplest directions, they'd say things like "Walk straight down this street sir, and when you have passed that elegant, magnificent bronze fountain . . ." If an Istanbul resident were to do likewise, he might find himself uttering such instructions as are found in the story, *Bedia and the Beautiful Eleni* by the great writer, Ahmet Rasim:

"Go past Ibrahim Pasha's hamam. Walk a little further. On your right, looking out over the ruin you've just passed (the hamam), you'll see a dilapidated house." Today's Istanbullu would be uneasy about everything the foreigner might see in those miserable streets.

A more confident resident might prefer to use the city's grocery stores and coffeehouses as his landmarks, now common practice, as these count amongst the greatest treasures of modern Istanbul. But the fastest flight from the *hüzün* of the ruins is to ignore all historical monuments and pay no attention to the names of buildings or their architectural particularities. For many Istanbul residents, poverty and ignorance have served them well to this end. History becomes a word with no meaning; they take stones from the city walls and add them to the modern materials to make new buildings, or they go about restoring old buildings with concrete. But it catches up with them: by neglecting the past and severing their connection with it, the *hüzün* they feel in their mean and hollow efforts is all the greater. *Hüzün* rises out of the pain they feel for all that which has been lost, but it is also what compels them to invent new defeats and new ways to express their impoverishment.

The *tristesse* that Lévi-Strauss describes is what a Westerner might feel as he surveys those vast, poverty-stricken cities of the tropics, as he contemplates the huddled masses and their wretched lives. But he does not see the city through their eyes: *tristesse* implies a guilt-ridden Westerner who seeks to assuage his pain by refusing to let cliché and prejudice color his impressions. *Hüzün*, on the other hand, is not a feeling that belongs to the outside observer. To varying degrees, classical Ottoman music, Turkish popular music, especially the *arabesk* music that became popular during the 1980s, are all expressions of this emotion, which we feel as something in between physical pain and grief. And Westerners coming to the city often fail to notice it. Even Gérard de Nerval (whose own melancholy would eventually drive him to suicide) spoke of being greatly refreshed by the city's colors, its street life, its violence and its rituals; he even reported hearing women laughing in its cemeteries. Perhaps it is because he visited Istanbul before the city went into mourning, when the Ottoman Empire was still in its glory, or perhaps it was his need to escape his own melancholy that inspired him to decorate the many pages of *Voyage en orient* with bright Eastern fantasies.

Istanbul does not carry its *hüzün* as "an illness for which there is a cure" or "an unbidden pain from which we need to be delivered": it carries its *hüzün* by choice. And so it finds its way back to the melancholy of Burton, who held that "All other pleasures are empty/ None are as sweet as melancholy"; echoing its self-denigrating wit, it dares to boast of its importance in Istanbul life. Likewise, the *hüzün* in Turkish poetry after the foundation of the Republic, as it, too, expresses the same grief that no one can or would wish to escape, an ache that finally saves our souls and also gives them depth. For the poet, *hüzün* is the smoky window between him and the world. The screen he projects over life is painful because life itself is painful. So it is, too, for the residents of Istanbul as they resign themselves to poverty and depression. Imbued still with the honor accorded it in Sufi literature, *hüzün* gives their resignation an air of dignity, but it also explains why it is their choice to embrace failure, indecision, defeat and poverty so philosophically and with such pride, suggesting that *hüzün* is not the outcome of life's worries and great losses, but their principal cause. So it was for the heroes of the Turkish films of my childhood and youth, and also for many of my real-life heroes during the same period: they all gave the impression that because of this *hüzün* they'd been carrying around in their hearts since birth that they could not appear desirous in the face of money, success, or the women they loved. *Hüzün* does not just paralyze the inhabitants of Istanbul; it also gives them poetic license to be paralyzed.

No such feeling operates in heroes like Balzac's Rastignac, who in his furious ambition, comes to convey, even glorify the spirit of the modern city. The *hüzün* of Istanbul suggests nothing of an individual standing against society; on the contrary, it suggests an erosion of the will to stand against the values and mores of the community, encourages us to be content with little, honoring the virtues of harmony, uniformity, humility. *Hüzün* teaches endurance in times of poverty and deprivation, it also encourages us to read life and the history of the city in reverse. It allows the people of Istanbul to think of defeat and poverty not as a historical endpoint, but as an honorable beginning fixed long before they were born. So the honor we derive from it can be rather misleading. But it does suggest that Istanbul does not bear its *hüzün* as an incurable illness that has spread throughout the city, as an immutable poverty to be endured like grief, or even as a perplexing failure to be viewed in black and white: it bears its *hüzün* with honor.

As early as 1580, Montaigne argued that there was no honor in the emotion he called *tristesse*. (He used this word even though he knew himself to be a melancholic; years later, Flaubert, likewise diagnosed, would do the same.) Montaigne saw *tristesse* as the enemy of self-reliant rationalism and individualism. *Tristesse*, in his view, did not deserve to be set in capital letters alongside the great virtues, Wisdom, Virtue and Conscience, and he approved of the Italian association of *tristezza* with all manner of madness and injury, the source of countless evils.

Montaigne's own sorrow was as solitary as mourning, eating away at the mind of a man who lives alone with his books. But the *hüzün* of Istanbul is something the entire city feels together and affirms as one. But for those Istanbul writers and poets who are excited by Western culture and wish to engage with the contemporary world, the matter is more complex still. Along with the sense of community that *hüzün* brings, they also aspire to the rationalism of Montaigne and to the emotional solitude of Thoreau. In the early years of the twentieth century, some drew upon all these influences to create an image of Istanbul that is, it must be said, part of Istanbul and so part of my story, too.

An abridged version which originally appeared in *Istanbul* (Faber & Faber, 2005): 81–96. It is printed here with the permission of the author.

FADWA EL GUINDI

The Veil Becomes a Movement

In Egypt the contemporary veil represents a movement that has passed through several transitional phases since the 1970s, spreading all over the Arab world and among Muslims worldwide. Today the Islamic movement continues to grow strong as it enters its third decade. Dress has played a pivotal symbolic, ritual and political role in this dynamic phenomenon. The new vocabulary and dress style embodies a moral/behavioral code. Islam has struggled to position itself vis-à-vis the Islamic veil. The response of secularists and feminists shows how threatening this trend is to their ideological position.

But by 1997, a quarter of a century later, Egypt (and other Arab countries) had accommodated the new movement and put effort into integrating it politically, despite initial attempts by the State to suppress it. Nonetheless, the veiled and unveiled continue to interact normally in daily life. Some mothers who originally objected to the veil have adopted it. The Islamic *ziyy* (dress) goes almost unnoticed in Cairo by the local population.

Islamic veiling in Egypt is somewhat different from the situation of the *chador* in Iran. In Iran the *chador*, a black head-to-toe wrap, is the body cover worn by rural and urban traditional women before the Revolution. The Shah, to Westernize the country, banned it, and the Islamic Revolution, to indigenize tradition, enforced wearing it. In Egypt, the Islamic dress worn after the mid-1970s by women replaced modern secular clothes and is part of a grass-roots activist movement. Unlike Egypt, both Iran and Turkey have long traditions of State-legislated dress reform for both sexes. Although State-discouraged in Egypt, veiling initially met with phenomenal success and spread throughout the urban centers. The authorities of Al-Azhar were silent about it.

As some young Egyptian women took up veiling in the mid-1970s, the government increasingly felt the threat of Islamic militancy and looked for solutions. In 1993, the education minister (Husain Kamal Baha' al-Din) sought to combat the spread of Islamic activism by imposing changes in the area of education, such as the transfer or demotion of teachers with activist leanings, a revision of the curriculum, and restrictions on the wearing of the veil (Barraclough 1998: 246). However, a ban on wearing the veil at universities was thrown out by the courts. By 1994, attempts to limit the wearing of the veil in schools to students who had their parents' permission were receiving heavy criticism. The minister of education started back-pedaling—conceding that schoolgirls could wear the veil even without parental consent. State interference focusing on the veil remains controversial in Egypt.

In Turkey and Iran there is a history of State legislation of dress, in the past mostly for men, but recently regarding the *hijab*. In the Ottoman world there were deep roots to the tradition of clothing laws—extending to the beginning of the empire. And as elsewhere

Ottoman clothing laws gave a particular emphasis to head coverings, which typically designated honor and rank. Turbans played a key role in mid-eighteenth century rituals surrounding the Ottoman coronation ceremonies in Istanbul. "In the procession, two horsemen each carried turbans of the monarch, tilting them to the right and to the left to receive the homage of the accompanying janissaries. The centrality of the headgear already was evident in the early 14th century." (Quataert 1997: 405).

According to Norton, Turks can judge people simply from appearances. They consider dress to be a marker of difference, devotion and defiance. "A glance at what a stranger is wearing is often enough to tell them that person's religious and political stance. Clothes can tell them the wearer's defiance of or devotion to the principles of Kemal Ataturk, the reformer who founded the Turkish Republic and banned the fez" (1997: 149). The present situation in Turkey, similar to that of most groups in the Islamic world, is such that dress has become the marker of "the front line" in the emergent battle between advocates of an Islamic society and extreme secularists. In secularist Turkey the women's veil had not been the subject of sartorial rules; the men's fez was. Norton observes that generally the veil was discouraged and in some places prohibited, but Turkey avoided an outright ban on the veil, the measure that the Shah took in Iran (Norton, 1997).

Interestingly, by the mid-1980s in Egypt some of the women who were reluctant at first to wear the *khimar* (a headcover that covers the hair and extends low to the forehead, comes under the chin to conceal the neck, and falls down over the chest and back) began to wear a turban-like headcover that had Turkish origins. It was seen as more chic.

Roots of Islamic Resistance

At some point the characteristically Islamic rhythm of daily life in Egypt by which Muslims weave ordinary moments with sacred time and space tipped toward a mode of permanent religiousness. Some observers referred to this state as escapist religiosity. It was not confined to Muslims—Copts had a similar experience.

This general mood in Egypt can be traced to two sociopolitical events: the 1967 defeat in the Six Day War, in which Israel attacked Egypt and swiftly destroyed its air force on the ground, and the 1973 victory in the Ramadan (or October) War in which Egypt attacked Israel and swiftly destroyed the Bar Lev Line, until then mythologized as invincible. Between 1967 and 1973 Egypt passed through several stages that, across cultures, typically characterize religious revival.

In the aftermath of the 1967 defeat a climate of intense religiousness developed in Egypt among the urban population in general, both Muslim and Coptic. People's faith in Nasser, then Egypt's President and until then an unshakeable symbol of pride, dignity, power and strength, shattered and was replaced by feelings of doubt, insecurity and diminished self-esteem. Confusion and gloom loomed over Egypt, a demoralized nation. Fantasy mixed with fact as war stories in graphic detail, real or imagined, circulated among the people. Egyptians at all levels and of all persuasions felt humiliated, betrayed and threatened by the destruction from the technological and military powers and threat from Zionist and Imperialist forces. No rhetoric could mask the profound impact of this defeat on the psyche and lives of Egyptians at that time.

Disbelief gradually turned to disillusion, anger to depression, and discontent to resignation. Defeat became interpreted as God's will to punish Egypt for the increasing decline in people's morals. Many joined Sufi orders during this period. And an image in light of the Virgin Mary allegedly appeared publicly in Zeitun, Cairo several months after the war and continued to reappear for several months afterward. El Guindi (1981) describes the apparition as related by a college student in a taped interview:

> We heard from many people; many were saying the Virgin appeared in Zeitun, near the Coptic church of Zeitun, the church is where the tree is, the tree under which Virgin Mary sat with Jesus in the same place a church was built. For a long time we hear the Virgin appears at night. So we went, we spent the evening: thousands and thousands went; important personalities also went. So we spent the night there once. It was like daytime—chanting and tunes, much activity there. It was 2.00 am, at dawn when the image of the Virgin appeared with lots of white pigeons around her. One person saw it first and got up. Everybody stood up then, stretching on tiptoes, standing on chairs. I only went once. My father went there daily. It is like a passing light, a flashing light.

Thousands of Muslims and Copts—men and women, young and old, from all strata— flocked to the spot where the Virgin Mary is purported to have once sat to rest with Jesus and Joseph under the tree and where her image was appearing in light. People waited hours and days to catch a glimpse of the "miracle". Men sat in coffeehouses listening to Umm Kulthum between prayers.

In October of 1973, the surprise Ramadan war brought about victory over Israel in the name of Islam. The Egyptian army destroyed the Bar-Lev line and with it the myth of the invincible Israel. Many Islamic signs and metaphors marked the military event. It took place during the holy month of Ramadan. The army troops roared "Allah Akbar" in unison at the moment of the attack, and the phrase "God is Great" was said to be scrolled across the sky as the troops crossed the Suez Canal.

From that moment an Islamic Movement was born, and evolved through various phases until the present time. Within the framework of Revitalization Movements, the religiousness of the 1960s represents a phase in the process. But there is no doubt that as an Islamic movement it began after the 1973 Ramadan war. Youth and college students began to dress differently in public from the majority of urban rising middle- and even upper-class Egyptians, who since the 1930s had worn modern Western clothing.

The Religious Movement

The term *mitdayyinin* (pl. form), which derives from the root *d-y-n* (religion), was coined in the context of this new visible trend and was used to refer to women and men who adopted a new austere appearance and behaved conservatively in public, in a near-ritualized manner different from the norm of most urban Egyptians. The word itself means "the state of being religious." Unrelated individuals who became *mitdayyinin* referred to each other as "brother" and "sister." They reached this state of religiousness by *iqtina'* (conviction). No overt pressure or force was exerted, only perhaps the indirect influence of a change in public moral climate in which some men and women became activist symbols of an "Islamic model" of comportment and dress. In general, they used no coercion to make others join. They themselves, small in number but strong in presence, became living models to emulate.

The dress adopted in the movement was distinctively austere in style and color, unfamiliar in historical and contemporary terms. Accompanying this dress, particularly during the movement's first decade, was a conservative comportment, what anthropologists would call cross-sex avoidance behavior. This does not mean that men and women stopped interacting in public, since the university campuses are co-educational and most public places in Egypt are shared. Rather, interaction was marked by reserve and austerity, almost ritualized. They were neither formally organized in associations nor were they secluded in one area or place. It did not take the form of a "cult-like" seclusion that physically separated them from mainstream society. They shared the bond of *iltizam* (discipline, compliance and commitment) after switching out of the ordinary secular way of life and into their innovated Islamic way of life, but they continued to live in their homes with their parents, dispersed among the many secular and religious university campuses and schools. They articulated and became exemplars of a shared behavioral, moral and dress code.

In the early phase of the movement, college students made up the core of its "informal membership." They described themselves as *mitdayyinin*. At the university they did not form their own separate organizations. Instead they continued as assimilated students interacting with the rest of the students and participating in university activities, although they were distinguishable by dress, manner, and public comportment. It was common at the time to find a secularly dressed student discussing how, slowly, she was becoming convinced of the new trend and how she was considering making the commitment. Friendships between the secularly dressed and the Islamically dressed continued as usual.

To participate in campus functions the *mitdayyinin* joined the student organizational structure already in existence. This provided a mainstream framework for campus politics and a base from which to organize among the rest of the students. The existing structure comprised the Student Union for governance and the *Osrah* (family)—clubs for various social and recreational activities. They successfully ran in student elections for governing offices. Their Islamic-based ideology countered that of Nasserite-leaning students. Through the *osrah* organization they formed clubs dedicated to religious activities to counter the recreational and social clubs. They slowly gained popularity, and Nasserite students were beginning to find an appeal in the new Islamic ideology, perhaps through its quality of resistance. As it grew stronger it spread beyond the campuses and penetrated the various sectors of society in Egypt. By the mid-1980s the word *mitdayyinin* was replaced by *Islamiyyin*, and it had become a major oppositional political force.

But there is more to it. This movement represented a major shift in the bi-rhythmic balance, the moving in and out from ordinary space to sacred space, from ordinary time to sacred time that characterized public street life and the social and cultural landscape of contemporary Islamic Egypt. The code embodied in the new movement was unidimensional—adopting it meant you were permanently in sacred time and space even when performing worldly activities. The balance tipped and the rhythmic pattern was challenged. Many Egyptians reacted against it. The sacred appearance that was reserved for the special status attained after pilgrimage in old age became standard and ordinary. It was no more a status enjoyed by one's grandmother or grandfather in their later years. Rather, these young college men and women forged their own permanent status of sacredness, thus challenging the Islamic life-cycle rhythm. Many of them, still in their twenties and thirties, performed *hajj* (pilgrimage) not once but several times. But even without the pilgrimage they had adopted a code in symbol and ritual that positioned them in this state of sacredness without any rite of passage, without the pilgrimage. *Al-Azhar*, the Islamic seat of learning and scholarship in Cairo and the university that produces the scholars of Islam, was not ready or prepared for an innovation of that magnitude and impact to emerge from below. And as much as the State wished it, *al-Azhar* could not condemn the new appearance. It was particularly difficult since the *mitdayyinin*, while maintaining their distinct appearance and a general aura of reserve and austerity, were assimilated into mainstream society. And although the dress, which men and women called *al-ziyy al-Islami* (the Islamic dress), was new to Egypt, it embodied a code they all equally shared with devout Muslims.

Al-Ziyy Al-Islami (The Islamic Dress)

The Code

Women's Islamic dress, known as *al-ziyy al-Islami*, is an innovative construction that was first worn in the mid-1970s by activists. It does not represent a return to any traditional dress form and has no tangible precedent. There was no industry behind it in Egypt—not one store carried such an outfit. Based on an idealized Islamic vision gradually constructed for the early Islamic community in the seventh century, it was made in their homes by the activists themselves. Privacy, humility, piety and moderation are cornerstones of the Islamic belief system. Luxury and leisure await Muslims in the next world. Some elements of this vision can be supported by reference to the Qur'an, others find support in the secondary source of Islamic information, the Sunna, through the Hadith. The "Prophetic vision" had become idealized through the ages, developing into a model to be emulated via recurring revivalist purifying movements within Islam, just as in the Islamic movement of Egypt in the 1970s.

In the Qur'an (considered the primary and divinely revealed source), but mostly according to the Hadith (a worldly source), evidence suggests that the Prophet Muhammad had paid much attention to a dress code for Muslims in the emerging community, with a specific focus on Muslim men's clothing and bodily modesty during prayer. By comparison, reference to women's body cover is negligible.

In the *Sura al-Ahzab* one *ayah* (33: 53) protects the privacy of the Prophet's wives from growing intrusions by male visitors and another (33: 59) distinguishes their status and that of all believers from all others.

Men and women in the contemporary Islamic movement read works by the ideologues Sayyid Qutb and Abu al-'Ala al-Mawdudi. They argue for the Islamic dress and behavioral code, using as support for their argument two specific *Suras* in the Qur'an—*al-Nur* and *al-Ahzab*. The two *ayahs* of concern in the *Sura al-Nur* (24: 30, 31) translate as follows:

> The believing men are enjoined to lower their gaze and conceal their genitals

[30] and the believing women are enjoined to lower their gaze and conceal their
genitals, draw their *khimar* to cover their cleavage [breasts], and not display
their beauty, except that which has to be revealed, except to their husbands,
their fathers, their husbands' fathers, their sons, their husbands' sons, their
brothers or their brothers' sons, or their sister's sons, or their women, or the
slaves, or eunuchs or children under age; and they should nor strike their feet
to draw attention to their hidden beauty. O believers turn to God, that you
may attain bliss.

(Qur'an 24: 30,31)

Islam links socio-moral behavior, sacred space and sartorial preferences. Two points can
be drawn from the text mentioned above: (1) the Arabic notions of *ghadd al-basar* (lower
the gaze) and *hifth al-furuj* (guard or cover the genitals) are central to the code; and (2)
men are first mentioned as having to abide by these two premises, to control their gaze
at women and suppress their passion and forwardness when interacting with "strange"
women. Likewise, in the Hadith men especially are enjoined to cover their genitals.
The phrase *hifth al-furuj* is used often in the Hadith regarding men's dress and bodily
modesty during worship. Next, the text similarly enjoins women to lower their gaze and
conceal their genitals. The significance of the specific message communicated in this text
lies in this relational context addressing men and women, and in the fact that men are
addressed first, and then women. To understand the message both text and context must
be considered.

Unlike other religions, orthodox Islam accepts sexuality as a normative aspect of both
ordinary and religious life and fluidly accommodates both sacred and worldly activity in
the same bi-rhythmic space. There is no contradiction between being religious and being
sexual. Sex is to be enjoyed in matrimony. However, outside marriage, behavior between
men and women must be desexualized. Both body and interactive space need to be
regulated and controlled and both men and women are required to abide by this temporary
desexualization to make public interaction between them possible. This presumes that
cross-sex interaction would potentially be sexually charged. Islam accepts sexualized,
reproductive men and women and guides them to regulate their public behavior. Having
chosen not to sublimate sexuality theologically or ideologically (as have, for example,
some major trends in Christian theology) Islam poses the opposite challenge to individual
Muslims, that is to accommodate both human qualities—sexuality and religiousness—as
normative while they strive to fulfill the ultimate ideal of sociomoral behavior.

Three other aspects in the same *Sura (al-Nur)* show how concealing and revealing are
very much tied to cultural notions of respectability, sexuality, eroticism and privacy. One
segment enjoins women to draw their *khimar* (head veil) over their *juyub* (breast cleavage).
Khimar is one of two clothing items for women referenced in Qur'anic text. The other
is *jilbab* (long shirtdress). Also *zina* (pronounced zeena), which means both beauty and
ornament, is integral to references about women's dress and comportment.

I contend that the reference to drawing the headveil to cover a woman's cleavage may
have been in reaction to the way contemporary women in the region (Arabia–Africa)
seem to have worn clothes that exposed their bodies. A visual analysis of images from
modern Yemen, for example, shows women from the low-status group of a (servants)

wearing clothing that reveals the breasts. The image evokes not seductive sexuality but slovenliness. Another prohibition concerns anklets. The admonition "that they should not strike their feet" is a reference to the practice in which women wore decorative jingling anklets made of heavy metal (silver or gold). It is not the anklet per se that is erotic, but the jingling that evokes erotic passions.

Within Islam, a woman's sexuality does not diminish her respectability. Islam in fact supports this combined image in womanhood. The Hadith mentions an incident in which the Prophet Muhammad told a woman to color her fingernails with henna so that her hands were not like the hands of men. What Islamic morality forbids is the public flaunting of sexuality. Dressing and moving in a way that draws sexual attention to the body is *tabarruj* (exhibitionist dress and behavior). It is associated in Islamic perception with Arabian women of *al-Jahiliyya* (the "Days of Ignorance," or pre-Islamic days) and was frowned upon during the formative years of the Islamic community in the seventh century.

The third aspect in the *Sura* (*al-Nur* 24: 31) deals with the context of heterosexuality, privacy and eroticism. It enjoins women not to reveal their *zina* (meaning "beauty" or "ornament") except in the presence of those who are in a position in which sexual relations are legitimate (such as their husbands), taboo or forbidden (culturally specified kin), or not possible (underage children or asexualized men). With a woman as the point of reference these relations are clearly specified: husband, father, husband's father, sons, husband's sons, brothers, brothers' sons, sisters' sons, brothers' wives' sons; or their wives' sons; slaves, eunuchs or underage boys. These constitute (except for the spouse) kinfolk (consanguineal and affinal) or domestic personnel who share the private space with women.

As to the other relevant *Sura* (*al-Ahzab*) there is reference in two *ayahs* to the Prophet's wives. One (33: 53) enjoins strangers who wish to speak to any of the Mothers of the Believers to do so from behind a screen or curtain. The term used in this context is *hijab*. It is noteworthy that *hijab* is not used in the Qur'an in the literal sense of women's clothing. The other reference (33: 59) enjoins the Prophet's wives, daughters, and all Muslim women, to don their *jilbab* for identification and protection from molestation. The other *ayah* (59) translates as follows:

> O Prophet tell your wives, daughters and believing women to put on their *jilbabs* so that they are recognized and thus not harmed (33: 59).

Jilbab refers to a long loose shirtdress. It does not connote head or face cover, although, as the ethnography of bedouins and rural Muslim Indians shows, veiling is not always accomplished through a fixed item covering the face. Often *jilbab* sleeves or headcovers are used situationally for covering part of the face. This passage refers to women directly connected to the Prophet (wives and daughters) in order to distinguish their status, and it extends the enjoiner of wearing *al-jilbab* to all believing Muslim women. It is interesting in this regard that in the Islamic movement in Indonesia, *jilbab* is more commonly used to refer to women's Islamic-style clothing, although it has no consistent meaning—some use it to refer to the head covering itself (An Indonesian-English Dictionary, 3rd edn). In the context of the early Islamic community I contend that the intent was to mark group identity (the community of believers), to achieve social distance for the Prophet's Wives, and to project an image of respect to avert harassment.

Significantly, in neither *Sura* referred to above, nor in any of their constituent segments, is there any explicit mention of face veiling or any cover solely for use as face cover for women. The two dress parts mentioned for women are *khimar* (the head veil) and *jilbab* (a long gown), which had not been newly introduced by Islam but were likely already to be part of the wardrobe of the time. Various forms of *jilbab* and head cover for men and women are items of Arab dress. Islam attached specific and characteristic meaning to their use, pertaining to privacy, respect and status.

Four themes can be identified from the various references in Hadith sources: (1) bodily modesty which pertains mostly to men in worship, (2) averting distraction in worship, (3) moderation in daily life, and (4) distinguishing the identity of the Muslim through aversion from certain forms of dress (hair, color, etc.).

A general theme that recurs in Hadith references is about the distraction caused by clothing during worship. This is expressed in a number of contexts in which Prophet Muhammad shuns wearing colorful designs on clothes. In this reference it is stated: the Prophet prayed in a *khamisa* (dress made out of fabric of silk or wool, striped and with decorative design), and then asked for its replacement with an *anbaganiyya* (opaque heavy cover without embroidery or decorative designs). He also referred to other distractions during worship, such as "the sheer patterned cloth hanging from 'Aisha's quarters," which overlooked the worship area and was therefore within the view of worshippers. Prophet Muhammad found this distracting.

Another theme is about general austerity and moderation in lifestyle, and it is suggested that men avoid wearing gold, fabric made out of silk, big rings, and colorful patterned fabric. There is a recurring reference favoring thickness and opaqueness of fabric for clothing and shelter.

The Notion of 'Awrah Reconsidered

'Awrah, a term mentioned a few times in the Qur'an and more in the Hadith, is among Islamic notions subjected to lay and expert interpretations considered unfavorable to Muslim women. The term's most common English translation is "blemish," and the reference is to a woman's body, parts of which are characterized in these interpretations as a blemish that must be concealed. Many publications on Muslim women in particular tend to use this connotation uncritically. Interestingly, major scholarly works on Islam do not address or critique the notion at all. The English translation "blemish" along with some other significations can be found in dictionary renditions. Etymologically, the term derives from the root *'a-w-r*. Consulting Wehr's *Arabic–English Dictionary* (1994) leads to two significations: (1) (sing.) defectiveness, imperfection, blemish, flaw; (2) (pl. *'awrat*) (a) pudenda, genitals; (b) weakness. Other derivatives range in meaning from blind in one eye, false or artificial (as in teeth or hair), and lending/borrowing, among others.

My anthropological analysis of the term as it is used in the Qur'anic text shows *'awrah* as neither confined to women nor to the body. Examining the primary source directly and in its original language, the Qur'anic text reveals the use of the term in the following passages: *Sura al-Nur*, 24: 31, 58 and *Sura al-Ahzab*, 33: 13. *Sura* 24: 31 refers in part to the males sharing the private space of women in whose presence women need not conceal certain parts of their bodies. The term *'awrat* is used as follows:

> ...and male slaves or eunuchs or underage boys not yet sexually mature for
> contact with women's 'awrat (genitals) in intercourse (24: 31)

In the above text *'awrat* connotes women's genitals. No valuation is put on the term. There is no sense of imperfection or blemish inherent in this context. The next passage is about privacy *(al-Nur*, 24: 58) as the text states:

> O believers, eunuchs and underage boys should not intrude upon your privacy
> on three occasions (at three times of day): before fajr (dawn) prayer, when you
> are resting at noon, and after 'isha (night) prayer. These are three 'awrat, outside
> of which interaction is not held against you or them. (24: 58)

The usage *'awrat* (pl.) in the above passage is interesting. It refers to a notion of privacy and private space and time, rather than a woman's body. The final passage in the Qur'an that uses the term is in the *Sura al-Ahzab*, in which the term is mentioned twice in the same segment. The context is a battle scene in which men joined the Prophet out of Yathrib (the seventh- century name for Madina). It states:

> ...if a group of them ask the Prophet for leave saying "truly our homes are
> *'awrah,'*" though they were not *'awrah*, then their intent was to flee the battle...
> (33: 13)

Again the term is not used in the sense of blemish or woman's body part. It connotes protection, safety, vulnerability, security, and privacy with regard to a home. There is a context in the Qur'an that is unambiguously about the genitals, which is in *Sura al-A'raf* (7: 26, 27), that relates the episode of creation and the first humans in the Garden. In these two instances the term used twice in two consecutive *ayahs* is not *'awrat* but *saw'at*, and it pertains to both sexes. The text states:

> O ye children of Adam! We have bestowed *libas* (dress) upon you to cover your
> *saw'at* (genitals) ... [and] ... stripping them of their raiment, to expose their
> *saw'at* (genitals) (7: 26, 27)

Taking all the Qur'anic text passages together, a range of contexts is revealed, all of which make sense if the meaning imbued to *'awrah* becomes "inviolate vulnerability" rather than the commonly assumed "blemish." Several contexts discerned are: women's genitals (sexuality), home, conjugal privacy, women's privacy. If we add Hadith text to the selected Qur'anic text we can further establish that the term *'awrah* (or *'awrat*) is often used with reference to men's immodesty when their genitals are exposed as they bend over during worship. Referentially, men's bodily immodesty during worship is in fact the most frequent context.

With regard to bodily modesty for men there are many references about clothing appropriate to ensure the concealment of men's genitals. First, there is bodily modesty for men during worship. One theme that re-emerges in different contexts is about layering clothes, or specifically "not wearing only a single item" that exposes men's genital area (men's *furuj* or *'awrah*) in certain reclining positions or while bending or crossing the legs. It is in this context of the inappropriateness of clothing worn by men as they learn the new practices of Islamic praying—bowing, bending, prostrating them selves, kneeling, etc.—that in a reference to worship women were told not to lift their heads until men had taken a "sitting position."

This leads us to two conclusions. First, that women and men shared space for worship during the Prophet's time. Secondly, owing to the inappropriateness of men's clothing for worship women were asked to avoid being in a position to "see" exposed men's body parts, or their *'awrah* (vulnerability). In other references women had complained to the Prophet about such awkward exposures on the part of men.

'Awrah, therefore, does not mean "a blemish on women's bodies," but rather the immodest exposure of men's genitals. It is better understood if situated in a more comprehensive paradigm that stresses its basic and original connotation of weakness and vulnerability. A more comprehensive paradigm will reveal connections with the broader notions of the Arabo-Islamic sanctity and privacy of the home and the family.

The Dress

Beginning in Egypt, in the Arabic-speaking region, the subject of the *hijab* was revived in the 1970s in the context of an emergent Islamic consciousness and movement that spread steadily throughout the Islamic East. The Qur'anic dress terms *khimar* and *jilbab*, and the notion of immoderate excess (*tabarruj*), and a contrasting opposition *tahajjub/sufur*, all reappeared as a revived contemporary vocabulary dominating daily discourse among the youth in the movement and around the nation.

This vocabulary framed the debate about Muslim women's and men's dress, conduct, morality and Islamic identity. *Hijab* became the object and the symbol for the new consciousness and a new activism. Arab dress again provided the conceptual and material tools for identity. This time, however, it was also for resistance; it was set forth in the name of Islam, and was born in a completely different historical context and sociocultural setting. The veil in resistance, for it or against it, is not new. It has recurrent precedents in Middle Eastern history.

In the contemporary revival, the dress code was translated this way: men and women wear full-length *gallabiyyas* (*jilbab* in standard Arabic), loose-fitting to conceal body contours, in solid austere colors made out of opaque fabric. They lower their gaze in cross-sex public interaction, and refrain from body or dress decoration or colors that draw attention to their bodies. The dress code for men consists of sandals, baggy trousers with loose-top shirts in off-white, or alternatively (and preferred) a long loose white gallabiyya. They grow a *lihya* (a full beard trimmed short), with an optional mustache. Hair is to be kept shoulder-length. (This last feature has not been sustained and was eventually dropped.) The general behavior code of austerity and restraint has support in Qur'anic segments that repeatedly stress the undesirability of arrogance and exhibitionist demeanor.

In women's dress there is a gradation: A *muhajjaba* (a woman wearing *hijab*) wore *al-jilbab*—an unfitted, long-sleeved, ankle-length gown in austere solid colors and thick opaque fabric—and *al-khimar*, a headcover that covers the hair and extends low to the forehead, comes under the chin to conceal the neck, and falls down over the chest and back. The common colors used by women during the first decade of the movement were beige, brown, navy, deep wine, white and black. This dress is worn while engaging fully in worldly affairs in public social space in which not only is her gender accepted, but also her sexual identity. Austere dress form and behavior are therefore not accompanied by withdrawal, seclusion, or segregation.

The voluntary informal dress code extends beyond clothing to a general demeanor characterized by serious behavior and an austere manner, an ideal applied to both sexes. A *munaqqabah* (a woman wearing the *niqab* or face veil) more conservatively adds *al-niqab*, which covers the entire face except for the eye slits; at the most extreme, she would also wear gloves and opaque socks to cover her hands and feet. This trend has been spreading throughout the Arab world, particularly among university students.

During the first decade of the movement in Egypt the dress code for women corresponded to the degree of Islamic knowledgeability and reading, as well as to a step on a scale of leadership among women. The more intensely covered the college woman, the more "serious" her public behavior, the more knowledgeable she was in Islamic sources, the higher she was on the scale of activist leadership among women. She would lead discussions, for example, in mosques and in women students' lounges between lectures. This correspondence dissolved as the movement spread outside the university campuses and as the *hijab* became part of normal life, mingling with secular life in Cairo and the other major cities.

This Islamic dress was introduced by college women in the movement and was not imposed by the al-Azhar authorities, who ordinarily prescribe Islamic behavior by issuing decrees. Instead, this was a bottom-up movement. By dressing this way in public these young women translated their vision of Islamic ideals by becoming exemplary contemporary models. Encoded in the dress style is a new public appearance and demeanor that reaffirms an Islamic identity and morality and rejects Western materialism, consumerism, commercialism, and values. The vision behind the Islamic dress is rooted in these women's understanding of early Islam and, as earlier presented, in primary and secondary textual sources. But it is a contemporary movement about contemporary issues.

Clearly, the movement is not simply about a dress code. Like early Islam in Madina, this activism espouses egalitarianism, community, identity, privacy, and justice. It condemns exhibitionism in dress and behavior, which was also characteristic of *jahiliyya* (the pre-Islamic era). *Jahiliyya*, then, is not just a historical moment, but a state and a condition of society that can occur at any time. Reserve and restraint in behavior, voice and body movement are not restrictions. They symbolize a renewal of traditional cultural identity.

References

Barraclough, Steven. (1998) "Al-Azhar: Between The Government and The Islamists." *The Middle East Journal* 52 (2), (Spring): 236-50.

El Guindi, Fadwa. (1981) "Veiling Infitah with Muslim Ethic: Egypt's Contemporary Islamic Movement." *Social Problems* 28 (4): 465-85.

Norton, J. (1997) "Faith and Fashion in Turkey." In Lindisfarne-Tapper and Bruce Ingham (eds.),

Languages of Dress in the Middle East, pp. 149–77, London: Curzon with The Center of Near and Middle Eastern Studies, SOAS.

Quataert, Donald. (1997) "Clothing Laws, State, and Society in the Ottoman Empire, 1720-1829." *International Journal of Middle East Studies* 29: 403-25.

Originally published in *Veil: Modesty, Privacy and Resistance* (Oxford, New York: Berg, 1999): 129–145. It is printed here with the permission of the publisher.

LARA DEEB

Women's Community Service in Beirut

During Ramadan afternoons in *al-dahiyya al-junubiyya*, the southern suburbs of Beirut, while most people are rushing through traffic to arrive home before *iftar*, a bustle of activity fills a warehouse on a prominent street corner. A crowd of over one hundred people waits impatiently on one side of the building. On the other side, separated by a colorfully wallpapered partition, fifteen well-dressed women volunteers rush around filling plastic containers with food and packing them into bags along with bread, soda, vegetables, and sweets. At a table along the partition's edge, two volunteers hand these bags to those in the waiting crowd. Another table is occupied by several wealthy donors, sitting with two more volunteers, who entertain them while keeping track of the many children rushing around trying to help. This is the scene one hour before sunset during Ramadan at the food distribution centre of the Social Advancement Association (SAA).

The SAA is one of the many Islamic *jam'iyyat*, or welfare organizations, located in *al-dahiyya*. The organization is active throughout the year, providing basic foodstuffs, clothing and shoes, essential household items, and health and educational assistance for approximately two hundred client families. The *jam'iyya* also conducts education programs on topics ranging from "correct" religious knowledge to how to store food properly or treat a child's fever.

All of this is done almost entirely with women's volunteer labor. Without the time and energy of women volunteers, neither the Ramadan centre nor any of the other activities and projects of this and the other *jam'iyyat* in the area would be possible.

Volunteering and Piety

Women's motivations for volunteering vary, but no matter how and why a woman initially joins a *jam'iyya*, it soon becomes an integral part of her life and identity, especially her identity as a pious member of the community. Volunteers understand faith as a ladder they must continually struggle to climb. One of the fundamental rungs on this ladder is *mu'amalat*, mutual reciprocal social relations. As the vehicle through which personal piety is most clearly brought into the public realm, community service is an important component of these social relations; a component that encapsulates both the personal morality and the public expression that together constitute piety in this community.

Taking this to an extreme, some volunteers have internalized these social expectations into an unorthodox conviction that community service is a religious duty on par with prayer.

As one volunteer put it, "[f]or us, it's not that it's a good thing for us to do this work—no, for us it's become an obligation, like prayer and fasting." Demonstrating a sense of social responsibility is a critical aspect of being a moral person for many volunteers, and it is important to fulfill that responsibility before oneself and God.

In addition, in order to be seen as a "good" Muslim woman in *al-dahiyya*, barring exempting circumstances, one is expected to participate in at least some of the activities of at least one *jam'iyya*. Community service has become a new social norm. This expectation is conveyed by volunteers to their relatives, friends, and neighbors in conversations about *jam'iyya* activities as well as outright attempts at recruitment. Once a *jam'iyya* network identifies a potential participant who is judged to be of good moral character—or occasionally when an interested woman herself initiates contact with a *jam'iyya*—she will receive a steady stream of telephone calls and invitations to attend fundraisers and other events. Gradually, she will be drawn into working with the *jam'iyya* more regularly.

As a social norm for women, community service provides an externally visible marker of a woman's morality. While not volunteering does not necessarily damage a woman's status or reputation provided she has good reasons for not participating and is not assumed to spend her time frivolously, participating in the activities of a *jam'iyya* adds significantly to public perceptions of her moral character. In this way community service has been incorporated into a normative moral system for women in *al-dahiyya*.

However, volunteers' prolific public participation is not without its critics. Despite its links to piety, a woman's volunteer activities are only met with approval if her household responsibilities are also fulfilled. Volunteers believe that with proper "organization" women should be able to manage the double shift of household and community work, and many take pride in their ability to do so. This too is linked to piety, as the energy and ability to complete one's work in both arenas tirelessly and efficiently are viewed as gifts from God, and often taken as further indication of a woman's religiosity.

Why Women?

As a public indicator of piety in *al-dahiyya*, community service is gender-specific, holding particular salience for women. To a certain extent, this obtains from the structure and method of the work itself. From among the myriad tasks and responsibilities fulfilled by volunteers, the most constant activity is regular visits to client families. During these visits, volunteers distribute material assistance, monitor changes in a family's economic, social, and health situation, draw on their personal networks to facilitate access to healthcare or employment, and provide advice and education. In essence, they function as liaisons between these families and the material and cultural resources managed and distributed by the *jam'iyyat*. In a community where a woman's- and her family's reputation would be severely compromised if she were to receive unaccompanied male visitors in her home, household visits are impossible for a male volunteer. Women volunteers, on the other hand, are able to enter homes readily. This is especially crucial as many of the households assisted by the *jam'iyyat* are female-headed.

Furthermore, women are believed to be inherently suitable for community work due to an understanding of essentialized sex differences that posits women as more nurturing than men. Both women and men in the community indicate that women's natural empathetic and emotional capacities equip them to handle the emotional stress of dealing with poverty, to contribute to the proper upbringing of orphans and the education of the poor more generally, and to be committed to community welfare.

Interestingly these essentialized sex differences are not necessarily interpreted as limiting women to domestically oriented roles in society. Many in *al-dahiyya* believe women have the potential to make excellent doctors, engineers, and politicians. The sole exception to this is the battlefield. Women are believed to be innately unsuited to military service, and taking up arms is considered inappropriate except in situations of self-defense. In the context of Israeli occupation of southern Lebanon (and after, as the border is still considered an active front), community work represents an appropriate way for women to participate in the Islamic Resistance without entering the battlefield. In this sense, the importance of community service is not gender specific, but the form that service takes is related to perceived gendered proclivities.

Finally, it is necessary to factor in a gender ideology that values men's work and time over women's, a valuation linked to the persistent notion that men are the primary providers. Women's employment is assumed to provide a secondary income to a household, and women's household duties are assumed to allow for more flexibility in time than men's work. Compounding this is the notion that paid employment in a *jam'iyya* does not carry the same weight with regard to piety as volunteering does, because it does not represent the same level of self-sacrifice. Volunteering, for many women, is seen as a form of martyrdom, paid in sweat instead of blood.

Women in the Public

So what does women's volunteerism in this community and its relationship to piety mean for gendered understandings of the public/private divide? As Suad Joseph (1997) has noted, researchers and theorists tend to view voluntary associations as a constituent aspect of civil society and to locate them in the public sphere. Coupled with assumptions about a gendered public/private divide, particularly in studies of the Middle East/North Africa, *jam'iyyat* and other such organizations are thereby associated with men. By their mere visibility in occupying public spaces and engaging in public work, women volunteers in *al-dahiyya* challenge these assumptions and conclusions. Yet the gendered divide between the public and private has been critiqued as overly dichotomous, particularly in the context of the Middle East. Women's community service in *al-dahiyya* reflects the porosity and the blurring of the division itself.

On the one hand, women in *al-dahiyya* are challenging traditional gendered boundaries through their active participation in the public sphere. This is the view of many SAA volunteers. For example, while expounding on the importance of the SAA as a women-only *jam'iyya* one afternoon, Hajji Amal observed that "[m]en think that women can't have a *jam'iyya* that works, because they think that when women gather we just gossip or fight." She went on to assert her hopes that through the work of the SAA they would be able to change men's views of women in the community by providing an example of a well-run and well-organized women's organization. At the same time, women's volunteerism draws on traditional gender roles and definitions.

Women's community service is also public with regard to the public marker of morality it carries. The understandings of piety that include community service as a constituent component are understandings produced in part by women in the community. Volunteers' argument that women have the same capacity for rationality as men is often extended to state that therefore, community service should be the rational choice for good Muslim women in the community and the logical extension of one's moral responsibility. While this argument draws upon notions of gender equity, it also contributes to the construction of a social norm that carries moral implications for women with regard to status and reputation. In this way, women are participating in the construction of community service as a social norm, and the proliferation of a broader normative moral system that may be as constraining as it is liberating.

Bibliography

Joseph, Suad. "Gender and Civil Society" (Interview with Joe Stork). In Joel Beinin and J. Stork (eds), *Political Islam: Essays from Middle East Report* (Berkeley: University of California Press, 1997): 64–70.

This essay is taken from *ISIM Review* (December, 2002): 27. It is printed here with the permission of the International Institute for the Study of Islam in the Modern World.

SUSAN SCHAEFER DAVIS

Growing Up in Morocco

Infancy

Male babies are preferred to females in Morocco. The preference is based on the function of each sex within the family. Since Morocco is a patrilineal society (in which descent is traced through males), the son will remain a part of the family and eventually be responsible for the support of his mother and father in their old age. The daughter, on the other hand, will marry and reside outside the group and is considered as someone who will be lost to the family at marriage.

Further, having a daughter is less desirable because the female offspring are considered a threat to the family honor, as was quite clearly revealed in an incident which occurred a few years prior to our residence in a Moroccan village. The daughter of one family had become pregnant by the son of the family next door. While both families seldom mentioned the incident, it was clear from local gossip that the girl was believed to be at fault and that her family had been more dishonored. The boy had left the village to study (his family was embarrassed enough to remove him from the scene), but his family suffered no great stigma. The girl had also left the area and was raising her baby in the city. Meanwhile, her mother and sisters were "snubbed" by the neighborhood women's groups and seldom participated in their activities but rather spent most of their time isolated inside their home.

At birth, preference for males is indicated by the larger celebration held for the naming ceremony of a boy. Otherwise, boys and girls are treated quite similarly from birth to two years of age. Both are constantly in the company of their mothers; baby sitters are an unknown institution. True, a small baby may be left in the care of a young girl for a few minutes, but only infrequently.

Since nearly all babies are breastfed, they are never far from their mothers. When the mother is working or walking, she carries the baby on her back in a cloth sling, which is tied in front, one end over the shoulder, the other under the opposite breast. This leaves her hands free for work or carrying and the baby seems to cause no inconvenience. Children are carried in this way, or ride on the hip of a younger sister when they are old enough, until they can walk well. Thus they are in nearly constant contact with their mothers and other members of the family. When they are sitting and visiting, women lay babies across their laps or on a cushion next to them; they are seldom held in the arms except when nursing. One is amazed when one sees several children sound asleep during an evening women's party with loud music and conversation, but they have learned early to sleep in any atmosphere.

It is interesting that, despite constant contact with her child, the mother appears to harbor no resentment toward it. One has no sense that she feels it a burden or that it hinders her from doing other things; whatever she does, the baby comes along, as do everyone's babies. Such tolerance may be partially due to the fact that babies do not appear to be a problem or nuisance. They are fed on demand (even three or four times an hour) and are never allowed to cry more than a few seconds without being pacified, usually with the breast. The baby is frequently wrapped with a cloth, used as a diaper but without pins, which is changed when soiled. Because of the almost constant bodily contact, mothers also learn to sense when babies are about to urinate or defecate and may then remove them from the back and hold them out over the (usually dirt) floor. One mother claimed that her son had been "trained" at six months—that is, he urinated and defecated only at specific times, and only when he had been "put aside" to do so. Accidents did occur, but women never seemed irritated or upset about their soiled *jellabas*.

One of the few times when babies do cry is when they are teased, and this usually does not occur until near the end of infancy; they are not teasable until that age. Adults seem to enjoy frustrating a child, perhaps holding a toy just out of reach until it bursts into tears, and then giving it both the toy and a big, warm hug. One does not have the sense they want to hurt the child or see it suffer but that the reaction to such teasing is one of the few varieties of behavior exhibited by the child and they want to see it perform. The hugs afterward are always very reassuring, and the child is never left to cry uncomforted.

When a child is in a group of people with its mother, it becomes the object of everyone's attention only if there is nothing else to talk about—that is, the baby will be held and cuddled and briefly admired, but it is not the focal interest of the group. Even when alone with its mother, the child is always attended to when it makes a demand, but otherwise it takes second place to other activities. One seldom observes women saying "Ma-ma, Ma-ma" and encouraging the child to repeat, or helping a child to stand and take its first steps. The child does these things when it is ready; it is not pressured or encouraged to be precocious. Conversations based on the accomplishments of one's children, so common among women in America, are not heard in Morocco. To a degree, Moroccan women do realize themselves through their children, especially their sons, but they place less emphasis on the process of childrearing than Americans do.

In infancy both sexes are dressed identically, in a little smock in the summer, with a sweater and long pants added in the winter. Babies also usually wear bonnets on their heads, knit in the winter, cotton with a ruffle (for boys and girls) against the sun in the summer. One must inquire to determine the sex of a child, and a mistake does not upset or offend the mother (which is surprising, in view of the great sex role differentiation of the society). In fact, what seemed most offensive to mothers was to be told that their baby was lovely; this was the only situation in which they would openly disagree with a visitor. Initially I thought a woman lacked affection for her child when in response to a compliment she replied, "She's not pretty at all. Look how wrinkled she is, and just as black as her father!" But when one understands the susceptibility of small babies to illness caused by "the evil eye," one learns either to agree with the mother that the baby is not perfect or to preface a compliment with the protective phrase *tbarek Allah* ("God bless").

Early Childhood

The early childhood period includes the second through fifth years in the child's life, when it is more mobile than the infant yet spends most of its time within the household rather than outdoors playing with peers. During this time the differential treatment of the sexes begins, the child learns to *hshim* (behave properly), and the events (important in traditional socialization studies) of weaning and toilet training occur.

Weaning could be said to occur in either infancy or early childhood, since it usually happens very close to two years of age. By the time of weaning most children are also eating bits of food from the table, but doing so occurs late in comparison to the American practice. A few children who were observed refused to ingest anything except their mother's milk; they spat out any other food offered. Only one such child appeared obviously malnourished; he was very scrawny and unable to walk although he was over two years old.

Because breastfeeding is believed to prevent pregnancy (a belief which has some basis in fact), it is continued as long as possible before the child is two, although I heard of (never observed) cases in which a child nursed until it was six or eight years old. Weaning also occurs when a woman becomes pregnant and her milk supply decreases. It is recognized that weaning is difficult for the child, and it often occurs on a holiday (*'id-as-seghir*), on which it is felt to be easier, or with a new moon. Nevertheless, women say of a newly weaned child, "Now he knows that *ghder* [treachery, betrayal] exists in the world." The feeling that before this time children are very close to the angels and unaware of worldly hardships in fact reflects, in metaphor, the real situation.

The process of weaning is very abrupt; the mother chooses a day, paints her breasts with liver bile or hot pepper to discourage the child, and from that point does not nurse it again. She binds up her breasts or her dress with the opening in back to be sure the child will not "steal" a sip while sleeping next to her. One might expect mothers to relent when they see how unhappy and upset the child is, but the culture bolsters their resolution through the common belief that their milk spoils and will poison the child once they stop nursing. One woman described how her baby girl had died at the time of weaning for just that reason. Although she had not given in and nursed the child, she thought the baby must have "stolen" some milk during the night. The next day the baby had diarrhea—her mother assumed it was from the "poison"—and she died a few days later. I suspect that diarrhea may indeed often occur with weaning, not from poisoned milk but because the infant is then more likely to drink the local water, which contains various germs. Adults are immune to most of them, and also strong enough to endure a round of dysentery, but the babies are much more susceptible.

Children will be fussy for the first few days after weaning, and some mothers try to pacify them with candy or cookies. Others object, however, saying that the children will then always crave sweets and not eat properly.

While weaning is quite precisely accomplished, toilet training is very relaxed. It was noted above that women can often sense when an infant is about to urinate or defecate and they then hold the child away from them, so that a child may be trained by early childhood. It appears that most children are toilet trained by three or four years of age, and some considerably earlier. When infants can sit but not walk they are often seated balanced on the mother's extended legs and defecate on the floor or ground. This is easily cleaned up and not noted, positively or negatively, by others present. When children are able to walk (at about one year), they wear only little smocks and no pants at all in the summer, so that they urinate or defecate wherever they happen to be standing. Again, no fuss is made, though they may be taken outside or to the toilet if they are noticed in time. When they are a little older, they learn to squat while defecating, further simplifying the process. Whenever seen squatting, they are taken to the proper place and quickly learn the association.

During this period, the differential treatment of the sexes becomes much more apparent. The slight amount of extra attention that infant boys receive becomes marked in early childhood. The attention of fathers increases at this time; infants are not particularly interesting to them. Their attention is directed mainly at boys; girls are given little. Children of both sexes are hugged and told that they are pretty, but boys more so than girls. Small girls do not cry or demand attention to show they resent being slighted, but just sit quietly and observe.

Another aspect of differential treatment is that little boys are allowed and sometimes encouraged to hit their older sisters, who are not allowed to retaliate. Little girls seldom strike anyone and are not encouraged to do so. Behavior that we would call "spoiled" (such as tantrums) is both exhibited more by boys and tolerated more with regard to them. While one seldom meets a spoiled little girl, spoiled youngest boys are the norm.

Moroccan children at this stage are much less sheltered than their American counterparts. They are allowed to roam freely about the house; there is no special concern to keep them away from the fire in the kitchen or to prevent them from falling down the stairs. It is not that the adults do not care; they are concerned when there is a reasonable danger, but they would see most American parents' behavior as overprotective. After a period of residence in Morocco, one comes to the conclusion that children are very durable and that they can assume a great deal of responsibility at an early age.

For example, one little girl was found toddling around on the roof where the rabbits were kept, ingesting their excrement. When the mother was informed, instead of rushing the child to the nearest clinic she merely smiled and remarked, "I guess she thinks those are vitamin pills." One local family used to laugh at the way I would nervously watch their five-year-old son whenever he rode his tricycle over to the top of a steep flight of cement stairs; he had not fallen down yet and they felt it unlikely that he would. The same boy failed to come home for dinner about 8 p.m., and his sister said, "He must be at his aunt's house—or somewhere. He'll come home sooner or later." Most American mothers would have considered the possibility of his falling in the river, wandering out into the hills, and other grim occurrences. The only time a family appeared worried about a child (for reasons other than illness) was when a local six-year-old was missing overnight, and he was later found staying with relatives in the adjacent town.

While American preschoolers are playing and being sheltered from the hardships of life, Moroccan children are enjoying more independence and learning pragmatic skills. Girls especially begin helping their mothers at this time. While boys sometimes run errands, such practice is regarded as "cute" rather than as a contribution to running the household. Girls, however, begin running errands, washing dishes, sweeping, and caring for younger children at this age. It is not unusual to see a five-year-old carrying a one-year-old on her back.

Children of both sexes begin to *hshim* at this time. *Hshim* and the related concept of *'qel* (discussed below) are both very important in Moroccan child-rearing; once children have mastered both, they are grown up. *Hshim* means literally "Show some shame!" or "Behave!" when spoken as a command, and is related to *hshuma* (shame). To *hshim* is to behave properly and not to exhibit bad manners or morals. Since the behavior expected of boys and girls varies, so does the meaning of *hshim* as applied to each. For a small boy it means to sit quietly; for a girl it demands bodily modesty in addition to quiet- ness. Three-year-old girls are encouraged to cover their legs with their dresses while seated, and strict parents do not even allow them to wear the short, French-style dresses. For a mother to say about her daughter "*Katshim*" (she's well behaved) implies an element of shyness, since proper behavior for girls includes a demure aspect. Often these girls would stare at the ground and blush while their mothers spoke (appropriate behavior when one is being discussed), leading me initially to understand *Katshim* to mean "she's shy or frightened." It should also be noted that *hshim* applies to observable behavior; it is more an external judgment by society of one's actions rather than something felt only internally and individually by a person. One can relate it to Western concepts of guilt and shame, where guilt is internalized self-punishment but shame is imposed on one by others. In Morocco shame (*hshuma*) is the most common means of control of behavior, whereas very little guilt appeared to occur. A child did not feel "bad" about stealing something because one should not steal, but felt "bad" only if he was caught, because then he would he publicly shamed. The effectiveness of shame as social control was revealed in a class of preschool children in the village. Because a child would not behave in response to directions or even slaps, the teacher stood him in the corner for a few minutes. He then cried as if his heart were broken is not understandable unless one realizes the impact of being publicly shamed.

Another aspect of child training that begins during early childhood and persists throughout may be related to the prevalence of shame over guilt. There is a striking inconsistency in the way in which children are disciplined. The first time a little girl takes a large lump of sugar from the tea tray and begins to suck on it, she may be laughed at or even admired, especially if guests are present. The next time she does it she may be soundly spanked; corporal punishment, while not very harsh, is frequent. There seem to be no concentrated efforts to teach children precisely what is right or wrong, and they are punished or rewarded indiscriminately. The main variable seems to be the mood of the parent rather than the nature of the particular act. Thus one would hardly expect the child to develop an internal sense of what is right and wrong, since it all depends on an exterior factor, the parent. Such methods lead directly to feeling only shame, imposed from outside, when caught. One might also speculate that herein lies the origin of the almost uncanny ability of many Moroccans to "psych out" people; it is a talent they develop early, in self-defense against their parents' moods.

Late Childhood

During late childhood further differentiation of the sexes occurs, with boys engaging in play and attending school while girls take on more and more responsibility at home. Probably partially as a consequence of their increased responsibility, girls begin to develop '*qel*, or more mature behavior, but boys do not do so until much later. During this stage (and sometimes earlier) boys undergo circumcision, which may have a disturbing psychological effect. Perhaps the most outstanding characteristic of late childhood is the fact that the boys are literally terrors outside the household, and one marvels to think that somehow they will be socialized into very restrained and proper men like their fathers.

Between the ages of six and twelve, girls are of maximum usefulness to the household. Although they further refine their housekeeping skills during adolescence, they are then no longer allowed to go out freely because one becomes concerned about their honor. The institution of "little girl maids" (*mta'llmat*) depends mostly on those in late childhood. Girls in this age category learn to do all the basic household tasks of washing, cleaning, cooking, and child care, and in addition run errands to buy food or deliver messages. More of these girls have been sent to public school recently, but many are too valuable as assistants for their mothers to spare them. One notes again the pragmatism of this training; it is difficult to imagine an American twelve-year-old as perfectly competent to run a household. These girls do play with peers, usually after dinner in the evening when all the work is done.

Boys, on the other hand, seem to spend most of their time playing. Most boys attend the public school for at least three or four years, but it must operate on split shifts because of crowding and thus occupies only a few hours of the day. The rest of the time is spent outside in unsupervised play; the only household task that might be asked of a boy is shopping or taking a message to his father, and that is infrequent. The most reserved or controlled game played by groups of boys is soccer, which is a great favorite. Another common game involves a gang of boys, each trying to kick one another in the pants. This seemed more typical of the play of these boys—very active and expressing a lot of aggression.

One wonders where all the aggression comes from, since girls do not seem to exhibit it at all. Is it related to the fact that small boys are spoiled but inevitably "dethroned" by the arrival of a new baby, whereas girls lack this experience? Yet girls receive less attention immediately after infancy than do boys, so that transition could be more difficult for them. Or perhaps it is related to the fact that girls' energy is channeled directly into household activities, whereas boys' energy lacks a productive or appreciated outlet. While all the above may be contributing actors, I suspect that the circumcision of boys between the ages of four and eight, with no prior warning or explanation to them, may also play an important role in explaining their aggression. There is no equivalent event for girls in Morocco.

For boys, however, circumcision (*tahar*) is a major event and the basis for a large celebration, to which friends and relatives are invited. In that regard, the circumcision is for boys what a wedding is for girls: the major ceremonial event to focus on them. Of course, the groom also celebrates his wedding, but the bride is the center of attention. Boys enjoy all the attention they receive at their circumcision, including wearing fancy clothing, parading through the streets on a white horse, and having musicians play in their honor, They also enjoy the feast, and at the men's party may be encouraged to smoke, drink wine, and dance with the dancing girls, revealing the initiatory aspect of the circumcision. Since most boys are still very young, their participation in the latter activities is more a charade than a reality.

However, all this celebration usually occurs before the actual circumcision. Mothers explain that it is wiser to wait, for if the child should fall ill as a result of the operation, the mother would have to attend to him and could not see to all her duties as hostess.

It seems that boys are aware of the more glamorous aspects but are not told in advance what the actual operation will involve. By eight years of age or so, children may discuss it among themselves, but younger boys are not prepared by their families.

When one assumes the naiveté of the boy, the actual circumcision must be quite frightening. After all the music, dancing, and eating are over, several women file into a house with the boy's mother. He is brought in by an uncle or other male relative (seldom by the father; one wonders whether he cannot bear it). The operation is usually performed by a barber-surgeon who specializes in it, although recently it has also begun to be available at health clinics. One village boy of five, waiting near the door as everyone filed in, showed a sense of what was impending when he said, "Well, I think I'll just wait here outside." But it was his circumcision and he had to go in. The male relative holds the child steady, the barber-surgeon removes the foreskin, and the women all sing loudly so that the mother will not hear the child cry.

After the operation, the child is placed on the back of his mother as if he were an infant, and she remains bent nearly double as she carries him to the room where he will recuperate for a few days. During this passage both mother and son are covered with a white sheet, one suspects as a defense against the evil eye. Friends and relatives then file in and each gives the child a little money and says something comforting. On one such occasion that I tended, the five-year-old boy cried heartbrokenly, a cry that suggested more than physical pain. He did not even pause when one of his visitors, an old midwife, said, "Don't worry, sonny; it'll grow back as big as this!" and displayed her forearm. One of my bigger regrets was that I did not interview this child in the next few days and ask him just what (he perceived) had happened; he was a very verbal child and would probably have had a lot to say. When I finally did ask him, about six months later, all he said was, "*Wellit sghir*" (I became small).

While boys seem to become wilder and less controllable during late childhood, girls have the opposite experience. Girls are allowed to laugh, run, and play in the streets (when they have time) as do their brothers. But as they approach adolescence, girls are encouraged to become quieter and more sedate. One little girl in particular comes to mind; at six she was almost as much a tease as her brother, with a twinkle in her eye and a ready laugh. But by ten she had become more restrained, and by twelve she was a "perfect little lady," seldom running or giggling, and the sparkle was replaced by a soberness and a sense of responsibility.

In fact, the greater responsibility borne by girls probably is one of the main factors in their development of '*qel* before the boys. '*Qel* or the more common *dir l'qel*, means literally to "develop a mind." It refers to the development of a person into an intellectually capable, or socially responsible, person. Abdelwahed Radi, a professor at Mohammed V University in Rabat, suggests that '*qel* involves internalizing the values of one's elders. One sees here an interesting contrast with the American concept of child development. We tend to perceive a child's development as linear through time, beginning in infancy, with each successive stage building on the previous ones. Moroccans do not share the concept of linearity; a child exists for a time, and finally one day it is discovered to have developed '*qel*. Girls act quite sensibly by the end of childhood and during adolescence most are recognized as having "become responsible." One can leave them in charge of the household and expect everything to be functioning smoothly when one returns. If it is not, they are held responsible and punished.

For boys, however, the picture is different. The first thing one would expect of boys at this age is that they would have *'qel*. Rather, they behave irresponsibly, sometimes even destructively, but are not blamed. People used to warn us never to allow children in our house because "they have not yet 'become responsible' and might steal something." We assumed the warning applied to children under seven, as was infact correct for girls; the boys they referred to were up to fifteen and evidently not yet held responsible for theft. These differences in the rate of assuming responsibility may be partly due to the fact that the realm of a woman lies inside the household and is fairly easily mastered when young, whereas that of a man involves many and varied interactions with the outside world that cannot be easily learned in the setting of the home, or at play, or in school.

Adolescence

During their teens girls exhibit relatively little change, except in the area of increased sexual modesty. Boys may begin to develop *'qel*, especially if they must work to support themselves or their families, but they are also expected to sow some wild oats at this time. Girls' socialization continues to be within the household, although they may also have friends in the neighborhood. With the onset of puberty girls begin to cover themselves more and are seen less frequently in the street. They quickly learn (most have already) that exchanging banter with boys or men is forbidden, and instead they pass by with eyes cast down. Most girls marry in late adolescence and are fully prepared to become wives and mothers.

Boys are still experimenting during this period, often with smoking, eating ham, drinking, and prostitutes. Obviously most of their socialization now occurs outside the home, with peer groups or with older males with whom they work. The son has a great deal of respect for the authority of his father, and the relations of the two are rather distant by this age. A son will not smoke in front of his father and would be very embarrassed to encounter him in a bar or a brothel. Thus the father is not responsible for much of the son's socialization, except as he represents a strong authority figure. The lack of dependable guidance for boys at this age probably contributes to their problems. Many perceive their fathers as old-fashioned and unsuccessful in the modern world. While I did not have enough contact with adolescent boys to be certain, it appeared that their main ideal was James Bond, but emulating him did not adequately prepare them to function in Moroccan society.

Mothers may threaten to tell fathers of a son's misbehavior, but in the final case the mother more frequently defends him to the father. Mothers hope their sons will love and respect them, and ultimately most do, but not until they are in their twenties. Teenage males often abuse both sisters and mothers, who are hurt but tolerate it. One young man of our acquaintance was very sharp with the female members of his family (he was brusque or silent with his father) and occasionally threw plates of food on the floor when he was especially irritated. Young men in Morocco today do face many problems, the main one being widespread unemployment. Given their position and lack of power in the society, women are the only available targets for their resentment. This particular young man was also very impatient with his six-year-old brother (who was otherwise the darling of the household), but one suspects it is less manly to pick on children than on women. All of this behavior worried his mother, but not because she saw her son as developing into a bad person—she knew how unhappy he was.

Boys manage to survive adolescence and are usually married in their early twenties. They develop *'qel* about the same time; few families would trust their daughter to an immature husband who had not yet developed *'qel.* The "socially responsible" couple then begin their own cycle of childrearing.

Originally published in D.L. Bowen & E.A. Early (eds.) *Everyday Life in the Muslim Middle East* (Indiana University Press, 2002): 23–33. Printed here with the permission of the author.

PART THREE

Negotiating Identities in Dissonant Worlds

Introduction

As noted earlier, one of the overriding existential issues that most Arabs are currently grappling with is a sustained effort to forge coherent and meaningful identities which allow one to function creatively in a changing and unsettling socio-cultural setting. All five essays selected for this chapter illustrate the poignant and problematic character of this process of negotiation and social construction.

Having been diagnosed with terminal cancer, the late Edward Said, arguably one of the most prominent Arab public intellectuals, reflects on his life and career to put, as he explains, some order in "fluid things." Over thirty years earlier, in his first book, *Joseph Conrad and the Fiction of Autobiography*, and then in an essay, "Reflections on Exile," Conrad, not surprisingly, served as a steady groundbass to much that Said experienced, both having acutely acknowledged the irredeemable loss of home and language in a new setting.

Disparity between his acquired Western identity and the Arab culture into which he was born and from which he had been removed, left Said feeling *Out of Place*, always a highly individualistic misfit. By the mid-seventies, he ironically found himself drawn into the Western debate between Israelis and Palestinians, two diametrically opposed constituencies, one Western, the other Arab, as much because of his ability to speak as an American academic and intellectual as by the accident of his birth.

For Said, assuming such a professional voice became a way of submerging his difficult and unassimilable past. He began to think and write contrapuntally, using the disparate halves of his experience as an Arab and as an American, to work with and against each other. Consequently, writing became a construction of realities that served one or another purpose. In his seminal works, *Orientalism and Culture and Imperialism*, he fashioned a self that revealed to a Western audience what had so far been either hidden or ignored. Moreover, his inability to live an uncommitted or suspended life fueled his insistence to declare an affiliation with an extremely unpopular cause, while reserving the right to remain critical when and if such a stance conflicted with what others expected from him in the name of national loyalty.

Amin Maalouf, the celebrated Lebanese novelist, begins his essay on "Damaged Identities and Violence," by asserting another fundamental premise which informs this anthology: that identity is not an essentialist pre-given and static phenomenon. One does not merely grow aware of his identity; it is acquired, step by step, and changes throughout a person's lifetime. More important, what determines a person's affiliation to a particular group is basically the influence of others; both his in-group and outer-group. While his in-group (i.e., relatives, fellow-countrymen, co-religionists) try to make him one of them, those of the outer-group do their best to exclude him.

To Maalouf, it is these wounds of exclusion which become irrevocable elements of our vulnerable identity that "at every stage in life determine not only men's attitudes towards their affiliations but also the hierarchy that decides the relative importance of these ties. When someone has been bullied because of his religion, humiliated or mocked because of the colour of his skin, his accent or his shabby clothes, he will never forget it."

He goes further to assert how such humiliation and fear can spark the cycle of retribution and vengeance.

I don't think any particular affiliation, be it ethnic, religious, national or anything else, predisposes anyone to murder. We have only to review the events of the last few years to see that any human community that feels humiliated or fears for its existence will tend to produce killers. And these killers will commit the most dreadful atrocities in the belief that they are right to do so and deserve the admiration of their fellows in this world and bliss in the next. There is a Mr. Hyde inside each one of us. What we have to do is prevent the conditions occurring that will bring the monster forth.

Rather than decrying the unsettling transformations inherent in globalization, Maalouf sees hope in the ever-accelerating intermingling of elements in which we are all caught up. Hence, he stresses the urgency for a new concept of identity in the age of globalization to replace the "tribal notion" that has been accepted and justified for centuries. Contrary to earlier views that reduce identity to one single affiliation, thus encouraging intolerance and distorted ideas, he calls for an identity composed of numerous allegiances and influences. Acceptance of a diverse identity will enable individuals to transcend prejudices leading to conflict and enter, instead, into tolerant relationships with the "other". By eliminating notions of "them" and "us" in communities and cultures, massacres and bloody wars can be avoided, whereas individuals who reject their own diversity, remain prepared to kill, attacking those who embody the part of themselves they struggle to suppress.

In "Living Between Worlds" Roseanne Khalaf provides a thoughtful account of coming to terms with the ambivalence and uncertainties inherent in the process of life in postwar Lebanon after a decade of imposed absence resulting from the ongoing atrocities of the Lebanese civil war. Her own confusion is described in language that can easily resonate with anyone who has experienced exile or the diaspora.

Upon her return, after eleven years in the US, Khalaf's sense of place was immediately thrown off balance. The country she had known and loved was no longer the same or perhaps it never actually "existed at all". The surreal and unsettling atmosphere in the country served only to increase her anxieties about this new chapter in her life. "This was not the Lebanon I had come back to in my mind, not the country I had revisited countless times in my imagination. Perhaps the country I had known and loved never really existed at all."

Sadly, on the political front, "the country was now more fragmented and volatile than ever before." Re-entry made Khalaf all the more aware of "the seething hostility that lurked below the surface, stemming from the fact that none of the major issues had been adequately addressed, nor were they likely to be in the near future."

Soon, however, she puts her bewildering experiences to good use by crafting stories about female characters all of whom share her sense of *suspended betweenness* for having lived lives midway between cultures. "They too were out of place; exiles, living and writing from the margins, experiencing *suspended betweenness* with all its pleasures, pains and anxieties."

As a professor of English at the American University of Beirut, she introduced the first creative writing courses, providing students, many of whom as returnees felt like outsiders in their own country, with a similar outlet, a space for creative expression otherwise unavailable to them at the university or in the wider public sphere. "Fate and circumstances had conspired to transform them into seasoned travelers, border crossers, outsiders. Living between two or more worlds simultaneously, without actually belonging to any one place in particular, is a fact of life for these young people."

Such opportunities for narrative engagement, Khalaf points out, enable students to truthfully explore issues that are of immense relevance to their lives. Moreover, the stories they craft, offer counter narratives or essential digressions from the official biography of a country like Lebanon. Ultimately student texts and discourse may provide more imaginative, tolerant and diverse ways of seeing for a country in dire need of innovative alternatives.

While the autobiographical sketches of Said, Maalouf and Khalaf deal reflexivity with their own personal encounters with the exigencies of identity construction, Mohammed Azzi focuses on the predicament of Maghrebi Youth as they oscillate between the forces of alienation and integration while confronting such encounters. The experience of the Maghreb is quite instructive, particularly since youth there have had considerable exposure to protest movements, actively participating in public demonstrations and political parties, yet remaining marginalized and alienated.

For example, despite increasing industrialization, workers continued to conform to the normative expectations of traditional culture. Likewise, despite considerable achievements in education, illiteracy rates, particularly among women, are quite high. Also, given the deficient quality of education, the passing rate for the baccalaureate examinations has rarely reached 20 percent which, in effect, means that a large segment of youth remain excluded from schooling.

Azzi invokes the views of the modernist Algerian elite to argue that the educational system has deviated from its original mission of molding citizens for the future; i.e., making them scientifically and technologically competent and culturally open to universal values. Instead, the system has become a pulpit for conservative forces to instill Islamo-Baathist ideologies, thus sowing the seeds of Islamic radicalism. Azzi, quite persuasively, goes further to argue that the Arabization of the system of education has had two inconsistent byproducts. It has enabled a generation of young people to have direct access to holy writings. Yet it has simultaneously marginalized the young from the administrative and economic spheres.

The Maghreb does not only suffer from a deficient educational system. Urban housing policies have also failed to integrate the large numbers moving into the cities and, hence, compounding forces of social disintegration and social anomie. Traditional quarters, Azzi tells us, are no longer sources of social cohesion. Instead, the streets, alongside the mosque, have become the cornerstones for informal gatherings and social networks.

Perhaps the most vivid is the portrait Azzi depicts of generation of *hittists*, the idle youngsters without resources who, literally, lean against walls days on end. "If idleness is the mother of all vices, *hittism* is one step below ... It is the total emptiness of the soul." Seething with bitterness, resentment and suspicion of the luxurious cars, clothes and opulent life styles of others, the *hittists* are not ready to integrate into a society they hold accountable for their marginalization and destitution. Indeed, they are driven instead by a longing to leave it or take revenge on it.

Those who do not become *hittists*, are drawn into the informal sectors of the economy such as the *trabendo* in Algeria. Unlike the *hittists* who are prone to remain disengaged and retreatists, the *trabendos* are engaged in smuggling, contraband and other nefarious activities.

In accounting for the venues the disenfranchised youth could resort to, in order to mobilize their discontent, Azzi speaks about a shift from the street corner to the mosque. As the traditional quarters and their supportive institutions and networks were becoming more obsolete and irrelevant to the needs of the young, Islamist movements started to gain in appeal. The enhanced social identity of the *imams* bestowed upon them a sense of worthiness. They began to overshadow and replace traditional groups of solidarity, such as the family, kinship, neighborhoods and social clubs.

In her informed and probing analysis of how the new generation of Saudi Arabians are currently caught up in the process of negotiating a coherent identity, Mai Yamani tells the story of three generations which embody the life experiences of a typical Saudi family. Over a period of about sixty years, a family would have lived through the three major landmarks or interludes in Saudi Arabia's twentieth-century history: grandparents born in the 1930s, parents in the 1950s and the new generation in the 1970s and 1980s.

The first generation would have lived during a period of great historical significance associated with state formation and national unity. The unification was a period of upheaval marked by civil war and the assertion of *Wahhabism* as a distinct religious ideology. During the youth of the grand-parents, the peninsula was mostly a vast desert of largely nomadic rural communities where kinship and tribal loyalties were the primal sources of identity. The horizons of the grandparents' generation, confined by the absence of vehicular transportation, rarely extended beyond the boundaries of their home town or village. Though the grandparents' generation came to adulthood as the discovery of oil started to make its effects felt, their consciousness and loyalties, remained rooted in pre-oil times.

The second generation, born in the 1950s, came to adulthood after the powers of the state became more firmly established. The stupendous flow of oil revenues reinforced national integration and facilitated the building of the infrastructure. With the advent of education, media, travel and employment opportunities, Saudis became increasingly dependent on state institutions. The dominant *Hanbali* school of jurisprudence was an added source of homogenization. The fathers' broader allegiance extended beyond the Saudi state and was inspired by Arab nationalist sentiments mobilized by the charisma of Jamal Abdul Nasser. Access to higher education, particularly in the US, also enhanced the power and grandeur of the state, since the bulk of the educated elite were absorbed by the government sector.

Another striking feature of the second generation was the role of women. Although educated at the new schools for women, the mother nonetheless maintained the traditional role of a woman of her generation by rearing children. However, she had the advantage of modern medicine and health care, and could make use of foreign nannies, spacious homes and modern comforts. This led to a reduction in levels of infant mortality and a baby boom that greatly increased the population.

The byproduct of this population increase is the third generation. Born during the peak of the 1970s oil boom and before the economic downturn of the mid 1980s, they have no recollection of anything prior to the oil bonanza. Indeed their memory of the past is largely mediated through the narrations of their grandparents and parents. Despite all the privileges available to them—mass education, foreign travel, mass media, particularly via the high tech of satellites and websites and mass consumerism—the exposure to modernity has been a source of ambivalence, uncertainty and fear.

Yet despite these dazzling cultural transformations, this young generation lacks the traditional certainties of their grand-parents and the economic security of their parents. Hence, they are embroiled in the need to negotiate a sense of self from among a set of overlapping and competing internal and external sources of loyalties. Internally, the Saudi today must negotiate between the expectations of religion, tribal belonging, family and the state. Externally, they have to grapple with the more compelling uncertainties of modernity and globalization. Somehow, Mai Yamani leaves us with a reassuring inference that despite the seeming anachronisms, "there is broad acceptance that there should be some fairly high level of congruence between an idea of what it is to be Muslim and what it is to engage in modern practices and to live with modern technologies and consumer goods."

Between Worlds

In the first book I wrote, *Joseph Conrad* and the *Fiction of Autobiography*, published more than thirty years ago, and then in an essay called "Reflections on Exile" that appeared in 1984, I used Conrad as an example of someone whose life and work seemed to typify the fate of the wanderer who becomes an accomplished writer in an acquired language, but can never shake off his sense of alienation from his new—that is, acquired—and, in Conrad's rather special case, admired, home. His friends all said of Conrad that he was very contented with the idea of being English, even though he never lost his heavy Polish accent and his quite peculiar moodiness, which was thought to be very un-English. Yet the moment one enters his writing the aura of dislocation, instability, and strangeness is unmistakable. No one could represent the fate of lostness and disorientation better than he did, and no one was more ironic about the effort of trying to replace that condition with new arrangements and accommodations—which invariably lured one into further traps, such as those Lord Jim encounters when he starts life again on his little island. Marlow enters the heart of darkness to discover that Kurtz was not only there before him but is also incapable of telling him the whole truth; so that, in narrating his own experiences, Marlow cannot be as exact as he would have liked, and ends up producing approximations and even falsehoods of which both he and his listeners seem quite aware.

Only well after his death did Conrad's critics try to reconstruct what has been called his Polish background, very little of which had found its way directly into his fiction. But the rather elusive meaning of his writing is not so easily supplied, for even if we find out a lot about his Polish experiences, friends, and relatives, that information will not of itself settle the core of restlessness and unease that his work relentlessly circles. Eventually we realize that the work is actually constituted by the experience of exile or alienation that cannot ever be rectified. No matter how perfectly he is able to express something, the result always seems to him an approximation to what he had wanted to say, and to have been said too late, past the point where the saying of it might have been helpful. "Amy Foster," the most desolate of his stories, is about a young man from Eastern Europe, shipwrecked off the English coast on his way to America, who ends up as the husband of the affectionate but inarticulate Amy Foster. The man remains a foreigner, never learns the language, and even after he and Amy have a child cannot become a part of the very family he has created with her. When he is near death and babbling deliriously in a strange language, Amy snatches their child from him, abandoning him to his final sorrow. Like so many of Conrad's fictions, the story is narrated by a sympathetic figure, a doctor who is acquainted with the pair, but even he cannot redeem the young man's isolation, although Conrad teasingly makes the reader feel that he might have been able to. It is difficult to read "Amy Foster" without thinking that Conrad must have feared dying a similar death, inconsolable, alone, talking away in a language no one could understand.

The first thing to acknowledge is the loss of home and language in the new setting, a loss that Conrad has the severity to portray as irredeemable, relentlessly anguished, raw, untreatable, always acute—which is why I have found myself over the years reading and writing about Conrad like a *cantus firmus*, a steady groundbass to much that I have experienced. For years I seemed to be going over the same kind of thing in the work I did, but always through the writings of other people. It wasn't until the early fall of 1991, when an ugly medical diagnosis suddenly revealed to me the mortality I should have known about before, that I found myself trying to make sense of my own life as its end seemed alarmingly nearer. A few months later, still trying to assimilate my new condition, I found myself composing a long explanatory letter to my mother, who had already been dead for almost two years, a letter that inaugurated a belated attempt to impose a narrative on a life that I had left more or less to itself disorganized, scattered, uncentered. I had had a decent enough career in the university, I had written a fair amount, I had acquired an unenviable reputation (as the "professor of terror") for my writing and speaking and being active on Palestinian and generally Middle Eastern or Islamic and anti-imperialist issues, but I had rarely paused to put the whole jumble together. I was a compulsive worker, I disliked and hardly ever took vacations, and I did what I did without worrying too much (if at all) about such matters as writer's block, depression, or running dry.

All of a sudden, then, I found myself brought up short with some though not a great deal of time available to survey a life whose eccentricities I had accepted like so many facts of nature. Once again I recognized that Conrad had been there before me—except that Conrad was a European who left his native Poland and became an Englishman so the move for him was more or less within the same world. I was born in Jerusalem and had spent most of my formative years there and, before but especially after 1948, when my entire family became refugees, in Egypt. All my early education had, however, been in elite colonial schools, English public schools designed by the British to bring up a generation of Arabs with natural ties to Britain. The last one I went to before I left the Middle East to go to the United States was Victoria College in Cairo, a school in effect created to educate those ruling-class Arabs and Levantines who were going to take over after the British left. My contemporaries and classmates included King Hussein of Jordan, several Jordanian, Egyptian, Syrian, and Saudi boys who were to become ministers, prime ministers, and leading businessmen, as well as such glamorous figures as Michel Shalhoub, head prefect of the school and chief tormentor when I was a relatively junior boy, whom everyone has seen on screen as Omar Sharif.

The moment one became a student at VC one was given the school handbook, a series of regulations governing every aspect of school life—the kind of uniform we were to wear, what equipment was needed for sports, the dates of school holidays, bus schedules, and so on. But the school's first rule, emblazoned on the opening page of the handbook, read: "English is the language of the school; students caught speaking any other language will be punished." Yet there were no native English-speakers among the students. Whereas the masters were all British, we were a motley crew of Arabs of various kinds, Armenians, Greeks, Italians, Jews, and Turks, each of whom had a native language that the school had explicitly outlawed. Yet all, or nearly all, of us spoke Arabic—many spoke Arabic and

French—and so we were able to take refuge in a common language in defiance of what we perceived as an unjust colonial stricture. British imperial power was nearing its end immediately after World War Two, and this fact was not lost on us, although I cannot recall any student of my generation who would have been able to put anything as definite as that into words.

For me, there was an added complication, in that although both my parents were Palestinian—my mother from Nazareth, my father from Jerusalem—my father had acquired US citizenship during World War One, when he served in the AEF under Pershing in France. He had originally left Palestine, then an Ottoman province, in 1911, at the age of 16, to escape being drafted to fight in Bulgaria. Instead, he went to the United States, studied and worked there for a few years, then returned to Palestine in 1919 to go into business with his cousin. Besides, with an unexceptionally Arab family name like Said connected to an improbably British first name (my mother very much admired the Prince of Wales in 1935, the year of my birth), I was an uncomfortably anomalous student all through my early years: a Palestinian going to school in Egypt, with an English first name, an American passport, and no certain identity at all. To make matters worse, Arabic, my native language, and English, my school language, were inextricably mixed: I have never known which was my first language, and have felt fully at home in neither, although I dream in both. Every time I speak an English sentence, I find myself echoing it in Arabic, and vice versa.

All this went through my head in those months after my diagnosis revealed to me the necessity of thinking about final things. But I did so in what for me was a characteristic way. As the author of a book called *Beginnings*, I found myself drawn to my early days as a boy in Jerusalem, Cairo, and Dhour el Shweir, the Lebanese mountain village which I loathed but where for years and years my father took us to spend our summers. I found myself reliving the narrative quandaries of my early years, my sense of doubt and of being out of place, of always feeling myself standing in the wrong corner, in a place that seemed to be slipping away from me just as I tried to define or describe it. Why, I remember asking myself could I not have had a simple background, been all Egyptian, or all something else, and not have had to face the daily rigors of questions that led back to words that seemed to lack a stable origin? The worst part of my situation, which time has only exacerbated, has been the warring relationship between English and Arabic, something that Conrad had not had to deal with since his passage from Polish to English via French was effected entirely within Europe. My whole education was Anglocentric, so much so that I knew a great deal more about British and even Indian history and geography (required subjects) than I did about the history and geography of the Arab world. But although taught to believe and think like an English schoolboy, I was also trained to understand that I was an alien, a Non-European Other, educated by my betters to know my station and not to aspire to being British. The line separating Us from Them was linguistic, cultural, racial, and ethnic. It did not make matters easier for me to have been born, baptized, and confirmed in the Anglican Church, where the singing of bellicose hymns like "Onward Christian Soldiers" and "From Greenland's Icy Mountains" had me in effect playing the role at once of aggressor and aggressed against. To be at the same time a Wog and an Anglican was to be in a state of standing civil war.

In the spring of 1951 I was expelled from Victoria College, thrown out for being a troublemaker, which meant that I was more visible and more easily caught than the other boys in the daily skirmishes between Mr. Griffith, Mr. Hill, Mr. Lowe, Mr. Brown, Mr. Maundrell, Mr. Gatley, and all the other British teachers, on the one hand, and us, the boys of the school, on the other. We were all subliminally aware, too, that the old Arab order was crumbling: Palestine had fallen, Egypt was tottering under the massive corruption of King Farouk and his court (the revolution that brought Gamal Abdel Nasser and his Free Officers to power was to occur in July 1952), Syria was undergoing a dizzying series of military coups, Iran, whose Shah was at the time married to Farouk's sister, had its first big crisis in 1951, and so on. The prospects for deracinated people like us were so uncertain that my father decided it would be best to send me as far away as possible—in effect, to an austere, puritanical school in the northwestern corner of Massachusetts.

The day in early September 1951 when my mother and father deposited me at the gates of that school and then immediately left for the Middle East was probably the most miserable of my life. Not only was the atmosphere of the school rigid and explicitly moralistic, but I seemed to be the only boy there who was not a native-born American, who did not speak with the required accent, and had not grown up with baseball, basketball, and football. For the first time ever I was deprived of the linguistic environment I had depended on as an alternative to the hostile attentions of Anglo-Saxons whose language was not mine, and who made no bones about my belonging to an inferior, or somehow disapproved, race. Anyone who has lived through the quotidian obstacles of colonial routine will know what I am talking about. One of the first things I did was to look up a teacher of Egyptian origin whose name had been given to me by a family friend in Cairo. "Talk to Ned," our friend said, "and he'll instantly make you feel at home." On a bright Saturday afternoon I trudged over to Ned's house, introduced myself to the wiry, dark man who was also the tennis coach, and told him that Freddie Maalouf in Cairo had asked me to look him up. "Oh yes," the tennis coach said rather frostily, "Freddie." I immediately switched to Arabic, but Ned put up his hand to interrupt me. "No, brother, no Arabic here. I left all that behind when I came to America." And that was the end of that.

Because I had been well-trained at Victoria College, I did well enough in my Massachusetts boarding-school, achieving the rank of either first or second in a class of about a hundred and sixty. But I was also found to be morally wanting, as if there was something mysteriously not-quite-right about me, When I graduated, for instance, the rank of valedictorian or salutatorian was withheld from me on the grounds that I was not fit for the honor—a moral judgment which I have ever since found difficult either to understand or to forgive. Although I went back to the Middle East during holidays (my family continued to live there, moving from Egypt to Lebanon in 1963), I found myself becoming an entirely Western person; both at college and in graduate school I studied literature, music, and philosophy, but none of it had anything to do with my own tradition. In the fifties and early sixties students from the Arab world were almost invariably scientists, doctors, and engineers, or specialists in the Middle East, getting degrees at places like Princeton and Harvard and then, for the most part, returning to their countries to become teachers in universities there. I had very little to do with them, for one reason or another, and this naturally increased my isolation from my own language and background. By the time I came to New York to teach at Columbia in the fall of 1963, I was considered to have an exotic but somewhat irrelevant Arabic background—in fact I recall that it was easier for most of my friends and colleagues not to use the word "Arab," and certainly not "Palestinian," in deference to the much easier and vaguer "Middle Eastern," a term that offended no one. A friend who was already teaching at Columbia later told me that when I was hired I had been described to the department as an Alexandrian Jew! I remember a sense of being accepted, even courted, by older colleagues at Columbia, who with one or two exceptions saw me as a promising, even very promising, young scholar of "our" culture. Since there was no political activity then which was centered on the Arab world, I found that my concerns in my teaching and research, which were canonical though slightly unorthodox, kept me within the pale.

The big change came with the Arab-Israeli war of 1967, which coincided with a period of intense political activism on campus over civil rights and the Vietnam War. I found myself naturally involved on both fronts, but, for me, there was the further difficulty of trying to draw attention to the Palestinian cause. After the Arab defeat there was a vigorous re-emergence of Palestinian nationalism, embodied in the resistance movement located mainly in Jordan and the newly occupied territories. Several friends and members of my family had joined the movement, and when I visited Jordan in 1968, 1969, and 1970, I found myself among a number of like-minded contemporaries. In the United States, however, my politics were rejected—with a few notable exceptions—both by anti-war activists and by supporters of Martin Luther King. For the first time I felt genuinely divided between the newly assertive pressures of my background and language and the complicated demands of a situation in the United States that scanted, in fact despised, what I had to say about the quest for Palestinian justice —which was considered anti-semitic and Nazi-like.

In 1972 I had a sabbatical and took the opportunity of spending a year in Beirut, where most of my time was taken up with the study of Arabic philology and literature, something I had never done before, at least not at that level, out of a feeling that I had allowed the disparity between my acquired identity and the culture into which I was born, and from which I had been removed, to become too great. In other words, there was an existential as well as a felt political need to bring one self into harmony with the other, for as the debate about what had once been called "the Middle East" metamorphosed into a debate between Israelis and Palestinians, I was drawn in, ironically enough, as much because of my capacity to speak as an American academic and intellectual as by the accident of my birth. By the mid-seventies I was in the rich but unenviable position of speaking for two diametrically opposed constituencies, one Western, the other Arab.

For as long as I can remember, I had allowed myself to stand outside the umbrella that shielded or accommodated my contemporaries. Whether this was because I was genuinely different, objectively an outsider, or because I was temperamentally a loner I cannot say, but the fact is that although I went along with all sorts of institutional routines because I felt I had to, something private in me resisted them. I don't know what it was that caused me to hold back, but even when I was most miserably solitary or out of synch with everyone else, I held onto this private aloofness very fiercely. I may have envied friends whose language was one or the other, or who had lived in the same place all their lives, or who had done well in accepted ways, or who truly belonged, but I do not recall ever thinking that any of that was possible for me. It wasn't that I considered myself special, but rather that I didn't fit the situations I found myself in and wasn't too displeased to accept this state of affairs. I have, besides, always been drawn to stubborn autodidacts, to various sorts of intellectual misfit. In part it was the heedlessness of their own peculiar angle of vision that attracted me to writers and artists like Conrad, Vico, Adorno, Swift, Adonis, Hopkins, Auerbach, Glenn Gould, whose style, or way of thinking, was highly individualistic and impossible to imitate, for whom the medium of expression, whether music or words, was eccentrically charged, very worked-over, self-conscious in the highest degree. What impressed me about them was not the mere fact of their self-invention but that the enterprise was deliberately and fastidiously located within a general history which they had excavated *ab origine*.

Having allowed myself gradually to assume the professional voice of an American academic as a way of submerging my difficult and unassimilable past, I began to think and write contrapuntally, using the disparate halves of my experience, as an Arab and as an American, to work with and also against each other. This tendency began to take shape after 1967, and though it was difficult, it was also exciting. What prompted the initial change in my sense of self, and of the language I was using, was the realization that in accommodating to the exigencies of life in the US melting-pot, I had willy-nilly to accept the principle of annulment of which Adorno speaks so perceptively in *Minima Moralia*:

> The past life of émigrés is, as we know, annulled. Earlier it was the warrant of arrest, today it is intellectual experience, that is declared non-transferable and unnaturalisable. Anything that is nor reified, cannot be counted and measured, ceases to exist. Not satisfied with this, however, reification spreads to its own opposite, the life that cannot be directly actualized; anything that lives on merely as thought and recollection. For this a special rubric has been invented. It is called "background" and appears on the questionnaire as an appendix, after sex, age and profession. To complete its violation, life is dragged along on the triumphal automobile of the united statisticians, and even the past is no longer safe from the present, whose remembrance of it consigns it a second time to oblivion.

For my family and for myself the catastrophe of 1948 (I was then 12) was lived unpolitically. For twenty years after their dispossession and expulsion from their homes and territory, most Palestinians had to live as refugees, coming to terms not with their past, which was lost, annulled, but with their present. I do not want to suggest that my life as a schoolboy, learning to speak and coin a language that let me live as a citizen of the United States, entailed anything like the suffering of that first generation of Palestinian refugees, scattered throughout the Arab world, where invidious laws made it impossible for them to become naturalized, unable to work, unable to travel, obliged to register and re-register each month with the police, many of them forced to live in appalling camps like Beirut's Sabra and Shatila, which were the sites of massacres 34 years later. What I experienced, however, was the suppression of a history as everyone around me celebrated Israel's victory, its terrible swift sword, as Barbara Tuchman grandly put it, at the expense of the original inhabitants of Palestine, who now found themselves forced over and over again to prove that they had once existed. "There are no Palestinians," said Golda Meir in 1969, and that set me, and many others, the slightly preposterous challenge of disproving her, of beginning to articulate a history of loss and dispossession that had to be extricated, minute by minute, word by word, inch by inch, from the very real history of Israel's establishment, existence, and achievements. I was working in an almost entirely negative element, the non-existence, the non-history which I had somehow to make visible despite occlusions, misrepresentations, and denials.

Inevitably, this led me to reconsider the notions of writing and language, which I had until then treated as animated by a given text or subject—the history of the novel, for instance, or the idea of narrative as a theme in prose fiction, What concerned me now was how a subject was constituted, how a language could be formed—writing as a construction of realities that served one or another purpose instrumentally. This was the world of power and representations, a world that came into being as a series of decisions made by writers, politicians, philosophers to suggest or adumbrate one reality and at the same time efface others. The first attempt I made at this kind of work was a short essay I wrote in 1968 entitled "The Arab Portrayed," in which I described the image of the Arab that had been manipulated in journalism and some scholarly writing in such a way as to evade any discussion of history and experience as I and many other Arabs had lived them. I also wrote a longish study of Arabic prose fiction after 1948 in which I reported on the fragmentary, embattled quality of the narrative line.

During the seventies I taught my courses in European and American literature at Columbia and elsewhere, and bit by bit entered the political and discursive worlds of Middle Eastern and international politics. It is worth mentioning here that for the forty years that I have been teaching I have never taught anything other than the Western canon and certainly nothing about the Middle East. I've long had the ambition of giving a course on modern Arabic literature, but I haven't got around to it, and for at least thirty years I've been planning a seminar on Vico and Ibn Khaldun, the great fourteenth-century historiographer and philosopher of history. But my sense of identity as a teacher of Western literature has excluded this other aspect of my activity so far as the classroom is concerned. Ironically, the fact that I continued to write and teach my subject gave sponsors and hosts at university functions to which I had been invited to lecture an excuse to ignore my embarrassing political activity by specifically asking me to lecture on a literary topic. And there were those who spoke of my efforts on behalf of "my people," without ever mentioning the name of that people. "Palestine" was still a word to be avoided.

Even in the Arab world Palestine earned me a great deal of opprobrium. When the Jewish Defense League called me a Nazi in 1985, my office at the university was set fire to and my family and I received innumerable death threats, but when Anwar Sadat and Yasser Arafat appointed me Palestinian representative to the peace talks (without ever consulting me) and I found it impossible to step outside my apartment, so great was the media rush around me, I became the object of extreme left-wing nationalist hostility because I was considered too liberal on the question of Palestine and the idea of co-existence between Israeli Jews and Palestinian Arabs. I've been consistent in my belief that no military option exists for either side, that only a process of peaceful reconciliation, and justice for what the Palestinians have had to endure by way of dispossession and military occupation, would work. I was also very critical of the use of slogan-clichés like "armed struggle" and of the revolutionary adventurism that caused innocent deaths and did nothing to advance the Palestinian case politically. "The predicament of private life today is shown by its arena," Adorno wrote. "Dwelling, in the proper sense, is now impossible. The traditional residences we grew up in have grown intolerable: each trait of comfort in them is paid for with a betrayal of knowledge, each vestige of shelter with the musty pact of family interests." Even more unyieldingly, he continued:

> The house is past... The best mode of conduct, in the face of all this, still seems an uncommitted, suspended one: to lead a private life, as far as the social order and one's own needs will tolerate nothing else, but not to attach weight to it as something still socially substantial and individually appropriate. "It is even part of my good fortune not to be a house-owner," Nietzsche already wrote in the *Gay Science*. Today we should have to add: it is part of morality not to be at home in one's home.

For myself I have been unable to live an uncommitted or suspended life: I have not hesitated to declare my affiliation with an extremely unpopular cause. On the other hand, I have always reserved the right to be critical, even when criticism conflicted with solidarity or with what others expected in the name of national loyalty. There is a definite, almost palpable discomfort to such a position, especially given the irreconcilability of the two constituencies, and the two lives they have required.

The net result in terms of my writing has been to attempt a greater transparency, to free myself from academic jargon, and not to hide behind euphemism and circumlocution where difficult issues have been concerned. I have given the name "worldliness" to this voice, by which I do not mean the jaded savoir-faire of the man about town, but rather a knowing and unafraid attitude toward exploring the world we live in. Cognate words, derived from Vico and Auerbach, have been "secular" and "secularism" as applied to "earthly" matters; in these words, which derive from the Italian materialist tradition that runs from Lucretius through to Gramsci and Lampedusa, I have found an important corrective to the German Idealist tradition of synthesizing the antithetical, as we find it in Hegel, Marx, Lukacs, and Habermas. For not only did "earthly" connote this historical world made by men and women rather than by God or "the nation's genius," as Herder termed it, but it suggested a territorial grounding for my argument and language, which proceeded from an attempt to understand the imaginative geographies fashioned and then imposed by power on distant lands and people. In *Orientalism* and *Culture and Imperialism*, and then again in the five or six explicitly political books concerning Palestine and the Islamic world that I wrote around the same time, I felt that I had been fashioning a self who revealed for a Western audience things that had so far been either hidden or not discussed at all. Thus in talking about the Orient, hitherto believed to be a simple fact of nature, I tried to uncover the longstanding, very varied geographical obsession with a distant, often inaccessible world that helped Europe to define itself by being its opposite. Similarly, I believed that Palestine, a territory effaced in the process of building another society, could be restored as an act of political resistance to injustice and oblivion.

Occasionally, I'd notice that I had become a peculiar creature to many people, and even a few friends, who had assumed that being Palestinian was the equivalent of something mythological like a unicorn or a hopelessly odd variation of a human being. A Boston psychologist who specialized in conflict resolution, and whom I had met at several seminars involving Palestinians and Israelis, once rang me from Greenwich Village and asked if she could come uptown to pay me a visit. When she arrived, she walked in, looked incredulously at my piano—"Ah, you actually play the piano," she said, with a trace of disbelief in her voice—and then turned around and began to walk out. When I asked her whether she would have a cup of tea before leaving (after all, I said, you have come a long way for such a short visit), she said she didn't have time. "I only came to see how you lived," she said without a hint of irony. Another time a publisher in another city refused to sign my contract until I had lunch with him. When I asked his assistant what was so important about having a meal with me, I was told that the great man wanted to see how I handled myself at the table. Fortunately none of these experiences affected or detained me for very long: I was always in too much of a rush to meet a class or a deadline, and I quite deliberately avoided the self-questioning that would have landed me in a terminal depression. In any case the Palestinian intifada that erupted in December 1987 confirmed our peoplehood in as dramatic and compelling a way as anything I might have said. Before long, however, I found myself becoming a token figure, hauled in for a few hundred written words or a ten-second soundbite testifying to "what the Palestinians are saying," and determined to escape that role, especially given my disagreements with the PLO leadership from the late eighties.

I am not sure whether to call this perpetual self-invention or a constant restlessness. Either way, I've long learned to cherish it. Identity as such is about as boring a subject as one can imagine. Nothing seems less interesting than the narcissistic self-study that today passes in many places for identity politics, or ethnic studies, or affirmations of roots, cultural pride, drum-beating nationalism, and so on. We have to defend peoples and identities threatened with extinction or subordinated because they are considered inferior, but that is very different from aggrandizing a past invented for present reasons. Those of us who are American intellectuals owe it to our country to fight the coarse anti-intellectualism, bullying, injustice, and provincialism that disfigure its career as the last superpower. It is far more challenging to try to transform oneself into something different than it is to keep insisting on the virtues of being American in the ideological sense. Having myself lost a country with no immediate hope of regaining it, I don't find much comfort in cultivating a new garden, or looking for some other association to join. I learned from Adorno that reconciliation under duress is both cowardly and inauthentic: better a lost cause than a triumphant one, more satisfying a sense of the provisional and contingent—a rented house, for example—than the proprietary solidity of permanent ownership. This is why strolling dandies like Oscar Wilde or Baudelaire seem to me intrinsically more interesting than extollers of settled virtue like Wordsworth or Carlyle.

For the past five years I have been writing two columns a month for the Arabic press; and despite my extremely anti-religious politics I am often glowingly described in the Islamic world as a defender of Islam, and considered by some of the Islamic parties to be one of their supporters. Nothing could be further from the truth, any more than it is true that I have been an apologist for terrorism. The prismatic quality of one's writing when one isn't entirely of any camp, or a total partisan of any cause, is difficult to handle, but there, too, I have accepted the irreconcilability of the various conflicting, or at least incompletely harmonized, aspects of what, cumulatively, I appear to have stood for. A phrase by Günter Grass describes the predicament well: that of the "intellectual without mandate." A complicated situation arose in late 1993 when, after seeming to be the approved voice of the Palestinian struggle, I wrote increasingly sharply of my disagreements with Arafat and his bunch. I was immediately branded "anti-peace" because I had the lack of tact to describe the Oslo treaty as deeply flawed. Now that everything has ground to a halt, I am regularly asked what it is like to be proved right, but I was more surprised by that than anyone: prophecy is not part of my arsenal.

For the past three or four years I have been trying to write a memoir of my early—that is, pre-political—life, largely because I think it's a story worthy of rescue and commemoration, given that the three places I grew up in have ceased to exist, Palestine is now Israel, Lebanon, after twenty years of civil war, is hardly the stiflingly boring place it was when we spent our summers locked up in Dhour el Shweir, and colonial, monarchical Egypt disappeared in 1952. My memories of those days and places remain extremely vivid, full of little details that I seem to have preserved as if between the covers of a book, full also of unexpressed feelings generated out of situations and events that occurred decades ago but seem to have been waiting to be articulated now. Conrad says in *Nostromo* that a desire lurks in every heart to write down once and for all a true account of what happened, and this certainly is what moved me to write my memoir, just as I had found myself writing a letter to my dead mother out of a desire once again to communicate something terribly important to a primordial presence in my life. "In his text," Adorno says,

> The writer sets up house... For a man who no longer has a homeland, writing becomes a place to live... [Yet] the demand that one harden oneself against self-pity implies the technical necessity to counter any slackening of intellectual tension with the utmost alertness, and to eliminate anything that has begun to encrust the work or to drift along idly, which may at an earlier stage have served, as gossip, to generate the warm atmosphere conducive to growth, but is now left behind, flat and stale. In the end, the writer is not even allowed to live in his writing.

One achieves at most a provisional satisfaction, which is quickly ambushed by doubt, and a need to rewrite and redo that renders the text uninhabitable. Better *that*, however, than the sleep of self-satisfaction and the finality of death.

Originally published in *Reflections on Exile* (Harvard University Press, 2000): 554–68. Published here with permission from the Wylie Agency.

Damaged Identities and Violence

Identity isn't given once and for all: it is built up and changes throughout a person's lifetime. This has been pointed out in numerous books and amply explained, but it is still worth emphasizing again: not many of the elements that go to make up our identity are already in us at birth. A few physical characteristics of course—sex, colour and so on. And even at this point not everything is innate. Although, obviously, social environment doesn't determine sex, it does determine its significance. To be born a girl is not the same in Kabul as it is in Oslo: the condition of being a woman, like every other factor in a person's identity, is experienced differently in the two places.

The same could be said of colour. To be born black is a different matter according to whether you come into the world in New York, Lagos, Pretoria or Rwanda. One might almost say that, from the point of identity we're not even talking about the same colour in the different places. For an infant who first sees the light of day in Nigeria, the operative factor as regards his identity is not whether he is black rather than white, but whether he is Yoruba, say, rather than Hausa. In South Africa, whether a person is black or white is still a significant element in his identity, but at least equally meaningful is his ethnic affiliation, whether Zulu, Xhosa or something else. In the United States it is of no consequence whether you have a Yoruba rather than a Hausa ancestor: it is chiefly among the whites—the Italians, the English, the Irish and the rest—that ethnic origin has a determining effect on identity. Moreover, someone with both whites and blacks among his ancestors would be regarded as "black" in the United States, whereas in South Africa or Angola he would be considered as "of mixed race."

Why is the idea of mixed race taken into account in some countries and not in others? Why is ethnic affiliation a determining factor in some societies but not in the rest? One could put forward various more or less convincing answers to both questions. But that is not what concerns me at this stage. I mention these examples only to underline the fact that even colour and sex are not "absolute" ingredients of identity. That being so, all the other ingredients are even more relative.

To gauge what is really innate among the ingredients that go to make up identity, we may make use of a mental exercise which is extremely revealing. Imagine an infant removed immediately from its place of birth and set down in a different environment. Then compare the various "identities" the child might acquire in its new context, the battles it would now have to fight and those it would be spared. Needless to say, the child would have no recollection of his original religion, or of his country or language. And might he not one day find himself fighting to the death against those who ought to have been his nearest and dearest?

What determines a person's affiliation to a given group is essentially the influence of others: the influence of those about him—relatives, fellow-countrymen, co-religionists—who try to make him one of them; together with the influence of those on the other side, who do their best to exclude him. Each one of us has to make his way while choosing between the paths that are urged upon him and those that are forbidden or strewn with obstacles. He is not himself from the outset; nor does he just "grow aware" of what he is; he becomes what he is. He doesn't merely grow aware of his identity; he acquires it step by step.

The apprenticeship starts very soon, in early childhood. Deliberately or otherwise, those around him mould him, shape him, instill into him family beliefs, rituals, attitudes and conventions, together of course with his native language and also certain fears, aspirations, prejudices and grudges, not forgetting various feelings of affiliation and non-affiliation, belonging and not belonging.

And soon, at home, at school and in the next street, he will suffer his first knocks. By their words and by their looks, other people will make him feel he is poor, or lame, short or lanky, swarthy or too fair, circumcised or uncircumcised, or an orphan; those innumerable differences, major and minor, that define every personality and shape each individual's behaviour, opinions, fears and ambitions. Such factors may act as formative influences, but they can also cause permanent injuries

It is these wounds that at every stage in life determine not only men's attitudes towards their affiliations but also the hierarchy that decides the relative importance of these ties. When someone has been bullied because of his religion, humiliated or mocked because of the colour of his skin, his accent or his shabby clothes, he will never forget it. Up till now I have stressed the fact that identity is made up of a number of allegiances. But it is just as necessary to emphasize that identity is also singular, something that we experience as a complete whole. A person's identity is not an assemblage of separate affiliations, nor a kind of loose patchwork; it is like a pattern drawn on a tightly stretched parchment. Touch just one part of it, just one allegiance, and the whole person will react, the whole drum will sound.

People often see themselves in terms of whichever one of their allegiances is most under attack. And sometimes, when a person doesn't have the strength to defend that allegiance, he hides it. Then it remains buried deep down in the dark, awaiting its revenge. But whether he accepts or conceals it, proclaims it discreetly or flaunts it, it is with that allegiance that the person concerned identifies. And then, whether it relates to colour, religion, language or class, it invades the person's whole identity. Other people who share the same allegiance sympathise; they all gather together, join forces, encourage one another, and challenge "the other side." For them, "asserting their identity" inevitably becomes an act of courage, of liberation.

In the midst of any community that has been wounded, agitators naturally arise. Whether they are hot-heads or cool schemers, their intransigent speeches act as balm to their audience's wounds. They say one shouldn't beg others for respect: respect is a due and must be forced from those who would withhold it. They promise victory or vengeance, they inflame men's minds, sometimes they use extreme methods that some of their brothers may merely have dreamed of in secret. The scene is now set and the war can begin. Whatever happens, "the others" will have deserved it. "We" can remember quite clearly "all they have made us suffer" since time immemorial: all the crimes, all the extortion, all the humiliations and fears, complete with names and dates and statistics.

I have lived in a country at war, in a neighbourhood being shelled from a nearby part of the same city. I have spent a night or two in a basement being used as an air-raid shelter, together with my young wife, who was pregnant, and my little son. From outside came the noise of explosions; inside, people exchanged rumours of imminent attack and stories about whole families being put to the sword. So I know very well that fear might make anyone take to crime. If, instead of mere rumours, there had been a real massacre in the neighbourhood where I lived, would I have remained calm and collected? If, instead of spending just a couple of days in that shelter, I had had to stay there for a month, would I have refused to take a gun if it had been put in my hand?

I prefer not to ask myself such questions too often. I had the good luck not to be put to the test; to emerge from the ordeal with my family unharmed, with my hands clean and with a clear conscience. But I speak of "good luck" because things could have turned out very differently if I'd been 16 instead of 26 when the war began in Lebanon. Or if I'd lost someone I loved. Or if I'd belonged to a different social class, or a different community.

After each new ethnic massacre we ask ourselves, quite rightly, how human beings can perpetrate such atrocities. Certain excesses seem incomprehensible; the logic behind them indecipherable. So we talk of murderous folly, of bloodthirsty ancestral or hereditary madness. In a way, we are right to talk of madness. When an otherwise normal man is transformed overnight into a killer, that is indeed insanity. But when there are thousands, millions of killers; when this phenomenon occurs in one country after another, in different cultures, among the faithful of all religions and among unbelievers alike, it's no longer enough to talk of madness. What we conveniently call "murderous folly" is the propensity of our fellow-creatures to turn into butchers when they suspect that their "tribe" is being threatened. The emotions of fear or insecurity don't always obey rational considerations. They may be exaggerated or even paranoid; but once a whole population is afraid, we are dealing with the reality of the fear rather than the reality of the threat.

I don't think any particular affiliation, be it ethnic, religious, national or anything else, predisposes anyone to murder. We have only to review the events of the last few years to see that any human community that feels humiliated or fears for its existence will tend to produce killers. And these killers will commit the most dreadful atrocities in the belief that they are right to do so and deserve the admiration of their fellows in this world and bliss in the next. There is a Mr. Hyde inside each one of us. What we have to do is prevent the conditions occurring that will bring the monster forth.

I shall not venture to propose a universal explanation of all the massacres, still less to suggest a miracle cure. I no more believe in simplistic solutions than I do in simplistic identities. The world is a complex machine that can't be dismantled with a screwdriver. But that shouldn't prevent us from observing, from trying to understand, from discussing, and sometimes suggesting a subject for reflection.

If the men of all countries, of all conditions and faiths can so easily be transformed into butchers, if fanatics of all kinds manage so easily to pass themselves off as defenders of identity, it's because the "tribal" concept of identity still prevalent all over the world facilitates such a distortion. It's a concept inherited from the conflicts of the past, and many of us would reject it if we examined it more closely. But we cling to it through habit, from lack of imagination or resignation, thus inadvertently contributing to the tragedies by which, tomorrow, we shall be genuinely shocked.

Murderous or mortal identities are those that kill. The expression doesn't strike me as inappropriate insofar as the idea I'm challenging—the notion that reduces identity to one single affiliation—encourages people to adopt an attitude that is partial, sectarian, intolerant, domineering, sometimes suicidal, and frequently even changes them into killers or supporters of killers. Their view of the world is biased and distorted. Those who belong to the same community as we do are "ours," we like to think ourselves concerned about what happens to them, but we also allow ourselves to tyrannise over them: if they are thought to be "lukewarm" we denounce them, intimidate them, punish them as "traitors" and "renegades." As for the others, those on the opposite side, we never try to put ourselves in their place, we take good care not to ask ourselves whether on some point or other they might not be entirely in the wrong, and we won't let our hearts be softened by their complaints, their sufferings or the injustices that have been inflicted on them. The only thing that counts is the point of view of "our" side; a point of view that is often that of the most militant, the most demagogic and the most fanatical members of the community.

On the other hand, when one sees one's own identity as made up of a number of allegiances, some linked to an ethnic past and others not, some linked to a religious tradition and others not; when one observes in oneself, in one's origins and in the course one's life has taken, a number of different confluences and contributions, of different mixtures and influences, some of them quite subtle or even incompatible with one another; then one enters into a different relationship both with other people and with one's own "tribe." It's no longer just a question of "them" and "us": two armies in battle order preparing for the next confrontation, the next revenge match. From then on there are people on "our" side with whom I ultimately have little in common, while on "their" side there are some to whom I might feel very close.

But to return to the earlier state of mind, it's easy to imagine how it can drive people to the worst kind of extremities: if they feel that "others" represent a threat to their own ethnic group or religion or nation, anything they might do to ward off that danger seems to them entirely legitimate. Even when they commit massacres they are convinced they are merely doing what is necessary to save the lives of their nearest and dearest. And as this attitude is shared by those around them, the butchers often have a clear conscience and are amazed to hear themselves described as criminals. How can they be criminals when all they are doing is protecting their aged mothers, their brothers and sisters and children?

The feeling that they are fighting for the survival of their own loved ones and are supported by their prayers; the belief that if not in the present instance at least over the long term they can claim to be acting in legitimate self-defense: these characteristics are common to all those who in recent years, throughout the world, from Rwanda to former Yugoslavia, have committed the most abominable crimes.

We are not talking about isolated examples. The world is full of whole communities that are wounded—either enduring present persecution or still overshadowed by the memory of former sufferings—and who dream of exacting revenge. We cannot remain unmoved by their martyrdom; we can only sympathise with their desire to speak their own language freely, to practice their own religion without fear, and to preserve their own traditions. But compassion sometimes tends towards complaisance: those who have suffered from colonialist arrogance, racism and xenophobia are forgiven for excesses they themselves have committed because of their own nationalistic arrogance, their own racism and xenophobia. This attitude means we turn a blind eye to the fate of their victims, at least until rivers of blood have been shed.

The fact is, it's difficult to say where legitimate affirmation of identity ends and encroachment on the rights of others begins. Did I not say that the word identity was a "false friend"? It starts by reflecting a perfectly permissible aspiration. Then before we know where we are, it has become an instrument of war. The transition from one meaning to the other is imperceptible, almost natural, and sometimes we all just go along with it. We are denouncing an injustice, we are defending the rights of a suffering people—then the next day we find ourselves accomplices in a massacre.

All the massacres that have taken place in recent years, like most of the bloody wars, have been linked to complex and long-standing "cases" of identity. Sometimes the victims are forever desperately the same; sometimes the situation is reversed and the victimizers of yesterday become victims of today; or vice versa. Such words themselves, it must be said, are meaningful only to outside observers; for people directly involved in conflicts arising out of identity, for those who have suffered and been afraid, nothing else exists except "them" and "us," the insult and the atonement. "We" are necessarily and by definition innocent victims; "they" are necessarily guilty and have long been so, regardless of what they may be enduring at present.

And when we, the outside observers, go in for this game and cast one community in the role of the sheep and another in that of the wolf, what we are unwittingly doing is granting the former community impunity in advance for its crimes. In recent conflicts some factions have even committed atrocities against their own people, knowing that international opinion would automatically lay the blame on their opponents.

This first type of complacency carries with it another, equally unfortunate form, whereby, at each new massacre arising out of identity, the eternal skeptics immediately declare that things have been the same since the dawn of history, and that it would be naive and self-deluding to hope they might change. Ethnic massacres are sometimes treated, consciously or otherwise, like collective crimes of passion, regrettable but comprehensible, and anyway inevitable because they are "inherent in human nature."

The laissez-faire attitude has already done great harm, and the realism invoked to justify it is in my opinion a misnomer. Unfortunately the "tribal" notion of identity is still the one most commonly accepted everywhere, not only amongst fanatics. But many ideas that have been commonly accepted for centuries are no longer admissible today, among them the "natural" ascendancy of men over women, the hierarchy between races, and even, closer to home, apartheid and the various other kinds of segregation. Torture, too, was for a long time regarded as a "normal" element in the execution of justice. For centuries, slavery seemed like a fact of life, and great minds of the past took care not to call it into question.

Then new ideas gradually managed to establish themselves: that every man had rights that must be defined and respected; that women should have the same rights as men; that nature too deserved to be protected; that the whole human race has interests in common in more and more areas—the environment, peace, international exchanges, the battle against the great scourges of disease and natural disaster; that others might and even should interfere in the internal affairs of countries where fundamental human rights are abused. And so on.

In other words, ideas that have hitherto prevailed throughout history are not necessarily those that ought to prevail in times to come. When new facts emerge we need to reconsider our attitudes and habits. Sometimes, when such facts emerge too rapidly, our mental attitudes can't keep up with them and we find ourselves trying to fight fires by pouring oil on them.

But in the age of globalization and of the ever-accelerating intermingling of elements in which we are all caught up, a new concept of identity is needed, and needed urgently We cannot be satisfied with forcing billions of bewildered human beings to choose between excessive assertion of their identity and the loss of their identity altogether, between fundamentalism and disintegration. But that is the logical consequence of the prevailing attitude on the subject. If our contemporaries are not encouraged to accept their multiple affiliations and allegiances; if they cannot reconcile their need for identity with an open and unprejudiced tolerance of other cultures; if they feel they have to choose between denial of the self and denial of the other—then we shall be bringing into being legions of the lost and hordes of bloodthirsty madmen.

A man with a Serbian mother and a Croatian father, and who manages to accept his dual affiliation, will never take part in any form of ethnic "cleansing." A man with a Hutu mother and a Tutsi father, if he can accept the two "tributaries" that brought him into the world, will never be a party to butchery or genocide. And neither the Franco-Algerian lad, nor the young man of mixed German and Turkish origin, will ever be on the side of the fanatics if they succeed in living peacefully in the context of their own complex identity.

Here again it would be a mistake to see such examples as extreme or unusual. Wherever there are groups of human beings living side by side who differ from one another in religion, colour, language, ethnic origin or nationality, wherever there are tensions, more or less longstanding, more or less violent, between immigrants and local populations, wherever there is a divided society, there are men and women bearing within them contradictory allegiances, people who live on the frontier between opposed communities, and whose very being might be said to be traversed by ethnic or religious or other fault lines.

We are not dealing with a handful of marginal people. There are thousands, millions of such men and women, and there will be more and more of them. They are frontier-dwellers by birth, or through the changes and chances of life, or by deliberate choice, and they can influence events and affect their course one way or the other. Those who can accept their diversity fully will hand on the torch between communities and cultures. They will be a kind of mortar joining together and strengthening the societies in which they live. On the other hand, those who cannot accept their own diversity may be among the most virulent of those prepared to kill for the sake of identity, attacking those who embody that part of themselves which they would like to see forgotten. History contains many examples of such self-hatred.

Originally published *In the Name of Identity: Violence and the Need to Belong* (Arcade Publishing, 2001): 23-36. Printed here with the permission of the author.

Living Between Worlds

> I could not Live in any of the worlds offered to me I believe one writes because one has to create a world in which one can live ... I had to create a world of my own ... in which I could breathe, reign, and recreate myself when destroyed by living.
>
> Anais Nin, *In Favour of the Sensitive Man*

We left Beirut in the fall of 1984 with the horror of war still fresh in our minds. While it was excruciating to leave family and friends behind, the senseless battles that raged on in the country only strengthened our resolve to distance our two young boys from the savage cruelties of a country torn apart by civil strife. Too many of our friends and acquaintances had become innocent victims of random violence. Besides, ten years of barely eking out an existence, of adhering to the numbing routine of survival was taking its toll on us. We had been witnesses to every atrocity imaginable: random shelling, street fighting, car bombs, sniping, kidnapping, torture, murder and massacres. Human suffering had reached immeasurable heights, the brutality was beyond description, and still, the violence continued to escalate. It was ongoing and relentless, with no end in sight. Obviously it would be sheer insanity to take any more chances especially as we had, on numerous occasions, barely escaped death. In the darkness of 1984, we finally took the agonizing decision to leave for what we thought would be a year's research leave, and I was immediately overwhelmed with despair. The war had brought so much fear and sadness to our lives that I was absolutely convinced we would never be able to shed it all and resume a normal existence.

Then in February 1995, after eleven years of involuntary exile, I found myself back in Beirut. Almost immediately my sense of place was thrown off balance. This was not the Lebanon I had come back to in my mind; not the country I had revisited countless times in my imagination. Perhaps the Lebanon I had known and loved never existed at all. Suddenly I was thrown into a state of confusion. One thing remained certain, the surreal atmosphere in the country only served to heighten my anxieties about this new chapter in my life. I was shocked by the visual images of a city I no longer recognized. The chaotic building boom paved the way for hideous, sprawling housing and commercial developments. To my horror, fast-food outlets and kitschy entertainment spots had invaded the Corniche that stretches along a once beautiful and unspoiled seafront. Concrete monstrosities, unzoned and illegally built structures now eroded the pristine landscape that used to surround the city. The downtown area, where some of the fiercest fighting had taken place, was being restored. Yet there remained, throughout the city, large pockets of bullet-ridden and bombed out buildings, a grim reminder of the senseless violence, brutality and destruction that had ravaged the entire country.

Clearly I had not realized just how distressing re-entry would be, although in reality, how could it have been otherwise? The sheer magnitude of the war, undoubtedly one of the bitterest civil wars in modern Arab history, was astounding. It had raged on for nearly two decades leaving 170,000 people dead, twice as many wounded or disabled, and approximately two-thirds of the population dislocated. Sadly on the political front, the country was now more fragmented and volatile than ever before. Below the surface lurked seething hostility resulting from the fact that none of the major issues had been adequately addressed, nor were they likely to be in the near future.

Upon my return two themes in particular seemed to take shape. The first centred on my academic life. For months I had looked forward to the prospect of seriously teaching again. Unfortunately, I was soon overwhelmed by my responsibilities that hardly allowed time for anything else. A heavy course load, endless and highly charged meetings, long office hours, and heaps of papers to grade left me anxiously wondering how I would ever get through the day. Happily, the second theme provided a much-needed respite from campus pressures. Almost instantaneously we were greeted by the gracious hospitality and warmth of old friends. Once again my husband and I stepped into a highly cosmopolitan way of life that brought together people of diverse interests and backgrounds. Our renewed encounters were enticing. I felt enormously enriched by my country's centuries old culture.

My desire to return to Lebanon had been strong, but I was unable to draw strength from it. Instead, a mood of dread hovered over me. I was gripped by a strange feeling of entering a world that is at once threatening and seductive. Desperately I searched for the charms and enchantments of the city, for its flavor, culture and mixture of civilizations. Then little by little, I began to isolate myself, to withdraw from all the ensuing confusion and focus my energies on work and writing. Sadly, this strategy was all too reminiscent of the ugly war years when isolation became a defense mechanism against the grotesque scenes of escalating violence. The challenge ahead now seemed daunting as I groped for meaning in a realm where memory had taken the place of reality but with time, I managed to focus on the simpler joys of life. It was sheer delight to take brisk walks on the Corniche in the twilight, to gaze at the flaming sun disappear into the glittering Mediterranean Sea. The choices and rhythms of my life had changed, but deep down I was convinced that creative possibilities abound in a country like Lebanon. After all, throughout the centuries it has remained a place to which travelers can return due to its vibrancy, cultural richness and diversity.

Finally I decided to write historical fiction, and I knew that my desire to spin tales again was in some inexplicable way connected to my return. I stole moments from my hectic schedule to shape thoughts, craft stories and polish prose. As my cast of characters came to life, it became obvious that the female protagonists shared similar attributes. Their suspended "betweenness" was a position that places them midway, as it were, between cultures. In unconventional ways it had equipped them with the fluidity necessary to merge multiple identities, and transcend the artificial boundaries of society and nationality. Undoubtedly such experiences are of immense value to those of us whose lives have been lived between worlds, who have welcomed the enriching texture of multiplicity, yet suffered its inevitable torments and confusions. My life, like the lives of my heroines, had been subjected to discontinuities and dislocations, to shifts and disruptions, to roles that must be invented again and again. Writing historical fiction, at least for the moment, satisfied my need to explore the creative potential of marginal lives, including my own. Suddenly it felt right to refocus and redefine my commitments and sense of self. Temporarily, these stories offered a meaningful escape into a realm rich with possibilities.

As winter gave way to spring, a neatly typed manuscript replaced the pile of handwritten papers on my desk and my narratives assumed personal significance. No longer did I feel distracted, disillusioned, doomed. Then, as it happened, I thought of how amazing it would be to offer a creative writing course, how refreshingly direct and of immediate relevance to the lives of numerous students, particularly returnees like myself, many of whom took refuge in writing as a redemptive pass-time. In addition to developing and refining their creative potential, it would address the need for significant literary production and a discourse around it. At first my colleagues in the English Department at the American University of Beirut were reluctant; after all creative writing did not fit into the traditional scheme of things. Besides, they doubted whether students would show any interest. Finally, after much deliberation, it was agreed that I should give it a try.

The response was overwhelming. Within the first hour of registration the course was completely filled. The eager students who crowded into my office were impressive, and contrary to all expectations they came from a variety of disciplines. Many were already avid writers with a profound desire to express themselves. One political science major asked if I would read a forty-page play she had completed over the summer. A history student explained that she was halfway through her second short story; and an aspiring medical student wanted my comments on a collection of poems he had been working on for some time. The following semester witnessed an even sharper increase in demand. Additional sections as well as advanced courses in fiction, poetry and drama were offered to accommodate the growing number of receptive students.

Initially, I was startled by how many of my students had a profound need to express themselves in their texts. Even more curious, was the realization that despite their diverse disciplines, ages and backgrounds, they had a great deal in common. As the semester progressed, it became clear that fate and circumstance had conspired to transform them into seasoned travelers, border crossers, outsiders existing on the margins of whatever society they happen to find themselves in. Living between two or more worlds simultaneously, without actually belonging to any one place in particular, was a way of life for these young people. "Because I have never lived in any one place for very long," wrote Yasmine, "I don't feel I belong anywhere. I also know I never will belong or feel completely at home in any one place." Ussama expressed similar feelings. "I guess I'll end up where I've always felt most comfortable, at that point in a large circle where everyone is in the circle but I'm on the circumference watching, rarely joining in the inner circle, just watching."

Almost immediately narratives began to echo similar themes and when students presented manuscripts for response and critique my academic world suddenly took on new meaning. The creative energy was contagious. Crafting and workshopping texts instigated an ongoing conversation that magically transformed our class encounters into charged happenings.

I vividly recall a gripping class discussion that took place one rainy afternoon. Ali said he was having difficulty writing an autobiographical narrative because he was unable to find the right words to describe what goes on in his head. For some reason, he sensed that whatever wording he used, they fell short of conveying the intensity of his feelings. What seemed to disturb him most was the feeling of being a complete stranger in his own country. "Life in Canada," he explained, had proceeded normally without any major upheavals. "It was not my country so it was normal not to fit in. Being an outsider did not bother me. Now the situation is entirely different." His returnee status sets him apart from mainstream Lebanese society. He is viewed with suspicion, and as he does not particularly adhere to social convention, he is perceived as being "different" from the rest, especially by an extended family that he cannot identify with, and that prides itself in maintaining "solidarity" or a "unified front". If Ali is "absorbed in a book" or "engrossed in writing", they become immediately agitated, fearing it might contain damaging or inappropriate ideas that he might use to "disgrace the family". With time, Ali has become a "tempting target" even to well-meaning relatives out of concern that he might make them vulnerable to social criticism within the community.

Curiously, as the discussion developed, students began to sound like comrades-in-arms, resorting to the use of military terms to conjure up a silent struggle. They talked about "winning" or "losing" the "battle" against suspicious and distrustful social moralists who increasingly "enforce" correct ways of behavior, and who are completely convinced they have all the right answers. Consequently, they "interrogate" and "enforce" their ways and values. Each one of them claims to be concerned about preserving the respectability of the family name.

I had, by now, become so fascinated by the animated discussion, that I began to write down what students were saying.

> Sana: If only they could get beyond the debunking phase and listen to what we have to say.

> Tariq: You must be joking. They don't give a fig for our views and feelings. Besides, I find them insulting. Usually they say, "Where were you during the war?"

> Sana: Exactly! I'm made to feel guilty for spending time in Europe when it was insane to remain here. They want to punish us for not being in the danger they were in.

This astonishingly frank discussion gave rise to amused and nervous chuckles of agreement. I listened in fascination as students expressed sentiments that had disturbed me for so long, sentiments I had been reluctant to translate into words or writing. Clearly they had no qualms about voicing their feelings on this matter. Remembering my role as an instructor, I attempted to ease the tension by summarizing their concerns. Extended family members, I suggested, seem to be fixated on looking outward instead of inward in order to eliminate the possibility of self-examination and tolerance. Instead, they narrow the focus to exclude rather than include human diversity, thus preventing people from living together in mutual respect and recognition. Generally such behaviour seems to stem from the fear of nasty gossip, what people might say, or how they might ostracize a particular family if one of its members appears to be different or strange. I was reminded of a quote I had jotted down in my journal a week before. It had to do with exiles returning to their country of origin. "Going into exile," Bauman (2002) writes, "has been recorded as their original sin, in the light of which all that the sinners may later do may be taken down and used as evidence of their rule-breaking."

The buzz of conversation was overwhelming. Rarely had I witnessed such a level of involvement and intellectual excitement. Yet today, troubled and questioning, students were alive to ideas concerning identity and belonging in ways that reflected an unusually high degree of concern and intensity. There was an urgency to communicate with non-mainstream, forward-looking individuals who touchingly believe they can give new shape and meaning to the society they live in. "We represent a silent invasion, but in reality we are the wake-up call that needs to be heeded before it's too late." (Nabil)

Students were quick to reject the romantic and nostalgic views fed to them by their parents while still abroad, dismissing these stories as wishful imaginings of homesick exiles whose emotional needs are satisfied by clinging to a vanished past. Nesrine laments the ability of her parents to reconnect at the expense of ignoring the tragic reality of a country torn apart by factional strife. "There is a part of me that accepts the need of my parents to reconstruct a perfect past; however, I wish they would stop living in denial and see how the war has destroyed Lebanon."

Disappointment aside, many students were perceptive enough to know that the fantasies parents instill in their children are to some degree necessary. However, the discrepancy in viewpoints continues to instigate ill feelings and friction. Understandably, the majority of students are unwilling to deny or escape reality by embracing the protective measures their parents wrap around themselves.

That evening as I sat on my balcony mulling over the frustration and disappointment felt by students, my gaze settled on a string of tiny fishing boats as they fanned out to dot the shimmering water with their lights. Overhead, a perfectly round moon hung low in the sky. Just for a moment, it crossed my mind how unreal and absolutely enchanting nature can be in this tiny, impossible country. And how absolutely essential it is, on occasion, to escape the ugly contradictions of one's society in order to cope with the taxing demands of daily life. Suddenly I was reminded of an episode that took place during the summer of 1992 when, taking advantage of an extended cease-fire in Lebanon, we returned from abroad for a brief visit.

Prior to our visit, our son, Ramzi, who is blessed with a playful and rich imagination, became so completely captivated by the breathtaking posters of Lebanon's scenic landscapes that he immediately conjured up a secret fantasy world. In his eagerness to explore the hidden mysteries of the city on our first day back, he convinced his father to take him on an early morning stroll through the busy streets of Beirut. At first, he skipped adventurously ahead of Samir, totally oblivious to the ravaged buildings until, little by little, reality seeped in, stealthily exchanging places with his dream world. Soon, paralyzed with fear at the sight of crumbling structures, dirt, chaos and noise, Ramzi clung tightly to his father's hand. It was indeed a rude awakening to discover that Beirut was a threatening place for a child, nothing like the beautiful spot he had imagined it to be.

Always a resourceful child, Ramzi was quick to devise a survival strategy. To begin with, he refused to leave our flat. Ingeniously, he converted our living room into a make-believe stage where all day long he performed his favourite Broadway musicals. He kept his belongings safely tucked away in his little blue backpack just in case we had to escape in a hurry. The ugliness he had witnessed outside was expertly blocked out of his imaginatively created space. During the war years, when Ramzi was still a toddler, he would crawl under the dining-table when severe episodes of shelling fiercely rocked our flat and inquire, in a petrified voice, whether the booms were thunder with or without water. Now, however, he was not asking questions. He knew the answers all too well and had opted to withdraw just like my students who sought new venues of expression in their writing; while their parents clung to nostalgically romanticized visions of what Lebanon used to be. Clearly writing offers students a kind of freedom from the external constraints of a threatening society in the same way that denial renders life infinitely less painful for their parents. Writing opens up spaces where students can shed the sentimental baggage and strictures that arise from unrealistic notions of the past.

Thoughts of my heroines immediately came to mind. As early as 1830 they had distanced themselves from stifling conventions in search of fresh and bold alternatives. All were future oriented, anti-tradition and richly imaginative. They too were out of place exiles, living and writing from the margins, experiencing suspended "betweenness" with all its pleasures, pains and anxieties.

The late-afternoon drizzle casts a silver-grey light on our classroom. Students have been frantically engaged in their autobiographical narratives for weeks, and understandably, we speak of little else. Each is consumed in the dramas and fantasies of who and what they are. All have fallen under the spell of their stories, and yet, a certain tension hangs in the air. There is a compulsion to share the numerous interruptions that have characterized their young lives. We play a game in which students describe the various identities they have acquired over the past few years. They are acutely aware that having to adjust to different places and ways of life, of not actually belonging to any particular place, is problematic. Juggling multiple identities, an inevitable part of the diaspora experience, means constantly losing and reinventing the self. Along with this comes isolation and confusion.

> I encompass a spectrum of personalities because my life has been interrupted so many times. I have never enjoyed continuity. My existence is choppy and disconnected. (*Maha*)

Students are positioned on the crossroads between cultures. Loss and reinvention is the mechanism used to cope with separateness yet there will never be any real or lasting feelings of belonging. Marginality is a condition taken for granted but sadly there seems to be so much pain at the centre of this kind of human experience. Often their honesty is disarming.

> I have been given a life rich with experiences but also filled with confusion and hardship. However, I need to keep moving, to keep going to different places. Otherwise I will suffocate. (*Karim*)

Ironically, students have no desire to alter their suspended "betweenness." In fact, in some inexplicable way, they welcome being kept off balance and grow accustomed to the condition of fluidity, presumably because it necessitates the constant and creative energy that accompanies the reinvention of self.

Once class is over, my thoughts send me scurrying down the deserted corridor, out the campus gate and into the narrow winding streets of the city. Amidst the bustle of my favourite market, surrounded by a profusion of enticingly displayed fruits and vegetables, I wait patiently as the ingredients of our evening meal are weighed on lopsided brass scales. Here there is everything to attract the eye and delight in.

Back in the welcoming quiet of our flat I start cooking to calm my dizzying ideas. The personal narratives students share in class give me the feeling that we are working side by side, combining the materials of our lives in order to shape something new. Together we chart different territory by relocating the personal in a way that allows for a more critical engagement with experiences that matter.

Students saw merit in the ability to remain detached; sustaining a high degree of emotional distance was viewed as an asset. The idea was not to shut out the rest of the world, but to observe from a safe distance. To achieve this, they place themselves in situations that are out of step with what is happening around them. Interestingly they opt to become situated observers who ultimately seek meaning from their gaze. Hence imagination becomes a crucial component especially since their particular ways of seeing carry narrative intentionality. Writing, to some extent, is a way of controlling the strangeness of the situation, but more importantly, hybridity can be utilized to create a liberating perspective.

> My father taught me to be extremely open. Throughout my sixteen years in Nigeria, I had friends from all classes, religions and nationalities, but I did not identify with any one group. This was easy for me to do because my parents never forced any religious or nationalistic beliefs on me. When we moved back to Lebanon I was distressed by the political and religious conflicts. Luckily I like to be alone and witness what is happening around me. Often I prowl the streets at odd hours just to observe and write about what I see. I don't like to be seen. In fact, I wish I could be invisible. (*Wael*)

For as long as I can remember my father struggled with a private and silent war that engaged conflicting loyalties and desires because it pitted his village roots against life in the US. As he grew older, the inevitable difficulty of moving from one culture to another became increasingly more demanding. The notion of a society governed primarily by work, speed and uniformity greatly troubled him. For all its problems, life in his Lebanese mountain village seemed, at least to him, more humane; it offered a set rhythm derived from continuity, tradition and sociability. In spite of this dilemma, for most of his life my father managed to hold his diverse worlds in balance by following an arrangement that divided the year equally between his two worlds.

Aboard the plane scattered fragments come to me. My head is filled with a haphazard jumble of disturbing thoughts of no particular importance to anyone but myself. My mind dashes from one agonizing image to another as the plane climbs steeply. Gradually the city lights grow fainter and I am deep in the silence of the night. My desperation is induced by far more than jet lag. Awake out of necessity, yet almost catatonic with fatigue after twenty-six hours of traveling, my suspension between one state and another is reminiscent of my father's precarious situation. Only a few days ago his voice had sounded calm and determined over the phone. Boisterously he joked about feeling imprisoned in the US. I was not to worry, though, because he had taken a firm decision to return to Lebanon early this year, by mid-February at the latest. Naturally I was immediately sworn to secrecy out of fear that my mother, who wanted to spend more time with her grandchildren, would most certainly thwart his plans. Now barely a week after his call, my father lay in a coma in some sterile, grey hospital thousands of miles away from the village where he had longed to be. The tests were conclusive; he was brain-dead.

From the corner of my eye I glimpsed a tiny tissue-thin woman who sat clutching a large object wrapped in an exquisite piece of cloth. Age had put deep wrinkles on her sun-beaten face and her head was crowned by a mass of snowy hair twisted into a perfectly round bun. She remained frozen throughout the flight, stared straight ahead and spoke not a word. I watched as the flight attendant inquired if she would like some dinner. When no answer came, he paused impatiently for a moment to check his exasperation. Then very rudely, he reached out and snapped down her tray onto which he aggressively plunked her evening meal, which of course, she never touched. I was irritated by what I perceived to be cultural insensitivity. Could he not see the anxieties that paralyzed this tiny Hispanic whiff of a woman? All alone, on probably her first flight ever, she was understandably intimidated by the rules of a society entirely unknown to her, let alone the fear of flying. My imagination flitted between the spoken, unspoken, and visual messages of different worlds. How much easier to be a detached observer viewing life with distant bemusement! My students were bravely mapping this different territory. Mentally they had positioned themselves to gaze and absorb from a safe distance in order to guard against the trappings of emotional involvement.

I thought of my father, of how reluctant he had been to leave his village. Now, in a cruel twist of fate, he would be brought back to Lebanon for burial and just as he had promised, he would return before mid-February. I watched the sunset dim. Too sad and strung out to sleep, I struggled desperately to toss out a host of dark thoughts that tumbled through my mind.

Spring in Lebanon is breathtaking. The campus is ablaze with flowers. From my office window a brilliant blue sea is visible behind a row of palm trees. Each passing seminar makes me all the more aware of how expansive and imaginative students are becoming. In the crafting of personal texts, they continue to break their silence by reversing the ability of society to render them invisible and voiceless. To do this with passion and dedication is evidence of how strong is their need to capture something different in the map of possible strategies, to bring new shape and meaning to their young lives. Above all, the desire to share experiences in the truthful exploration of what it essentially means to live between worlds is, in the final analysis, immensely important for individuals whose lives must constantly be re-invented. Certainly these stories offer essential digressions from the official and encouraged biography of a country like Lebanon. Ultimately they may even hold the key to innovative, tolerant and diverse ways of seeing for societies that are desperately in need of viable alternatives.

Reference

Bauman, Z. (2002) *Liquid Modernity*. Madden: Blackwell.

Originally published in *Transit Beirut* (Saqi Books, 2004): 58-67. It is printed here with the permission of the publisher.

MOHAMED FARID AZZI

Maghrebi Youth:
Between Alienation and Integration

Recent Maghrebi history has been marked by upheavals led by the young people, who burst onto the social and political stage and have continued to play a decisive role on that stage. All Maghrebi societies have experienced grave disturbances since the 1980s. The most striking example of those disturbances occurred in Algeria in October 1988. Riots shook the country for three days and caused considerable human injury and property damage.

In Morocco, even earlier than in Algeria, the cycle of protest and rioting involved a majority of young people. Indeed, since its independence in 1956, Morocco has experienced violent protests involving large numbers of young people. After a short respite lasting from the mid- to late seventies, the cycle of protests, which involved more than just young people, resumed. In June 1981, riots in Casablanca resulted in the deaths of two hundred young protesters. The riots broke out after the government reduced food subsidies. Tunisia experienced similar disturbances. For instance, at the end of 1983, a violent uprising took place following an increase in the price of bread. The demonstrators attacked the state's institutions and the symbols of wealth. Scores of people died during the confrontation between the police and rioters.

Youth movements have not always been limited to violence. For example, in the Algeria of the seventies, young people—especially students— were much involved in politics. They again became intensely involved during the short-lived period of democratization (1989–91). The youth constituted a significant proportion of the membership of the newly formed political parties and associations; many of the top positions in some major political parties were held by young leaders. Therefore, it is not difficult to understand why young people reacted strongly to the interruption of the democratization process. The cancellation of the legislative election in January 1992 and the annulment of the results of the first round of elections have led to an open war between the state security forces and armed Islamist groups, the membership of which is dominated by persons between the ages of eighteen and thirty. Although young people in Morocco and Tunisia have also alternated between participation and alienation, Algerian youth have suffered the most from alienation and marginalization.

The October 1988 events in Algeria and riots in Tunisia and Morocco have been examined in great detail. However, most of the analyses have focused almost solely on the most obvious aspects of the conflict, such as the army, the Islamists and the political parties. Indeed, few studies have analyzed the factors affecting social change, leaving the youth of the Maghreb and their influence underanalyzed.

This chapter briefly examines some of the dimensions of the complex, multidimensional reality of Maghrebi youth and analyzes the socioeconomic conditions, which constituted the primary ingredients of the turmoil. This study is based on observation and on the primary findings of an opinion survey conducted in 1995 on social and demographic change in the urban milieu.

Ambitious plans were undertaken to create the "man of tomorrow," the citizen of a modern nation. The "man of tomorrow" would evolve while modernizing society through culture, industrialization, and education. Young persons became the foundation of the postindependence modernization because of their numbers and because of the youthfulness of the political elite.

Induced Social Change

A certain degree of "willfulness" (voluntarism) characterized the three Maghrebi states in their quest for modernization and social change. The will of the state to induce social change and to modernize society has determined, to a greater degree, the destiny of a whole generation.

The willfulness of government policies was most pronounced in Algeria, where authorities sought to generate social and cultural change through rapid and planned economic development. Those authorities aimed to transform Algerians, as stated in the "National Charter", into "conscientious citizen[s] of a modern nation." The concomitant objective of the government's policies was to eliminate tribal, patriarchal, and semi-feudal structures of the old society.

An elite was entrusted with the task of modernizing society through a demiurgic state. The industrialization launched in the early 1970s began the modernization. Industrialization was to fulfill such economic, social, and cultural goals as creating jobs, inculcating industrial cultural norms, and, eventually, producing consumer goods. Rapid industrialization (from 1967 to 1978) absorbed many workers. According to the technocratic elite, industrialization would acculturate the populace through the factory. The elite believed that the modern setting of the new place would instill new cultural values and norms in the workers, who, in turn, would diffuse the new culture into society at large. Studies by Algerian scholars on industrialization and industrial culture have shown, however, that the workers continued to conform to the traditional culture rather than to adapt to the industrial culture. Those studies concluded that the acculturation within the factory did not engender the modern industrial worker, but rather another type of worker, whom they called the "majority worker" (*ouvrier majoritaire*). Such a worker was young, of peasant origin, and attached to an Islamic cultural reference. Finally, industrialization failed to achieve its economic and acculturative missions.

In Tunisia, the voluntaristic approach apparent in the declared objectives of a vast program of social and cultural reforms and designed to prepare the Tunisian citizens for a better future set, as a priority, the change in culture. The main priority was to persuade the population to abandon traditional values and beliefs through a cultural and psychological revolution. Important reforms were implemented in order to modernize the society, emphasizing education, legal reforms, and the encouragement of new attitudes.

Education was to enhance social and cultural change. Indeed, in the last thirty years, the Maghreb has made considerable progress in expanding educational opportunities. In the mid-1970s, Algeria, for example, allocated as much as 30 percent of its national budget to education. Tunisia and Morocco, too, devoted substantial portions of their national budgets to education. Because of the substantial investment in education, school enrollment swiftly increased: at the primary level, enrollment reached 99 percent in Algeria, 120 percent in Tunisia, and 69 percent in Morocco (compared with 83 percent in 1980, which marks an important decrease). Secondary education also increased between 1980 and 1992 from 33 to 59 percent in Algeria, from 27 to 46 percent in Tunisia, and from 26 to 35 percent in Morocco. During the same period, college enrollment increased from 6.2 to 11.8 percent in Algeria and from 5.7 to 10.7 percent in Tunisia. In Morocco, however, while the ratio was increased at the same rate as the rates of the two neighboring countries during the 1970s and the 1980s, it has dropped significantly in the 1990s.

Upon independence, the new Maghrebi states opened the gates to secondary and college education nearly as widely as they opened those to primary education. The "democratization" of education was, in fact, carried out at the expense of efficiency and quality, resulting in a disparity between the system inputs and the technical and social requirements of economic development. Despite considerable achievements in education in the Maghreb, many shortcomings developed, as shown by the unjustifiably high illiteracy rate. Half of Morocco's adult population is illiterate, as is more than one-third of Algeria's and Tunisia's. Illiteracy in the Maghreb is more widespread among women than men; Morocco has the highest women's illiteracy rate.

Teachers are subjected to poor working conditions and do not enjoy high social status. In recent years in the Maghreb, education is no longer regarded as a means for social mobility as it had been regarded in the 1960s and 1970s; hence, it has lost much support, lowering the morale of teachers and students alike. This led the late Algerian president Mohammed Boudiaf to declare that "the educational system is disaster-stricken." Aside from the low quality of education, Maghrebi education has become a machine for exclusion. In Algeria, for example, although 27.64 percent of the total population is attending school, the passing rate for the baccalaureate examination has barely reached 20 percent in the last ten years, meaning that over three hundred thousand young persons are excluded from school every year.

Education also lies at the center of society's debate as well as its frustrations. The Algerian cultural and ideological elite argue about the educational system and the content of its programs. The modernist elite argue that the educational system has deviated from its original mission of molding citizens for the future: making them scientifically and technologically competent and culturally open to the universal values of the modern world. Instead, they argue, the system has become a pulpit for conservative forces, who have used the schools to instill their Islamo-Baathist ideologies, thus sowing the seeds of radical Islamism, which they helped transform into a major political and ideological force in the 1980s. The conservatives counter that schools have not done enough to enhance the authentic Algerian personality. Schools have instead introduced alien values, such as socialism, into society. A question was asked in that same survey about whether religious teaching in schools was sufficient or insufficient. As many as 50 percent of those under thirty (as compared with 40 percent of those over thirty) thought that the amount of religious teaching was insufficient.

In Algeria, the debate on the educational system also concerns Arabization, a much smaller issue in Tunisia and Morocco. In Algeria, the debate has become overideologized and politicized. As explained by an observer: "Arabization cannot be reduced to a linguistic problem only. It expresses clashes between opposed cultural and ideological trends." Technical and linguistic constraints related to Arabization do, in fact, exist, but the criticism and the resistance of the francophone elite to its implementation obscure the issue of privileges and status. In reality, French is still the working language in most government services, especially in those related to the economy, whereas most college classes are conducted in Arabic. Arabization has accomplished two things: it has enabled a generation of young people to have direct access to the holy writings and their interpretations, and it simultaneously has marginalized those same young people from the administrative and economic spheres. The result has been an enormous frustration easily channeled by the Islamic opposition parties, who skillfully used the issue of Arabization to mobilize the monolingual generation.

The educational system is not the only cause of frustration and social exclusion of young people. A more precarious situation has prevailed in the employment sector. Industrialization was propitious for job creation; the unemployment rate had dropped from 22 to 18 percent between 1978 and 1984, but it rose to 25 percent in 1990 and to 28.1 percent in 1995. Because of the combined effects of the contracting economy and the implementation of stabilization and structural-adjustment programs, the number of unemployed reached 2,104,700 in 1995, as compared with 1,552,000 in 1992. About 80 percent of the unemployed are under thirty years of age. According to that last survey, only 7.3 percent of the unemployed have no education at all; 55.7 percent have primary and secondary education; 11.25 percent have professional training; and 4.4 percent are college graduates. Arabic degree holders are the most affected by unemployment.

In Morocco, the rate of unemployment among urban youth was 30 percent in 1989, among whom 5 percent were university graduates and 47 percent had received secondary education; only 7.03 percent were illiterate.

In Tunisia, unemployment among young people (ages fifteen to twenty-nine) reached 26 percent in 1989, representing 72 percent of the unemployed population. As in Algeria and Morocco, more and more young unemployed Tunisians have secondary or college education. The statistics confirm the failure of the economic integration of the Maghrebi youth and their unmet growing demands.

Inadequate housing conditions are as crucial as the lack of jobs for the young. In fact, if they had a choice, many would prefer to have housing than to be employed. Overcrowded apartments (fifteen persons in two-room apartments in some populated areas) pose a grave problem because of the cultural code, which segregates men from women in domestic space. Despite efforts aimed at alleviating the housing shortage, construction cannot keep pace with growing demands. The housing deficit is estimated at 2 million units.

Parallel to rising unemployment and to the deterioration of the overall socioeconomic conditions of the lower and middle classes in the 1980s, an excessive concentration of wealth occurred. One observer noted: "In the midst of the present economic and managerial crisis, a few people succeeded in not only increasing their wealth but also in displaying it in the form of late model cars, new villas and new businesses."

The convergence of such skewed socioeconomic conditions has contributed greatly to the wave of disturbances in the Maghreb since the mid-1980s, but those conditions themselves do not "justify" the depth or the intensity of the crises. The method by which those crises are subjectively interpreted instead explains the reaction of the social actors. Their perceptions and attitudes toward those whom they judge responsible for their frustrations and alienation have, to some extent, determined the method by which Maghrebis, especially the young, have manifested their discontent. In other words, sociological factors may broaden our understanding of the complex Maghrebi reality.

Young People: Deficient Socialization

The process of urbanization in the Maghreb, which started during colonial rule and accelerated after independence, has had disrupting effects. The authoritarian, but unfulfilled, modernization and the uncontrolled urbanization have greatly affected the pattern of traditional social life and its institutions of socialization in the Maghreb. The three Maghrebi countries adopted urban and housing policies, which have failed to integrate the large numbers moving into the cities. The consequences of those policies have resulted in social disintegration and social anomie.

In Algeria, social interaction and socialization processes in the cities took place and were regulated by social institutions, such as the family, peer groups, the neighborhood, or in the "native" quarters (*houma*). In fact, the *houma* is where most of a youth's social life takes place. Most Maghrebi cities are marked by the role that each quarter plays as a social unit with its own particular identity. During colonial times, those quarters served as refuges for the native population. After independence, and despite the massive arrival of newcomers from rural areas, those quarters continued their integrative role; however, because of rapid urbanization and continuous rural exodus during the 1960s and 1970s, peripheral new quarters mushroomed. To those new quarters the newcomers brought with them their lifestyles and often settled with or near their families and people from the same region. Most of the youths' activities and interactions, sports competitions, music, and concerts take place in the quarter. The quarter thus serves as the community of belonging, the place where the individual is well integrated.

In view of the worsening socioeconomic conditions, the demographic pressure, and the withdrawal of the state (insufficient social services), the community no longer can function as a safety valve. Erosion of the social cohesion has thus occurred. In a fieldwork study on the famous quarter the Casbah of Algiers, the author noted that the *houma* (quarter) is no longer a factor of urban integration. From a place of social harmony and solidarity, it has become a place of disorder, insecurity, and violence. Social links have weakened; vertical relations do not function anymore. The process of desocialization experienced by traditional groups has given way to new forms of sociability and new groups of young people. The street has become the cornerstone around which those groups revolve. The street is now the space within which informal political and economic activities and informal gatherings take place. In other words, the street is the same physical spatial entity, but it is less entrenched within the social network as the old quarter used to be. New forms of sociability have emerged, forming a network built essentially around the mosque.

The phenomenon of the "street" is common to all the Maghrebi countries. In Algeria, in particular, in the early 1980s, new social groups of young people appeared on the social scene. The better known are the *hittists*—youngsters, without resources, who lean against walls all day long. An Algerian politician has described them, rather contemptuously, as "abandoned human beings, not attached to any social group, not concerned by what is happening around them." Or worse yet:

> [I]f idleness is the mother of all vices, *hittism* is one step below. It is the total emptiness of soul. It is a look full of suspicion of others' luxurious cars, clothes ... [The *hittist*] is ready for any adventure, for he sincerely believes that he has been dispossessed. He, silently, execrates the state that did not employ him and will not accommodate him ... He is not ready to integrate into society; on the contrary, he is seeking ways to leave it or take revenge on it.

Not all the socially marginalized young people stand against walls; a large number are involved in the informal economy, known in Algeria as *trabendo* (smuggling). Those involved in the *trabendo* show a high social and economic dynamism; their activities have acquainted them with the outside world, from France to Thailand. With little or no education, they have learned how to manage their way through the complex international trade and customs regulations. They have gained social status within their quarters and families, for whom they have become young breadwinners, thus displacing the role of the father or the older brother.

Like the *hittists*, the *trabendists* (smugglers), albeit for different reasons, resent the state. In their daily activities, they face continuous harassment from state agents, forced into bribery and corruption in order to survive.

Among the social groups that have become visible in the 1980s is the group of well-to-do young people known in Algeria as *tchi-tchi*. They are the offspring of the *nomenklatura*, rich traders, and private industrialists living in the shadow of the state. Their ostentatious lifestyle has sharpened the sense of social inequality among the lower social groups.

Amid the profound social change which generated new social actors, new ways of being, and (especially) a great number of unmet social demands, neither the state nor civil society has been able to structure those new social groups or channel their demands into a peaceful process.

The traditional institutions and quarters have become obsolete and no longer can fulfill aspirations or ease mounting frustrations. The Islamist movement, however, has succeeded where the traditional institutions have failed. The Islamist movement has also succeeded in the other Maghrebi societies. The movement began in the mid-1970s on university campuses, which provided the first cadres and activists for Islamist preachers. Initially, the leaders directed their efforts to the inner-city areas and peripheral quarters.

The new space of efficient sociability shifted from the street corner to the mosque, where, in addition to religious themes, matters related to professional, family, and even emotional life could be discussed and some times resolved. The key figure in the mosque was the imam, often self-proclaimed, who offered new models of behavior to young people and provided them with new reason, purpose, and ennobling myths.

The mushrooming of Islamist associations and parties further enhanced the social identity of the imams' young followers and bestowed upon them a sense of worthiness. The high mobilization of Islamist parties (particularly in Algeria in 1989–91) strengthened the sentiment of belonging to the community of the faithful, which overshadowed and replaced the traditional groups of solidarity, such as the family, kinship, neighborhoods, and sports clubs. The strength of the new order was demonstrated during the local and legislative elections (1990–91), in which FIS candidates outstripped others, even though the others were better rooted in their quarters and towns.

Some scholars believe that the Islamist movement has gained strength partly because some individuals' desire to escape from traditional communities has left no room for personal life. The adoption of Islamist symbols and behavior by many young people has been interpreted as an attempt to break the patriarchal model. Youngsters suddenly gained new status and challenged the authority of the elders; for example, young women took the veil to escape the authoritarian male model. The young clearly found a response to their aspirations and expectations in the Islamist movement, which imparts a sense of worthiness to the marginalized young person. The movement made them discernible (beard, *qamis*) and useful (assisting the elderly and distributing aid). However, the new identity is paradoxical, because once the individuals are detached from their traditional milieus, they become members of a new community in which personal differences among the faithful are strictly prohibited.

Faced with social and cultural change, which coincided with major economic difficulties and important changes in the international environment, Maghrebi regimes undertook significant political and economic reforms. Those reforms, however, did not last long: they ended in Tunisia in 1989 and in Algeria in 1992, with the halt of the electoral process. The resulting violence and counter violence that followed have forced society into a low profile. In Algeria, the youth responded differently and adopted opposite attitudes. Many formed or joined the armed groups to fight the regime, which they believe robbed them of their victory. Others returned to their original milieus, within which they sought protection and the means for survival. Given the continuous degradation of socioeconomic conditions (much worse than in 1988), the primary solidarity groups did not greatly help this group. A deep feeling of loneliness followed. The suicide rate rose—unusual in times of war, where the struggle for survival is supposed to give meaning to life. A considerable increase in psychiatric care and psychotropic drug consumption has also been reported. Some young people affirm that there are now two parties: "the party of the mosque" and "party of the drug."

Youth's Political Attitudes

Scholars and students alike often have emphasized two main features that characterize the political attitudes of Maghrebi youth: apathy and alienation. Although these attitudes might be considered a common denominator of the political orientation of young people in the Maghreb, some differences among countries should be qualified.

Algeria, until the late 1980s, lived under the rule of a single party and enjoyed a relatively stable political life. Many studies were undertaken to analyze Algeria's economic and political system, with emphasis on the economic changes, but little attention was paid to general public opinion or to political attitudes. No cumulative figures on political attitudes exist. Nonetheless, from the general political studies and participant observation, one can discern the pattern of political opinion and attitude in four periods.

The years that followed independence were marked by a close identification with the regime. Independence, newly won after a long revolutionary war, mobilized the population for government-oriented tasks. Following the military coup d'etat in 1965, opposition and critics rose among the governing elite and extended to leftist student organizations. After the initial repression, the regime succeeded at the beginning of the 1970s in co-opting most of its opponents. The students were mobilized in economic and ideological campaigns, such as the agrarian revolution. The workers were involved in participatory management—for example, socialist self-management.

The first signs of a challenge to the political regime and anti-system political attitudes appeared in the late 1970s. Those culminated in April 1980 with the Berber uprising, during which serious disturbances shook the Kabylie region. The natives of that region demanded cultural emancipation and democratic rights; and Islamic activism appeared on university campuses. The reaction of the political regime was repression and cooptation.

The most politically alienated social groups among the youth expressed themselves by rioting many times during the 1980s, culminating in the general revolt of October 1988. The political changes that occurred between 1989 and 1991 prompted political participation, symbolized by such manifestations as a growing number of civic associations, political parties, and high turnouts in various elections.

More recently, and conducted during a time of intense political violence and great uncertainty, a survey in 1995 revealed a low level of personal involvement in political activities and public life in general. A mere 6 percent of the respondents in the survey claimed that they belonged to an association of any kind, and only 13 percent participated in some type of public-service work.

In spite of the proliferation of associations and political parties since 1989, Algerian men and women seem to have returned to political passivity and apathy. The violence of armed groups and the legal constraints imposed by the regime on politics (a ban on demonstrations, a state of emergency) discouraged any participation.

In Morocco, antiestablishment grievances and political alienation of its young people date back to the 1960s. The period between 1960 and 1972 was punctuated by confrontations between the opposition and the regime. In those confrontations, the youth, especially students, played leading roles. Surveys taken during that period showed that many Moroccan students exhibited strong refractory feelings, as demonstrated by the riots in Casablanca in 1965, during which hundreds were killed. Unrest and rioting have continued until the present. Unlike the Algerian regime, which succeeded in mobilizing the population around economic and social policies in favor of the masses at large, especially in the 1970s, the Moroccan monarchy undertook no significant social or economic policies in favor of the populace. This partly explains Moroccan young people's relative lack of participation in politics.

This apparent indifference did not mean that young people were depoliticized; on the contrary, they tended to be well informed and highly attentive to politics but unwilling to participate in political life. The alienation of so many young people results from their attitudes toward the politics of the country. Moroccan youth, for example, fear politics because of a traditional reverence for the Makhzen. In Algeria, however, "doing politics" or talking about it is no longer taboo, perhaps because of the different histories of state building and dissimilarities in the legitimizing mechanisms of political power in the two countries. In Morocco, politics is considered to be beyond the sphere of ordinary citizens. Even among those few who show some interest in politics, much skepticism exists; politics is considered to be reserved for the governing elite, who strive to satisfy their own interests in the name of the people. As a young Moroccan stated, "He [the king] bought off all of them; once you are in the parliament, you are bought off. He offers you a villa or a farm, you will say, 'Long live my lord,' and that's it. This is the truth."

The governing elite is thus stigmatized through the disrepute of the political institutions, which are conceived of as private clubs. That disrepute could explain the lack of interest in politics and public affairs of the majority of young people. A Moroccan researcher conducted a survey in which only 25 percent of those interviewed expressed some interest in politics. Almost the same proportion of Algerian young people expressed the same attitude: in response to the question "How do you perceive politics?" a mere 30 percent felt they understood the subject. Antiregime feelings are also widespread among Algerian youth. Only 38 percent held positive views on the performance of the regime, and 51 percent of interviewees believed that the regime rarely or never cared about the needs of the citizens.

That alienation partly resulted from radical leftist movements of the 1970s and early 1980s, in which the workers' and students' unions played an important role. Discontent among most social groups grew in the mid-1980s and the early 1990s. Islamist groups, which found support among the educated fringe of society, voiced society's grievances.

Antiregime feelings, political alienation, and Islamist sympathies best characterize the attitudes of most Maghrebi youth during the last fifteen years. A new political culture among the politically alienated youth has emerged and expanded. It has been expressed in Islamist ideologies, and those ideologies have won their widest support in Algeria.

Maghrebi young people who feel alienated from politics and do not share the political culture have perceptions and values regarding society and politics. Their beliefs highlight some values and attitudes, and reshape and redefine some others. The Algerian young people interviewed in 1995, in a context of political violence and economic hardship, emphasized values and aspirations such as social peace, solidarity, social justice, and strong political leadership. Other values, such as democracy and pluralism, do not seem to constitute a high priority. Only 18 percent of respondents answered the following question affirmatively: "Should the establishment and development of democratic institutions be an immediate task for the government to be concerned with?" In the last legislative elections, held in June 1997, the democratic parties registered a low 12 percent, confirming the low priority assigned to democratization.

Some basic cultural traits and values persist and characterize Algerian political culture. Egalitarianism is one of those values; it is rooted in the long struggle against colonization and amplified by the official populist ideology since independence. The value of egalitarianism has also compromised the legitimacy of wealth and authority. The October 1988 riots, for example, were not so much hunger riots as they were demands for social justice. The youths' feelings that they had been deprived of their rights to enjoy their part of the national wealth motivated their violent rejection of the political system and of the governing elite. Among Algerians, there is a strong conviction that their country is immensely rich but that corruption and incompetence among its leaders have made the country poor.

In the qualitative study on Morocco mentioned earlier, one may detect some attitudes among the Moroccan youth similar to those among their Algerian peers concerning expectation and political views. In Morocco, too, Western regimes are looked upon as the best in serving the interests of their citizens. What is most valued in those regimes are, on one hand, their economic development and their strength and, on the other hand, the social justice achieved through the welfare state, which provides all kinds of social assistance, such as social security and unemployment benefits. Also emphasized were the sense of civic responsibility and the respect for human rights that characterize Western societies. France is often mentioned as the model that best represents those rights.

Like their Algerian and Tunisian counterparts, young Moroccans stress the value of social justice and egalitarianism. That emphasis seems to be one of the most common feelings among Maghrebi people in general, perhaps explained by the widening gap between the rich and the poor, egalitarian traditions which uphold a long struggle against foreign occupation, and the populist promises formulated at independence. Morocco is the Maghrebi country in which inequalities are the most striking, where misery cohabits with opulence, and where high walls separate sprawling, overpopulated shantytowns from wealthy districts. The gap between the poor and the rich has also been widening in Algeria, especially during the last decade. In the Algerian opinion survey discussed earlier, 82 percent of the respondents thought that such a gap between the rich and the poor was widening. In Algeria, a populist, egalitarian ideology coupled with a redistribution policy has greatly contributed to the sharpening perception of inequality and thereby the sense of injustice that arose in the 1980s. The violence prevailing in Algeria for almost a decade may be explained partly by idealistic aspirations of egalitarianism and social justice.

As an alternative to an unjust state, Maghrebi youth have espoused democratic or Islamist values and attitudes. Democracy and Islam do represent to a majority of young people the ideals of social justice. Those ideals are reinterpreted and given additional meanings to suit expectations of the young and to express their frustrations. Democracy, Islam, and respect for human rights are seen as lacking in the Maghreb.

Conclusion

Significant and rapid change has occurred in the Maghreb during the last three decades. That change has resulted from state-led development based on mass education, urbanization, and the institutionalization of a salaried society. The first two decades seemed to favor the population in general, and the young generation in particular, as far as their integration in society was concerned. The last three decades were times of ascending social mobility and political mobilization, at least for Algeria and Tunisia.

Mounting economic difficulties, persistently high birth rates (at least up to the mid-1980s), a hindrance to social and professional mobility, the lack of significant political reforms, and unmet social demands have resulted in the marginalization of many youth. Young people periodically express their alienation and their anger by descending into the streets, destroying on their way what they believe are the sources of their alienation.

When Maghrebi youth are not rioting, they are negotiating the terms of their integration into society. Their economic integration has followed a tortuous path. They use all available resources: the family, the state, and the informal economy. They also negotiate their cultural integration through syncretism and some patching up of models. The attitudes adopted by young people who try to reconcile a pragmatism and a normative order have resulted in tensions when they were denied participation in the mass-consumer society. The integration of the Maghrebi youth has been particularly difficult at the political level.

The dilemma that faces Maghrebi governments is the convergence of differing demands of different natures. On one hand, Maghrebi governments confront socioeconomic grievances; on the other, they are pressed by demands for political participation and more government account ability. The socioeconomic demands can be partly met only if resources are efficiently managed—presupposing, among other things, institutions of control and an accountable government.

Economic reforms have been instituted without any accompanying social policies, posing dire consequences on vulnerable people. Too much repression has been used to stifle demands of the youth without any effort to reform politics or to integrate young people into society. Much is to be feared; the reasons for discontent and violence still exist, and if no genuine effort is made to resolve them, violence and rioting will continue to be the only means of expression left to the young.

Originally published in Yahia Zoubir (ed.) *North Africa in Transition* (University Press of Florida, 1999): 109–126. It is printed here with the permission of the publisher.

MAI YAMANI

Saudi Identity:
Negotiating between Tradition and Modernity

Since its creation in 1932 Saudi Arabia has undergone rapid and continuous social, economic and cultural transformation. The three generations of the population that have lived under the rule of a specifically Saudi state have seen every aspect of their lives touched by the development of a unified state and the integration of that state into the world economy. What makes the new generation different is its size and potential influence. In order for Saudi Arabia to continue to prosper as a stable state the majority of the population that the new generation represents feel that they must be given jobs but also demand the social and political space to express their hopes and fears about the situation in which they find themselves.

This new generation perceives itself to be located between the institutions of the previous generation, most conspicuously those it views as "traditional"—the family and religion—and the newer modem institutions of the market and state. It is the members of the new generation who, like their parents and grandparents, will go on to re-examine just what is considered "traditional" and "modern". It is they who will redefine the role of religion within a society that cannot avoid the gathering economic and social forces of a globalized world. Their views of the world they inhabit show that notions of tradition and modernity have become contested, with no single definition having common currency. The future of Saudi Arabia will, to a large degree, be decided by which of the competing definitions will triumph and guide the population as they reshape their lives and their relationship to the state.

The perceptions and attitudes of the new generation have been formed by an engagement with a wider range of possibilities than was available in recent times: travel for both work and leisure, education at home and abroad a broad array of technological consumer goods, print and electronic media. Many of those interviewed for this study experienced struggles with their family or the state over access to these possibilities as a result of which they developed an acute awareness of the conflicting social and political interpretations among Saudis. There is, however, virtual unanimity over the characterization of the global market-place as the bearer of modernity and of the communities to which they belong as traditional. Modern life is frequently associated, for good or ill, with the West in general and specifically with the United States of America.

For most of those at the heart of this study, there is a sense of inevitability about the growth of the modern in their lives. Problems arise from the need to negotiate between the "traditional" Saudi social basis to their lives and the modern pressures seen as emanating from outside. Preexisting cultural identities seem less and less able to encompass the kinds of social practices and social relations to which the state and market have increasingly given rise. The task facing the new generation is the need to negotiate a sense of self in these new and unfamiliar circumstances. All the new generation, indeed all members of Saudi society, irrespective of their political and social affiliations, face the problems that modernity throws up. But depending on their understanding of the negative and positive effects of such interaction, their responses vary greatly. Under these conditions, cultural identities tend to range across a spectrum of positions from what could be called conservative or insular to liberal or eclectic. Whether conservative or liberal, cautious or expansive, insular or cosmopolitan, almost all express some ambivalence and a hybrid of complex reactions, attitudes and evaluations.

For "conservatives", the new activities should, whenever possible, be subordinated to a moral sensibility more in keeping with tradition. These new activities should be encompassed by existing familial and religious institutions and they should be subject to higher authorities, including the state where appropriate. Those at the conservative or more cautious end of the spectrum also tend to see a pattern of moral decay spreading through society and are pessimistic about the effects of expanded market opportunities. They tend to promote traditional institutions as places from which people can acquire the traditionally based wisdom that will enable them to judge adequately the character of the opportunities provided by the market.

Those identified by their opinions as occupying the middle ground avoid proscribing social practices and shift towards a dilution of moral precepts so that their emerging conceptions of the good life encompass a widening range of novel activities. The largest constituency may be termed the "pragmatists", those who through exposure to outside education and travel see the need for social change and reforms but are aware of limitations and inefficiencies in implementing this process. They tend to settle for the present situation as they consider it preferable to the uncertainty of radical change. Fearing social upheaval, the pragmatists believe a balance must be maintained between innovation and tradition.

"Liberal" opinion attempts to marginalize the sphere of tradition and is more optimistic about the moral implications of the new opportunities. More inclined to use a language of individual achievement than a language of the moral community, liberal thinkers tend in this context to minimize the scope of identity reference to the group. Liberals are more open to change and are keener to join a global economy.

Despite the differences, however, there is broad acceptance that there should be some fairly high level of congruence between an idea of what it is to be Muslim and what it is to engage in modem practices and to live with modern technologies and consumer goods. In fact, some conception of what it means to lead a virtuous life and some appreciation of what it means to have standards by which the individual, others and communities might be judged are more or less explicit in all the evaluations made of contemporary life. Naturally, conservative opinion is more restrictive, usually expressing a stronger sense of the dangers of engagement with the modem and emphasizing the role of community. Liberal opinion tends towards more market-oriented and individualist assessments of status which will be judged in terms of the practical skills and efforts which make for success in the market. The standards by which moral status is to be judged, however, have clearly entered a period of intense debate. This contest is the terrain on which identities of the new generation in Saudi Arabia are negotiated and reinvented.

The Evolution of Saudi Society:
The Story of the Three Generations

The best way to portray the extent to which society and the cultural references of ordinary Saudi Arabians have been transformed is by taking an "ideal type", in this case the life experiences of a typical Saudi family. This family would have lived through the major landmarks of Saudi Arabia's twentieth-century history, the establishment of national unity, the oil era and globalization. The effects of modernization can best be judged by looking at a family in which the grandparents would have been born in the 1930s, the parents in the 1950s, and the new generation in the 1970s and 1980s. The story of such a family can explain the cultural identity and political consciousness against the backdrop of changing economic and political circumstances. Over a period of some sixty years the horizons of each successive generation have expanded, from the purely local to those bounded by the state and then to the present generation whose horizons are global.

The grandparents of this archetypal family would have been born in a decade of great historical significance for the Kingdom, namely that of political unification in 1932. The area that is now Saudi Arabia, prior to unification, encompassed separate territories with distinct political heritages: the southern region, Asir; the central region, Nejd; the eastern province, Ahsa; and the western region, the Hijaz. Before unification, the Hijaz had three schools of Islamic law: the *shafi'*, following the teachings of imam al-Safi'i; the *hanafi*, following the teachings of imam Abu Hanifa; and the *maliki*, following the teaching of imam Malik; while the Nejd had the *hanbali* school of law, following the teachings of imam Ahmed bin Hanbal, and specifically its interpretation by the wahhabi *'ulama* or religious scholars. (Wahhabism is a particular interpretation of the *hanbali* Islamic school of law, founded by Muhammad bin Abdul Wahhab (1703–87). Wahhabis, who prefer to call themselves Muwahhidun, are strictly monotheistic. The aim of the founder of the movement was to abolish all innovations (*bid'a*) which came after the third Islamic century.)

The unification was a period of upheaval marked by civil war, especially between the Kingdom of Hijaz and the Sultanate of Nejd, and the assertion of a distinctive religious ideology, wahhabism. During the youth of the grandparents, the peninsula was mostly a vast desert of largely nomadic rural communities. Identity was based on the family or tribe. Regional belonging was the basis of political identity, with variation of dialect, social behaviour, religious rituals, cuisine and dress. The grandfather wore his locally specific dress and the grandmother her distinctive clothes and jewelry. These and their dialect would have identified their origins. They also had a distinctive cuisine reflecting the physical environment and access to trading routes. As far as macro-political allegiances, the transition that the central government sought, from loyal ties based on a tribal and/or regional identity to a national one, did not impact on the daily existence of the vast majority of the population. National homogeneity was certainly the objective of the newly established government under the Al-Saud family but this goal was unrealized in the 1930s and 1940s. The founder of the Kingdom, Abdul Aziz Al-Saud, aimed at a gradual integration and political unification, knowing that the gap between the regions was too wide to be bridged in a short time or by military coercion. The first vehicle of unification was wahhabi hanbalism as the official Saudi dogma.

The practical (as opposed to religious) horizons of the grandparents' imagination did not extend beyond the boundaries of their home town or village. The grandfather's only means of transport was on foot or camel and later by truck; extended journeys were usually undertaken only once in a lifetime, and then to Mecca for pilgrimage. This reflected the economic circumstances of the time, characteristic of a country with almost negligible or as yet untapped resources, with the only major source of external income deriving from pilgrimage. Subsistence farming was dominant, with life organized around the scarcity of water. Villages outside main trading centres and ports were feebly connected to the areas surrounding them, let alone to the world economy. Trade was limited to the ports of Jeddah and those in the Ahsa. As far as education, the grandfather's knowledge did not go beyond religious education at the *kuttab* (schools for the memorization and study of the Quran) as well as tribal and local affairs. In modern terminology, one would describe him as semi-literate. The exception was Hijaz, where there were more liberal educational centres, both in the great mosque of Mecca and in that of Medina, which accommodated diversity.

The typical man of the grandfather's generation had one wife—unlike a minority of men who were better placed tribally and/or economically and had more. His wife was from the same lineage and more particularly the same extended family. The grandmother's major occupation in life was to produce and rear the offspring—an average of seven children, though the high infant mortality rate meant several others did not survive. The only help she had in raising her children were members of her extended family. Wealthier families may have also depended upon slaves to carry out domestic tasks (slavery was abolished by King Faisal in 1965). The grandparents' generation came to adulthood when oil revenues had started to make their effects felt, but they still remembered pre-oil times. Oil brought non-Muslim foreigners to the newly established Saudi Arabia. The grandfather began to come into contact with non-Muslims for the first time in his life, particularly as American oil workers not only visited but started to have a quasi-permanent presence in the country.

The parents, those of the second generation, were born in the 1950s. They came to adulthood after the institutional structures of the state had been firmly established. National homogeneity became the norm with the unification of dress (all Saudi men adopted the national *thoub* and head-dress and all Saudi women the black '*abaya* in public), a national education curriculum and the beginnings of mass communication through the first national newspapers and radio. With these innovations it became possible to speak of the emergence of a Saudi Arabian identity. The process of integration became effective with the flow of oil revenues. Oil money accelerated the building of an infrastructure that in turn facilitated political integration. Travel throughout the Kingdom was commonplace. Saudis began to come into regular contact with and depend on state institutions. They began to read in national newspapers about their fellow citizens and hear the pronouncements of a national government on the radio. There was also a homogenizing of religious practice under the dominant *hanbali* school of jurisprudence as prescribed by the established religious elite. The father's broader allegiances became synonymous with the Saudi state and beyond that with the wider causes of Arab nationalism which he would have heard articulated in Jamal Abdul Nasser's speeches on the radio. Social and geographical mobility was widespread by comparison with the previous generation. Oil money resulted in major shifts and changes in people's socio-economic status. Some became impoverished in relation to others who became very rich. Likewise, people moved from one region to another for the first time. Hence, a Hijazi might go to live in Riyadh, in the heart of Nejd, or to the Ahsa to work in the oil industry.

If the father of the family went on to higher education he probably did so at a university in the United States, where he was supported by government grants. When he returned to the Kingdom he worked in the government sector, where he was guaranteed a job. The rapid growth in government bureaucracy during the 1950s meant these newly educated workers could easily be absorbed, with the government becoming the largest employer. In the 1930s there were only two ministers, the Minister of Foreign Affairs and the Minister of Finance. During the 1950s the governing structure at the pinnacle of the Saudi state was partly institutionalized with a cabinet of over twenty ministers. During the 1970s, the wages paid by state employment in the administration or the petroleum industry allowed a man to provide for his wife, children and other dependents in the extended family—a standard of living far in excess of anything that the average member of his parents' generation could have imagined. The rapid growth of the economy owing to oil production also caused an increased demand for skilled foreign workers, who began to enter the country in large numbers for the first time since the discovery of oil. The oil economy led to large sections of the Saudi population coming into contact with Westerners and non-Muslims for the first time, as well as with other Arabs from Egypt, Palestine, Jordan, Syria and Iraq. The latter had political influence as advisers to the king and social and educational influence as teachers in schools. During the 1950s, many of these Arabs from neighboring countries acquired Saudi citizenship. However, this trend was drastically curtailed in the 1960s, when citizenship became nearly impossible to acquire, given an attempt by the government to confine the definition of "Saudi" to the indigenous population. This was not only a form of nationalism but also a technique of social exclusion directed at other Arabs and Muslims.

During the father's time, the state represented power and grandeur. This marked a transformation in the nature of political authority. The state acquired legitimacy and loyalty through the distribution of wealth. The response was no longer political submission but gratitude towards the generous and wealthy political patrons. Authority began to rest on the just distribution of Allah's wealth.

The "mother", although educated at one of the new schools for women, nonetheless maintained the traditional role of a woman of her generation by rearing children. However, she had the advantage of modern medicine and health care, and could make use of foreign nannies, spacious homes and modern comforts. This led to a reduction in levels of infant mortality and a baby boom that greatly increased the size of the population.

The result of that population increase is the third generation. The members of this new generation were born during the peak of the oil boom of the 1970s (1973–9) or at least before the downturn of 1984. They do not remember anything prior to oil; all notions of "tradition", of a Bedouin past, indeed of a life lived primarily in the desert, have been handed down to them through the stories and recollections of the two previous generations.

During their upbringing the members of this new generation took for granted mass education, regular travel abroad, radio and television, including, more recently, satellite broadcasts. Foreign "servants" were a key part of their life, including nannies who assisted in bringing them up. They have been left to grapple with a very uncertain set of beliefs about "modernity". They know much more than their parents' generation because of their exposure to wider influences and education, but this knowledge creates problems. They have more opportunities than previous generations, but they also have more fears. They are still expected to follow their parents' "traditions" and to listen to their instructions, but exposure to the wider world poses an increasing challenge to their fathers' authority. Change has been so swift that they still do not have the cultural terms of reference to put this new society and their role within it into perspective. The dress they wear and the food they eat represent the complexity and tension of this situation. Western fashions inspired by satellite television and the US-dominated global culture compete with Saudi culture and national dress. The music available to them through various channels is officially banned by the 'ulama. The youth have even encountered war in 1990–91, which added to their uneasy sense of identity. The unanswered questions that trouble the new generation are many: will they be given the chance to apply usefully the new skills and concepts learned in a greatly expanded and generously funded education system? Will they even have the guaranteed employment and the same living standards as their parents? And, crucially, who are they—what is the basis and location of their identity?

Following this amazing cultural transformation, young people lack the certainties of their grandparents, the villagers whose position and role in life appeared stable and predictable. They also lack the economic security of their parents, who grew up in a time when oil delivered plenty. The choices and uncertain future that face the new generation are seen as threatening. There are still numerous benefits (houses, food and other material goods); however, rapid urbanization has created a sense of dislocation. The move, in the space of two generations, from a self-supporting village, weakly connected to the outside world, to the cities of a modern state at the heart of a region undergoing the effects of globalization has assaulted the identity of these young people, leaving them ambivalent and troubled by an apparently superficial way of life.

The uncertainty that modernity brings can be challenged and placed in perspective by confronting its effects and questioning the outcomes. These young people, however, have not been given the personal autonomy to question a profoundly disorientating experience because of basic beliefs, traditions and religious customs that constrain and censor their thoughts and actions. One can identify two broad categories of problems with which they are grappling: first, and most noticeably, the economic transformations; and, second, the increasing questioning of their cultural values and norms, which are criticized as anachronistic.

Nation, Family, Religion and Belonging: Notions of Tradition among the New Generation

The sense of identity of the young people of Saudi Arabia described here has been taken primarily from their own thoughts and comments as expressed in their own words. Identity is key to any individual, allowing one to place oneself within the family, community and wider society. An individual's identity has many strands, each assuming different importance depending on the situation. These strands or forms of identity range from the most pervasive—the family—to the tribe, the region and, more recently, the city.

Despite state-driven attempts to foster Saudi national identity and even to develop a "Gulf" identity, Saudi Arabia, though united in a single national unit in 1932, remains a heterogeneous country. National and wider "Gulf" identity must compete with and often comes second to the family and the four regions as prime units of allegiance.

Those interviewed attach a high significance to the persistence of institutions that are familiar to their parents and grandparents and that remain important to the new generation's self-conceptions. Tradition is seen by the new generation in terms of religion and culture. Young people deploy these values alongside the sense of belonging to the state and the wider Arab community. The use of the term "nation" is problematical in this regard: although portrayed by the institutions of the state as traditional and unchanging, it is for many a novelty with ambiguous connotations. However, this ambiguity the youth sometimes express has not prevented the emergence of a strong sense of national belonging. A shared sense of cultural difference from both Westerners and others in the wider Arab world has fostered a cultural commonality at both the national and wider Gulf levels that overshadows regional or tribal distinctions.

Tradition is represented through vivid images, usually drawn from family life. For example, when I asked Saad (16), from the Hijaz, to describe aspects of tradition he said, "Tradition is family reunion," and "It is when the *zabiha* (the whole lamb) is presented to eat." Asma (28), from Jeddah, defines tradition as "the things people always do as their parents and grandparents did". Said (27), from Tabuk, said that tradition was following the prophet Mohammad's practices through his authenticated *hadith* (sayings). Linking tradition to their parents' way of life not only means obedience to family and religion but seems to lessen fears about change and uncertainty. The new generation appears to have created a sense of being rooted in what it sees as the traditional institution of the family, which provides a link to the continuity of the past. At times of serious change in their way of life, young people's link with "tradition" gives them a sense of security and a sense of identity. Adnan (24), from Mecca, said that "tradition is respect shown towards older people". Malak (17), from Jeddah, says that she admires the *ihtiram* (respect) of tradition. However, she worries that the respect paid to the past is rapidly diminishing. She says that it used to be important to be *bint an-nas* ("the daughter of good people") and to follow tradition, but now people do not necessarily admire self-respect and good lineage. Concerned about the pace of change, she agrees that "in order to be part of the global village, we need to become more international". But she hastily adds that "we must keep something for ourselves". In other words, she thinks that local identity has to be maintained to give coherence to both the individual and society in the midst of changing circumstances.

Hamad, from a southern tribe in Asir, voices a more critical opinion about tradition: "The older generation generally does not allow the younger to take over, basically because fathers are very jealous of their sons." But Hamad qualifies and dilutes this assertion by saying that he likes tradition, especially some "beautiful traditional rules such as the respect for elders and other customs that prevent calamities and provide security". But there are for Hamad some traditions which should be swept away; for example, if a man dies his brother should not have to marry his widow. Despite this, "marrying one's first cousin is a good thing, as long as the woman is not obliged to marry against her will".

Said wants to emulate the values of his parents' generation. "I want to be just like my father. I admire his wisdom, his reactions and the way he handles problems. There is so much to learn from the older generation." This is despite the fact that Said's father is illiterate, "but he has always had an instinctive ability with numbers, making him a good businessman".

The symbolism of Islam combined with the unique heritage of Saudi Arabia based on the guardianship of Mecca and Medina continue to be central to the Saudi identity and therefore to many Saudis' sense of political and social stability. Adnan is typical of many who link tradition and their sense of belonging to religion. When asked about his family background, he says that they were *'ulama* who taught at the Great Mosque in Mecca. "I wish that I were living in the days of my grandfathers to learn from them." When asked where his values and morality come from he refers to them being specifically Muslim values. Nouf is more specific in her definition of tradition and religion. It is "*salafi* and pure desert Nejdi culture". She criticizes Sufi practices because "they efface the individual, which *salafi* Islam celebrates."

The new generation tries to relate the various and sometimes competing communities to which it feels it belongs. Although family is the most important unit of identity it is accompanied by an increasing sense of national belonging. Religion is often given greater prominence than both nation and family because it allows for other competing allegiances to be subsumed into the larger category. However, there is an ambiguity in the general appeal of "tradition" among the new generation. The Saudi state since 1932 has not only used a notion of "tradition" to legitimate itself, but through actively sponsoring cultural, religious and political unification has also created a new, distinctly national notion of tradition. When questioned during group interviews about the importance of values, many of the respondents attached importance to Islamic identity first and then a national identity. Many in the new generation see religion as the primary defining factor of their lives, giving them a moral purpose.

Exposure to Modernity

There is widespread participation among the new generation in social practices that have been introduced since their parents' day or that have become more available. People have far greater access to print arid electronic media, including satellite as well as domestic television, the Internet and a variety of publications. Participation, however, is far from uniform. There are differences related to wealth, education and language acquisition. For the new generation the idea of progress is associated with the need to absorb modern technologies into practical life. Some social relations are associated with modernity: the democratization of family life, for instance, and other matters relating to gender can often be seen in terms of Western social values. The young people interviewed have two main ways of encountering the wider world—the media, including the internet, and foreign travel. Restrictions on access to the media within Saudi Arabia are a persistent source of controversy.

Access to the media is ubiquitous among those interviewed. There are some expected differences between them all based on language, interests, and exposure to other countries. Some young people place a higher value on the media for the access it gives them to information and the help it provides for their education. Mansour travels between Saudi Arabia and London, but he has also been to the United States, Europe, other GCC countries and Egypt. He watches television, especially programmes that deal with the mind, such as BBC shows and Imad Al-Din talk shows on Orbit. Mansour reads *Al-Hayat*, *Al-Sharq-Al- Awsat*, the *International Herald Tribune* and *Time* magazine. He uses the Internet and believes it is generally very beneficial. Mansour believes that technology is important and rates the different sources of information in order: television first, then newspapers, magazines and radio.

The issue of censorship is perplexing for Hamad (29), whose favourite television channel is Al Jazira, a political satellite broadcast from Qatar. He considers that Al Jazira fills a gap and makes people aware of political debates that concern them. "Four years ago we did not know about oil problems, or two years ago about the stock exchange crisis. People now receive this information from Al Jazira." Interestingly, he has a low opinion of Western satellite television. It "has negative effects on the youth, because many blindly imitate what they see, from clothes and appearances to dancing to a song that you don't even understand the words to. People have lost their identity. It is as if a spell has been put on them, transforming them into distorted figures."

Travelling abroad is an option available to many of the new generation. In many ways, travel has an impact on their views and opinions, especially when they can speak English. However, closer contact with other cultures often reinforces a sense of belonging to one's own community.

There is no doubt about the considerable enthusiasm among many in the new generation for what modernity has to offer. Twenty-four-year-old Adnan's feelings about travelling to the United States encapsulate this more expansive view. He values it because he "can find anything there", as well as enjoying the beaches and entertainment. However, he likes Dubai because "you can get a taste of what you are missing in Saudi Arabia but still feel at home". Saad is constantly using the Internet. He mostly likes television programmes that have music. He thinks that "technology in Saudi Arabia will contribute to breaking down barriers, especially the Internet as it becomes cheaper to be exposed to different people".

There is a deep and widespread unease that modernity may well entail more than just the acquisition of technology. For many, modernity brings Western values that threaten Saudi traditions. Despite this enthusiasm for the goods and opportunities made available through the development of increased market access to the West, there is a general apprehension of possible contradictions between what the new generation values as traditional and modern cultures. Some young people gave accounts of their personal experiences of struggle over the introduction of new practices and social innovations, largely located within the family and political arenas.

The home is the site of greatest impact of the new electronic media technologies. There are evident tensions between the modern and the traditional which affect life within the home. This can be the case regardless of wealth or status. Nouf finds that she is still searching for a balance between being a Saudi princess and all the "rebellious ideas" she is exposed to in the West. At the moment, she describes herself as rebellious but says her immediate family is understanding. Said, on the other hand, comes from a rural village where his parents are illiterate. Sources of cultural exposure were extremely limited, with the radio providing the main window on the outside world until 1977, when television arrived. New forms of media were not welcomed by his mother, who used her "strength and dominance in the family" to oppose the latest intrusion, a satellite dish.

At a time of major changes in the social structure, the question of tradition and modernity obviously preoccupies the youth, whatever their economic or regional background and irrespective of gender. Salman explains the tensions in the system realistically. "There are tensions here between modernity and tradition. There was tension with the 'ulama when radio was successfully introduced. There is still tension over women's education and satellite dishes but the wheels of evolution will not stop, cannot stop turning."

There are deeply conflicting pressures from contemporary political and economic forces. The state and religious authorities show great reluctance to permit general access to some forms of modem communication. Yassir, when asked about the Internet, replied jokingly, "What is the Internet?", referring to the official reluctance to introduce it in Saudi Arabia. However, he acknowledged that the Internet and satellite television were "a double-edged weapon". But when asked whether Saudi society should open up more, he said it had already opened up to the outside world.

Despite state-sponsored efforts to restrict what can be watched on domestic television, there is nonetheless a greater variety available on satellite television, both Western and Arab channels. The state-run media have lost their dominance over young people. The drab presentation and limited scope of issues covered on Saudi television mean that it has increasingly been rejected, and attention has also been drawn to the issue of censorship.

The ambivalence among most young people is captured by Mish'al, who comments: "I like tradition. I like to sit like this and eat with my hands. Why should I pick up my cup of tea in an English fashion? It has no history in my country." But he goes on to comment: "For Saudi Arabia to become part of the global society, it needs to open its borders, and strict social rules should be abolished. People must be given more opportunities.

The real threat to the lives and experiences of members of communities in Saudi Arabia posed by the new technologies is nonetheless taken quite seriously by most of the young. There is no blanket acceptance of new technologies, even by those who have unrestricted access to them.

Direct contact with Westerners or things perceived to be Western can also raise difficult questions. When Ayman (16) was asked whether travelling to Europe and the United States had a significant impact on his values, he said that it had advantages and disadvantages. "It is good to learn English, to get away from one's own world and to forget problems as well as to relax, but the disadvantage could be losing Islamic values."

Ayman believes that "even when abroad a person must preserve his identity by being in touch with the country and heritage". That said, embers of the new generation think that maintaining Saudi identity is difficult when contact with the West is needed in order to advance.

There is a wide recognition that modernity involves being judged according to alien standards as cultures increasingly share, even compete for, the same physical spaces. Precisely which standards should be applied to others or which are being applied to one's own conduct is a problem.

For conservatives, modern social practices appear to be incompatible with virtues. The very term "open-minded" seems to capture a sense of profligacy of personality, persons without restraint or practical control over themselves and their relations with the world.

A large number of those interviewed are aware of the tensions but they do not regard modern goods as bad in themselves. There is a widespread feeling that these goods and practices can be put to good use, provided they are approached in the right spirit. For some, especially among those who have had the exposure to the West, having been educated in English and having adopted liberal terminology as well as practical goods, the direction of tensions is reversed. For liberals, the need to survive and achieve in the contemporary world requires a more open-minded attitude.

These general attitudes can be investigated in relation to the issues of indirect contact between groups through technology and the media, of direct contact between groups via travel, tourism and immigration, and of attitudes towards relations between generations. The comments of the new generation are increasingly expressing a more individualistic morality of personal achievement while recognizing and lamenting a falling off of social solidarity. The market, as opposed to the family or community, takes on greater significance and the terms in which evaluations are made are increasingly oriented towards that market mentality, rather than the community.

Conclusion

Over the past few years, pre-existing economic, political and religious behavioural standards have come under increasing pressure within Saudi Arabia. This has resulted in old standards of behaviour being either discarded or modified, a process that has inevitably resulted in the reinvention of new levels and forms of identity. This has generated an ambiguity of outlook, embracing technology and the information it brings while seeking security in a modification and reinvention of the tradition that permeates the identity of the new generation. For some, their perception of tradition allows them to interact with a changing and possibly threatening world from a position of certainty. The shift towards market-oriented practices has had a considerable effect on attitudes towards what the young conceive of as older institutions. The heightened awareness of the family as a unit of reference can be related to this. Families are no longer the dominant sphere of socio-economic life; their role appears to be becoming gradually marginalized. Valorizing the family is a recognition of its diminished role in life. Something similar can be said of religion. There is a shift in the relationship between religion and the more market-based social life. Religion either adjusts to this by becoming less concrete and more permissive, or adopts a more rigorous enforcement of certain concrete social practices.

Those who take tradition and community seriously argue that the state and family should see to it that the tensions between the old and the new are minimized. To this end, they argue for measures to reinforce a sense of national community. Respect for tradition and the older generation means that people should not be exposed to things that will "shock their minds". Amina (18) enjoyed her travels and Western exposure but does not believe that too much questioning is good. "In Saudi Arabia you can learn how to control your behaviour and to respect. Most of the time you cannot say what you think, which is good."

Yet others see no alternative to some form of convergence between themselves and the West. Adnan did not accept that social distance should be maintained between foreigners and Saudis. When asked with which categories of expatriates he thought Saudis ought to have closer contact, he responded that "this decision should not be based on nationality but rather on profession". Asked whether he thought Saudi Arabia was isolated and needed to open up to the outside world, he answered affirmatively. Ahmed's view of relations with the expatriates is that "we should learn from their experiences and absorb what is beneficial from their cultures".

On the one hand, as mentioned above, there is a tendency towards the marginalization of the significance of the family as a socio-economic force. Saad believes that in Saudi Arabia there is much more modernity than tradition. Saad sees that tradition is not a static concept and must change with social developments, even if this means reducing the significance of family just to occasional gatherings.

On the other hand, there is the marginalization and diminution of the significance of religion. Ayman believes that there is no future for those who study *sharia* at university and that the development of a more secular national identity is important. Naif believes that "all we should maintain from tradition is the Islamic theological nucleus, and that's all".

Identity, whether conceptualized as "given" (natural) or "constructed" (social), is that which endows groups and individuals with a place, a function, a purpose and, in the modern world, with the capacity for action. So identity is indivisible from modern politics. The basis of an individual's identity within a given society is over-determined, being created from numerous sources. Each input gains or loses importance depending on the individual's social circumstances the individual is in. Since the founding of the state, Saudi identity has been determined by overlapping and competing sources. Internal sources of competition have included religion, tribal belonging, family and the nation. External sources have encompassed the forces of Western modernization. The direction of this evolving sense of identity has been linked to the processes of economic development and government policy. The ruling elite has sought to control the process in ways that support its own political agenda and strengthen its position at the heart of the state. In times of economic growth, the Saudi population, optimistic about the future and supported by a financially strong state, has received ideas from the outside world with a degree of confidence that facilitates their coherent assimilation. However, in times of economic uncertainty and government austerity (the current Saudi context), the population as a whole tends to seek cultural reassurance in notions of tradition. They become preoccupied with the mosque and public displays of piety or the home village from which their grandparents came, or else they transfigure the meaning of tradition so that it fits more easily with the new world. Either way, this retreat into certainty is an attempt to interact with a rapidly changing and uncertain world from a secure and recognizable base.

Originally published in *Changed Identities: The Challenge of the New Generation in Saudi Arabia* (The Royal Institute of International Affairs [Chatham House], 2000): 1–25. It is printed here with the permission of the publisher.

PART FOUR

Behavioral Departures and Alternative Lifestyles

Introduction

Discussions of deviance, over the past decade or so, have been undergoing something akin to paradigm shifts. There has been a marked shift from the earlier, positivist, essentialist approach which regarded deviance as something objective, predetermined and inherent in normative violations on which there is a large residue of consensus. Instead, what has gained prominence is a move away from the focus on the origins, causes or what predisposes individuals or groups to engage in deviant behavior to how such violations are defined, labeled and socially constructed.

Since modern society is characterized by considerable diversity, uncertainty and ambivalence regarding what constitutes cherished and agreed upon values or normative expectations, it is certainly more realistic and meaningful to adopt a neutral and comparative perspective which talks about behavioral departures and alternative life styles. All the manifestations of social "deviance" we are considering in this chapter—from female circumcision and honor killing to prostitution, homosexuality and sexual harassment—are characterized by normative dissonance and uncertainty as to how they should be treated and controlled.

The practice of circumcision or female genital mutilation, despite concerted efforts to control some of its barbaric and harmful effects, is still common in countries like Egypt, Sudan, Yemen and some Gulf states. Underlying the survival of this practice is naturally the persistence of sexual modesty and, more particularly, an intact hymen as cherished values in society. It is reinforced by the belief that by removing parts of the girls' external genital organs, sexual desire is curtailed. This is also a reflection of patriarchal fears that when young girls reach the "dangerous age" of puberty, there is a need to safeguard the honor of the family by protecting the girls' virginity.

Nawal El-Saadawi, a veteran rural physician and human rights activist, herself a victim of cultural cruelties, is in a fitting position to extract confessions and intimate personal accounts from girls and women who have also been subjected to similar misfortunes. In her paper she makes judicious use of her sustained research, medical practice and feminist advocacy to expose the manifest and latent cruelties inherent in such aberrant practices and their lifelong psychological consequences. El-Saadawi identifies some of the economic, political and socio-cultural circumstances which reinforce the practice and compound its ominous byproducts, decrying the outmoded views and taboos which distort and mystify the nature of sexuality. The archaic religious and moral authorities of these misbegotten beliefs are blamed along with the indifference and lethargy of her colleagues in the medical and academic professions.

Her instructive conclusion could well apply when reflecting upon other manifestations of human departures considered in this chapter:

> ...There are still a large number of fathers and mothers who are afraid of leaving

the clitoris intact in the bodies of their daughters. Many a time they have said to me that circumcision is a safeguard against the mistakes and deviations into which a girl may be led. This way of thinking is wrong and even dangerous because what protects a boy or a girl from making mistakes is not the removal of a small piece of flesh from the body, but consciousness and understanding of the problems we face, and a worthwhile aim in life, an aim which gives it meaning and for whose attainment we exert our mind and energies.

... In the life of liberated and intelligent women, sex does not occupy a disproportionate position, but rather tends to maintain itself within normal limits. In contrast, ignorance, suppression, fear and all sorts of limitations exaggerate the role of sex in the life of girls and women, and cause it to swell out of all proportion and to end up by occupying the whole, or almost the whole, of their lives.

Ghasalat al-arr literally means washing away the shame by killing a girl or woman, often on the mere suspicion of her sexual conduct. Her actual or alleged misconduct, particularly if associated with the loss of virginity, is seen by her family and community as an unbearable stain or stigma on the honor of her male relatives. Once this familial sexual shame has been "washed," the offense is often quickly forgotten. As in other Arab countries, an honor killing, often dubbed as a crime of passion, is not by law considered a criminal offence. Indeed, the offender, usually a brother, cousin or close relative, is set free shortly afterwards without any conviction. Often the culprit chosen to carry out the deed is deliberately a minor so as to guarantee lenient retributive reaction.

Reliable statistics on the incidence of honor crimes are hard to come by. The United Nations Population Fund estimates that about 5,000 such crimes take place every year around the world particularly in rural areas. Some human rights advocates claim that Syria suffers from comparatively high numbers, ranking it as second or third in the world. It is also widely agreed that the incidence of honor crimes in Muslim communities (e.g. Bangladesh, Egypt, even Great Britain) is disproportionately higher than elsewhere.

The tragic life and death story of Zahra, as graphically told by Katherine Zoepf, is unusual because it has some striking and compelling elements to it. First, and unlike other such episodes, it was not willfully washed away. Indeed, it evolved into something of a cause célèbre in Damascus with much media attention and public debate. A group of young human rights activists, lawyers, Islamic scholars and Syrian officials, sparked by the aroused public sympathy for Zahra's young widower, used the notoriety of the case to lobby for a change in the criminal code which protects the perpetrators of such aberrant crimes. Also credit must be given to Fawaz, her bereaved husband and cousin who, in defiance of local custom and tribal traditions, has filed a civil lawsuit against Zahra's brother and killer.

The case is also instructive because it highlights the conflict and tension generated by the dissonance between two sets of cultural scripts. Syria since 1963 has been governed by a secular Baathist regime which purports to support sex equality. The magnitude of literacy among women is almost equal to men. So is the rate of high school and university graduates and those who have access to employment opportunities in the professional and public sectors of the labor market. Such seemingly liberal and secular manifestations are contested by the survival of traditional and tribal norms which continue to be apprehensive about the sexual life of women. Indeed, the Baathist ruling elite have been cautious lately not to offend the revivalist expectations of conservative Islamist groups. The ongoing debate regarding Article 548 in the Constitution which is lenient in condemning an offender who commits such a crime, is proof that the public is still divided on this matter.

The more persuasive proof is, of course, the high incidence of honor crimes. Women's rights advocates estimate that about 300 girls and women are victims of *Ghasalat al-arr* every year. The figure, incidentally, would have been much higher had not police authorities sustained the practice of placing minors and potential targets in prisons or under public custody for their own protection. Judges usually extract sworn statements from male guardians that the girls will not be harmed when released. Such promises, however, are often in vain. Even a cousin marriage—a valued betrothal arrangement in tribal communities—did not protect Zahra. In the words of Fawaz, by marrying Zahra he was restoring her honor and lost virtue. The honor was short-lived. The blissful life she was enjoying lasted barely five weeks. One early morning, moments after Fawaz had left Zahra soundly asleep on the carpeted floor, her brother walked in and in cold blood brutally stabbed his sister five times, "tearing thrusts that shattered the base of her skull and nearly severed her spinal column." Leaving the door open he calmly walked to the police station and turned himself in, informing the officers on duty that he had just killed his sister to cleanse the stain and dishonor she had brought to the family by losing her virginity.

To human rights activists, in Syria and elsewhere in the Arab world, such aberrant crimes are likely to survive as long as the basic cultural scripts regarding women's virginity and sexual modesty are not earnestly challenged. Some liberal advocates may question the ethics in private, but are hesitant to do so publically. Hence to many activists men today continue to "feel pressed by their communities to demonstrate that they are sufficiently protective of their female relatives' virtue. Pairs of lovers are sometimes killed together, but most frequently only the women are singled out for punishment."

This is clearly an indication that chastity as a social capital is still a cherished value, along with reinforcement of patriarchal authority and the rationalization of double standards where the victim is blamed rather than protected. Many of the tensions today in a score of countries in the Middle East between ruling elites and religious conservatives are largely an expression of these conflicting perceptions of how to monitor the conduct of women in public. For example women advocates in Jordan, with the tacit support of the royal family, launched efforts to establish harsher punishments for men who commit such crimes. Yet, the parliament rejected the proposed legislations in 2003 because of opposition of conservative groups. The same took place in Morocco.

Slight as they are, there are some promising signs of change. Recently, the top Shiite cleric and spiritual leader of Hezbollah—Mohammad Hussein Fadlallah—issued a *fatwa* banning honor killing. A more telling example is the *fatwa* upheld by the grand mufti of Egypt which permits women to restore their virginity through hymen surgery. This is certainly predicated by the belief that such measures will enhance prospects of marriage and, hence, eliminate the need for *Ghasalat al-arr* by way of cleansing the family honor.

Not only are the cruelties of honor crimes being mitigated, some of the abusive features of prostitution as a sexual outlet, particularly the confinement of women in brothels, are also being allayed. By tracing the origin and transformation of prostitution in Beirut, Samir

Khalaf elucidates on how the inevitable commodification of legal prostitution generated circumstances which rendered it more human and less alienating to both the women who are supplying the services and the men who demanded them.

Using historical records and autobiographical sketches, Khalaf tells us that brothels or houses of prostitution were in existence in Beirut as early as 1880. It was not, however, until 1920 that laws were promulgated as a public health measure to control the outbreak of an epidemic among French troops. Not only prostitutes (*al-mumsat*) but dancers, singers and other so-called "artists" were required to register with the police. They were issued identification cards, went about their work in designated brothels and were subject to medical inspection twice a week. No doubt, the presence of French troops played a part in increasing the demand for commercial prostitution.

The first decree to recognize and regulate prostitution (*al-da'arah*) as a legal profession was introduced by the Ottomans in 1931. The law defined a prostitute as any women who submitted to sexual intercourse (*irrtikab al-fasha'*) in return for a monetary reward. It also distinguished between "public houses" and other "places of assignation." Because of these restrictive measures, the number of registered prostitutes was reduced by more than half: from 1250 to 624. Also the number of licensed brothels was confined to about sixty. Though limited in number, the prostitutes and the district in which they were located, east of the Bourj, became more visible and notorious. Like much of the traditional city center of Beirut, it was the period when virtually all enterprises and entertainment ventures were becoming commercially minded and receptive to novel modes of marketing and gentrification. "The enterprising *patronas* gave the maligned image of their tainted and damnable quarter the face-lift it needed to transform it into a welcoming place."

Khalaf dwells on the epic-like story of Marica Espiredone, the Greek emigrant who managed to cast her mythical shadow over the entire Red Light district of the Bourj for over half a century. Her rags-to-riches biography is riveting precisely because she epitomizes the circumstances associated with the metamorphosis of commercial prostitution. In fact, one could easily extract from her story defining features in the textbook analysis of prostitution that was to become salient in the 1990s. "She was transforming herself from a *sex object* to a *sex worker*: from a quintessentially passive and resigned victim of male domination and manipulation to a willful agent who actively constructed her work life."

The fact that the notorious red-light district was becoming so compelling and visible in the very heart of the nation's capital did not go unnoticed. As in the reaction to other forms of behavioral departures—i.e., genital mutilation and honor crimes—the public perception of prostitution was not consistent or uniform. Khalaf identifies three distinct reactions or groups: First, traditionalists, particularly heads of religious communities, were inclined to regard prostitution as a necessary evil; a safety valve for the release of the superfluous sexual energies of the young. In their view the prostitute protects the virtue of the family and the sanctity of marriage. Second, there were those who were more inclined to condemn prostitution because it involved the commodification of sexual intimacy, the confinement of women and the restriction of their freedom. Finally, there are those who recognized the need for regulated brothels but who wished to relocate them away from the heart of the city. Given the persistent demand for licensed prostitution, and the unlikelihood of its disappearance with the liberalization of sexual mores, this group is of the view that outlawing prostitution carries the risk of shutting off an expedient safety valve. The prostitute, through the help of pimps and procurers, will be driven underground and forced to resort to clandestine and more nefarious means.

The results of a rare empirical survey of the state of legal prostitution in the mid 1960s, based on personal interviews with virtually all the sample of resident prostitutes in the red-light district, confirm the above projections. While the prostitutes remained comparatively busy, they were already beginning to complain about the decline in the quality of their business. They were also astute and prophetic in attributing this inevitable demise to changing life-styles associated with the advent of stereo-clubs, mass consumerism, international migration and sexual tourism.

The destruction of the red-light district during the early rounds of the civil war for control of the city center in 1975–76 was "altogether a propitious windfall." Already, manifestations of clandestine prostitution, part of the bourgeoning global industry, were beginning to permeate society. Khalaf's concluding inferences merit being quoted in full:

> By then and perhaps more than other societies in the region, Beirut had not been spared some of the aberrant consequences of globalization and mass consumerism. International migration has carried with it a dramatic change in the sex industry, particularly in the manner with which a growing number of consumers are now purchasing their sexual services and products. As in other societies, particularly those where tourism is likewise a viable sector, prostitution is now part and parcel of a thriving adult entertainment industry. The accessibility of X-rated videos, adult cable shows, computer pornography, adult magazines, even commercial telephone sex has, like elsewhere, invaded the inner sanctum of the home. In this respect, the globalization of sexuality has paradoxically contributed to its privatization. Porn, in both its "soft" and "hardcore" varieties, existed in some of the run-down and dilapidated movie houses in Beirut during the war and shortly after. The past decade has, however, seen porn migrate from the movie houses to the privacy of the viewers' own living rooms. Little can be done to avert or control such an aggressive and tenacious invasion.

The commodification of sexual outlets has not only affected the character of prostitution. The emergent and fluid features which characterize homosexuality as a community, or a sub-culture, within the context of postwar Beirut, have also begun to reflect some of the broader changes associated with regional and global transformations. Indeed, the very liberal and permissive setting at the time Jared McCormick was conducting his survey (spring of 2005), is symptomatic of the fact that homosexuality is no longer a taboo topic unavailable for exploration.

Discussions of homosexuality and the often sensational attention it was being given by the media was an indication that it had already become part of the public discourse. More compelling, Lebanon could already boast of being the first country in the Arab world to establish a gay rights voluntary association (*Helem*, the Arabic word for dream and acronym for *Himaya Lubnaniyya lil Mithliyien* [Lebanese Protections for Homosexuals]). While states in the region are still prosecuting gays (in Iran and Iraq they are still executed), *Helem* has a regular periodical (*Barra*), its own website and a guide which offers inventories of gay-friendly clubs, bars and safe cruising areas. As a result, the number of gays who have recently 'come out' and are actively engaged in defending their lifestyle and associated freedoms are becoming more audible. Moreover, the recently installed website is inundated with over 50,000 hits and postings every month.

Despite the overt liberalization and less inhibitive socio-cultural setting, the evidence McCormick extracts from his recorded interviews reveals that most Lebanese are still averse to considering a gay way of life as acceptable. This is why many of his twenty informants lead portions of their lives covertly, particularly in relation to their family. Usually, the father is kept in the dark. At least he is the last to know. Hence, the delicate balancing act—being "in/out" of the closet—is still riddled with tension, ambivalence and personal anguish. It is interesting to point out in this regard that the six men who returned from at least eight years of experience abroad clearly show less dissonance between their lived and gay identity. In fact, quite a few who have come out recently appear to display many of the Western gay archetypes as a guide and role model in validating their own gay identity. They are also the ones who assume leadership roles in the affairs of Helem.

McCormick devotes the bulk of his essay to demonstrating how three circumstances have had a transforming effect on the process or redefining global transplants to accommodate local realities: the establishment of *Helem*; the role of the internet, chat-rooms and other electronic and digital networks and information technologies; and, finally, the advent of globalization, particularly the changing of consumerism and marketing.

McCormick ends with a fairly positive conjecture; i.e., that this quest to forge a local gay identity is groundbreaking. It is bound, despite the travails it is currently embroiled in, to play a transforming role in the advancement of sexuality and gay rights in Lebanon and perhaps elsewhere in the Arab world.

NAWAL EL SAADAWI

Circumcision of Girls in Egypt

The practice of circumcising girls is still a common procedure in a number of Arab countries such as Egypt, the Sudan, Yeman and some of the Gulf states.

The importance given to virginity and an intact hymen in these societies is the reason why female circumcision still remains a very widespread practice despite a growing tendency, especially in urban Egypt, to do away with it as something outdated and harmful. Behind circumcision lies the belief that, by removing parts of girls' external genital organs, sexual desire is minimized. This permits a female who has reached the "dangerous age" of puberty and adolescence to protect her virginity, and therefore her honour, with greater ease. Chastity was imposed on male attendants in the female harem by castration which turned them into inoffensive eunuchs. Similarly, female circumcision is meant to preserve the chastity of young girls by reducing their desire for sexual intercourse.

Circumcision is most often performed on female children at the age of seven or eight (before the girl begins to get menstrual periods). On the scene appears the *daya* or local midwife. Two women members of the family grasp the child's thighs on either side and pull them apart to expose the external genital organs and to prevent her from struggling—like trussing a chicken before it is slain. A sharp razor in the hand of the *daya* cuts off the clitoris.

During my period of service as a rural physician, I was called upon many times to treat complications arising from this primitive operation, which very often jeopardized the life of young girls. The ignorant *daya* believed that effective circumcision necessitated a deep cut with the razor to ensure radical amputation of the clitoris, so that no part of the sexually sensitive organ would remain. Severe hemorrhaging was therefore a common occurrence and sometimes led to loss of life. The *dayas* had not the slightest notion of asepsis, and inflammatory conditions as a result of the operation were common. Above all, the lifelong psychological shock of this cruel procedure left its imprint on the personality of the child and accompanied her into adolescence, youth and maturity. Sexual frigidity is one of the after-effects which is accentuated by other social and psychological factors that influence the personality and mental make-up of females in Arab societies. Girls are therefore exposed to a whole series of misfortunes as a result of outdated notions and values related to virginity, which still remains the fundamental criterion of a girl's honour. In recent years, however, educated families have begun to realize the harm that is done by the practice of female circumcision.

Nevertheless a majority of families still impose on young female children the barbaric and cruel operation of circumcision. The research that I carried out on a sample of 160 Egyptian girls and women showed that 97.5% of uneducated families still insisted on maintaining the custom, but this percentage dropped to 66.2% among educated families.

When I discussed the matter with these girls and women it transpired that most of them had no idea of the harm done by circumcision, and some of them even thought that it was good for one's health and conducive to cleanliness and "purity". (The operation in the common language of the people is in fact called the cleansing or purifying operation.) Despite the fact that the percentage of educated women who have undergone circumcision is only 66.2%, as compared with 97.5% among uneducated women, even the former did not realize the effect that this amputation of the clitoris could have on their psychological and sexual health. The dialogue that occurred between these women and myself would run more or less as follows:

"Have you undergone circumcision?"

"Yes."

"How old were you at the time?"

"I was a child, about seven or eight years old."

"Do you remember the details of the operation?"

"Of course. How could I possibly forget?"

"Were you afraid?"

"Very afraid. I hid on top of the cupboard [in other cases she would say under the bed, or in the neighbour's house], but they caught hold of me, and I felt my body tremble in their hands."

"Did you feel any pain?"

"Very much so. It was like a burning flame and I screamed. My mother held my head so that I could not move it, my aunt caught hold of my right arm and my grandmother took charge of my left. Two strange women whom I had not seen before tried to keep me from moving my thighs by pushing them as far apart as possible. The *daya* sat between these two women, holding a sharp razor in her hand which she used to cut off the clitoris. I was scared and suffered such great pain that I lost consciousness at the flame that seemed to sear me through and through."

"What happened after the operation?"

"I had severe bodily pains, and remained in bed for several days, unable to move. The pain in my external genital organs led to retention of urine. Every time I wanted to urinate the burning sensation was so unbearable that I could not bring myself to pass water. The wound continued to bleed for some time, and my mother used to change the dressing for me twice a day."

"What did you feel on discovering that a small organ in your body had been removed?"

"I did not know anything about the operation at the time, except that it was very simple, and that it was done to all girls for purposes of cleanliness, purity and the preservation of a good reputation. It was said that a girl who did not undergo this operation was liable to be talked about by people, her behaviour would become bad, and she would start running after men, with the result that no one would agree to marry her when the time for marriage came. My grandmother told me that the operation had only consisted in the removal of a very small piece of flesh from between my thighs, and that the continued existence of this small piece of flesh in its place would have made me unclean and impure, and would have caused the man whom I would marry to be repelled by me."

"Did you believe what was said to you?"

"Of course I did. I was happy the day I recovered from the effects of the operation, and felt as though I was rid of something which had to be removed, and so had become clean and pure."

Those were more or less the answers that I obtained from all those interviewed, whether educated or uneducated. One of them was a medical student from Ein Shams School of Medicine. She was preparing for her final examinations and I expected her answers to be different, but in fact they were almost identical to the others. We had quite a long discussion which I reproduce here as I remember it.

"You are going to be a medical doctor after a few weeks, so how can you believe that cutting off the clitoris from the body of a girl is a healthy procedure, or at least not harmful?"

"This is what I was told by everybody. All the girls in my family have been circumcised. I have studied anatomy and medicine, yet I have never heard any of the professors who taught us explain that the clitoris had any function to fulfill in the body of a woman, neither have I read anything of the kind in the books which deal with the medical subjects I am studying."

That is true. To this day medical books do not consider the science of sex as a subject which they should deal with. The organs of a woman worthy of attention are considered to be only those directly related to reproduction, namely the vagina, the uterus and the ovaries. The clitoris, however, is an organ neglected by medicine, just as it is ignored and disdained by society. "I remember a student asking the professor one day about the clitoris. The professor went red in the face and answered him curtly, saying that no one was going to ask him about this part of the female body during examinations, since it was of no importance."

My studies led me to try and find out the effect of circumcision on the girls and women who had been made to undergo it, and to understand what results it had on their psychological and sexual life. The majority of the normal cases I interviewed answered that the operation had no effect on them. To me it was clear that in the face of such questions they were much more ashamed and intimidated than the neurotic cases were. But I did not allow myself to be satisfied with these answers, and would go on to question them closely about their sexual life both before and after the circumcision was done. Once again I will try to reproduce the dialogue that usually occurred.

"Did you experience any change of feeling or of sexual desire after the operation?"

"I was a child and therefore did not feel anything."

"Did you not experience any sexual desire when you were a child?"

"No, never. Do children experience sexual desire?"

"Children feel pleasure when they touch their sexual organs, and some form of sexual play occurs between them, for example, during the game of bride and bridegroom usually practiced under the bed. Have you never played this game with your friends when still a child?"

At these words the young girl or woman would blush, and her eyes would probably refuse to meet mine, in an attempt to hide her confusion. But after the conversation had gone on for some time, and an atmosphere of mutual confidence and understanding had been established, she would begin to recount her childhood memories. She would often refer to the pleasure she had felt when a man of the family permitted himself certain sexual caresses. Sometimes these caresses would be proffered by the domestic servant, the house porter, the private teacher or the neighbour's son. A college student told me that her brother had been wont to caress her sexual organs and that she used to experience acute enjoyment. However, after undergoing circumcision she no longer had the same sensation of pleasure. A married woman admitted that during intercourse with her husband she had never experienced the slightest sexual enjoyment, and that her last memories of any form of pleasurable sensation went back twenty years, to the age of six, before she had undergone circumcision. A young girl told me that she had been accustomed to practice masturbation, but had given it up completely after removal of the clitoris at the age of ten.

The further our conversations went, and the more I delved into their lives, the more readily they opened themselves up to me and uncovered the secrets of childhood and adolescence, perhaps almost forgotten by them or only vaguely realized.

Being both a woman and a medical doctor I was able to obtain confessions from these women and girls that it would be almost impossible, except in very rare cases, for a man to obtain. For the Egyptian woman, accustomed as she is to a very rigid and severe upbringing built on a complete denial of any sexual life before marriage, adamantly refuses to admit that she has ever known, or experienced, anything related to sex before the first touches of her husband. She is therefore ashamed to speak about such things with any man, even the doctor who is treating her.

My discussions with some of the psychiatrists who had treated a number of the young girls and women in my sample, led me to conclude that there were many aspects of the life of these neurotic patients that remained unknown to them. This was due either to the fact that the psychiatrist himself had not made the necessary effort to penetrate deeply into the life of the woman he was treating, or to the tendency of the patient herself not to divulge those things which her upbringing made her consider matters not to be discussed freely, especially with a man.

In fact the long and varied interchanges I had over the years with the majority of practicing psychiatrists in Egypt, my close association with a large number of my medical colleagues during the long periods I spent working in health centres and general or specialized hospitals and, finally, the four years I spent as a member of the National Board of the Syndicate of Medical Professions, have all led me to the firm conclusion that the medical profession in our society is still incapable of understanding the fundamental problems with which sick people are burdened, whether they be men or women, but especially if they are women. For the medical profession, like any other profession in society, is governed by the political, social and moral values which predominate, and like other professions is one of the institutions which is utilized more often than not to protect these values and perpetuate them.

Men represent the vast majority in the medical profession, as in most professions. But apart from this, the mentality of women doctors differs little, if at all, from that of the men, and I have known quite a number of them who were even more rigid and backward in outlook than their male colleagues.

A rigid and backward attitude towards most problems, and in particular towards women and sex, predominates in the medical profession, and particularly within the precincts of the medical colleges in the Universities.

Before undertaking my research study on "Women and Neurosis" at Ein Shams University, I had made a previous attempt to start it at the Kasr El Eini Medical College in the University of Cairo, but had been obliged to give up as a result of the numerous problems I was made to confront. The most important obstacle of all was the overpowering traditionalist mentality that characterized the professors responsible for my research work, and to whom the word "sex" could only be equated to the word "shame". "Respectable research" therefore could not possibly have sex as its subject, and should under no circumstances think of penetrating into areas even remotely related to it. One of my medical colleagues in the Research Committee advised me not to refer at all to the question of sex in the title of my research paper, when I found myself obliged to shift to Ein Shams University. He warned me that any such reference would most probably lead to fundamental objections which would jeopardize my chances of going ahead with it. I had initially chosen to define my subject as "Problems that confront the sexual life of modern Egyptian women", but after prolonged negotiations I was prevailed to delete the word "sexual" and replace it by "psychological". Only thus was it possible to circumvent the sensitivities of the professors at the Ein Shams Medical School and obtain their consent to go ahead with the research.

After I observed the very high percentages of women and girls who had been obliged to undergo circumcision, or who had been exposed to different forms of sexual violation or assault in their childhood, I started to look for research undertaken in these two areas, either in the medical colleges or in research institutes, but in vain. Hardly a single medical doctor or researcher had ventured to do any work on these subjects, in view of the sensitive nature of the issues involved. This can also be explained by the fact that most of the research carried out in such institutions is of a formal and superficial nature, since its sole aim is to obtain a degree or promotion. The path of safety is therefore the one to choose, and safety means to avoid carefully all subjects of controversy. No one is therefore prepared to face difficulties with the responsible academic and scientific authorities, or to engage in any form of struggle against them, or their ideas. Nor is anyone prepared to face up to those who lay down the norms of virtue, morals and religious behaviour in society. All the established leaderships in the area related to such matters suffer from a pronounced allergy to the word "sex", and any of its implications, especially if it happens to be linked to the word "woman".

Nevertheless, I was fortunate enough to discover a small number of medical doctors who had the courage to be different, and therefore to examine some of the problems related to the sexual life of women. I would like to cite, as one of the rare examples, the only research study carried out on the question of female circumcision in Egypt and its harmful effects. This was the joint effort of Dr. Mahmoud Koraim and Dr. Rushdi Ammar (1965). It is composed of two parts, the first of which was printed under the title Female Circumcision and Sexual Desire, and the second, under the title Complications of Female Circumcision. The conclusions arrived at as a result of this research study, which covered 651 women circumcised during childhood, may be summarized as follows:

1. Circumcision is an operation with harmful effects on the health of women, and is the cause of sexual shock to young girls. It reduces the capacity of a woman to reach

the peak of her sexual pleasure (i.e. orgasm) and has a definite though lesser effect in reducing sexual desire.

2. Education helps to limit the extent to which female circumcision is practised, since educated parents have an increasing tendency to refuse the operation for their daughters. On the other hand, uneducated families still go in for female circumcision in submission to prevailing traditions, or in the belief that removal of the clitoris reduces the sexual desire of the girl, and therefore helps to preserve her virginity and chastity after marriage.

3. There is no truth whatsoever in the idea that female circumcision helps in reducing the incidence of cancerous disease of the external genital organs.

4. Female circumcision in all its forms and degrees, and in particular the fourth degree known as Pharaonic or Sudanese excision, is accompanied by immediate or delayed complications such as inflammations, haemorrhage, disturbances in the urinary passages, cysts or swellings that can obstruct the urinary flow or the vaginal opening.

5. Masturbation in circumcised girls is less frequent than was observed by Kinsey in girls who have not undergone this operation.

I was able to exchange views with Dr. Mahmoud Koraim during several meetings in Cairo. I learnt from him that he had faced numerous difficulties while undertaking his research, and was the target of bitter criticism from some of his colleagues and from religious leaders who considered themselves the divinely appointed protectors of morality, and therefore required to shield society from such impious undertakings, which constituted a threat to established values and moral codes.

The findings of my research study coincided with some of the conclusions arrived at by my two colleagues on a number of points. There is no longer any doubt that circumcision is the source of sexual and psychological shock in the life of the girl, and leads to a varying degree of sexual frigidity according to the woman and her circumstances. Education helps parents realize that this operation is not beneficial, and should be avoided, but I have found that the traditional education given in our schools and universities, whose aim is simply some certificate, or degree, rather than instilling useful knowledge and culture, is not very effective in combating the long-standing, and established traditions that govern Egyptian society, and in particular those related to sex, virginity in girls, and chastity in women. These areas are strongly linked to moral and religious values that have dominated and operated in our society for hundreds of years.

Since circumcision of females aims primarily at ensuring virginity before marriage, and chastity throughout, it is not to be expected that its practice will disappear easily from Egyptian society or within a short period of time. A growing number of educated families are, however, beginning to realize the harm that is done to females by this custom, and are therefore seeking to protect their daughters from being among its victims. Parallel to these changes, the operation itself is no longer performed in the old primitive way, and the more radical degrees approaching, or involving, excision are dying out more rapidly. Nowadays, even in Upper Egypt and the Sudan, the operation is limited to the total, or more commonly the partial, amputation of the clitoris. Nevertheless, while undertaking my research, I was surprised to discover, contrary to what I had previously thought, that even in educated urban families over 50% still consider circumcision as essential to ensure female virginity and chastity.

Many people think that female circumcision only started with the advent of Islam. But as a matter of fact it was well known and widespread in some areas of the world before the Islamic era, including in the Arab peninsula. Mohammad the Prophet tried to oppose this custom since he considered it harmful to the sexual health of the woman. In one of his sayings the advice reported as having been given by him to Um Attiah, a woman who did tattooing and circumcision, runs as follows: "If you circumcise, take only a small part and refrain from cutting most of the clitoris off ... The woman will have a bright and happy face, and is more welcome to her husband, if her pleasure is complete" (El Barkouky, 1945).

This means that the circumcision of girls was not originally an Islamic custom, and was not related to monotheistic religions, but was practiced in societies with widely varying religious backgrounds, in countries of the East and the West, and among peoples who believed in Christianity, or in Islam, or were atheistic ... Circumcision was known in Europe as late as the 19th century, as well as in countries like Egypt, the Sudan, Somaliland, Ethiopia, Kenya, Tanzania, Ghana, Guinea and Nigeria. It was also practiced in many Asian countries such as Sri Lanka and Indonesia, and in parts of Latin America. It is recorded as going back far into the past under the Pharaonic Kingdoms of Ancient Egypt, and Herodotus mentioned the existence of female circumcision seven hundred years before Christ was born. This is why the operation as practiced in the Sudan is called "Pharaonic excision".

For many years I tried in vain to find relevant sociological or anthropological studies that would throw some light on the reasons why such a brutal operation is practiced on females. However, I did discover other practices related to girls and female children that were even more savage. One of them was burying female children alive almost immediately after they were born, or even at a later stage. Other examples are the chastity belt, or closing the aperture of the external genital organs with steel pins and a special iron lock (Morris, 1967). This last procedure is extremely primitive and very much akin to Sudanese circumcision where the clitoris, external lips and internal lips are completely excised, and the orifice of the genital organs closed with a flap of sheep's intestines leaving only a very small opening barely sufficient to let the tip of the finger in, so that the menstrual and urinary flows are not held back. This opening is slit at the time of marriage and widened to allow penetration of the male sexual organ. It is widened again when a child is born and then narrowed down once more. Complete closure of the aperture is also done on a woman who is divorced, so that she literally becomes a virgin once more and can have no sexual intercourse except in the eventuality of marriage, in which case the opening is restored.

In the face of all these strange and complicated procedures aimed at preventing sexual intercourse in women except if controlled by the husband, it is natural that we should ask ourselves why women, in particular, were subjected to such torture and cruel suppression. There seems to be no doubt that society, as represented by its dominant classes and male structure, realized at a very early stage that sexual desire in the female is very powerful, and that women, unless controlled and subjugated by all sorts of measures, will not submit themselves to the moral, social, legal and religious constraints with which they have been surrounded, and in particular the constraints related to monogamy. The patriarchal system, which came into being when society had reached a certain stage of development and which necessitated the imposition of one husband on the woman whereas a man was left free to have several wives, would never have been possible, or have been maintained to this day, without the whole range of cruel and ingenious devices that were used to keep her sexuality in check and limit her sexual relations to only one man, who had to be her husband. This is the reason for the implacable enmity shown by society towards female sexuality, and the weapons used to resist and subjugate the turbulent force inherent in it. The slightest leniency manifested in facing this "potential danger" meant that woman would break out of the prison bars to which marriage had confined her, and step over the steely limits of a monogamous relationship to a forbidden intimacy with another man, which would inevitably lead to confusion in succession and inheritance, since there was no guarantee that a strange man's child would not step into the waiting line of descendants. Confusion between the children of the legitimate husband and the outsider lover would mean the unavoidable collapse of the patriarchal family built around the name of the father alone.

History shows us clearly that the father was keen on knowing who his real children were, solely for the purpose of handing down his landed property to them. The patriarchal family, therefore, came into existence mainly for economic reasons. It was necessary for society simultaneously to build up a system of moral and religious values, as well as a legal system capable of protecting and maintaining these economic interests. In the final analysis we can safely say that female circumcision, the chastity belt and other savage practices applied to women are basically the result of the economic interests that govern society. The continued existence of such practices in our society signifies that these economic interests are still operative. The thousands of *dayas*, nurses, para-medical staff and doctors, who make money out of female circumcision, naturally resist any change in these values and practices that are a source of gain to them. In the Sudan there is a veritable army of women who earn a livelihood out of the series of operations performed on women, either to excise their external genital organs, or to alternately narrow and widen the outer aperture according to whether the woman is marrying, divorcing, remarrying, having a child or recovering from labour (Oldfield, 1975).

Economic factors and, concomitantly, political factors are the basis upon which such customs as female circumcision have grown up. It is important to understand the facts as they really are, and the reasons that lie behind them. Many are the people who are not able to distinguish between political and religious factors, or who conceal economic and political motives behind arguments in an attempt to hide the real forces that lie at the basis of what happens in society and in history. It has very often been proclaimed that Islam is at the root of female circumcision, and is also responsible for the under-privileged and backward situation of women in Egypt and the Arab countries. Such a contention is not true. If we study Christianity it is easy to see that this religion is much more rigid and orthodox where women are concerned than Islam. Nevertheless, many countries were able to progress rapidly despite the preponderance of Christianity as a religion. This progress was social, economic, scientific and also affected the life and position of women in society.

That is why I firmly believe that the reasons for the lower status of women in our societies and the lack of opportunities for progress afforded to them are not due to Islam, but rather to certain economic and political forces, namely those of foreign imperialism operating mainly from the outside, and of the reactionary classes operating from the inside. These two forces cooperate closely and are making a concerted attempt to misinterpret religion and to utilize it as an instrument of fear, oppression and exploitation.

Religion, if authentic in the principles it stands for, aims at truth, equality, justice, love and a healthy wholesome life for all people, whether men or women. There can be no true religion that aims at disease, mutilation of the bodies of female children, and amputation of an essential part of their reproductive organs.

If religion comes from God, how can it order man to cut off an organ created by Him as long as that organ is not diseased or deformed? God does not create the organs of the body haphazardly without a plan. It is not possible that He should have created the clitoris in woman's body only in order that it be cut off at an early stage in life. This is a contradiction into which neither true religion nor the Creator could possibly fall. If God has created the clitoris as a sexually sensitive organ, whose sole function seems to be the procurement of sexual pleasure for women, it follows that He also considers such pleasure for women as normal and legitimate, and therefore as an integral part of mental health. The psychic and mental health of women cannot be complete if they do not experience sexual pleasure.

There are still a large number of fathers and mothers who are afraid of leaving the clitoris intact in the bodies of their daughters. Many a time they have said to me that circumcision is a safeguard against the mistakes and deviations into which a girl may be led. This way of thinking is wrong and even dangerous because what protects a boy or a girl from making mistakes is not the removal of a small piece of flesh from the body, but consciousness and understanding of the problems we face, and a worthwhile aim in life, an aim which gives it meaning and for whose attainment we exert our mind and energies. The higher the level of consciousness to which we attain, the closer our aims draw to human motives and values, and the greater our desire to improve life and its quality, rather than to indulge ourselves in the mere satisfaction of our senses and the experience of pleasure, even though these are an essential part of existence. The most liberated and free of girls, in the true sense of liberation, are the least preoccupied with sexual questions, since these no longer represent a problem. On the contrary a free mind finds room for numerous interests and the many rich experiences of a cultured life. Girls that suffer sexual suppression, however, are greatly preoccupied with men and sex. And it is a common observation that an intelligent and cultured woman is much less engrossed in matters related to sex and to men than is the case with ordinary women, who have not got much with which to fill their lives. Yet at the same time such a woman takes much more initiative to ensure that she will enjoy sex and experience pleasure, and acts with a greater degree of boldness than others. Once sexual satisfaction is attained, she is able to turn herself fully to other important aspects of life.

In the life of liberated and intelligent women, sex does not occupy a disproportionate position, but rather tends to maintain itself within normal limits. In contrast, ignorance, suppression, fear and all sorts of limitations exaggerate the role of sex in the life of girls and women, and cause it to swell out of all proportion and to end up by occupying the whole, or almost the whole, of their lives.

References

El Barkouky, Abdel Rahman. *Dawlat El Niss'a*, first edition, (Renaissance Bookshop, Cairo, 1945).

Morris, Desmond. *The Naked Ape*. (Corgi, 1967).

Oldfield, Rose. "Female genital mutilation, fertility control, women's roles and patrilineage in modern Sudan." *American Ethnologies*. Vol. II, No. 4, 1975.

Originally published in *The Hidden Face of Eve* (Zed Press, 1980): 33–43. Printed here with the permission of the publisher.

A Dishonorable Affair:
Chastity and Honor Killing in Syria

The struggle, if there was any, would have been very brief.

Fawaz later recalled that his wife, Zahra, was sleeping soundly on her side and curled slightly against the pillow when he rose at dawn and readied himself for work at his construction job on the outskirts of Damascus. It was a rainy Sunday morning in January and very cold; as he left, Fawaz turned back one last time to tuck the blanket more snugly around his 16-year-old wife. Zahra slept on without stirring, and her husband locked the door of their tiny apartment carefully behind him.

Zahra was most likely still sleeping when her older brother, Fayyez, entered the apartment a short time later, using a stolen key and carrying a dagger. His sister lay on the carpeted floor, on the thin, foam mattress she shared with her husband, so Fayyez must have had to kneel next to Zahra as he raised the dagger and stabbed her five times in the head and back: brutal, tearing thrusts that shattered the base of her skull and nearly severed her spinal column. Leaving the door open, Fayyez walked downstairs and out to the local police station. There, he reportedly turned himself in, telling the officers on duty that he had killed his sister in order to remove the dishonor she had brought on the family by losing her virginity out of wedlock nearly 10 months earlier.

"Fayyez told the police, 'it is my right to correct this error,'" Maha Ali, a Syrian lawyer who knew Zahra and now works pro bono for her husband, told me not long ago. "He said, 'It's true that my sister is married now, but we never washed away the shame.'"

By now, almost anyone in Syria who follows the news can supply certain basic details about Zahra al-Azzo's life and death: how the girl, then only 15, was kidnapped in the spring of 2006 near her home in northern Syria, taken to Damascus by her abductor and raped; how the police who discovered her feared that her family, as commonly happens in Syria, would blame Zahra for the rape and kill her; how these authorities then placed Zahra in a prison for girls, believing it the only way to protect her from her relatives. And then in December, how a cousin of Zahra's, 27-year-old Fawaz, agreed to marry her in order to secure her release and also, he hoped, restore her reputation in the eyes of her family; how, just a month after her wedding to Fawaz, Zahra's 25-year-old brother, Fayyez, stabbed her as she slept.

Zahra died from her wounds at the hospital the following morning, one of about 300 girls and women who die each year in Syria in so-called honor killings, according to estimates by women's rights advocates there. In Syria and other Arab countries, many men are brought up to believe in an idea of personal honor that regards defending the chastity of their sisters, their daughters and other women in the family as a primary social obligation.

Honor crimes tend to occur, activists say, when men feel pressed by their communities to demonstrate that they are sufficiently protective of their female relatives' virtue. Pairs of lovers are sometimes killed together, but most frequently only the women are singled out for punishment. Sometimes women are killed for the mere suspicion of an affair, or on account of a false accusation, or because they were sexually abused, or because, like Zahra, they were raped.

In speaking with the police, Zahra's brother used a colloquial expression, *ghasalat al arr* (washing away the shame), which means the killing of a woman or girl whose very life has come to be seen as an unbearable stain on the honor of her male relatives. Once this kind of familial sexual shame has been "washed," the killing is traditionally forgotten as quickly as possible. Under Syrian law, an honor killing is not murder, and the man who commits it is not a murderer. As in many other Arab countries, even if the killer is convicted on the lesser charge of a "crime of honor," he is usually set free within months. Mentioning the killing—or even the name of the victim—generally becomes taboo.

That this has not happened with Zahra's story—that her case, far from being ignored, has become something of a cause célèbre, a rallying point for lawyers, Islamic scholars and Syrian officials hoping to change the laws that protect the perpetrators of honor crimes—is a result of a peculiar confluence of circumstances. It is due in part to the efforts of a group of women's rights activists and in part to the specifics of her story, which has galvanized public sympathy in a way previously unseen in Syria. But at heart it is because of Zahra's young widower, Fawaz, who had spoken to his bride only once before they became engaged. Now, defying his tribe and their traditions, he has brought a civil lawsuit against Zahra's killer and is refusing to let her case be forgotten.

Nashweh, where Zahra al-Azzo was born in 1990, is the sort of Syrian town that seems literally to crumble at its edges—its squat cinder-block houses giving way to heaps of decaying construction materials, then to stubbly wheat fields strewn with garbage. The quantities of laundry drying on wires strung above the houses suggest vast extended families. Nashweh is small enough and remote enough that if a stranger steps out of a car, it is a matter of seconds before a troupe of small boys wearing dirty *galabias* circles round and begins shouting invitations home for tea. Before last year Zahra had spent her entire life there, but recently, when asked if they had known her, a half-dozen town women—uniformly dressed in head scarves and thin velour house dresses, most over 40 with blue Bedouin facial tattoos—simply looked away.

By local standards, the circumstances of Zahra's life in Nashweh were perfectly ordinary. In her early childhood the family earned a good living raising Arabian horses, but the Azzos had lately fallen on hard times, and Zahra's father, according to social workers who talked to Zahra in prison, was rumored to be having an affair.

According to the lawyer Maha Ali, who met Zahra in prison, Zahra first heard the rumors from a friend of her father's. The man threatened Zahra, telling her that he would reveal the scandal if she didn't join him outside her house, itself a grave transgression in her conservative society. That Zahra did so, disobeying her family and going out with a man unaccompanied, even under duress, is so scandalous to many Syrians that advocates working on Zahra's case have tried to obscure this fact, preferring to describe what took place as a simple kidnapping. They also say that at 15 she was naive in the extreme, so young for her age that she took a teddy bear to bed every night in prison.

Zahra was frightened by the man but apparently believed that if she came out with him, briefly, she could ensure her family's reputation and safety. Instead, says Yumin Abu al-Hosn, a social worker at the prison, she was taken to Damascus, held in an apartment and raped. Terrified, in a strange and crowded city she had never visited, Zahra didn't try to run away. She was in the capital with the man for about a week when a tip from a neighbor took the police to the door. The man was taken to jail, where he now awaits trial for kidnapping and rape. Zahra, meanwhile, was taken to a police station for a so-called virginity exam, the hymen examination that, however unreliable at establishing virginity, is standard procedure in Syria in rape cases and common when women are taken into police custody.

In the United States, a whitewashed, heavily guarded building like the one where Zahra was then sent for her protection would probably be called a juvenile-detention center, but Arabic offers no such euphemism, so the words for "prison" or "institution" are used. Syria does not have shelters where girls or women can go if they are threatened with honor killing; instead, minors are often placed in girls' prisons for their protection. Like many of the teenagers who arrive there, Zahra felt humiliated at having gone through the forcible genital examination and tried at first for a show of defiance, according to Maha Ali. "I came in and met Zahra," Ali said. "And she just looked at me and said, 'God, do I have to tell the story all over again?'"

For girls like Zahra, prison is only a temporary solution. Even the most murderously inclined families often issue emotional court appeals to have their daughters returned to them. Judges usually try to extract sworn statements from male guardians, promises that the girls, if released, will not be harmed. But those promises are often broken.

Among Syria's so-called tribal families—settled Bedouin clans like the one that Zahra belonged to—first-cousin marriage is common. So it wasn't a shock when her family, looking for some-one who could marry her while she was in prison and help secure her release, turned to one of her cousins, Fawaz. But Fawaz hadn't intended to marry a cousin, he told me recently, and was startled when Zahra's brother Fayyez showed up one day at his home.

"Fayyez started telling us that his sister, Zahra, had been kidnapped," said Fawaz's mother, who is usually addressed by the honorific Umm Fawaz, meaning "mother of Fawaz." She was sitting cross-legged, along with her son and husband, in the front room of the family apartment outside Damascus. The shades were pulled down to keep out the searing late spring heat, and the room was lighted by a single fluorescent tube. Umm Fawaz pointed out the place on the cushions—arranged, Arab-style, on the floor against the walls—where Fayyez had sat.

The mere fact that Zahra had been taken from her home for a few days signaled dishonor for the family. "'Oh, Auntie, I don't know what to say,'" Umm Fawaz recalled Fayyez saying as she adjusted her hijab with one hand and dabbed her eyes with a tissue in the other. "I said: 'Don't be ashamed for your sister. Even in the best families, something like this can happen.'" Fayyez claimed that despite having been kidnapped, his sister was still a virgin. Slowly, he broached the subject he had come to discuss. Would Fawaz consider marrying Zahra in order to secure her release?

At first, Fawaz, a shy, wiry man, politely demurred. He felt sorry for Fayyez, he told me, but he couldn't help recoiling a little at the story, which in his community constitutes an ugly sexual scandal. Besides, he was already engaged to another girl. After Fayyez left, though, Fawaz and his mother talked over Zahra's situation. "We decided to visit the girl, just to see," Umm Fawaz said. And so several days later the two of them took a taxi to the girls' prison. They walked past a heavy steel gate, and a guard led them to an office.

Fawaz smiled as he recalled the moment Zahra was brought in. It would be indelicate for him to comment on Zahra's appearance, so it was Umm Fawaz who talked about Zahra's beauty ("As lovely as Sibel Can!" she exclaimed, mentioning a Turkish singer popular in the Arab world).

"I liked the girl," said Fawaz, who seemed embarrassed to have admitted such a personal thing in public, and he quickly corrected himself. "I mean, here we fall in love with a girl after we marry her. But I decided to leave my fiancée for Zahra. I felt that a normal girl like my fiancée would have other chances. With Zahra I thought, my God, she's such a child to be stuck in this prison."

Fawaz's father disapproved, suspecting from the outset that Zahra's family would kill her once she left prison. But when, months later, Zahra's family begged the other family to reconsider, Fawaz's father relented, and Fawaz eventually accompanied Zahra's father to court to sign her release papers. Zahra and Fawaz were married in a civil ceremony at the prison on Dec. 11, 2006, and then a week later in a formal celebration for the neighborhood, held in the bride's new home. The few photographs of the wedding were taken with cellphones so the prints have a blurry, ephemeral quality. In them, Zahra looks stunned and a bit sulky, her hair teased high on her head, her childish features thickly coated with foundation, shocking pink eye shadow and frosted lipstick.

The marriage, by all accounts, was happy. "Zahra used to call me even after her wedding," Ali, the lawyer, recalled. "'How is Fawaz?' I'd ask her. And she'd say, 'Oh, Auntie Maha, we're spending all night up together, talking and having fun.' Once, her aunt called me. She said: 'Don't tell Zahra I called, but can you talk to her? You have influence on her. Fawaz can't get up for work because Zahra keeps him up all night.'"

Fawaz told me that, according to his interpretation of Islam, he was "honoring Zahra again"—restoring her lost virtue—by marrying her. In this decision he was supported by his sheik, or religious teacher, who according to Fawaz subscribes to a progressive school of Koranic interpretation. Fawaz and his immediate family, though not well educated, are proud of their open-mindedness, and he boasts about Zahra's intelligence and literacy. Even so, he and the family rebuffed Zahra's efforts to describe her ordeal to them, so that to this day they know the details only secondhand. "So many times, when we were married, she wanted to talk to me about what had happened to her," Fawaz said. "But I refused. I told her, 'Your past is your past.'"

According to Fawaz, Zahra had been married just five weeks when her brother, Fayyez, arrived on an unannounced visit, saying he planned to look for work in Damascus. Zahra was happy to see her brother, but Fawaz described feeling painfully torn between his duties to hospitality, a cardinal virtue in Bedouin culture, and his feeling that Fayyez—sleeping just upstairs in Fawaz's parents' apartment—was a danger to his wife. On the morning Zahra was attacked, Fawaz recalls going upstairs before leaving for work to find Fayyez awake and tapping nervously at his cellphone.

"He couldn't afford to have a mobile," Fawaz said. "I'd been wondering about that. It turned out that his uncle had given him the phone so that he could call and tell the family that he'd killed his sister. We learned later that they had a party that night to celebrate the cleansing of their honor. The whole village was invited."

Most honor killings receive only brief mention in Syrian newspapers, but Zahra al-Azzo's death has been unlike any other. Dozens of articles and television programs have discussed her story at length, fueling an unprecedented public conversation about the roots and morality of honor crimes.

In May, hoping to gauge public feeling about Zahra's case, I spent a couple of hours walking around a crowded lower-middle-class neighborhood in Damascus. In the wealthiest areas of the city, half the people on the streets might be female, but here, in the late evening, there were very few women to be found. In shawarma sandwich shops and juice stalls, most men had heard of Zahra, but more than half of them believed that the practice of honor killing is protected—or outright required—by Islamic law. A man named Abu Rajab, who ran a cigarette stall, described it as "some thing that is found in religion" and added that even if the laws were changed, "a man will kill his sister if he needs to, even if it means 15 years in prison."

Yet the notion that Islam condones honor killing is a misconception, according to some lawyers and a few prominent Islamic scholars. Daad Mousa, a Syrian women's rights advocate and lawyer, told me that though beliefs about cleansing a man's honor derive from Bedouin tradition, the three Syrian laws used to pardon men who commit honor crimes can be traced back not to Islamic law but to the law codes, based on the Napoleonic code, that were imposed in the Levant during the French mandate. "Article 192 states that if a man commits a crime with an 'honorable motive,' he will go free," Mousa said. "In Western countries this law usually applies in cases where doctors kill their patients accidentally, intending to save them, but here the idea of 'honorable motive' is often expanded to include men who are seen as acting in defense of their honor.

"Article 242 refers to crimes of passion," Mousa continued. "But it's Article 548 that we're really up against. Article 548 states precisely that if a man witnesses a female relative in an immoral act, and kills her, he will go free." Judges frequently interpret these laws so loosely that a premeditated killing—like the one Fayyez is accused of—is often judged a "crime of passion"; "witnessing" a female relative's behavior is sometimes defined as hearing neighborhood gossip about it; and for a woman, merely speaking to a man may be ruled an "immoral act." Syria, which has been governed since 1963 by a secular Baathist regime, has a strong reputation in the region for sex equality; women graduate from high schools and universities in numbers roughly equal to men, and they frequently hold influential positions as doctors, professors and even government ministers. But in the family, a different standard applies. "Honor here means only one thing: women, and especially the sexual life of women," Mousa said. The decision to carry out an honor killing is usually made by the family as a group, and an under-age boy is often nominated to carry out the task, to eliminate even the smallest risk of a prison sentence.

Some advocates claim that Syria has an especially high number of honor killings per capita, saying that the country is second or third in the world. In fact, reliable statistics on honor killing are nearly impossible to come by. The United Nations Population Fund says that about 5,000 honor killings take place each year around the world, but since they often occur in rural areas where births and deaths go unreported, it is very difficult to count them by country. Some killings have been recorded in European cultures, including Italy, and in Christian or Druse communities in predominantly Muslim countries. But it is widely agreed that honor killings are found disproportionately in Muslim communities, from Bangladesh to Egypt to Great Britain.

The Grand Mufti Ahmad Badr Eddin Hassoun, Syria's highest-ranking Islamic teacher, has condemned honor killing and Article 548 in unequivocal terms. Earlier this year, when we met for a rare interview in his spacious office on the 10th floor of Syria's ministry of religious endowments, he told me, "It happens sometimes that a misogynistic religious scholar will argue that women are the source of all kinds of evil." In fact, he said, the Koran does not differentiate between women and men in its moral laws, requiring sexual chastity of both, for example. The commonly held view that Article 548 is derived from Islamic law, he said, is false.

With his tightly wound white turban and giant pearl ring, the grand mufti is one of Syria's most recognizable public figures. He is a charismatic and generally popular sheik, but because he is appointed by the state, many Syrians believe that his views reflect those of the ruling party, and they may find his teachings suspect as a result. In downtown Damascus, one man I interviewed on the street declared that the grand mufti was not a "real Muslim" if he believed in canceling Article 548. "It's an Islamic law to kill your relative if she errs," said the man, who gave his name as Ahmed and said that he learned of Zahra's story on Syrian television. "If the sheik tries to fight this, the people will rise up and slit his throat."

There are religious figures who defend the status quo. At a conference on honor killing held this year at Damascus University, Mohammed Said Ramadan al-Bouti, one of Syria's most esteemed clerics, maintained that the laws should not be changed, defending them on the principle in Shariah law that people who kill in defense of their property should be treated with lenience (he is believed to have moderated his stance since). When, at an earlier conference, the grand mufti announced that he didn't believe protecting a woman's virginity was the most important component of honor, many attendees were upset. In response, a group of about a dozen women, all dressed in the long black *abayas* that in Syria are usually worn by only very conservative women, walked out of the room.

In our interview, the grand mufti told me that he believed Article 548 would be struck down by the Syrian Parliament within months, and given his government ties he might be expected to know. Still, women's rights advocates are not so optimistic. They point out that Syria's educated elites have long opposed honor killing, though there is often a squeamishness about discussing a practice that is embarrassing to them. They say that some conservative Syrians are having second thoughts about the custom thanks to the efforts of their Islamic teachers, but that their numbers are small.

Bassam al-Kadi, a women's advocate, told me that Zahra's case made an ideal rallying point. "We have hundreds of Zahras," he said. "But there are some stories that you can campaign with, and others that you can't." Zahra, in other words—extremely young, a victim of rape, married at the time she was killed—makes a sympathetic figure for a broad Syrian public in a way that, say, someone older who was killed after being seen with her boyfriend in a cafe might not.

With tensions like these in play, Syrian women's advocates are careful to phrase their criticisms of tribal traditions of honor and Article 548 in Islamic terms. Though some will privately admit that they are secularists, even feminists, they keep it quiet. It would be politically impossible to suggest in public, for example, that women have the right to choose their sexual partners. The basic culture of chastity is in no way being publicly rethought. Some advocates say that their cause is damaged if they are perceived as sympathetic to "Western values," and even that honor killing is seen by some conservatives as a bulwark against those values. Where 15 years ago Syria banned the import of fax machines and modems, today the Internet is widely accessible. "There's been a very complicated reaction to the new availability of Western media in this part of the world," Kadi, the women's rights advocate, explained. "We're going through a transition, and our values are changing dramatically."

"Our parents tell us that there was an earlier day when honor meant that you were honorable in your work, that you didn't take bribes, for example," Kadi said. "But now, the political and economic situation is so bad that some degree of corruption is necessary to survive. People will say that you're a good earner for your family; they won't blame you. Historically speaking, all our other ideologies have collapsed. No one talks about loyalty to country, about professional honor. Now it's just the family, the tribe, the woman. That's the only kind of honor we have left."

Syrian activists say that while many in government would like to see Article 548 changed, the government, which is led by a tiny religious minority, the Alawites, may be afraid to risk offending the more conservative elements of Syria's Sunni majority. In other parts of the Middle East, too, tensions between ruling elites and religious conservatives have complicated efforts to combat honor killing. Rana Husseini, a Jordanian women's advocate, told me that though an effort to establish harsher punishments for men who kill female relatives received support from members of the royal family, Jordan's Parliament rejected the law in 2003 after conservative groups opposed it. In Morocco, a campaign to stop honor killing resulted instead in a ruling that, if anything, endorsed the practice, by extending to women who kill in a fit of sexual jealousy the same protection under law that men had.

Yet there are signs of change. In Lebanon last month, Grand Ayatollah Mohammed Hussein Fadlallah, the top Shiite cleric and spiritual leader of Hezbollah, issued a *fatwa* banning honor killing and describing it as "a repulsive act, condemned and prohibited by religion." And earlier this Egypt's grand mufti upheld a *fatwa* stating that Islam permits a woman to have her virginity "refurbished" through hymen surgery, which would allow her to marry and would eliminate the need to cleanse the so-called stain on her family's honor. He even appeared on national television to advise Egyptian women considering the procedure. Although the ruling has been assailed by conservative scholars, it has been welcomed by those who hope it will prevent future honor killings.

In Syria activists say that the existence of a case like Zahra's—which has remained open in part because of the bad blood between Fawaz and Zahra's family—has proved essential to keeping up momentum in the campaign to change Article 548. The civil suit brought by Fawaz claims that Fayyez conspired to deceive him, and the existence of the civil case means that, under Syrian law, the criminal case is unlikely to be dropped as quickly as similar ones. Fayyez is in custody awaiting trial (no lawyer has been appointed for him yet), and if Zahra's death is ruled a murder rather than an honor crime, he could go to prison for

12 to 15 years. Activists say that penalty, whether or not Article 548 is struck down, would stand as a powerful warning to other would-be killers in the name of honor. Fawaz and his family are under enormous pressure from their tribe to drop the case. They have been in touch with Zahra's family members—who, they say, do not deny the crime, nor having celebrated it. Zahra's family has offered Fawaz money and another daughter to marry he says, if he will abandon the lawsuit that is now the cause of so public scrutiny.

"It's a big scandal now, in the whole neighborhood, the whole community," Fawaz said. "I can't even have coffee now with my best friends, because they're afraid for their sisters."

But Fawaz told me that he didn't understand his own feelings about honor killing until Zahra's death, and that he hoped the publicity surrounding her case would help other men to re-evaluate theirs. "In Zahra's case, the girl was basically kidnapped," Fawaz said. "If she'd been a bad girl, if she'd decided to run away with a man, I'd say, maybe. It's a brutal solution, but maybe."

His father broke in. "Even then! When a girl does something wrong like that, especially a girl that young, I don't think that she is responsible. The family is responsible. The father is responsible. I don't want to give anyone excuses for murder."

Fawaz nodded. "I start thinking about Zahra lying there, dying, and I don't think I can believe in that set of values any longer."

Originally published as "A Dishonorable Affair" in *The New York Times Magazine*, September 23, 2007: 22–29. Printed here with the permission of the author.

SAMIR KHALAF

The Commercialization of Sexual Outlets in Lebanon

The public imagination of those who knew the Bourj existentially, before its beleaguering destruction during the civil war, was not only intimately associated with their initiation into the novel adventures of movie-going, street cafés, boisterous restaurants, bars, nightclubs and street demonstrations. The Bourj was also the only place where one could have been initiated into the shady and stigmatizing world of prostitution. From its inception as an unregulated outlet for commercial sex, the Bourj has been notorious, even infamous, for sheltering the houses of ill repute; derisively and popularly known as *Souk al-Awadem* (literally, "the Market of the Virtuous"!).

Initially, the area or *souk*, had no special identity. Historical records are not very definitive with regard to either its exact location or time of appearance. Some sources merely referred to *"Nazlet al-Pore"* or *"Khalf al-Bank"*: in other words, "the passage down to the port" or "the area behind the Ottoman Bank". Others maintain that it was located in *Souk al Khammarine* ("the wine sellers' market") between the Petit Serail and the port, east of the Muslim cemetery. Actual dates as to when it started to be frequented by regular customers are also a bit hazy. One source traces this back to 1880. Another, to 1895, after the enlargement of the port when some of the *"maisons de tolerance"*, as they started to be called, had to move up in the direction of the city's growing commercial and administrative centre.

What is fairly certain, however, is that with the return of the French army in 1920, the number of prostitutes *("al-mumsat")* increased to about 1,250: 400 of whom being Turkish, Greek, French, English and the remainder Palestinian, Syrian and Lebanese. This sudden preponderance of prostitutes—and journalistic accounts of the day were already declaring it as the "golden age"—aroused the concern of public health officials with regard to the transmission of venereal diseases. Indeed, the first measures were promulgated in 1921 to combat the outbreak of one such epidemic among French troops stationed there. Not only prostitutes, but dancers, singers and other so-called "artists" were required to register with the local police. They had to carry identification cards, attend to their work in designated brothels and be subject to medical inspection twice a week. Special dispensaries or clinics were established within the district for that purpose. Those who absented themselves from such examinations were taken to court. Exit from the district was also closely monitored. For those who wished to abdicate their work, arrangements were made to have them live with a guardian.

In 1931 the Ottomans introduced the first decree to recognise and regulate prostitution (*al-da'arah*) as a legal profession. The law defined a prostitute as any woman who submitted to sexual intercourse (*"irtikab al-fahsha"*) in return for a monetary reward, overt or covert. It also distinguished between "public houses" and other "places of assignation" and declared all secret and unregulated prostitution illegal and subject to prosecution. Because of these restrictive measures, the number of registered prostitutes was reduced to 624, distributed among sixty-two houses. This is more than half the number the district was drawing during its heyday. Paradoxically, although depleted in number the prostitutes and the district were becoming more visible and notorious. Like elsewhere in the Bourj, this was the period when all enterprises and entertainment ventures were becoming commercially minded and attuned to novel modes of advertising, marketing and promotional design.

The enterprising "patronas" gave the maligned image of their tainted and damnable quarter, at least in the public imagination, the face-lift it needed to transform it into a more welcoming place. The prostitutes were identified with particular houses. They acquired "brand names" which popularised the commodity they were marketing. Selling sex, in other words, was being increasingly commodified. With the advent of neon lights and other forms of imaging and public display, the district was festooned with decorative billboards advertising the "stars" and celebrities of the house. To this day, regular habituates of the district, or those who made inquisitive but furtive sojourns into it, can still recollect the glittering names. Sometimes the labels reflected a special personal attribute (*"Leila el Chacra"*: "the blonde"), or an identity of a particular place (*"Zbeidi al Mizranieh"*) or a particular city (*"Hoda al-Halabie"*) or a national identity (*"Hikmat al Misrie"*) or the "French Antoinette" or the "English Lucy". The most interesting were those that bore their maternal identity: (*"Faride Im Abdou"*).

Of course, the most notorious was Marica Espiredone, the Greek emigrant who managed to cast her mythical shadow over the entire district for over half a century. Her epic rags-to-riches biography is riveting and has been told and retold scores of times. The little orphaned Greek girl, still in her early teens, disembarked at the port in 1912. She had nothing except a few pieces of currency tucked under her sparse garments and her nubile beauty, which instantly attracted the attention of a Turkish officer. Overwhelmed by her reception at the port, dense with fierce-looking and desirous Turkish soldiers and with no woman in sight, she had no choice but to accept the officer's offer to go home with him to assist his wife as a household help. From then on her story is a rerun of a most familiar theme in the recruitment and induction of prostitutes into the profession.

Already scarred and traumatised by an early initiation into sex by her mother's lover in Greece, Marica was a hapless victim of further such abuse in her new life in Beirut. In no time, the wife discovered her husband in bed with Marica. She was summarily dismissed and had to drift aimlessly in search of shelter. A handsome French officer, single this time, offered her the shelter she desperately needed. Again taken by her exceptional beauty, he lavished her first with loving attention and gifts. Soon, however, the relationship turned sour and violent. This time she ran away. After days and nights of roaming around the city in search of shelter she ended up on a sidewalk of the Medawar neighbourhood next to the Bourj. It is there that Maria al Halabieh, a prominent patrona and pimp, was instantly attracted by her potential, given her good looks and foreign accent.

From then on her story departs markedly from the conventional and hackneyed prototypes of innocent and gullible young girls being taken in by city slickers who live off their earnings from prostituting their bodies. Marica was much too shrewd and enterprising to fall victim to such devious foils. In less than a year she became so popular and widely sought by prominent men who became her regular clients that she managed to break away from Maria's house and establish one on her own. Street-smart, savvy and quick-witted, she applied her business acumen to convert her house into a salon-like lounge—almost a drawing room—for the rich and famous. She recruited a team of resourceful and ruthless pimps and procurers who solicited prize recruits to meet the growing demand for her services. Her business was so lucrative that she was able to rent one of the most spacious and attractive buildings on Mutanabi Street: a three-storey walk-up suburban villa with Italian-style arches and elaborate balconies and balustrades.

With remarkable foresight and business sense, she went about mapping out the twelve rooms as though eager customers were purchasing sex as if it were any other ordinary commodity. Hence blondes, brunettes, lean girls or those more substantial in size and endowments and of different age group etc were placed in separate, well-defined quarters. More appealingly, she converted part of the ground floor into a lounge and bar, thereby adding an aesthetic and non-mercenary dimension to her brothel. Indeed, during the l940s and 1950s her house in that infamous quarter became a meeting place for the rich and famous. The memories of those who felt privileged being part of her intimate entourage are replete with nostalgic tales about the engaging and spirited discussions they conducted there, often unaware that this was also a public space associated with debauchery and the commercialisation of sexual encounters. They also spoke admiringly of her selfless generosity, benevolence for church-sponsored charity and concern for the poor and downtrodden.

One could express this in more conceptual terms. Marica displayed very early in her career symptoms of a paradigm shift in the analysis of prostitution that was to become salient to the early 1990s. She was transforming herself from being merely a "sex object" to a "sex worker": from being a quintessentially passive and resigned victim of male domination and manipulation to being a willful agent who actively constructed her work life.

The fact that the red-light district, with all the sordid and disreputable activities it was attracting, was becoming so compelling and visible in the very heart of the nation's capital did not go unnoticed. By the late-1940s and early-1950s, judging by the extensive press coverage, the whole issue of legal prostitution was beginning to provoke public concern. The fact that the main street in the district was often named *"al-Mutanabbi"*, after one of the most celebrated Arab poets, compounded the outrage and contempt of the public even further. In their view, this was clearly not a fitting tribute to such a distinguished cultural legacy.

In their reactions to legalized brothels, moralists at the time harboured different ethical dispositions. Traditionalists, particularly heads of religious communities and sectarian associations, were inclined to regard prostitution as a necessary evil; a safety valve for the release of the superfluous sexual energies and untapped libidos of the virile, youthful segments of the population. In this regard, the prostitute protects the virtue of the family and the sanctity of marriage. If such outlets were unavailable, the purity and chastity of women would be, in their view, threatened. Others were more inclined to condemn prostitution because it involved the commodification of sexual intimacy, the confinement of women and the restriction of their freedom in prison-like sanctuaries.

By the early-1950s, it must be recalled, more and more countries were already closing their medically inspected brothels. The French, for example, who for many years were chief proponents of regulated prostitution, abolished it in 1946. Their famed *"maisons de tolerance"* were all outlawed. It was this system. by the way, under Napoleon I, which they brought over to Lebanon. In the US—with the exception of the state of Nevada – prostitution was, for all practical purposes, also made illegal. Likewise, Italy and Japan, among others, also closed their licensed houses in 1958. The British adopted perhaps the most realistic response. Rather than directing their attention to the futile efforts of suppressing prostitution, they were more concerned with preventing some of its harmful consequences and byproducts. Although it was not licensed, prostitution in Britain was not illegal and the Wolfenden Report of 1957 argued against making it so. As such, no prostitute was punished for what she is, but if she did something to promote her trade, such as street solicitation or advertising, then she was penalised.

A third group, while recognising the need for regulated brothels, were proposing their relocation to a less visible or prominent place. With the gradual liberalisation of sexual mores, more of the upper and middle strata of society were already enjoying greater access to more natural and humane outlets for sexual encounters. A fairly large number, however, for a variety of considerations, were still in need of licensed prostitutes. As long as such a demand persists—and it was not likely to disappear overnight in Lebanon—supply always has a way of meeting it: by fair means if possible, and foul means if necessary. Outlawing prostitution carried the risk, this group felt, of shutting off an expedient safety valve. In so doing, we could well be encouraging nonprostitution outlets as an underground and disguised activity: the profession will only change its form, and the prostitute her tactics. In most cities, for example. the few remaining brothels and houses of assignation were already becoming massage parlours, escort bureaus, Turkish baths and the like. The prostitute, through the help of pimps and procurers, was driven underground and forced to resort to clandestine means.

It is for such reasons that methods of dealing with prostitution were at the time undergoing a fundamental change. Historically, all such methods were steered in the direction of penalising or stigmatising the prostitute. By the early 1950s, at least in most Western societies, efforts were being made to legislate against third parties and to punish those who live off the earnings of prostitutes.

The prostitutes in the Bourj were already beginning to feel such pressures and were, hence, becoming legitimately anxious about their future prospects in the district. Manifestations of such changes had, in fact, appeared earlier and were, in part, associated with the regulative measures introduced by the UN in 1948. Alarmed by the proliferation of "white slave" traffic and other forms of involuntary prostitution, the UN issued a declaration urging all member countries to abolish legalised prostitution. Lebanon concurred but requested a timeframe before they could comply with the intent of the prohibitive declaration. A decade elapsed before the Municipal Council of Beirut could issue their regulative decree of 1958. In it, the Council promised to suspend issuing any new licenses and to close any house after its "patrona" or proprietor retired or gave up the premises. Hence, by the 1950s the number of licensed houses was fixed at seventy-five, accommodating 207 prostitutes. Incidentally, the number of houses was determined by the number of permits issued. As such, there may well be more than one "house" on the same floor, let alone the same building.

If and when clandestine streetwalkers were accosted, because of the UN decree they were issued a permit without being accommodated in the brothels. This rather unusual form of prostitution was defined as "*Mumis Sirriyeh*": that is, as a secret but licensed prostitute. Although operating outside the red-light district, they were subject to municipal control and surveillance. By the mid-1960s these numbered about 175: an indication that there was still, despite the presumed liberalisation of sexual mores, an appreciable demand for commercial prostitution. The results of a rare empirical survey of legal prostitution in Lebanon, based on personal interviews with virtually all the sample of resident prostitutes in the red-light district at the time, are very revealing and instructive in this regard.

First, the Bourj prostitutes were still comparatively active. The typical prostitute was investing around nine to ten hours per day in her work and was receiving, on average, almost one client per hour. Considering the perceptible increase in amateur and freelance prostitution, this fairly high estimate is clearly an indication that there was still a relatively substantial demand for the type of services the Bourj prostitute was offering at the time. For example, a comparable London prostitute was, around the same time, receiving not more than twenty to twenty-five clients per week; rendering her counterpart in the Bourj three times as busy.

Second, although Marica and her colleagues were fairly busy, around 85 per cent of the prostitutes were already beginning to complain that their business had been declining. Clearly, their "golden age" was a thing of the past, and they often evoked those days with considerable nostalgia and reverie. They were equally astute in attributing the decline in the volume of their business to three sources of societal competition: the preponderance of "stereo-clubs" and bars, the car and the moral looseness and licentious predispositions of the so-called *bint 'ayleh* (well-bred family girl). With equal bitterness, they were also lamenting the decline in the socio-economic standing of their clients. Gone were the days when the elite of the upper bourgeoisie would drive into Mutanabbi Street with their mule-driven carriages or chauffeured limousines and their accompanying retinue of well-groomed and well-mannered men! These, along with a growing number of their counterparts in the new middle class, were already enjoying easier access, more natural, "nobler" and adventurous outlets for satisfying their sexual urges. The proliferation of "*garçonieres*" and single men's apartments in Hamra and West Beirut were tangible evidence of such a relaxation in sexual lifestyles.

The destruction of the red-light district during the early rounds of fighting for control of the city centre in 1975 and 1976, although it eradicated a few of the noteworthy architectural emblems in the neighbourhood, was altogether a propitious windfall. If judged by the quality of the industry and the expectations of those providing the services within it, there was little that could have been revived. The district was in the throes of its own tortuous demise. The prostitutes themselves were beginning to be aware that their life in a confined brothel was misbegotten and short-lived. They were also embittered by the alienating character of their work. Indeed, the bulk of the superannuated prostitutes still tending their declining trade were simply awaiting their imminent retirement and indemnification. Early in the 1960s the government was in fact already considering the prospects of moving the brothels to Sid al Bushriyyeh, a neighbourhood in the north-eastern suburbs of Beirut. Clandestine prostitution, part of the early manifestation of the bourgeoning global sex industry, was already beginning to permeate society.

By then, and perhaps more so than other societies in the region, Beirut has not been spared some of the aberrant consequences of globalization and mass consumerism. International migration has carried with it a dramatic change in the sex industry, particularly in the manner with which a growing number of consumers are now purchasing their sexual services and products. As in other societies, particularly those where tourism is likewise a viable sector, prostitution is now part and parcel of a thriving adult entertainment industry. The accessibility of X-rated videos, adult cable shows, computer pornography, adult magazines, even commercial telephone sex has, like elsewhere, invaded the inner sanctum of the home. In this respect, the globalisation of sexuality has paradoxically contributed to its privatisation. Porn, in both its "soft" and "hardcore" varieties, existed in some of the run-down and dilapidated movie houses in Beirut during the war and shortly after. The past decade has, however, seen porn migrate from the movie houses to the privacy of the viewers' own living rooms. Little can be done to avert or control such an aggressive and tenacious invasion.

In tandem with such incursions, perhaps even because of them, clandestine prostitution in its various forms is now a thriving and income-generating industry. A recent study claims that the industry is worth an estimate of 140 million dollars annually and employs over 4,000 people. As in other sectors of the post-war economy, its good fortunes are, it seems, part of the unintended fallout from 9/11. The marker is clearly in an upscale mode, reminiscent of the heydays of the "*maisons de tolerance*" during Marica's notorious tenure in al-Mutanabbi Street. The industry, with all its X-rated tourist attractions, caters now to a wealthier and more discerning set of clients demanding a level and variety of services comparable to those found in other capitals in the world notorious for jet-set prostitution, call-girl rackets and other nefarious outlets.

Taking advantage of a loophole in the country's public-health laws dating back to 1931, which penalises those who facilitate, encourage or live off acts of prostitution but not the prostitute herself, bevies of shrewd entrepreneurs emerged to exploit the potential inherent in such a laissez-faire setting. The most thriving part of this largely global industry is represented by the "super nightclubs" that dot the coastline between Jounieh and Maameltein. There are somewhere between eighty and ninety such upscale joints in those tourist neighbourhoods. Each club is entitled to employ up to sixty hostesses, mostly girls from Eastern Europe or the former Soviet Union. Others of lesser quality, and not as concentrated, can be spotted around Hamra, Ain Mreysseh, Mansourieh, Sin El File, Hazmieh and mountain resorts like Aley. To qualify as a "super nightclub", the establishment must offer a cabaret and the hostesses are recruited as "artistes" for six-month renewable periods. Only a few of the larger clubs provide such artistic performances or entertainment, however.

The main attraction is the opportunity to spend time with a girl of one's choice; the fee—ranging from $60 to $100—depends on the quality of the drink and the time spent, not exceeding ninety minutes. The clubs are not bordellos, and the girls are not allowed to provide any sexual favours. Undercover policemen or Sureté Generale officers are expected to monitor the premises by making unannounced spot checks. In principle, customers are not permitted to leave with girls from the club. For a certain fee however, a man is entitled to "ask the girl out" during her "off" hours, from one o'clock to seven o'clock. It is during these interludes that the girls tend to their trade. Depending on their personal appeal and resourcefulness, the business could be exceedingly lucrative, even though by the terms of their contract they are expected to share a stipulated portion of their earnings with the club proprietor and, often, the hotel manager for paying off security officers.

The "super nightclubs", generating an estimated $100 million annually, is by far the most lucrative sector of the expanding sex industry in post-war Lebanon. Since the bulk of the workforce providing the services in this stigmatized profession are itinerant trans-nationals, some of the ethical reservations that traditional moralists continue to hold with regard to prostitution are partly allayed. Lebanon, however, like other countries involved in the illegal trafficking of women for sexual exploitation, has a questionable record on human rights which on occasion prompts the government to be more prohibitive in its restrictive measures.

Although not as visible or lucrative, the tourist sex industry has other outlets that cater to the eroticized needs of customers. Most prominent are massage parlours, often euphemistically labelled as anti-stress centres. Technically, the parlours are legal since licenses are usually sought for a hygienic "treatment centre". Under such a therapeutic guise, they openly advertise in the local press, and their premises are located in respectable residential or business quarters. They generate over $20 million annually. Given their accomplished ethnic skills in this regard, most employees are Filipino or Asian women who attend to about seven customers per day. The session, lasting thirty to forty minutes, usually costs around $20—plus all the other additional services, up to $30—which are kept by the masseuse.

The three other conventional outlets, the closest to those offered by the traditional brothels, are the bar-girls, call-girls and freelancers. Together they generate another $20 million annually. There are about two dozen such bars, recognisable by their traditional red lights, in the Hamra and Ain Mreysseh districts. They are usually managed by mature, enterprising patronas and employ about four women, mostly Egyptian and North African. The cost of a drink is no different from other ordinary bars. Unlike "super nightclubs": the women are available—for about $50—for sexual encounters in a secluded modest room behind the bar or elsewhere in the premises. Since these establishments are unlicensed, the police have to be kept quiet and at a distance.

More upscale and glamorous are the rings of fearsomely popular Lebanese girls, often aspiring models, singers, dancers or those seeking marriage partners, who ply their trade in hotel lobbies, lounges and other fashionable resorts. The more ambitious advertise their "escort" and other services in the many glossy magazines in the hope of being picked up by one of the agents who arrange, under a rich variety of proxies, regular weekend party charter flights between Beirut and the Gulf states.

The lowest on the totem pole of commodified sex, and the most accessible and affordable component, are the ordinary streetwalkers. They are generally Lebanese, Syrians and Africans who may be seen on highways, Raouche, Janah and popular intersections. Others might be domestic help moonlighting on their days off. As of late, many are frequenting cafés, bars and open meeting spaces of downtown Beirut: their original abode of old!

Originally published in *Heart of Beirut* (London: Saqi Books, 2006): 211–222.

JARED McCORMICK

Transition Beirut:
Gay Identities, Lived Realities –
The Balancing Act in the Middle East

The new global economy and the flow of goods that inevitably succeed it have transformed local markets. These trades, sparked by liberal capitalism, are applauded for shoring up development and economic integration, though they are often berated for their increasing homogenizing effects. Note how the widespread prevalence and growth of technologies, of the new world order, such as satellite television channels and the internet are threatening the very fabric of local social hierarchies by altering not only how we access information, but more importantly, what we choose to access. Moreover, particular ways of living, ideas and values are becoming linked to an internationalized standard through global integration. Therefore, it is no surprise that with the increasing inroads of globalization, "sexuality becomes the terrain on which are fought out bitter disputes" (Altman, 2001: 1).

Sexuality, and its effects, remains, notwithstanding a few recent exceptions, a relatively unexplored phenomenon in the context of Arab societies. Given the emotionally charged and contested nature of sexuality, any open treatment or recognition of this highly sensitive issue is tabooed and stigmatized. This is more so of homosexuality; an even greater proscribed topic. Other than a few journalistic, sensational accounts and feature stories, empirical and grounded studies are very scant, if not non-existent. In contrast, Lebanon, particularly since the millennium, has experienced a growing gay social scene. Discussions of homosexuality have become part of the public discourse. More compelling and certainly unprecedented elsewhere in the Arab world, Lebanon can now boast of establishing the first gay rights voluntary association—*Helem*, the Arabic word for "dream". Interestingly, this is the acronym for *Himaya Lubnaniyya lil Mithliyien* (Lebanese Protections for Homosexuals). Statistically, there has been a perceptible increase in gay men who are not only openly gay but defend their "lifestyle" with more audible voice.

Fieldwork for this essay was carried out in the fall of 2005 and conducted using multiple interviews with twenty Lebanese men who all self-identified as gay. The term "gay" is employed to mean the existence of a "social life: not only same-sex desires but gay selves, gay neighbours, and gay social practices." The intention was to examine the processes by which they graft this way of living and the beliefs it connotes with their lived reality. This process of grafting was of particular relevance to those who had discovered and acted upon their inclinations while outside of Lebanon.

Six subjects were Lebanese who, in some capacity, had been in the West for at least eight years working/studying or were born/raised in Europe or America, most having dual citizenship. Their gay identity was characterized by more openness, clarity and general acceptance in comparison to those born and raised exclusively in Lebanon. Still they had to face the painful task of renegotiating an identity in a comparatively unreceptive socio-cultural setting. It became evident from the remaining fourteen that their gay identity was not entirely locally produced but rather was greatly inspired by the imported paradigm of the "global gay" character.

Today, self association with the term gay does not translate to a precise tailor-made set of behaviours or a common ethos, yet both groups of men have ongoing challenges with the cultural import of the gay identity that undoubtedly requires a juggling act with the subject's lived reality in Lebanon. Incidentally, the informants were religiously mixed, representing virtually all the major sectarian groups: Shi'i, Sunni, Maronite, Catholic, Greek Orthodox and Druze. This juggling act is most clearly seen by the balance of being "out" of the closet while still being "in". Family members—especially fathers—were almost always not privy to the subject's sexual history, whereas many of the subject's friends and perhaps a sister might know.

The social context of sexuality in Beirut is rapidly changing and the precursors and outward manifestations of a gay identity are increasing. The gay community is gaining momentum, aided by technology and the growth of *Helem*. Given such, it is worthwhile to pause for a moment and consider not only the importance and consequence of coming out, but also what local and international forces are influencing this phenomenon. With the transfer of the modern gay identity, which has never existed as a way of life in the Middle East, so begins the complex negotiation and appropriation of the individual's identity between their local identity and the values of their imported identities.

It is hoped that this exploratory study will provide an instructive case study observing a portion of the transition that "out" Lebanese men are facing as they negotiate their masculinities and validate their gay identities among friends and family. Hence, it could well provide some grounded and instructive instances of how they are forging and validating their own identities with the increasing interconnectivity of modernity.

Local Negotiation of Identity

In order to explore the changing character of sexual identity being caught, as it were, in the process of reformulating itself, it is necessary to view the process within three historical contexts: the post-independence interlude; the massive number of worldwide Lebanese emigrants who return, in some form, with a hybrid set of cultural, economic and social pressures; and the religious and ethnic diversity which characterizes Lebanon. These factors are offered to illustrate, albeit very briefly, how Lebanon's landscape, in comparison to neighbouring Arab countries, helped lay the groundwork for the ostensibly liberalizing social situation witnessed today.

Additionally, in 1989, the Taif Agreement effectively ended the Lebanese Civil War which ravaged the country. The abating wartime mentality created fertile grounds to redefine some of the social boundaries repressed during combat, including a tacit exploration of sexual definitions. Around the millennium, with the prevalence of the internet, coupled with the foundation of *Helem*, the scene became more conducive to the development of a gay identity; or at least access to identified places where a small community of men could assemble.

Today, Beirut has an international reputation as a decadent and outlandish postwar hotspot. To some extent, this characterization also applies to the gay scene. A recent feature article in *Out Traveler* focusing on Lebanon declares Beirut "the Arab World's most gay-friendly city". The article normalizes the homosexual scene in Beirut and in essence only mentions venues which are accessible to the economically predisposed. This may be misconstrued to mean that socioeconomic status could be a major consideration in accounting for one's gay identity. Yet the overall profile of informants selected for this research does not support such deterministic impressions or monocausal interpretations. If anything, they reflect a plurality of characteristics and predisposing circumstances. It is possible, however, to single out a few common experiences which my informants converge upon or share in, of course, to varying degrees. First, access to capital may indeed be a factor as nearly all the men interviewed *self*-perceived their families as upper to middle class compared to the average Lebanese family. Moreover, all those interviewed were working towards their bachelor's degree, at the minimum, while most were starting or had finished higher degrees of learning. Their access to education clearly precipitated more exposure to contemporary ideologies and surely it offered greater access to foreign languages, as all spoke English. The third palpable theme was how well-travelled the men were. All, save two individuals, had travelled outside the Arab world, with most having visited Europe at least once. This is not to imply that wealth led directly to their open formation of a gay identity, yet it might be inferred that their economic status allowed them access to many spheres of life unviable to one without economic resources.

Interestingly, the group of six who spent at least eight years outside Lebanon clearly showed less dissonance between their lived identity and their gay identity. The disjunction between sex life and private life was less manifest and more of their friends, associates and family knew they were gay. These men who returned to Lebanon also had fewer difficulties translating their desires into action in comparison to their counterparts who remained. Though the evidence might be limited, one could nonetheless infer that the significant amount of time they have spent in the West influenced their ability to bridge their biculturalism in favour of the "global gay" model.

In contrast, a number of the men born and raised in Lebanon whom I attempted to interview were ambivalent, hesitant and often uncertain while talking about their sexual identity. Many, in fact, did not unequivocally identify themselves as "gay" despite their vast and varied connections in numerous pockets of the homosexual scene. Many would say "yes" in the beginning, only to later recant their responses. Rather than believe they were trying to dissemble their gay identity, it illustrates the struggle of navigating between various identities inwardly and externally. The schism of this negotiation was most often observed in their responses to preferred/ assumed sexual role as the active or passive partner. The informants expressed frustration in finding an equalitarian homosexual relationship, in terms of sexual and emotional reciprocity and support, because of the strict adherence to a sexual dichotomy which stresses a role based on the subject's function as "active" (masculine) or "passive" (feminine). One quite effete informant seemed insulted by my research, believing my goal was to make everyone with homosexual inclinations come out. Rather, I alerted him to the fact that nearly three-quarters of my informants said that coming out was less than totally liberating because of the other drawbacks it created, especially as Tahir noted, "having people know is a liability, you can't control it ... and Lebanon is small."

Effects of Gay Identity in Lebanon

> Beirut has a gay scene, Lebanon doesn't.
> (Kamal, twenty-six years old)

Inevitably a major point of departure for those who adhere to the term "gay" begins with migration to Beirut. The informants in this study originally came from all over Lebanon but currently live in greater Beirut for studies or work. However, because of Lebanon's size, it is conceivable that one could "migrate" to the city, not to reside, but for the city's social networks and for an outlet to the gay scene.

Among my informants the very idea of a gay community remains amorphous. While some felt part of a tightly knit group, others questioned the existence of a few clubs, bars and chat rooms as a viable or meaningful definition of a community. There seems to be little, if any, semblance of a full community outside of *Helem*. By and large, the homosexual community consists of small groups of men of varying identities in a secretive web. The different conceptions of community became visible as some subjects compared Beirut's gay community to Europe, while others equated community to mean the "gay scene". There does indeed exist a community in the sense of a group of men sharing a characteristic. It lacks though a cohesive meaning and contains little depth in comparison to the Western model which emphasizes it as a shared struggle. As one informant put it:

> [There is] no community in the sense of the European communities. It's very fragmented and underground. It is repressed because it's such a small country and people only do this kind of stuff in Beirut.
> (Marwan, twenty-three years old)

The estrangement between a homosexual lifestyle and the full gay identity accounts for the lack of community. Hani, a nineteen-year-old Shi'i noted, "people see gays as just a way to have sex. Not a lifestyle. If it is a lifestyle then it clashes with our Lebanese lifestyle." Forging a gay identity seemed a complex process for most informants. Though the incorporation of some element has had an impact in informing the advocacy character of the movement, it has had its problems; as it is ultimately incompatible with parts of their lived experience in Lebanon. When asked, for example, if they looked to the West to define their meaning of being gay, one responded it was "automatic." Another quipped "of course, what else would it be?" Others "took it as [a] guide to start discovering their identity", while an insightful returnee to Lebanon, who studied in an American high school and state university, perhaps shed light on what people find in the foreign gay identity by replying, "America allowed me to be who I am. It said who I am was OK."

Such reflections might appear like a natural progression to adopting the global gay identity since Lebanon lacks any rubric or local framework to support the meaning that a modern gay lifestyle has taken. However, this prompts one to question the underlying beliefs which might have pushed them to this foreign paradigm and pulled them away from their local identity formation. Likewise, in reference to gay men acting "Americanized" one informant from the American University of Beirut suggested that "people need to take risks, but remember to be Lebanese." This only supports, by his own admission, that the gay identity is not of Lebanon and conceivably unable to meld with the local ideals.

Modernity and globalization appear to have advanced the prospects of overall worldwide sexual acceptance. In spite of that, Lebanon's values in general are not advancing at the same rate. One difficulty each member the gay population in Lebanon negotiates is the role they play in the public sphere as gay men. The matter ultimately rests on the degree of their openness with their homosexuality. Hence the basic question: "should more men come out in Lebanon?" generated many unexpected responses. The opinions of the informants varied and did not converge on a set of common expectations.

While there were a variety of replies, many seemed to overlap on the realistic necessity of being in Beirut for exposure of the "community." There were divergences of opinions, however, as some expressed coming out as less than they had "bargained for". Nader, an eloquent twenty-seven-year-old, expressed his apprehension of coming out because it is practically irreversible and comes with such high stakes that "affect the rest of your life." It was most bluntly put by Loay, a twenty-five-year-old Lebanese, born and raised in America: "only come out if you can make it without your family." All of the informants actively supported others to come out, but having done so themselves they understood the costs associated with it and implicitly seemed to understand any apprehension.

Hesitation exists, as there is obviously a high cost to coming out. It looks as if a number of consequences are an expression of the primacy and centrality of the family as an agency of socialization for enforcing societal norms. To fully understand how these men are grappling with their identity transformation, one must appreciate what is to be lost by positively identifying as gay. The rights and responsibilities of being a man are threatened by straying from Connell's (1987) idea of a "hegemonic" masculinity. Most Lebanese still do not consider a gay "way of life" as an acceptable or viable identity. From my interviews, it seems that the continuation of such a view might well account for the predispositions of many informants to lead sections of their lives in secret, especially in relation to their family.

As a result, the psychological cost of living such diametrically opposed realities cannot be demeaned. Many felt they did not have a balancing act of being "out/in" the closet, but through accounts of their actions around older/immediate family members gave the impression that sometimes their behaviour reverted to something more socially acceptable, whether they were conscious of it or not. Hussein said his conduct did not change when he spent time in his village in the south, but he continued to act "normal." This indicated his belief that gay behaviour is unorthodox yet his own is not; thereby expressing the conflict between his gay identity and his family life. One could easily infer from this that in cultures where family loyalty is not as intense, the conflict might not assume such forms. Donham (2005) noted in a study of the South African gay community that the "gay identity is different to the degree that it does not rely upon the family for its anchoring, indeed if anything, it has continually liberated itself from the effects of family socialization." It seems that the gay identity did not draw the subjects away from their families but did alienate them in some regards because of the covert lifestyle they have been inclined to assume outside the home. The anxiety and fear that the family might somehow discover their true identity remains one of their most menacing concerns. Therefore their homosexual life is kept tightly private.

Given such realities one can begin to understand and appreciate the circumstances which sustain the apprehensions against coming out. They are largely a byproduct of economic considerations and the security the family continues to provide in this regard. Considering all emotional involvement aside, their support comes through financial means and family connections which are subject to change should such a status-changing event, such as coming out, disrupt the balance of their own gender/sex paradigm in their family. Imagine funding one's own education without family support or finding a job with no *wasta* (favours). There are too many compelling pressures for men not to reveal any non-heteroseuxal proclivities until they can be more financially independent of their families. It is within this context that the prospects of coming out remain inextricably associated with the survival of the family as a venue for economic security.

Unyielding as these circumstances may seem, it is not difficult to discern that there are additional trends/phenomena that have become apparent in Lebanon that are changing the lived and perceived realities of homosexual men. Three such realities stand out: the establishment of *Helem*, the role of the internet and the changing character of growing global consumerism/marketing. An explanation of these will help us understand the predicament that homosexuals are facing in forging and validating their sexual identities.

Helem

"Fight to Exist' because 'Silence is Death'"
(Helem slogans, from printed material)

Helem, founded in 2001, is effectively the first non-governmental organization (NGO) fighting for LGBT rights in the Arab world. There is indisputably no other place in the Middle East from which *Helem* could operate besides Beirut. *Helem* is jointly registered in Quebec, Canada and Lebanon. Nonetheless, it has not, as of yet, received an official registration number from the Lebanese Ministry of Interior. George Azzi, the coordinator of *Helem*, said, "according to the current jurisprudence, the fact that we have paid and received an acknowledgment of registration will be accepted in courts as proof of state recognition." This does not mean *Helem* has *carte blanche* to push and propagate its agenda and all its alleged objectives. It is significant that they have followed the proper protocol with the Lebanese government, which has granted. in a way, tacit approval through the absence of any restrictions.

Currently, there exists an internal debate regarding the strategies the group should pursue; i.e. should they subscribe to a more politically expedient mission or work on grassroots development and public opinion? They have set up a lobbying subcommittee to work not only on the removal of law 534 from the Penal Code but also to seek positive modifications that would actively protect homosexuals. There are two lawyers who advise *Helem* on legal issues, and they seem to be on the brink of making a slight dent into the political realm for gay rights. Some members acknowledge that even if—by some stroke of luck—the law was changed, it would do little to transform the overall mentality against homosexuality. Certainly some members believe a legal framework to safeguard homosexuals is necessary before it will be feasible for more people to come out. A minority, on the other hand, prefer to stress the social acceptance and understanding needed to change public opinion.

Another goal of *Helem* is to raise the general discourse surrounding homosexuality. Advocating such a sensitive issue in public within the Arab world is seen by Massad (2002) as an "incitement to discourse." The Lebanese are generally tolerant, yet increasing dialogue on homosexuality might have unfavourable consequences. A member of *Helem*, Ahmed, expressed his view that *Helem* walks a fine line between increasing awareness and pushing the limits too quickly. The latter is unavoidably, in his view, to spark a backlash against the NGO or gay-frequented establishments. One might indicate in this regard that the last police raids of two gay-frequented nightclubs happened at Acid on 12 November 2005, when seven were arrested, and roughly a week later at X-OM with no arrests. One could cite this as evidence of a backlash; however, it does not provide a convincing case of "cracking down" as both clubs are flourishing more than ever. There was admittance of underage individuals and suspected drug use at both.

Ahmed's apprehensions are legitimate as *Helem* and the gay community must strive to support men as they struggle to reconcile the desired elements inherent in a global gay identity model in light of the morals and ways of life in Lebanese society. Put another way, can the local society and culture sustain and absorb *Helem*'s professed goals and objectives?

Interestingly, *Helem*'s incitement of public discourse has been recently aided by their development of a gay press (another first in the Arab world) with the publication of the magazine *Barra*, meaning "out" in Lebanese colloquial Arabic. Launched in 2005, *Barra*'s content is mixed between French, English and Arabic and provides analysis and commentary on current issues that assail the gay community. It is distributed in limited locations around Beirut and also online. The publication has grown so much that they are hiring a freelance sales representative to handle advertising and the March 2006 issue includes nearly eighty pages, of which most is Arabic with some English and French additions. The previous two issues, which were roughly thirty pages, are available on the *Helem* website and 5,000 have been downloaded thus far. *Barra*, along with *Helem*, may eventually help to solidify the "internationalized" gay identity, as was observed in Bolivia when an outreach clinic opened to support HIV education to the homosexual community.

Moreover, *Helem* must overcome the financial and socioeconomic divides that split the homosexual community to attract a diverse following and membership in addition to the sectarian rifts already omnipresent in Lebanese society. One informant, for instance, remarked that because out gay men were already on the fringes of Lebanese society, he believed the close association with "gays and the West" allows one to de-emphasize his confessional identity, thereby entertaining the prospects of supplanting one for the other. However, I do not have sufficient data to substantiate this interesting inference.

Helem is struggling to solidify a gay identity within the fabric of local content—which is predominately a homosexual community of men having sex with men (MSM) with little or no association with the gay identity. They aspire to increase public awareness, move the community to a more solid common ground regarding sexual openness, and address issues that beset the gay community such as HIV and hate crimes.

Recently, the Dutch embassy provided funding that will sponsor production of a booklet on positive sexual health for the LGBT community. This booklet will be the first of its kind in the Arabic language and will serve as a comprehensive resource on sexual health. While I do not question the necessity of the information on sexual health, it raises issues of how the gay community and their individual values are being shaped to conform to the global gay identity as "a product of foreign imaginations, being invented, as it were, in the service of obscure international agendas" (Donham, 2005:289). The emergent outlines or emancipatory efforts to formulate a gay identity appear to ride on the coat tails of globalization as Western countries continue to advocate rights for this way of life, their policies and by granting aid money to NGOs. One informant, as Westernized as he was, considered the encroaching "global gay identity" as another form of imperialism. Even though the Lebanese are eager to invoke conspiracy theories, his perceptions might carry some weight. At the least, it deserves further verification and validation to examine how the manifestations of this global gay identity are being reflected in beliefs and lifestyle throughout the world. Incidentally, other studies have shown the delicate balance between such global identities and their local counterparts.

Role of Internet in Gay Identity Formation

I'm straight but I make exceptions for foreigners.
(Man outside Acid nightclub)

The "internet revolution", by allowing access to material otherwise deemed inappropriate, has shaped many modern trends in terms of sexual identity. The dilemma of how agents, living in a culture that is ostensibly repressive towards their identity, can adapt to find ways to express themselves is partially solved by the internet serving as an accessible and expedient outlet.

The expansion of the internet has created a new avenue to explore one's sexuality, and at present, there are roughly 600,000 (or 13.4 percent of the population of Lebanese) online with 100 percent growth rate from 2000 to 2005 (Internet World Stats, 2005). The role of the internet is of utmost importance in the Middle East as it allows a negotiation and flexibility of the inner and outer identities of an individual. It also allows the subject to "role play" and briefly experience something outside of himself in a clandestine manner. It may allow a subject to explore various possibilities, while maintaining a safe distance from those possibilities and their consequences. Because of this safety it is likely that authentic feelings come out online and the true gender is performed.

This elicits questions of whether Lebanese who have experience online become more predisposed to come out. From the twenty informants for this research, the fourteen raised within Lebanon all seem to recognize the internet as a major factor in their gay identity. So much so, in fact, that I would consider internet access as a possible prerequisite on the path of entering the homosexual subculture in Lebanon. Many said it started with curiosity, but as chat-rooms served as a viable and socially less intimidating way to meet men, they found an easy gateway to the homosexual community all the while circumventing the associated social disgraces.

A large majority of informants, more exclusively the youngest ranging from seventeen to twenty-three years old, are regular chat-line users. Almost all admitted to meeting men "offline", some declaring that they had recently stopped. Bassam, a very thoughtful twenty-four-year-old, cast doubts on the internet when he said it is "not healthy, not social. This does not form a community. It should be a phase as it's helpful to discovery. But it has to move to something real off the computer." His thoughts add to the argument of the missing gay community. People are not willing to accept coming off the "anonymous" internet to bear the social costs of association with the identity or are unwilling to place themselves in this archetype.

The importance of the internet for *Helem* is also noteworthy. By far the majority of the information on homosexuality and gay issues available on the web is written in languages other than Arabic. While the Lebanese are known for their polyglot predisposition, which would allow them to access material in French or English, it is a watershed that the *Helem* website is in both English and Arabic. The English site hosts full content while the Arabic, currently under construction, covers the majority of the subject matter. It is also curious that the message boards and discussions are almost exclusively in English, save a few transliterated words from Arabic. It is feasibly one of the first sources of gay material in Arabic and surely one of the first from an NGO on Arab soil. One can imagine many Arab nationals viewing the growing collection of coming out stories, news updates or message boards, bearing in mind that the traffic reaches over 50,000 hits per month. Roughly 6 percent of those visitors are from Saudi Arabia and only an estimated 5 percent are from within Lebanon. This illustrates the importance and function of *Helem* in the changing sexual context of the Arab world. Therefore, it is no surprise that during religious holidays hundreds of "Gulfies" (citizens from the Arab Gulf countries) are visible in the clubs/bars as Beirut is a growing destination for tourism. The expanding sexual flexibility affords "breathing space" and brings neighbouring Arabs flocking to Beirut because it is familiar and physically closer than Europe, while curious non-Arabs enjoy it as an exotic new playground.

The final ground-breaking facet of the *Helem* website, and perhaps the most explicit, is how openly they disclose gay venues. Under the "Queer Lebanon Guide", *Helem* has an exhaustive list of gay friendly clubs, bars and "theatres" in Beirut. There are maps to clubs/bars including descriptions of the crowd, music, time and costs. Furthermore, the guide lists public cruising areas like Ramlet El Baida and "theatres" where it is possible to pick up men and how to connect to gay chat lines on IRC (Internet Relay Chat)— all the while warning the would-be participant to "beware of thieves and undercover police." It is only that much more significant considering the geospatial location of Beirut in the Middle East. By publishing this information *Helem* appears to be trying to bridge the dissonance and stigma between the gay and straight realities in Lebanon, but in presenting information from the same perspective as a Western gay rights NGO it may cross the line of social tolerance in Lebanon.

Consumerism and Marketing

There is a growth in identity-based movements, and there is an impact of the global gay identity where people throughout the world are seeing themselves as part of a larger global movement.
(Cary Johnson, 2005)

The global gay identity in Lebanon is also being reinforced by imminent consumerism and marketing. Take for example the possibility of downloading the latest issue of *Barra* online for just $5 in addition to purchasing items from affiliates' ads on *Helem*'s webpage. Raynbow, an online store selling gay pride merchandise printed and manufactured in the USA but shipped worldwide, is Lebanese-owned and donates a portion of their proceeds from each sale to *Helem* (www.raynbow.org). One of their recent additions, the "Lebanese Hunks Calendar" for just $17.99, offers semi-clothed men in a graphic facsimile of similar such global marketing ventures. Not to undermine the mission or question the sincerity of their fundraising, it is, however, interesting to cite the experiences of the American gay community. Research has noted many websites strive to gain from constructing an image of community. Raynbow, along with others, are embracing and purposely marketing to the homosexual Lebanese community. It is forming a small, albeit growing, industry by outwardly playing off of gay pride and Lebanese pride with men becoming the sexualized object, as is quite visible in the "Lebanese Hunks Calendar."

Another example is the travel company LebTour, which arranges and runs tours throughout Lebanon (www.lebtour.com). They advertise on the *Helem* website and apparently seem to specialize in serving a gay clientele as rainbow flags adorn every side of their website. In addition to the religious and eco-tourism tours there is a section offering "gay tours" throughout Lebanon. It could indeed serve as an easy access point for foreigners into the Lebanese gay scene.

Yet, the larger question remains: how tolerated will the gay identity become in Lebanon even in view of such symptoms of commercialization? Apparently, from a service standpoint, it is bound to become more accepted. Take for instance the billboards of the chic department store Aishti. In 2005 they produced a full ad campaign around Lebanon tited "Vote for Tolerance", which showed models re-enacting the colors of the gay pride flag and included two male models in a near embrace. Furthermore, the number of "gay nights" at various bars/clubs/cafes in Beirut currently accounts for five nights of the week. All subjects for this study responded positively to frequenting some of these establishments that either market or cater to the homosexual community.

Another case in point is a club, UV, near the infamous Monot Street. In 2005 it offered an "Oriental Night", "Halloween Party", or an extra drink ticket for guests who arrived before a certain time. The means of communication was via SMS from cellular phone numbers they collected at the door. I offer this instance to illustrate a new balance of tolerance in some parts of Beirut as managers and owners use subtle marketing ventures and embrace technology to promote their businesses. Perhaps gay marketing will increase in Beirut as the homosexual community is viewed as an economic entity to serve. Interestingly, the importance of homosexuals' betrayal of the hegemonic masculinity in Lebanon may well become obscured by the size of their wallets.

Conclusion

The development of a homosexual identity is dependent on the meanings that the actor attaches to the concepts of homosexual and homosexuality, and that these meanings are directly related to the meanings that are available in his immediate environment; and the meanings that are available in his immediate environment are related to the meanings that are allowed to circulate in the wider society. The commitment to a homosexual identity cannot occur in an environment where the cognitive category of homosexual does not exist. (Henderson, 2006).

I offer this example of the Lebanese community as further proof of Dank's argument while at the same time revealing transformations he had not anticipated. Even though *Helem* has started to provide the context and support needed in the "immediate environment" for a gay identity to develop, I suggest the role of the internet is crucial and has added an unforeseen component to homosexual identity negotiation in Lebanon. The "immediate environment" of the subject is altered by the cyber world, which allows one to stretch the limits and borders of local reality. Accessing the global gay identity, something historically unavailable, allows them to transcend the values of their immediate environment. One significance of the internet becomes more pronounced when we recognize that to virtually all the younger subjects the internet was singularly instrumental in their exposure to aspects of the global gay identity.

Another important theme, which was not considered, is the role of the Lebanese government. In nearly any Arab state an open gay rights group advocating a public agenda of acceptance would have only existed for a few days at best. While the Lebanese authorities are not particularly friendly to *Helem* they have done little by way of constraining them. Should this be taken to signify an implicit or tacit approval from the leadership—or a more pragmatic speculation, is the state too strained by other weighty concerns to really care? It is interesting to note that the intense political situation in 2005 coincided with *Helem*'s largest growth; however, linking the two is pure conjecture. Yet the magnitude of the political crisis might have distracted the concerns or public gaze of certain governmental agencies. Likewise, declining tourism might also account for this seemingly lax and permissive attitude of public officials who are anxious not to disrupt the crucial flow of revenue from tourism.

Regardless of the internal situation in Lebanon it is important to question on a larger scale how this global gay identity spreads across the world with Lebanon as another "convert". It provides little or no room to express a same-sex identity without the rubrics of the Western gay model, therefore it is no marvel that a foreign term denotes something not-of-Lebanon. I argue that the imported global gay identity has been embraced by a small number in the homosexual community and will continue to grow along with *Helem*'s support. Most "out" men have taken the Western gay archetype as a guide. Hence, the "re"-localization of their identity cannot occur until a more liberal socio-sexual setting begins to contain some of the elements associated with a homosexual identity.

It is interesting to note in this regard that a few informants, particularly those who had not been abroad, admitted that, in the absence of such local venues, those in the midst of forging meaningful and coherent sexual and gender identities have little choice but to revert to the borrowed and mediated role models, transmitted through the global media.

The experience of Beirut, though still in a formative period, is quite useful. Throughout Beirut's checkered socio-cultural history, it has managed by virtue of its mixed and hybrid composition to evince a greater readiness to experiment with novel and cosmopolitan lifestyles. The relatively accommodating, at time felicitous experience of homosexuals in grafting a coherent identity, is a case in point. At a time when their counterparts elsewhere in surrounding countries are being demonized, repressed and incarcerated (and at times sent to their deaths, as in Iran), the gay community in Lebanon has succeeded in creating a voluntary association, a media (print and virtual) and numerous public venues.

It is hoped this brief study has touched upon the greater significance of a gay identity in Lebanon. The outward development of this identity involves many "firsts" in the Arab world. *Helem* is inciting discourse, engaging in civil society and hopes to gain more active members. There are also expanding resources in Arabic regarding sexuality and a diversifying scene in Beirut.

In closing, it is not being suggested that the development of a gay identity in Lebanon is strictly limited to the influences and experiences of the West through the "global gay" identity. Altman (1996:85) notes: "It seems clear that some form of gay and lesbian identity is becoming more common across the world. The global gay identity has arrived and those who have adopted it have grafted this to their other identities due to their education, experience online and more extensive travel experience. Indisputably this quest for a local gay identity is ground-breaking and will play a large role in the advancement of sexuality in Lebanon, while Beirut is the apposite location for the entry of gay rights into the Arab world.

References

Altman, Dennis. "Rapture or Continuity? The Internationalization of Gay Identities." *Social Texts*, No. 48, Duke University Press, 1996.
——. *Global Sex*, Chicago: university of Chicago Press, 2001
Connell, R.W., *Gender and Power*, Oxford: Polity Press, 1987.
Dank, Barry. "Coming Out in the Gay World." *Journal for the Study of Interpersonal Process*, vol. 34, 1971.
Donham, Donald L., "Freeing South Africa: The "Modernization" of the Male-Male Sexuality in Soweto." In Robertson, Jennifer, ed. *Same-Sex Cultures and Sexualities*, Oxford: Blackwell, 2005. Internet World States, Internet Usage in the Middle East, 31 December 2005.
Massad, Joseph. "Re-Orienting Desire: The Gay International and the Arab World." In *Public Cultural Journal*, vol. 14, no.2, 2002.

Originally published in Samir Khalaf & John Gagnon (eds.) *Sexuality in the Arab World* (London: Saqi Books, 2006): 243–260.

PART FIVE

The Empowerment of Marginalized Groups

Introduction

Much of the literature on social change and development, often epitomized as the interplay between the forces of tradition and modernity, has been the byproduct of two major theoretical perspectives: Developmentalism and Marxism. Proponents of the former assumed that traditional ties and loyalties, particularly those which sustain the cohesion and resilience of kinship, tribal, confessional and communal groups and institutions, are an obstacle to modernity. So-called traditional societies, in other words, were expected to break away and disengage themselves from such relics of pre-modern times if they are to enjoy the presumed fruits of modernity or to become full-fledged nation states.

Likewise, to Marxists, communists and socialist regimes were seen as "giant brooms" expected to sweep away pre-existing loyalties. If non-class attachments and parochial interests survive, they are treated as forms of "false consciousness" to mask fundamental economic and social contradictions. In other words both agreed that primordial ties and loyalties are destined to disappear. Both, of course, have been wrong. For neither in the developing world, nor in advanced societies have presumably irresistible secular and liberalizing forces of modernization been so overwhelming in eroding the resilience of some of the local and segmental loyalties. Indeed, in times of social unrest, political strife and uncertainty, such loyalties are bound to become sharper and more assertive.

Samir Khalaf employs the metaphors of *roots and routes* to provide further evidence in support of such a dialectical view of the interplay between tradition and modernity. By re-examining the socio-cultural and political history of Lebanon during the past three decades, he has been able to explore both the enabling and disabling features of primordialism to reassess their impact on Lebanon's political culture. He does so by focusing on three related dimensions. First, he makes an effort, within the context of the unsettling internal, regional and global transportations, to identify the circumstances which have reinforced communal and sectarian cleavages. Second, and more concretely, he examines how familism, communal and confessional solidarities have been responding to the forces which undermine their cohesion and collective identities. Finally, he demonstrates how this longing to reconnect with one's *roots* may be transformed into *routes* for the articulation of new cultural identities more relevant for safeguarding civil and peaceful forms of pluralism and tolerance.

For example, during the war years (1975–92), a larger number of people found themselves, willingly or otherwise, enfolded within the family. By their own testimonies, they were drawn closer to members of their immediate and extended family. Much like a "haven in a heartless world", the family had to reinvent and extend itself to assume added functions. It became almost an exclusive outlet to absorb a larger share of the leisure, recreational, welfare and benevolent needs of its members. It also served as an economic and commercial base and continued to have a decisive impact on political succession and circulation of the parliamentary elite.

The boundaries and horizons within which people have been circulating were also becoming more constricted. It is inevitable, in times of uncertainty, fear and paranoia, that such bonding in exclusive spaces should become breeding grounds for heightening communal and territorial identities. Khalaf goes further to argue that in this sense:

> The community, locality, neighbourhood, or quarter are no longer simply a space to occupy or a place to live in and identify with. They have become akin to an ideology—an orientation or a frame of reference through which groups interact and perceive others. It is then, that the community is transferred into a form of communalism.

Symptoms of the reassertion of religious and confessional consciousness are also becoming more visible. This is particularly interesting since it manifests itself in seemingly paradoxical and inconsistent features. Curiously, people indicated that their religiosity—as measured by the degree of changes in the intensity of their spiritual beliefs, religious commitments and observation of rituals, practices, and duties of their faith—was declining. Their confessional and sectarian identities were however becoming sharper. This is dismaying in a more poignant sense. A surprisingly large proportion of what presumably is a literate, cosmopolitan and sophisticated sample of professionals, university and college teachers, intellectuals, journalists, and the like, displayed strong confessional biases, and a distance from and intolerance toward other groups. This clearly implies, among other things, that religion "is not resorted to as a spiritual force to restore one's sense of well-being, but as a means of communal and ideological mobilization."

Khalaf is fully aware of some of the unsettling consequences of the revitalization of primordial allegiances, particularly since they are inclined to engender and sustain the growth of self-sufficient and guarded communities and neighborhoods. Yet, he is also of the view that when stripped of their bigoted and intolerant features, they became the bases for equitable and judicious forms of power sharing and the articulation of new cultural identities germane for co-existence and multiculturalism.

Miriam Ghazzah extends her analysis to the area of popular culture and music to show how Moroccan youth in Dutch society make efforts to forge a meaningful and coherent Moroccan-Dutch identity by incorporating elements from both cultures. The *Shaabi* musical genre allows them to connect with and incorporate elements of their parents' culture. By doing so, they create occasions to reinforce ingredients of an ethnic past and celebrate a Moroccan identity.

The *Shaabi* traditional musical genre is infused with nostalgia for Morocco's past. During regular festivals, concerts, dance parties which attract famous *Shaabi* artists, Moroccan-Dutch youths can glorify part of the culture of their parents and, thereby, retain their autonomy and independence. Ghazzah is keen on reminding us that the Dutch-Moroccan community is far from homogenous. The majority represent Berbers from the Rif, while the others are a mix of Arab speaking groups from different regions. The frenzy and exhilaration experienced during these highly charged events allow the youth to transcend their local identities. Somehow, this "losing of oneself in the atmosphere of dancing enhances the feeling of solidarity." At least, internal differences seem to temporarily disappear. Youth can construct a meaningful identity which focuses more on being Moroccan in the Netherlands rather than on being Moroccan in Morocco.

Hip-hop music, on the other hand, exposes youth to another genre of popular music with a distinctly different history and effect. "Hip-hop is an eclectic music known for its bricolage of sounds, beats and text fragments. It originated in African American neighborhoods in New York when, in the 1970s, youths started the genre by rapping over drumbeats." They became effective tools for marginalized youths to create prestige and status. Hence, as Ghazzah concludes, "self-definition in Maroc-hop is based both on creating links with American or global hip-hop culture and on creating alliances with a local ethnic community."

There is more to such popular outlets than their expressive and entertaining features. They are also transformative in a more fundamental sense, since they raise consciousness by addressing sensitive global issues such as 9/11, the war in Iraq, racism, the Palestinian-Israeli conflict.

The role of Islamic voluntary welfare associations (NGOs) in providing services to subaltern groups such as the poor, orphans, widows, disabled and other underprivileged communities continues to be contested and debated. Some scholars and observers regard such associations as primarily agencies for fostering cooperative ties to enhance the solidarity of Islamist movements. Their contribution to the actual empowerment of marginal and dispossessed groups is not recognized.

Egbert Harmsen in "Between Empowerment and Paternalism" investigates the activities and conduct of a score of such associations in Jordan and advances a more enabling and reconciliatory assessment of their impact. In other words, rather than seeing an anachronistic relationship between the survival of certain paternalistic features, sacred and ritualistic notions of Islamic piety and the secular demands inherent in modern and global forms of mobilization, Harmsen recognizes the possibility of blending and hybridization between the two. He cites concretes and persuasive instances of such blending in the service of empowerment. For example, in one women's association in a poor suburb of the industrial city of Zarqa, Harmsen shows how the Islamic concept of *Karma* (dignity) is mobilized to enhance notions of self-esteem and empowerment of school-dropout girls of their mothers from broken homes and socially weak families. In another association—Al-Faruq Welfare Society for Orphans—social workers were able to use Quranic precepts such as *himaya* (protection), *rahma* (compassion), *tasamuh* (forgiveness and tolerance), *sabr* (patience) to redirect communication "in line with globally formulated rights principles, and on an active cooperation with transnational development actors. On the other hand, fear of losing one's independence and cultural authenticity in the face of western-dominated globalization processes is widespread."

On Roots and Routes :
The Reassertion of Primordial Loyalities

"Most societies seem allergic to internal anonymity, homogeneity and amnesia."

Ernest Gellner (1988)

Almost 40 years ago I preambled an essay I wrote, on the interplay between primordial ties and politics in Lebanon, with the following salient characterization:

> By the admission of many dispassionate observers—indigenous and foreign alike—the political system in Lebanon stands as a curious but happy phenomenon. A pluralistic confessional society, it enjoys a parliamentary system of government with a freely elected Chamber of Deputies. Outwardly the country appears to be bolstered by liberal and democratic traditions, yet Lebanon hardly possesses any of the political instruments of a civil polity. A National Pact, a sort of Christian-Moslem entente, sustains its so-called national entity—*al-kayan*, yet this sense of identity is neither national nor civic. Its politicians, masterminds at the art of flexibility and compromise, are local *zaims* not national heroes.

> The few parties that do exist are so closely identified with sectarian groups and so unconcerned with a larger national identity that they can easily engender political disintegration. Likewise, its political blocs and fronts are so absorbed with parochial and personal rivalries that they fail to serve the larger national purpose of mobilizing the population for the broader aims of society. Politicians and pressure groups alike have not been able to transcend their petty personal feuds to grapple effectively with the public issues of the country.

I went on to argue that precarious as the political system was at the time, it had nonetheless managed to maintain a balance of power among its heterogeneous, confessional, kinship and communal groups. Except for the crisis of 1958, for nearly a century the country's pluralistic allegiances and loyalties had been relatively stable and viable. It also demonstrated a noted resilience in resisting the ideological and political turmoil that had overwhelmed its adjacent Arab states. Writing at a time when perspectives of developmentalism and comparative modernization were still in vogue, it was argued that political modernization in Lebanon need not involve a transfer of sovereignty from primordial allegiances to secular, liberal and ideological commitments. Given the persistence of primordial sentiments, the metamorphosis of political life in the country may never involve such a sharp transformation. Adopting a dialectical rather than a dichotomous relationship between the forces of tradition and modernity, the paper cast doubt as to whether Lebanese society can ever be a duplicate of a purely rational, secular and egalitarian society based exclusively on achievement-oriented and universalistic criteria. Nor can it be a reactionary throwback on an ossified, unbending and incompliant social order where traditional norms and practices are mindlessly adhered to. Instead the problem boils down to a question of fusion and assimilation: how to assimilate certain selective features of traditional culture into the culture of a rational and secular society without undermining both.

Prefiguring much of the subsequent concerns with issues associated with the so-called "crisis of identity", the paper advanced another caveat: given the survival of traditional ties and loyalties, it is not surprising that the average Lebanese citizen should continue to elicit greater satisfaction and security from his primordial attachments than from his involvement or participation in purely rational and ideological associations. Within such a setting, and contrary to what is often proposed, this perpetual crisis of identity cannot be resolved by fiat. Legislation cannot turn a confessional, kinship and personalistic society into a nation-state overnight. Nor can a wilful sense of government legitimacy be created by constitutional arrangements and a representative electoral system alone.

Such realities, I maintained in 1968, cannot or should not be wished away, bypassed or dismissed as futile nostalgic gestures to seek shelter in the relics of a dead, disinherited or imagined past. These hybrid entities, often a viable fusion of seemingly disparate ties and networks, have proved to be—particularly when their inhibitive and intransigent elements were contained or neutralized—effective mediating agencies.

By documenting the resilience of primordialism, I was not proposing that the system was a paragon of political virtues. The country's shortcomings and pitfalls were readily recognized. Yet throughout its checkered political history, Lebanon I argued, has been fairly successful in integrating its pluralistic factions, guaranteeing a modicum of freedom of expression and civil liberties, evolving a coherent foreign policy, protecting and encouraging a liberal economy and most of all safeguarding a free, independent, prosperous and peaceful society. In subsequent research (Khalaf, 1991, 2002), I advanced five further inferences regarding the primacy and survival of primordialism:

1. The sweeping changes Lebanon has been subjected to, from internal insurrections to centralized and direct rule by foreign powers or the more gradual and spontaneous changes associated with rapid urbanization, spread of market economy, and the exposure of a growing portion of the population to secular, liberal, and radical ideologies, etc., did little to weaken or erode the intensity of primordial loyalties. Indeed, in times of social unrest and political turmoil such loyalties are inclined to become sharper and often supersede other ties and allegiances. Hence, it is not uncommon that protest movements and other forms of collective mobilization of social unrest, sparked by genuine grievances and unresolved public issues, should be, as was frequently the case in such episodes, deflected into confessional rivalries.

2. Primordial loyalties have not only survived and retained their primacy; they continue to serve as viable sources of communal solidarity. They inspire local and personal initiative and account for much of the resourcefulness and cultural diversity

and vitality of the Lebanese. But they also undermine civic consciousness and commitment to Lebanon as a nation-state. Expressed more poignantly, the forces which motivate and sustain harmony, balance, and prosperity are also the very forces which on occasion pull the society apart and contribute to conflict, tension and civil disorder. The ties that bind, in other words, also unbind.

3. From the aborted accord of Shakib Effendi (the partition scheme of 1843) to the current discourse over the "Ta'if Accord", Lebanon grappled with successive strategies, pacts, covenants, concordats, and other political and territorial rearrangements to identify and safeguard the country's sovereignty and autonomy as a plural society. To a large degree, the most viable of these efforts were more the byproduct of volition, collective acts of will, consent, habits of discussion, and compromise— even courtesy—rather than coercion, force or cruelty. Cruelty only begot further cruelty.

4. Clearly, not all the persisting internal disparities which have plagued Lebanon for so long, should be attributed to foreign intervention. Nor were they exclusively generated by unplanned and fortuitous circumstances. Foreign powers, by virtue of their preferential and shifting patronage of different communities, must have also contributed to the accentuation of such gaps and dislocations. This is most visible in their direct involvement, often as principal architects of covenants and pacts or in negotiating terms of settlements on behalf of their client groups or protégés. Such willful and deliberate involvement carries their intervention to its ultimate degree. Without exception all pacts in Lebanon, particularly those coming in the wake of armed struggle, were brokered by foreign governments either unilaterally or through their trusted local or regional allies.

   Despite sharp differences in their visions, all the foreign powers involved in the various settlement schemes ended up, willfully or otherwise, by consolidating the confessional foundation of the political order. I wish to argue that the schemes which were fairly successful (particularly the *Règlement Organique* of 1861 and the *Mithaq* of 1943) had recognized the realities of confessional affiliation but sought to secularize sectarianism in such a manner as to encourage harmonious coexistence between the various confessional groups. In short, they made efforts to transform some of its divisive and pathological features into a more enabling and constructive system.

5. When external sources of instability were contained and neutralized various Lebanese communities were able to evolve fairly adaptive and accommodating strategies for peaceful coexistence. The last and, perhaps most successful of these was the 'National Pact' of 1943 which survived for over 30 years. The ideology or philosophy which inspired the Pact perceives Lebanon neither as a society "closed against the outside world, nor a unitary society in which smaller communities were dissolved, but something between the two: a plural society in which communities, still different on the level of inherited religious loyalties and intimate family ties, co-existed within a common framework" (Hourani 1976:38).

Two decades of displaced and protracted collective violence along with the unsettling consequences of globalization, consumerism and popular and mass culture have reawakened interest in the character and role communal and primordial groupings are playing today. Of all such ties, confessionalism appears to elicit the most acute and contentious polemics. Most observers have been predisposed to document its disruptive and abusive features. Hence, the literature abounds with references to the evils of confessionalism, such as the bankruptcy of ideological parties and pressure groups, deficient civility, the paralysis of the parliament, excessive meddling of religious leaders in the political life of the community, and the sacrifice of competence and efficiency on the altar of sectarian balance. Most damaging perhaps, recurrent cycles of political violence are often perceived as byproducts of crazed fanatics, or a reawakening of the deeply-rooted confessional bigotism lodged in the collective unconscious of warring communities, locked in and driven by little else other than the imagined or real hostility and intolerance they harbour towards others.

Eager to highlight the abuses of such tendencies—and they certainly cannot be minimized or dismissed—observers have nonetheless often misread their sources and consequences. Confessionalism in Lebanon is often made an expedient scapegoat for abuses whose roots lie elsewhere. For example, in my view, the abuses of *marja'yah* or *taba'iyah* (i.e. clientelism) are far more egregious in their character and pervasive implications. Indeed, the seemingly sanctimonious and self-righteous communal predispositions underlying sectarian loyalties become expedient disguises for the more aggrandizing and self-seeking interests which sustain patron-client ties.

Have the abusive features and manifestations of primordialism (particularly confessionalism) become so subversive that they are beginning to undermine whatever supportive or rehabilitative functions they might have once served? I wish instead, to argue that roots, to invoke the metaphor of the essay's title, have been thus far effective routes for socio-cultural and psychological mobilization. At least during certain interludes, when stripped of their bigoted and intolerant features, they became the bases for equitable and judicious forms of power sharing and the articulation of new cultural identities germane for co-existence and multiculturalism.

The paper is a reconsideration of both the enabling and disabling features of primordialism, to reassess their impact on Lebanon's political culture in the context of the unsettling internal, regional and global transformations the country has been subjected to during the past three decades. It explores three related dimensions. First, and by way of framing the discussion within a comparative conceptual context, an attempt is made to identify the circumstances which have reinforced communal and sectarian cleavages. Second, this is followed by a more concrete and substantive documentation of how the three salient forms of primordialism (kinship, communal and confessional solidarities) have responded to the forces which undermine their cohesion and collective identities. Finally, I explore the prospects of how this longing to reconnect with one's abiding but threatened roots may again become routes for the articulation of new cultural identities more germane for civil and peaceful forms of pluralism and guarded co-existence.

Three Salient Modes of Primordialism

For some time mainstream theoretical paradigms—i.e., those associated with modernization, Marxism and their offshoots—were quite tenacious in upholding their views regarding the erosion of primordial ties and loyalties. Despite the striking ideological differences underlying the two meta theories, they shared the conviction that ties of fealty, religion and community—which cemented societies together and accounted for social and political distinctions—were beginning to lose their grip and would, ultimately, become irrelevant. Indeed, to proponents of modernization theory, notions like familism, tribalism, confessionalism were not only pejoratively dismissed and trivialized, they were seen as obstacles to modernity. So-called "traditional" societies, in other words, were expected to break away and disengage themselves from such relics of pre-modern times if they were to enjoy the presumed fruits of modemity or to become full-fledged nation states.

Likewise to Marxists, communist and socialist regimes were perceived as "giant brooms" expected to sweep away pre-existing loyalties. If non-class attachments and interests survive or resurface, they are treated as forms of "false consciousness" to mask or veil fundamental economic and social contradictions. In short, ethnic and primordial loyalties were treated as transitory phenomena by modernization theorists and as epiphenomenon by Marxists. Both agreed, however, that primordialism was destined to disappear. Both, of course, have been wrong. It is a blatant misreading, if not distortion, of history in both advanced and developing societies.

Lebanon's political history, in both good and bad times, reinforces this self-evident but often overlooked or misconstrued reality. Throughout its epochal transformations—the emergence of the "principality" in the seventeenth and eighteenth centuries, the upheavals of the mid-nineteenth century and the consequent creation of the Mutesarrifate of Mount Lebanon (1860–1920), down to the creation of Greater Lebanon in 1920, the National Pact of 1943, the restoration of unity and stability after the civil war of 1958, and the aftermath of almost two decades of protracted violence—some salient realities about the ubiquity of recurring "retribalisation" are reconfirmed.

As the cruelties of protracted violence became more menacing, it is understandable why traumatized and threatened groups should seek shelter in their communal solidarities and cloistered spaces. Confessional sentiments and their supportive loyalties, even in times of relative peace and stability, have always been effective sources of social support and political mobilization. But these are not, as Lebanon's fractious history amply demonstrates, unmixed blessings. While they cushion individuals and groups against the anomie and alienation of public life, they also heighten the density of communal hostility and enmity. Such processes have been particularly acute largely because class, ideological and other secular forms of group affiliation have been comparatively more distant and abstract and, consequently, of less relevance to the psychic and social needs of the uprooted and traumatized. Hence, more and more Lebanese are today brandishing their confessionalism, if we may invoke a dual metaphor, as both emblem and armour. Emblem, because confessional identity has become the most viable medium for asserting presence and securing vital needs and benefits. It is only when an individual is placed within a confessional context that his ideas and assertions are rendered meaningful or worthwhile. Confessionalism is also being used as armour, because it has become a shield against real or imagined threats. The more vulnerable the emblem, the thicker the armour. Conversely, the thicker the armour, the more vulnerable and paranoid other communities become. It is precisely this dialectic between threatened communities and the urge to seek shelter in cloistered worlds which has plagued Lebanon for so long.

Massive population shifts, particularly since they are accompanied by the reintegration of displaced groups into more homogeneous, self-contained and exclusive communities, have also reinforced communal solidarity. Consequently, territorial and confessional identities, more so perhaps than at any other time in Lebanon's history, are beginning to converge. It is in this sense that "retribalisation" is becoming sharper and more assertive. Some of its subtle, implicit and nuanced earlier manifestations have become much more explicit.

Recently such symptoms of "retribalisation" have become more pronounced. Ironically, during the pre-war and pre-Ta'if periods when confessionalism was recognized, its manifestations and outward expression were often subtle. Groups seemed shy, as it were, to be identified by such labels. More so during the decades of the 50s and 60s when nationalism and often secular and so-called progressive and ideological venues for group affiliation had special appeal (see Melikian, L. and L. Diab, 1974). Today, as the sectarian or confessional logic is consecrated by Ta'if and, to the some extent, by public opinion, the overt expression of communal and sectarian identities has become much more assertive.

Universities, colleges, research foundations, voluntary associations, special advocacy groups, radio and TV stations are all being established with explicit and well-defined communal identities. So are cultural and popular recreational events and awards to recognize excellence and encourage creative and intellectual output. Even competitive sports, normally a transcending and neutral human encounter, have been factionalized by sectarian rivalries.

As the scares and the scars of war became more savaging and cruel, it is understandable that traumatized groups should seek refuge in their most trusted and deeply embedded primordial ties and loyalties, particularly those which coalesce around the family, sect, and community. Even in times of relative harmony and stability, kinship and communal groupings were always effective as mediating agencies. They have served as accessible and often innovative venues or routes for sociopsychological support, political mobilization and cultural change.

Among other things the cruelties of protracted and diffused hostility had drastically rearranged the country's social geography. Massive population shifts, particularly since they involved the reintegration of displaced groups into homogeneous and exclusive communities, rendered territorial identities sharper and more spatially anchored. It is in this sense that "retribalisation" became more pervasive. The term is employed here loosely to refer to the reinforcement of kinship, confessional and communal loyalties—especially since they also converged on tightly knit spatial enclosures. Lebanon, in other words, is being retribalised precisely because in each of the three basic groupings (i.e. family, community, and sect) loyalties and obligations and the density of social interaction which binds groups together are increasingly becoming sources of intense solidarity. A word about each is in order, by way of elucidating some of the salient manifestations and consequences of such resurgent primordialism.

Familism

The Lebanese family has always been a resilient institution. Despite the inevitable decline in the sense of kinship the family experienced in the prewar years—generated by increasing urbanization, mobility, and secularization—it continued to have a social and psychological reality that pervaded virtually all aspects of society. As repeated studies have demonstrated, there was hardly a dimension of one's life which was untouched by the survival of family loyalty and its associated norms and agencies. To considerable extent, a person's status, occupation, politics, personal values, living conditions and life style were largely defined by kinship affiliation. So intense and encompassing were these attachments that the average Lebanese continued to seek and find refuge and identity within close family circles. This was most apparent in the emergence and survival of family associations—perhaps unique to Lebanon. Even when other secular and civic voluntary associations were available, the family was always sought as a mediating agency to offer people access to a variety of welfare and socioeconomic services (Khalaf, 1971).

The war years have shored up the family's prominence. A significantly larger number of people found themselves, willingly or otherwise, enfolded within the family. By their own testimonies, they were drawn closer to members of their immediate and extended family than they had been before the war. They were also expending more effort, resources, and sentiments on family obligations and interests. As a result, the traditional boundaries of the family expanded even further to assume added economic, social, and recreational functions.

The concept of kin, or 'ayhleh, became more encompassing and extended beyond the limited confines of a nuclear family. The results of an empirical survey conducted in 1983, in the wake of the Israeli invasion of 1982, reconfirms the manifestations of such resurgent familism. For example only 12 percent of the respondents perceived the boundaries of their family to be limited to spouses and children. Almost 40 percent extended their definition to include both parents. Another 22 percent stretched it further to include paternal and maternal uncles. The remaining 27 percent extended the boundaries even further to encompass all relatives. The family was not only becoming more encompassing. It was also becoming more intimate and affectionate, reinforced by repeated visits and mutual help. 60 percent evaluated their family relations in such highly positive terms. The remaining 38 percent considered them as moderately so. Only 2 percent admitted that their family relations were distant, cold and had no sign of any mutual help or support.

As shown in Table 1, more than 58 percent of the respondents stated that their ties and relationships with their immediate families had been strengthened by the war. The incidence fell to about 23 percent for relatives and dropped to as low as 18.8 percent for colleagues. The respondents were also asked to indicate, on the conventional 5-point scale, the degree of their involvement in domestic and family affairs. More concretely an effort was made to assess the extent to which such family concerns were becoming more, remaining the same or becoming less important since the outbreak of civil hostilities. Here as well, and for understandable reasons, more than 60 percent of the respondents indicated that they had become more preoccupied with domestic and family affairs. Thirty-eight percent felt that there was no change in such relations during the war, and only 2 percent reported that domestic and family-centred interests became less important for them.

Given the large-scale devastation of state and other secular agencies and institutions, the family was one of the few remaining social edifices in which people could seek and find refuge in its reassuring domesticity and privacy. It became, to borrow Christopher Lasch's apt title, a *"haven in a heartless world"* (Lasch, 1979). During the war the family had to reinvent and extend itself to assume added functions. For example, beyond absorbing a larger share of the leisure, recreational, welfare, and benevolent needs of its members, it also served as an economic and commercial base. Many, particularly lawyers, craftsmen, retailers, and agents, were forced to convert their homes into offices for business operations. Housewives, too, were known to have used their homes to conduct a variety of transactions and to sell clothing, accessories, and other such items.

Table 1: Impact of the War on the Nature and
Identity of Social Relations

	Immediate family	Relatives	Friends	Colleagues
Strengthened	58.2%	22.9%	27.6%	18.8%
About the Same	39.4%	65.4%	57.5%	68.6%
Weakened	2.4%	11.7%	14.9%	12.6%
Total	100.0%	100.0%	100.0%	100.0%

Their longing to take shelter in the security and emotional sustenance of family ties and ancestral roots, in times of uncertainty and ambivalence, is understandable. Persisting uncertainties of the post-war interlude along with the unsettling transformations generated by the forces of globalism, consumerism, popular culture and mass entertainment have had added strains on the family. Demographic pressures, associated with the disproportionate outmigration of young professionals, skewed sex ratios, postponement of marriage, are generating acute tensions and sharper dissonance between parental authority and the liberalization of sexual norms and conduct youthful groups are prone to be receptive to.

Another inveterate feature of the resilience of kinship solidarities is the manner with which family ties and personalistic loyalties continue to shape the political process. In more than one respect, I argued in 1968, the whole political history of Lebanon can be described in terms of a handful of prominent families competing to reaffirm their name, power and privilege in their respective regions or political constituencies. Competition for political succession, particularly as it manifests itself in contentious electoral campaigns, remain the broadest arenas where such factional rivalries vent themselves. Nothing has transpired over the past three decades to dilute or undermine such elements.

Virtually all the prominent political families manage to find the circumstances to perpetuate their re-election into the parliament. I have elsewhere provided evidence to substantiate the magnitude and survival of such a reality (Khalaf, 1980). Indeed, over the entire span of fifty years of parliamentary life (1920–72), 425 deputies belonging to 245 families have occupied a total of 965 seats in 16 assemblies.

It is revealing that only 129 deputies (28 percent) of all parliamentary representatives are unrelated to other parliamentarians. The remainder, with the exception of approximately 10 percent of the earlier pre-Independence cases whose family ties could not be ascertained, bear some close or distant relation to other deputies. 45 percent of all parliamentarians can be considered closely related, through direct kinship descent or marriage, to other colleagues in the Chamber. Another 17 percent might be considered distant relatives. Altogether, in other words, 62 percent of the entire universe of deputies have some kinship attachments to other parliamentary families.

That there are oligarchic or "dynastic" tendencies is also apparent in the disproportion ate share of parliamentary seats a few of the prominent families have enjoyed. Altogether, not more than twenty-six families have monopolized 35 percent of all parliamentary seats since 1920. What this means in more concrete terms is that 10 percent of the parliamentary families have produced nearly one-fourth of the deputies and occupied more than one-third of all available seats.

A few other striking features of family succession are worth noting. Once initiated into political life, almost all the families have virtually had uninterrupted tenure in all successive Chambers. With the exception of one family (Gemayel), which entered the parliament in 1960, the majority had initiated their political career in the 1920s. This is quite telling, considering the prominent and decisive role the Gemayels, Pierre, his two sons Amin and Bashir, and grandson and namesake, came to play in the political life of the country during the past three decades.

In some instances, it is one man (Sabri Hamadeh), or fathers and sons (Arslan, Edde, Karameh, Ghusn, Khazin, As'ad, Skaff, Khuri, Zayn, Zuwayn, Gemayel, Tueni), brothers (Zayn, Edde, Shahin, Skaff), cousins (the five Solhs, four Khazins, two Gemayels, two Sihnawis, and two Kayruzes), or brothers-in-law (Hamadeh-As'ad, Salam-Karameh, Arslan-Junblat, Safiuddin-Arab) who perpetuate family succesion. In three particular instances—Frangieh, Gemayel and Khatib—three successive generations of grandfathers, fathers, and sons have already ensured the continuity of their family mandate in parliament. This is rather remarkable given the comparative recency of Lebanon's experience with parliamentary life.

The staying power of the family is particularly demonstrated during by-elections. In several instances when a parliamentary seat is vacated in mid term, the deputy is succeeded by a son, if he has an apparent successor, or relative. Magid Arslan, Kamel al As'ad, Antoine and Suleiman Franjieh, Zahir al-Khatib, Bahij al-Fadl, Maurice Zuwayn, Myrna Bustani, Abdallatif al Zayn, Amin Gemayel, Philip Taqla, Ma'rouf and Mustapha Saad—to mention a few—have all inherited their seats from a father, brother, or uncle.

Nearly all other *aqtab*, with an eye on their imminent retirement, have made manifest and unhesitant efforts to bequeath their political capital and influence to their children. Camille Chamoun, Saeb Salam, Suleiman Frangieh, Pierre Gemayel, Kamal and Walid Junblat, Ma'rouf and Mustafa Saad, among others, encouraged their sons to assume more visible public roles and delegated to them some of their official and unofficial responsibilities.

The above evidence is hopefully sufficient to confirm the continuity of kinship ties in political succession. In terms of both the number of seats they occupied and the successive assemblies they served in, it is clear that a disproportionately small number of families have been able to retain and extend their power positions. Expressed differently, at least a significantly larger number of families have demonstrated staying power in comparison to those whose political fortunes have suffered sudden set-backs. The political casualty rate among prominent families, in other words, is remarkably low. Only nine such families—Daouk, Beyhum, Sad, Thabet, Trad, Munthir, Nammur, Istfan, Abdel-Razzag—who were prominent politically in the pro-Independence era have since lost or disinherited their positions.

A caveat is in order. Opportunistic and unprogrammatic as most personal relation ships are, it is erroneous to assume that the whole structure of the body politic is sustained by personal and kinship alliances. The radicalization of the Shi'ites in the south, Beirut's suburbs, the Beqa'a or elsewhere, clearly speak otherwise. So does the divisive rift between those who differ regarding the presence and implications of Syria's intractable hegemony over Lebanon. What these and other such instances suggest is that the continuing dominance of personalistic loyalties does not preclude the existence of ideological rivalries. The political history of Lebanon—both remote and more recent—is replete with instances where purely personal and kinship rivalries are transformed into doctrinal conflicts and, conversely, where doctrinal and political issues have been reinforced by kinship loyalty. Despite the avowed and celebrated expressions and tokens of family solidarity, instances of political divisions and discord within families are legion.

Virtually all prominent political families, particularly those with perpetual seats in the Chamber of Deputies, cannot claim that they are the uncontested political spokesmen of their respective families. For example, the political standing of families such as Franjieh, al-Khazin, Murr, Lahhoud, Hrawi, Asaad, Zein, Salam, Karameh, Khalil—to mention a few—have all been splintered by inveterate schisms.

Communalism

Manifestations of resurgent primordialism have also been resurfacing at the communal level with, perhaps, greater intensity. Since the boundaries and horizons within which groups have been circulating are becoming more constricted, it is natural that these tightly knit localities should become breeding grounds for heightening communal and territorial identities. Inevitably, such bonding in exclusive spaces was bound to generate deeper commitments towards one's community and corresponding distance from others. In-group/out-group sentiments are consequently becoming sharper. Segmental and parochial loyalties are also more pronounced. So have the sociocultural, psychological, and ideological cleavages. In this sense the community, locality, neighbourhood, or quarter are no longer simply a space to occupy or a place to live in and identify with. They have become akin to an ideology—an orientation or a frame of reference through which groups interact and perceive others. It is then, that the community is transferred into a form of communalism.

Two unsettling, often pathological, features of such "retribalisation" are worth highlighting again. More and more communities, in the wake of protracted hostilities, started to assume some of the egregious attributes of "closed" and "total" entities. The two are naturally related. Comparatively mixed, hybrid, and open communities were becoming more homogeneous and closed to outsiders. Such polarization was bound to engender and sustain the growth of almost totally self-sufficient communities and neighbourhoods.

Since early in the initial stages of the war the traditional city centre and its adjoining residential quarters witnessed some of the fiercest rounds of fighting and destruction, the episodes were accompanied by a quickening succession of massive population shifts and decentralization. In no time business establishments and virtually all the major public and private institutions—including universities, schools, banks, embassies, travel agencies, and the like—took measures to establish headquarters or branch offices in more than one district. This clearly facilitated the proliferation of self-sufficient urban enclaves. Before the war, people by necessity were compelled to traverse communal boundaries to attend to some of their public services and amenities. Gradually the urge to cross over became superfluous and undesirable. As a result, a rather substantial number of Lebanese are now living, working, shopping, and meeting their recreational, cultural, medical and educational needs within constricted communal circles. More compelling, generations of children and adolescents have grown up thinking that their social world could not extend beyond the confines of the ever smaller communities within which they have been entrapped.

Some of the sociopsychological and political implications of such reversion to "enclosed" communities are grievous. The psychological barriers and accompanying sociocultural differences are becoming deeper and more in-grown. More and more Lebanese have been forced over the past two decades to restructure and redefine their lives into smaller circles. What is rather unsettling in all this is that they don't seem to particularly resent such restrictions.

A few results of the empirical survey we conducted in 1983, particularly those which reinforce the proclivity of groups to seek shelter in cloistered spatial enclosures and their corresponding inclination to maintain distance from other communities, are worth noting. Around 70 percent of the respondents indicated that their daily movements are restricted to the area or neighbourhood they live in. Surprisingly, a slightly larger number desire to live, work and confine their movements to such restricted areas. Only 22 percent were moving at the time, albeit furtively, between different sectors of the city.

The religious composition of the three broad communities from which the samples were drawn (Ras Beirut, Basta, and Achrafieh), must have, no doubt, enhanced their receptivity to sustain and encourage feelings of communal solidarity and to entertain unfriendly and hostile feelings toward other groups. The sectarian composition of our respondents corresponds to the religious profile we generally associate with those urban districts. Ras Beirut is the only fairly mixed district. The majority (40%) are Orthodox, followed by Sunnis and Protestants. The rest are almost equally distributed among Maronites, Catholics, Shi'ites, and Druze, with a few Armenians and other Christian minorities. On the whole, however, Ras Beirut is more than two-thirds Christian and around 27 percent Muslim. On the other hand, Basta is almost exclusively Muslim in composition, just as Achrafieh is almost exclusively Christian. The proportion of Maronites, Catholics, and Protestants is as negligible in Basta as is the proportion of Sunnis, Shi'ites, and Druze in Achrafieh. The only exception is perhaps the Orthodox. It is the only sect which is represented in the three communities, although to a much lesser degree in Basta.

It is natural that residents of such closely knit and homogenous communities should begin to display particular attitudes towards other sectarian groups. The war, judging by some of our preliminary results, has apparently sharpened such sentiments. The respondents were asked: "How do you evaluate your present feelings and opinions towards the groups listed below? Do you feel closer to them now than before the war, or do you have unchanged feelings, or do you feel more distant?"

The results reveal some obvious and expected tendencies that reflect the roles the various communities played during the war at the time of the survey and the consequent social distance between them. If we take the sample as a whole, 39 and 38 percent have grown more distant from the Kurds and Druze respectively and harbour hostility toward them. Next come Maronites (29%), Shi'ites (26%) and Sunnites (23%), followed by Syriacs (18%) and Armenians (17%). The rest, namely Catholics, Christian minorities, Orthodox, and Protestants evoke little or no hostility or negative feelings. Conversely, the respondents feel closer to Maronites (22%), Orthodox (19%) and Sunnites and Shi'ites (15%). Groups that elicit least sympathy are Druze (8%), Armenians (5%) and Kurds (1.6%).

It is interesting to note that, with the exception of the Druze, attitudes toward belligerent sects (Maronites, Sunnis, Shi'ites) invite both extremes. Nearly the same proportion who indicate that they have grown closer to a particular sect also display enmity and distance toward them. They are equally admired and admonished. It is also interesting in this regard, to observe that attitudes toward nonbelligerent groups or those who were not directly involved in the fighting, (i.e. Protestants, Christian minorities, Catholics, and Greek Orthodox) remained largely unchanged.

Confessionalism

Symptoms of primordialism are, doubtlessly, most visible in the reassertion of religious and confessional consciousness. What makes this particularly interesting is that religious and confessional loyalties manifest a few paradoxical and seemingly inconsistent features that reveal the sharp distinctions between them. Clearly religiosity and confessionalism are not and need not be conterminous. Indeed results of the 1982–83 empirical survey revealed some sharp distinctions between the two.

Curiously, as respondents indicated, their religiosity—as measured by the degree of changes in the intensity of their spiritual beliefs, religious commitments, and observation of rituals, practices, and duties of their faith—was declining. Their confessional and sectarian identities however were becoming sharper. When the respondents were asked whether the war had had an impact on the religious practices and activities, the majority (85%) admitted that they had not changed in this regard.

One could infer from such findings that the Lebanese are not taking recourse in religion in an effort to find some spiritual comfort or solace to allay their rampant fear and anxiety. To a large extent this kind of refuge is better sought and served in the family and community. Religion is therefore clearly serving some other secular—indeed socioeconomic and ideological—function. Some of the results clearly support such an inference. It is, in a way, revealing that when it comes to matters that reflect their religious tolerance and their willingness to associate and live with other sectarian or religious groups—such as the schooling of their children, their attitudes toward interconfessional marriages and their residential preferences—confessional considerations begin to assume prominence.

When asked, for example, whether they would agree to send their children to a school affiliated with a sect other than their own, close to 30 percent of the respondents answered in the negative—i.e. a preference to educate their children in schools with similar sectarian background. Their attitudes toward mixed sectarian or religious marriages—for both males and females—reveal much of the same sentiments. Close to 28 percent disapprove of such religiously mixed marriages for males and 32 percent for females. Similar predispositions were expressed regarding their preferences to live in a locality that has a majority of people from their own sect. Around 21 percent were sympathetic with such a prospect.

Altogether, a surprisingly large proportion of what presumably is a literate, cosmopolitan, and sophisticated sample of professionals, university and college teachers, intellectuals, journalists, and the like, displayed strong confessional biases, and a distance from and intolerance toward other groups. This was apparent in their disapproval of interconfessional marriages, their preference for parochial schooling for their children, and their reluctance to associate and live with other sectarian and religious groups. More poignant, perhaps, it was also becoming increasingly visible in this rather narcissistic preoccupation with one's community, with its corresponding exclusionary sentiments and phobic proclivities towards others. This heightened confessional consciousness, understandable in times of sectarian hostility and fear, started to assume fanatic and militant expressions of devotion to and glorification of one's group. The relative ease with which the various communities were politically resocialised into militancy was largely an expression of such aroused sectarian consciousness.

It is understandable, given the depth of such sentiments and their inherent association with feelings of collective security, solidarity and well-being of various groups, that they could be readily aroused in times of public discourse over the contested issues of power-sharing, electoral reforms, national identity, foreign policy, civil marriage and the like. But virtually all other debates, with no direct or visible link to sectarian interests or loyalties, become embroiled nonetheless in such overriding consciousness. In earlier epochs the expressions of confessional sentiments were nuanced, subtle and furtive. If and when invoked, it was always perceived as a pathology to be wished away or contained. Today the dissonance between its rhetorical expressions and explicit behaviour manifestations are more acute and poignant. It has also become much more invasive. It intrudes virtually every national discourse or public issue, substantive or prosaic. Hence, not only debates over electoral reforms, civil marriage, foreign policy, school curricula but even common-place and quotidian parliamentary debates on the budget, economic rehabilitation, monopolies etc... become suffused with confessional undertones.

Incidentally, the whole *sine-qua-non* of the Ta'if Accord was supposed to allay such visceral fears. Its legacy thus far has not been very felicitous in this regard. Ta'if, it must be recalled, was predicated on the effort not only to put an end to 15 years of protracted and displaced hostility, but to bring about a more balanced and equitable formula for power-sharing among the belligerent communities. Accordingly, while Ta'if preserved the custom of the Maronite presidency, the Shi'a speakership and the Sunni premiership, it greatly undermined the powers of the Maronite president while enhancing those of the prime minister, the council of ministers and the speaker. More unsettling are the explicit transformations which engendered the further marginalization of the Christian community.

Given such reawakened fears, more so since these are being exacerbated by the unsettling regional and global transformations, it is understandable that marginalized communities should seek shelter in their tested cloistered, communal and territorial solidarities. Indeed, this compulsion to huddle in compact, homogeneous enclosures has been reinforcing

Lebanon's "balkanized" social geography. There is a curious and painful irony here. Despite the many differences which divide the Lebanese, they are all in a sense homogenized by fear, grief and trauma. Fear, as it were, is the tie that binds and holds them together—three primal fears, in fact: the fear of being marginalized, assimilated, or exiled. But it is also those fears which keep the Lebanese apart. This "geography of fear" is not sustained by walls or artificial barriers as one observes in other comparable instances of ghettoisation of minorities and ethnic groups. Rather, it is sustained by the psychology of dread, hostile bonding and ideologies of enmity. Massive population shifts, particularly since they are accompanied by the reintegration of displaced groups into more homogeneous, self-contained and exclusive spaces, have also reinforced communal solidarity. Consequently, territorial and confessional identities, more so perhaps than at any other time, are beginning to converge. For example, 44 percent of all villages and towns before the outbreaks of hostilities included inhabitants of more than one sect. The sharp sectarian redistribution, as Salim Nasr (1993) has shown, has reshuffled this mixed composition. While the proportion of Christians living in the southern regions of Mount Lebanon (i.e. Shouf, Aley, Upper Metn) was 55 percent in 1975, it shrunk to about 5 percent by the late 1980s. The same is true of West Beirut and its suburbs. Likewise, the proportion of Muslims living in the eastern suburbs of Beirut has also been reduced from 40 percent to about 5 percent over the same period (Nasr, 1993).

Within urban areas, such territorial solidarities assume all the trappings and mythology of aggressive and defensive "urban '*asabiyyas*'" which exist, Seurat (1985) tells us, only through their opposition to other quarters. In this sense, the stronger the identification with one's quarter, the deeper the enmity and rejection of the other. Seurat's study also suggests that, once such a process is under way, a mythology of the quarter can develop. In it, the quarter is seen not only as the location where a beleaguered community fights for its survival, but also as a territorial base from which the community may set out to create a utopia, a world where one may live a "pure" and "authentic" life, in conformity with the community's traditions and values. The neighbourhood community may even be invested with a redemptive role and mission (such as the defence of Sunni Islam in the case of Bab Tebbane in Tripoli which Seurat was studying). Hence, the dialectics between identity and politics may be better appreciated. Politics implies negotiation, compromise, and living side by side with 'the other'. Heightened feelings of identity, however, may lead one to a refusal to compromise, if negotiation comes to be perceived as containing the seeds of treachery that may undermine the traditions, values and "honour" of one's community. In such a context, violence and polarization become inevitable: precisely the phenomena that have plagued Lebanon for so long.

To assert that sectarian affiliations have been reinforced by the war is, in many respects, documenting the obvious. It is, nonetheless, an affirmation worth belabouring, given some of the curious and pervasive features and consequences of Lebanese confessionalism. Lebanon's political history is replete with instances where sectarian loyalties evolved a dynamic of their own and became the most compelling forces underlying some of the major socio-cultural and political transformations in society. Even during periods of relative stability and normality, confessional allegiances have almost always operated, touching virtually all dimensions of everyday life. All the momentous events in a person's life cycle continue to be shaped by sectarian affiliation. It is a reality one cannot renounce. Early socialization, access to education, employment, welfare, hospital care, as well as many other vital services and personal benefits, are mediated through or controlled by sectarian foundations or agencies. Even a person's civil rights and duties as a citizen are, largely, an expression of one's sectarian identity. The *sine qua non* of the state is, after all, an embodiment of a pact—transfigured at times into a sacred covenant— between the various sects to preserve this delicate balance.

Although the two decades of rapid socio-economic change which preceded the outbreak of the war had ushered in some of the inevitable manifestations of secularization, the residues of seventeen years of civil unrest and random violence have eroded many of them. At least, the burgeoning class identities depicted, and at times heralded, by many observers prior to the outbreak of the civil war, have been grossly undermined. Indeed, sectarian sentiments and their associated clientelistic loyalties appear to have reaffirmed themselves more powerfully than ever before.

More pressing perhaps, is the role of sectarian organizations in dispensing relief and shelter and attending to much of the war-stricken needs of the homeless and traumatized. In this context, it is scarcely surprising that sectarian mobilization and the accompanying exacerbation of religious tensions and passions should become more pronounced. Indeed, confessional loyalties have become so intense that they now account for much of the bigotry and paranoia permeating the entire social fabric. More surprising, they bear an inverse relationship to the degree of religiosity. As we have seen, while religiosity, measured by the extent of changes in beliefs and the practices of religious duties, has been declining, confessional and religious biases and prejudices are becoming more pronounced. This implies, among other things, that religion is not resorted to as a spiritual force to restore one's sense of well-being, but as a means of communal and ideological mobilization.

Equally enlightening is the way Ta'if enshrined intercommunal consensus to sustain its solemn pact of communal coexistence (*al aysh al-mushtarak*) and safeguard the strained features of power-sharing and distributive justice as the defining elements of its political culture. This is at least a tacit recognition on the part of the architects of the Accord that nearly two decades of civil strife had done little by way of undermining the intensity of communal and sectarian loyalties in society. Ta'if, in other words, has judiciously opted to embrace, as Joseph Maila has argued, the "consensual, sectarian logic and accepted its dictates." This, once again, renders Lebanon "more of a contractual, consociative country than one based on a constitution. According to this tradition, the formal, legal framework is always subordinate to pragmatic, consensual approach to mitigating conflict within the country, and to managing national and communal strains" (Maila, 1994:31).

References

Hourani, Albert. "Ideologies of the Mountain and the City." In Roger Owen (ed.) *Essays on the Crisis in Lebanon* (London: Ithaca Press, 1976): pp. 33–41.

Khalaf, Samir. "Family Association in Lebanon." In *Journal of Comparative Family Studies* (Autumn 1971): pp. 235–250.

——. "The Parliamentary Elite in Lebanon." In Jacob Landau and Ergun Osbudun (eds.) *Electoral Politics in The Middle East* (London: Croom Helm & Hoover Institution, 1980): pp. 243–71.

——. "Ties that Bind: Sectarian Loyalties and the Revival of Pluralism in Lebanon." In *The Beirut Review* 1 (1) (Spring 1991): pp. 12–61.

——. *Civil and Uncivil Violence in Lebanon* (New York: Columbia University Press: 2002).

Lasch, Christopher. *Haven in a Heartless World: The Family Besieged* (New York: Norton, 1979).

Maila, Joseph. "The Ta'if Accord: An Evaluation." In Deirdre Collings (ed.) *Peace for Lebanon: From War to Reconstruction* (Boulder: Lynne Rienner, 1994): pp. 31–44.

Melikian, L. H. and L. N. Diab. "Stability and Change in Group Affiliations of University Students in the Middle East." In *The Journal of Social Psychology* 93 (1974): pp. 13–21.

Nasr, Salim. "New Social Realities and Post-War Reconstruction." In Samir Khalaf & Philip S. Khoury (eds.) *Recovering Beirut* (Leiden: E. J. Brill, 1993): pp. 63–80.

Seurat, Michel. "Le Quartier de Bab Tabane a Tripoli (Liban): Etude d'une Asabiyya Urbain", in C.E.R.M.O.C. (ed.) *Mouvements Communautaires et Espaces Urbaines au Machreq* (Beirut: C.E.R.M.O.C, 1985): pp. 45–86.

Abridged article from Theodore Hanf and Nawaf Salam (eds.) *Lebanon in Postwar Limbo* (Bader: Nomos Verlagsgesslschaft, 2003): 87–106. Printed here with the permission of the publisher.

MIRIAM GAZZAH

Maroc-Hop: Music and Youth Identities

Music and Youth Identities

Two musical forms highly popular among youths of Moroccan origin in the Netherlands, "Moroc-hop," and *shaabi*, permit youths to express specific and multiple identities in local contexts. Whereas these youths are often identified primarily as "Muslims" in the debates on integration and minority issues, they identify themselves according to very different categories.

Dutch-Moroccan hip-hop, or "Maroc-hop," was put on the musical map in the Netherlands in 2002 with the release of the hit-record, "K*tmarokkanen" ("F*king Moroccans") by the 25-year-old Dutch-Moroccan rapper, Raymzter. He wrote the song in reaction to a Dutch politician's remark that was accidentally picked up by a microphone and aired on national television in which he referred to Moroccan youths as "those f*king Moroccans." The enormous success of Raymzter's rap cleared the way for other rappers of Moroccan origin who have been active in the production of a growing hip-hop musical scene. In addition to hip-hop, a vibrant subculture has been constructed around Arab/ Moroccan popular folk music known as *shaabi* and which includes dance events, websites, and magazines. Maroc-hop and *shaabi* contribute in different ways to the construction of identity of Dutch-Moroccan youths within the specific context of contemporary Dutch society. While *shaabi* music gets used as a way to reinforce elements of an ethnic past and celebrates a Moroccan identity, Maroc-hop is infused with angst and is becoming an important means for youths to voice their frustrations with Dutch society.

Shaabi Music

The word *shaabi* is the Arabic word denoting "of the people," and refers, when describing music, to "popular" music. In the specific context of Morocco, *shaabi* represents a category of music consisting of different genres from different regions including, for instance, *reggada* music from Oujda and Berkane, and *rewaffa* music from the Rif. Various factors contribute to the popularity of *shaabi* music in the Netherlands: its musical composition, its lyrics, its availability, and, more especially, the events organized around it.

Shaabi music is readily available in the many Moroccan music shops in major cities of the Netherlands. Dance events are also key to *shaabi's* popularity among mainly second generation Dutch-Moroccans aged between 18–30. Organizers of these events attempt to create a Moroccan and Arab-Islamic environment by providing, for example, Moroccan food and the famous mint tea stands where people can sell Moroccan and Arab music, books on Islam, or jewellery. At most occasions there is no alcohol sold and people who are intoxicated are refused entrance. Dance parties, festivals, and concerts of famous *shaabi* artists such as Najat Aatabou, Senhaji, or Daoudi which can attract crowds of up to 3000, occur regularly.

Different types of *shaabi* events take place, among which are women-only parties, or "*Hafla Annisa.*" Mothers, friends, daughters, children, aunts, and nieces find in these women-parties a space where they can enjoy themselves, dance, sing, and interact with other women without any kind of male interference, Although the main attraction of these gatherings is the performance of *shaabi* music by both female and male musicians, the ingredients of these parties are somewhat different from the regular *shaabi* events. For example, there might be a fashion show demonstrating the newest Moroccan fashion or a workshop on how to apply *henna*.

Why does this music mobilize such large crowds of young people? If you ask young Moroccans why they go to these parties or listen to *shaabi* music, the answer often includes phrases such as, "I feel Moroccan when I hear this music. It evokes a sense of solidarity with other visitors!" Thus, these events satisfy a desire to be in, or return to, Morocco, even though it is only for a short time. *Shaabi* parties, in other words, represent a celebration of Moroccan identity.

The actual musical performance does not appear to be the central concern of the audience. The audience is usually more caught up in interacting with each other and often dance with their backs to the performers, seemingly not interested in what is happening on stage, but more concerned with becoming absorbed in the atmosphere and losing oneself in the moment. The performance of the artist thereby becomes part of the background while the performance of the crowd moves to the foreground. This losing oneself in the atmosphere of dancing enhances the feeling of solidarity. *Shaabi* musical events therefore enable youth to create a kind of coherent Dutch-Moroccan community. The emphasis here is on "coherent," because outside the context of concerts and dance events, one can hardly speak of a unified and coherent community The Dutch-Moroccan community is quite heterogeneous with the majority representing Berbers from the Rif, and the others a mix of mainly Arab-speaking peoples from different regions. Historically the Berber-speaking population has had a strained relationship with the Arab population. When Dutch-Moroccan youths come together in these musical contexts, internal differences seem to temporarily disappear.

Shaabi music also allows young people to incorporate elements of their parents' culture into their own youth cultures. *Shaabi*, a traditional musical genre, is infused with nostalgia for Morocco. In such a way *shaabi* music plays a significant role in the assertion and preservation of a Moroccan identity among Moroccan-Dutch youths, some of whom have never even been to Morocco. By means of music and events, these youths can express an identity that focuses more on being Moroccan in the Netherlands than on being Moroccan in Morocco. Additionally, they can glorify part of the culture of their parents without actual interference of their parents, and thereby retain their autonomy and independence.

Maroc-Hop

Hip-hop music occupies another important arena of popular music for Moroccan youths in the Netherlands, yet with a distinctly different history and effect. Hip-hop is an eclectic music known for its bricolage of sounds, beats, and text fragments. It originated in African American neighbourhoods in New York when, in the 1970s, youths started the genre by rapping over drumbeats. Hip-hop often incorporates bits and pieces from other songs, films, TV programmes, commercials, and street sounds, a technique referred to as "sampling." Nowadays hip-hop can be divided into several sub-genres: the so-called "boast rap" which thrives on materialism, and "message rap" which is characterized by social engagement and social criticism. Minority groups worldwide have found in "message rap" a vehicle to articulate frustration about their oftentimes difficult position in society.

The type of hip-hop that has been growing among Dutch-Moroccans can be called "Maroc-hop," since it has appropriated and adapted many elements from American hip-hop culture in specifically local ways. The emphasis on self-definition, for example, whereby the artist chooses a stage name that defines his role and persona, is emblematic of general hip-hop. Many hip-hop scholars consider these names to be a tool for marginalized youths to create prestige and status. They argue that most hip-hoppers come from lower class communities and have limited access to legitimate forms of status attainment in society and consequently resort to taking on new identities and names that enable them to obtain "street credibility" or prestige from below.

Rappers usually choose names that relate to their coolness, power, street smart, or supreme qualities as a rapper such as Ali Bouali (Ali B.), Brainpower, or Ladies Love Cool James (LL Cool J). Sometimes names relate to local neighbourhoods or cities (Den Haag Connections/The Hague Connections). Also, some artists choose self-mocking names or names that implicitly comment on society. For example, Ali B. chose this name referring to the way Dutch media speak about criminal suspects by reporting a first name and last initial, mocking the stereotypes about Moroccan youths as criminals.

Self-definition in Maroc-hop is based both on creating links with American or global hip-hop culture and on creating alliances with a local ethnic community. Many rappers have adopted an American style of self-naming, using abbreviations and American hip-hop terms, for example MC (i.e. Master of Ceremony) Berber. On the other hand, others have deliberately decided to maintain their "Moroccan" names, affirming an alliance with their ethnic background. For example, Soussi B, refers to the southern Moroccan Souss region. Yes-R is a wordplay on the Arabic name Yasser. Equally interesting is that these stage names often refer to hometowns of the rappers, signifying a connection with a Moroccan and a Dutch background.

The Messages

Among the recurrent themes of Maroc-hop are racism, Dutch politics, the war in Iraq, 9/11, and the Israel-Palestine conflict, revealing a considerable political consciousness. Many rap bands have written songs about Bush and Sharon in especially angry terms. In the repertoire of underground bands whose music largely circulates on the Internet such as Nieuwe Allochtoonse Generatie (New Foreign Generation) and The Hague Connections, several tracks blame Bush, Sharon, and the Jewish people in general for the misery of the Arab world. These songs reveal a strong identification with the Arab and Palestinian people and with Muslims in general. Islam is passionately defended by rappers who lash out at everyone who "attacks" Islam in whatever form. Moreover, there are many songs dealing with local topics such as Dutch politicians Pim Fortuyn and Ayaan Hirsi Ali. Both Fortuyn (murdered 6 May 2002 by an animal rights activist) and Hirsi Ali are known for their critical attitude towards Islam. Other rappers try to invalidate stereotypes about Moroccan youth, such as Ali B.'s song "Geweigerd.nl" ("Refused.nl") criticizing the policy of many Dutch discotheques to refuse entrance of groups of young Moroccans. Others have a more humorous way of addressing social issues, as illustrated in Samiro's rap, "Couscous." This song hilariously tackles stereotypes harbored by both the Moroccan and Dutch communities of each other. In the below verse (translated to English from the original Dutch), Samiro sings in a broken Dutch accent typical of a Moroccan migrant:

> *He is fed up and only wants couscous*
> *No French fries with chicken and no applesauce either (typical Dutch food)*
> *He is fed up and only wants to eat couscous*
> *They say: low fat but that is just on excuse*
> *I do not like French fries or Brussels sprouts (typical Dutch food)*
> *That is not good for me and I will never eat it again*
> *My friend invited me over for a fondue Bourguignon*
> *Afterwards I spent the night on the toilet*
> *Me, stomach-ache and nauseous, me shout: oh, no!*
> *I have to buy couscous, thank you very much, yes please*

A great deal of Maroc-hop's repertoire could thus be seen as a reaction to the exclusion of Moroccans in public debates about Islam, particularly since 11 September 2001. It represents an "artistic," if sometimes blunt, contribution to the debates. Maroc-hop, however, does not limit itself to political topics. Many songs glorify sex, violence, crime, drugs, love, and women. Rather than present themselves primarily as "Muslim," or "Moroccan," these rappers invoke identities based on local areas and "boast and brag" about their group of friends, their rap crew, and their rap qualities ("flow"). Members of this music culture, in other words, exhibit a strong identification with their Dutch context. Maroc-hop has attracted a growing audience because of its ability to offer its listeners a repertoire of identities as a hip-hopper, a foreigner, a Muslim, a young Moroccan, or just a young person in the Netherlands. Maroc-hop can simultaneously support, strengthen, and deny all of these identities, offering listeners the choice to select whichever identities suit the mood or the times.

This article is reprinted from *ISIM Review*(Autumn 2005): 6–7. Reprinted with permission of the Institute for the Study of Islam in the Modern World.

EGBERT HARMSEN

Between Empowerment & Paternalism

Do Islamic charities empower their beneficiaries or rather induce new forms of paternalism? The author argues that these options are not mutually exclusive. Dissecting the ideals and practices of Islamic charities in Jordan, he shows that empowerment and paternalism should be understood in their socially and ideologically informed contexts. While blind pursuance of self-interest is discouraged, the goals of improving society may have empowering implications.

The role of Islamic voluntary welfare associations providing services to subaltern groups such as the poor, orphans, widows, and disabled is—in academic as well as media discourse and debates— often emphasized in the frame of political trends of Islamic revival occurring in the Arab world. A few political scientists, Janine Clark in particular (2004), regard such associations as instruments of an effort of religious and moral colonization of underprivileged segments of Muslim societies employed by Islamist movements. She attributes much significance to the function of these associations in fostering cooperative ties among actual as well as potential Islamists from the middle classes. In other words, she focuses on the instrumental function of Islamic associations in the service of Islamist movements. The degree to which voluntary associations affiliated to political Islam may contribute to the empowerment of subaltern groups is hardly mentioned by them. Analyzing the role of Muslim NGOs in terms of the empowerment of the underprivileged, this article takes a closer look at this matter.

Voluntary welfare activism

The Muslim Brotherhood is by far the most prominent formally organized Islamist movement in Jordan. Unlike in Egypt or Syria, the Muslim Brothers are officially recognized by the Jordanian state and may, to a certain extent, undertake religious, social, and political activities openly and legally. Establishing voluntary associations that deal with the daily problems of the underprivileged segments of the society is an important strategy to spread Islamist ideology and influence in society. Jordanian legislation knows, however, many restrictions preventing such service-providing NGOs from playing too overt an oppositional role in the public sphere. Transgressions of these regulations may result in the arrest and imprisonment of NGO members as well as in the dissolution of the NGO in question (Wiktorowicz, 2002). This makes it impossible for these associations to mobilize subaltern groups into political struggle in order to improve their lot. Below, the example of an Islamist welfare institution serving orphans and their families will be given to discuss the question whether its activities are still contributing to the empowerment of subaltern groups, and if so, how.

The Islamist welfare institution in question is a centre for the poor and orphaned in Al-Hussein, the Palestinian refugee camp in Amman that I regularly visited in 2003. It belongs to the Islamic Centre Charity Society, the biggest Muslim Brotherhood-affiliated NGO in Jordan. This Society runs many such centres, in addition to medical centres, hospitals, schools, and even some institutions of higher education, all over the country. The centre gives financial and in-kind assistance to so-called orphan families, i.e. fatherless and mostly single-parent families that lack a regular income-provider. The centre offers educational, social, and cultural activities to the same target groups.

The dependency relationship between workers of the centre and the target group was underlined during my observations of the distributions of financial and in-kind aid. The mothers of the orphan families had to wait patiently and quietly in rows in a hall until they were called upon to receive their modest benefits. This was obviously not an example of self-organization by the underprivileged fighting for their own rights. Rather, this was a welfare initiative established and implemented by Muslims from the middle class delivering services to the needy. The centre receives the sources of financial and in-kind assistance mostly from local individual donors and sometimes from donors in the Arab Gulf States.

Many of the ethical messages in folders, brochures, and pamphlets are addressed to potential donors and supporters. The latter are called upon to give selflessly to the poor and orphans *fi sabilillah*, for the sake of God. Fulfilling this duty is supposed to counter one's greed and egoism, to have a morally purifying effect, and to enhance chances for divine reward in the afterlife. The poor recipients, in turn, are told to find inner peace in God by being thankful for that which He provides them, and by cultivating a patient attitude in life, In specific terms, this entails countering their greed and jealousy vis-à-vis the better off, The perfectly just Islamic society is supposed to be realized through a pious mentality or attitude of all the believers, regardless of rank, status, or wealth. Such an attitude has to be translated into honest, selfless, and helpful behaviour.

This orientation on duty is also reflected in the way the centre uses its financial and in-kind assistance as a means of pressuring the orphans and their mothers to participate in its educative and cultural programme. Religious ideology, in my experience, plays a central part in these educational efforts.

During a language class for orphan boys that I attended, for instance, only religious material was used. Among this material was a poem about the life of the prophet Muhammad. The teacher drew a parallel between levels of aggression against the Prophet and his first followers in Mecca and the present situation, during which Muslims were once again humiliated and threatened by others, especially the United States and "the Jews." The message was that Muslims had to regain power by restoring their mutual solidarity as a community of believers with its common faith in God and in His revelation. Similar political messages were expressed in a satirical play that the orphan girls at the centre were staging. In this play, they mock Arab rulers who betray their own people by collaborating with the Americans and the Israelis. At that occasion, the orphan girls and the centre's women workers also sang a song about Eid al-Fitr, the feast which concludes Ramadan. A message of social solidarity as well as protest is clearly discernible in the song. It deals with the fate of an orphan family that is economically unable to celebrate while wealthier people celebrate the feast in luxury.

Interviews with workers as well as orphans reveal that reading and reciting the Quran and the Hadith, and following the behavioural injunctions contained within both sources, play a central role in the activities and group discussions at the centre. Duties and responsibilities in the field of rituals, civilized and pious eating habits, ways of communication and modest dress, especially in the case of women, and the duty of older children to take care of smaller ones and of children in general to respect and obey the elderly or their older siblings are stressed.

In the view of the workers of this centre, religious duty is clearly connected to change and empowerment. Conversations with the orphan girls reveal that they understood the Islamic injunctions in terms of notions of dignity, taking one's responsibility, and developing and utilizing one's capabilities for the sake of beneficial purposes. There is a strong emphasis, for instance, on the importance of knowledge and education and high school achievements. The centre also tries to tutor orphan children in their homework for school. It emphasizes the value of work as a means of self-sustenance, and tries to obtain jobs for the older orphan boys by using its social networks. Furthermore, it offers the older orphan girls and their mothers training and some income in a sewing workshop and a bakery.

This example shows a blending of a paternalistic approach toward clients with certain ideas related to empowerment. Such empowerment, however, is here derived from a vision emphasizing duty toward God and toward the development of a strong and harmonious Islamic society.

Islamic piety and development

Other Muslim welfare NGOs that were visited and even some other centres of the Islamic Centre Charity Society are more obviously willing or able to cooperate with global and Western development actors, including non-Muslim ones. Such NGOs usually base their philosophy and practice of empowerment on global human, women's, and children's rights discourses that are enshrined in international treaties. Such an orientation is not necessarily at odds with a devotedly religious attitude, however. An Islamic women's association in a poor suburb in the industrial city of Zarqa, for instance, is working for the empowerment of school-dropout girls and their mothers from broken and socially weak families. Methods used by this association are literacy courses, a creative handicraft project, confidential discussions of personal and social affairs, and recreational outings. It is led by a woman who is also working as a religious teacher and social worker in a mosque. She wears orthodox Islamic dress, including the niqab or full veil, She was, at the same time, trained by Questscope, a British development organization supporting projects for "children at risk." In the name of the Islamic concept of *karam* or dignity, this association endeavours to enhance the self-esteem of the girls and their mothers, and to counter traditional habits that discriminate against females regarding their social and educational opportunities, Here we have a clear example of a process of hybridization between the discourse of Islamic piety and a modern and global development approach as promoted by Questscope.

Another example is the Al-Aqsa Association led by Nawal al-Fauri. She is an Islamist activist for women's and children's rights who left the Muslim Brotherhood in the 1990s out of frustration with the conservative and patriarchal attitudes among the organization's leadership. The Islamic message means for her that one should adopt a positive, friendly, and constructive attitude toward outsiders, including non-Muslims, and look for beneficial cooperation with them. With the support of several Western embassies, her association has implemented micro-credit projects enabling needy women to set up agricultural and stockbreeding farms. In the name of the Islamic message, the association carries out awareness raising activities for underprivileged women on social, cultural, and political issues, including gender. Again in the name of Islam, al-Fauri stresses that women have a right to participate in economic, social, and political life that is equal to that of men, and that a husband has to assist his wife in household tasks and the upbringing of children. Women, she states, should follow the will of God as it is revealed in the Islamic sources, and not the arbitrary and self-interested traditional habits and beliefs invented by men. In my experience, especially females belonging to Muslim, including Islamist, voluntary welfare associations are often critical of traditional gender habits discriminating against women.

Al-Faruq Welfare Society for Orphans, that is mainly active in the Palestinian refugee camp of the northern city of Irbid, is not Islamist in orientation. It provides nonetheless the same type of services to orphan, or fatherless families as the Muslim Brotherhood-affiliated centres for the poor and orphans are doing. Its educational and cultural programmes, however, are much less one-sidedly based on a religious doctrine. They pay as much attention to globally formulated human, children's, and women's rights. Their methodology toward orphan children and their upbringing is to an important extent adopted from UNICEF. This approach is focused on letting children discover their own individual qualities and taking their individual feelings and thoughts seriously, rather than on conformity with strictly conceived religious injunctions. However, the Society organizes Quran courses as well, and uses Islamic concepts in its discourse. A female social worker of the Society, for instance, saw in the Quranic principle of *himaya*, or protection of the woman, a basis for the struggle against women's abuse and domestic violence. The social workers use religious concepts like *rahma* (compassion), *tasamuh* (forgiveness and tolerance), and *sabr* (patience) to redirect communication within client families in the direction of mutual empathy, understanding, and respect and to counter practices of verbal and physical violence.

Between empowerment and paternalism

In the more conservative Islamist view, rights and empowerment are not primarily based on the assertive autonomy of individuals, groups, or classes, They can be realized only when Muslim society as a whole achieves an environment of social harmony and solidarity, thus implying that one's rights are necessarily embedded in social relationships of dependency. In this view, a Muslim's duty necessarily fulfils another Muslim's rights. A truly pious lifestyle, Islamists reason, will lead to true social harmony. prosperity, and justice. Concomitantly, they insist that blind pursuance of self-interest and "one's own rights" by any separate individual, group, or class will lead to the undermining, disruption, and disintegration of Muslim society. Such a worldview implies a confirmation and legitimation of existing social hierarchies and dependency relationships along the lines of class, age, and gender, even though the "stronger" are called upon to exercise their power with good care and consideration for the "weaker." Such a combination of power and care creates a relationship of paternalism and patronage. On the other hand, the stress of the Islamist discourse on shaping and improving one's actual behaviour and fully utilizing one's capabilities in a wide range of social fields, including ritual discipline, interpersonal relationships, education, training, and work, may have empowering implications on an individual level for men and women alike.

The Islamic message may also be used to criticize traditional practices often perceived as oppressive, for instance toward women or children, and as negative in terms of social cohesion and well-being in modern society. Muslim NGOs and Islamist social centres with more liberal orientations focus on the reinterpretation of the Islamic message in line with globally formulated rights principles, and on an active cooperation with transnational—including Western—development actors. On the other hand, fear of losing one's independence and cultural authenticity in the face of Western-dominated globalization processes is widespread. Islamist ideology is the most outspoken and dogmatic expression of this fear, but the same sentiment is shared by other Muslim associations as well. Generally speaking in Jordanian society, Islam stands for what is good —hence, working for a better social environment is often perceived first and foremost in Islamic terms. This may have implications for the choices international development partners have to make in the selection of local development partners. Secularist biases in the Western-dominated international development community may have to be critically rethought.

References

Clark, Janine A. *Islam, Charity and Activism: Middle-Class Networks & Social Welfare.* in *Egypt, Jordan and Yemen* (Bloomington & Indianapolis: Indiana University Press, 2004): 161.

Wiktorowicz, Quintan. "Embedded Authoritarianism, Bureaucratic Obstacles & Limits to Non-Governmental Organizations in Jordan." In *Jordan in Transition* (ed.) George Joffe (London: Hurst & Company, 2002): 115–122.

Originally published in *ISIM Review* (Autumn 2007): 10-11. It is printed here with the permission of the International Institute for the Study of Islam in the Modern World.

PART SIX

Gender Revisited

Introduction

One of the striking demographic features of Arab society is the disproportionately large size of its youthful population. Given the persistence of pro-natalist sentiments and high fertility rates, some of the Arab countries are handicapped by comparatively high portions (over 40 per cent) of the population who are 15 years and under. The implications of such an imbalance in our human resources are grievous. Among other things, it implies that fairly large segments of the population are still dependents, demanding sizeable investment and attention without contributing much in return. They are still largely parasitic and feel, since large segments of the youthful population remain unemployed and disengaged, correspondingly marginalized from and bitter towards a system that does little to allay their fears and apprehensions. In the language of Salwa Ismail, Arab youth masculinities today suffer from pervasive feelings of being "marginalized" and "injured".

In her essay on "Youth, Gender and State in Cairo", Salwa Ismail draws on the ethnographic fieldwork she conducted on young men and women in Bulaq al-Dakrur, a lower-class neighborhood. Her central argument is that young Egyptian men's construction of their masculine identity is shaped by a set of interrelated factors: the changing position of women in the household and in public, antagonistic relations with state agencies and the rising role of women as mediators with state institutions. To substantiate her thesis, she explores the following dimensions: first, she dwells on the role of fraternities (*Gam'iyyat*) in shaping masculine identity, their social engagements and political activism. Second, she focuses on the character of gender relations, particularly with regard to women's role as mediators with the state and their contributions to the finances of the household. Finally, she examines young men's everyday-life encounters with the state to show how these encounters undermine and disrupt their masculine identity.

Foremost, the fraternities or *Gam'iyyat* the young men establish serve their basic need for sociability. By appropriating street corners and workshop areas, they manage to produce a territorialized identity as *awlad al-Hara* or *awlad al-Hitta* (sons of the area). Their sense of masculine identity is largely a byproduct of cherished qualities and values of generosity and open-handedness with other fraternity members. Traits of *shahm* (dependable), *gada'* (tough and brave), and *kasib* (earner), which recall the classical *Ibn al-balad* masculine virtues are also celebrated.

Another aspect of fraternity relations involve an esteemed masculine attribute, labeled by Kandiyoti (1994) as "male nurturance":

> Through fraternal relations, young men secure needs both material and emotional. Their exchanges include help with getting a job, finding a bride, securing purchases, and subverting state regulations. Many of the young men I interviewed found jobs through the help of male friends from the neighborhood. They usually start working at a young age, while still in school or after dropping out. The bonds, ties, and exchanges between the men are constructed around

norms of trust, loyalty, and obligation. These relations take precedence over other considerations such as issues of legality.

In addition to sociability, fraternal relations also develop around religious associations, often with *Wahabi, Jihadist* or Islamist ideological orientations. These provide outlets for participation in religious activities such as reading groups, preaching, musical bands, and other pietist and activist organizations.

Another major issue of concern to men was declining morality and how to shelter women from such rampant demoralization. Hence, matters relating to the dress code (veiling) and the deviant conduct of women (restriction on their mobility and employment), assumed importance in asserting their masculine authority. Naturally, what is at stake here is the eagerness of men to exercise their authority as moral guardians of women's conduct; not only at home but also in the community.

Historically, young men from popular quarters fashioned themselves in valorizing terms as *awlad al-balad* (sons of the country). This masculine self came to be associated with the figure of the *futuwwa*. The *futuwwa* was a strong-bodied male who displayed physical strength and exhibited his manliness through acts of honor and courage—watching out for his female neighbors, intervening in neighborhood disputes, and so on. *Futuwwa*, in its etymology, signals an exultation of youth; its root, *fata*, means a male youth.

To Salwa Ismail perhaps the most vital aspect of her fieldwork was when she became aware of the role of women as mediators with state agencies, particularly with regard to how they can mobilize their manly attributes (*hiyya ragil*) to extract privileges and benefits. As one of her respondents told her: "The *harim* are tough. They can take the abuse at government offices, put up with being told off, and spoken to badly for the sake of getting the service." Also, women have acquired the *cultural capital* needed for negotiating the bribe, learning who gets it and how much to pay. In describing her performance as mediator with state agents, Um Hasan constructed womanhood in terms of strength, resilience, and appreciation of household responsibility.

Christa Salamandra, in her "Consumption, Display and Gender", considers an entirely different form of cultural and social capital, one which has direct bearing on women's sexuality and which also remains shrouded from public recognition or concern. Making judicious and creative use of Pierre Bourdieu's analysis of distinction, taste, and image-consciousness, Salamandra draws on her probing ethnographic fieldwork to explore how upper-class Syrian women manipulate the appearance of sexual purity and chastity as forms of social capital.

In a shame-oriented culture where sexual modesty is a highly cherished and jealously guarded expectation, any threat to it can have ominous implications for a woman's marriage prospects, let alone the honour and social standing of her family. Salamandra is fully aware that this longing of the Syrian woman to cultivate an attractive outward appearance and sex appeal—how they comport themselves, the spaces and encounters they seek to display and enhance their bodily endowments—is clearly not unique to the upper-class Damascene women she was studying. By treating, however, the phenomenon as a "chastity capital", a few of its unusual Syrian manifestations become more pronounced. First, there are symptoms of growing conflict generated by the dissonance between the burgeoning access to novel trends and venues of consumerism and the surviving traditional values of sexual modesty, family honour and patriarchy. The seeming preponderance of fashionable clothing, cosmetic stores, beauty parlours and the like should not be taken to mean that these venues and what they request are now widely accepted. Indeed, Syrian women seem more taxed than their cohorts elsewhere in the Arab world by the process of negotiating a coherent and workable identity that reconciles the virtues inherent in both sets of expectations and cultural scripts.

Salamandra's grounded ethnographic data allows her to suggest that at least in contrast to Cairo, where a thriving industry in ornate *hijab* clothing offers an alternative to the bland styles worn in Syria, Damascene women are left with the more cumbersome task of forging reconciliatory strategies that incorporate both stylistic features. Such efforts have not been very comforting. Indeed, as she argues, "women find it difficult to maintain a stylistic middle ground between the invisibility of *hijab*, and the flamboyance of the coquette". As one Damascene woman put it (in English), "we have cockteasers and *muhajjbat*, and nothing in between!"

Second, the obsession with safeguarding and enhancing one's "chastity capital" also accounts for the competition, often assuming intense rivalry, between women in pursuit of this scarce and cherished resource. This competitive display is so pernicious that it moves beyond public gatherings to intrude into the sanctuary of close communal networks and circles. Since prospects for any intimate encounters or liaisons are still tabooed, the gaze assumes special prominence. Hence the stakes and public regard for the representational self, to invoke Goffman (1959), become very high indeed. Incidentally, it is not only the gaze of men that is important. Given the pivotal role mothers, sisters and aunts play in finding an eligible young man a suitable bride the attention of other women is crucial.

So engrossed are women in the competitive struggle to acquire the outward trappings of the coveted "chastity capital," that little else seems to matter. Their behavior casts doubt on the alleged inferences feminist anthropologists often make regarding the social harmony and genial comradeship they believe still prevails among Middle Eastern women. Behind outward sociability lurks bitterness and jealousy that makes it difficult for Syrian women to sustain genuine and trusting friendships with other women.

Finally, and perhaps most central to Salamandra's overriding concern with "chastity capital," particularly within the context of an acute marriage market, are her central premises that sexual appeal, how to procure it and gain access to spaces in which to display it, are surpassing other conventional measures of social worth and esteem. Such consuming negotiating strategies naturally come with a cost. Women, much more than men, remain "victims" of the inconsistent demands inherent in two salient cultural scripts: they are expected first to be sexually attractive. This abiding norm is internalized during early childhood socialization when young girls are encouraged to be coquettish, coy, even flirtatious. Peer pressure during puberty and tantalizing media images of global consumerism, which place a high premium on sensuality and eroticized images, accentuate such expectations. But this is in stark opposition to another more impermeable cultural script; a taboo-like condemnation of any form of sexual conduct or intimacy. This, if anything, is a textbook instance of anomie. Syrian women, in other words, like elsewhere in the Arab world, must negotiate an identity which reconciles these two dissonant demands. They are revered for being sexually attractive but admonished if they resort to any form of sexual activity.

The poignant narrative of the late Mai Ghoussoub that tells the story of her birth as a second daughter as told by her mother, is suffused with juxtaposed values and contradictions. Her parents, much like other emancipated middle-class Lebanese families who shuttled between their mountain resorts (in her case *beyt shabab*) and the Christian neighborhoods of East Beirut, lived at a time of transition. Though educated and keen about the virtues of westernized nuclear family, liberal schooling and bringing up free and responsible children, they still displayed more than just a ritualistic belief in the traditional values of family honor and the sexual modesty of young girls, salient in the 1940s and 1950s. At least her parents were clearly more emancipated than the family doctor who delivered her. He felt that his social standing and self-worth as a gynecologist was undermined every time he ushered another female into the world!

Little wonder that Ghoussoub's adolescence was beset by her "desperate, not always unhappy, effort to reconcile at least two epochs, two modes of behavior, two value systems that prevailed simultaneously and very concretely in prewar Lebanon." The emancipation of her parents notwithstanding, she grew up with the tainted and damaged label of a "*garçon manqué*"; not just a tomboy, for the French expression is more compelling—literally, a "boy missed." To Ghoussoub, already a precocious social rebel, being a *garçon manqué* epitomized the predicament of her country; a precarious republic which had missed its democratic and tolerant potentialities.

SALWA ISMAIL

Youth, Gender, and the State in Cairo: Marginalized Masculinities and Contested Spaces

This chapter examines the interplay between young men's interaction with the Egyptian state, their constructions of masculinities, and gender relations. More specifically, it interrogates how gender relations, state practices of control, and constructions of masculinities, as sites of power and domination, traverse one another and contribute to a state of flux that may open up possibilities for challenge and defiance on the part of differently situated subordinate subjects. Gender as a social category, mediates interaction with the state. In turn, state practices—themselves gendered—shape gender constructions in terms of negotiating masculinity and femininity. Drawing on fieldwork I conducted among youths in Bulaq, I inquire into how their daily encounters with the state interact with the social construction of gender and the enactment of masculinity. I argue that by virtue of their class position and their experience of subordination, young men locate themselves in the power hierarchy through constructions of masculinity that not only express their marginalized position but seek to reproduce hegemonic masculinity. I draw attention to the fact that this construction is contextually shaped and takes the expression of an "injured masculinity" that youths negotiate through acts designed to reproduce their dominance at home and in their circumscribed public space. Meanwhile, the spectacle of injured masculinities combines with ongoing changes in gender relations in the family and in public to open up a space for women to question hegemonic masculinities. The disruption in gender relations and the experience of injured masculinities also inevitably shape young men's meditations on relations with the state. The terms in which they incorporate this experience may be read as ranging from submission to rebellion.

Gender relations and class position are central to understanding the trajectories of youths, their terms of political engagement, and their social activism. For young men the construction and assertion of their masculinity is articulated in terms of the preservation of the patriarchal relations of domination over women. These relations are also imbricated in their households' interaction with state agencies and their own relations with the state. My central argument is that young Egyptian men's construction of their masculinity is shaped by a set of interrelated factors: the changing position of women in the household and in public, antagonistic relations with state institutions involving violence, and the rising role of women as mediators with state institutions. As a counterpoint to young men's narratives, women's views on norms governing gender relations, their position in the family, and their role as mediators with the state enhance our understanding of the politics of everyday power relations in the family, and social hierarchies.

The analysis is situated in the context of the shift in state–society relations in Egypt, from the politics of welfare to the politics of security. With the state's withdrawal from its role of development agent and welfare provider, its apparatuses of violence expanded their reach and intensified their activities. Indeed, violence was a hallmark of the state's response to Islamist activism and challenge in the 1980s and 1990s. By the middle of the 1990s, with the Islamist challenge contained, more diffuse strategies of state control were put into effect. These included the normalization of the country's emergency laws by writing them into the legal system, as was the case with the law on combating terrorism. They also included passing laws targeting young men from popular neighborhoods, namely *Qanun al-Baltaga* (the law on thuggery) of 1998, as well as the expansion of surveillance and monitoring by the police in the form of security campaigns (*hamalat amniyya*) carried out in these neighborhoods.

Youths in the Middle East, especially young men, have been important actors in oppositional movements in the region, particularly in Islamist movements. However, the literature on social forces and the state in the Middle East tends to leave youths out or to incorporate a discussion of youth into wider analyses focused on class or family. Yet, we know that youths have engaged in developing their own forms of organization and modes of activism. These are inscribed in their everyday-life structures and are deserving of closer scholarly attention. Studies of Islamist movements have focused largely on the socioeconomic conditions and ideological beliefs motivating activism. My interest here is not to investigate the factors that have contributed to the rise of such movements. Rather, I argue that an understanding of male activism must inquire into everyday forms of male social organization and sociability such as fraternities as well as changing dynamics of gender relations and how these factors come to bear on young men's positioning vis-à-vis the state.

The chapter draws on my ethnographic work with young men and women, aged between fifteen and thirty years, in Bulaq al-Dakrur. The first section explores the role of fraternities in shaping masculine identity and young men's social engagement and political activism. Young men's membership in a variety of Islamic organizations, such as *al-Tabligh wa al-Dawa* and *Ansar al-Sunna al-Muhammadiyya*, and in religious musical bands, as well as the fraternal relations they develop in workshops and in the neighborhood, contribute to a sense of solidarity and to the building of social networks beyond the family. It will be argued that work relations, spaces of sociability, and patterns of spatial mobility reinforce a spatial identity that is quarter-based and linked to a lifestyle and a particular set of social norms. Against this background we can comprehend the constructions of masculinity, gender relations, and interaction with the state.

In the second section, the discussion is structured around young men's discursive constructions of gender relations and the ongoing negotiation of these relations. Two factors are of particular importance to understanding these relations: women's role as mediators with the state and their contributions to the finances of the household. The final section examines young men's everyday-life encounters with the state. My objective here is to show how these encounters disrupt the dominant masculine construct while instituting men in oppositional positions to the state. This disruption helps explain the ongoing process of renegotiating gender relations in the family and in public. Further, these encounters are important to any investigation of the potential for organization and activism among young men.

Fraternities, Sociability, and Family Obligations

Young men develop fraternal relations and establish fraternities around a number of social activities and institutions, depending on their life trajectories and on their position in these trajectories (e.g. employed/unemployed; married/single) at a given point in time in their life cycle. For example, fraternities may take shape in school or, more commonly, develop around workshops among young men who have dropped out of school. In Bulaq, neighborhood fraternities are linked to work, religious activities and quotidian practices of sociability. These tend to overlap as bases of association. Young men working in various crafts or skilled occupations belong to the same networks because of the spatial proximity of their work. Thus, on *Gam'iyya* Street, one of the main commercial arteries of the area, a group of mechanics, grocers, and house painters belong to a common fraternity.

What do fraternities and fraternal relations involve? First, there is a great deal of sociability among the men. They share their meals and spend leisure and break time together. They buy their meals from shops in the area and eat together in their workshops. Sharing a meal entails mutual obligations of loyalty and generates relations of trust as it establishes the bond of *'aysh wa malh* (bread and salt). Spending leisure time together in coffee shops or in their workshops reinforces fraternal bonds. For example, Sameh, Fathi, and Nagi spend their Sundays on *Gam'iyya* Street in front of Sameh's shop. They congregate there, even though shops are closed on Sundays, because of familiarity, a feeling of safety, and the sense of having a place that is theirs. Thus, the shop and the street serve as spaces of sociability. This particular fraternity comprises Sameh, Fathi, Nagi, Muhammad, Ra'fat, Sabri, and Hamdi.

By appropriating the street corners or the workshop areas and investing them as safe and familiar spaces, young men produce a territorialized identity as *awlad al-hara* or *awlad al-hitta* (sons of the area). This practice is grounded in the organization of the *hara* as a basic social and political unit. The issue of the territorial identity of youth deserves closer attention when examining questions of activism and youth relations with the state. Territorial markings are lines drawn in contest. Thus, to produce a territorial identity is to establish spatial title in relation to others, including the state. In Algiers, *oulad-al-houma* (sons of the quarter) constituted the rank and file of Islamist gangs in the period of confrontation with the state (Martinez, 2000).

A great deal of the daily lives of the men in fraternities is spent on the street. For example, Sabri's workplace is in the street, on the corner of a little alley and *Gam'iyya* Street. He parks the motorcycles that are brought to him for repair under the window of his grandmother's first-floor apartment, located in a building along the alley. He does the actual repairs at the corner where the street and the alley meet; in effect, the street corner is his workshop. He worked in this spot for a number of years. Repairing motorcycles is noisy work, but because of Sabri's social relations with the neighbors and his close contacts with other workers in the area, the noise is tolerated. He had at one time relocated to rented premises outside the neighborhood. However, he did not get a permit for the business and was forced to close the shop. He subsequently returned to the alley. Although his home is in the alley where he works, he spends his break times at the nearby coffee shop, buying drinks for himself and his friends. He goes home to sleep. Indeed, a significant portion of Sabri's earnings is spent in the coffee shop. In contrast, he makes a contribution of only ten pounds per week to his grandmother's household.

Sabri's own trajectory illustrates the importance of workshop-based ties. He began as an apprentice with a motorcycle mechanic who had a shop in another alley, not far from the street corner where he now conducts most of his business affairs. Sabri says that this mechanic was like a father to him—he taught him the trade and looked after him. Sabri recalls that whenever he would run away from home, his *usta* (master craftsman) would go looking for him and bring him back.

Like Sabri, most of the young men I interviewed spend some part of their income on sociability within the *hara*. Generosity and open-handedness with other fraternity members are qualities that are given importance in these young men's conception of the masculine self. Also important are the traits of *shahm* (dependable), *gada'* (tough and brave), and *kasib* (earner), which all recall the classical *ibn al-balad* masculine construct of the popular-class male who embodies the spirit of the country (see El-Messiri, 1978). This aspect of the masculine construct may exist in tension with the household responsibilities identified with being a man, particularly with the role of provider. The demands of sociability and fraternity compete with family obligations. Many of the young men stated that they had family responsibilities and that they had to contribute to their household income. However, as will be shown below, in many instances, sociability demands took precedence over family expectations.

The young men in the workshops were the ones in their families who took a trade in support of parents or siblings. For example, Sameh, at twenty-one, is his family's main breadwinner. He has a high school level diploma in commerce and completed two years of a college level degree before dropping out. He is in charge of the family-owned bicycle repair shop, being the only child who learned the trade from his father. His older brother is a cab driver and is married, so he takes care of his own family. Sameh also has two younger brothers for whom he feels responsible. This includes helping them with their schooling expenses and, eventually, with their marriage expenses. Similarly, Fathi, who earns between twenty and twenty-two pounds per day from his job as a furniture painter, believes that he must assume the expenses for his sister's marriage because he became the household head following his father's death.

Other dimensions of fraternity relations have to do with what Deniz Kandiyoti (1994) refers to as expectations of male nurturance. Through fraternal relations, young men secure needs both material and emotional. Their exchanges include help with getting a job, finding a bride, securing purchases, and subverting state regulations. Many of the young men I interviewed found jobs through the help of male friends from the neighborhood. They usually start working at a young age, while still in school or after dropping out. The bonds, ties, and exchanges between the men are constructed around norms of trust, loyalty, and obligation. These relations take precedence over other considerations such as issues of legality. For example, Ali hired Ahmad as a driver of a minivan that he owns even though Ahmad does not have a driver's license (he needs a literacy certificate to obtain one). In Ali's view, trust in a male friend is more important than the legal regulation. Also, Ali introduced Ahmad to his fiancée and influenced him to quit drugs. In turn, Ahmad agreed to guarantee the installment payments on furniture purchased by Ra'fat. He also helped to find and convince a marriage registrar to contract Ra'fat's marriage, despite the fact that the latter does not have an identity card. These exchanges confirm moral obligations and norms of reciprocity. The young men exercise influence over each other—through advice and moral pressure they may succeed in getting one to quit drugs or another to attend lessons in the mosque.

Drug consumption organizes an alternative form of sociability. There is a widespread view that the majority of young men in the area have, at some point, experimented with or been addicted to drugs. Among the men I interviewed, some were addicted to drugs while others had successfully fought off their addiction. This, to some extent, parallels what Luis Martinez (2000) highlighted about young men in popular neighborhoods in Algiers. There Martinez points out youths were confronted with two choices: to join either *hizb al-zalta* or *hizb al jami'* (the party of drugs or the party of the mosque).

Drug dealing and abuse have become sources of conflict in the area. For example, failure to pay dealers, competition between dealers and drug addiction itself are all causes of fights in which knives and other weapons are used. In fact, several drug-related criminal cases have involved murder and grave injuries. This situation is viewed as threatening. Area residents think the government is doing little to control the problem and, in some instances, identify the police as part of the problem. As will be shown in the following section, activities of moral regulation are central to both pietist and militant religious groups. Furthermore, the management of public morality, as such, constitutes common ground for much youth activism.

Religious Networks and Fraternities

Fraternal relations also develop around religious practices and associations. The narratives of the young men participating in religious activities indicate that much of the recruitment is neighborhood-based and tied in with relations of sociability. My findings also point out that there is a multiplicity of religious groupings and discourses invoking different understandings of religion. At the same time, the articulations of a personal view of what it means to be a Muslim, a believer, and *multazim* (person who is religiously observant) are linked to general ethical concerns while also entering into the constitution of moral selves. Through their daily practices, social relations, and interaction, the youths are engaged in the construction of moral selves. In what follows, I situate this construction in relation to the various life trajectories of young men participating in a variety of religious groupings such as *Ansar al-Sunna al-Muhammadiyya, al-Tabligh wa al-Da'wa,* and religious musical bands.

Ayman and Mamduh are members of *Ansar al-Sunna al-Muhammadiyya,* a religious association known for its *wahabi* ideological orientation. Ayman is twenty-six years old. He dropped out of preparatory school and is now a manufacturer of leather jackets. After his apprenticeship in leather-goods manufacturing, he moved into sales, procuring goods on credit from leather manufacturers. He used the profits from sales to start his own manufacturing business, which he set up on the first floor of his mother's house. His younger brother Muhammad works with him. At the time that I met him, Ayman had been a *multazim* for three or four years. He had been recruited into a religious fraternity by his friend, Mamduh, who took him to hear a preacher at an Ansar-run mosque. Following that, Ayman, Mamduh, and other friends went from one mosque to another to attend religious lessons given by Ansar preachers. They consider themselves to be followers of Sheikh Muhammad Hasan, a preacher whose taped sermons and religious lessons are in wide circulation. Ayman and Mamduh share their readings and adopt a similar posture in their social relations in the *hara*—abstaining, for instance, from "speaking idly to women." The subjects of their readings underline their concern with issues of ethics and morality and the growing influence of conservative Islamist discourses.

Ayman, along with the other members of his reading group, preaches on morality issues. The group was in control of the *Gam'iyya al Khayriyya* mosque. Ayman's membership in the group integrated him into the family of a preacher whose daughter became his fiancée. He is now a disciple who aspires to become a preacher. He calls his friends to do the prayer and leads all-night prayers called *tahajjud* which commence at one o'clock in the morning and continue until the dawn prayer. The *tahajjud* consists of prolonged prayers in which the worshiper is expected to show profound humility before God. As noted by Hirschkind (2001), these practices of self-discipline and piety enter into the constitution of moral personhood.

Ayman advises his family on religious matters. He has also recruited his brother Muhammad into the group. Their preaching activities involve sharing readings with others and distributing tapes of their favorite preachers. However, Ayman stressed that they do not put pressure on others nor use force.

M. Sayyid, a twenty-five-year-old accountant, is a member of a religious musical band that plays percussion instruments only, such as *tabla, duf,* and *simbala* (tambourine), in the belief that electronic instruments are un-Islamic. He joined the band upon the encouragement of a university friend. The friend is a *multazim* whom M. accompanies to the mosque to attend religious lessons. They are not involved in preaching activities, but in *'ibada* (worship) which M. sees as a form of action, namely "doing good". The band performs at weddings, beginning with Quranic recitations and followed by religious songs. The idea is to promote *halal* (licit) practices. He says he is indebted to his friend for encouraging him to pursue a life of good deeds. Such expressions of gratitude, as well as the confirmations of fraternal bonds among male friends, were enunciated by the majority of my male informants. According to M. Sayyid, income from the performances is used to "do good." For example, the band uses part of the money to pay the *Hajj* (pilgrimage) expenses of one of their members, selected by means of a lottery draw.

The pietist groups to which the youths belong are often seen as passive and sometimes as opponents of militant action and *jihadist*-type Islamism. However, this view of the groups does not address the central question of how the cultivation of piety shapes self-positioning in social and political terms. I do not wish to argue that religiosity and devoutness create a predisposition to militancy. Rather I want to draw attention to the possible passage from *multazim/mutaddayyin* (observant/devout) to active Islamist.

If we look at the practices of the youths in religious fraternities and musical bands, we find signs of the ongoing processes of re-Islamization whereby signs and symbols from Islamic traditions are reinvested in various domains of social life. For example, the grid of *halal* and *haram* (licit and illicit) is applied to musical instruments and adding celebration rituals. Also, the Islamic position on the permissibility or impermissibility of various practices is developed. This ongoing re-Islamization attests to the sociality of Islamism and to the fact that its significance cannot be assessed only in terms of the fortunes of militant Islamist groups.

Members of religious groups follow particular preachers, listen to their sermons, and read their pamphlets. They may invoke their authority in choosing a course of action or determining the appropriateness of an act. Undoubtedly, the re-Islamization of cultural practices and the interpretative frameworks articulated in reference to Islamic traditions are variables that help make Islamist movements appealing. A good example of this is the control of women's conduct. Islamists' involvement in the monitoring of gender interaction and the management of relations between the sexes is inscribed in realms of governance that continue to be important (Ismail 2004).

The socio-political position of Mahmud, and of many other young men, confirms that the micro-context of mobilization is favorable to protest activities and movements. An important factor here is that oppositional positioning vis-à-vis the state is shared by many youths. At the same time, there are constraints on mobilization. First, state policing of protest presents serious constraints on the broadening of collective action beyond the neighborhood. Second, militant groups' confrontational and violent strategies foreclosed other courses of action that were necessary to widen their base of mobilization (e.g., the jama'at was not open to entering into an alliance with the Muslim Brotherhood on university campuses; rather, its members clashed with MB members). These kinds of constraints help explain the current impasse of militant Islamism. We should also take into account the strategies adopted by official Islam to discredit the militants.

Youths and Gender Relations: Marginalized Masculinities and the Community of Women

In my discussions with young men, issues surrounding gender relations appeared to be of utmost concern. While discussing problems of the quarter; young men spoke repeatedly of declining morality. Occasionally, this assessment was qualified in comparative terms, by reference to well-off districts of the city where, they observed, there is less morality. The sign of immorality evoked most often was the dress and public conduct of women. The narratives of women's transgression tended to follow a common line of girls and young women dressed immodestly and going out with boys. Fathi noted that women wear a "body" (a tight-fitting top, *'biyilbisuh al-body'*), stretch pants, and tights, in addition to makeup. He commented that "a girl speaks to one boy and ten more." Nagi stated that girls were too forward in their interactions with boys—they approached or would "go after" boys. Similarly, Mahmud's main criticism with respect to morality was focused on women's attire and loose behavior. He gave examples of women in coffee shops in Muhandissin "smoking shisha" and women in Bulaq "using bad language."

A number of young men did not think the veil was a guarantee of women's morality and good behavior. In fact, they related abundant stories of women using the veil as a cover for compromising conduct. The motif of women removing their veils in particular settings is not present only in the narratives of Bulaq male youth, however. It is incorporated into other men's commentaries about women and sexual morality. For instance, I have been told similar stories by taxi drivers referring to the conduct of women clients in their taxis. The predominant motif of this imaginary is of women as potential transgressors and as strong candidates for breaking the moral code.

Another recurrent theme in the men's narratives is that of intervention to correct transgressive conduct by young women. Young men recounted instances of approaching young women and admonishing them for what they consider improper behavior. This performance constitutes a public enactment of their manhood, by which masculine identity is territorially inscribed: the young men perceive their assertion of their masculinity in taking steps to reinstitute the moral order in their neighborhoods. For this enactment to take place, other performances are undertaken, including the monitoring of the comings and goings of women in the neighborhood. From the vantage point of their workshops and the coffee shop, Fathi and Mahmud appear to be performing this monitoring of young women. If they see them immodestly dressed or speaking to a stranger, they talk to them. Here they find another sign of moral decline. This emerges in the responses of the young women's families to their interventions. A number of young men said parents objected to their intervention or accused them of trying to sully their daughter's reputation. One young man said he did not walk out with his sister for fear that others may mistake him for a boyfriend.

Let us recall that the Islamists' appeal to young men had to do with this kind of masculine enactment. A common practice of Islamist activists was to patrol the streets together as a group with the aim of managing public morality by enforcing the veil, ensuring the separation of the sexes, and punishing transgressions. In the absence of this kind of organized monitoring, the men expressed concern in terms of the effects that parents' objections to this practice of intervention would have on women's morality. The main worry, as stated by Nagi, Fathi, and Sameh, is how to find a good wife. They represented the search for a moral partner as a bigger problem than getting a flat. Given how difficult it is to obtain an affordable flat in Cairo, it would seem that these young men consider it almost impossible to find a good wife. In this respect, their monitoring of neighborhood women is also designed to locate a potential partner, someone who has not been out with another man and who, in principle, would not go out with them either.

The majority of the married young men in the area chose their wife after a period of monitoring or upon the recommendation of a trusted friend. Most of the chosen marriage partners come from the area and are part of the family network.

These views on gender relations are shared by both educated and uneducated young men. The desire to restrict women's mobility is also expressed in these young men's rejection of having working partners. The men framed their rejection of women's work in terms of familial roles; that is, women are seen as child raisers and men as breadwinners. They also did not wish to have wives out in public, seen by or interacting with other men. It is also within the familial role of women as child raisers that they explained their preference for having educated wives. They all thought that the education of women was important and wanted to have educated wives who can help the children with their schoolwork and be good mothers. Many of the men were uneducated, yet they married women with intermediate levels of education. They will also educate their daughters, but would leave it up to their future sons-in-law to decide on the work question.

Young women's views on the need for the social control of women were diametrically opposed to those expressed by young men. They considered talk about young women's conduct, especially among young men, as gossip and as a social practice designed to control them. They did not see any harm in speaking to boys from the area, although they had reservations about interacting with outsiders. In many respects, young women engaged in activities that challenged notions of male authority in the household and confronted male practices of control. Dunya, an eighteen-year old who studies crafts in high school and sees a boy from the *hara*, took judo lessons and believed herself to be a man's equal. Huwayda, a divorced single mother, sought financial independence through employment and securing social security from the Ministry of Social Affairs to support her children. She viewed financial independence as important to her freedom of movement, especially her ability to go out without being asked by her brothers about her comings and goings. She went back to night school in order to improve her employment opportunities. Raga', a young divorced woman who lives with her brothers, accused neighboring men of gossip and objected to their interventions regarding the fact that her brothers received male friends in their house. For these young women, work and education helped them achieve their independence in the family.

How should we interpret young men's denial of women's contributions and their elevation of the problem of finding a suitable marriage partner to an overarching level, high above the challenge of finding housing or secure employment? In puzzling out the youths' emphasis on the need to control women's morality and sexuality, the concept of marginalized masculinities sheds light on the apparent tensions in male youth narratives. "Marginalized masculinities," as R. W. Connell (1995, 80–81) defines it, refers to a configuration of practices through which men in subordinate positions negotiate their position in the power hierarchies of class, gender, and race. Through a reassertion of practices of patriarchy, they seek to reproduce the dominant position of men, that of hegemonic masculinity. In response to my inquiries as to why they identified this or that person as a figure of power in the community, my informants narrated tales of sexual transgression on the part of the named person or a member of his family. One tale told of a powerful person's son having harassed a woman in the neighborhood and then going so far as to commit an act of aggression against her in her home. The community failed to support the woman's demand for retribution and she was constrained to move out of the neighborhood. This theme in men's narrative of power, as symbolized and enacted in sexual transgression, bears the marks of marginalized masculinities. Figures of power, then, are identified as those who can get away with transgressing the sexual code. The violence of sexual dominance is linked with a higher power and, in this instance, is a confirmation of the inability of dominated men to stand up to a violation of their masculinity. In this tale there is recognition that money and connections support a patriarchal hierarchy.

Marginalized masculinities are inflected with the humiliation experienced at the hands of agents of the state and with the absence of any shield from state repression such as higher class status. The role of women in mediating this experience of state domination is pushed out of men's narratives. Rather, male youths insist that women are idle gossipers, doing little but displaying their feminine wiles. In contrast to the denial of women's work, male youths affirmed through their narratives the male's responsibilities in the family. Lower-class men's masculinity is constructed in relation to their position as providers for the families and as guardians of their women. Women's work could be seen, thus, as a challenge to this construction, especially when women become the main breadwinners of the household. Indeed, women have articulated this challenge by deploying a critique of husbands who fail to contribute and thus do not live up to the image of the masculine self. Failing to provide for household needs disrupts the masculine construct. This failure has its costs, such as the questioning of male prerogatives of control. Married women whose husbands fail to provide financial support have felt that their spouses' sexual expectations are inappropriate. A husband who fails to provide should not expect compliance with sexual "obligations" within the marital bond (el-Kholy, 2002). Women's questioning of their sexual obligations by invoking husbands' inadequacy as providers may be interpreted as women finding an opening, in a context of changing social conditions, to interrogate patriarchal terms of domination.

The position of youths in the urban setting and their construction of masculinity under conditions of subordination should be contrasted with earlier constructions of masculinity by subordinate urban youths. Historically, young men from popular quarters fashioned themselves in valorizing terms as *awlad al-balad* (sons of the country) (el-Messiri 1978). *Ibn al-balad* (son of the country) was the ideal male figure. This masculine self came to be associated with the figure of the *futuwwa*. The *futuwwa* was a strong-bodied male who displayed physical strength and exhibited his manliness through acts of honor and courage—watching out for his female neighbors, intervening in neighborhood disputes, and so on. *Futuwwa,* in its etymology, signals an exultation of youth; its root, *fata,* means a male youth.

Young men's narratives about their interventions in cases of women's transgressions highlight the actions taken by men to reinforce the moral order of hegemonic masculinities. What is at stake is the exercise of male authority not only in the home but also in the community If the fraternities have no formal political power, they have disciplinary power in which checking the potentially transgressive conduct of women is an important dimension. In other words, the monitoring of women emerges as a technique of internal governance that is continuous with the patriarchal dominance of hegemonic masculinities.

Women as Mediators

I became aware of the role of women as mediators when I asked Um Hasan why it was she who did all the running around to process her application with the water authorities to get a water connection. Um Hasan responded: "The *harim* are tough. They can take the abuse at government offices, put up with being told off, and spoken to badly for the sake of getting the service." Also, women have acquired the cultural capital needed for negotiating the bribe, learning who gets it and how much to pay. In describing her performance as mediator with state agents, Um Hasan constructed womanhood in terms of strength, resilience, and appreciation of household responsibility. This construction should, however, be put in the wider frame of Um Hasan's family arrangements and the broader gender narratives of the family. Through her earnings as a peddler, she managed to acquire the home in which her family lives. Her husband, meanwhile, is an *arzuqi* (daily laborer) with an irregular income. He used to drink heavily, which meant that this income was mostly unavailable to the family. Similarly, the sons' position in the household does not conform to the public narrative. In Um Hasan's words, one son is a bum *(sayi')*. He does not have a steady job and does not make any contribution to the household. The second son is enlisted in the army and is engaged to be married. To help him with marriage expenses, Um Hasan has set up a small business in her home. The youngest son peddles with her. Um Hasan's view of the *harim* (a word used to refer to women in a patronizing way) as "tough" inverses the conventional gender assignations of strength and weakness. Women striving to get basic public services in the face of hostile and abusive authority place higher value on family needs than on an individualized articulation of honor and self-respect. Self-respect, in Um Hasan's narrative, is about meeting the needs of the household.

In opposition to the practice of masculine concealment, women question the terms of their subordination and point to the contradiction built into the claims of marginalized masculinities. I think that Shirin's understanding of her position in the family with respect to the male members—her father and brother—points to this questioning. Shirin is a fifteen-year-old peddler selling sunglasses on a main boulevard in Giza. She was set up in this trade by her father who was selling out of a street stand until the police forced him to shut down for lack of a permit. Shirin now sells the goods for him, displaying them in the street. Her father sits close by for part of the day. On her way to her place of work, she passes by her mother, who sells paper tissues by the railway crossing in Nahya. This daily encounter with her mother's own harsh reality and struggle captures her imagination as well as her love and sympathy for her mother and other struggling women. In Shirin's account of the different roles assumed by the members of her family, her father appears as an irresponsible parent. He plays dominos and gambles in a coffee shop, spending, and some times losing, the money earned from sales. He has been trying to get a permit for a vendor's kiosk but has not yet succeeded. She thinks that her father uses the kiosk permit as an excuse for not working. As trust is absent in their dealings, she keeps some of the profit from sales to give to her mother to help with household expenses. Her withholding of some of the earnings from the proceeds is sometimes discovered, resulting in beatings from her father.

Shirin thinks she was taken out of school to educate her brothers. She has come to question this preference for her male siblings after starting to attend night school, where she has learned from her teacher that women are just as important as men and that they will change society one day. She is now determined to continue her schooling and is helping her younger sister, who has dropped out, to enroll in school again. She teaches her what she learns. Out on the street, Shirin is exposed to different situations, including being harassed by men. The experience has taught her to stand up to her father and tell him what she thinks of him. She says this shows that she is courageous and better than her older brother, who beats her up if she is out late but does not stand up to his father. She critically notes: "he acts as a man dominating me" *('amil alayya ragil)* pointing out the contradiction in his behavior. Shirin's contribution to the household and her work on the street have repositioned her in relation to the men in her family. She feels morally justified to question patriarchal claims. Her exclamation about her brother's conduct aims at the heart of masculine enactments of domination.

By assuming a greater role in public and contributing to their household expenses, women have also opened up spaces for questioning constructs of femininity anchored in frames of domesticity and banishment from public space. In response, social practices aimed at managing this change attempt to hold on to older constructs of femininity. I read the terms in which my key informant was cast by her family and neighbors as representing such practices. Manal is a local activist and a quintessential mediator who has taken on a public role that involves supporting women in their pursuit of social services, mediating local disputes, and presenting herself as a resource person. Her role, and her family's and neighborhood's acceptance of it, is framed in terms of gender crossing. "She is a man" (hiyyya ragil), they say, to justify her public engagements, her interventions to resolve disputes, and her social activism. But her undertakings are precisely those from which men have withdrawn. She accompanies women on their visits to various government departments, because, as she puts it, their men folk have no stomach for government. But acceptance of her role comes at a cost—the negation of her femininity and the conferral on her of a symbolic and honorary masculinity.

In tracing transformations in the city globally, Manuel Castells remarked that what has emerged is "the city of women," where women are workers in the informal sector and heads of households. As I reflect on the narratives of men and women and on my observations of the daily practices, I am led to think that I have encountered the community of women—a collectivity that transcends sisterhood and sororities and that is by no means in opposition to the male fraternities. Rather, the community of women is about resistance against the grinding conditions of everyday life; it is about overcoming. The women's return to school, as in the case of Sawsan, Manal, Nihmaduh, Samia, Raga', and Karima, is illustrative. Each of these women viewed education as empowering, as a means to improve their employment prospects, to learn and broaden their intellect, and to allow them to speak to men and to answer them. Further, by rejecting gossip as a strategy of social control and by taking up work as domestics or peddlers in defiance of social sanctions, these women challenge practices of control aimed at their subordination.

Raising capital through marriages to Gulf Arabs has become a more common practice among women of poor neighborhoods like Bulaq. The practice of women marrying wealthy men from oil-producing Arab countries has become a strategy of raising family income, a transaction that benefits other members of the family. As a new family member, the husband is asked to invest in a business venture or an existing enterprise such as a mechanic shop or a bookstore. On the whole, young men were silent on the idea of women being used as asset raisers if not as asset substitutes.

The changes in marriage arrangements have contributed to further questioning of gendered roles. Marriage remains an important social institution that engages the efforts of many families especially for raising the necessary capital. This has traditionally put most of the responsibility on prospective male partners who were to pay a dowry, make an engagement offering, and buy the substantial items of household furnishings. In addition, procuring housing had been the man's responsibility. These arrangements are now changing as women are making major contributions to the financing of the marriage, buying household furnishings, and selling their engagement offerings to pay the housing down payments. The contribution of women changes the power relations in the households. In fact, women seek to increase such contributions to enhance their position in the household vis-à-vis their husbands and in-laws (el-Kholy, 2002). One indication of the ongoing changes is the decision among young men to contract marriages with older women. Such marriages reduce the engagement offerings and other contributions that men must make to ward the union, since the women usually have residences and furnishings of their own.

Youths' Everyday-Life Encounters with the State

In this section, I want to sketch out the quotidian encounters between young men and the state. These encounters take place in markets, coffee shops, and alleyways. As residents and workers in a popular neighborhood that developed as a result of people's initiative, the youths, along with other residents, are the object of state regulatory practices aimed at bringing them under control. Such practices include raids on markets by the utilities police as well as patrols by other police departments, including the security police. Here I focus on the practices aimed at young men.

As part of Cairo's informal economy, young men work in unlicensed shops and use public space in contravention of utilities regulations. For example, Nagi set up an unlicensed kiosk on *Gama'iyya* Street to sell audiotapes. He called the kiosk *'mashru' shabab* in reference to a state-sponsored program designed to support young people who want to establish their own businesses. In many instances, the spatial dimension of these informal economic arrangements brings the "irregular" nature of their work into public view, open to inspections and monitoring practices of the state; indeed, the management of young men's public presence is a particular preoccupation of state authorities, especially the police. Undoubtedly this has to do with the fact that Islamist activists are drawn primarily from the ranks of young men in popular neighborhoods. Thus, the monitoring of young men's activities and conduct has been integrated into the general security objectives of state. Practices of territorialization are a related concern. They are seen as potentially oppositional tactics, as when youths form gangs or groups that encourage challenging authority. Much spatial maneuvering occurs on all sides.

Young men's encounters with the state follow the general patterns found in their communities' relations with state institutions, but also have their specificities. Youths in the markets and on commercial axes share the experiences of older vendors and traders in dealing with police raids and utilities police campaigns. However, they face additional and particular forms of police repression, discipline, and monitoring that have to do with their age and certain state policies targeting youths. For example, police raids on coffee shops and "campaigns to arrest suspects" have young men as a primary target. Also, the practices of requesting identity cards and "suspicion and investigation" (*ishtibah wa tahari*) procedures are concentrated in popular neighborhoods and aim at the control of young men's presence in public.

A number of my male informants were of conscription age but did not present themselves for military service as required. As a result, they try to avoid contact with the police out of fear of being arrested. This same is true for youths who drive without license. The experience of arrest is not limited to those whose status and licensing papers are not in order. Young men are also arrested because of their 'suspicious appearance', for example, bearded and wearing white *gallabiyyas*. The situation for young men is described as being marked by persistent fear that the police will exercise their powers of suspicion and investigation (*ishtibah wa tahari*) against them.

The arrest procedures and the new regulations relating to public order appear to target young men. In 1998, the law of *baltaga* (thuggery) was passed in Parliament. One intent of the law is to deal with young men's presence and conduct in public. Under its provisions, displays of physical strength for the purpose of intimidation are identified as acts of thuggery punishable by up to five years in prison. This should be situated in relation to the history of confrontation between the state and the Islamists. From the standpoint of state authorities, young men in popular quarters embody opposition. Drawing on its own experience, and a particular reading of it, the state deals with young men as a potential oppositional force that must be tamed. Young men's lifestyles during this period are seen as potentially threatening. Recall that this state, under emergency rules, considers a gathering of three or more people as potentially seditious, having outlawed all public gatherings and requiring a permit for any public meeting. By congregating on street corners and forming fraternities of sorts, young men are engaging in acts that could be unruly from the state's point of view.

To manage this public presence, the state deploys a wide range of practices of control. The state's management of young men draws on its experience with Islamist activism, reworking strategies and practices deployed against the Islamist activists. The Islamist activist as a lawless, violent enemy of the state was, in the ideal type constructions, a young man from popular quarters. The Islamist activists were viewed, in blanket terms, as terrorists. With the 1998 law on thuggery, the Islamist terrorist was replaced by the young *baltagi* (thug)—a social terrorist—as the rising threat to national security. This representation underwrites the official violence inflicted on young men in public. The objective of the police raids on coffee shops, stop and investigate operations, arrests, and beatings are to render the potentially resistant bodies into obedient bodies restrained by fear of physical sanction, public abuse, and humiliation. This framing is intended to deny young men the more positive image of the *futuwwa*. The effect of such policies marks both the discourse of young men and their practices. The young men of Bulaq, for instance, avoid crossing to "the other side", retreating instead to their neighborhood alleyways and staying close to their homes. They also avoid presenting themselves in public offices. As noted previously, the spatialization of sociability practices takes the form of a territorialization of activities in the quarter and the creation of safe zones in alleyways and around workshops. For young men, urban space is mapped out in terms of zones of relative safety or danger. The map guides them through their everyday-life movements. Yet the evasion and concealment designed to shield their injured masculinity and, indeed, humanity deepen the injury. The wounded masculine self seeks recovery/restitution in the home and alleyway through enactment of control over women's mobility and over their presence in public.

Young Men: Between Submission and Rebellion

How are the daily encounters with the state incorporated into the construction of the self, in particular, the masculine self? How are these encounters negotiated in relation to criteria of manhood? Unlike the beatings experienced by Palestinian youths when confronting

Israeli soldiers, the humiliating and violent encounters between Egyptian youths and police have not been turned into "rites of passage." Unlike the Palestinian male youths studied by Julie Peteet (2000), the Egyptian males do not seek confrontation. Rather, their agency takes the form of evasion—staying away from public thoroughfares and only frequenting coffee shops in their neighborhood alleys. They narrate the experience in terms of humiliation and injury and not as an experience of sacrifice that must be endured. The tactics of evasion do not exhaust the responses of the youth, and there are instances of defiance. For example, a number of young men refused to act as informants for the police. In turning down police offers of remuneration in the form of farmed out positions of dominance within their neighborhoods, they rejected co-optation as an option. In their view, police informants are thugs who betray the ethic of fraternity and the values of manliness associated with the traditional manhood of the *futuwwa*.

Two particular episodes of encounter highlight the complexity of determining positions of submission and rebellion. The first episode involves a young man, M. Abu Zayd, a third-year law student and manager of a family business on a commercial thoroughfare in Bulaq. From the vantage point of his shop, Abu Zayd witnesses the daily police campaigns in the market. In his account of the police presence in the area, he told of one intervention in which the police arrived and sought to confiscate the weight scales used by an eighteen-year-old woman vendor. When the young woman resisted and tried to prevent the seizure of the scales, she was beaten up by a police soldier. As he watched the assault, Abu Zayd felt angry and was indignant at the aggression. However, he stopped himself from intervening. He reasoned that his intervention would bring him into conflict with a police officer in uniform, an action that would jeopardize his career prospects. We may read this response as one of submission or at least of feigning submission and of engaging in a public performance scripted in the culture of fear.

In another encounter, Ayman was standing outside his home early one evening when a police patrol passed along the street. Ayman and one of the officers exchanged looks. The next day, the police patrol came by again and, once more, Ayman and the officer exchanged looks. Then, the officer approached Ayman and asked to see his identity card. Following that, he ordered Ayman into the police car. Ayman was arrested, charged with drug possession, and brought before the prosecutor. He interpreted his arrest as a result of daring to look back and failing to keep his head down. Here, it would appear that Ayman, when challenged to be submissive, responded with defiance.

Abu Zayd's and Ayman's responses are mediated by the logic of the situation and do not necessarily reveal the positions of submissive or rebellious subjects in the abstract. What the episodes show is that the young men occupy antagonistic positions vis-à-vis the state. I want to end this section with Ayman's reflections on the state and collective action. During our discussions, Ayman expressed the view that the idea of changing government through elections was unrealistic and that people of his background would never get elected. When he watches broadcasts of the People's Assembly, Ayman said, he sees there the ineptness of government and the lack of representation. This lack is also reflected in the images of public institutions and in hosts and guests who appear on TV talk shows and news programs. Ayman pointed out that no one like him is interviewed on these shows, except on rare occasions and, then, only briefly. This extends to sports, especially football, where coaches are chosen by manipulation and with disregard for the fans. Ayman attributes economic problems to corruption and adds that "if government was conducted according to God's edicts, there would be no problem." Although he is not religious, he still thinks that the *shari'a* should be applied. He does not pray, but would do so if government was conducted according to the *shari'a*. Ayman has never elected an MP or a local councilman. He does not have an electoral card and suggests that most people in his *hara* do not have electoral cards. In reflecting on how change would come about, Ayman said, "One day we will all rebel like 'Urabi, but we need a leader, a Salah al-Din to guide us." The construction of the relation to the state in Ayman's reflections clearly expresses antagonism. His narrative anticipates confrontation of a revolutionary nature. It may be that in invoking the eventual arrival of a leader, the narrative displaces the confrontation indefinitely. However, it highlights the oppositional positioning that he, along with other young men, occupies vis-à-vis the state.

Conclusion

In looking at the lifestyles of young men in popular quarters of Cairo, we gain insights into their position from the state and the potential for action. The youths inhabit a space of dissidence that can become a space of confrontation. Their presence contradicts official rules of law and order such as congregating on street corners and working in the middle of the street. Their presence is intensely public. Their narrative of their experience of interaction with the agents of the state is organized around values of self-respect and dignity and feelings of humiliation and injury. The encounters with the state destabilize their masculine constructs and necessitate a renegotiation of their masculinity.

In addressing the question of young men's activism and opposition to the state, I suggest that we need to examine how gender constructions mediate their relations with the state. The humiliation they experience in dealing with state agents threatens their dominance at home, exposing their powerlessness and bringing women in as mediators with the state. At the same time, changes in marriage arrangements and in women's employment challenge hegemonic masculinities. The young men experience social change in the family as threatening to their position of power and dominance and the terms that define their masculinity. Public discourse and practices of socialization into masculinity construct manhood in terms of guardianship of honor and responsibility for providing for the family. Yet the exigencies for lower-class women's work, documented in the late 1980s by Arlene MacLeod (1991), continue to unfold in the early 2000s. Women are household heads in the absence of husbands who have deserted them or become migrant workers. Further, ongoing changes to the cultural and ideological organization of space undermine the principles of a gendered separation of space. Yet, women continue to appear as the ultimate boundary of community in the young men's narratives. In the young men's accounts of women's transgressive conduct, as evidenced by their attire, their mobility, and their appropriation of public space, we find enactments of masculinity that seek to reinstitute an alternative construction of acceptable femininity, harking back to visions of female domesticity that are central to hegemonic masculinities.

My analysis of the intersection of youth activism, gender relations, and state power rests on a particular reading of the wider field of state—society interaction. In this reading, I propose that there has been a shift from welfarism and corporatism toward an articulation of security politics with neoliberal politics.

References

Connell, R. W. 1995. *Masculinities*, Berkeley: University of California Press.

Hirschkind, Charles. 2001. "The Ethics of Listening: Cassette-Sermon Audition in Contemporary Egypt." *American Ethnologist* 28, 3: 623–49.

Ismail, Salwa. 2004. "Islamist Movements as Social Movements: Contestation And Identity Frames." *Historical Reflections* 30, 3: 385–402.

Kandiyoti, Deniz. 1994. "The Paradoxes of Masculinity: Some Thoughts on Segregated Societies." In *Dislocating Masculinities: Comparative Ethnologies*, ed. Andrea Cornwall and Nancy Lindsfrane, 197–213. London: Routledge.

Kholy, Heba Aziz el-. 2002. *Defiance and Compliance: Negotiating Gender in Low-Income Cairo*. New York and Oxford: Berghan Books.

MacLeod, Arlene Elow. 1991. *Accommodating Protest: Working Women, the New Veiling, and Change in Cairo*. New York: Columbia University Press.

Martinez, Luis. 2000. *The Algerian Civil War 1990-1998,* trans. Jonathan Derrik. London: Hurst &Co.

el-Messiri, Sawsan. 1978. *Ibn al-Balad: A Concept of Egyptian Identity*. Leiden, Holland: E. J. Brill.

Peteet, Julie. 2000. "Male Gender and Rituals of Resistance in the Palestinian Intifada: A Cultural Politics of Violence." In *Imagined Masculinities: Male Identity and Culture in the Modern Middle East*, ed. Mai Ghoussoub and Emma Sinclair-Webb, 103–26. London: Saqi Books.

Originally published in *Political Life in Cairo's New Quarters: Encountering the Everyday State.* (University of Minnesota Press, 2006): 96–128. Printed here with the permission of the publisher.

CHRISTA SALAMANDRA

Consumption, Display, and Gender

> In my imagination young women were divided into two classes; those who were to be purchased, and those who were to purchase.
>
> Maria Edgeworth, *Castle Rackrent*

> We make conversation: we husbands talk about production; the ladies, about consumption.
>
> Italo Calvino, *Time and the Hunter*

In Damascus social identities are increasingly negotiated and contested through competitive consumption. Women emerge as central players in contests over position and prestige; what they wear, where they dine, and who they marry may signify, reinforce, and even create class affiliation. The commodification of social life engenders a context in which Damasceneness is continually invoked, and some times undermined.

The ability to purchase expensive consumer goods, and to be seen in fashionable venues, has long been an important mark of elite status for women in Damascus. Under the socialist economic policies of the 1960s, 1970s, and 1980s, minimal domestic industry combined with import bans to render commodities scarce. Access to consumer goods, such as fashionable clothing, distinguished those with connections to powerful individuals (for whom sanctions against smuggling did not apply) and the wealthy who traveled abroad. The Ba'th Party attempt to rid Syrian society of social hierarchy not only failed, but actually produced new class divisions. During the 1990s, a boom in local production and loosening of import regulations led to an increasing availability of both locally produced and foreign consumables on Syrian store shelves. The commodification of many aspects of social life accelerated as more commodities and public leisure sites widened opportunities for social distinction through consumption.

The kind of consumption in which people in Damascus engage both reflects and constructs social differences. My exploration of this phenomenon draws on Pierre Bourdieu's (1984) analysis of distinction, which links preferences in cuisine, art, music, and home furnishings to income, educational level and social background. Bourdieu's once groundbreaking and now commonplace argument demonstrated that taste is a matter not of individual proclivity but of social position. "Good taste," the socially acquired preference for high over low cultural forms, serves as cultural capital, an asset not directly material but enhancing and reinforcing class position.

The relationship between consumption, display, and social identity is explored in a significant body of recent literature. Much of this material shows how the range of commodities now available allows the differentiation and ranking, by presentation and consumption, of persons who have no "natural" relations, such as kin or locality, but instead must state their social position before an audience who otherwise might know little of them. Elite Damascus presents a seeming paradox. Style, leisure activities, and displays of wealth have become increasingly significant with economic liberalization. As one informant puts it, elites in Damascus are "inventing occasions to show off their wealth." Yet these have not eclipsed the importance of family name. Damascus is still very much like a small town for the middle and upper classes; all appear to know one another. But like the inhabitants of Herbert Gans's "ethnic village" urban enclave Damascenes do not actually know one another. They know of and about one another (1962: 15, 75). Damascenes often have at their fingertips detailed information, or speculation—family background, income, profession, education—about persons they have never met. Information networks are vast; social networks are much smaller. Because people may not know one another personally, may only know about one another, seeing and perceiving others become significant. Here consumption comes into play. Elite names remain elite, and new names become elite through public displays of wealth. Older forms of social identification are not disappearing but are being reworked, through consumption in a new arena, a public culture of hotels, restaurants, and cafés. To paraphrase a line from Lampedusa's *The Leopard,* things are changing so that things can remain the same (1960:40).

In a "community" where people may not know one another but do see one another, appearances take on great importance. Syrian men are image conscious—those who can afford it wear expensive clothing, cologne, and gold jewelry and drive flashy cars; but it is women who most often represent familial wealth and status through physical beauty and adornment. Feminist critics in the West argue that with the continual bombardment of narrowly defined images of female beauty in the contemporary media, physical appearance has become the most important measure of a woman's worth. Such comments are made in the context of advanced industrial societies, where the pressure on women to reach unattainable heights of physical perfection is perceived by some as part of a backlash against feminist successes (Wolf, 1991). In Syria, a similar situation is developing, as increasing access to Western media combines with ever tightening restrictions on women's social presence outside the home, although Western-style feminism has never occurred.

The Syrian media's commodification of women's bodies is swiftly catching up with that of Western counterparts. With the privatization of the Syrian economy over the past decade, a rapidly growing domestic advertising industry has developed. When the Arab Advertising Institute (*al-Mu'assasa al-'Arabiyya lil I'lan*) was set up in 1990, there were only three Syrian television advertising agencies; by the middle of 1991 this number had increased to sixty-five. In addition, four international agencies set up offices in Damascus in the mid 1990s. Televised images of heavily made-up, tightly clothed women now join those long depicted on the pages of Arabic women's magazines. Between advertisements, foreign and locally produced serial dramas convey a similarly homogeneous, exaggerated, hyper real feminine ideal—the glossy mouths, lacquered hair, and power shoulder pads of 1980s American soap operas adopted by Syrian women of all ages and social groups. Holding center stage in consumption and display contests, women provide an ideal focus for a discussion of the commodification of image and identity.

Chastity as Capital

Compounding the importance of image for Syrian women is the premium placed on the appearance of chastity. An unpopular subject among gender specialists who prefer to emphasize Middle Eastern women's empowerment, the issue of control over female sexuality is profoundly affecting Syrian society in novel ways. Elite Syrians themselves are reluctant to discuss this situation, even in forums focusing on gender. A lecture on feminism at the American Cultural Center provides a case in point: a young Syrian female Ph.D., adorned with the emphasized femininity of a Hollywood starlet, discussed Simone de Beauvoir and Hélène Cixous. Neither she nor the post-lecture commentators mentioned the local obsession with female sexual purity. Instead, a young actor spoke passionately about the need to preserve the family. A long debate, reminiscent of American notions of "political correctness," centered on whether or not male authors are able to write from a woman's point of view, and whether or not a writer could depict experiences he or she had not had. A Damascus University professor spoke of sexism in language. No one mentioned the vast majority of women who are forbidden—by parents, brothers, husbands, or the watchfulness of neighbors—to attend a lecture like this one, held in the evening, since returning home after dark prompts suspicion.

The appearance of sexual purity becomes a form of capital for a young woman. Its absence can be disastrous for her future prospects. It can also become ammunition for opposing families to hurl at their enemies. In order to preserve their chastity capital, young women should not be seen interacting with men, particularly one-to-one, before they are engaged. Their moving about the city alone, especially after sundown, is frowned upon. The economic implications of these sanctions are profound. To paraphrase Bourdieu (1979), women's subjective situation—restricted movement outside the home--is both a precondition and a product of their material dependency.

Although premarital social and even sexual contact between men and women is not unknown, discretion is key. Elite districts of Damascus—which provide relative anonymity—are peppered with small, dark, heavily curtained coffee shops where courting couples can sit together unnoticed. Headscarf-clad young women hold their boyfriends' hands as they speak intensely over inexpensive cups of coffee and tea. Dates take place either surreptitiously or under the guise of fictional marriage engagement.

Young women for whom interaction with men is restricted adopt strategies of attraction through display. Semi-public spaces provide venues for showing oneself to others. The Health Club in Abu Rummaneh, for instance, is an entirely unisex workout place in a neighborhood largely populated by upper-middle-class, conservative Damascenes. The women who can afford to go there drive or are driven. They tend not to walk on the streets, even in conservative clothing. Yet inside the club they wear heavy makeup and skimpy leotards—often with spaces cut to reveal large sections of bare stomach, back, or thigh—and leave flowing their invariably long hair. In contrast, non-Syrian women appear in leggings or sweat pants and long baggy T-shirts, their faces bare of makeup and hair tied back. The club's single, brightly lit, mirror-paneled room seems designed with display in mind, as aerobic classes take place in a cleared area in front of the weights and exercise machines. Those pumping iron— mostly men—can watch the bobbing behinds, delineated clearly in thong-backed leotards, of the women taking step aerobics or body-toning classes, as technopop blares in the background. All the leotards sold in the club's small boutique have low-cut scoop necklines and thong-backed bottoms. The Health Club is one of the arenas between public and private where young women, and to a lesser extent young men, take advantage of the in-between-ness to show off as much body as possible. This contrasts sharply with the hidden intimacy of the curtained coffee shop, as Health Club patrons hide themselves from sight on the way to and from a space specifically designed to reveal.

Most semi-public spaces, including professional ones, provide opportunities for attraction. Flirtatiousness is the norm. A Damascene professional told me that a diplomat from the American Cultural Center had suggested starting classes in office conduct for Syrian women. She told the diplomat that no one would attend them, as women who work do so to attract husbands, not build careers. Most jobs open to women, however prestigious, do not pay enough to enable them to become economically self-sufficient. Unmarried women, even wealthy ones, rarely set up independent households. Jobs are seen as temporary measures on the way to marriage or as supplementary income afterward. For young single women, they are primarily a venue for display, the ultimate aim of which is to secure a successful future in the private, rather than public, sphere. For married women, they supply extra income, social contact, and a chance to exhibit their husbands' affection and economic status through self-adornment.

Beauty and Wealth on the Marriageability Scale

In elite Damascus, competitive display is often geared toward attaining desirable marriage partners. Marriages, like the wedding ceremonies commencing them, signify and engender social position. A daughter who obtains a prestigious mate raises, or at least reinforces, her family's lofty rank. Brides are chosen for a variety of assets, among which beauty and wealth are most significant.

Damascenes value feminine beauty, and associate it with the city. A beautiful woman is said to have drunk the water of Damascus *(sharbaneh mayat al-sham)*. As notable author Rana Kabbani notes, Damascene beauties are "famous for their bedroom eyes and alabaster skin" (1998: 134). Yet wealth sometimes eclipses beauty, as great fortunes can now obliterate distinctions between new and old money. A young Damascene professional woman from an old elite family described these standards to me:

> If there's a lot of money involved, beauty makes no difference. It matters when they are of average wealth, or borderline. For example, you have *bayt* (family) X, who are not Damascenes. Their daughters are ugly *(bisha'at),* by the beauty standards of the country. They're not attractive, they all have hairy complexions. But they have lots of money, so they married *awlad 'ayal* (Damascene elites).

When I asked if *awlad 'ayal* also consider money the most important characteristic, my informant replied:

> Of course! They are even more interested in money. Sons of old noble families are more interested in new money, in the new money classes. It's the opposite

of what you might think. The interest in money among upper classes is equal, new money or old. It's more important than anything else.

Such a characterization from an articulate informant with a wealth of local knowledge contradicted my own assumption, and many Syrians' contention, that the old urban elite marry only among themselves. I asked my informant how intermarriage occurs, given that, as she had told me earlier, the Old Damascenes "consider themselves superior":

> How does this work? A boy (shabb) of the rich classes—new money—marries an old money girl (bint). If he has a lot of money, her family won't consider it a problem, even if this money has come through different means. If an old money boy marries a new money girl, the matter is different. If she's not pretty, she must be very, very rich.

Damascene author Raria Kabbani concurs:

> For all their feminine wiles, Damascene women are hardheaded when it comes to the beneficiaries or victim of their beautification: men. Given the choice between Romeo and rich Count Paris, they will choose the latter. Their perfectly sugared arms need gems to show them off. (1998: 135)

While beauty is a key asset for women, wealth is what renders a groom desirable. As my Damascene informant observed: "Boys' looks don't matter. A boy, old or new money, may be short and bald, but if he has a lot of money, he can marry the prettiest girl in the country. So looks are only important for girls."

Syrian women of elite classes are aware of and not always complacent about this double standard. At a dinner party of middle-aged couples, one of the husbands called his wife—ten years younger than himself—an old hag. Suddenly all the women disappeared into the back rooms of the flat, then re-emerged with all the portable mirrors they could find and handed them to their husbands.

Beauty remains important, yet wealth is beginning to replace other attributes of desirability. Complex distinctions are made between beauty, money, and status, as a middle-aged Damascene housewife explained:

> For example, X [elite old Damascene] wanted to marry a girl from a very, very rich family—you can call them one of the millionaire families. But she wasn't at all pretty. But here her family begins to calculate: ok, he's a good-looking boy, and their daughter is ugly, and he's not poor, he has money, so it's an appropriate match. Had she been pretty, they would have engaged her to someone a bit better than him, someone richer. So the girls of this family all married good-looking boys who had less money than they. They do a trade-off—those who have money want beauty. Now, given the country's standards, if an old money boy can choose between a very, very pretty girl and one who is very rich, he will choose the richer. It didn't used to be this way. Fifteen years ago, when my husband's [old elite] brothers got engaged, they were looking for pretty girls. Pretty young girls, in order to have pretty children. But those who are becoming engaged now are always looking for very rich girls ... Standards have changed. Before, the best they could have was a pretty girl, a young daughter-in-law.

Now they chose a very rich girl. There's been a change in people's thinking with respect to wealth.

Location of the family house is a key class indictor. The housewife continued:

> Recently my husband's youngest brother went to meet a girl who lived in Suwaiqa. She was amazingly beautiful, the standard of a beauty queen, and a nice girl—he himself said all this about her—a fourth-year English literature student, who speaks English and has been to America. And she was 21 or 22, an appropriate age. But his family refused. My husband was shocked, such a pretty, nice, educated girl of an appropriate age. But they want someone who lives near West Malki, the closer the better.

A mate's desirability is not defined by the groom alone; choosing a partner is a family matter in which mothers and sisters are central.The marriage market in elite Damascus exists within a male-dominated economic system, but is not itself male controlled; powerful matrons direct the movement of people and statuses. Contemporary Damascus here resembles nothing so much as the drawing rooms of Jane Austen and Maria Edgeworth. Beauty and fortune are explicitly weighed and measured—usually by women themselves—to determine a woman's worth. Indeed, one Damascene informant, like Lady Bertram of Austen's *Mansfield Park,* repeatedly expressed surprise and indignation at an acquaintance who, although neither attractive nor rich, had married well. Not unlike nineteenth-century Britain, contemporary Syria is undergoing rapid social and economic transformations, with older kinship-based forms of distinction giving way to materially based ones, or at least a material idiom replacing that of kinship. Elites are redefining themselves, yet some things remain the same: the centrality of marriage and kin and the basis of family honor. The contrived chastity of contemporary Syria parallels the contrived gentility of Austen's England.

Clothing Makes the Woman

For all women in Damascus, the ability to purchase a look that highlights beauty, and suggests wealth, is crucial. For single women, appearance is central to obtaining a desirable spouse. But the pressure to present a stylish image does not disappear after marriage, since a wife's grooming and attire then signify her husband's and family's status. Competitive display is evident at elite in-spots: at the Sheraton Hotel pool, wealthy women change bathing suits several times during an afternoon of sunbathing. A married woman, expensively coiffed and dressed, is one who has made an enviable match. Wedding rings are a clear status marker. The Damascene professional observes:

> I was at a party recently, sitting at a round table with ten other people. When I saw their hands on the table, I could tell immediately what class they belong to, from the diamond rings on their fingers. When a woman is very rich, she always wears diamond rings; one with five large diamonds and one a solitaire, a big, clear diamond. And that's it, even if she is from a different governorate, she's clearly from the very rich. These two rings alone would cost a million SP.

> You'll find it is a very important in thing among the richest girls in the country, how much their solitaires cost. It means the bridegroom can afford everything else. Even if I don't know anything else about you, without asking you anything, I can tell your class from your ring.

Here style marks intra-elite distinctions:

> Also, someone may have a ring as heavy as a diamond ring, but which has no diamonds in it, and it's immediately clear that she is new money, not from old money. Gold [alone] indicates that she does not have nobility [*'araqa*] in her family. Diamonds are higher. Why? Because diamonds are a luxury, while gold is a means of saving. Diamonds are 100 percent luxury. They show that your husband can spend a million lira on just a ring.

Acquisition practices among the elite are ranked, with those who can afford to shop in France or Lebanon at the top, those who buy at the better Damascene stores in the middle, and below them those who must resort to the cheaper synthetic local imitations of European catwalk fashions available in less expensive boutiques. Natural fabrics are rare and worn only by the uppermost stratum, or sometimes the Western educated. Certain fabrics mark old elites from their newer counterparts, as my young professional informer notes:

> Upper-class, old-money Damascene girls wear *guipere* dresses. Then it's known how much was spent on the fabric for the dress, even if its style is ugly. *Dentelle* (lace) as well. And of course, mink. It must be a long black coat, with recognizable sections in it.

Women move beyond superficial adornment of clothing to resculpt their bodies. Rana Kabbani argues:

> For plastic surgery, Damascus must rank second to Rio in terms of popularity. A new monied generation is heavily into liposuction, facelifts, breast enhancement, eyebrow, eyelid, and lip tatooing, and other cosmetic improvements. The richest surgeon in town is the nose-job king whose motto is "the husband is the last to nose." (1998: 35)

The Problem of What to Wear

Competitive self-adornment, the essence of social display in most major Middle Eastern cities, has received scant scholarly attention. My own work is not intended as the extended treatment that clothing in the Middle East warrants; instead I examine sartorial statements as strategies for social mobility.

Young women dress to impress not only men, but even more importantly, other women, given the central role mothers and sisters play in finding a young man a bride. All-female social events are opportunities to introduce a marriageable daughter, niece, or sister. An extraordinary amount of time and money is spent thinking about, talking about, and purchasing new clothes and hair styles.

Dress style among both young and middle-aged women tends to run to two extremes. On the one hand, there is a strong tendency toward highly marked sensuality or sexuality: tight, figure-hugging, and sometimes cleavage-revealing clothing in vivid colors—red and black are a favorite combination—heavy makeup, teased and moussed long hair, high heels, multiple gold or gilt accessories. One evening, as we sipped coffee in the Sheraton's *al-Nawafeer* Café, one of my two women companions glanced around at the parade of glitter and bemoaned the recent changes in taste. "The aristocracy used to have class," she remarked; "now everything must be bigger, busier, heavier, and shinier." On the other hand, there is an increasing number of *muhajjabeh,* who, with their white headscarves and simple blue or gray overcoats, eschew all local conventions of attractiveness. Women find it difficult to maintain a stylistic middle ground between the invisibility of the *hijab* (Islamic dress) and the flamboyance of the coquette. As one Damascene woman put it (in English), "we have cockteasers and *nuhajjabeh,* and nothing in between."

The following anecdote illustrates this sartorial dilemma. A young, unmarried Syrian woman, working among foreign men at the UN Observer Forces Headquarters, told me she tries to dress conservatively at work to avoid attracting sexual attention. She is Christian, so the scarf for her is not an option. But when she goes out in the evening, more flamboyantly dressed, her women friends always compliment her and ask why she does not dress that way all the time. In this context, the choice to eschew makeup and wear an overcoat and scarf can be seen as a socially acceptable form of retreat from the endless pressure to objectify oneself. The wearing of the *hijab* signifies a dignity and moral authority placing the wearer above display contests. There is very little middle ground. To affect an understated style is to invite criticism from all sides.

Wolf quotes a long series of comments made about women's clothing in the Western workplace, arguing that any style is open to criticism (1991: 38-47). This problem is acute in Damascus, where appearance is so often and so openly discussed. Only a few women manage an in-between-ness, often those who have professional and social contacts with the French. For the old elite of Damascus, proficiency in French language and culture represented refinement and cultivation. Just as the study of French literature is giving way to business and technical English at Damascus University, the Francophone and Francophile circles are shrinking in a swell of strongly marked materialism.

Display Cases

For married women, the tradition of the afternoon reception, *istiqbal,* provides an opportunity for displays of skill, taste, and wealth. On the same day each month, a woman invites her circle of friends to her home for an *istiqbal.* The afternoon is preceded by a flurry of activity, as the matron, her daughters, daughters-in-law, and household servants clean the house thoroughly and bring out the best china and silver. Women of the extended family and their guests dress in their finest and most fashionable clothes. Most often light refreshments are served, sometimes a full meal. Whatever is offered is as elaborate, expensive, and labor intensive as possible. Freshly squeezed juice, homemade preserves, sweets laden with *samneh* (sheep's milk butter), and nuts are standard. An *istiqbal* is intended to reveal a woman's beauty, taste, and housekeeping skills, and her husband's wealth and position. Guests arrive wearing their own status markers. Husbands take part in both shopping for the event, and discussing it afterward, thereby gaining a glimpse of their colleagues' fortunes: "A woman serves the most expensive foods and drinks that she can, according to her husband's ability and position. Hospitality (*al-diyafeh*) is important because it demonstrates how much he is worth." As a Damascene proverb holds, "a wife is a man's face" *(martu wajihto)*. "The *istiqbal* is his advertising agency," as one Damascene informant put it.

More frequently, competitive display takes place beyond such domestic spaces. Major gathering spots, such as the big hotels, also provide venues for seeing and being seen. Many upper-middle-class families—those who cannot afford villas in Marbella—vacation at the Meridien or the Cham Côte d'Azur hotels on the Syrian coast, at Latakia, during the August peak season. In the evenings, people stroll from one hotel to the other, so as not to miss any action. At dusk, throngs of holiday-makers pass one another on the tree-lined avenue connecting the two. These hotels provide little in the way of activities or entertainment; their lobbies, restaurants, bars, and cafés are packed with vacationers who at first glance appear to be doing nothing at all. They are actually very busy, doing an important part of the work of contemporary elites: looking and being looked at, talking and being talked about. Everyone dresses carefully in new clothing. Young women take advantage of the resort atmosphere to display every curve in fluorescent Lycra mini-dresses.

This mating game continues year round at the Sheraton pizzeria, where up-to-date fashions reveal cleavage and thigh. Young men and women gaze at each other from the safety of groups; they rarely converse one-to-one publicly. Young women are allowed, indeed encouraged, to attract men, but are forbidden to socialize with them. The aim is to attract a husband with her body, since young people of opposite sexes are rarely permitted enough time together for anything else to matter. Discouraged from openly attracting male attention through wit, warmth, intelligence, or charm, women become silent images. Display, contained within certain spaces, is more acceptable than interaction.

The decision to wear a headscarf in public—which a growing number of women are making—can be seen as retreat from a competition that is becoming increasingly unaffordable, as economic liberalization swells inflation and floods the market with luxury goods out of reach for most. Yet given that many relatively well-to-do young women have adopted the scarf, economic explanations alone do not account for the phenomenon. Nor does it always reflect a newfound religiosity. Rather, the scarf is often a way of opting out of the display game and its objectification. Several Damascene women I met opted for the *hijab* after traumatic encounters with men. It is here that standard sociological explanations of veiling as political protest intersect with personal histories. As public culture's objectification and commodification of women's bodies mirror their abuse in private, women increasingly shrink from both spheres.

In a context where image rather than achievement determines status, the presentation stakes are high. Every aspect of a woman's appearance is subject to scrutiny and evaluation by other women. Losing or gaining a pound, drying one's hair differently, wearing a skirt instead of trousers or a slightly thicker line of eyeliner, all elicit comment; sometimes, but not always, in compliment form. A song by the Iraqi heartthrob Kadhim al-Sahir that was wildly popular during my second year of fieldwork set to music a comment I heard throughout my stay in Syria:

That color looks great on you (*Hadha al-lawn 'aleiki yujanin*)
It matches the color of your eyes (*Yashbah lawn 'ayunak*)

Elusive Friendship

At Damascus's exclusive *Nadi al-Sharq* (Oriental Club), two young women greet each other with high-pitched excitement and kisses on both cheeks. "They are not on good terms," whispers my companion into my ear. In marked contradiction to the social harmony among Middle Eastern women often depicted by feminist anthropologists, behind the appearance of intimacy often lurks bitterness and hostility. Syrian women have confided in me the difficulty they have making female friends amid continual rivalry. The constant competitiveness is wearing; nothing about the other goes unnoticed. Women compare themselves continually and mercilessly in an agonistic mode of sociability tinged with hostility.

In elite Damascus, women alternate flattery with criticism, cruelty with kindness, and as one put it, "build you up in order to knock you down again." Cutting remarks are sandwiched between grand gestures of affection and generosity, so one seldom knows where one stands. One favorite form of female sparring is the backhanded compliment: "You've gained weight, but it looks good on you"; "You look better in skirts than in trousers"; "You don't look short because you're fat." Outright insults are also not uncommon. Once I was with a friend on holiday in Latakia when she met an acquaintance she had not seen since the previous year. "Are you pregnant?" asked the woman. "No, just heavier," my friend replied. Instead of cowering in embarrassment the woman continued, "But this is really quite a change, isn't it? You really have gained weight!"

Knocking others down alternates with propping oneself up. Self-congratulation is standard. It is not uncommon to hear Syrians recounting their many suitors, describing the beauty of their singing voice, showing off things they have made, repeating compliments they have received. It is statistically impossible for me to have met so many people who, they claim, graduated first in their class in all of Damascus, all of Latakia, all of Syria.

Such "off the record" remarks by women reflect an essential quality of Arab women's interaction. Status consciousness, competition, and one-upmanship are among the most salient features of female social life. Unsurprisingly, many of these contests are played out over physical appearance. This is true even in Oman, a society considered unique in the Middle East for its social reserve and lack of open conflict (C. Eickelman 1984: 112; Wikan 1982:10, 14).

The intensity of relationships among women is often misread as social harmony, but closeness does not always involve mutual support. As Georg Simmel notes, "the extreme violence of antagonistic excitement is linked to the closeness of belonging together" (1955: 50). Anthropologist Suad Joseph includes in an edited collection on the Arab family an anonymous contribution from a Syrian painter whose fraught relationship with her sister was captured in a biographical film:

> The interview with my eldest sister, Isabelle, came to me as a shock. She expressed all intense involvement with me that I had not previously noticed. I

knew, of course, that she had been hovering over me, but what I did not know
was that this concern came from an irrepressible jealousy and not from the
normal concern an older sister would have for her younger sister. That she had
always interfered, that she had always been there to comment, report, fuel all
arguments I had with my mother as I was growing up—this hostile behavior
had been prompted by jealousy. (Scheherazade 1999: 93)

Writing from exile, the Aleppine painter now recasts her sister's behavior in American
pop psychological terms, as "abuse."

My sister abused me both physically and mentally. And to tell myself that that
abuse came from her jealousy of me did not make it any less painful— a jealousy
that did not relent and ruined years of my life. When I complain about it to
my mother, she says, "No, no, you are the only one she ever loved." But what is
love in that case? It is forever mingled with manipulation (ibid.: 105)

Intensely emotive power struggle, rather than warmly supportive bonding, often
characterizes relations among women in the strongly patriarchal societies of the Middle
East. Ethnographers often present striking interactions of discord with little comment,
and fail to reflect upon their implications for a presumed harmony among women. This
silence may reflect a deep ambivalence on the part of the anthropologists sensitive to the
portrayal of groups who, like Arabs and Muslims, have been so vilified in the Western media
and popular culture. Indeed, much of this writing comes in the wake of Said's *Orientalism*,
a study of negative imagery and stereotyping in literature and scholarship on the Middle
East. Said's excursion into Foucauldian questions of knowledge and power in colonial
and post-colonial academia has often been so literally read that a political correctness
has arisen, making it controversial to portray Arabs or Muslims in anything but the most
positive light. Competition and contestation must therefore be downplayed.

Some recent material moves beyond assumptions of sisterhood. Susan Waltz's (1990)
study of political efficacy among Tunisian women points to ways in which women
themselves reinforce patriarchal structures. Here the most effective and successful women
politicians recounted distance or hostility from their mothers and encouragement from
male role models such as fathers and brothers.

Anne Meneley's work on Yemen (1996) and Unni Wikan's early work on Cairene
women are the only extended ethnographies dealing with female competition in the Middle
East. "Nobody here wishes anybody any good," says one woman of her community (Wikan
1980: 5), and Wikan's informants articulate what mine express through display: "I'm
better than you! I eat drink and dress better than you!" She describes a context in which
differences in material possessions are perceived as differences of human value. Friendships
are volatile and short lived. Wikan attributes these women's pervasive materialism, mutual
distrust, frequent slander, and self-praise to the difficult and degrading conditions of
poverty: yet all are prevalent among the elite of Damascus. I argue that such agonism
also serves as response to the pressures facing elites, who, in ever changing circumstances,
fear falling down the social scale.

References

Austin, J. *Mansfield Park*, London: Penguin, 1966; original 1814.

Bourdieu, P. 'The Disenchantment of The World." In *Algeria 1960*, Cambridge: (Cambridge University Press, 1979).

——. *Distinction: A Social Critique of the Judgment of Taste*. (London: Routledge and Kegan Paul 1984).

Eickelman, C. *Women and Community in Oman*. (New York: New York University Press, 1984).

Kabbani, R. "Global Beauty: Damascus." In *Vogue*, Vol.164, no. 2394, (January 1998).

Lampedusa, Giuseppe di. *The Leopard*. (New York: Pantheon Books, 1960).

Meneley, A. *Tournaments of Value: Sociability and Hierarchy in a Yameni Town*. (Toronto: University of Toronto Press, 1996).

Scheherezade. " My Sister Isabelle." In *Intimate Selving in Arab Families: Gender, Self, Identity*, edited by Suad Joseph, 92-105. (Syracuse, N.Y.: Syracuse University Press 1999)

Simmel, G. "Conflict." In *Conflict and the Web of Group Affiliations*, (New York: Free Press of Glencoe, 1955; original 1908).

Waltz, Susan E. 1990. "Another Way of Feminine Networks: Tunisian Women and the Development of Political Efficacy." *International Journal of Middle East Studies* 22:21-36.

Wikan, Unni. *Life Among the Poor in Cairo*. Translated by Ann Henning. (London: Tavistock 1980).

——. *Behind the Veil in Arabia: Women in Oman*, Md.: (Johns Hopkins University Press 1982).

Wolf, Naomi. *The Beauty Myth: How Images of Beauty Are Used Against Women*. (London: Vintage 1991).

Originally published in *A New Old Damascus: Authenticity & Distinction in Urban Syria*. (Indiana University Press, 2004): 48–64. Printed here with the permission of the publisher.

Missed Opportunities: Me and My Gender

It took me a long time to understand why my mother loved to tell the story of the doctor who delivered me. Whenever there was a willing audience, she would tell it. I must have heard it a thousand times.

For her story to make sense, you need to know that I am the second female born to my parents and that my sister and I are their only progeny. "When Dr Razook left the delivery room, his face was tense and he walked past your father without looking at him. Your father was waiting anxiously for the baby to be delivered so that he could join me. (In those days, husbands were never allowed to witness the birth of their child.) The attitude of the doctor terrified your father, who thought that something terrible must have happened to me and to our baby. When he knew that I had given birth to a healthy baby girl, he was delighted. Dr Razook did not like to deliver girls, especially if the parents were his friends, and he felt his reputation as a gynecologist was perturbed by every female he brought into the world. As for your dad and me, we did not care one way or the other, boy or girl."

The story of my birth as told by my mother is a perfect metaphor for my country of origin. It is the story of juxtaposed values and contradictions. Yes, it is OK to be born a girl but the story never ends here. There is a "but", a Mediterranean "but" and a westernized OK that have to coexist, and modernized citizens somehow have to juggle and survive within the spaces of this coexistence. And they have to do it with grace and honour. My parents are from the generation of Middle Easterners who lived at the time of transition from the traditional values of large families to the westernized nuclear family with a maximum of two children, raised and educated in the best schools you could afford. They dreamt of bringing up free, responsible individuals—individuals who were nonetheless constantly reminded that they were the custodians of their family's honour, especially if they stood on the female side of the gender border; individuals who had to watch constantly for "what the neighbours say" about them and their parents, their uncles, cousins and other relatives.

My story, the way I tried to live my life, is a desperate, not always unhappy, effort to reconcile at least two epochs, two modes of behaviour, two value systems that prevailed simultaneously and very concretely in prewar Lebanon.

Let me come back to my mother. A clever woman, she was considered very marriageable thanks to her good looks and was consequently withdrawn from school, in the late 1940s, by her parents at the age of sixteen. She had loved her school and treasured the knowledge she had acquired there, mainly in the sciences. She had no say about her parents' decision and anyway she had fallen in love with my father. My father, a modern young man, cared very little about the difference in their religious confessions and courted her openly because he had "good intentions". They fell madly in love and married when she was seventeen and he twenty years old. They despised marriages of convenience or calculation, believed in true love and had the Hollywood movies, already triumphant over the screens of Beirut, to confirm the rightness of their romantic choice.

There were a few couples like them in Lebanon in those days, but they were not the rule. Nine months after their wedding, they brought my older sister into this world. They were delighted; they adored her. One only has to look at the infinite number of pictures they took of her, and at the journal my mother kept, in which she recorded every smile, every tooth that appeared on the baby girl's face. It occurred to me once that the same Dr Razook had delivered my sister, and that he may have been as disappointed by his deed as he was when it was my turn to show up. But, for some unexplained reason, it was only my appearance that seemed to be a worthy story for my mother to narrate. The reason should have been obvious to me. It may not matter to the parents if the newborn is male or female, but in the wider society there is nothing to boast about when you bring only girls into this Middle Eastern world. You have to be very keen on bringing up a small, well-cared-for family to stop after the second child and not try for that special one that will perpetuate your name and speak for the virility of the father and the blessing of the mother.

Garçon manqué was the term I kept hearing about me, tomboy. The French expression is more revealing. A boy missed. An opportunity missed. But the values that the post-industrial societies had introduced in our Levantine reality were tangible enough and no third child was to be expected. So my story meets that of my society. I am female, accepted as such but unconsciously or very silently wished different. The context in which I was born, the Lebanon of the 1950s, was a paradigm of this dichotomy. Some named the two poles in this combination modern and traditional, others used the labels east and west, now the term post-modern is frequently used.

I can think of a perfect metaphor: *un garçon manqué*, a missed boy, and *une opportunité manquée*, a missed opportunity. A country that has missed its democratic and tolerant potentialities. A happy alternative. But ...

To go back to my gender and its implications: like any child who finds him/herself at the centre of attention, I started to play the role that made me successful among the members of my family and their friends. I started to behave as a tomboy. I wrote to Father Christmas asking him for a cowboy outfit. When I played with my dolls I did so discreetly, for the pleasure of mothering or dressing them was hampered by a sharp feeling of guilt and the fear of disappointing the grown-ups. I joined the boys in the courtyard after school to play football and all was free and fun until Sit Zalfa, an imposing old neighbour, saw me fighting physically over the score with one of the boys. She used to terrify us with her severe chignon and her Turkish and Italian vocabulary. "Pronto," she screamed, pointing her stick at me and then in the direction of my home. She visited my parents and told them that it was not "right" for a nine-year-old girl to mix with the boys of the neighbourhood. That was the end of my street life. What the neighbours said proved more powerful than the cute image of a *garçon manqué*. The neighbours' opinion had a decisive influence on my parents, who still insisted that it did not matter to them if I were a girl or a boy. We were already in the early 1960s, and Lebanon enjoyed the rule of a functioning parliament; a coup d'etat had been defeated and my mother as well as my aunts dressed in the latest Parisian fashion. My mixed school was preparing to separate the girls from the boys: yes, even the French Lycée adapted its rules to the Arab-Mediterranean reality of Lebanese society. Religion and religious teaching were not allowed inside the secular institution, but girls who were approaching puberty had to be separated from boys. A *garçon manqué* in a girls' school did not make much sense. A segregated secular lycée would have been an anomaly in France, but we were not in France, even though we spoke French and believed in the values of the Enlightenment.

I had heard my parents calling me a tomboy, and now I started hearing my mother asserting that I was very good in the sciences, the objective ones. Accordingly I became good at mathematics and physics. My grades in French literature, a subject I adored, did not impress my mother, whereas her face would beam with joy whenever she saw me resolving some geometry or calculus problem. This was a safer way of replacing the boy that was never to be born; safer than playing and fighting with the boys over a football kick. For sciences do not jeopardize virtue or reputation. At school, when I was not yet fourteen years old, I read *The Mandarins* by Simone de Beauvoir and heard of free love, but a concert by Johnny Halliday, the French pop star, was cancelled by the Minister of Interior, the "progressive" Kamal Jumblatt, who believed that 'western degenerate images' did not suit our moral values and might be harmful to our youth. Along with all the citizens of the Lebanon in the 1960s, I learned to live with these conflicting attitudes and values. Jugglers we became: with more or less graciousness, sometimes over some broken eggs, we wove our way through mini skirts and scarves, chanting anti-imperialist slogans as well as the Beatles. The kitsch singer Taroub sang for an Arab public, while her sister Mayada set Arabic words to western pop songs. When a dance called the Hully Gully invaded the night-clubs of Lebanon, the famous Diva Sabah sang *"Hully Dabke Yaba Of."*

> *Hully Gully est connu chez tous les occidentaux,*
> *Hully Dabke Yaba Of est connu chez*
> *Les Orientaux, presque le même et tout le monde l'aime.*

Neither we nor Sabah could have guessed that the Occident and the Orient were going to sing to totally different tunes. From Radio Cairo the mesmerizing voice of *Umm Kulsum* was asking for a rifle—A'tini Bunduqiya'—a rifle to liberate Arab land. We were reading Jean-Paul Sartre and starting to demonstrate for the liberation of Palestine.

By the early 1970s I was studying mathematics and French literature. Male and female subjects. Feminism was on the agenda: George Tarabishi translated Sheila Rowbotham, Germaine Greer's *The Female Eunuch* was available in the bookshops and Sonia Beiruti, a TV broadcaster, invited a few of us to her TV show to debate women's emancipation. Two scenes from that period keep recurring in my memory. First scene: on this TV show, I said I wanted to be a free woman and to be independent, to work so that I would not live off my father's or a future husband's money. My father, who was watching the programme, felt deeply humiliated. He took these words as an insult to his honour. Second scene: during a student demonstration, a few women jumped on the shoulders of their colleagues to lead and chant revolutionary slogans. Everybody in this demonstration had seen the pictures of May 1968 in France and the dynamic images of the women lifted above the crowds by their co-objectors. "Scandalous," screamed some passers-by, as well as a few demonstrators. The women were put down very quickly. We may have been influenced by May 1968 but we were not in the Latin Quarter of Paris; we were still on the shores of the Mediterranean.

We were a parliamentary democracy, we had no kings and no army generals ruling over us, but many of our politicians were the sons of landowners or sons of other politicians. They all spoke of democracy and we called for our right to independence as women while armed militias were being formed and operations to restore women's virginity were easily available. Somehow, I see a parallel between my studying mathematics at the American University and French literature at the Lebanese National University, between my gender that held me responsible for the family's reputation on one hand and my county's coexisting contradictions on the other.

Feminism was an obvious route to follow for somebody like me—a woman who had believed that men's spaces were not totally impermeable, nor mysterious or difficult to handle. You play with boys, enter their classrooms, obtain better grades than many of them and then you are asked to obey them or accept an inequality that places them above you? This was very difficult to swallow, especially if Simone de Beauvoir's *The Second Sex* has been widely read among your French-educated friends and her assertion that '*on ne naît pas une femme, on la devient*' (one is not born a woman, one becomes so) is a cool slogan to raise. Old feminism, that of the pioneers such as Hoda Sha'rawi or the active lawyer Laure Meghayzel, felt inadequate to our youthful impatience. We did not want only equality, the right to be professional while ensuring that we were first and foremost "good mothers": we wanted to claim loudly and shamelessly that nothing could stop us from realizing our wishes and that our bodies belonged to us.

Engels, Reich and Alexandra Kollontai's teachings gave a social dimension to our belief that "all is possible". The country itself believed that its rise as the financial-tourism heaven of the Middle East and its enriched Gulf region was unstoppable, that the Palestinian resistance fighters were the local expression of the Vietnamese freedom fighters. We spoke out loudly against the hypocrisy of our society. We were getting more radicalized in our beliefs, and so were the contradictions and the conflicts in Lebanon.

A time came when, in the middle of the bloody and cruel sequences of the civil war, I started to miss the so-called hypocrisy of pre-war times. The feeling that "I want everything and I want it now" dissipated. I looked with different eyes on the liberalism of my parents who had to bite on their Mediterranean wound and let me be. They tolerated my freedom of movement, even though my tomboy image was long dead and buried under the powerful influence of Sitt Zalfa and her ilk.

I moved to the other side of the Green Line, where I thought people would be free from the prejudices of my own milieu. There I found a reversed mirror detonating with the same kind of intolerance. What we called hypocrisy before the war was the best form of compromise people had found for living together. The taboo preventing one from spelling out one's dislike for the other had been a good discipline. Look around you and see how ugly it all becomes when people feel no inhibition in their intolerance. I am not calling for censorship, far from it. People have the right to express their feelings, however despicable we may think them, but this should not discourage us from doing all we can to relate hatred for the other's colour, race or sexual choice to the notion of bad, uncivilized and immoral and to link the violent expression of this hatred to legal judgment and action.

Yes, it took me a long time to realize why my mother loved to tell the story of Dr.

Razook and my birth. It took me longer to realize that the contradictions my parents had to live through opened great new spaces for me. And if they had not hoped for me to jump over the limiting fences my gender imposed on me, I may have been confined to living, all my life, on one side of the border(s) and I would have never learnt that we were all as human or as bad as "the other" during the ugly years of our civil war. If my mother had not told this story, would I have had the confidence, some eighteen years ago, to face the London bank manager who was reluctant to deal with me as one of the directors of Saqi Books and "would rather see my male boss"? Would I have had the courage to bend the long aluminium rod that holds my sculptures, would I have been capable to be "the other", to integrate among the others without pain and often with plenty of fun? I may have been a missed opportunity for Dr Razook and others like him; but I still believe that I am better off missing the narrowness of the choice that would have been my secure lot and instead taking the risk of following my individual routes.

Originally published in Hazim Saghie (ed.) *The Predicament of the Individual in the Middle East* (Saqi Books, 2001): 211–216. Printed here with the permission of the publisher.

PART SEVEN

Shifting Family Patterns

Introduction

Despite being one of the most venerable and vital social institutions in Arab society, the family, and its cherished kinship obligations and loyalties, is not always coherent. While it is enabling by virtue of the reinforcing functions it continues to provide by way of socio-cultural, psychological, and economic supports, it could also be in some significant dimensions quite disabling. By analyzing the premarital strategies and the factors which influence people's choice of marriage partners, Homa Hoodfar provides some persuasive evidence in support of her central thesis; namely, that the marriage institution and gender ideology provide a framework within which both sexes operate, manipulating the norms and conventions to promote their own interests, in both marriage and society. By doing so, asymmetric gender and gender ideology, to the disadvantage of women, are often reproduced.

In an overwhelmingly kinship culture where family ties and loyalties remain resilient sources of psychological wellbeing, social welfare and economic security, it is not surprising that marriage continues to be the most important social event in the lives of Middle Eastern men and women. It is through marriage and procreation that adulthood and self-realization are validated. Particularly in a precarious urban setting replete with insecurities, the idea of remaining unmarried by choice is very rare. Indeed, it is the epitome of deprivation.

Given such realities, it is understandable why parents, almost the moment their children are born, become obsessed with strategies for improving prospects for their successful marriages. For example, among low-income groups, where men often depend on their wives' labor, men are reluctant to enforce their paternalistic prerogative to restrict women's movements. During the last few decades, particularly in the wake of *infitah*, economic liberalization and social change, women and their families have developed initiatives and strategies to circumvent the legal and ideological restrictions imposed on them.

Like elsewhere in Arab society, marriage in Egypt is regulated by customs, religion and legal requirements. Matters like choosing a suitor, arranged versus love marriages, grounds for divorce, multiple wives and the exacting character of negotiating the terms of marriage remain contested.

Perhaps the most arduous are the marriage negotiations which normally cover two major components: First, the material contributions of each side to the marriage (such as the size of the bride's *mahr*) and second, other relational arrangements between the bride and the groom after marriage. For example, matters regarding veiling, divorce, multiple wives and employment prospects have assumed importance in recent years.

The bulk of the interviews Hoodfar conducted in a lower-class neighborhood in Cairo focused on the strategies women developed to manipulate and rearrange the norms which enhance their sense of autonomy and bargaining power within the marriage and the household. Such strategies, she concluded, do not always work to the advantage of women. Indeed, such strategies often reproduce the structural constraints which are the source of their asymmetry and marginalization in society.

Suad Joseph, a prominent Lebanese-American anthropologist, arrives at similar conclusions as she shifts her analysis to matters of gender, sexuality, love and power within a working-class neighborhood in the eastern suburbs of Beirut. By focusing on the evolving patterns of brother-sister relationships, she too reveals how some of the salient symptoms of Arab patriarchy are preserved and reinforced. As an ethnographer Joseph had the opportunity to intimately observe and revisit her research site over an interlude of close to a decade (1970–78). The conclusions she made in this regard cannot be dismissed as casual and impersonal reflections extracted from passing and episodic instances. The relationship between Hanna (the oldest son of the family) and his younger sister (Flaur), particularly during her pre and post adolescence, epitomize the survival of patriarchy and other associated manifestations which all members of the household willingly reconfirm in their everyday life.

Astute and probing researcher that she is, Joseph did not just exclusively focus on the testy and emotionally charged relationships between Hanna and Flaur, engaging as the evolving dynamics between the two siblings were. Instead, the graphic story she constructs revolves around three sets of processes. First, by focusing on love, power and dimensions of connectivity, she depicts peculiarities of brother-sister relationships. Second, she looks at marriage and inheritance to pronounce their implications for cross-sibling mutual dependence and obligations. Finally, she considers how cultural norms associated with honor and shame reinforced the sense of selfhood both Hanna and Flaur came to observe and celebrate.

One of Joseph's inferences deserves highlighting that by feminizing Flaur, Hanna "was teaching her to accept male power in the name of love. His family supported his learning that loving his sister meant taking charge of her and that he could discipline her if his action was understood to be in her best interests." Hanna was also teaching his sister how to present her feminine sexuality. "By feminizing Flaur, Hanna was masculinizing himself. He was using his culturally acceptable control over his sister to challenge his father's authority in the family."

While Hoodfar and Joseph explored some of the double-edged significance of the dynamics of family relations, particularly as embodied in marriage, inheritance and sibling rivalry, Najla Hamadeh extends her observations to another inveterate feature of the traditional Arab family; namely polygamy and the character of relationships between co-wives. Here, as well, Hamadeh elucidates the dual and contested nature of women trapped in the fabric of polygamous marital arrangements.

Though polygamy as a form of marriage is not as prevalent today in most Arab societies, an analysis of the experience of co-wives ,and the strategies they evolve to cope with such situations, may be instructive for understanding the vulnerabilities and strength women derive from sharing a husband with another women. Much of the literature on polygamy, extracted from both academic studies and popular opinion, is inclined to depict the relationship between co-wives to be characterized by considerable resentment and friction. The thrust of the literature is based on the view that the victims of such marriages are trapped in arrangements not of their choosing and that they are compelled to suffer all the misbegotten miseries of sharing a husband with other women.

Hamadeh's grounded fieldwork and the three case studies she explores question such negative perceptions. Her vivid portraits also provide evidence which challenge salient premises regarding how so-called traditional values and institutions are reacting to some of the unsettling incursions associated with modernization and global transformations. For example, calls are occasionally made by a score of scholars that a move towards the nuclear family and the undermining of patriarchy are prerequisites for the achievement of democratic relations must not be accepted without some qualifications. Likewise, the fact that the experience of Western urbanization has been associated with some desirable elements, should not lead us to assume that societies in the Arab World will display similar supportive tendencies. The ethnographic data Hamadeh collects from two distinct socio-cultural settings—tribal Bedouins in the Bekaa' valley and nuclear families in an urban district in Beirut—reveal some interesting findings. Women living within nuclear families seem to fall under a more oppressive patriarchy than those in tribal communities. Patriarchal power among the Bedouin tribes resides within a few elders who are usually chosen for their wisdom and superior moral standing. The authority of the elders, together with the watch that tribes keep on the behavior of their members, ensures some rights for women and a modicum of fairness in the way they are treated. In contrast, under urban patriarchies, women are more vulnerable since they are subject to the whims of their single husbands regardless of their discretion and moral standing.

Marriage, Family, and Household in Cairo

In Egypt people rarely live alone by choice. Individuals move out of their natal households when they form their own households through marriage. A household may include extended and nuclear family members, and other kin on occasion, though membership is rarely extended to nonkin. In the lower-income neighborhoods of urban Egypt, most households are formed around the nuclear family and marriage plays a significant role in shaping the structure of a household and the position of individuals within it. Moreover, marriage practices in Egypt (and generally) play an important role in reproducing gender ideology.

In practice, at the outset of marriage, a bride and groom together with their families generally negotiate agreements that enhance their positions and their bargaining power within the marriage and the household. In addition to emotional and social factors, economic considerations are of prime importance in the choice of a marriage partner and in the stipulation of the conditions of a marriage contract, since the material well-being of individuals—particularly women and children—is closely tied to the economic situation of their households. After briefly outlining the rights and responsibilities of husbands and wives in Muslim marriage as it is practiced in Egypt, this chapter reviews the major premarital strategies and the factors that influenced people's choice of marriage partners.

Marriage in its Cultural Context

Marriage is probably the most important social event in the lives of Middle Eastern men and women. It is through marriage and having children that adulthood and self-realization are achieved. Particularly in the urban setting, the beginning of married life often coincides with the couple setting up their own household. Almost from their children's infancy, parents are preoccupied with improving the prospects for successful marriages. While marriage is often delayed because of financial hardship, the pursuit of education, or family circumstances, the idea of remaining single by choice is beyond the imagination of almost everyone in the neighborhoods of Giza (Greater Cairo)—young or old, male or female. "How could anyone choose not to follow the custom of the Prophet?" an elderly woman responded to my innocent query about the possibility of remaining unmarried by choice. In the neighborhoods and in Egypt generally, like most other parts of the Muslim world, marriage is the only acceptable context for sexual activity and parenthood and provides the primary framework for the expression of masculinity and femininity and the fulfillment of gender roles.

Marriage in Egypt is regulated by custom, religion, and the legal system, which dictate different roles and responsibilities for men and women. Muslim marriage gives certain rights to a husband in return for his expected contribution to the family. Men are responsible for providing for their families which includes their current wives and underage children and may include aged parents, unmarried sisters, younger brothers, and the orphaned children of their brothers. In return for these responsibilities, a husband is assumed to have the unilateral right to end his marriage without the consent of his wife.

He also has the right to have as many as four wives on the condition that he can provide adequately and equally for all of them and treat them equally. Furthermore, at least according to the cultural interpretation of Islamic marriage mores and the legal codes in Egypt, a husband has the right to restrict his wife's physical mobility. This has come to be understood as the husband's right to prevent his wife from being employed. Should a marriage end in divorce, husbands have the guardianship and custody of their children beyond a certain age, usually five to seven years for boys and puberty for girls. In recent decades in Egypt, as in other Muslim countries, there has been some attempt to legally limit some of men's rights by favoring a more liberal interpretation of Islamic *shari'a*. Nonetheless, women, particularly those with children, are aware that they stand to lose more than men should the marriage fail.

In a Muslim marriage, in addition to providing for the family (regardless of his wife's financial status), a husband is expected to satisfy his wife sexually. Failure in any of these responsibilities gives a woman grounds for divorce with or without her husband's agreement. She is also entitled to her *mahr,* which is a sum of money or tangible property agreed on before marriage. Muslim women have always had the right to control and dispose of their own property, including inheritances or any wages they may earn, without having to contribute to the household. While women may inherit from their blood kin, they inherit only a negligible part of their husband's property. In the case of divorce, however, a wife is entitled to only three months alimony, her *mahr,* those possessions she brought with her at the start of the marriage, and what she may have acquired with her own income during the marriage. For these reasons, the security of marriage is an important factor for women and their natal families—who are responsible for supporting a woman whose marriage fails—and thus they strive to arrange secure marriages for their daughters.

The reality of the institution of marriage is much more complex than its accepted ideology indicates. For example, among low-income groups, in which men often depend on their wives' labor, men rarely use their prerogative to restrict women's movements, and women are generally free to perform their errands and social activities. As well, the relatively low incidence of divorce, particularly after children are born, suggests that marriage is a relatively stable institution in Egypt. In general, most women enjoy more rights than are traditionally ascribed to them, and hence they are unlikely to resist or question the status quo on gender relations, despite being very aware of their restricted legal rights in marriage. While the more powerful, wealthier classes have advocated legal reform as a means of social change, the less privileged groups try to protect their interests through manipulation of the resources and avenues they can control. During the last few decades of rapid social change, women and their families have developed initiatives and strategies to circumvent the legal and ideological limitations imposed on them. For instance, kin and in-group marriages have historically been the most common strategies for protecting women from abuse by their husbands. More recently, women have been demanding a larger *mahr,* and among low-income communities detailed and rigorous premarriage negotiations that cover most aspects of married life are becoming the accepted norm.

Social and economic change has given rise to much higher material expectations, which place greater pressures on men, the ideologically designated breadwinners. For young men, the legal and religious privileges that marriage historically afforded come at a greater cost than for previous generations. Hence many young men try to find ways to minimize these responsibilities. For example, they may marry women who have some cash income, or they may marry women from much lower social rankings whose expectations may not be so high.

Choosing a Suitor

Both Islam and tradition provide channels for devising strategies for secure and successful marriages. Since marriage is viewed not as a partnership between individuals but rather as an alliance between two families, the equation to determine the best marriage partner is very complex and not easy to disaggregate. All but four women in my sample said that it was best for women to marry kin because their economic status and background are known, leaving no room for deception. Furthermore, they pointed out that should there be a problem between the groom and the bride, the families would try to help patch up the differences, as the consequences of divorce or domestic violence would be grave for both sides of the family.

Women and most younger members of the communities almost always viewed members of their mothers' kin as the most suitable for marriage partners, as opposed to the norm of patrilineal and especially cross-cousin marriage. This choice may stem from the fact that most families in the neighborhood more commonly interacted with their mother's kin. Fathers, however, often said that the ideal marriage was between parallel cousins from the father's side, but they frequently qualified that statement by saying that in their own case their relatives were not suitable.

While men also expressed preference for kin marriages, their underlying logic was very different. Both young men and their fathers said that kin marriages are best because they are less expensive. Neither the bride nor the groom can demand many gifts or a high mahr, making these marriages less of a burden for the fathers of both bride and groom. Ironically, many women, particularly younger ones, counted this aspect of kin marriages as a disadvantage. Fatin explained:

> In Egypt men do not work at home. In fact they do not spend much time at home. Once a man is married and has a wife who cooks and cleans for him, he no longer has a vested interest in providing household goods and so does not work as hard. But if he has to provide these as a condition of marriage, then he probably is more eager to do that... . But when one marries a relative the bride's family places fewer demands on the groom. Consequently kin marriages give women less economic leverage and a wife has to endure more hardship to improve her standard of living.

Many daughters observed that the eagerness of their fathers to marry them to relatives stemmed from a desire to lessen their own financial responsibilities while ensuring safe marriages.

Great emphasis was put on the credentials a spouse ought to have. In addition to a pleasant appearance for suitors of both sexes, a potential wife should be a clever homemaker and a good mother, while a potential husband should be able to provide for the family, be a responsible and loving father, and respect his wife. Azza's mother, who had four daughters, explained the difficulties most parents face.

> In the old days most people married their relatives or neighbors who were of the same social class. But now there is much more contact between different people and one's daughters may have a chance of marrying into a much higher income group. But this also means that the daughter may not be treated with respect by her husband and in-laws. For my daughters, I wish to find good self-made suitors, educated men who have good jobs but come from similar family and social backgrounds.

Whereas most young and educated unmarried girls in the neighborhood expressed a desire for rich, modern, educated, and handsome men, more traditional and less educated women were skeptical of marrying up. At the age of sixteen, against the wishes of the uncle who was her guardian, Mona married Nasser, a handsome man from a family considered relatively well-to-do. She had no education; he had a high school diploma. Ten years into her unhappy marriage, Mona told me,

> If only I had the sense to marry someone like myself, I would not be treated the way Nasser treats me. You have seen how he treats me, I don't feel like his wife, he makes me feel I am his and his children's servant. And there is nothing I can do now because if I ask for a divorce, I would have to become a maid to support myself. Worse yet, he may take my children away from me and then I will have nothing in life. So I have to put up with being a servant in my home, as the alternative is being a servant to other people.

Young women from families who proudly associated themselves with *baladi* (urban traditional) or *fallahi* (peasant) culture were inclined to accept the conventional wisdom and marry among their own class. However, they were often considered "backward" by the more educated young men.

There were other factors that women pointed out as important elements of a successful marriage. All women in my sample said that men have to be more educated than their wives. Younger and urban-born women insisted that a husband should be older by at least five or six or even ten years. When I asked why that was, they explained that a wife should obey and listen to her husband, and, since men do not mature as fast as women do, a woman cannot heed a man of her own age whose judgment is not as sound as hers. This would create problems for a marriage and might even result in divorce. Women consistently used this justification for their preference for older men. Mona, a seventeen-year-old high school student, told me,

> I would never marry someone of my own age, education, income, or social stature. The problem is that in our society men like to think they are wiser

than women, though if they are equal in age and education it is always the woman who is more clever, as you can see all around you. On the other hand, according to our religion a wife has to obey her husband. But no one can obey someone who is not as wise as she is, and consequently there would be lots of arguments and the marriage will fall apart and what would happen to the children? Therefore, it is better for a woman to marry someone who is older, more educated, who has much more experience in life than she has, and so it would not be illogical for her to obey him.

What this kind of universal justification indicates is that women not only do not consider themselves inferior to men but also see themselves, under equal conditions, as wiser and more capable. Therefore, to cope with the religiously legitimized male expectation that a wife has to obey her husband, women deliberately marry old more experienced men.

Urbanization, social change, and the trend toward nuclear households have strengthened women's conviction that it is best to marry an older man. A middle-aged woman who was older than her husband explained to me,

> In the village age wasn't important; if the families decided the couple was right for each other and if they had the means to live, they could marry. My parents agreed with my mother's brother that I should marry his son, who was about two years younger, so we married. But in the village, men used to do their own work on the farm and women did their own tasks. Men and women did not spend time with each other. One spent more time with one's mother-in-law and should have a good rapport with her more than with one's husband. But things have changed, even in the village.

Men's description of the ideal wife and circumstances of marriage mirrored women's views. Men felt strongly that to be accepted and respected as heads of the household, they had to be older and more educated than their wives. None of my male informants expressed any inclination to marry women of higher social standing since such a marriage was viewed as a continuous test of their dignity. Some men acknowledged that the option of hypergamy (marrying up) was not usually open to men because of financial constraints. But the more successful men in the neighborhoods expressed outright hostility to the idea, saying that even when the couple truly loved each other, marrying up meant a man would be a "henpecked husband."

One of my middle-aged informants told me that while he was at university he fell in love with a classmate. The love was mutual, but she came from a rich and vastly different background, so he decided to marry a young woman from the neighborhood instead.

Generally, men were aware that society awarded them privileged status within the family, and they were conscious of placing themselves in socioeconomic positions within marriage so as to avoid situations that might cause women to question the status quo. Some of the more traditional older men from upper Egypt said as soon as women earn money, the marriage institution is spoiled and men are no longer men. Other, younger men said they would never marry a woman who earned more money than they do because in that case "the husband becomes a wife" and gave examples of such couples from the neighborhood. Men saw a direct link between their masculinity and their role in marriage as the major breadwinner; any deviations would leave their masculinity and adequacy open to question.

In other words, gender ideology and, the marriage institution provide a framework within which both genders try to manipulate the norms and promote their own interests, within marriage and outside it.

Arranged Marriages versus Love Marriages

Ideally, parents chose their children's partners with the tacit agreement of the prospective couple. The groom's father directly or indirectly contacted the bride's family, and if the response was positive, he then visited them and proceeded with marriage negotiations. By this stage the potential bride and groom have usually seen each other and agreed to the match. Although one hears about women who were married against their will, apart from a young Coptic woman who was married at the age of fourteen, I never came to know of any and none of my informants knew of any such marriages, though a few women had not been sure and their mothers and relatives had persuaded them by reminding them of the groom's attributes. One thirty-two-year-old woman who was always amused by my interest in their lives and views jokingly told me,

> Write for your professor at American University that we were poor and we all had to marry among the poor. For our parents, one good responsible poor man was the same as another poor man. They had no reason to force us to marry against our will ... Maybe if we were rich it would be very different.

When asked how they chose their partners, women invariably answered that their familes or fathers decided whom they would marry. However, after I got to know them better, a different picture emerged. Several older women said that their fathers or brothers had found them rich suitors, thinking that it was in their best interest. But through their mothers and aunts the girls expressed opposition to the matches and they were canceled. Many educated women who married in the 1970s chose their husbands from among their colleagues. At least five in my sample had married for love and had decided on their marriage before their parents met the groom, and two of them had married against the wishes of their parents. Others had asked friends to find them suitors among their families or brothers. Many of the older couples had married relatives or neighbors or someone from their village. Younger and more educated people had found their marriage partners through their network at home or through contacts outside the neighborhoods. However, in all cases, formal steps were taken and the bride's family negotiated the marriage conditions, even in the two cases in which the family had opposed the marriage.

Although an ideology of marriage based on love is gaining popularity, it is compatibility and harmony that are viewed by both men and women as the key to a successful marriage. Love is said to be blind and irrational, as one educated woman who herself had an unhappy marriage based on love told me.

> Love may make the best subject for a pleasant song or the basis of a film. Maybe it is good for dreams when you are fifteen, but it surely should not be the only

or even the major basis for marriage. How can physical attraction, which is all love really is, be the basis of a marriage?

Marriage in Egyptian culture, as several observers have noted, is supposed to be primarily for survival, for cooperation between two parties, not for the unification of two souls. This view was conveyed to me by many men and women in the neighborhoods. Umm Shadia, an elderly woman, mother of four sons and four daughters, and a respected community leader who was often consulted by others about marriage and marital disputes, decided to teach me the principles and importance of marriage among Egyptians. She explained,

> Here one does not marry a person, but a family. Therefore marriage is much too important to be left in the hands of two kids who have lost their heart to a pair of beautiful eyes or nice hair, who think life is like love films they see on television. What do they know about the difficulties of life? A marriage should be based on compatibility of the couple and their families. Husbands and wives should be respectful of each other and perform their respective duties within the marriage ... A marriage based on respect and harmony brings love, but a love marriage that lacks harmony ends in fights and disaster.

Although a few men said they would marry a woman they fancied as long as she was from a good family and was decent and modest, even if their parents disagreed, all women, including the younger women who thought love is essential for marriage, said they would not marry without their parents' complete approval. Samia, a very bright eighteen-year-old known for her rebellious nature, told me,

> I think loving my husband is essential for me. In marriage, life is tougher for a woman than for a man. At least if one loves one's husband it makes it easier to obey him... But I will not marry a man if my parents do not agree. I may tell my parents it is either him or nobody, but if a daughter does not have the blessing of her parents, her husband is not going to treat her with respect. He will think a woman who does not respect her parents' wishes after all they have done for her will not respect him, a stranger, either.

This attitude is reinforced by observing the lives of those who deviated from traditional marriage practices. Those who had married without their parents' approval were the first ones to point out the problems. Sadia's marriage provides an excellent illustration of this point. Sadia, a white-collar worker, told me,

> When I was a teenage schoolgirl in the 1960s we were told about dreams of modern Egypt, not the Egypt of the rich, but our Egypt. Women were going to be educated and free themselves from the traditional binds. Like all my classmates at the time, I took that to heart. I believed in love and wanted to marry the man I chose. I fell in love with the brother of one of my friends who was tutoring us. I agreed to marry him and I announced this to my parents, who had already found me another suitor and were waiting for me to complete high school and then marry us off. They were shocked but finally agreed, but they told me that I had to take 100 percent responsibility for the marriage, that if tomorrow I had problems with him, I could not complain to them. So

I married him, before receiving my high school diploma, and since he had very little money, we had to move to his mother's at first. There I quickly realized that I was dreaming that marriage was just about love but in fact it was about harmony and mutual respect—that society and parents, too, have to approve of the marriage. I could not go to my parents, as they had warned me, and worse, I became pregnant almost immediately. However, my first child, a son, died. I decided to finish my studies, and had my second child the same year. I got a job at the Ministry of Education, and immediately after that my husband refused to pay any money to me for house expenses because he wanted to spend all his money on himself. Since I married without my parents' support, he believed I could not turn to my parents and indeed it was hard for me to do so, but I did and they forgave me. I also felt stronger because I had what was then considered a good job. I almost got a divorce over this matter. However, I went back to him. Life is different when you have children ... My parents helped us to get a small flat and now he pays a little money. But our relationship is not healthy. The love died long ago and the harmony and respect was never there, but I only came to discover this after I had married him. Now, when I take a look at my sisters' marriages arranged by my parents, they are happier and have their husbands' respect. I married for love, but I want my three daughters, who are the apples of my eye, to marry in the traditional arranged way so that I can negotiate on their behalf and make sure they have a good start. I want them to be happy and not suffer the way I did.

Some thought that women should show respect for their husbands, but never love, even if they are in love with them. One afternoon, after a few of us watched an old Egyptian movie on television, we had a lively debate on the role of love in marriage. Haleh, a happily married twenty-eight-year-old woman, concluded our long discussion by saying, "One should never demonstrate her love for a man because he will take her for granted. The right way is that men should love their wives much more." Others agreed with her. This view stems in part from many women's belief that expressing such love for their husbands undercuts women's bargaining power. As one middle-aged woman commented, "Men want what they don't have; why would they do anything for you if you are already at their feet?"

Ideologically and religiously, the most important responsibility for any parent was to assure that their children, both male and female, were happily married. However, despite strong views on these matters by all, few parents from low-income households actually were involved in their sons' marriage arrangements, or rather their involvement was more formal than real. Only the richest and, sometimes, the poorest parents in the neighborhoods had a say in the marriages of their sons. This gap between ideology and practice was due in part to parents' inability to pay or substantially contribute to the soaring cost of marriage, which traditionally in Muslim cultures is largely borne by the groom and his family. Also, a large number of parents were from rural backgrounds and felt they no longer possessed the experience and expertise needed to advise their sons or find them suitable wives. Sons, therefore, enjoy much more freedom in choosing partners. Some men considered this a mixed blessing as they believed only a woman could get to know another woman, and without the support of their mothers and sisters they would find out little about the true nature of the woman they intended to marry. Many men under forty had found their wives through their own networks.

While parents can withdraw from involvement in a son's marriage without great social consequences, particularly if there is a legitimate reason, no parent can choose not to participate in a daughter's marriage arrangements. A family's honor and self-respect are very closely tied to the daughter's. Allocating resources to the marriage of a daughter is probably the only time she receives priority over her brothers. However, the cost of a daughter's marriage is much less than a son's. While the parents are expected to provide her with a suitable trousseau, consisting of clothing and personal items, the contribution of other items is much more flexible and is considered a gift, not an obligation. What is important is that the bride's parents play an effective role in negotiating the groom's contribution to the cost of the wedding and establishment of the new household.

Marriage Negotiations: Strategies to Reduce Marital Conflicts

Marriage negotiations are considered the most important element in setting a marriage on the right path. As one woman who was helping her husband to build their very first small flat put it,

> Marriage negotiation is just like a plan for a building. You have to realistically assess your resources and think of every little detail that is important for your comfort and the safety of the flat. If parents conduct a good and smart marriage negotiation for their children, it is most unlikely that the marriage would end in disaster.

Among low-income Egyptian families, in addition to financial matters, every detail of married life considered important by the parties is up for negotiation. Some mothers will even go so far as to negotiate whether the bride should use contraception the first year or have a child and then use contraception.

After an initial meeting, when the groom or his family visits the bride's home and both sides indicate their consent, additional meetings take place to negotiate the details. Ideally, negotiations should take place between the elders from both sides: fathers and uncles, mothers and aunts, and grandmothers. However, in the neighborhood, negotiations often began between the bride's parents and the groom, who might take a friend along. I know of only one case in which the groom's father participated and another in which the groom's mother, who paid for the wedding herself, negotiated all the aspects of the marriage with the bride's father. The groom's mother and sisters may be present at the final stage of negotiation to formally give their blessing, The exceptions were instances in which the two families were very close and the women of both sides played the key roles in negotiations.

The primary player in the negotiations is the mother of the bride, who, depending on her position in the household, may participate actively and openly or may sit more quietly and note the details being discussed and afterward convey her opinions to her husband. During formal discussions the bride's father, while making his wishes known, chooses his words very carefully, remaining noncommittal until later in the negotiations.

Negotiations start with the groom revealing information about his family and himself, such as the details of his education, job, income, worldly possessions, and future plans. The bride's father or his representative indicates his demands. Neither side expects that this first serious meeting will end in any concrete agreement, beyond the sharing of several pots of tea. Ideally, if the groom is not well known to the bride's family, after this meeting the bride's mother and friends set out to learn about the man and his family from his neighbors, colleagues, and employers. However, the degree to which families take this character investigation seriously varies substantially. In fact, since nowadays there is typically an engagement period of several years during which the bride's family has the opportunity to know the groom better, the importance of character investigation has diminished.

Marriage negotiations have two components: first, the material contribution of each side to the marriage and the new household; and second, other relational arrangements between the bride and the groom after the marriage. For the most part, the first includes the size of the bride's *mahr*. This is usually a considerable sum that varies with the social status of the bride's family. Theoretically a bride can demand all or part of the *mahr* at the time of the marriage or reserve it until some time during the marriage or in the event of divorce. In Egypt, the *mahr* is customarily divided into two sums. The first payment, called the *muqaddama,* is given by the groom to the bride before the marriage and is used to buy furniture for the couple. Sometimes the groom buys the furniture, which he then puts in the bride's name when the marriage contract is signed. The second payment, called the *muakhkkara,* religiously and legally may be demanded at any time after the signing of the contract but usually is used as a deterrent for divorce, since if a man wishes to divorce his wife he would first have to pay her this remaining sum. Therefore, the larger the sum, the more effective the wife's leverage.

Anyone over the age of forty can tell you that marriage expenses have increased since the 1970s. Elderly women told me that at the time of their marriage, a bed and canopy, a wardrobe, and a few other major items were provided by the groom, while the bride's family provided bedding, cooking facilities, and a small trousseau of personal items. Often they just rented a room near their parents and expanded their quarters as the family grew, but times have changed. Parents, and young people themselves, expect that each generation will have a higher standard of living. A couple preparing to marry now needs a gas stove, a television, a matching bedroom set, settees and a table, an electric washing machine, a food mixer, and a refrigerator. The bride's trousseau includes many nightgowns and enough clothing and personal items to assure she will not need to ask her husband for personal items for at least five years. The greatest expense incurred in setting up a household is the key money needed to rent a small flat, which runs from 1,500 to 3,000 pounds even in the most distant neighborhoods. This means that the groom has to work hard for a few years before he can get married. By contrast, as soon as a daughter is born many families start accumulating items for her trousseau.

The negotiation includes details of all items that both sides have agreed should be provided before marriage, what share the bride's family will provide, and what the groom's responsibilities will be. Once the items are accumulated and the marriage takes place, everything is carefully detailed in the marriage contract as the property of the bride. If the marriage dissolves for whatever reason, the groom must see that all nonperishable items are returned to the bride. All women agreed that this was important, to remind men to treat their wives well. This custom led to deferred marriage and encouraged potential grooms, who normally live with their parents and have few housekeeping expenses, to work hard and save money so that they can begin married life with a higher standard of living.

Many young women expressed bitterness about waiting as long as four years to get married, They were torn between wanting to have most of the basic household goods before marriage and not wanting to wait so long, particularly since many engagements were broken after a couple of years. Women are very conscious that during a long engagement they miss other marriage opportunities. As one mother pointed out, men can always find someone to marry whereas a woman's options diminish with age, particularly since men prefer to marry younger women.

This new trend in marriage practices has caused the average age of marriage to rise considerably for women and men. While the state, family planners, and some feminists may consider this a positive indicator for population control or women's increase in status, most women in my sample viewed it negatively. Women who were neither students nor employed resented having to postpone building their family. Many women agreed to marry older grooms who had worked and saved up enough to be able to marry. One young bride said, "I would rather marry a man just five or six years older than I am, but they don't have the means to marry. So my groom is fifteen years older. But my parents and I felt this was a better choice." The age and experience of the husbands and the gap between men's and women's monetary contributions to the household place women in an even more subservient position in the marriage partnership. It also means that they will spend long years as widows who will most likely be financially dependent on their children. This in turn has ramifications for population policy as women try to have more sons to secure their chances for later economic as well as emotional support. Many young men find a fiancée and, after an agreement is reached, migrate to the Gulf to work for a couple of years and save money to be able to marry. I asked women why they do not make smaller demands on their fiancés so they could marry sooner. They insisted that such strategies would mean poverty forever. One young woman, engaged to be married, said,

> Today I can demand to have a gas stove before marriage. But once I am married, he will not buy it. He wants his lunch, but whether I cook this on a kerosene burner or a gas stove is not his problem.

Financial arrangements include the amount the groom should pay as housekeeping money, what expenses this covers, and what he can expect from his wife. Some negotiations are so detailed as to specify whether he should expect one meal a week with meat, or two. Fatin had divorced her husband at the age of nineteen. Now in her thirties she had not expected to marry again. But she found a suitor, the *mahr* was successfully negotiated, and everybody was excited and preparing for the engagement ceremony. But the engagement came to a halt because the potential groom had agreed to pay 90 pounds per month but would not consent to buy food or clothing for her. After family members consulted, they decided that if he agreed to bring home a kilogram of meat every week they would agree to the arrangement, but he refused. Fatin had worked as a semiprofessional seamstress in the neighborhood for many years, had bought all her household goods, and had a rented flat of her own. This liberated the groom from providing or paying for all those items. She thought that he was taking advantage of her, that he wanted a wife, a comfortable home, and good food but did not want to contribute very much.

Women are keenly aware of the importance of these negotiations for relationships with their husbands. Some of the younger women who were experiencing problems with their husbands over financial affairs blamed their mothers for not having negotiated well. Many men try to get out of their obligations, but a good negotiation before marriage helps assure a woman's security. "It hurts a woman's dignity if she has to talk money with a husband she has just married," said one unhappy bride.

Men generally felt an agreement before marriage was fair, because if the conditions are not acceptable, a groom is free to end the negotiations and look for another bride. Premarital negotiations may also include how often the bride should be able to stay with her family. I never heard of this matter being written in the legal marriage contract, but such a discussion was intended to help ensure a smoother marriage with little room for conflict.

According to my older informants, detailed negotiations regarding the daily life of a married couple have emerged only in the last few decades. In the past, people married within their communities, where customs and norms were shared, but now people may marry across regions and social classes with vastly different customs and expectations. Moreover, life is changing very rapidly, and most young couples do not live the way their parents did. Some young women whose mothers were not very influential in the family or had little experience in such matters would ask a relative or a neighbor to participate in the negotiations. On the whole, as a result of social changes, the bride's mother is taking a more prominent role.

Although most negotiations focused on the demands of the bride and her family, increasingly men bring their own conditions to the negotiating table. For instance, more men, especially educated men who choose to marry educated women, are now objecting to their wives working outside the home, particularly if the job is located outside their area of residence. This even includes men who have chosen their brides from among their colleagues. This demand often creates a dilemma for some women who, to increase their chances of finding a secure job, finished high school at great sacrifice to their parents and sometimes their siblings. Men's objection to their future wives' employment is often framed in terms of the costs involved and the threat to a husband's honor. Though not always successful, women try to make compromises by agreeing to stay home after having children or if they feel they cannot cope with both domestic responsibilities and their jobs. Occasionally they also suggest taking up the veil to protect the family's good name and honor. This situation has encouraged many younger women in the neighborhood to return to more traditional female activities such as tailoring or hairdressing, since these skills allow them to operate from home and circumvent their husbands' objections.

A second, now common, condition men attached to their marriage proposal is that the bride take up the veil. Although until 1986 only a few educated women in the neighborhoods wore the veil, the practice is now quite widespread. It is now rare for women who get married to remain unveiled, particularly if they are educated or aspire to be considered modern (though not *afrangi,* which implies Westernized) as opposed to *baladi* (traditional). Husbands' demands to this effect are now far less controversial from women's point of view than they were a decade ago. During the first few years of my fieldwork, women felt very strongly that veiling should be done of a woman's free will and that a husband had no right to impose it on his wife. Nahed, for example, was excited because her friend had found her a handsome, educated suitor who had the financial means to marry within a few months. However, her excitement soon withered away after a couple of meetings with her suitor because he demanded that she take the veil at once. Nahed, disillusioned and disappointed, explained to me,

> If he had put forward any other condition I would have accepted to marry him because he is from a very decent family and I liked him. However, his demand for me to veil because he wishes and not because I might decide it is best for me indicates that he will not respect his wife as an equal partner and also that he has not understood what Islam is all about. I have thought from time to time that I might like to veil and I admire women who do it, but I feel I have not reached that point yet. I will veil when God wants me to and when he gives me the strength, but not when a man demands it of me as a condition of marriage.

Though taking up the veil no longer seemed to be a major issue during marriage negotiations, the question of employment remains quite significant for educated women. In the face of rapid social change, women and their families feel they should try to safeguard their future and old age by having a secure formal sector job. However, the salary for low-level clerical jobs in the formal sector has not kept up with the rate of inflation, and many men felt that their wives' employment would not contribute much to the household income but would cause great inconveniences. Some men added that women's wages may also make them "big-headed" and lead them to question men's authority as head of the household. Other men framed their objections in terms of not wanting their honor tested for nothing.

Polygynous Marriages

According to conventional Muslim ideology, if a man can fairly, equitably, and adequately provide for each wife, he can marry up to four wives. The assessment of the ability to provide equitably has, however, been left to men's conscience rather than to legislation. Historically, though polygyny has been practiced mainly by economically privileged men, at times it also occurs among the less affluent. The marriage of a man with few resources to another wife has far-reaching effects on the family. Many men stop or drastically reduce contributions to the first family. Polygyny was thus an issue both women and men discussed frequently, often with reference to the polygynous households in the neighborhoods. While women tended to condemn polygyny outright, particularly for poor men, men were reluctant to condemn the practice even when they themselves believed they would never enter a polygynous marriage. "I am happy with my wife and I will never marry another woman, nor could I afford that. But there must be a good reason for its existence if the Qur'an has recognized that right," one middle-aged man told me.

Some men in the neighborhoods had married a second wife because the first wife could not have any children, and in one case that I knew of, it was the first wife who chose the second wife for her husband. The first wife, a middle-aged woman, defended polygyny, saying if it were not for such arrangements, women like her (who did not produce children) would have to sleep in the street. However, there were other cases in which the husband and wife were reputed not to get along well and therefore the husband finally left and married a second wife.

Men invariably said a man in a happy marriage would not marry another woman, thereby indirectly blaming the women. Some women accused men of being greedy and shortsighted, thinking only of their own pleasure. Otherwise, they argued, why would a poor man marry a second wife when he cannot even afford to keep his first wife? Women insisted that for this reason they must be clever and manipulate men to prevent them from exercising their right to marry a second wife. Some younger women said if a man wished to take additional wives, his first wife must be as much to blame as he, since the cost of marriage is so prohibitive that no man would want to go through marriage twice.

Women's reluctance to consider divorce stems from two major factors. First, children legally belong to their fathers and women do not want to risk losing them. Second, women often lack the financial means to survive; even when they have a paid job, their income is often too meager to support the family. Women are also very aware that divorced women with children have little chance of remarrying, because men rarely accept other men's children in their home. Therefore, the practical choice for a first wife is to stay married to her husband and try to secure support from him. Moreover, women also benefit from the legitimacy of marriage, which affords them more freedom in the community.

Some women became second wives unwittingly and found out about their husbands' domestic arrangements only after the marriage. However, a woman who knowingly becomes a second wife, particularly in a close-knit neighborhood, is often treated badly by other women, unless they see that she had no choice in the matter. Umm Sabah, who sells vegetables in the local *suq,* is a second wife and is liked by her neighbors. She explained her marriage story to me.

> I came from a very poor family and my father was sick most of the time. He had a stand where he sold vegetables and I used to help him with his business. Every time a suitor came along, my father refused. For one thing they didn't have money to buy me a trousseau, and second, the family could not survive without my labor. In the end, my parents died and my brother went to do his military service and I managed to marry off my younger sister and later my brother also married and left me. I ended up living by myself in a dark and damp room even worse than the one I live in now, and I survived by selling vegetables and greens in the local market. I barely earned enough to pay rent and eat. I was very sad, not because I was poor, but because I, like all other women, so much wanted to have children, but no one would marry me because I was poor, old, and not pretty. One day a neighbor said the butcher wants to marry a second wife and get away from his first wife. He asked me if I would marry him, and I said yes. Before I knew it, I was married to him and I had two children. That is all I wanted from God. He is not the best husband, but he pays 10 pounds a week and I earn around 5 or 6. He visits twice a week and brings the children some meat. I think, given my situation, this is the best arrangement. I do not want more children, but I am glad that my children have another five brothers and sisters, and sometimes they go there to play with them. I have also lived by

myself and have become stubborn and do not really want a husband all the time who I have to obey and cook for and clean after. Now I only have to cook for him twice a week, and almost never do any cleaning or wash his clothes. And he is a good father, and very kind to my children. It suits me fine, and my co-wife, though initially upset, has become more friendly and accepts my children.

Umm Sabah was very content, and glad that her children had more siblings. "Eventually, they [the half-siblings] will support them more than a stranger. They are of the same blood, and blood pulls," she said.

Summary

In Egypt households are formed on the basis of marriage and kinship. While blood ties remain important, marriage is a domain within which individuals can influence whom they want to marry or be related to. Hence among the poor (as well as the rich) marriage choices and conditions are important life and survival strategies. The ideology of marriage and gender roles, legitimated by law and by conventional understandings of Islam, prescribes different rights and responsibilities for men and women. This assymetry encourages women and their families to develop marriage strategies to circumvent legal and social limitations.

Unable to challenge the social and ideological constraints that treat women as inferior to men, women, who generally see themselves under equal conditions as equal if not always superior to men, have opted to marry men who are older and have higher social and economic credentials. While this made it more logical for men to act as the head of the household, as they were more educated and more experienced, and for women to obey them, it also meant that through marrying up women translated their social and ideological inferiority to men into socioeconomic advantages. Men felt that they should marry women with lower credentials so as their privileged position as the head of household would not be questioned by their wives. Hence gender inequality and the ideology of inferiority of women are continuously reproduced with little pressure for social and legal change.

Because of the parents' inability to contribute to the cost of the marriage traditionally borne by the groom and his family, men in low-income neighborhoods increasingly choose their partners without their parents' influence. However, women's awareness of their unequal social and legal status in marriage diminishes the appeal of love marriages. Women of modest means prefer to have their parents and in particular their mothers involved in their marriage negotiations. Marriage contracts, demand for a substantial *mahr* (in cash and household goods), which they keep in the event of divorce, and other strategies are used to circumvent the legal limitations women face.

Similarly, men motivated by their desire to retain their privileged position in marriage devise strategies and bring conditions to the negotiations. In the 1980s they frequently asked their potential brides to wear the veil, which at least symbolically communicated that they accepted the conventional gender ideology. Since veiling has become much more widespread and most women, especially those with careers, wear some kind of veil, it is no longer a sensitive issue in marriage negotiations. However, more and more suitors demand that women give up their employment. This demand conflicts with women's, particularly educated women's, concerns regarding financial security in the event of divorce or widowhood, and yet many women feel obliged to acquiesce as most eligible suitors give this demand high priority in the marriage negotiations.

In short, the marriage institution and gender ideology provide a framework within which both sexes operate, manipulating the norms and conventions to promote their own interests, in both marriage and society. In the process, asymmetric gender and gender ideology, which often disadvantage women, are reproduced.

*Originally published in *Between Marriage and the Market: Intimate Politics and Survival in Cairo* (University of California Press, 1997): 51–79. Printed here with the permission of the publisher.

Brother-Sister Relationships:
Connectivity, Love, and Power in the Reproduction of Patriarchy in Lebanon

The Yusifs were a working-class family living in the urban neighborhood of Camp Trad, Borj Hammoud, a part of the Greater Beirut area of Lebanon. Abu Hanna, the Lebanese Maronite father, was a man who, even on the rare occasions when he was angry, spoke with the soft, slow lull of someone who had just awakened from a deep sleep. Um Hanna, the mother and a Palestinian Catholic, graced an abundant figure and a shy yet welcoming smile. A caring family with five boys and two girls, the Yusifs were respected as peace-loving, honorable folks by their neighbors. I lived next door to the Yusifs from 1971 to 1973 and came to know them well over a decade (Joseph, 1993a, 1993b). When I first met them, I sensed a harmony in the family. I never heard a raised voice. I developed close relationships with all members of the family, taking on the role of sister with the parents and aunt with the younger children.

I was particularly close to the oldest son, Hanna. With soft, wavy brown hair and roguish brown eyes that seemed always poised to make an assertion, Hanna, at nineteen, was seen as a highly attractive marriage choice. Very conscious of his grooming and masculine self-presentation, he ritually combed his hair with a comb kept in his back pocket. His medium build and height seemed to expand as he walked with firm yet graceful movements that appeared planned. There were few college students in this street, and Hanna was already in the eleventh grade in 1972.

A politically active bridge-builder with friends across ethnic and religious groups, Hanna was viewed as peace loving and conscientious.

I was shocked, therefore, one sunny afternoon to hear Hanna shouting at his sister Flaur and slapping her across her face. Flaur, at twelve, was the oldest daughter and the third oldest child. She seemed to have an opinion on most things, was never shy about speaking her mind, and welcomed guests with boisterous laughter and dancing light brown eyes that invited visitors to wonder what she was up to. With a lively sense of humor and good-natured mischief about her, Flaur was thought, by neighbors, to be a live wire despite the fact that she did not conform to Lebanese ideals of feminine beauty.

Hanna played father to Flaur, even though she helped care for the younger siblings who looked to her for mothering. Hanna repeatedly instructed Flaur to comb her hair, dress attractively, and carry herself with grace. In a local culture in which self-grooming occupied young women, Flaur seemed to pay no attention to her clothing, hair, body, or comportment. Her curls fluttered around her face, her clothes were often wrinkled and worn, and when you hugged her, you could feel a few preadolescent rolls adorning her hips and waist. This irritated Hanna considerably. His ire at her peaked, though, whenever he caught her lingering on the street corner near their apartment building gossiping with other girls. He would forcefully escort her upstairs to their apartment, slap her, and demand that she behave with dignity. No doubt the charge in their relationship came in part because Flaur was entering puberty as Hanna was reaching manhood.

Perhaps because of my special relationship with the family, I was stunned at Hanna's behavior. Flaur sometimes ran crying into my apartment. A few times I heard Flaur screaming, and I ran across the hall. Um Hanna watched. No one, myself included, questioned my right to intervene.

Hanna took it as his right and responsibility to mold and discipline his sister. Neither Um Hanna nor Flaur appeared to appeal to Abu Hanna about Hanna's behavior. Flaur's seventeen-year-old brother, Farid, might have protected her, but he deferred to Hanna. Family members, including Flaur, agreed that Hanna was acting within his brotherly role.

Hanna regarded me as an older sister, consulting me on personal, social and political matters. I had accepted that role and felt comfortable speaking to him about his behavior. When we talked, he said he knew what the world was like and she did not. It was his brotherly responsibility to train Flaur to be a lady. I suggested he might teach rather than beat her. He responded, with a smile in his eyes, that Flaur could not understand words and he did not hurt her. With authority, he added, he did it "*minshanha, minshan mistakbilha*" (for her, for her future).

When I discussed Hanna's behavior with Um Hanna, she found the matter amusing. I was surprised. She claimed that Hanna was doing his brotherly duty. She continued that Hanna cared deeply about Flaur. Besides, she added, Flaur provoked Hanna and brought his violence upon herself. Maybe, she chuckled, Flaur even liked it.

Flaur, for her part, seemed not unmindful of her own power over Hanna. Although she admired her brother, she teased him about his constant grooming or the romantic interests of neighborhood women in him. She was aware that her behavior would provoke Hanna. There was a willful element to her behavior that I thought was either an attempt to assert her own identity or to involve her brother intimately in her life.

On one occasion when Um Hanna, Flaur, and I were discussing Hanna's behavior, Um Hanna repeated, in Flaur's presence, that Flaur invited and enjoyed Hanna's aggression. With a mischievous smile in her eyes, Flaur laughed and agreed. She added, with bravado, "It doesn't even hurt when Hanna hits me." On another occasion, she indicated that she would like a husband like Hanna.

When I returned to Camp Trad in 1978 during the civil war, I stayed for a couple of days with the Yusifs Flaur was married and had a one-year old baby. Although taller, more voluptuous, and womanly, she still seemed a bit disheveled. Her husband was quiet, thin, and pale to the point of seeming unhealthy. Um Hanna asked me what I thought of Flaur's husband. I responded that I thought he was '*akil* (well mannered). Um Hanna noted that before her marriage, Flaur had lost weight and had become quite pretty. In the pocket-size wedding picture she showed me, Flaur did look beautiful and like a perfect size eight. She had had a number of suitors, Um Hanna went on, and could have gotten a better-looking man. She asserted, "*Wayn Hanna wa wayn hada*" (Where is Hanna and where is this one), implying that the best match for Flaur would have been someone like Hanna.

The relationship between Hanna and Flaur is a prime example of the connective love/power dynamic between brothers and sisters in these Arab families. That dynamic was critical to Hanna's empowerment and masculinization and Flaur's domestication and feminization; Hanna was teaching Flaur to accept male power in the name of love. His family supported his learning that loving his sister meant taking charge of her and that he could discipline her if his action was understood to be in her best interests. Flaur was reinforced in learning that the love of a male could include that male's violent control and that to receive this love involved submission to control. She was learning that her brother was both a loving protector and a controlling power in her life.

Hanna was additionally teaching Flaur how to present her feminine sexuality. She was learning to become a sexual person for her brother. Given Abu Hanna's absence and the interest that Hanna took in her, her brother was the most involved male sexual figure during her puberty. By feminizing Flaur, Hanna was masculinizing himself. Hanna also was using his culturally acceptable control over his sister to challenge his father's authority in the family. By taking charge of his sister, with the blessings of his mother and siblings, he highlighted his father's failures as head of the household. Hanna was learning to become a patriarch by becoming the man of the house in relation to his sister, mother, and younger siblings. Hanna and Flaur's relationship socialized each other into the links between gender, sexuality, love, and power. Their mutual dependency, underwritten by patriarchal connectivity inscribed as love. Their relationship reveals psychodynamic, social structural, and cultural processes through which the brother-sister relationship contributes to the reproduction of Arab patriarchy, a role that scholars of the Arab world have yet to unravel.

Brother-Sister Relationships: Arab Contexts

Although brother-sister relationships have received anthropological attention in the literature on a number of societies, relatively little of the work on Arab societies has considered the centrality of brother-sister relationships to the reproduction of family life and patriarchy. This lacuna comes in part from the relative lack of studies problematizing the internal dynamics of Arab family life. With the "Arab family" becoming increasingly the center of controversy in the literature and popular culture of the Middle East, new efforts have been made to more closely scrutinize the familial issues on both Arab and national bases. Most of the research on family in the Arab world, stressing the cultural ideals of patriarchy, patrilineality, patrilocality, and patrilineal endogamy, has focused on relationship among males. Scholars have paid less attention to brother-sister or other key male-female relationships. Research on Lebanon also offers insights into family life but does not address the brother-sister relationship in detail.

The little work that does exist on brother-sister relationships in the Arab world tends to regard it as either romantic or patriarchal, focusing respectively on "love" or "power." Scholars who focus on "love" aspects of the relationship are often attuned to psychodynamics but usually do not link them with social structural and cultural process (El-Shamy, 1981), or do not focus on the Arab world (Gilmore, 1987). Scholars identifying the "power" aspects of the relationship tend to be interested not in brother-sister relationships per se but in family structure and culture. These scholars often neglect psychodynamics or inadequately connect them to social structural and cultural processes (Peristiany, 1966; Pitt-Rivers, 1977). Few studies effectively link psychodynamic, social structural, and cultural processes. Most, therefore, do not recognize the connectivity that charges the love/power dynamics underpinning the central role played by the brother-sister relationship in the reproduction of Arab patriarchy.

Cultural Processes: Honor and Shame

For both brothers and sisters in Camp Trad, connective identities and mutual love were linked to family honor. The ideal of brother-sister relationships in Camp Trad was based on a cultural promise: a brother will protect his sister; a sister will uphold her family's honor. Men saw themselves as their sisters' protectors. Invested in their sisters' behavior, their sense of their own dignity and honor was tied to their sisters' comportment. They were permitted by their parents and the culture to see sisters as extensions of themselves and, thus, to be molded to fit their sense of self. This included the cultural sanction to discipline their sisters when their behavior was considered improper.

Sisters identified with their brothers as their security. A woman without a brother was seen as somewhat naked in the world. A brother's achievements opened opportunities for his sisters, just as his failures closed doors. Sisters understood that to receive the protection and support of brothers they had to address their brothers' expectations. They were socialized to accept their brothers' authority over their lives and to see it in their own interests to accept that authority. Even when they might have disagreed with their brothers, sisters acknowledged their brothers' "rights" over them as a central vehicle for maintaining family honor.

Thus, connectivity was an underlying psychodynamic process supporting the enactment of the cultural practices entailed in maintaining family honor. It is, I argue, because their connectivity encouraged brothers and sisters to view love and power as parts of the same dynamic that their relationship was so critical an instrument of the reproduction of Arab patriarchy. It is also because love and power were experienced as part of the same dynamic that these patriarchal relations had such hold on the members of Arab families. That is, patriarchy seated in love may be much more difficult to unseat than patriarchy in which loving and nurturance are not so explicitly mandated and supported.

My data is presented around three sets of processes. After describing the local community, I first discuss psychodynamic processes in brother-sister relationships focusing on the love and power dimensions of connectivity. Second, I analyze social structural processes of family, marriage, and inheritance, drawing out the implications for cross-sibling mutual dependence and responsibility. Finally, I consider how cultural processes, working through notions of honor and shame, linked brothers' and sisters' senses of self. The processes I discuss below did not characterize all brother-sister relationships at all times in Camp Trad. Yet they constituted such a significant pattern of relationality in discourse and in practice that one could see, and I demonstrate, a fundamental intertwining of connectivity, love, and power in psychodynamic, and social structural, and cultural processes.

Local Community

Borj Hammoud is an urban working-class municipality in the Greater Beirut area. In the early 1970s almost all of the religious sects and ethnic groups of both Lebanon and the neighboring Arab countries were represented in Borj Hammoud. About 40 percent of the population was Lebanese Shi'a. Forty percent were Armenian Orthodox, Armenian Catholic, or Armenian Protestant. The remaining 20 percent were Maronite, Roman Catholic, Greek Orthodox, Greek Catholic, Arab Protestant, Syrian Orthodox, Syrian Catholic, Sunni, Druze, Alawite. The population included Lebanese, Syrians, Palestinians, Greeks, Jordanians, and Egyptians.

My fieldwork in the Camp Trad neighborhood of Borj Hammoud just before the outbreak of the civil war in 1975 captured a unique moment in modern Lebanese history. It was a period of change, escalating tensions, and potentials. Camp Trad experienced an unprecedented high degree of heterogeneous relationships among peoples of different religious sects, ethnic groups, and nationalities. Its residents, primarily Arab, included members of all of the communities mentioned above. Many shared patterns of family life developed across religious, ethnic, and national lines.

Most of the families in Camp Trad were recent migrants to the area. A Lebanese Maronite agricultural area at the turn of the twentieth century, the neighborhood became gradually urbanized, particularly in the 1940s with the influx of Armenian refugees. Palestinians entered the area after the creation of Israel in 1948. Syrians and rural Lebanese began settling in the 1950s for economic opportunities or to escape political insecurities. In the early 1970s few household heads had been born in Camp Trad or Borj Hammoud. Almost all the residents had come from rural backgrounds where extended families ties remained vital. Some, like Palestinians and Armenians, were cut off from their places of origin whereas others, like the Lebanese, Syrians, Jordanians, and Egyptians, had access to natal family and village ties. A number of the residents had managed to reconstitute parts of their extended families within Camp Trad and Borj Hammoud. Sociologically, there were many household forms: nuclear families, joint, extended, duo-focal, single parent, single individual. Yet, culturally, Arab family ideals of patrilineality, patriarchy, and patrilocality were relatively strong for most residents.

In the early 1970s, when I began fieldwork, Lebanon was in the midst of economic, political, and social crises. Banking, trade, and tourism were being undermined by the Arab-Israeli conflict fought on Lebanese soil. Inflation, unemployment and underemployment, and worker strikes fueled the sense of economic crisis. Rapid urbanization had left the infrastructure of Greater Beirut ill equipped to respond to the mass demand for basic services. A "ring of poverty" circled Beirut.

The Lebanese state system was being challenged from within and without. Lebanon had become the primary site for attacks by Israel against the Palestinians and vice versa. Political minorities, such as the Shi'a, were organizing to demand equitable representation in government. Bribery and brokerage became necessary for most political transactions. Stalemated, the minimalist Lebanese state could not provide the services and protection citizens wanted.

In this economic, political, and social pressure cooker, individuals were thrown onto their families for help finding jobs, financial assistance, political protection, and emotional support. Family had always been central to social, economic, and political life in Lebanon. Ruling elites recruited followings and distributed services to their clienteles on the basis of kinship. Non-elite individuals relied on their families for brokerage and protection in a state that was perceived as untrustworthy and inefficient. Although it was not new for individuals to rely on their families, such dependence was precarious because the same pressures were limiting the avenues through which family members lived out their obligations. So although individuals needed, turned to, and believed in their families as the repositories of their identities and securities, family members found it increasingly difficult to carry out familial obligations.

The conditions of the early 1970s in urban Lebanon, therefore, in many ways were undermining the foundations of patriarchy. It was struggle for brothers and sisters to live out the roles and responsibilities for which they were socialized. Under these pressures, it is remarkable that brother-sister relationships remained powerful. It is only by linking psychodynamic, social structural, and cultural processes that one can understand the ongoing struggle to live out brother-sister relationships even under conditions that were undermining the family system that gave them meaning.

Psychodynamics of Connectivity

Connectivity as Love

In Camp Trad, connectivity was taken to be an expression of love. Brothers and sisters were taught to bond with each other and to see themselves mirrored in each other. Brothers saw their identities and sense of self wrapped up with their sisters' attributes and behavior. Sisters saw their dignity and security tied to their brothers' character and fortunes. Brothers and sisters were expected to love and look out for each other through adulthood. Parents and other relatives encouraged brothers and sisters to idealize and romanticize each other. They supported their using each other as standards for judging potential spouses. I had a sense something precious was undermined by the marriage of either. Um Hanna's (above) concern that Flaur's husband was not as handsome as Flaur's brother was, in cultural terms, an acceptable criticism of Flaur's husband. Idealization of the brothers and sisters was expressed through sayings that children learned. "*Al-ikt hanuni*" (the sister is sympathetic) was a frequently repeated saying in Camp Trad. Sisters referred to their brothers as "*akh al-hanun*," "*al-ʿatuf*", "*al-aziz*", "*al-habib*" and "*al-ghali*" (the brother is sympathetic, sensitive, dear, beloved, and priceless). The idealization of cross-siblings continued after marriage. Brothers and sister named their children after each other at times. Nimr Zahr, a seventy-three-year-old Lebanese Shi'i from Kfar Dunin in Southern Lebanon, had had a sister who died when she was about twenty. Five years later, when he had his own firstborn child, a girl, he named her after the deceased sister. His second son was named after his wife's brother.

Sonia Fraij was a thirty-five-year-old Lebanese Maronite married to a thirty-six-year-old Greek Orthodox bus driver's aide. Two of her brothers lived next door to her. She had named her oldest son after the younger of these two brothers and her youngest son after her youngest brother, who was living in Australia. A strong-willed and outspoken woman, she continually praised her brothers, described them lovingly, and compared them favorably to her husband. In interviews she subtly, in his presence, put her husband down in relation to her brothers. The older brother traveled frequently. The younger, John, a strikingly handsome twenty-year-old, was a chronically unemployed construction worker. Sonia had a loving relationship with John. As his apartment was right across the hall from hers, he spent much of his leisure time with her in one of the apartments. John spoke in the most affectionate terms of Sonia, gazed her lovingly, and seemed to hang on her words. The expressions of devotion were among the most pronounced in the neighborhood. They were together all the time. She both served him and took charge of his life in some ways. She cooked for him, washed his clothes, went shopping with him, received her house visitors with him, and at times took him with her when she paid some of her formal calls. In some ways, John acted as a husband in the absence of her husband, who worked long hours. Having a brother nearby whom she loved, served, and to some degree managed and who also protected her, empowered her.

A number of neighborhood women seemed to compare their husbands to their brothers. Yasmin Unis, a forty-seven-year-old Lebanese Shi'i, married for love, yet said her brothers "*bi nawru hiyyati*" (light up my life). Her sense of identity came from her natal family. She and children referred to her brothers repeatedly when speaking of themselves. Her marriage was relatively stable, yet she spoke of her husband as *maskin* (poor, humble), a mixed compliment and criticism.

I found this idealization/romanticization of brother-sister relationships in other social classes in Lebanon, particularly the Beirut middle classes. Among the families I observed, married and unmarried brothers and sisters talked of each other affectionately. Middle-class brothers and sisters went together to parties, movies, theaters, and other social occasions. They danced together, escorted each other in cohort group events, traveled together, and often walked arm in arm in the streets. Brothers, by accompanying their sisters, might have been giving them access to activities they might not have had otherwise. In playing the dual role of sister's protector and partner, they contributed to the romanticization of the relationship.

Unmarried women often devoted themselves to their brothers and their brothers' children. Unmarried men often relied on their sisters to provide emotional support and household service. Unmarried adults usually lived with their natal families, so unmarried brothers and sisters became each other's primary caretakers. In one case, a married Maronite woman with no children had raised her brother's two children while he was working in West Africa with his wife. The children called their aunt "*Mama*" and her husband, "*Baba*" (father).

Although there is little research on sexuality in brother-sister relationships in Arab societies, my own fieldwork indicates that the brother-sister relationship was sexually charged. Boys and girls in Camp Trad practiced sexual presentation with each other in socially approved ways. They seemed to groom themselves as much, if not more, for each other as for other opposite-gender individuals. Brothers paid attention to and commented on sisters' clothing, hair styling, and makeup. Sisters sought their brothers' approval for their self-presentations and offered their own evaluations of their brothers' presentation. Brothers defined their sexuality in part by asserting control over and lavishing attention on sisters. Sisters defined their sexuality in part by acceding to their brothers and/or by affording resistance.

Among a number of middle-class Beiruti families, also, I noticed that brothers and sisters were very involved in each other's attire and comportment. Brothers in these families often participated in purchasing their sisters' wardrobes. Sisters, although not having similar control over the brothers, often, nevertheless, significantly influenced their style by their evaluations.

On festive occasions, when Camp Trad young people dressed up and could engage in sexual play-acting, brothers and sisters seemed particularly involved with each other. Few families had much in the way of fancy attire. Going to church on Sunday or the mosque on Fridays, visiting neighbors and family on Christian and Muslim holidays, and attending weddings and funerals were among the few occasions during which Camp Trad youth could parade themselves. On these occasions brothers and sisters often escorted each other or went in the company of their families. On such occasions they usually spent more time in the company of each other than with nonfamily individuals. Brothers and sisters, besides the rest of the family, were on display to each other and seemed to take great interest in the opportunity for expression that such occasions provided.

I noticed in other parts of Beirut and surrounding suburbs that festive occasions were similarly occasions for constructing sexualities. Here, too, brothers and sisters seemed to use each other for role playing. For example, in family gatherings brothers and sisters danced with each other from a young age. On one occasion I observed two preadolescent middle-class siblings (children of a Syrian Christian mother and an Italian father) dancing together in their home in a suburb of Beirut during a festive gathering. The boy was advancing toward his younger sister. With roars of approval and great laughter the men and the women in the room (all Arab, except the father) shouted, "*bi hajim, bi hajim*" (he attacks, he attacks). The little boy, appearing somewhat confused, accelerated the behavior. The little girl, seemingly as confused, was ignored and continued dancing. Such occasions were prime times for learning culturally appropriate sexual behavior.

The romanticization/sexualization of the brother-sister relations appeared to have had concrete expression at times. There was one half-sibling marriage reported by Camp Trad informants. Sa'da Hamid was a fifty-five-year-old Lebanese Shi'i from Bint Jbeil in Southern Lebanon. Both her parents had been married twice. She reported a marriage between her sister by her mother and her full brother, that is, the couple shared a mother, but had different fathers. In 1972 Sa'da's brother, eighty-two, and his wife/half-sister, seventy-eight, were living in their village of birth. In a more ambiguous case, Yasmin Unis, a Lebanese Shi'i, reported a marriage between her step-siblings, who did not share parent.

Connectivity as Power

Romanticization and sexualization differentiated the brother-sister relationship from other familial cross-gender relationships. The relationship was differentiated, also, in terms of its role in gender socialization. Training for relationships of power organized around gender; brothers and sisters were used in the family system and used each other to learn culturally appropriate hierarchal masculine and feminine roles and identities. Additonally, young males emerging into their manhood might compete with their fathers for control over the family, using relationships with their sisters as a base of power—at times with the cooperation of their sisters and mothers.

Brothers and sisters learned early that love and power were parts of the same dynamic. Love meant acceptance of the power asymmetry and culturally approved assertions of the asymmetry were taken as expressions of love. Parents taught daughters that loving their brothers included serving them and taught brothers that loving their sisters included some control over them. Families may have preferred brothers to fathers as sisters' protectors because their secondary positions relative to fathers would burden them with less responsibility should violence occur. Little girls practiced modesty, seductiveness, and serving authoritative males with their brothers, thereby learning how to be feminine. Brothers practiced sexual assertion, receiving feminine nurturances, and protecting and take charge of the life and sexuality of females. Although connective love/power dynamics were enacted in parent-child and other family relationships, the mutual gender socialization distinguished the brother-sister relationships.

Young men also distinguished themselves from their fathers in relation to sisters by being physically present in the house. Fathers were often absent working long hours six days a week. Brothers usually did not work if they were still in school and spent much of their non-school time at home. When they did work, they often spent more time at home or around the neighborhood than did their fathers. Married brothers could play their cultural roles toward their sisters more effectively if they lived in proximity to their sisters. A remarkable number of Camp Trad adults indicated that they did have siblings in other parts of Borj Hammoud or neighboring districts. Those whose cross-siblings lived further away still expressed similar attitudes toward their siblings.

For young males living with their families, adolescence was the period to shape their manhood. Taking charge of the lives of their sisters and, at times, those of their mothers and younger brothers, was an avenue of empowerment for some males. Mothers often deferred to their older sons' control over younger children. Some fathers deferred to their sons, whereas others resisted. The degree of power the brothers took, then, was affected by how much power the father asserted. The more controlling the fathers, the less power the brothers could assert. In the case of the Dawuds, a Palestinian Catholic family (discussed below), the eldest son exerted considerable authority including defying his parents to help his sister marry the man she loved. In the case of the Rafik family, Abu Mufid, a Syrian Sunni, exerted patriarchal control to such a degree that the oldest son could assert little.

Differences in the brother's view and the sister's view of their relationship or in their reading their own and each other's needs could create spaces for resistance. Yet when resistance occurred, the challenge most often was not to the basic premises (love/power) of the brother-sister relationship. Rather, it usually centered on whether the sibling was acting on those premises properly, or it was understood as miscommunication or was explained away as flukes of character. Flaur's persistence in her behavior, despite Hanna's response, might be seen as resistance, except for the fact that she did not challenge his right to have authority over her or that he loved her and that she loved him. Instead, she and her family brushed it off as the consequence of her feistiness.

Structure of Family, Marriage, and Inheritance

Family and Marriage

Some of my informants stated a preference for non-kin marriage. The cultural norm of marriage between relatives, however, was still valued as an ideal by most of my Muslim informants. Although expressed as an ideal less frequently by Christians, endogamy was nevertheless practiced among them as well. Sa'da Hamid, the Lebanese Shi'i whose brother and half-sister had married (above), was herself married to her father's brother's son. Five of her seven married children were married to relatives, including two sons who had married two sisters. Two other sons had not married relatives, but their wives were related to each other. All but one of her children lived in Borj Hammoud and were very involved each other's lives. Four of Sa'da's siblings had married relatives and of them (a brother and sister) lived in Camp Trad.

Brothers and sisters were involved also with each other's children. The father's brother ('am) was viewed as a formal authority often feared second only to the father, but the khal (maternal uncle) was seen to be affectionate, loving, warm, and playful. He could become a substitute father in the absence of the father. The khal could also shelter the sister's children from their father. In one incident a young Camp Trad Maronite man had a heated dispute with his father after which the son took refuge in the home of his khal. The children of the khal, both sons and daughters, were also sources of emotional support and compassion, at times in contrast to the children of the father's siblings. In the cultural ideal a similar relationship was expressed with the mother's sister (khalta) and her children. The sister as the 'amta (paternal aunt) was expected to be affectionate to her brother's children. A common saying in Camp Trad depicted this relationship: "ya 'amti ya ikt bayyi hamm min ummi 'aliyyi" (my aunt, my father's sister, worries for me more than my mother). At the same time, as a member of the patriline, the 'amta also occupied a position of authority vis-à-vis her brother's children. Hanan, a Lebanese Shi'i, lived two stories below her brother's daughter, Dalal. Visiting each other daily, more than they each visited anyone else, Hanan helped Dalal by watching the three children (the oldest of which was four), shopping for her, and cooking with her.

Inheritance

Inheritance and property issues impacted the brother-sister and the husband–brother-in-law relationship. Women often did not take their inheritance from their natal families. Leaving their inheritance with their brothers could offer them insurance should they need protection from families of origin. A woman's attitude toward inheritance could change as she and her family of procreation matured. She might want the inheritance to help support her children. As her sons grew older, she might rely more on them than on her brothers. Husbands and brothers could compete over a woman's inheritance.

Najat, a thirty-two-year-old Lebanese Sunni married to a forty-one-year-old Lebanese Sunni (son of a Tunisian Sunni), had three brothers between twenty-six and thirty-six years old. Najat's siblings (married, divorced, and single) all lived with their mother in nearby Sin il Fil except for a married sister in Aley. Her father had died earlier in 1972, shortly before my interview. Najat claimed that she had refused to take any inheritance from her father's property. She had left it with her brothers. As she said, "My brothers' and mine are the same. It will always be there for me."

Family Culture: Honor and Shame

Ideally, brothers continued to be responsible for their sisters' behavior and welfare throughout their lives, even after marriage although the practice was often contradictory in the 1970s. Should a woman commit a shameful act or be compromised in any way her brothers shared responsibility with her father in disciplining or avenging her. The range and limits of brotherly responsibility for protecting and controlling adult sisters can be seen in the following example. The whole neighborhood street became involved in this dramatic enactment of the brothers' roles as protectors of their sisters' and families' honor. The key actors included the Dawuds, a Palestinian Catholic family, Amira Antun, a recently widowed Lebanese Chaldean Catholic of Syrian origins, Amira's son Edward and brother Francis; Abu Mufid, a Syrian Sunni discussed above; and Abu Mufid's brother's son, Adnan.

The Dawuds were a close family. The parents and sisters were bonded in devout admiration of their sons/brothers. They saw the sons/brothers, especially the oldest, Antoine, as heroes (*abtal*). The parents and sisters outdid each other in superlatives describing Antoine. They emphasized his strength and courage. Active in the Fateh wing of the Palestine Liberation Organization, Antoine was frequently armed, which no doubt added to the family's sense of his fearsomeness.

Antoine had helped his sister Antoinette elope against their parents' opposition. Antoine was 19 when Antoinette, 18, decided she wanted to marry their mother's father's sister's son. Their parents opposed the marriage because Fadi was poor. Antoine was interested in marrying Fadi's sister. Overriding his parents, Antoine had helped his sister elope with the intention that Fadi would then help arrange Antoine's marriage to his sister. Later, Antoine decided that Fadi's sister was too demanding and did not marry her. Antoinette's marriage was still intact, however. Antoine and Antoinette had a close relationship, and she continued to think of him as her protector.

Antoine and his brothers appeared to derive pleasure and personal pride from the beauty and comportment of their sisters. The sisters also felt their security and dignity were linked to their brothers' involvement with them. The Dawud sisters boasted continually about their brothers. Twenty-one-year-old Therese often said that if she could only find a man like her brothers, she would marry instantly.

In the spring of 1973 Adnan, a young Sunni, had his eyes on an unidentified young woman living on the street. Neighbors thought it was Therese. In a manner considered inappropriate, Adnan drove repeatedly in front of her house. He sped his car screeching through the street. Given the narrow streets and the fact that small children usually played outside unsupervised, neighbors complained. Adding to this concern was the fact that although intermarriages did occur in the neighborhood, they were usually arranged in a more discreet manner. It was a breach of etiquette for courting to take place in this manner, particularly given the intersectarian character of the relationship. Therese's brothers

(Antoine twenty-four, Jacque, nineteen, and Michel, fourteen) discussed the matter with several male friends living on the street, including Edward Antun (the twenty-year-old son of Amira Antun), Rafik Abdullah (the eighteen-year-old son of a Maronite woman divorced from her Shi'i husband), and Hanna and Farid Yusif (Hanna's seventeen-year-old brother). They decided to stop Adnan.

One afternoon late in March, Adnan sped through the street several times. Michel Dawud and Edward Antun were at home. During his next pass, they stopped his car and told him they did not want him to drive through the street because there were children playing. Adnan had a friend with him. He replied that he was free to come and go as he wished and, furthermore, that they were not to speak with him but could speak with his friend. The friend had a long knife and made "teasing" or "threatening" looks at the young men. Michel Dawud became irritated and hit Adnan's friend in the face. Adnan sped away.

The commotion attracted the attention of a number of residents. Rafik Abdullah was home ill but came down to the street in his pajamas. Farid Yusuf was coming down the stairs from his apartment and went to join his friends. Abu Antoine (Therese and Michel's father) had overheard the conversation and had come to try to make peace. 'Adil and Zaynab, close Shi'a friends of Amira Antun (Edward's mother), stepped out as well. Within a few minutes, more than fifty people had gathered in the street, and many stood on their balconies or rooftops watching.

Adnan, in the meantime, had collected his friends and relatives from the predominately Shi'i neighborhood of Nab'a. They returned to the street in two cars. At an apparently prearranged whistle, the two cars drove through the narrow street at top speed, aiming right at the crowd. Most of the people jumped out of the way, but Edward Antun was slightly injured. A car parked at the end of the street blocked Adnan's escape. Neighbors began beating the cars and breaking the windows. Within a few minutes, though, the two cars sped away.

It was early evening by this time, and I heard the commotion at my end of the street. I had been helping Um Hanna who was ill. I went down the street to find members of nearly every household talking excitedly. Um Antoine was arguing with Zaynab. Um Antoine shrieked, "This is the fault of the Muslims. The Muslims are coming to get us!" Zaynab, a Shi'I shouted, "Don't make this sectarian!" Hanna Yusif told me that his brother Farid had noticed that one of the two cars had been that of Mufid (the son of the Syrian Sunni, Abu Mufid) and that he thought he had seen Mufid with them, but he could not be sure.

Edward Antun was rushed to the hospital by 'Adil Zaynab's husband and Amira Antun's good friend. Amira became hysterical, tearing at her clothes and screaming uncontrollably. Amira was a forty-one-year-old mother of ten children ranging in age from five to twenty-two. Her husband had died in 1971 just as I was beginning my fieldwork. She had six sons (her four oldest children were all male), including a married son, but she turned to her second oldest brother, Francis, as a father-substitute for her children. Francis, thirty-four, married with no children, owned a pin-ball arcade two short blocks away from Amira's apartment.

When Edward was injured, Amira's neighbors gathered around her, particularly her good friends, Zaynab and 'Adil. Amira had excellent friends in the neighborhood; however, the primacy of the brother was apparent. Francis was informed of the incident and came quickly. When arrived on the street, the crowds parted to let him through. I vividly member the hushed silence as he approached his sister and embraced her. There was a stirring sense among the neighbors that Amira was now in the care of the most honorable of protectors—her brother. The silence among the neighbors added to the drama and the authoritative voice with which he spoke. He turned to the people and demanded to know what had happened to his nephew. As her brother stood there next to her there seemed to be a feeling that now justice would be done.

Abu Antoine sent for his son, Antoine. The tension noticeably increased as Antoine arrived almost immediately with a motorcade of armed Palestinian guerrillas dressed in civilian clothes. The neighbors now felt bold and invincible. The presence of Therese's brother Antoine, backed by the Palestinian guerrillas, and Amira's brother Francis, along with nearly all the men of the neighborhood, enhanced the incredible sense of neighborhood solidarity.

The crowd gathered around to tell the story of the incident. Some of the young men of the neighborhood had run after the car. Later, a couple of the culprits were found in a shop near Francis's pin-ball machine store. Francis was among the neighborhood men who found them. They beat the culprits and called the police. The families of the Shi'a young men were mistakenly told that one of their sons had been killed. Several cars from the Shi'i neighborhood of Nab'a, filled with men and guns, came immediately to Camp Trad. The Nab'a families arrived just as the police pulled in, so they drove away. The one person who was still in custody was taken to the police station. Within minutes, a phone call came from a *za'im* (political leader), and he was released.

Adnan's paternal uncle, Abu Mufid, deflated the conflict. He lived on the same street as the Dawuds and was highly respected. Abu Mufid told me that he thought his nephew was a bit wild and he would rather not have gotten involved. He felt he had no choice but to intervene for the sake of neighborly good will and to protect his own name. Arranging a meeting between Adnan and the Dawuds and Antuns, Abu Mufid forced his nephew to apologize.

The incident provoked a neighborhood crisis. Across religious, ethnic and national lines, neighborhood people supported the brothers' actions. It was uniformly discussed in terms of the brothers protecting the honor of their sisters and families. Men and women seemed to agree that the incident was primarily about honor, not religion. Therese and her parents extravagantly praised Michel and Antoine while Amira heaped praise on her son Edward and brother Francis. The men were described as *abtal* (heroes). The neighborhood men, in general, appeared to take great pride in their manly display of solidarity. And the women glowed in admiration of the men. In the immediate days after the incident, there was noticeable swagger in the walk of the men directly involved. Displays of boasting by both men and women created a sense of possession: they owned this street. Brothers had protected their sisters and men had protected their women—the ultimate social boundary of the community. The community was reminded of the importance sisters had in their brothers' lives. For all the participants the incident reinforced the cultural belief that brothers were the foundation of sisters' security. The culture had been supremely upheld in a most honorable manner.

Arab Brothers and Sisters:
Connectivity, Love, and Power in the Reproduction of Patriarchy

In Camp Trad the brother-sister relationship was central to the reproduction of patriarchy. It contributed to socializing young males and females into appropriate gender roles. Young females learned feminine roles by submitting to brothers. Young males learned to be patriarchs by practicing first on their sisters and younger brothers. Brothers could also use their relationships with their sisters to contest their fathers' authority and attempt to build a sphere of influence from which they would mature as patriarchs.

The sister paid a price for the protection of the brother. She served the brother, to some degree shaped herself into his image, at times put her brother before her husband. Sisters had some power in this relationship because their conduct directly affected their brothers' and families' standing. The tensions around the issues of honor, protection, and control at times led to violence.

At the same time, the brother-sister relationship was one of love. Brothers and sisters reported deep caring and concern for each other. They were expected by others and expected themselves to protect and nurture each other for all their lives. Brother-sister love was romanticized. Their masculinity and femininity were defined and practiced in a connective relationship that was often sexually charged.

Complexity is missing in much of the literature. As my analysis suggests, the brother-sister relationship was a connective relationship built on the duality of love and power expressed psychodynamically, social structurally, and culturally. It was second only to the mother-son relation in evoking love, and yet it was premised on a power asymmetry—the subordination of the sister to the brother. The intense involvement of brothers and sisters in each other's lives invested each in their natal family and its reproduction. Life-long connectivity organized around love and power gave the brother-sister relationship a forceful role in the reproduction of Arab patriarchy. By the early 1970s, Camp Trad brothers and sisters were living with external stresses that made achievement of cultural prescriptions concerning their relationships more difficult. The instability of family life; the economic, political, and social uncertainty; and the limitations of the Lebanese state in providing services and protections thrust people onto their families for support at a time when it was increasingly for family members to help each other. It is striking that, under these conditions, men and women, nevertheless, still made the effort to embrace their cross-siblings and the patriarchy and patrilineality their siblingship supported.

References

Gilmore, David, ed. 1987 *Honor and Shame and the Unity of the Mediterranean.* Washington, D.C.: American Anthropological Association.

El-Shamy, Hasan 1981 "The Brother-Sister Syndrome in Arab Family Life, Socio-Cultural Factors in Arab Psychiatry: A Critical Review". *International Journal of Sociology of the Family 2.* pp 313–23.

Joseph, Suad 1993a "Connectivity and Patriarchy Among Urban Working Class Arab Families in Lebanon." *Ethos* 21, no. 4 (Dec). pp. 452–84.

——1993b "Gender and Relationality Among Arab Families in Lebanon." *Feminist Studies.* 19, no 3 (Fall) pp. 465–86.

Peristiany, J.G. 1966, *Honor and Shame: The Values of Mediterranean Society*. Chicago: University
    of Chicago Press.
Pitt-Rivers, Julian 1977 *The Fate of Shechem or the Politics of Sex: Essays in the Anthropology of the
    Mediterranean*. London: Cambridge University Press.

*Originally published in Suad Joseph (ed.) *Intimate Selving in Arab Families:Gender, Self and Identity*
(Syracuse University Press, 1999): 113–140. Printed here with the permission of the publisher.

An earlier version of this article has been published in *American Ethnologist* 1994.

NAJLA S. HAMADEH

Wives or Daughters:
Structural Differences Between Urban and Bedouin
Lebanese Co-wives

Polygyny has ancient roots in Arab society, having existed alongside monogamy and other types of marriage since pre-Islamic times. Because polygyny is still permissible in contemporary Islamic communities of the Arab world, many Muslim Arab women have to deal with the possibility, if not the actuality, of having to cope with a co-wife (or co-wives) despite the fact that nowadays households that include more than one wife for a husband are far from the prevalent norm. Analysis of the women's ways of coping when they do find themselves in such a situation may yield significant insights concerning the vulnerabilities or strengths in the women's psychosocial baggage. A comparative study of the variation of such relationships between communities with different social norms enables an assessment of the impact of each type of society on the construct of the selves of women and on the efficacy of the type of subjectivity exhibited by these selves.

In Arabic the co-wife is referred to as *al-durrah*, "the one who harms." The popular saying is "*al-durrah murrah*" (the co-wife is a bitter taste). Both usages suggest that popular opinion expects the relationship between co-wives to be one of resentment and antagonism. Moreover, most writers about polygyny record mainly the discord between co-wives and the misery that a woman experiences as she finds herself obliged to share her husband with another, and sometimes with more than one, woman.

I was enticed to study the relationship between co-wives by the discrepancy between the way such relationships are depicted in popular attitudes and in the vast majority of literature and what I have sometimes observed. I have sometimes witnessed in my patrilocality, in the Bekaa' valley, co-wives who maintain friendly, and occasionally affectionate, relationships with one another. One can surmise that popular sayings and stories neglect friendly relations between co-wives because it is the unfriendly ones who are colorful, problematic, and good material for rich plots. Because popular wisdom tends to promote the moral and the beneficent, it is understandable that it tends to portray the perils of polygyny to deter people from practicing it. Moreover, the neglect in books and studies of friendly relations among co-wives results from the fact that urban life receives the most interest and is more easily accessed by writers, and such friendly relations, as confirmed by the current study, are rarely found in urban society.

I briefly describe my fieldwork and recount my findings, giving a detailed account of three cases that represent a variety of the most typical findings. I then analyze what the gathered data and the described case studies reveal concerning structural differences in the self-constructs of urban and Bedouin Lebanese women and their relevance to a study of Arab women or to the specificity of women's self-constructs in general.

The Field Study

The area I come from in the Bekaa' valley is frequented during the summer season by Bedouin tribes who spend the rest of the year in the Syrian Desert. A considerable proportion of the sedentary population of the area are of Bedouin origin. The latter call themselves *asha'ir* and take pride in their Arab (Bedouin) ancestry. They are careful to preserve many of their Bedouin traditions and values although their houses and their economic means of survival and some other aspects of their practical lives, such as electricity television, and motorized transportation, are akin to those of other peasants in the area. Because my study is concerned primarily with psychological variations influenced by social traditions, I consider the nomads and sedentary *asha'ir* as one group, referring to them as Bedouin. These peoples I compare to a sample of urban co-wives that I interviewed in Lebanese cities. Limited by time and scope and the specific aims of the present study, I exclude the peasants of the Bekaa' who are not considered to he descendants of known Bedouin tribes. The peasants are considered to be of "inferior" lineage, and their social norms and values differ from those of the Bedouins.

Aside from the data gathered by the field study, my analysis draws from earlier observations. I live simultaneously in two types of environment. I was born and have lived most of my life in the city of Beirut; at the same rime, I have always had access to the Bedouin and peasant-Bedouin communities in my patrilocality in the Bekaa' valley where I have frequently visited and sometimes spent summer holidays. This situation gave me the opportunity to witness relationships between urban, as well as Bedouins, co-wives.

I began conducting my survey of Bedouin co-wives in the summer of 1992 and continued the fieldwork in the summer of 1993. For this purpose, I spent most of these two summers in the Bekaa' valley. During the interval between the two summers and in the winter of 1995, I interviewed a number of urban co-wives in the cities of Beirut and Tripoli and in the town of Baalbeck. My research covered eighty-five women, each of whose husbands had either one or two other wives. Twenty-eight of these were Bedouin, thirty-five were sedentary of Bedouin origin, and twenty-two were urban. The main reason for the restricted number of subjects was the scarcity of polygynous households, especially in the cities.

One of the case studies I include comes from outside the survey. It is an account of the relationship between my late paternal grandmother and her co-wife, also deceased. I include this case because it coincides with several characteristics of some relationships between Bedouin co-wives and because this case provides, within the scope of my experience, a unique example of polygyny in a higher social class. My account is based on direct observation that predates this study by many years and on what was recounted to me, recently, by people who had lived in my grandfather's house.

Each co-wife covered by the survey was interviewed alone, often several times. Sometimes, I also talked to the husbands or other family members. During the fieldwork, some husbands insisted that I include their points of view. One urban husband of three young wives told me: "Why do you talk to them?", indicating his wives. He added: "They will only tell you lies. If you want the truth, you can only get it from me." This husband, and other husbands, seemed to want to talk to vindicate a condition that caused them a measure of shame or, perhaps, of guilt. Several, like the afore-mentioned husband of three, seemed to feel a mixture of pride and shame about their multiple marriages. The shame or guilt is understandable: polygyny is infrequent, and the Qur'an discourages polygyny even in the very verses that permit it.

I interviewed forty-one first wives and forty-four second or third wives. Approximately one-third of the women lived in the same household with their co-wives. When asked how they felt about their co-wife (or co-wives), 26 percent said that they loved and/or had friendly feelings toward her (or them), 14 percent said that they had neutral feelings, and 59 percent said that they hated, were jealous of or felt both hatred and jealousy toward their co-wife (or co-wives). Those who claimed to have friendly or neutral feelings toward their co-wives were mostly Bedouin (51 percent of the Bedouins and 5 percent of the urban). As might be expected, second or third wives seemed to be more kindly disposed toward their co-wives than were first wives. One significant finding was that the first wife tended to feel less hatred for, and/or jealousy of the subsequent wife (or wives) when she believed that her husband took another wife for reasons other than love. When the husband married again in order to have offspring or because his first wife had borne only daughters or because his counterpart in an exchange marriage *(muqayada)* took another wife, the wife took more kindly to the new wife. Even when she believed that the husband married another woman because of an excessive sexual drive, she tolerated the co-wife much better than when she thought that love propelled him toward the new marriage. [I thank Monique Chaaya for computing the percentages after recording gathered answers to questionnaires.]

To illustrate the types of relations that exist among the co-wives, I portray three sets: urban, nomadic Bedouin, and sedentary rural of Bedouin origin. In line with the collected data, the chosen illustrations depict antagonistic relations between urban co-wives and neutral to friendly relations between Bedouin co-wives. The three portraits are drawn from a middle-class, a lower-class, and an upper-class set of co-wives, respectively.

Wadad and Lama (Urban Co-wives Living in Beirut)

Wadad is the only daughter among five brothers of a well-to-do textile merchant. She finished high school and oscillated for a few years between helping her father and brothers in the shop and idling around, waiting for an appropriate husband. She was physically unattractive but probably had expected that her father's wealth and social position would help her procure a husband. At twenty-five, she married Mounir, a self-made man who had recently earned a Ph.D. Soon after their marriage, he was appointed to teach at a university. The marriage produced three children. When I met her, Wadad was in her late forties.

Lama, the co-wife of Wadad, was fifteen years younger than she. She was a tall, black-eyed beauty, who had grown up fatherless. Her mother had worked as a housekeeper to support her and her one sister and two brothers. The mother had instilled in her children the value of education as their only means to rise from the state of squalid poverty they were reared in to a more comfortable and respectable station. Lama and her siblings, who seemed to have been endowed with high levels of intelligence and vitality, had fulfilled their mother's dreams by acquiring university educations. As a student at the Lebanese University, Lama had taken courses taught by Mounir. She had found herself drawn to discuss with him some of her emotional and financial problems. Eventually, a love relationship had developed between them, which had led to their marriage. Soon after their marriage, Mounir installed Lama in a separate house, and weeks later, he broke the news of his new marriage to Wadad.

Lama believed that Mounir kept his first wife because he hoped to benefit from what she would eventually inherit. She also believed that her husband did not appreciate her enough because of her poverty. She tried to get around her co-wife's advantage and her own weak position by becoming economically productive. Thus, she worked as a teacher and later as a school administrator.

I visited the two households. The ways each of the two women dressed and decorated her home were noticeably informative about her view of herself and her mode of relating to life. Wadad's house gave the impression of a poorly organized antiques shop. In the small apartment, in a fairly respectable neighborhood, the imitation Louis XV armchairs looked out of place. On shelves and on tables stood several silver frames containing family photographs and many other silver ornaments. Several hand-stitched *aubusson* (embroidery on canvas) pieces, portraying little girls and wild animals, were displayed on the walls. She insisted on treating me to juice, cookies, nuts, coffee, and chocolate every time I visited her. The cups she served coffee in were gold-rimmed with an elaborate design. She had dyed her hair an unbecoming yellowish blond and was once wearing what appeared to be an expensive designer dress, a size or two too tight for her.

Lama's apartment was in a newer building in a modest populous neighborhood. The furniture in the living room included formica tables and other cheap, practical items. The overall impression was that of a temporary residence. The colors were dark. Tin pots containing wilted plants stood on the window sill and on tables in the living room. It was probably the impact of Lama's story that made me see that everything looked sad and longing to be elsewhere. Lama was dressed in the extremely plain "Islamic costume," which has recently become popular among women of some pious Muslim groups. Her costume consisted of a shapeless gray suit and a white scarf that enveloped the head and covered part of the forehead.

Wadad related to me that when her husband told her of his new marriage, she felt as though the walls of her house were closing in on her. She fell to the floor and for three days refused to get up or to eat. When her husband attempted to reason with her, she drove him out of the house with her hysterical shouting. Later, she thought that if she allowed her grief to overwhelm her, she would die, and that would please the couple whose happiness was being built on her ruin. She thought that her death would hurt only her children. From then on, she decided to do whatever she could to hurt Mounir and Lama while fighting to keep Mounir as father to her children. Thus, when he proposed to divide his time equally between the two households, she accepted. She even accepted resuming sexual relations with him "although I hated him like the devil. But I wanted to do anything that would spite her," Wadad said.

At one point during the Lebanese civil war (1975–91), Lama's house was destroyed; thereupon, she moved into Wadad's house. Wadad described the ensuing period as "hell."

She confessed, "When the two of them stayed in their room, with the door closed, I felt I was losing my sanity." She said that Lama kept teasing her and invading all her space. She added: "She kept peering into my closets and criticizing my clothes. She made fun of my style in setting the table, saying that I wasted all my time doing elaborate things that are totally useless."

In 1984, during a round of fighting, a piece of shrapnel entered through the living-room window and hit Lama's five-year-old daughter in the head. The child was reduced to a vegetable-like state, and there was no hope her condition would improve. "After the injury to her daughter," continued Wadad about Lama, "she was transformed. She quit her coquettish ways, starred praying five times a day, and tried to be civil to me and to my children. But sometimes I feel that it was better the other way. When she visits me with my husband, I feel awkward and humiliated. When somebody refers to her as 'Mrs. Mounir,' I feel that she is erasing my very existence."

When I talked to Lama, she sounded like one who considered her life shattered. She shed many tears as she recounted her story. She explained that she had always wanted to live a great love. She added that when she and Mounir became attached to one another, she thought that she was going to live the love for which she had always yearned. She was not much bothered by his being already married because she was sure that the true and strong feeling that bound them together would lead him to divorce his first wife. When time passed and he did not divorce Wadad, Lama felt that the love between them was being smothered.

Um Hussein and Amira (Nomadic Bedouins)

Um Hussein (the mother of Hussein) and Amira are co-wives in a nomadic tribe that spends most of the year in the steppe areas adjoining the Syrian Desert and the summers in the Bekaa' valley. During the summer season, the women work in the fields as day laborers. They also tend live stock and attend to the usual housework. I was told that they consider their sojourn in the desert as an easier time during which they are freed from working as farmhands.

Their Bekaa' abode, in which I visited them, consisted of three tents: one for receiving guests, one for cooking and washing, and one for sleeping. The woman with whom the husband was spending the night would sleep in the tent allotted to receiving guests. The other wife would sleep in another tent with Abu Hussein's sister Ghazaleh and the teen-age daughters of Um Hussein and Abu Hussein. The area around their tents was kept clean. The guests' tent was the best furnished, with imitation Persian rugs, a huge copper coffee maker, and embroidered cushions used to seat visitors or as back supports. That tent was referred to as Um Hussein's.

The women wore long, loose robes and very attractive headgear that made their eyes and the bone structure of their faces appear to advantage. Um Hussein was plainly and soberly dressed in dark colors, and Amira wore colorful fabrics, an embroidered vest and a great deal of makeup and jewelry. Ghazaleh, the independent businesswoman (she made and sold cheese), wore a more practical shorter dress with long pants underneath. She was the first to engage me in conversation about her life, commenting on the treachery of men: 'If you trust the love of a man, you are like one who entrusts a sieve with holding water." She had married for love against the wishes of her family. She had worked hard before successfully convincing her father and brothers to break her engagement to her cousin and to accept her marriage to the man she loved. After a few years of happiness, her husband married another woman from a neighboring tribe. He married the girl against her family's wishes, fleeing with her on horseback from her family's quartets to his own. Ghazaleh reacted by asking for a divorce, which the husband refused to grant. But Ghazaleh went back to her family "to live *mu'azzazah mukarramah*" (loved and respected). Having told her story, she went off to attend to her business, leaving me to interview her brother's wives. As she was recounting her story, I was struck by the good taste with which she could string together her words and sentences. In fact, most of the Bedouins interviewed were impressive conversationalists.

Um Hussein, a high cheek-boned classical beauty, was thirty-five when I met her in 1992. Her father used to be a sheep merchant. She had three brothers and two sisters. She described her family as "a respectable one, whose members did not blaspheme and did not slander other people." She illustrated the high moral caliber of her kin by telling me that although one of her sisters had been dead for ten years, her husband still refused to re-marry, saying that he could never find another woman like his late wife.

Um Hussein had married at the age of nineteen. She and her husband had had three daughters and one son. Her youngest child and only son, Hussein, had drowned in a pond when eight years of age. About one year before the death of Hussein, her husband expressed a desire to take another wife "in order that the daughters will have more than one brother to protect them when their father is no longer there for them." A few months after the boy's death, Urn Hussein proposed that she herself find a new wife for her husband.

She visited a family that had three daughters of marriageable age and chose the youngest, Amira, a beautiful girl of seventeen. When the family of Amira set as a condition for their consent that one of the daughters of Um Hussein be given in an exchange marriage (*muqayada*) to Amira's brother, Um Hussein consented despite her daughter's aversion to the young man. The arrangement concluded, Um Hussein took Amira to the town of Baalbek to buy her trousseau. When Amira expressed her desire to wear an urban white bridal gown rather than the usual Bedouin wedding costume, Um Hussein bought her one.

On the wedding day Um Hussein, still in mourning for her son, baked and cooked for the wedding feast. When she noticed that the neighbors were boycotting the celebration out of respect for her mourning, she changed her black garments and made a round of the neighbors, asking them to join in the festivities. In the evening, she spread carpets, a mattress, and cushions for the newlyweds in a separate tent. She adorned the tent with flowers, filled a plate with fruits and a pitcher with fruit juice.

Amira is the third daughter in a family of six boys and eight girls. Her father also is a sheep merchant. She looked perfectly happy. Before and after my interviews with her and her co-wife, she sat close to Um Hussein, a little behind her. She seemed unquestioningly willing to do her bidding and be guided by her. When I asked her why she had agreed to marry Abu Hussein, she answered, "Because they liked me and chose me from among my sisters, I also liked them." When I pressed her about why she had consented to marry a man old enough to be her father, she repeated that he was respectable and that she felt that

Um Hussein could make of her a better person. She also said that she liked the company of Um Hussein's daughters. From fragments of phrases punctuated by much giggling, I gathered that she was enjoying her sexual encounters with Abu Hussein and that she did not feel guilty or awkward toward Um Hussein on that account. She seemed to feel that her youth and her co-wife's mature age entitled her to be preferred sexually and entitled Um Hussein to take precedence over her in other domains.

Um Hussein expressed regrets about her new situation: "Who would like to see her husband in the arms of a girl of seventeen?" she asked. She added: "The new wife is like a new dress. Nobody likes to wear an old garment when one has acquired a new one." Yet, despite that, she treated her co-wife with maternal affection. She appeared to take Abu Hussein's new marriage as destiny, dictated by circumstances for which nobody could be blamed. She said that her faith in God remained a great solace and that what she really hoped for were God's grace and the respect of the community.

When I revisited them in the summer of 1993, I found some change in the attitude of Um Hussein toward Amira. I was told that during the winter Abu Hussein had divorced Amira and that he had taken her back only after much pleading from Um Hussein. The older co-wife explained, "Respectable people like us do not take other people's daughters, impregnate them, and send them back to their folks." When I asked Abu Hussein about the reason for the divorce, I was told that Amira's mother had caused it by urging her daughter to demand that he divorce his first wife. This made Abu Hussein so angry that he divorced Amira instead. He added, "I respect all the family, but Um Hussein has in my esteem a special position, before everyone else, because she sacrificed for the sake of the family and because she is the mother of my daughters and bears the name of my late son."

Um Hussein admitted that although she still considered Amira a good girl, relations between them had changed: "I no longer draw her to me and kiss her cheeks as I would my own daughters," she said. Amira, however, pleased to be carrying her newborn daughter in her arms, insisted that she still loved, respected, and obeyed Um Hussein. I witnessed Um Hussein giving her orders concerning what to do for the baby and saw that Amira was prompt in doing her co-wife's bidding. Yet, Um Hussein had during this last interview the attitude of a chastising, rather than of an approving and encouraging elder, which she had had the summer before. Amira seemed to respond by trying her best to regain the affection and the confidence of her co-wife although her main effort was directed toward tending the precious bundle that she carried about on her back, held in a cloth-basket dangling from her shoulders. Probably the lack of anxiety in her attempts to appease her co-wife resulted from the deep satisfaction that she appeared to feel because of the little one in the basket.

Almaza and Ward (Sedentary of Bedouin Origin)

Almaza was my paternal grandmother, who passed away at the age of one hundred and four in 1964, and Ward was her co-wife, the second wife of my paternal grandfather. She passed away in her mid-nineties in 1988. Although the families of both women, the Hamadehs and the Harfushes, respectively, have been well known in Lebanon for several centuries, the two families identified with their ancient Bedouin descent. They were very proud of their origin and maintained many of the old Bedouin traditions and values.

Almaza was a tall blonde, daughter of a *pasha*, who in her early twenties married her paternal first cousin. Her father was proud of her, believing her to be of exceptional intelligence. Encouraged by her marked interest in politics, he used to discuss with her political matters that the other women knew only generally and vaguely. This interest and her habit of conversing with politically active kinsmen about issues related to their work remained with Almaza all her life. Strongly identifying with the family's political role, she did not seem to he bothered by the fact that being a woman prevented her from engaging in politics directly. She had a poetic talent by means of which she sublimated her need to express herself in the field of her interest by composing songs and poems about events happening on the political scene.

Rivalry over political leadership existed between Almaza's father and, later, her brother, on the one hand, and her husband and, later, her son, on the other. Almaza always took the side of her family of birth (father and brother). She became eager for the advancement of her son's political career only after the death of her brother. Almaza showed the same type of preference when she undertook to use what she inherited from her parents to educate the children of one of her brothers, who had died young, depriving her own children.

When Almaza's brother, who was married to her husband's sister, took another wife, Almaza's husband retaliated by taking another wife, a traditional retaliation in such circumstances, to avenge his sister. The second wife, Ward, was a short, dark-eyed, lively, and intelligent woman. Even in her old age, she had a knack for saying things that made people laugh, regardless of how solemn the occasion might be. She was orphaned before her teens and grew up with her sisters and young brothers in a household run in harmonious collaboration between her mother and her mother's co-wife. Growing up among women and little boys, Ward probably yearned for the security that the presence of a man in the house brings, for when she married, she lavished on her husband more explicit appreciation than the traditions of their community permitted.

Before Ward's inclusion into the family, Almaza used to supervise the household, including care of the children. Afterward, however, she gladly relinquished such tasks to her co-wife. Ward took over, adding some sophistication in housework that she had learned as she grew up closer to the town of Baalbek. She taught the women ironing and the use of certain utensils. Ward was also the one to manage finances.

Ward had no children, yet her maternal love added warmth to the lives of several generations of her husband's family. She lavished care and attention on Almaza's children. Her stepdaughter grew to love her more than she did her own mother. Later, when the wife of one of her stepsons died in childbirth, she took care of his numerous children. She also saw to it that what she inherited from her husband would go, upon her death, to her husband's children and not to her nephews and nieces, who were her legal heirs by Muslim law.

The house they lived in was a large, airy mansion that combined the Ottoman and the Mount Lebanon styles of architecture. It featured a large hexagonal reception area, wide balconies in the background of which stood arcades partially covered by colorful tainted glass, and a red brick roof. Except for the men's reception area, where the seating arrangement was in divan style, the house was furnished like the inside of some Bedouin tents: rugs and cushions spread on the floor and big wooden chests adorned with oriental designs that functioned as closets for clothes and other items. The women wore clothes that also combined Bedouin, Lebanese, and Ottoman elements, choosing from those what were more becoming and more convenient for their various purposes. The young women kept an eye on fashion in Istanbul, and the older ones maintained the fixed traditions of Bedouin and Lebanese female attires.

Almaza and Ward openly communicated to each other, in word and action, their thoughts and feelings, including their occasional jealousies of each other as co-wives. I was told that once, when their husband upon returning from a trip, went directly to Ward's room, Almaza expressed her anger by staying up all night and keeping a fire ablaze in the open court. After that, he always greeted her first before going to see Ward. As a child, I often heard them bickering about whom their late husband had favored. Sometimes, they laughingly teased each other over who was going to die first and thus gain the privilege of lying in the grave closest to their husband. They also used to express their fondness of each other, each telling the other how lost she felt when the other was away for a day or more.

During their husband's lifetime and after his death, they used to sit in the afternoons for long hours on the same cushion, smoking the *narguila* (water pipe) and discussing various issues. They often slipped into competitive discussions of the history of their respective families. Yet, behind each other's backs, each used to remind the younger folk not to overlook their duties to the other. They also attended to each other in times of sickness and confided in each other their innermost thoughts and feelings. Ward used to repeat the songs that Almaza composed, and Almaza's eyes used to glitter, as her face became wrinkled with merriment, upon hearing Ward's witticisms.

Structural Differences in the Attitudes of Urban and Bedouin Women Towards Co-wives

As revealed by the statistics cited earlier, the vast majority of urban co-wives feel hatred toward one another, whereas Bedouin co-wives exhibit a variety of affective connections to their respective co-wives. The feelings toward one another explicitly voiced in the interviews were, to a great extent, corroborated by observation of behavior and conversations heard outside the scope of the interviews. Urban women's claims were generally of hatred toward co-wives, and their behavior, even when the perpetrators seemed to think that they were being neutral, polite, or even humane, conveyed the enmity they professed.

By contrast, the Bedouin women expressed, when questioned, and exhibited in their behavior toward their co-wives a variety of feelings that ranged between the extremes of hatred and love. The ones who did not hate their respective co-wives seemed to attempt to adjust to their polygynous marriages by taking into account the co-wife's (or co-wives') disposition and preference.

Bedouin women who claimed in the interviews to hate each other tended to justify the hatred by referring it to the actions or the character of the co-wife. In so doing, they appeared not to believe that her being the co-wife was enough justification for hating her. This was evidenced by Bedouin women's tendency to give reasons for any antagonism that they professed to feel toward their co-wives. They would say that they hated her because "she is a liar"; or because "she is a hypocrite"; or because "she is greedy, always trying to get more than her share." A frequent cause of the declared hatred was laziness. Two of the Bedouin co-wives claimed to hate a co-wife who "fakes sickness every time we have an overload of work." Urban women were comparatively less prone to give such explanations, frequently appearing surprised when asked for reasons for their hatred. Their attitudes indicated that partaking of a woman's husband was clearly a sufficient and very good reason for the woman to hate her co-wife.

The prevalence of enmity in the relationships between urban co-wives and the failure to see anything in the co-wife other than a threat indicate the existence of structural factors in urban women's lives and/or psychological formation that lead to their view of their role as a wife as the cornerstone of their existence and the most central determinant of their identity.

In the following two sections I argue that (1) the basis of this structural difference lies in the fact that the husband occupies a more central position in the practical and social lives of urban women than in those of Bedouin women and (2) the self-construct of urban girls is built around their future roles as wives, whereas that of Bedouin girls is more enmeshed with their situation as daughters of their families (or tribes or *ashirahs*).

Reasons Why Husbands Are More Central in the Lives of Urban Women than in those of Bedouin Women

Economic and Social Factors

The economic factor in Bedouin life displaces the husband from the center of his wife's life. Possessions among large tribal groups impede the couple from forming an economic unit. The woman's assured claim on support by her consanguine close relatives gives her a measure of economic security apart from her husband. Moreover, the Bedouin woman's work on the land and in tending livestock and in weaving tents and blankets, all of which are basic for the survival of the group, give her a sense of economic worth and as such enhance her psychological independence.

In contradistinction the usual family unit in urban localities is nuclear. Nuclear families are economically self-contained units. They do not usually expect or receive external financial help. This situation makes a wife who does not have her own economic resources totally dependent on her husband, and often when she does work, her earnings are recognized as secondary and are frequently used for items that the family can dispense with rather than for the basics. It is interesting to note, in this connection, that urban husbands are pressured by the community to be the main breadwinners, whereas among Bedouins a competition between husband and wife over productivity is nearly unheard of, a fact supported by the great numbers of "male Bedouins of leisure" who spend their days making coffee and chatting with guests while the women and children attend to matters of livelihood.

Even when city women are economically independent, as in the cases of Wadad and Lama, their independence from the husband remains thwarted by the fact that a woman on her own in an Arab city is an uncommon and an ill-tolerated phenomenon. Had these two women been Bedouin, their kinsmen would have claimed them away from an unhappy marital situation.

The urban woman's choice is restricted because although Arab tradition and Islamic law dictate that unmarried or divorced females should be financially supported by their closely related kinsmen, conditions of life in the city, including small apartments and the difficulty of coping financially in a consumer society, make the practice of such a tradition and law cumbersome for both sides. Women often are pressed to get married or to stay married because they feel that they cannot rely on their brothers for support or because they fear they will inconvenience their brothers' families.

In traditional Bedouin communities it is usual for brothers to repay the sister's husband with violence if he is violent with her and in *mugayada,* which is a far from infrequent form of marriage among Bedouins, when a husband divorces a man's sister or brings home another wife, the brother retaliates by divorcing the sister of that husband or by marrying another wife in order to get even with the brother of his wife for hurting his sister. Even a woman's disgrace, according to Bedouin tradition, is punished and otherwise borne by her family of birth (and later by her children) and not by her husband or his family. All this changes with urbanization, tying the woman more closely to her husband and loosening her ties to her family of birth.

For companionship and emotional exchange Bedouin women often rely a great deal on other women. The lifestyle of the Bedouins causes them to spend most of their time with members of their own sex. The women, especially when young, because the older matrons often join the men's gatherings during meals and for social interaction, share work and amusement with other women. Friendships are exclusively with members of their own sex. This makes the co-wife, sometimes, a more likely candidate for enriching and sharing a woman's life than the husband is.

By comparison, women in the city rely heavily on their husbands for companionship and emotional exchange and support. City life limits the woman's daily contact, to a large extent, to members of her nuclear family and to her work associates if she happens to work outside the home. Life in the city is often too fast and too busy to permit spending much time with friends or relatives.

The Difference in Value-Systems

The most crucial value, in Lebanese urban society, is material success. For the vast majority of Lebanese urban women, the way to such success is via a rich husband. The few women who manage to achieve political or intellectual prominence often suffer from not being taken seriously as professionals and from being blocked from reaching the truly satisfying elevated levels of success, which society seems to collaborate in allocating only to men.

Where social status is concerned, the main value according to which women in Lebanese urban society are measured is their marital status. Professional or not, a woman is judged by whether or not she has achieved the status of wife and mother. Condescending smiles and sometimes suppressed giggles are often seen or heard when an older woman, although professionally successful, is introduced as "Miss." When professional women miss out on the roles of wife and mother on the way to professional achievement, they often suffer from a feeling of inadequacy caused by prevalent social values.

The more "modern" urban women's need to express individual talents and choices, added to the internalized social values that emphasize marriage as a necessary condition for women's recognition and acceptability, results in women having to juggle the two roles— professional person and mother, who has to bear, often unaided, the sole responsibility for housework and child care. This leads to the devaluation of women's right to enjoy a free space in which they can recharge their spirits and unleash aspects of their need for the artistic and the playful.

By comparison, Bedouin women (and men) derive their social status and value primarily from their lineage. In fact, a Bedouin woman with a no prestigious lineage would not experience a significant change in her social status, even if she were to marry into an old and powerful tribe. Apart from lineage, the achieved worth of the individual, in Bedouin society, is determined by the larger community, especially the elders in that community. The elders' criteria usually have to do with moral uprightness and usefulness to the community.

Moreover, shared household responsibilities and seasonal variation in workloads coupled with a value system still not totally consumed by materialistic criteria of wealth and success leave the Bedouin women time and scope to attach value to the enjoyment of the playful and artistic aspects of life.

Comparing urban and Bedouin basic values, one finds that they are divisible into three categories: (1) value outside the woman's control, mainly marriage for urban women and lineage for Bedouins; (2) value within the woman's control, consisting of possible careers for urban women and room for morally appreciated conduct for Bedouins; (3) value attached by the woman to her personal happiness, which is seen by urban women to be a function of love-based marriage, whereas Bedouin women view happiness as deriving from play, art, and friendship and not solely from matrimonial bliss. Where values 2 and 3 are concerned, Bedouin women have more control over factors that impact their happiness and factors that lead to the acquisition of society's appreciation.

Development of the Self in Urban and Bedouin Women

The conditions and values in urban Lebanese society cause the woman's self-construct to be structured around the axis of her future role as a wife. The psychosocialization process continues to be affected by social pressure and by practical aspects of a quotidian life that push the woman to identify herself primarily as a wife. Unlike the urban ways, lifestyle among and values of Bedouin groups cause the woman's self-construct to be based on her continued identification as the daughter of her family of birth. The husband's position in a Bedouin woman's life is comparatively less pivotal because socioeconomic factors keep her strongly connected to consanguine relatives and to other women, even after marriage.

The difference in the two groups' sense of identity is verified by the fact that the vast majority of wives in Lebanese cities such as Beirut, Tripoli, and Sidon socially assume, when they get married, the family names of their husbands. They add the husband's family name to, or substitute it for, that of their own families, whereas rural and Bedouin wives continue to call themselves by their maiden family names.

The urban tendency to psychosocially identify women as wives rather than daughters entails, especially in communities that permit divorce and polygyny, that urban women feel vulnerable at the very source of their self-construct. This tendency causes a growing urban girl to fear that she may fail to acquire, in the future, this necessary ingredient to complete her identity. The urban girl grows as a plant with no fixed roots. She waits to acquire, in the future, perhaps, a vulnerable anchor (a husband) and can consider that she has developed fixed roots only when she has children grown and male, a factor that comes too late in life to help her secure a psychologically integrated sense of self. What adds to the psychological misery that comes as a package deal with the urban type of female self-identity or self-construct is the fact that although becoming, or staying, a wife is a psychosocial necessity for these women, initiating and keeping the marriage are totally dependent on the men. Moreover, the prerequisites for being sought after as a wife are often qualities that are outside the women's control, such as beauty, youth, a rich father or a prestigious lineage. She usually has to wait passively or maybe pray or use magic (two "activities" that spring from the recognition of her lack of power to control her destiny), hoping that this effort may procure a husband for her.

Because urban women's selves are constructed around their role as wives, which places the husband in the central position of what is required to make them feel whole and adequate, a competitor for the husband is seen as a colossal and devastating threat. The person embodying such a threat, namely the co-wife, can only be met with aggression and hatred. Hatred or aggression can be effective, however, only if the one driven by them possesses a measure of autonomy and recognizes the availability of some space for the manipulation or transformation of reality in accordance with one's desires. The urban women of this study seemed helpless, behaving as though, for them, the scope for decisively effective action was nonexistent.

In comparison, the Bedouin women relating to, or identifying with, their respective families of birth, hold the advantages of continuity and unalterability. It guarantees a sense of belonging that structures their self construct from the very beginning to have firm and secure roots. Moreover, Bedouin women's more accessible control over what decides their mobile or achieved social status, which in Bedouin communities derives from their evaluation in terms of moral uprightness or social contribution, gives them a stronger sense of self-determination. The feeling of security and of having a measure of control over their social image create in Bedouin women a greater efficiency in dealing with situations realistically and in solving problems. In this study Bedouin women were more capable of adjusting to their marriages and of relating to their co-wives. They were also more likely to leave the marriage when staying in it made them unhappy.

That Bedouin women see themselves as effectively autonomous is reflected in their outlook toward their co-wives as persons and not just as rivals. This is evident in the lack of uniformity in their feelings toward the co-wife and in the fact that Bedouin co-wives' feelings toward one another were subject to change in accordance with the behavior of the one toward the other, more so than the feelings of urban co-wives.

Indeed, I venture to claim that although urban women have much more of a say in the choice of a husband, yet, with so much conditioning, their choices tend to be largely society induced. The Bedouin women often succumb to arranged marriage, yet they can maneuver other aspects of their lives to place more emphasis on what they enjoy from a few choices of occupation and a wider range of recreational activities. Indeed, if linguistic expression is considered a possible means of genuine self-expression or a surrogate desire fulfillment, Bedouin women's constant recourse to poetry and to songs and to imagination-enriched tales and legends is expected to give them a considerable scope for cathecting urges and desires.

The urban women lack initiative in the pursuit of free, individually determined, sources of enjoyment of life such as friendship, nature, play, and art. By comparison, the Bedouin women's choices arise from a deeper relating to the self and its desires. Maybe the latters' closeness to nature is a factor. Because Bedouin women are more secure in their identity, they are more capable of acting freely, and because they are more deeply and genuinely integrated into the community into which they are born, the structurally permeable boundaries of their selves enable them to be more capable of identifying with the joys and miseries of others.

Conclusions

In the Arab world Bedouin norms are generally the origin, or the past, which is being infiltrated, to varying degrees, especially in the Middle East and North Africa, by Western norms. Because this infiltration is taking place to a greater extent in the urban centers, the positive valorization of urbanity is often reflected as looking favorably on the imported changes. Moreover, because the West is the nest of power and the source of the most pervasive media transmission, its ways are gaining ground and appeal in various regions of the world. A hasty consideration of urban as positive and desirable and of the Western impact as positive and desirable seems to cause an oversimplification in the light of which the impact of imported changes on an Arab or Islamic world with certain characteristics that remain unchanged (multiple marriages, restrictions on women, a closely controlling patriarchy) is taken to be a move in the right direction. The findings of this study encourage a more holistic scrutiny under which the above-mentioned infiltration may be better judged with respect to the impact of its outcome on the status and happiness of women.

In the light of these findings, the calls occasionally made by a score of scholars that a move towards a nuclear type of family and the undermining of patriarchal authority are essential prerequisites for the achievements of democratic relations, must not be accepted without some qualifications. Instead, the thrust of my argument is in line with Leila Ahmed's recommendation that reform be pursued in a "native idiom" and not in one appropriated from other patriarchies found in other cultures. It is essential to avoid biases and generalizations; for example, the fact that urbanity or Western ways hold many desirable traits should not lead to the assumption that any motion in their direction is desirable and completely positive.

Whether Arab women live in extended or in nuclear families, they remain under patriarchal hegemonies. The surveyed women living within a nuclear Arab family seemed to fall under a more oppressive form of patriarchy than the tribal one, insofar as patriarchal power in the tribe concentrates decision making and the assessment of individuals in a few elders who are usually chosen for their wisdom and their superior moral standing. Such power to make decisions and to pass judgment on women accrues within a nuclear family, to every husband, regardless of his moral or mental caliber. In Bedouin communities, the authority of the elders, or sheikhs, together with the watch that tribes keep on the behavior of their members, ensure some rights for women and a measure of fairness in the way they are treated, whereas under urban patriarchies women's sense of security has to depend on civil society and its willingness to afford women a measure of protection.

Unless civil society in each Arab country becomes a deterrent to the "nuclear" patriarch, the conditions of the life of an Arab woman under such absolute patriarchy are very precarious. Often, neither religious laws—*shari'a* often depart from the word and spirit of the Qur'an as a result of self-serving biases of the patriarchs who draft religious law—nor civil laws effectively protect the interests of women or safeguard their dignity. In Lebanon the sectarian regime is incapable or fearful of implementing change or of adequately enforcing rules. Such a regime prevents imported or locally devised new social ways from being woven into the fixed social realities to form a more efficient or more equitable society.

At the level of the discussion of the psychosocial conditions under which women in general live, and not just in Lebanon or the Arab world, the above investigates the problematic of women having to shift families between the ones of birth and those of marriage. A man is identified with one family, one locale, and one name from birth to death. But a woman's self-construct has to prepare her to live as a "nomad," not only in the geographic sense but also where her psychological identity and social adjustment are concerned. This "nomadic" existence may be the cause behind several of the so-called "feminine" characteristics that are detrimental to women's status and to women's ability to hold the reins of their lives and to steer them in directions advantageous to themselves and/or promoting the fulfillment of their desires. It is ironical that my investigation reveals that in Lebanon Bedouin women have a more "settled" self-construct than that of urban women!

Psychology has demonstrated the importance of every detail of the "family drama" in the formation of the child's personality. The tone and type of the family drama determine whether the child is expected to grow to be more individualistic with more strictly defined borders between self and others or whether he/she is socialized to be more caring for others and more dependent on them. This study indicates that Lebanese urban women seemed to be lost between the two patterns.

At an even more general level that embraces women and men, this study questions the wisdom of attaching value to items that are not related to, or that have a negative impact on, happiness, whether it is happiness of the individual and/or that of society. Valorization of success and of material achievement, which reinforces a closely bound construct of the self, is shown to obstruct allocating space for the enjoyment of pursuits that favor the individual's happiness and obstruct higher moral commitment where the latter often leads to bestowing happiness on others. Indeed, because socialization in any form of upbringing is geared to form social individuals, a socialization that creates individuals with closely-bound self-constructs is one that, in a sense, is not in harmony with its own purpose. For to produce individuals with clearly demarcated and closely guarded boundaries, is, in some sense, tantamount to creating asocial personalities. Clearly, such individuals would be more likely to interact with others superficially, in a socially acceptable and functional fashion, without becoming socially committed at the deeper or more affective, and perhaps more effective, levels.

People with closely bound self-constructs ruled by material values may carry a latent threat for social and global aims, owing to their lack of social integration and commitment. They also have a type of self-construct that sabotages its own access to happiness in play, in friendship, and in deriving joy vicariously by means of contributing to the happiness of others. It seems, from the types recorded and analyzed here, that by shutting out others from the self one tends to shut out access to the pulse of the general vital force, which is the more reliable source for attuning to the world and for seeking, and finding, happiness.

Originally published in Suad Joseph (ed.) *Intimate Selving in Arab Families: Gender, Self and Identity* (Syracuse University Press, 1999): 141–173. Printed here with the permission of the publisher.

PART EIGHT

Religion and Ritual

Introduction

Islam, as a set of religious beliefs and rituals, as repeatedly asserted by a score of observers, is far from being monolithic. Other than some of its revealed, divine and essentialist attributes, virtually everything is subject to questioning and interpretation; particularly its popular manifestations of everyday life.

As we have seen, the cosmopolitan segments of Egyptian youth seem averse to accepting the patronizing and austere edicts and *fatwas* of Azharite pulpits. Instead, they are more receptive and feel psychologically more at ease with the genial and convivial messages delivered and staged by star-like performers and media icons like Amr Khalid.

The way Islam is perceived and lived by Muslim immigrant families and their children is, likewise, a variant entity. To children in diaspora, religion is not just a matter of faith and belief. It is a venue for communal belonging and the validation of identity and self-image.

The young muslims Nadia Hashmi interviewed in London, mostly second and third generation British subjects of Muslim parents, did not just passively accept the religious beliefs they inherited from their parents. They were active in constructing a new religious identity, incorporating both the values of their parents' home country with those of the host country that were more meaningful to their new needs. As such, many of Hashmi's respondents willingly recognized themselves as "Muslims". Yet whether they pray, fast during the month of Ramadan, drink alcohol or eat pork can vary. Likewise, while many admitted to never going to the mosque, and not being a member of an Islamic association, they still fasted with their family and friends.

As a transnational identity, being a European Muslim does not simply mean that they are "in-between" a country of origin and Western European society. Within the context of being a Muslim in Europe, particularly for the children of immigrants, lies the ability for such displaced and uprooted groups to construct new identities which are formed as a transcultural hybridization.

For example, in France the word *Arabe* was originally seen as slightly derogatory, in that as Hashmi maintains, it was used to define indiscriminately immigrant groups of Arab origin which otherwise might not be seen as being so close (such as those from Maghreb, including the Berbers, from Egypt and the Middle Eastern countries). The word *Arabe* or *beur* is often used interchangeably to mean Muslim, since the majority of Muslims in France are, in fact, Arab. It is interesting in this regard that the words *beur* and *beurette* are adopted by immigrant children to refer to themselves. Their parents, incidentally, refuse to be labeled as *beurs*.

One central implication of this transnational identity must be kept in mind: immigrant identity is unique since it involves a re-definition or re-evaluation of oneself and one's identity when being situated in a strange environment and surrounded by different customs, traditions and language to which the immigrant is expected to adjust. This is also, in part, a generational problem. For the first generation of immigrants in Europe still retained a clear memory of their country of origin. They can still define themselves as being from that place. Their children, however, are not seen as being *from* anywhere, other than *here*. Like other victims of transnational migration, they suffer a double alienation. Their ties with their parents and country of origin are quite often tenuous. In fact, even though many might not have ever visited their country, they are still recognized as "Others," since they are perceived as being different by the host population.

In her conclusion Nadia Hashmi draws another interesting inference that the second generation of immigrants is not merely an "in-between" or liminal identity; separated from their country of origin and not assimilated into a Western European society. Rather, within the context of being Muslim in Europe lies the ability of this group to develop new identities which are formed as a transnational hybridization. Naturally, this involves considerable negotiation in order to construct a new sense of self.

In the US and Canada the ritual evocation of Karbala (the commemoration of the Martyrdom of Husain, the Prophet Mohammad's beloved grandson), serves to enhance a sense of piety for Shi'i Muslims. More important, perhaps, it also helps them to construct a unique and meaningful collective identity as they struggle to cope with the alienating circumstances of the diaspora.

Being members of a marginalized religious minority has been an inveterate feature of the Shi'i throughout their checkered history. Even in most parts of the Muslim world they continue to live their lives in the midst of other communities who do not share many of their religious beliefs, rituals and practices.

Vernon James Schubel conducted his ethnographic research at the Ja'ffari Islamic Center in Ontario (1990), which attends to the spiritual needs of immigrants from East Africa. His central thesis is very compelling and is consistent with the experience of other displaced groups in the diaspora. The commemoration of the battle of Karbala, doubtlessly the most momentous cosmic drama of profound historic significance, is vital to the way Shi'i Muslims reinforce their unique identity within the larger *ummah*. The importation of the rituals in the re-enactment of Karbala also serves, according to Schubel, to facilitate the community's adaptation to the Canadian environment. The devotional rituals of *Ashura* allow the Shi'i community to claim space in North America that is both North American and Islamic. By doing this they Islamize North American culture while creatively adapting Islam to the North American environment.

Devotional activities serve not only to reinforce the unique authority of Shi'i Islam but also to encourage the creative adaptation of the community to changing circumstances. For example when the Ja'ffari Center was built in 1978, an architect was hired with explicit instructions to construct a recognizably Islamic building that was devoid of characteristic features such as domes and minarets, in order to prevent it from standing out. The completed building is a remarkable edifice, which is recognizably Islamic and yet part of the Canadian architectural landscape.

After 9/11 the image and public perception of Islam underwent something akin to a paradigm shift. Islamism as a political project with a contentious agenda that appealed to constituencies drawn largely from an impoverished middle class, started to evolve into an agency of active piety concerned with personal salvation and popular culture. The shift also involved a change in the direction, appealing more to fragmented adherents, including privileged groups.

In the US, and elsewhere in Europe, the unprovoked attack reinforced Western anxieties to the threat of Islamic militancy. This surge in "Islamophobia," bolstered by widespread anti-Muslim prejudice, was bound to beget radical and extremist reactions of various forms in the guise of Islamic activism. These range from global terrorist organizations like al-Qaida, suicide bombers, revivalist mass protest movements to the more quietist sub-cultural expressions of popular Islam, concerned with matters like personal piety, salvation, ethics and culture.

To Asef Bayat the causes underlying this change and compounding their unsettling consequences are multiple and grievous. They converge, however, on two overriding realities: the crisis of Islamic governance, be it where it was put into practice (i.e. Iran or Sudan) or where it failed in its belligerent strategies (i.e. Egypt and Algeria); and the persistence of Israeli hostilities. In the face of such disheartening realities, it is understandable that disillusioned masses begin to find shelter in new visions of the Islamic project.

In his essay, Bayat focuses on one recent manifestation of change in Egyptian religious mobilization—the popularity of new genre of lay Muslim evangelism. To him, among many others, the so-called "Amr Khalid Phenomenon", the celebrated Egyptian preacher, represents this paradigm shift. Almost everywhere we can observe a clear shift from the earlier emphasis on Islamist polity with a belligerent and confrontational agenda to a more ritualistic and expressive Islam; a form of active piety concerned with personal well-being and culture.

Amr Khalid, the closest analogue to the prototype of an American televangelist, has become a household name not only among the affluent classes of Cairo but also among the privileged and cosmopolitan youth in Arab society. He began by preaching his flavored sermons in private homes and exclusive social clubs. He quickly rose to fame by employing state-of-the-art websites, audio and videotapes to become a star and dazzling performer. Unlike the stern and fierce-looking orthodox preachers who deliver their austere sermons in a joyless moralizing tone, Khalid comes on as a compassionate, congenial, easygoing companion. By ingeniously combining faith and fun, he manages to convey simple, ethical messages, in colloquial Arabic, about the moralities of everyday life. Nothing is spared. He particularly addresses issues of concern to contemporary youth who seem eager to entertain change and assert their individuality yet remain within the fold of salient norms and expectations. Hence matters such as gender relationships, consumerism, dress codes, adultery, drunken driving, the *hijab* and the sins of sexual tourism are approached candidly and with heightened emotional intensity. Khalid does not issue admonishing *fatwas*. Rather, and much like the public therapist of American talk-shows, he addresses the spiritual and psychological needs of those groping to forge a meaningful identity which allows them to live comfortably in both worlds.

NADIA HASHMI

Immigrant Children in Europe:
Constructing a Transnational Identity

Fast is East and West and ne'er the
Twain shall meet

R. Kipling, *The Ballad of East & West*

It has been history—stories of the Crusades, the Mogul Emperors and colonial rule—that has shaped the way in which the Orient is seen in the West. As noted by Edward Said in *Orientalism* (1978), Westerners are always shown as being peaceful, rational human beings, whereas Arab Orientals are none of these things. In this way, Orientalism is seen by Said as a way of legitimizing Muslim poverty and disadvantage.

Jenine Abboushi Dallal (1998) points out that one of the ironies of multiculturalism is how parochial it is, and how it remains limited to American culture. Dallal analyses literature as an example of this, and argues that the increase in literary translations from Eastern developing countries does not indicate that Western readers are becoming more interested in Eastern writers. On closer examination, there is evidence that suggests that the books were written with the Western audience in mind. Arab culture is explained in detail, whereas many aspects of Western culture which would be unknown to those unfamiliar with it, are not. In the same way, the Self is portrayed by these Arab writers through the eyes of, and for, the Other. She goes on to say that this was also the case with Rushdie's *Satanic Verses*, in that Islam was seen as having been parodied for the sake of the Western audience.

For many people in Europe, it is only through post-war immigration that they have contact with the "East". The specific circumstances of the immigrant mean that he or she will inevitably be compared to and be spoken of in relation to another, usually the majority. As Green points out, "The immigrant represents the Other in the nation-state [...] The immigrant embodies an implicit comparison between past and present, between one world and another, between two languages, and two sets of cultural norms."

With its origins lying East of Europe and the United States, Islam was originally seen as an "immigrant religion". This is now changing due to the generation of Muslims who have been born and who have grown up in Europe. In a way, the meeting of "East" and "West", religion and secular society, the traditional and the modern, all presented as virtual dichotomies, can be seen to be embodied in the biographies of the children of Muslim immigrants in Europe. These individuals see both the world of their parents and the world of their majority counterparts through the eyes of an outsider, and yet also from the perspective of one who can understand both categories of life experience. The lives of the members of this group are different from those of their parents. They have had no experience of migration, and yet still have to assess and deal with the significance of their parents' origins—which, for many, have not been experienced first-hand—and also of being Muslim while also being a resident of Europe. For these, who make up the so-called "second generation", it is suggested here that Islam can play a different role than it does for their parents. Whilst it will certainly have a specific personal meaning, it can be taken on as a collective marker of difference which can incorporate what they have from their parents as well as their own experiences. Whatever their "identity" is—a term that is overused in academic writing—it is far more complicated and complex than simply a mixture of the elements of each of these two cultures.

The issue here is not one concerning the macrostructuration of group dynamics through collective identity. Rather, the approach is focused on an analysis of the potential of a cross-cultural synthesis originating through the microstructures of the immigrant situation. Collective identity is therefore a by-product, a factor of stabilization, but not something that, in itself, creates dilemmas faced by second generation European Muslims. Issues of inclusion versus exclusion in European societies are then subordinated to the level of the multiple, simultaneous, and more flexible procedures of distinction and identification. This chapter will look at the idea of identity formations of a minority group and consider why the children of immigrants incorporate the ideas of the Self and the Other and the way in which the image is adopted as a self-image.

The ideas of multiple and hybrid identities have been examined by various writers including Modood (1994) and Werbner (1997). I take these studies as a point of departure for my own research, which involves interviews with young Muslims of immigrant origins. I concentrate most specifically on religion as a marker of identity, something more than a faith which is also a vehicle of "belonging". This chapter investigates how, in this way, religious belonging might be a specific tool of identification for the children of immigrants. It looks at the mechanisms linking personal choice to communal references which highlight how these various identities are negotiated and accommodated in a specific social space of second generation European Muslims, and how the ideas of the Self and the Other are incorporated within the individuals of this group.

Religion as an Identifier

I shall consider the concept of religion as a key variable in the development of an identity. The religion in question is Islam—in part because it is the religion of many of the post-war immigrant populations in Europe, and in part because it is, in principle, originally a non-European religion that has subsequently been transplanted to Europe. Religion is sometimes used as an autonomous variable in studies of immigrant groups, or otherwise incorporated within culture or ethnicity. The central idea of the research from which this chapter is partly derived is that religion can be considered as a separate variable from culture or ethnicity.

Religion in contemporary modern societies might be seen as a case of believing or of belonging. Islam is definitely significant for Muslim immigrant families and their children in both instances. It represents something that can be inherited in an almost primordial way; "it is not something that one chooses", said two interviewees.

To take the idea a step further, a minority religion can be a signifier of one's difference, with a more personal meaning attached. Having been born into a religion and taking it on in an almost automatic way is one thing, how the younger generation practise it, is another. It can be redeveloped in order to place an emphasis on different aspects, incorporating both the parents' home country values and new meanings. This opens up a space of reflection on what it means to be a Muslim including issues of religious practice; and in relation to Muslim identity. In the interviews that were conducted for this research, numerous variations within the definition of being Muslim were found through a distinctive practice, or a more or less consciously managed lack of practice. Many people willingly call themselves "Muslim" of their own accord, yet whether they pray, fast during the month of Ramadan, drink alcohol or even eat pork can vary. While many of the respondents admitted to never going to the mosque, and not being a member of an organization, they still fasted with their own family or friends, or even on their own. This might result from parental or peer pressure, but perhaps it is still partly related to the will to carry on a part of an inherited past, along with belief, and the desire to feel part of a wider, historical community.

Like ethnic background, religion is perceived to form a significant part of one's sense of self. The definition of the self can be seen to come from the way in which others perceive the individual. These definitions are internalised by the individual in keeping with the way he or she believes to be seen by others within social interactions. Cooley emphasized this idea through the notion of the "looking-glass self". The fact that people do not have direct access to the viewpoint of others, and will therefore only see themselves as they believe others see them, is known as the "metaperspective", that is, the generator of self-images. Further to this is the fact that, once a self-image is established, subsequent categorizations and social comparisons are needed between oneself and others in order to develop a stable sense of one's own self and a positive evaluation of the group to which one belongs. An individual can subsume him or herself under a variety of social categories, but the greater the number of categories, the greater the chance of ambiguity and inconsistency amongst them, thus causing internal conflict and a very uncomfortable psychological state. In this sense, fitting into a collective identity is not a straightforward process, but rather the result of a tortuous work of reassembling a self-identity. One sees one-self as a personal construction and, in comparing oneself to others, sees them as being "like me" or "not like me". This construction of the self is the necessary platform from which one constructs other superordinate patterns of belonging, and in this way the construct system of the individual will affect his or her subsequent actions. Through the complexity of experience, one's personal construction of the self will have to be revised and renegotiated according to the way in which the "self" wishes to be presented and in an uninterrupted, processual way.

Group Categorization: The Image and the Self-Image

Specific to the situation of Muslim migrants and a powerful agent of recomposition of a stable sense of belonging, are the xenostereotypes produced by entrenched processes of social categorization. For a large amount of empirical research, including the present, the categorization of subjects into groups is inevitable for the purpose of clarity of results.

It is the categorization of people into social groups that leads others to predict the behavior of a group. In the case of immigrant populations they are perceived to be a single homogenous group, and different from the host population. It is interesting to note that the usual criticism of multiculturalism is that defining groups through the external imposition of categories upon them simply accentuates differences. In this way, boundaries are seen as being even more rigid and less permeable than they might previously have been. The perceived homogeneity of shared characteristics and interests attributed to the group from the outside will have an influence on group feelings. Thus, this perception will shift onto the group itself and, possibly, lead to increased cohesion within the collectivity. An example of this is observable in Britain and the USA, where the classification into ethnic groups for monitoring equality in areas such as recruitment applications has become common practice by the groups themselves, not just in the original context, but to the point where the classifications have become auto-definitions, e.g. Asian, Afro-Caribbean, Hispanic. Although Muslims have yet to be recognized as a "racial" group in the terms of the Race Relations Act of 1976 in England and Wales, nevertheless, in a similar way, religion is something that can become an identifying marker by virtue of the fact that it demarcates a group of which one believes one is perceived as being a member by others. In turn, one chooses to assert oneself according to this marker.

As noted, in some theories of group identity, and especially on the micro level, there is also a presumption that the individual from a minority group, or who is a member of a group that is perceived as being inferior, will actually attempt to pass into the majority group and assimilate. Only if this individual tries and is unsuccessful will he or she return to their own group and reevaluate this into an identity which is assessed positively. This assumption is criticized. The idea that the individual aspires to assimilate into the majority group as well as the idea that she or he will only achieve the necessary favourable self-evaluation in relation to their own group if they fail to assimilate with the majority and are thus forced to return (on a social-psychological level) to the group of origin is an over-simplification.

Whilst many of the respondents recognized the fact that Islam has a negative portrayal in the media, "[They think] that it is a barbaric religion. That it's backward". When asked if this made them angry most replied that, no, in fact they realized that those people who bother to be better informed and form their own opinion do not believe everything that they read; "If they are stupid enough to take in what is said on television, too bad for them [...] they are stupid [...] it's them who are the idiots.. They don't know how to make a difference, they take everything said on TV as the final word." For those interviewed, it seemed that despite an acknowledged consciousness of Muslims being a disadvantaged group in Europe due to their minority status, this situation did not make them any more reluctant to identify themselves as Muslims who face prejudices. Some of the fiction written by authors such as Hanif Kureishi, Azouz Begag and Meera Syal offer a good insight into the perceptions from the point of view of the children of immigrants.

In several EU countries, immigration is linked to a colonial history, whereby, for example, many migrated to France in order to fill a gap in the mainly manual labour market, and, as a consequence, had to face not only socio-cultural, but also socio-economic marginalization. Many of those who came lived in lodgings for immigrant-workers. When they were joined by their families they were usually forced to look for larger accommodation, and so lived in poor housing conditions in tower blocks or in estates in areas of high immigrant concentrations, often in the suburbs of large cities. In France, the term *banlieue* is used to refer to such suburbs of a city, with a connotation of it being a socio-economically deprived area. A *banlieusard* is one from an area like this, who is caught in a vicious circle in which schooling is of a lower standard, people are less well off, and crime is perceived as being higher. The stereotypes that are formed are also reflected back onto the population. Although it may not only be ethnic minority groups who are in these areas and who experience such a situation, it is frequently the case.

In this way, the social position of the *arabe*, the *beur*, the *bicot*, the *bougnaule*—all terms which are used interchangeably for a young immigrant from the suburbs—is also set on a cultural level. They are seen, or expected, to commit petty crimes, hang about in the streets, drop out of school, and have low employment prospects. The fact that this is the way in which they think they will always be perceived creates the vicious circle where there is no incentive to try harder, to look for a better job, as the outcome will be the same. Many thus preempt the inevitable prejudices that they have already experienced or that are known to exist.

The word *beur* offers one of the best examples of how the image is taken on as the self-image. It is derived from the word *arabe* which in *verlan* becomes *beur*. The word *arabe* was originally seen as slightly derogatory in that it was used to define indiscriminately immigrant groups of Arab origins but which otherwise might not be seen as being so close—those from the Maghreb (Algeria, Tunisia, Morocco) including the Berbers, from Egypt and from other Middle Eastern countries. The word *arabe* or *beur* is often used interchangeably to mean Muslim, since the majority of Muslims in France are, in fact, Arab (although some Arabs are Christian or Jewish). There seems to be an automatic presumption that one is also the other. For this reason, statistics regarding religious groups are also estimates taken from non-French and North-African numbers rather than official statistics from any religious monitoring. The words *beur* and *beurette* have been adopted by the children of immigrants to refer to themselves. In the interviews conducted in Paris, the exact meaning and use of this word was investigated. Some said they would use the word for a certain type of person, the young Arab boy or girl who had a specific way of talking and dressing that was particular to that group, and who conveys a new, young identity that has little to do with their parents' culture and is more of a street youth culture, but one different from that of their French counterparts. Most, however, said they would use the word in general to denote any Arab boy or girl. Their parents, said one, would not be classified as *beur*; "Mes parents, ils ne sont pas beurs" as this was specific to the younger generation.

In this way, a new label has been found which has been derived from the perceived difference of the group from the *Français de souche*. The fact that the label exists and is used as a sort of auto-identification is a demonstration of how, by virtue of this word, the group is recognized by others and also by itself. All the same, the extent to which its contemporary use is automatic is arguable, in that it was neither used as freely nor as often as the word *arabe* in the interviews.

Islam as a Transnational Identity

Religion takes on added significance when it is taken out of the context of its original surroundings and is threatened—something which can occur when placed in the minority context of the immigrant. Whilst it is agreed that immigrants of the second generation are not able to reproduce the identity of their parents, but have to create a new one of their own, for many of the younger generations and the offspring of immigrants, Islam is being re-evaluated in a new socio-cultural context. Young people call themselves Muslims and, indeed, wish to be seen as such. Yet some observers would say that being a non-practising or partly practising Muslim is a contradiction in terms. In interviews it was frequently noted that one should not really call oneself Muslim unless one was practicing, and yet so many people do call themselves Muslim despite this. This mirrors Olivier Roy's description of the way in which the *néofondamentalistes* see others who are non-pacticing as not really being Muslims, or as being bad ones.

It is often the same groups of Muslim activists who maintain that only those countries that have adopted the *shari'a* as their national law are suitable or correct places for Muslims to live, and that Muslims who do not live in such countries should move just as *muhajirs* have done historically. This term is used to describe those who leave their non-Islamic territory in order to migrate to an Islamic one. Of course, there are countries that have a Muslim majority, but have secular or non-Islamic laws, or only partially incorporated *shari'a* law. In Islam, a country can be *dar al-harb*, a land open to war and conquest, or *dar al-islam*, a land where Islam can be practised freely. Paradoxically, countries that are seen as being traditionally Muslim are sometimes not seen as being *dar al-islam* due to the fact that Muslims are not always free to practice as they might wish, whereas many European countries are seen as being so, in the sense that Muslims arc safe and freedom of practising is guaranteed. For this reason, it is often groups and movements maintaining these views that have grown in popularity in Europe.

The situation of the immigrant referred to here is a specific one. The immigrant only becomes aware of that which is different about him or herself from the majority, when faced with his or her situation in the context of immigration. A sense of peer group and family pressure adds to this heteroidentification. In itself, immigrant identity is a particular one since it involves the re-evaluation of oneself and one's identity when being situated in a strange environment and surrounded by different customs, traditions, and language to which the immigrant is expected to adjust. Often the result is a reassertion of differences and a re-identification with others from the same origins with whom one might not have felt any specific bond, had immigration not taken place. Factors such as socio-economic situation, employment, housing and education will all affect the extent to which the individual will or will not feel accepted by the host society.

On a different register, Valerie Amiraux has discussed the way in which the Turkish immigrant community in Germany has used the opportunities that are available there to its advantage. The *laissez-faire* attitude of the German state towards its immigrant populations who are usually not seen as being part of the mainstream ethnic German culture or citizenship has been used in a positive way. Networks have been formed between small businesses and associations in Germany and those of the country of origin, the result being that the immigrant can benefit from being a political and social actor in both countries.

This situation might be specific to the group in the Kreuzberg area of Berlin, and with regard to the situation in Germany and in Turkey. There are similar cases of ties formed between immigrant groups and the country of origin in cities in other countries. With advanced communication systems and increased ease of travel, the sending of remittances or, indeed, other forms of money is facilitated.

On a more basic level, one can look around any large city with a significant immigrant population and see the way in which immigrants have tailored their environment to their needs. In Southall, West London, restaurants, *halal* butchers, clothes shops and supermarkets cater to the needs of the local Sikh Indian and Pakistani communities. Areas such as this exist all over London—in the centre, Edgeware Road provides a similar plethora of Arab restaurants, cafés, shops and banks. Similarly, a walk through the Rue Jean-Pierre Timbaud in Paris' 11th *arrondissement* reveals a street where *halal* butchers, Muslim bookshops and *maghrebian* bakeries are found. A few years ago there was a business on this street offering insurance for people so that, on their death, their bodies could be flown back to North Africa for burial (despite the fact that they can be buried in certain cemeteries in Paris). That people still wish to be buried in their country of origin is something significant and only time will tell if subsequent generations will do the same, despite having lived in Europe all their lives. These services can be seen as the natural course of urban immigrant development in major cities, as is the demand for specific services relating to food, religion, travel, and burial. However, it can also be seen as occurring due to the opportunity that the immigrant context creates or, arguably, necessitates.

This ability to make use of one's resources is notable for the benefits one incurs and for making transnational links, although there is a certain hesitance in this area on the part of European institutions, following the assumption that the outside influences are not helping to create a truly "European" Islam. This is partly due to the fear of fundamentalism, which is perceived to originate in the very same countries with which ties are maintained by the immigrant populations.

Conclusions

As we can see, identity patterns are more complex for the children of immigrants. Indeed, for the first generation of immigrants in Europe, there is still a very clear memory of their country of origin. They can still define themselves as being from that place. For them, having such opportunity and resources is important in order not to miss certain things that they would have obtained in their home country. Their children, however, are not seen as being "from" anywhere, other than here. In this way, much of their definition does come from the supposed "Other". Their ties with their parents' country of origin might be tenuous, indeed many from this generation might not have ever visited their country. And yet members of this group are seen as being different from the majority population and are thus supposed to have a clear-cut explanation for their personal history and how they define themselves in relation to that history. However, they are not "in-between" a country of origin and Western European society. Within the idea of being Muslim in Europe lies the ability for members of this group to develop new identities which are formed as transcultural *hybridization*, the result of which is completely different from the original components. The generational gap adds to this phenomenon of altering and transgressing boundaries of the self and community.

In this sense, the cases of liminality discussed by Anja Hansch in her chapter are extended and intensified at the passage from the first to the second generation of immigrants. The works of fiction examined by Hansch largely prefigured a sociological reality that came to full maturation with the second generation. More than a case or an occasion for normalization, the second generation further complexifies the liminal situation, but also builds upon the accumulated resources of transnational ties and multiple identities of the previous generation to be factored into profiles of "European Muslims". The transnational links might continue to thrive, but there will also be the need for a different kind of space. With regard to the second generation, this idea of space is a vital one, in that it is here where identity negotiation and expression will be able to take place in order to gain a sense of self.

References

Dallal, J. A. "The Perils of Occidentalism: How Arab Novelists Are Driven to Write for Western Readers." In *The Times Literary Supplement*, April 1998.

Modood, T, *Changing Ethnic Identities*, London, Policy Studies Institute, 1994.

Roy, Olivier, *The Failure of Political Islam*, Cambridge, Mass: Harvard University Press, 2001.

Said, E., *Orientalism*, London, Routledge, 1978.

Werbner, P., & Modood, T.,(eds.), *Debating Cultural Hybridity: Multicultural Identities and the Politics of Anti-Racism*, London, Zed Books, 1997.

Originally published in A. Höfert and A. Salvatore (eds.) *Between Europe & Islam* (P.I.E.-Peter Lang, 2000): 163–173. Printed here with the permission of the publisher.

VERNON JAMES SCHUBEL

Karbala as Sacred Space among North American Shi'a

"Every Day is Ashura, Everywhere is Karbala"

Karbala holds a place of central importance in the piety of Shi'i Muslims. As the place where the Prophet Muhammad's beloved grandson Husain was martyred in 680 C.E., Karbala is simultaneously the site of a particular historical tragedy and the location for a metahistorical cosmic drama of universal significance. In the United States and Canada, the ritual evocation of Karbala helps Shi'i Muslims construct a unique and meaningful identity in the midst of an "alien" environment. By creating spatial and temporal arenas for the remembrance of Karbala, the Shi'a consciously adapt and accommodate existing institutions such as lamentation assemblies and processions in ways that allow them to claim space through the expression of central and paradigmatic symbols.

This essay explores the role of Karbala as a "sacred center" for Shi'i Muslims in the context of a particular North American community. The research was conducted primarily at the Ja'ffari Islamic Center in Thornhill, Ontario, in July and August 1990. The Ja'ffari Center is a Shi'i institution whose buildings are located on a major traffic artery in the Toronto suburbs. It serves the spiritual needs of a large community of Urdu and Gujarati-speaking Shi'a, consisting largely of immigrants from East Africa. The community's members live dispersed throughout the Toronto area. The community is relatively affluent, the majority of its members having successfully made the transition to become suburban residents in the modern Canadian "ethnic quilt".

Living as members of a religious minority group is nothing new for the Shi'a. In most parts of the Muslim world, the Shi'a constitute a religious minority who live their lives physically surrounded by other communities who reject many of their beliefs and practices. The Shi'a of the Ja'ffari Center are also an ethnic, as well as a religious, minority, a situation familiar to the Gujarati Khojas, the majority of members of the center, who migrated from East Africa. They must decide which elements of the cultures of their countries of origin they will preserve. For most, their Shi'i identity is primary.

The remembrance of the battle of Karbala as a significant historical and religious event is crucial to the way in which Shi'i Muslims maintain their unique identity within the larger *ummah*. The importation of rituals for the remembrance of Karbala has also facilitated the community's adaptation to the Canadian environment. The remembrance and re-creation of Karbala allow the Shi'i community to claim space in North America that is both North American and Islamic: they thus Islamize elements of North American culture while creatively adapting Islam to the North American environment.

The Nature of Shi'i Piety

Shi'i piety is firmly oriented toward a historically focused spirituality that seeks to understand the divine will through the interpretation of events that took place in human history. Important events in the early history of Islam, such as the battle of Karbala, are understood as "metahistorical," in that they are seen to transcend and interpenetrate ordinary reality, providing definitive and dramatic models for human conduct and behavior. While this is true to some degree for all Muslims—as well as for Jews and Christians—the Shi'a place a distinctive emphasis on this aspect of piety, evident in rituals like the one described below.

Shi'i Islam can be described as the Islam of personal allegiance and devotion to the Prophet Muhammad. As one important Shi'i thinker in Pakistan explained it to me, whereas both the Sunni and the Shi'a accept the authority of the Prophet and the Qur'an, the Shi'a believe that the Qur'an is the Book of God because Muhammad says that it is, and he can never lie; in contrast, the Sunni believe that Muhammad is the Prophet of God because the Qur'an identifies him as such. Thus, although Sunni Islam emphasizes obedience to the Qur'an as the fundamental basis of Islam, the Shi'a, who also fully accept the authority of the Qur'an, categorically reject Umar's statement at the deathbed of the Prophet that "For us the Book is sufficient." The Shi'a argue that the Qur'an can only be properly interpreted by Muhammad and his family *(Ahl al-bayt)*, who specifically include the Prophet's daughter Fatima, his son-in-law 'Ali, their two sons Hasan and Husain, and, for the *Ithna'ashari* majority of the Shi'a, a series of nine more imams (the first three being 'Ali, Hasan, and Husain), culminating in the hidden twelfth imam, who will eventually return to establish justice in the world. For them, Islam requires allegiance, not only to Muhammad, but also to the twelve imams, to whom God has given divine responsibility for the interpretation of the Islamic revelation.

The Shi'a also typically claim to be distinguished by their special emphasis on the necessity of love for the Prophet. Muhammad is the beloved of God *(Habib Allah)*. Thus, if one wishes truly to love God, one must also love the Prophet whom God loves; one must further demonstrate that love by expressing love and allegiance for those whom the Prophet loved. This is particularly true of those closest to the Prophet in his own lifetime—Fatima, 'Ali, Hasan, and Husain. For the Shi'a the events of their lives form the ultimate commentary upon the Qur'an. These events carry with them a reality and a meaning that transcend and encompass all of human and spiritual history.

The most important of these events is undoubtedly the martyrdom of Husain at the battle of Karbala. Vastly outnumbered and cut off from food and water, the last remaining grandson of the Prophet was brutally slain in combat at Karbala, having first watched his close family members killed by the troops of Yazid b. Mu'awiyah, the man who claimed to be the rightful caliph of Islam. Husain, who as a child had climbed and played upon the back of the Prophet, was decapitated; his body was trampled on the desert floor. The women of his family, the surviving witnesses to the slaughter, were marched in shackles before Caliph Yazid in Damascus. Husain's head was carried into Damascus on a pole. Given the atrocities committed against the Prophet's family, from the Shi'i perspective, the community of Islam divided once and for all at Karbala between those who accepted the necessity of allegiance to the *Ahl al-bayt* and those who rejected it.

The importance of Karbala for the Shi'a finds its fullest articulation in numerous rituals that orient the community toward the events that took place there. Indeed, many South Asian cities contain areas called "Karbalas" in which ritual objects such as *ta'ziyehs* (replicas of Husain's tomb) are buried. Annual commemorations of Husain's martyrdom at Karbala during the first ten days of Muharram are essential to Shi'i piety. These include mourning assemblies (*majlis-i 'aza*) and processions (*julus*). Such activities, collectively known as *'azadari*, are occasions for the ritual re-creation of Karbala. Karbala is ritually portable, and South Asian immigrants have carried it with them to the North American environment.

Karbala is linked to both a place and an event. As such, its re-creation involves the transformation of both time and space. The re-creation of the place of Karbala is typically accomplished through the establishment of buildings dedicated to Husain called *imambargahs*, which are community centers where a number of functions are carried out, including devotional rituals, community education, and the preparation of the dead for burial. The re-creation of sacred time is accomplished by the cyclical commemoration of important events in the lives of the *Ahl al-bayt* as they appear on the Shi'i calendar through rituals of *zikr* (remembrance) and *shahadat* (witness).

As Professor Abdulaziz Sachedina—an important figure in the community—stated during a *majlis* in Toronto, the Shi'a believe that it is incumbent upon Muslims to remember the *ayam-i allah* (Days of God), For the Shi'a, of course, these *ayam* include the days of Karbala. Optimally, the remembrance of Karbala should be integrated into the everyday lives of the Shi'i community. From the Shi'i perspective, the whole world continuously participates in Karbala; it is as if the events of Karbala are always taking place just below the surface of ordinary reality. Devotional ritual allows devotees to cut through the veil that separates them from Karbala so that they can actually participate in it. "Every day is Ashura, and everywhere is Karbala," banners carried in the Muharram processions in down town Toronto declare.

The ritual re-creation of Karbala creates an environment that provides opportunities for individual and communal reflection. Devotional activities serve not only to reinforce the unique authority of Shi'i Islam but also to encourage the creative adaptation of the community to changing circumstances.

The Imambargah as "Sacred Space"

Imambargahs in North America serve both to evoke Karbala and to publicly claim space by creating an Islamic presence in the midst of the alien "West." Imambargahs are tied to Karbala as a sacred place by decorative symbols that draw one's attention to God, the Prophet, and the *Ahl al-bayt*. When imambargahs are established in buildings originally designed for other purposes, only the interiors of these buildings are transformed into recognizably Islamic places.

On the other hand, when a community has the opportunity to build its own structure, it must decide to what extent the building will participate in a "Western" aesthetic. In the case of the Ja'ffari Center, which was built in 1978, an architect was hired with explicit instructions to construct a recognizably Islamic building, arid yet one lacking such characteristic features as domes and minarets, which might make it stand out too abruptly from the local architecture. The completed building is a remarkable edifice, which is recognizably Islamic and yet part of the Canadian architectural landscape. It represents all Islamization of local architecture that mirrors other attempts by the community to find ways to Islamize the local environment—for example, using English in *majlis*. Imambargahs are therefore places where an indigenous North American Islamic aesthetic is being created.

The Jaʿffari Center is situated amidst other religious edifices, including a Chinese Buddhist Temple and a Jewish synagogue—both of which provide extra parking for the center during Muharram. On its main level, the center contains a large hall for *majlis*, called the Zainabia Hall, and a *masjid* (mosque). Upstairs are a library and a large room for women with children. Women can participate in *majlis* from a large room located downstairs.

The centrality of spiritual history and allegiance to the *Ahl al-bayt* is clearly evident in the architecture and decoration of the building. The very names of the component parts of the structure evoke the presence of the *Ahl al-bayt*. For example, the *majlis* hall is named for Husain's sister Zainab. This is significant, since the hall is used for the purpose of bearing witness to the events of Karbala just as Zainab, as a survivor of Karbala, bore witness to the generation of Muslims immediately following those events.

The importance of sacred names and words is evident throughout the building. The *majlis* hall is flanked on one wall by ten glassed-in arches. The rear wall contains four more—two each on either side of a large arch-shaped window—for a total of fourteen. When I first saw the structure in 1982, these arches held bare glass. Within the past few years, stained glass bearing the word "Allah" in Arabic script and one of the names of the fourteen *masumin* (those protected from error)—Muhammad, Fatima, and the twelve imams—has been installed at the top of each arch. This hall is laid out towards the *qiblah* (the direction facing Mecca). At the end of the hall closest to the *qiblah*, there is a large archway connected to a skylighted alcove, which forms an open boundary between the hall and the *masjid*.

Recently, ornate pieces of Arabic calligraphy have been installed in the center. At the *mihrab*, there is a piece containing many of the ninety-nine names of God. In the hall itself, on either side of the archway leading to the *masjid*, there are two large pieces of calligraphy. One depicts the hadith in which the Prophet designated ʿAli as his successor, the other a qurʾanic verse reputed to refer to Husain. During the first ten days of Muharram, the *zakir*, or person who delivers the *majlis*, sits upon the *minbar* (a wooden staircase of about six or seven steps that serves as a pulpit near the *qiblah*) between these two signs of the *Ahl al-bayt*'s authority to deliver his *majlis*.

At one end of the hall, there is a room labeled *zari*, which contains replicas of the tombs of the imams (*taʿziyahs*) and other pictures and objects evocative of the *Ahl al-bayt*. There are also containers for making monetary offerings in the name of the imams, ʿAli, or the *Ahl al-bayt*.

All these features serve to evoke the central paradigm of Shiʿi piety—allegiance to the *Ahl al-bayt*. The physical environment of the building continually draws one's attention to the necessity of that allegiance by constantly evoking Karbala in both the spatial geometry and the decoration of the center. Karbala is thus always present within the imambargah.

During the first ten days of Muharram, the presence of Karbala is intensified through the performance of devotional rituals.

Muharram 1411: Devotional Activities at the Ja'ffari Center

Large crowds of people came to the center for the Muharram activities—an estimated three thousand people attended on Ashura day, the tenth, alone. They came to attend the religious performance called *majlis*, when people gather to remember and mourn in a structured way the deaths of the *Ahl al-bayt*. *Majlis* may be held quite frequently, but they are most intense during the first ten days of Muharram immediately following the evening prayer. The crowd assembles in the *majlis* hall facing the *minbar*. Immediately before the actual *majlis*, poetry *(marthiyah)* recalling Husain is recited in Urdu.

The *zakir*'s sermon from the *minbar* seeks to inspire his audience with a sense of mournful devotion to the *Ahl al-bayt*. The *majlis* begins with the quiet communal recitation of *Sura Al-Fatiha*, the first chapter of the Qur'an. This is followed by the *khutba*, a formulaic recitation in Arabic consisting of praise of God, the Prophet, and the *Ahl al-bayt*. At the center of the *majlis* is the *zakir*'s presentation of a religious topic. This portion of the *majlis* generally begins with a verse from the Qur'an, with the rest of the *zakir*'s discourse acting as an exegesis of that verse.

The last portion of the *majlis* is the *gham*, or lamentation, recitation of an emotional narrative of the sufferings of the family of the Prophet. During each of the first ten days of *Muharram*, the content of the *gham* is traditionally linked to a specific incident at the battle of Karbala, which is recounted by the *zakir*. For many people, the *gham* is the most important portion of the *majlis*. Members of the congregation begin to sob and wail at the beginning of the *gham*. The mourning becomes more and more intense as the incidents of Karbala are recounted. People may strike their chests and foreheads. The *gham* ends with the *zakir* himself overcome with tears and emotion. On certain days, the *gham* is followed by matam, the physical act of mourning.

On the last four days of these rituals, the matam is preceded by small *julus*, or processions, within the imambargah itself. Symbols that evoke the stories of the martyrs of Karbala are carried through the crowd in the *majlis* hall. These take many forms: coffins draped in white cloth colored with red dye, as if bloodstained; a cradle representing the infant martyr 'Ali Asghar; a standard bearing the five-fingered Fatimid hand, representing both the severed hand of the martyr Abbas and the five closest members of the Prophet's family—Muhammad, Fatima, 'Ali, Hasan, and Husain. The *matam* concludes with the recitation of *ziyarat* (visitation), in which the entire congregation turns in the directions of the tombs of the *Ahl al-bayt* and recites salutations to them. *Ziyarat* is the word used for pilgrimage to the tombs of the imams. As used here, however, it refers to Arabic recitations that serve as metaphorical visits to the tombs of the Imams. This is often followed by the communal sharing of food and drink before the congregation disperses.

These rituals focus the attention of their participants on the *Ahl al-bayt* and the necessity of allegiance to it. The didactic portions of the *majlis* are reinforced by the emotional power of the *gham*, matam, and *julus*, which follow. Through the *gham*, the community emotionally enters into Karbala. The fact that the ritual concludes with a metaphorical *ziyarat,* or visitation, of the places where the *Ahl al-bayt* are buried is significant. The *majlis* creates an actual encounter with Karbala and challenges the community to live up to its standards.

The Blood of Husain

In addition to *majlis*, the re-creation of Karbala took other dramatic forms, such as the annual blood drive. Blood is an important symbol connected with Muharram. Husain is linked by blood to Muhammad, and the spilling of his blood on the field of Karbala is an act that is seen by the community as essential to the salvation of Islam. In South Asia, acts of ritual flagellation, called *zanjir ka-matam,* are commonplace; however, this spilling of blood in remembrance of Husain is seen as problematic in the Western context.

Recent *fatwas* have shown that flagellation—while considered permissible—is nevertheless an act that is allowed only with the provision that it not be done in such a way as to bring embarrassment to Islam. When I attended Muharram observances in 1986 at an imambargah located near a fast-food restaurant in New York City, the private practice of *matam* drew a large crowd of confused North Americans. The initial derision and amazement of American students when I lecture on this subject have demonstrated clearly to me the problem of explaining *zanjir ka-matam* in the West. Some of the people I talked to at the Ja'ffari Center stated that they believed that such a practice was illegal in Canada. In any event, *zanjir ka matam* was not performed at the center.

Instead, East African communities in both Pakistan and North America have engaged in an interesting transformation of blood-shedding in the memory of Husain. For many years, they have encouraged people to shed blood by donating it to blood banks. At the Ja'ffari Center on the day of Ashura, the community set up a Red Cross blood bank and donated over 163 units of blood. Many more people were turned down because in view of the AIDS crisis; the Red Cross would no longer accept blood from people from sub-Saharan Africa.

One of the most interesting discussions within the community addressed from the *minbar* had to do with the issue of whether or not this blood could be given to non-Muslims. Dr. Sachedina, a renowned scholar and professor in the Religious Studies Department at the University of Virginia, argued on the basis of hadith that the imams had given water and food to people in need without asking first if they were Muslim or non-Muslim; thus blood donation to non-Muslims was allowable. The majority of the community seemed to share his opinion.

During the Ashura period, a scale model of Karbala was erected outside along the rear wall of the center building. I was told that this custom had recently become popular in Tanzania and had made its way to North America in the past few years. The model battlefield was laid out in a wooden box filled with sand. A trench was dug through the sand to represent the river Euphrates. The tents of the forces of Husain, as well as those of Caliph Yazid's general, 'Umar, were erected in the relevant locations and marked with signs. Toy soldiers and horses were placed in different positions on different days to represent the changing circumstances of the combatants. Signs identifying the location of important events of the battle such as "Martyrdom place of Imam Hussein, Son of Ali and Fatema, Grandson of the

Holy Prophet," "Place of Amputation of the Left Arm of Hazrat Abas Ibne Ali," and "Place where Ali Ashgar was Buried" were placed on the model battlefield. A roof was erected over the entire area, and a sign was hung over the model battlefield that stated "This is Karbala." A large map on the back wall of the model showed the route Husain and his followers took from Mecca to Karbala.

Public Rituals: Julus in Toronto

The remembrance of Karbala not only serves to educate the community (particularly the younger generation), it also provides for the education of outsiders, as a means of calling them to the "true" Islam—the Islam best exemplified in the lives of the *Ahl al-bayt*. From the perspective of the participants, Karbala speaks to the humanity of all people, drawing them not only to ethical action, but also to the eventual acceptance of Islam. To this end, the community stages a yearly procession through downtown Toronto.

The julus was held on the 6th of Muharram. It began at roughly 3:00 P.M. on a Sunday afternoon, when the community gathered at Queen's Park. Most of the community members, especially the women, were dressed in black. People carried banners and staffs, distributed water and other beverages, and handed out literature.

As in South Asia, the *julus* serves a number of important and interrelated functions. It enables the community both to reenact the Karbala paradigm and to display its religion to outsiders through such acts as distributing water, food, literature, and the presentation of speeches bearing witness to Karbala and its meaning. In Canada, this audience of outsiders is not only non-Shi'a, but non-Muslim as well. Witnessing to this audience is problematic, given the ubiquitous stereotypes about Islam in American culture. The Muslim community is well aware of these stereotypes and the general lack of knowledge concerning Islam that produces them. It was no coincidence that the banner that led the procession read "Islam Stands for Peace," a clear rebuttal of Western stereotypes about Islam as an inherently militaristic religion.

The use of *julus* as an act of public ritual illustrates an interesting juncture between Shi'i and North American culture. The *julus* has its origin in the Muslim world, and yet the act of people marching with banners in the downtown of Toronto seemed curiously familiar. In many ways, the *julus* of the Shi'a could be seen by outside observers as simply another version of a secular activity, the parade. On one level, the community was simply bringing a ritual to Canada, but on another it was Islamizing the already familiar North American ritual of ethnic groups parading.

As a part of the educational function of the *julus*, members of the procession passed out a pamphlet entitled *Islam: The Faith That Invites People to Prosperity in Both Worlds*, which was clearly aimed at non-Muslims with little or no knowledge about Islam or Shi'ism. It stressed the notion of peace in Islam and emphasized the common elements of the three monotheistic religions of Judaism, Christianity, and Islam. It clearly elaborated a Shi'i perspective, noting the need for an "authoritative leader in Islam who will guide the believers on the right path." It further stressed the necessity of people rising in defense of God's laws on earth, even to the point of martyrdom if necessary. The paradigmatic example of this martyrdom is, of course, that of Husain: throughout Islam history, as a result of the battle of Karbala, "When rulers became oppressive, Muslims arose following the examples of Imam Husayn to demand Justice."

This pamphlet presents its argument in a manner common in Shi'i polemics; that is, it appeals to the universal human values expressed in the incident at Karbala. The root paradigms at the heart of the Karbala drama include such virtues as courage, honor, self-sacrifice, and the willingness to stand up against injustice and oppression. There is the conviction that the universality of these virtues may ultimately attract people to embrace Islam.

The procession, briefly diverted to avoid a gay and lesbian rights parade, made its way to a central downtown square, where a grandstand had been erected, from which speeches were read. There were few non-Muslims in attendance, but the ones who were there watched somewhat bemusedly from a distance. The presence of black-clad, modestly dressed women bearing a huge banner proclaiming, "Every day is Ashura, everywhere is Karbala" was, from the standpoint of non-Muslim Canadians, strikingly juxtaposed against the ultramodern architecture of downtown Toronto.

Conclusion

One night while I sat waiting for the *majlis* to begin, I overheard a small boy running into the center and shouting to a friend, "Karbala is here. It's really here; it's out back." On one level, he was simply referring to the model of the battlefield outside of the center; but on another level, what he was saying was quite profound: the devotional activities at the center during Muharram indeed seek to re-create Karbala. For this child, a life-time of participation in the paradigm of Karbala had begun.

The re-creation of Karbala allows Shi'i Muslims to focus their attention on the necessity of allegiance to the *Ahl al-bayt*. For them, Karbala resonates as a beacon in what would otherwise be spiritual darkness, challenging all who encounter it. The ethical life of the community is continually measured against the lives of the participants in Karbala. For example, the first page of a pamphlet promoting a plan organized by the community for sponsoring orphans in the name of Hazrat Zainab states:

> In the name of the great lady who looked after so many children under so much pressure after the event of Karbala, let us fulfill some of our duties as Muslims by actively helping one particularly needy child to enjoy the basic opportunities of life. As Muslims our struggles must go on. Helping the needy is one of the struggles whose results are satisfying. If we remember, "Every day is Ashura and every place is Karbala," then we will not forget the needy.

Karbala in this context not only serves as a point of reference for the maintenance of group identity, it is also a continuous call to creative ethical action. The Shi'i community faces a number of problems common to all religious groups in North America: the impact of secularism, the temptations of materialism, and the often uncaring individualism of a capitalist economy. *Majlis* functions as a kind of Islam revival meeting, calling people back to an ethical standard exhibited by Husain and his companions in the battle of Karbala.

In a sense, "sacred spaces" such as the Ja'ffari Center are problematic for the very act of creating a sacred environment carries the risk of thoroughly secularizing the world outside of that space. The real "sacred space" in this interpretation of Shi'ism is Karbala itself, as it is continually encountered in the hearts and lives of each succeeding generation. This focus on the creation of an inner ethical and spiritual life, fostered above all by devotional assemblies, proves to be a common thread in the religious lives of many of the diaspora communities.

Originally published in Barbara Daly Metcalf (eds.) *Making Muslim Space in North America & Europe* (University of California Press, 1996): 186–203. Printed here with the permission of the publisher.

ASEF BAYAT

Piety, Privilege and Egyptian Youth

Understandably, the 11 September terrorist attacks in the USA have reinforced more than ever Western anxieties over the threat of "Islamic fundamentalism". The perpetrators' Islamic identity and the subsequent mass street protests in the Muslim world during the US bombings of Afghanistan left little doubt that political Islam in the Middle East is here to stay. However, the picture conceals some significant changes that Islamism in the Middle East has been undergoing in recent years. There is a clear shift from the earlier emphasis on Islamist polity to one on personal piety and ethics; from constituencies centred around impoverished middle classes to more fragmented adherents including the privileged groups.

Specificity of individual Muslim countries notwithstanding, there seems to be a change from Islamism as a political project with a contentious agenda into an active piety concerned with personal salvation and culture. The causes of the change are complex, but broadly include the crisis of Islamic rule wherever it was put into practice (as in Iran and Sudan), the failure of violent strategies (e.g. in Egypt and Algeria), more hostile Israeli policies which overshadow domestic conflicts in Muslim countries, and thus the emergence of new visions about the Islamic project.

This essay concentrates on one aspect of change in Egyptian religious activism—the popularity of a new genre of lay Muslim preachers. In particular, the focus is on what is currently described in Egypt as the "Amr Khalid phenomenon". As the most popular preacher since Sheikh Sha'rawi, Amr Khalid exemplifies a transformation of Islamism into a post-Islamist piety—an active piety which is thick in rituals and scriptures and thin in politics. It is marked and framed by the taste and style of the rich, in particular, affluent youth and women; and sociologically it embodies the views of Georg Simmel. Thus, the convergence of youth sub-culture, elitism, and a pietistic Islam together produce this new genre of *da'wa* and its appeal. It has grown against a backdrop of a crisis of political Islam, and a profound stagnation in Egypt's intellectual and political landscape.

Since 1999, Amr Khalid, an accountant-turned-preacher, has become a household name in wealthy Cairo. Khalid followed the leads of fellow lay preachers Umar Abdel-Kafi and Khalid el-Guindy, but surpassed them in popularity amongst the well-to-do youth and women. A gifted orator—televangelist style—he began by lecturing in private homes and exclusive social clubs, but soon rose to stardom at the pulpit of El-Hossari Mosque in the trendy Muhandesin urban district before he was forced by the authorities to move to Sixth October City, a new posh community in the outskirts of Cairo. His weekly lessons have become a spiritual staple for thousands of young people who flock from throughout the city's affluent districts to hear him. Crowds arrive hours in advance of the sermons to get a spot, filling the lecture halls, the surrounding streets and sidewalks, often causing heavy traffic congestion. In 1999, Amr Khalid delivered up to 21 lessons a week in socially prominent households, peaking at 99 during Ramadan. The tapes of Amr Khalid's sermons were the un-paralleled best sellers in Cairo's massive Book Fair in 2002, and have travelled as far as the back-street markets of East Jerusalem, Beirut and the Persian Gulf cities.

Faith and Fun

The new preachers deliberately target youth and women of the elite classes, "the people with influence", because "they have the power to change things", according to Khalid el-Guindy. Since the elite families generally kept away from the traditional mosques located in the lower class areas, the young preachers brought their message to their doorsteps, to the comfort of their private homes, social clubs and the stylish mosques of their posh neighbourhoods. More importantly, in addition to face-to-face sermons, Amr Khalid utilizes a full range of media to disseminate his message, including satellite television channels such as Dream T.V., *Iqra'a* and Orbit, the internet with his state-of-the-art website, and audio and videotapes—media which particularly reach the middle and more affluent classes. For some time a popular state-sponsored magazine, *Al-Ahram al-Arabi,* distributed his tapes as gifts to readers. Khalid el-Guindy established a paid "Islamic Hotline" to be used by the public to seek advice from the sheikh. Within the period of one year daily calls increased from 250 to 1,000. For his part, Amr Khalid travelled with his message to the stylish Agami and other upper middle class north coast resorts, and has more recently gone on speaking tours to Arab Gulf states where his fame had already spread. The colorful décor and a talk show-like aura of his lecture halls, in contrast to the austere *Azherite* pulpits, reflect the taste of his main audience—males and females from 15 to 35 years of age, never before exposed to religious ideas in such an appealing and direct manner.

Amr Khalid's style resembles that of his young, affluent audience; he appears cleanly shaven in blue jeans and polo shirts or in suit and necktie. Khalid simultaneously embodies the hip-ness of Amr Diab (Egypt's most revered pop-star), the persuasion power of evangelist Billy Graham, and unsubtle therapy of Dr Phil, American popular talk-show host. For the young, Khalid, in the words of a female fan, is "the only preacher that embraces and tackles our spiritual needs", someone who "makes us psychologically comfortable", "who treats us like adults, not children". Unlike more orthodox preachers known for their joyless moralizing and austere methods, Khalid articulates a marriage of faith and fun. Speaking in a sympathetic tone, compassionate manner, and in colloquial Arabic, Khalid and his colleagues convey simple ethical messages about the moralities of everyday life, discussing issues that range from relationships, appearance, and adultery, to posh restaurants, drunk driving, the *hijab,* and the sins of summer vacations in Marina. In a sense, the new preachers function as "public therapists" in a troubled society which shows little appreciation for professional psychotherapy. Emotional intensity, peace, and release (crying) often symbolize Khalid's sermons.

From the likes of Khalid, the young hear the message that they can be religious and still live a normal life—work, study, have fun and look like anyone else in society. More importantly his words assure the audience that they can be pious while maintaining their power and prestige. Khalid's message operates within the consumer culture of

Egypt's *nouveau riche* where piety and privilege are made to cohabit as enduring partners. Analogous to the Methodist church of the well-to-do in the American Bible belt where faith and fortune are happily conjoined, Khalid's style makes the Egyptian rich feel good about their fortunes.

Of course, adherence to religious ethics and the search for spirituality are not new among Egyptian Muslims, including the wealthy youth. But theirs was a passive religious attachment. That is, as believers, they unquestioningly carried out their religious obligations. However, what seems to be novel (since the late 1990s) is that affluent families, the youth and women in particular, have begun to exhibit an active search for religious devotion, exhibiting an extraordinary quest for religious ideas and identity. Not only do they practice their faith, they also preach it, wanting others to believe and behave like them.

Scriptural Cosmopolitanism

Khalid is not a scholar or interpreter of the Qur'an, and does not issue *fatwas*. Rather he is devoted to correcting individuals' ethical values and everyday behavior, fostering such values as humility, generosity, trust, loyalty, and repentance. However, he is not a liberal Muslim thinker. Some of his ideas remain highly conservative, and his methods manipulative. Khalid advances a religious discourse which contains passion, clarity, relevance, and humour, but lacks novelty, nuance and vigour. While his style is highly imaginative, his theology remains deeply scriptural, with little perspective to historicize, to bring critical reason into interpretations. On the *hijab,* for instance, Khalid begins by basing the "integrity of society on the integrity of women" and the latter on "her *hijab*". This is so in his view because "one women can easily entice one hundred men, but one hundred men cannot entice a single woman." Since, according to this logic, unveiled women are promoters of sin, a "complete, head-to-toe *hijab* is an obligation in Islam". The unconvinced Muslim women are not really Muslim, he claims, because Islam, in the literal terms, means simply "submission" to the words of God.

In fact, Khalid's doctrinal views hardly differ from those of orthodox *Azharite* sheikhs who dismiss him despite, and perhaps because of, his popularity. Rather, in the current juncture in Egypt where religious thought in general possesses little sign of innovation, Khalid appears as an innovator, if only in style. The mass appeal of the likes of Khalid is a by-product of Egypt's mass education, one that valorizes memorization, fragmenting knowledge, revering printed words, and nurturing authoritarian mentors. Compared to the patronizing manner typical of *Azhari* sheikhs, the amiable and passionate Khalid appears as a true democrat. For those who have learnt to take short cuts in seeking knowledge, or are trained to be docile learners, Khalid emerges as a superior source of wisdom. "He is easy to understand" echoes what the young admirers Khalid invariably express.

Yet this new genre of *da'wa* is as much initiative of the sermonizers as a response to the appeal of the increasingly globalizing youth. In a sense, Egyptian cosmopolitan youth fostered a new religious sub-culture, one which is expressed in a distinctly new style, taste, language and message. It is resonant of their aversion to patronizing pedagogy and moral authority. This globalizing youth display many seemingly contradictory orientations. They are religious believers but distrust political Islam. They swing back and forth from Amr

Diab to Amr Khalid, from partying to prayers, and yet they feel the burden the strong social control of their elders, teachers, and neighbours. As the Egyptian youth are socialized in a cultural condition and educational tradition which often strain individuality and novelty, they are compelled to assert them in a "social way", through "fashion".

Thus, from the prism of youth, this religious sub-culture (ideas, emotions, and identities) galvanized around the "Amr Khalid phenomenon" is partly an expression of "fashion" in the Simmelian sense, in the sense of an outlet that facilitates a simultaneous fulfillment of contradictory human tendencies: change and adaptation, difference and similarity, individuality and social norms. Adherence to active piety permits the Egyptian youth to assert their individuality, undertake change, and yet remain committed to collective norms and social equalization. In the social juncture in Egypt characterized by the decline of organized Islamism, intellectual stagnation and political closure, Khalid ingeniously took his *da'wa* literally to the sitting rooms of his audience. By doing so, Khalid and his colleagues became catalysts for a gradual shift in Egyptian religious politics.

This essay is taken from *ISIM Review* (July 2002): pp 23–24. It is printed here with the permission of the International Institute for the Study of Islam in the Modern World.

PART NINE

The Construction of Space: Local and Global Identities

Introduction

As in other manifestations of socio-cultural change, the nature of urban spaces and character of social relations in urban areas in the Arab world depart from patterns and realities observed elsewhere. The comparative massive and rapid *urbanization* as a physical phenomenon, as seen in high densities, demographic shifts, high proportions of unanchored urban masses and depletion of residential space is not consistent with *urbanism* as a cultural and psychic phenomenon. Even in primate cities like Cairo and Beirut, where disproportionate segments of the country's population are concentrated in their capital cities and expanding suburban fringe, they continue to be sustained by non-urban ties and loyalties. In other words, people might be *in* the city but not *of* it. Hence their life in the city is perceived as a passing interlude to be sustained by periodic visits to their ancestral rural towns and villages. Or, and more likely, by their proclivity to recreate rural ties and associations in the city.

These rural-urban disparities have been compounded by the advent of global and post-modern transformations associated with the telecommunications revolutions, mass consumerism and multimedia conglomerates which operate across regional and national boundaries. Such sweeping transformations have weakened the link between the physical place one lives in and one's cultural experiences. As a result, people have access to worlds and cultural products which challenge the autonomy and authenticity of their local attachments. But just as the Cairean and Beiruti can adapt to city life by recreating their village ties and loyalties, they have likewise been able to preserve some of their local identities by resisting global incursions. In other words, the conventional conceptualization of the world becoming a monolithic "global village" and that local identities are inevitably undermined and destroyed in the process, is certainly inconsistent with the findings and inferences of the essays in this chapter extracted from the studies of Lara Deeb, Farha Ghannam and Samir Khalaf. In different ways, they demonstrate how local identities are reinforced and reformulated through a variety of outlets and juxtapositions.

Lara Deeb focuses on one of the most notorious suburban districts of Beirut—Al-Dahyyiah—to explore the interplay between religious piety and political mobilization. Sandwiched between Beirut's International Airport and the Mediterranean sea, it occupies one of the most visible and coveted sites of the city. Its maligned history and dreaded public image are largely a byproduct of the unsettling circumstances associated with its checkered and uncontrolled urban growth: a successive inflow of impoverished and displaced Shi'i immigrants from South Lebanon, illegal construction and a sizeable pool of embittered youth receptive for radicalization. To both the foreign media and other residents of Beirut, Al-Dahyyiah continues to elicit, particular after the July war of 2006, the typical misbegotten stereotypes and misfounded clichés.

In her paper Deeb makes a persuasive effort to demystify al-dahyyiah's image as a

"Shi'i Getto." She reconsiders the history of the area by revealing its mixed sectarian and confessional origins and how the successive incursions in 1978, 1982 and 1993, fleeing Israeli bombardments and invasions, altered its sectarian composition. Graphically, she illustrates how the communal solidarity of Al-Dahyyiah can be easily extracted from its temporal, visual and aural textures, by employing the three S's (Sight, Sound and Season), to demonstrate how the district shares many attributes with other regions of Beirut. Yet it also embodies some distinctive features which set it apart from other neighborhoods. Naturally, the religious images, iconography, sacred sounds, the seasonal celebrations of *Ashoura, Mawlid* and *Iftar*, among others, all amplify the particular mix of Shi'i piety and politics and account for its emergence as a pious-modern urban neighborhood.

Farha Ghannam also focuses on a particular suburb—al-Zawiya al-Hamra in Northern Cairo—to explore the changing character of religious identity within a new urban setting. Much like al-Dahiyyah, al-Zawiya al-Hamra was also composed of displaced and uprooted groups. But while residents of al-Dahiyyah come from the peripheries and fringes of the South and Beqa, those of al-Hamra were decentered as a result of the state's efforts to "modernize" and "gentrify" part of Cairo's traditional quarters to accommodate the emergent needs of upper-class Egyptians, international tourists and transnational groups.

The basic theme of Ghannam is to demonstrate that this interplay between the local and global is not as dissonant and conflicting as often portrayed in the literature. Rather, residents of al-Hamra seem adept at redefining their local and communal sentiments and loyalties to accommodate national and global exigencies. Indeed, religious identity, as a hegemonic identity, was consolidated by the changes brought by the global as experienced by the people and filtered by national policies.

Just as al-Dahiyyah was characterized as a "pious modern" urban space with a particular mix of politics and piety, the newly established suburb in Cairo also epitomized this dialectical interplay between local and global encounters. Ghannam traces this to the open-door policies (*Infitah*) of Anwar al-Sadat in 1974, in opposition to Nasser's policies which kept Egypt isolated from the rest of the world.

Within policies of urban planning, *Infitah* had two distinct manifestations. The first attempted to incorporate elements of Egypt's glorious past (e.g. Islamic monuments, the Pyramids) into the modern areas of the city. The second attempted to reconstruct the "less desirable" parts of the popular quarters to render them more appealing to tourists, transnationals and upper classes. The old traditional quarters of Bulaq were replaced by modern buildings, luxury housing, multi-storey parking lots and five-star hotels.

Such displacement often meant uprooting entire urban quarters from their traditionally recognized crafts, informal economy and social networks. Indeed, the massive riots of 1977 were largely a protest against such disruptive measures. It is here that displaced groups found shelter in religious identity as a powerful alternative to coercive state authority or the seductive but elusive appeals of modernity and mass consumerism. Hence Egyptian displaced groups do not experience the global as a coherent, unified set of discourses and processes. Nor should globalization be reduced glibly to "Americanization" or "Westernization". Instead, it is experienced as fragments and contradictory pieces that are filtered through local vectors and agencies.

Ghannam, as such, argues that the global, as an analytical concept, should be expanded to include a mixture of images, discourses and goods that are brought to people through various channels such as state-controlled media, commercial video and audio tapes distributed by Islamic activists and consumer goods brought to al-Zawiya al-Hamra by migrants to Arab countries. *"Islam, thus, is becoming a force in localizing the global and globalizing the local."* What this has meant is that religion, rather than nationalism, neighborhood or village of origin, became powerful in articulating and socially grounding the various identities of the different groups residing in al-Hamra. Displaced families—Ahali, Massakin, Fellahin, Saidis—can all find commonality in religion that is expressed in practices such as dress code and decoration of shop and houses.

In "The Bourj as a Cosmopolitan Public Sphere," Samir Khalaf elucidates the three defining features of the historic center of Beirut; namely pluralism, receptivity to change, and tolerance to account for its emergence and survival as a cosmopolitan public sphere. He employs Habermas's concept of public spheres to account for how such open forums for public debate—clubs, coffee houses, newspapers and periodicals—proliferated. He argued that such public forums were of particular relevance to dislocated groups seeking to forge new identities and consolidate anchorage in the social fabric of the new social order. Like other vibrant and adaptive public spheres, the Bourj, throughout its eventful history, managed to resist the overwhelming threats of an inept and unresponsive government bureaucracy and the distant forces of globalism and mass consumerism.

Within this context, the essay explores two related dimensions: the genesis and evolution of the Bourj as a public sphere are explored first followed by an attempt to document and account for how it managed, over the years, to reinvent its identity and public image. In highlighting its historic evolution, a few distinctive features stand out.

Foremost and because of its compact size and predominantly commercial character, the collaboration between the various communities were both inevitable and vital for their coexistence and survival. Typical of a so-called "merchant republic", traders and entrepreneurs of various communities were partners in private business ventures. They assisted each other in times of austerity and financial need. More importantly, they perceived themselves as members of an urban merchant elite, resisting the hostile elements that threatened their common economic interests.

Likewise, during the emancipatory struggle for independence and subsequent mass protest movements and demonstrations in support of labour unions, women suffrage, Palestinian mobilization and other dispossessed groups, the Bourj always served as a vector and rallying ground for giving voice on behalf of neglected and marginalized segments of society. Student demonstrations, often with heightened confrontational strategies, reserved their most virulent outcries for the Bourj. Another unusual feature also accounts for the role it played as meeting place for itinerant groups. At a time when transport, telephone, electronic and other virtual forms of communication were nonexistent, the outlets the Bourj provided for such valued access were both inventive and functional. For example, the mushrooming hotels, pensions, locandas and residences were used as transit stops and meeting grounds. A nascent hotel industry, as early as the 1830s, had already developed to accommodate the growing stream of foreign travelers.

Not only hotels, but also bus and car terminals, transport agencies, especially coffee houses, served as meeting points for villagers. It was common for Beirut residents to deliver and receive their mail, messages and parcels of personal effects via such venues. To villagers seeking jobs, contacts and other city chores, these places became expedient stopgaps and surrogate homes and offices. Some coffee houses placed makeshift mailboxes for such purposes. Others became intimately associated with particular groups. This is, doubtlessly, the interlude in Beirut's urban history when displaced and uprooted groups—largely because of the quickening pace of urbanization—felt the need to reconnect by seeking refuge in urban spaces amenable to such informal and associational contacts. Virtually all such collective public amenities were converted into public spheres. For example, at a time when recognized clubs, galleries, auditoriums and other formal public venues were still rare, coffee houses, restaurants and bars became expedient haunts for intellectuals, artists, poets, journalists and politicians. As early as the 1930s such places gained notoriety precisely because they became meeting places for particular groups.

The bulk of Khalaf's paper is devoted to an explicit documentation of how the Bourj had to reinvent itself repeatedly to accommodate the relentless succession of imperial occupations. Although the labels and collective identities of Beirut's center were in perpetual change, at different interludes it assumed over a dozen such names which can be meaningfully regrouped into four general categories: First, as a *maidan*, *sahl*, *sahat* or *muntazah* in reference to it as an open space; ranging from an untamed, wild, natural and organic plain or field to a fairly regulated, landscaped and bounded courtyard or public garden. Second, as *Place des Canons* connoting its colonial legacy; in view either of the brief Russian presence during the Crimean War or of the extended hegemony of the French Mandate. Third, during the Ottoman period it witnessed at least four successive changes in its popular identity in reference to epochal events or political transformations—*sahat al-Itihad*, *al-Hamidiyyah*, *Hadiqat al-Hurriyah*—and finally as Martyrs' Square to commemorate martyrdom and, hence, the felicitous nationalist sentiment by way of celebrating the country's liberation from Ottoman control. Fourth, as a *Bourj*, the most lasting and enduring label, in reference to the one remaining relic of its ancient medieval walled ramparts.

While Lara Deeb, Farha Ghannam and Samir Khalaf were mainly concerned with documenting how local urban communities redefined their spatial identities to accommodate broader structural forces and global transformations, Aminah McCloud shifts her analysis to show how Muslim spatial identities, particularly private homes and places of religious congregation, situate themselves and validate their identity within an American city.

She prefaces her paper on the Muslim home in the African-American row houses in Philadelphia, by stating that despite wide variations in the cultural lives of Muslims, much of their defining religious and ritualistic practices are dependent on space. The act of submission by the Muslim believer to the will of God is, after all, dependent on the reappropriation of space for spiritual purposes. Formal prayer (*salat*), fasting (*soum*), pilgrimage (*hajj*), the call for prayer (*adhan*) and signal movement from one reality to another (*iqamah*) all demand temporal and spatial readjustments. Her study is in two distinct but related parts: she first describes the congregational spaces of the Muslim communities in Philadelphia before turning to a vivid representation of the Muslim home focusing on its distinctive architectural attributes and decorative artefacts.

If one is to judge the Muslim communities of Philadelphia by their congregations, then the city seems like a microcosm of virtually all Muslim groups in America. Though they all share the overarching concepts of *umma*, their edifices reflect their sectarian divisions and their conception of American hostility to the Muslim world. McCloud traces their origins to as early as 1913 with the founding of the Moorish Science Temple, as a divine national monument, which stood for the grand principles of love, truth, freedom, peace and justice. This was followed by a succession of missions and associations, most prominent among them are the American Muslim Mission (AMM) and *Darul Islam*. In all their places of congregation, they uphold *Hadith* and observe all the divine prescriptions for prayer, fasting, *zakat*, and performing the *Hajj* to Mecca. They assemble in large houses with strict adherence to the code of gender separation. Walls are usually decked with Arabic calligraphy, decorations and furnishings reflecting a variety of Muslim sources.

But it is their "Muslim Home," located in close proximity to the *Masjid*, which is distinctly marked as a space of difference and separation by a bold sign on the door instructing visitors: *"This is a Muslim Home/Please Remove Your Shoes."* McCloud argues that the African-American Muslim deliberately and self-consciously organizes the use of domestic space in the light of teachings found in the Qur'an and *Hadith*, as well as through the example of immigrant Muslim homes and homes in the Muslim world.

One of the classical divisions known in Islam, between *Darul Islam* (the House of Islam) and *Darul Harb* (the House of War), translates in American usage as the domestic space and the outside community. Domestic space is consciously separated from the space of the House of War, which is viewed as a space of religious intolerance and racism. The use of domestic space creates moreover a sense of shared spirituality with Muslims elsewhere in the Muslim world while fostering a sense of well-being in an environment perceived as hostile.

McCloud is careful to point out that although the typical Muslim home is replete with Arabic calligraphy, oriental rugs, brassware, latticed screens and the like, it is usually not tied to any particular country. They tend to draw upon the entire Muslim world for items of interior design. Yet a few district features stand out: window shades, curtains, closed drapes to exclude the view of outsiders. In kitchens, dietary restrictions are strictly adhered to. Muslims, we are told, do not linger in bathrooms (*hamam*) where *jinn* are thought to be present. The bathroom is a space of both pollution and purification. The believer wearing special shoes or slippers enters left foot first, acknowledging the danger of the space with a *da'ua* before performing the necessary acts. Leaving to re-enter prayer space must be on the right foot. Finally, unlike Muslims elsewhere, African-American Muslims try to avoid television and radio to "shut out Western values and open the door to Muslim values."

McCloud concludes by arguing that African-American Muslims have clearly found that their American nationality is but one small aspect of their identity as prescribed by Islam.

They are part of the larger Muslim world and interact with immigrant Muslims, while at times clashing with them and even encountering racism. African-American Muslims are likely in the near future to seek a greater blending of African Islam with African-American Islam and thus to engender an even more distinct African-American Islam. Then, as now, the home will be central to its expression and will be seen, whether explicitly sign-posted or not, as a separate explicitly Muslim space.

LARA DEEB

Al-Dahiyya:
Sight, Sound, Season

Residents and outsiders alike refer to the southern suburbs of Beirut as *"al-Dahiyya"*—a word that simply means "the suburb" in Arabic, but that connotes "the Shi'i ghetto" to many in other parts of the city. More a conglomeration of multiple municipalities and neighborhoods than a single suburb, al-Dahiyya is bounded by the city to the north, Beirut International Airport to the south, the Mediterranean on the west side, and an agricultural area to the east. It used to be that due to this location al-Dahiyya was unavoidable. To get from the rest of Beirut to the airport or anywhere south of the city, you had to drive through it. Until recently, outsiders passing through caught glimpses of the area from the old airport road or from the coastal highway that leads south to Saida (Sidon) and Sour (Tyre). Today new highways, built to bypass al-Dahiyya, connect Beirut to the airport and to the south, allowing visitors and Lebanese alike to avoid acknowledging its presence.

The residents of this often ignored or maligned area of Beirut who were my interlocutors often referred to *al-bi'a*, the milieu, of al-Dahiyya as a critical factor in their religious, social, and political understandings, identities, and practices. The visual, aural, and temporal textures of this milieu are the focus of this chapter, and frame the spaces of those that follow. These textures layer religion and politics into public space, and are pointed to as evidence of the spiritual progress of the community and of its recent visibility in Lebanon.

To focus is to allow the surrounding context to blur into white. Before permitting Beirut to fade like this, a few paragraphs are necessary to capture this city that—despite its betrayals and violences—is fiercely claimed as home by Lebanese of all persuasions.

Beirut is a balance of constant stimuli and contagious ennui. The former assault your senses and drains your energy, the latter emerges in the omnipresent hopelessness and a slow rhythm of bare motion. There is no way to capture the essence of Beirut: the romance, the dirt, the reality. It is a word the international media have turned into an epithet for destruction and that Lebanese expatriates have turned into the whimsy of a golden past. Much has been written about Beirut, its deaths, and resurrections, but this is not the place for me to recap that. Instead I simply highlight three aspects of the city that begin to give a sense of its rhythms: size, resilience, and traffic.

Lebanon, at a mere 10,400 square kilometers (roughly seven-tenths the size of Connecticut), is tiny relative to most countries in the world. Barring horrible traffic, you can drive its length along the coast in four hours, and its width in less than two. Centrally located Beirut is accessible from anywhere in the country. This smallness of scale creates a density of activity and relationships that intensifies and localizes experiences. At the same time, the fact that places are within easy reach of one another amplifies the impact of the immense psychological and ideological distances that divide them. Many residents of areas of Beirut I traveled between daily had never set foot in the "other" neighborhoods simply because they were "other." Samir Khalaf, among others, has discussed this retrenching of sectarian identities in space:

> This compulsion to huddle in compact, homogenous enclosures further "balkanized" Lebanon's social geography. There is a curious and painful irony here. Despite the many differences that divide the Lebanese, they are all in a sense homogenized by fear, grief, and trauma. (Khalaf, 2002: 247).

Beirut is also a city of unbelievable resilience. Surviving years of war is the city's greatest testament to this. I witnessed a much smaller example on the morning of February 8, 2000. The night before I had awakened to the sounds of Israeli planes breaking the sound barrier and bombing infrastructure around Lebanon. They destroyed three power plants, leaving fires you could see burning from balconies in the city. Despite this, early the next morning a friend of mine picked me up for a meeting in al-Dahiyya. The only discernible differences during that day and those that followed were the dark circles underneath people's eyes, the extra sweaters worn to guard against the cold in places that would have been heated with electricity, the flashlights carried to light the way up stairwells when elevators were not running, the simmering anger in voices discussing the events, and the constant whir of generators that had sprung up overnight. After a few days of darkness, electricity was rerouted and rationed throughout the country, generally on a six-hour on-and-off cycle.

Chaotic traffic, resilience, and compactness are notions that could describe almost any area of Beirut. Yet Lebanese who do not live in al-Dahiyya often assume these general characteristics to be especially true of al-Dahiyya. I had a hard time convincing many Lebanese, especially but not only those who were not Shi'i, to accompany me to al-Dahiyya, and sometimes even to give me a ride to an organization or an acquaintance's house in the area. This reluctance sometimes stemmed from fears and false assumptions about what it meant to be in an area controlled by Hizbullah. For others, however, it was simply an unwillingness to navigate the narrow roads, dead ends, and one-way streets that inevitably led to a headlock situation where one driver was forced to drive backwards the way she came, hoping there would be no other traffic behind her. A similar reluctance was expressed by many I knew in al-Dahiyya with regard to other areas of Beirut, particularly Ashrafiyye, the mostly Maronite Christian suburb to the east. Again, for some, it was a hesitation based in fear and stereotypes, while for others it was the same unwillingness to navigate the gridlock of an unfamiliar part of the city.

To non-residents mention of al-Dahiyya often elicits such responses of discomfort, ranging from caution mingled with curiosity to outright trepidation: responses built on stereotypical associations of "al-Dahiyya" with poverty, illegal construction, refugees, armed Hizbullah security guards and secret cameras, and "the Shi'i ghetto." Such stereotypes obscure al-Dahiyya's complexity. Before moving on, it is necessary to address this complexity in order to undo some of these common assumptions.

Assumptions Undone: Al-Dahiyya is not Uniform

Al-Dahiyya encompasses several municipalities and a number of very dense neighborhoods, with a combined population of approximately five hundred thousand people in an area of sixteen square kilometers. Mona Harb el-Kak (1988) divides al-Dahiyya into eastern and western zones, with the former made up primarily of older villages that were incorporated into the urban fabric of the city and a few illegal sectors along the edges, and the latter consisting of a combination of dense illegal sectors and less urbanized areas (1998, 2000). Within these multiple municipalities and neighborhoods, there is immense variation with regard to class, length of residency in the area, and political leanings, as well as some religious diversity.

One of the characteristics of stereotypes is that they homogenize. As a real space, al-Dahiyya was not uniform; it was not only "poor," "illegal," or "Hizbullah." The region signified by the term included areas where Harakat Amal was the principal political party rather than Hizbullah, and there existed older legal residential districts as well as newly built illegal neighborhoods, some lingering Christian residents, "original" residents mingled in among more recent arrivals displaced by the wars, and an emerging Shi'i "middle class" living in constant contact with its poorer neighbors. During my field research, the *ra'is baladiyya* (mayor) of one municipality, Haret Hrayk, was a Maronite Christian who worked in close cooperation with Hizbullah. And on some streets, elaborate homes and the latest model BMWs indicated wealthy residents, as did the shops selling European fashions that existed alongside internet cafés, vegetable stands, and corner markets.

Al-Dahiyya has a History

Stereotypes also belie the fact that this area has not always been predominately Shi'i or (sub)urban. Thirty years ago, much of it was semirural, its population a mix of Shi'i Muslims and Maronite Christians. A quarter century and a civil war later, this had become the second most densely populated area of the country, exceeded only by the Palestinian refugee camps, and it was predominately Shi'i Muslim.

Prior to the end of World War I and the subsequent French mandate in Lebanon, al-Dahiyya was rural and several of its current municipalities were villages. By 1970, one of these villages, Chiyah, had become two suburbs with a population of thirty thousand people and four thousand more households than had existed forty years earlier (Khuri, 1975). Much of this growth was due to the wave of rural to urban migration that occurred throughout Lebanon in the 1950s and '60s, though the southern areas of Beirut were mostly settled by Shi'is from the south and the Beqaa.

Writing in 1975, Fuad Khuri described the suburbs thus:

> A glance at the suburbs gives the impression that nothing is placed where it is supposed to be. The observer is immediately struck by the lack of planning, zoning, a center to the town, straight streets, and standardized buildings. Apartment buildings of various sizes and indistinct style blotch the horizon. They are often separated by one-floor houses with concrete pillars on the roof to suggest that the unfinished part of the building will be completed soon; or

by small, neglected orange or olive orchards; or by well-cultivated vegetable
gardens. Goats and sheep are often seen roaming around the twisted streets,
looking for garbage to feed on. Chickens are more frequently heard and are
seen caged in small poultry runs in gardens, beside houses, or on house-top.
(1975:37)

Soon after the remnants of village life vanished with the arrival of thousands of Shi'i
refugees from the northeastern suburbs of Beirut, the south, and the Beqaa during the years
of war. Refugees continued to pour into al-Dahiyya, as it grew southward and westward,
throughout the violence, and especially in 1978, 1982, and 1993, as villagers from the south
and the Beqaa fled Israeli invasions and bombardments.

These consecutive surges in migration altered the sectarian makeup of the suburbs.
The original village of Chiyah had a Maronite Christian majority and a Shi'i Muslim
minority, a ratio that was gradually reversed over the next few decades through both Shi'i
migration to the area and Maronite emigration to South America (Khuri, 1975). Before
the wars began, there was still a slight Maronite majority in the southern suburbs. By the
late 1990s, approximately 70–80 percent of the population was made up of Shi'is who
were displaced during the wars.

At the beginning of the twenty-first century, when you enter al-Dahiyya from many
other areas of Beirut, there is generally no clear marker of division, but there is a palpable
change. Your senses clearly indicate that you have entered an area that is dominated by a
particular mix of politics and piety. The recent demographic changes that have occurred
in al-Dahiyya marked a new visibility for many Shi'i Muslims as a presence in Lebanon,
and especially in Beirut, inscribed on public space and time. In what follows, I render the
temporal, visual, and aural textures of al-Dahiyya that contribute to the sense of community
cohesion held by those located within the pious modern.

Although most of my interlocutors resided in al-Dahiyya and it was their shared
values that dominated public space in the area, al-Dahiyya was not coterminous with
Shi'i "Islamism" or piety in Lebanon. On the one hand, while urban Lebanese Shi'i
Islamism was concentrated in this suburb, its roots and reach extended throughout the
country, and especially into the south and the Beqaa Valley. On the other hand, there
existed within al-Dahiyya other political perspectives, religious beliefs and identities, and
lifestyles. Yet my focus lies with those who both claimed a particular religious identity
based in authenticated Islam and were active participants in shaping their social landscape
in accordance with that religious identity.

As I move to describing what pious Shi'is called al-bi'a (the milieu), I want to emphasize
that the forms I discuss are those that were both ubiquitous and hegemonic, both at first
glance to an outsider and to the particular public of the pious modern. So, for example,
in describing the plethora of signs that papered al-Dahiyya's streets, I focus on images
of orphans, religious leaders, and Resistance martyrs. There were also pictures of other
political figures and candidates, especially around election times. And there were other
sorts of images—building names, signs advertising commodities and services—but these
were not what were perceived to set the cityscape apart from other areas of Beirut. Nor
were these images the ones people pointed out to me when describing the positive changes
that had occurred around them over the past few decades.

Additionally, the rapid growth shifts in population, and surges in building that have come to characterize al-Dahiyya were experienced by many residents as the making of an area of Beirut that was explicitly Shi'i—essentially as the creation of a place for the religious-political-social movement they were working to forge. For them, the various textures of al-Dahiyya's milieu that I describe in this chapter were significant because they represented the rooting of the uprooted, and because they were evidence of the "rise" of "the Shi'a" as a critical community in Lebanon.

Textures of al-Dahiyya

Sight

The first time I entered al-Dahiyya, I went by taxi. My luck was with me that day, as my driver was both loquacious and from one of the neighborhoods that would eventually become part of my field site. After I explained that I would be working with the *jam'iyya* (social welfare organization) where I had an appointment that day, he began to point out landmarks to help me get my bearings. As we turned off the old airport road, we joined a slow stream of traffic, with men pushing vegetable carts wandering between the cars, and pedestrians crossing at will. *Services*—ubiquitous shared taxis that are always old Mercedeses—held up the flow, and young men on motorbikes whizzed loudly around, weaving closely between cars. The buildings looked taller, something I immediately attributed to less regulated construction, and there seemed to be a lot of billboards with pictures of children on them. Similar pictures dotted many of the electrical poles, alongside posters of Nasrallah, another sayyid who looked a lot like him to me, and Khomeini. When the driver saw me looking at a huge canvas painting of Khomeini that leaned against the side of a building, he gestured to it and said simply, *"qa'idna"* (our leader).

Several months later, I was driving myself around al-Dahiyya with relative ease, though I still dreaded parking and frequently had to ask for directions. I had learned that that other sayyid who had looked a lot like Nasrallah was in fact Sayyid Abbas al-Musawi, the previous Secretary General of Hizbullah who had been assassinated by Israel along with his wife and five-year-old son. And I now knew that those children's faces were the faces of need, of orphans representing the many charitable organizations that worked in the area.

I had also learned that, contrary to what some people from other Beirut neighborhoods had indicated, in certain ways al-Dahiyya looked a lot like many other regions of the city. Some of the buildings were indeed taller and more closely spaced, and that did have to do with unregulated building. But this was not unique to al-Dahiyya. Nor was the high level of pedestrian traffic in the streets unique to this particular part of Beirut, although the especially high population density was probably reflected here to a certain extent. Yet in other ways, there was something that set al-Dahiyya apart. This was the presence of a particular politics of piety, a sense of publicly displayed and claimed piety: what my friends at the American University of Beirut glossed as "Hizbullah" but what was in fact far more complicated than a political party.

This public piety appeared in the higher prevalence of women who wore Islamic dress and the *hijab* than in perhaps any other part of the country, and certainly in the numbers of women in Iranian style *'abayas*. It was also manifested in the ease with which I and other women could walk through the streets. Al-Dahiyya was the only area of Beirut where I was never subject to a single catcall. The only comment ever made to me by a strange man was a singular occasion when someone said *"Allah yahdiki"* (May God give you guidance), apparently in reference to my modest but unveiled appearance, something that my (at the time) new Shi'i acquaintances found quite amusing. Another area where public piety appeared was in the pervasiveness of certain images: portraits of orphans, religious leaders, and martyrs.

In al-Dahiyya, a person would sometimes point to a poster of a martyr while describing her solidarity with the Resistance, or to a portrait of a religious figure while explaining "how far the community had come." For many, the iconographic salience of orphans, martyrs, and religious leaders lay in the ways these images claimed and defined the space of al-Dahiyya as belonging to their community. Through these visual signifiers, al-Dahiyya was claimed as a place for the Shi'i Islamic movement and a place within which (a particular) piety would be nurtured. At the same time, the presence of these particular portrait images exemplified the freedom pious Shi'is felt within al-Dahiyya to claim this piety publicly. As will be discussed later, many felt strongly that they were part of a communal group that had always been dispossessed in the Lebanese polity. The images that filled al-Dahiyya were evidence to them of the progress their community had made within the nation-state. Increased piety—visible spiritual progress—was linked to political success.

Images of orphans, martyrs, and religious leaders were read differently by those who felt a part of the Shi'i Islamic pious modern than by those who did not. Outsiders sometimes saw photographs of orphans as children being used for fund-raising purposes. Depending on one's political leanings, portraits of sayyids and shaykhs might be read as frightening evidence of an insistence on an Islamic state, or as a distressing reminder of the failures of the secular left, or as elements in an internal iconographic war among Shi'i political parties. Responses to the renderings of martyrs often seemed to vary with the political climate and latest events; in the months leading up to and following Israeli withdrawal in 2000, they were regarded by many as national heroes who liberated the south.

Portraits of sayyids and shaykhs are not solely religious images, rather they are part of the plastering of public surfaces with the images of prominent political figures that is common to all of Lebanon and much of the Middle East. In Jordan, posters and large paintings of the late King Husayn and the current King Abdullah fill public space. In Syria one finds omnipresent images of late President Hafez al-Asad and his successor and son, President Bashar. Similarly in Morocco images of the king are mandatory in all public buildings and often appear in homes and offices as well. The lack of one dominant political persona in Lebanon, the lack of a singular face confronting spectators at every turn, reflects the sectarian political system in the country and underscores the usage of portrait images as weapons in a continuous turf war. The prominence of particular leaders declares political loyalties and produces the effect of territorial claims that may, whether intentionally or not, influence the fears and resegregation of Lebanon's various communities. In al-Dahiyya, the dominant faces were those of Hizbullah political leaders, with competition in some areas from Harakat Amal.

The political, rather than religious, significance of these images is reinforced by who was not represented among them, namely Sayyid Muhammad Husayn Fadlullah. Those who were represented were all religious leaders who had clear political roles: Ayatollah

Khomeini and his successor Ayatollah Khamenei; Secretary General of Hizbullah Sayyid Hasan Nasrallah; his martyred predecessor Sayyid Abbas al-Musawi; Shaykh Raghib Harb, another martyred Hizbullah leader; Sayyid Musa al-Sadr, the original mobilizer of the Lebanese Shi'a; and even Shaykh Subhi Tufayli, whose movement split from Hizbullah during an internal conflict in the early 1990s. But there were no posters of Fadlullah hanging from electrical poles or balconies. Many of his followers had framed photographs of him in their offices or homes, but this was a personal statement of religious allegiance and admiration, rather than part of the political iconography of the area.

A similar negative association was expressed to me by a close relative of Sayyid Musa al-Sadr, perhaps the religious leader most frequently pictured in posters and paintings in the country:

> He said that it really upsets him, "the whole thing with the pictures," and tears welled up in his eyes. He continued, saying that he has thought about this a lot and that it is clear to him that these pictures are being used for political goals, to help people win elections, because they always put a picture of Berri [Amal's political leader], of the exact same size, next to al-Sadr's image. He then added that he thinks some people just put the pictures up everywhere out of ignorance, because they loved [al-Sadr] and think this is a good way to show it: "It's an ignorant expression of love."

This man resented both the political uses to which al-Sadr was being put and what he perceived as the misplacing of admiration in political postering. Indeed, al-Sadr is perhaps one of the most contested faces in al-Dahiyya. The turf wars expressed through these portraits are often strongest among political parties affiliated with the same sect.

Turf wars also emerge in less sanctioned images. In a few streets in al-Dahiyya, small spray-painted stencil images of renegade Shaykh Subhi Tufayli covered the cement walls of buildings. This was not official postering associated with a party, but an expression of loyalty to the shaykh and his movement by area residents. Again, it is the political leadership of the shaykh that is emphasized through his representation, rather than his religious position.

Like pictures of religious leaders, portraits of martyrs work to indicate political loyalties and claim territorial space. Yet these images also carry a duality that emerges from their memorializing aspect. This duality is related to "the tension between personal identity and social identity, individual and type, a tension integral to portraiture" (Kratz, 2002: 119). But just as martyr photographs are individualized and localized, at the same time they facilitate mourning on the community level, and promote and declare community solidarity and political loyalties. Any display of martyr photographs in al-Dahiyya contained an element of homogenization of form.

One did not have to have a personal relationship with a martyr, religious leader, or orphan to understand his image as part of one's "family." The smallness of social scale that heightened the chances that one would actually have such a personal relationship served to intensify a sense of community solidarity, but that sense was there nonetheless. At the same time these portrait images were public: displayed in such a way as to provide an iconography of community, incorporated into a narrative of collective identity, one in which leaders, ideal participants, and those in need were all represented.

Like images anywhere, martyr, religious leader, and orphan portraits in al-Dahiyya did not possess inherent meanings. Nor were meanings solely determined by the production and display of these images, which frequently was controlled by *jam'iyyas,* political parties, and other institutions. Instead, the meanings carried by these photographs and paintings were situated in a wider social and narrative framework. In al-Dahiyya, the particular iconography associated with the Shi'i Islamic movement dominated the visual landscape, facilitated by the hegemonic character of its narrative framework in the area. It emerged from a complex context that included social welfare and political institutions, the residents of al-Dahiyya, Lebanese national polity and public(s), and the global order. Spectators played a crucial role in this process. Through the meanings they brought to the images around them—whether personal mourning, solidarity, a sense of belonging in a place, or something else—pious Shi'is were participating in the creation and maintenance of the context within which the images carried meaning: the framework of the pious modern. I now turn to another key element in its manifestation, moving from the visual to the aural.

Sound

Along with images, the cityscape of al-Dahiyya is textured with sound. This soundscape had regular features. Most prominent, after the din of the streets, were sacred sounds, again reinforcing the sense of public piety that characterized this area of the capital. Perhaps the most constant feature of the soundscape were the regular calls to prayer, the *adhān,* projected five times a day over loudspeakers from each of the many mosques in the area. One effect of the *adhān* is to sacralize space. In al-Dahiyya, this transformation was acknowledged through gesture: even if she was not going to pray at the time, a person would often shift her posture, uncrossing crossed legs, and straightening her back, and would touch her hand to her head quickly when the *adhān* began.

The *adhān* also marked time in al-Dahiyya. Rather than, "I'll meet you there after lunch," or "I'll meet you at 12:30," I was often told, "I'll meet you there right after the noon prayer." The significance of the *adhān* to the daily rhythms of life was highlighted for me when we set our clocks back an hour in the fall for daylight savings time. I had noticed, as I always do, darkness creeping in earlier, but for Aziza the change was even more striking "I can't believe it's only 11:35 a.m. but it's already *al-dhuhr* (time for the noon prayer)!" she exclaimed upon hearing the call to prayer. The sound of the *adhān* is what divided morning from afternoon and afternoon from evening. Because the *adhān* is set by the path of the sun, and not the clock, daylight savings had the jarring effect of abruptly bringing afternoon an hour earlier, shifting the divisions of the day. For Aziza, afternoon began shortly after 11:35 a.m. that day.

In addition to marking space and time in al-Dahiyya, *adhān* in Lebanon marks sectarian space and identity. There are areas of Beirut where it has always been typical to hear churchbells and *adhān* sharing the soundscape, but most neighborhoods of al-Dahiyya did not fit this description. Moreover, in Lebanon, the details of the *adhān* declare the sect of the mosque. Shi'i mosques are distinguishable by an added line bearing witness that Ali is the *wali* (deputy) of God.

Other related sounds do not mark daily time, but are instead weekly, like the sermons, Qur'anic recitations, and noontime prayers that emanated from many mosques on Fridays. This mosque-based soundscape also included seasonal elements, discussed further below. Also important are occasional manifestations of sound that can be read by residents, such as the Qur'anic recitations that took place when someone had died. On several occasions I would be visiting someone in al-Dahiyya when the recitation slipping in the window prompted her to wonder aloud who in the area had passed away. Ears would then strain to hear the announcement that would follow, informing the community of who had died and when the burial would take place.

Sound in al-Dahiyya marked time, transmitted religious and community knowledge, and engendered or facilitated emotion. Most crucially, elements of the soundscape underscored the indissolubility of religion from everyday life, linking the mundane to the sacred. These sacred sounds were everyday sounds, part and parcel of the spaces where people live.

In the contemporary moment, the mosque is not the only source for pietistic sound in al-Dahiyya. It has been joined by cassette tapes of sermons and Qur'anic recitation, as well as two major radio stations and a television station. The radio stations—al-Basha'ir (the Messenger or Herald) affiliated with Fadlullah, and al-Nûr (the Light) affiliated with Hizbullah—broadcast a variety of programming, the former primarily religious and social, and the latter a mix of religion, politics and current events/news updates. The television station, Al-Manār (the Lighthouse), is affiliated with Hizbullah, and also has a wide variety of programming, ranging from news updates and in-depth current events discussions, interviews, and debates, to children's shows and fictional serials, often based on religio-historical events.

All these media pause their programming in order to sound the call to prayer, and to broadcast Friday sermons and prayers. Many commented on the importance of these media, emphasizing their contribution to the religious milieu as well as their educational value. Neither the soundscape nor the visual cityscape were uniform throughout the year in al-Dahiyya. It is to the cycle of seasons and the related shifts in texture that this chapter now turns.

Season

The standard visual and aural textures of al-Dahiyya were supplemented by seasonal additions, following the ritual cycle of the Hijri, or Islamic calendar. The first month of the year is Muharram. For Sunni Muslims, 1 Muharram is celebrated as the beginning of the New Year. Yet for Shi'i Muslims, the year begins in tragedy. The first ten days of Muharram are commemorated as days of hardship for the Shi'i leader Imam Husayn and his followers, leading to their martyrdom on 10 Muharram.

Imam Husayn was the grandson of the Prophet, the son of his daughter Sayyida Fatima and his cousin and son-in-law Imam Ali. In 680 CE, Husayn was killed in battle by an army sent by the Caliph, Yazid, on the plain of Karbala, now in Iraq. This was perhaps the most major of a series of conflicts over succession to the leadership of the Islamic community that divided Shi'i and Sunni Muslims. A group of Shi'is in Kufa, also in Iraq, had called upon Husayn to lead them in revolt against Yazid. He agreed and set out on the first of Muharram, taking with him armed guards and his family. They were intercepted and besieged at Karbala. The battle began on the tenth of Muharram, and by the end, all the men except one of the Imam's sons had been killed and the women and children taken captive. The entire ten-day period that culminates in the commemoration of the battle and martyrdom on the tenth of Muharram is referred to metonymically in Lebanon as "Ashura."

For Shi'i Muslims, Ashura ushers in a season of mourning and darkness. It is important to note the general atmosphere of solemnity that pervaded al-Dahiyya during Ashura and for several weeks following it. People generally dressed in somber clothing—black, perhaps navy after the tenth of the month. Celebrations, such as weddings or birthday parties, were frowned upon. Ritual mourning gatherings were held throughout the season, continuing for forty days after the day of the martyrdom, and many in al-Dahiyya considered the second month of the calendar, Safar, to be a time of year as sober, if not more sober, than Muharram itself.

The religious seasons in al-Dahiyya were reflected in the imagery and soundscape of the area. During this period of solemnity, it was common to hear the lamentative strains of at least one *majlis 'aza* (mourning gathering, plural, *majālis*) radiating from a mosque, *husayniyya*, street corner, or private home. The recent use of microphones in privately held *majālis* has increased this in the past decade. Many pious individuals listened to tapes of *majālis* or *nudbas*, which are like dirges, mourning songs commemorating the events around the martyrdom. Radio and television programming on the Fadlullah and Hizbullah frequencies also reflected this mood, broadcasting *nudbas* or educational programming about the life of Husayn and the meanings of Ashura.

The standard portrait imagery was supplemented with black banners hung from buildings and balconies, strung across roads, and attached to streetlights and electrical poles. Written on these banners were texts commemorating Husayn's martyrdom: sayings of the Prophet, verses from the Qur'an, or quotes from Khomeini and other important figures, all of which highlight Ashura's importance to the contemporary era. While some of these carried no political insignia, and were erected by mosques or religious organizations, others were clearly linked to territoriality and political affiliation. In 2000, two black bridgelike structures spanned a highway south of Beirut a short distance apart, one clearly marked with Amal signs and the other Hizbullah. In Hizbullah territory, the standard yellow flags of the party are usually replaced by red and black ones.

After the season of mourning, the rest of the year is one of neutrality marked with joy. Some people insisted that Shi'i Muslims exist in perpetual shadow, in a state of constant sadness. However, they were rare individuals whose piety approached asceticism. Two other major commemorative times mark the Hijri calendar: Ramadan and the *hajj*, both of which are shared by Shi'i and Sunni Muslims alike. Before turning to them, however, I want to touch upon the smaller celebratory moments, the *mawlids*. During the last week of the month Safar one year, I was at a *jam'iyya* while some volunteers were planning a fund-raiser. They had wanted to hold this event for some time, but were waiting for *"mawsim al-mawālid,"* the season of *mawlids* (birth celebrations), as one woman put it, to do so. When I asked why, she responded: "Just as God gave us Ashura which is a sad occasion, he gave us the *mawlid*, the happy occasion of the Prophet's birth."

A *mawlid* commemorates the Prophet Muhammad's birth (in Rabi 1) in a celebratory event that often includes professional religious singing in his honor. Shi'i Muslims also hold *mawlids* to mark other occasions, like the birthdays of Imam Husayn (in Rabi 11), Imam Ali (in Rajab), and Imam al-Mahdi, the twelfth Imam (in Shaban). The fund-raiser this particular *jam'iyya* was planning was to coincide with the anniversary of Imam Ali's marriage to Sayyida Fatima, the Prophet's daughter, one of the numerous annual commemorative dates that are noted in al-Dahiyya. *Mawlids* generally did not affect the public sound or cityscape in al-Dahiyya, because they were usually held as private gatherings.

The next major moment in the religious calendar is the month of Ramadan, the ninth month of the year and one whose importance is emphasized by all Muslims. Ramadan is the month in which the Qur'an was revealed to Muhammad. The night on which this is believed to have occurred, the twenty-seventh of the month, is commemorated as *laylat al-qadr* with special prayers. For all Muslims, observing Ramadan involves prayer and fasting—meaning abstaining from food, drink, smoking, and sex—between sunrise and sunset throughout the month. At sunset, the fast breaking meal, or *iftār,* has become a lavish undertaking for many, though this has been criticized by those who fear that Ramadan is losing its religious significance. The end of Ramadan is celebrated as *Eid al-Fitr,* also called *Eid al-Saghir* (the minor holiday).

Because Ramadan is a month of reflection and generosity, many *jam'iyyas* conducted their primary fund-raising activities during this time. Some held large banquet *iftārs,* placing an envelope underneath each plate for donations. Others placed advertisements asking for donations, and reminding pious individuals of their religious duty to help the less fortunate. Ramadan fund-raising made use of a wide variety of media, and contributed to the particular textures associated with the month. This is the season during which the orphan as icon took center stage. Billboards and signs showing forlorn yet happy orphans sprouted up all around al-Dahiyya as well as other parts of Beirut, often accompanied by a verse from the Qur'an or a *hadith* enjoining passersby to remember the orphans during the month of generosity, or reminding them that those who help orphans will secure their place in heaven. The radio waves were not immune to this either, as various *jam'iyyas* placed ads that combined children singing with requests for donations.

The other seasonal markers that appeared with Ramadan were celebratory lights and decorations reminiscent of Christmas in the suburban United States. Strings with colorful lanterns, lightbulbs, and paper decorations hung across intersections in al-Dahiyya, and neon lights, including some of the Hizbullah symbol, lined many roads. In 1999 and 2000, the coincidence of Ramadan and Christmas prompted the trimming of Hamra Street—a major road outside al-Dahiyya in Ras Beirut—with neon blue and pink signs alternating *"Ramadan karim"* with "Merry Christmas" and "Happy New Year." Those same years, Hizbullah constructed a large nativity scene in an al-Dahiyya neighborhood.

The two months following Ramadan are relatively quiet, as people resume their normal schedules. Around this time a flurry of banners began to appear, advertising different *hajj* organizers, called *hamlāt.* The *hajj*—the pilgrimage to Mecca required for Muslims who are able to go once in their lifetime—takes place during the first ten days of the last month, *Dhu al-Hijjah.* At the end of the pilgrimage is *Eid al-Adha* (the holiday of sacrifice), also called *Eid al-Kabir* (the major holiday), during which families slaughter a sheep or other animal and distribute the meat to the poor in commemoration of Abraham's willingness to sacrifice his son Ishmael at God's command and God's mercy in substituting a lamb for Ishmael. During these festivities, which like most holidays include feasting and visiting, the houses of people on the *hajj* were decorated with streamers, often extending across the street or over balconies. Driving through al-Dahiyya, one could easily identify many of the households who had a member on the *hajj*. When family members returned, dressed in white to signify their completion of this sacred duty, they were welcomed by celebratory crowds at the airport. Visiting then commenced for weeks, as friends, family and acquaintances came to greet the new *Hajj* or *Hajjeh*, who had brought tokens of the voyage to distribute, including prayer beads, Qur'ans, jewelry, and *may al-zumzum* (water from the sacred Zumzum well in Saudi Arabia).

For Sunni Muslims, this *Eid* and the close of the *hajj* season marks the last major moment in the Hijri calendar until the new year a couple of weeks later. Shi'i Muslims, however, mark one more day, the eighteenth of *Dhu al-Hijja*, or *Eid al-Ghadir*, on which they quietly acknowledge the moment Muhammad made Ali his successor. From that point, the calendar begins its shift from the seasons of joy to the season of mourning, as Muharram and Ashura approach once again and black returns to shroud al-Dahiyya.

The creation and claiming of a place for the Shi'i Islamic movement and its constituents in al-Dahiyya, a place where the milieu is established in part through the various textures of piety and politics described in this chapter, is crucial to the totality of progress. Yet places and communities are not claimed or created through texture alone, but also through a shared sense of history and shared practices and meanings.

References

Harb el-kak, Mona, 1998, 'Transforming the site of dereliction into the urban culture of modernity: Beirut's southern suburb and Elisar project.' In *Projecting Beirut: Episodes in the construction and reconstruction of a modern city*, ed. Peter Rowe and Hashim Sarkis, 173–82. Munich: Prestel.

Khalaf, Samir, 2002, *Civil and Uncivil Violence in Lebanon: A History of the Internationalization of Communal Conflict*. New York: Columbia University Press.

Khuri, Fuad, 1975, *From Village to Suburb: Order and Change in Greater Beirut*. Chicago: University of Illinois Press.

Kratz, Corinne A., 2002, *The Ones That Are Wanted: Communication and the Politics of Representation in a Photographic Exhibition*. Berkeley: University of California Press.

A slightly abridged version adapted from *An Enchanted Modern: Gender and Public Piety in Shi'i Lebanon* (Princeton University Press, 2006): 42–66. It is printed here with the permission of the publisher.

FARHA GHANNAM

Re-imagining the Global:
Relocation and Local Identities in Cairo

Short of a certain threshold of likelihood, only magical solutions remain.
Magical hope is the outlook on the future characteristic of those who have no
real future before them.

(Bourdieu 1979: 69)

"Praise the Prophet. Once upon a time, there was an old woman who used to live in an
apartment that was as small as that tiny table [pointing to the small table in their living
room]. Each time the old woman swept the floor, she found either one pound or 50
piasters [an Egyptian pound is worth around 34 cents] that she kept hidden in a place in
her window. The old woman was saving to buy a larger apartment. But one day, a thief
stole all the money that she saved. She was very sad. An *afriit* [demon or ghost] appeared
and asked the old woman what she would like to have. She asked for a larger apartment.
The *afriit* asked her, 'Would you like the apartment to have a balcony?' and she answered
yes. He asked her, 'Would you like a television set, a fan and a bottle of water?' [describing
some of the things that were in front of us in the living room]. The old woman said yes.
Then he asked her, 'And would you like some pictures of Samira Said and Latifa?' [two
popular female Moroccan and Tunisian singers whose posters were decorating the wall of
the living room]. The woman again answered yes. The *afriit* brought all these things for the
old woman. She was very happy and cried out of joy. In the same day, however, she smelled
the *birshaam* [a type of drug believed to be produced by the USA and Israel] that was
hidden behind the television set which caused her heart to collapse (*gham ala albaha)* and
the old woman died." (A story told to me by the five-year-old Amal in Cairo, 1994).

Amal's narrative was contextualized by her family's attempts to find a larger housing unit
to move into from the one-bedroom apartment that she, her four sisters and their parents
have been occupying since 1980, when the family was displaced from their home in the
centre of the city and relocated in al-Zawiya al-Hamra in northern Cairo. Amal's images
of the desired home are constructed, as is the case with many other children, from global
images transmitted to them through television programmes, school textbooks and visits to
different parts of the city. Her dreams, as well as those of her sisters, of the future apartment
are informed by the movies and soap operas that they like to watch: a big apartment with
a balcony, a spacious kitchen, modern furniture and organized spatial arrangements inside
and outside the unit. These images contradict the objective realities of Amal's tale and create
desires that cannot be satisfied even through some magical means. Like the dreams of many
other low-income people, Amal's discourse "proceeds in a jagged line, the leaps into daydream

being followed by relapses into a present that withers all fantasies" (Bourdieu 1979: 69). Death and destruction is the ultimate answer.

Amal, her family and the rest of their neighbors are not fax-users, e-mail receivers, jumbo jet travellers or satellite-owners. They are part of Cairo's working class whose experience of "the global" is structured by their economic resources and position in social space. In addition to the many consumer goods, especially television sets, that are desired by people and are becoming signs of distinction, Amal's family and many other families experienced the force of the global in their displacement from their "locality" in the centre of the city. Their houses were demolished to be replaced by buildings and facilities that cater to upper-class Egyptians, international tourists and the transnational community. In this chapter, I focus on relocation, utilized as part of the state efforts to "modernize" Cairo and its people, to show how global discourses and forces are articulated in contradictory ways at the national and local levels. In the first section, I present a brief review of the history of the relocation of roughly 5000 working-class families from 1979 to 1981 and the state public discourse utilized to justify the project. This discourse strategically appealed to the global in the state's attempts to implement its different economic policies and to construct a modern national identity. In the second part, I draw on my recent ethnographic research in Cairo, or *Umm al-Dunya* (the mother of the world) as Egyptians like to refer to it, to map some of the identities that are attached to and formed by Amal's group to show how the displacement of the local by global processes and national policies brought new changes that paved the way to redefine local communal feelings in ways that help people live in the modern world. I argue that religious identity, as a hegemonic identity in the formation, was consolidated by the changes brought by the global as experienced by the people and as filtered in national policies.

Modernity and the struggle over urban space

In *Search for Identity* (1978), Anwar el-Sadat presents a strong critique of Nasser's policies that kept the country isolated from its neighbors and the rest of the world and destroyed Egypt's economy. To remedy the country's chronic economic and financial problems, Sadat reversed Nasser's policies by suspending relationships with the Soviet Union and reorienting Egypt towards the West. He turned to the United States in particular for aid in resolving Egypt's conflict with Israel as well as the economic and technological development of the country. After his victory in the 1973 war (at least it was a victory for him), Sadat crystallized his new visions and ideas in declaring "the open-door policy" or *infitah* in 1974. This policy aimed to "open the universe ... open the door for fresh air and remove all the barriers *(hawajiz)* and walls that we built around us to suffocate ourselves by our own hands" (Sadat, 1978: 12). As he explained to a group of young Egyptian men, Sadat's infitah was motivated by his belief that each one of them would like to "get married, own a villa, drive a car, possess a television set and a stove, and eat three meals a day" (Sadat, 1978: 12).

Sadat's policy strived to modernize the country through speeding planned economic growth, promoting private investment, attracting foreign and Arab capital, and enhancing social development. Private local and international investments were expected to secure the capital needed to construct modern Egypt. Egyptians were encouraged to work in oil-producing countries and invest their remittances in the building of the country. At the same time, laws were enacted to secure the protection needed to encourage foreign investors and to facilitate the operation of private capital. Investments in tourism were especially important because they were expected to "yield high economic returns and provide substantial foreign exchange and well-paid employment".

This orientation to the global, the outside, or the "universe" as Sadat describes it, required a "distinctive bundle of time and space practices and concepts" (Harvey, 1990: 204). Many changes were needed to facilitate the operation of capital and meet the new demands that were created. For example, the growing demand for luxury and middle-class housing for the transnational community and Egyptians who work in oil producing countries inflated the price of land, especially in the centre of the city, and increased the cost of construction materials. The promotion of private and foreign investment also increased the demand for offices and work-oriented spaces. High-rises proliferated around Cairo, using Western design principles and Los Angeles and Houston, Sadat's favourite American cities, became the models that were to be duplicated.

Two tendencies were expressed in the discourses and policies of urban planning that aimed to promote the *infitah* policies and to rebuild modern Cairo. The first tried to integrate into the modern city areas of significance to Egypt's glorious past (for example, the pyramids and Islamic monuments), which Sadat loved to emphasize and which were visited by tourists. The second tendency, which is the subject of this chapter, attempted to reconstruct the "less desirable" parts, especially popular quarters, that did not represent the "modern" image of Egypt and were not fit to be gazed at by upper-class Egyptians and foreign visitors.

The State, the Global and the Creation of the "Modern" City

Faust has been pretending not only to others but to himself that he could create a new world with clean hands, he is still not ready to accept responsibility for the human suffering and death that clear the way.

(Berman 1988: 68)

As part of Sadat's larger plan to restructure the local landscape and build "modern" Cairo, around 5000 Egyptian families were moved during the period from 1979 to 1981 from Central Cairo (Bulaq) to housing projects built by the state in two different neighbourhoods: 'Ain Shams and al-Zawiya al-Hamra. Bulaq, once the site of the winter houses of the rich, then a major commercial port and later an industrial centre, had become unfit for the modern image that Sadat was trying to construct. This area, which over the years had housed thousands of Egyptian low-income families, is adjacent to the Ramsis Hilton, next to the television station, around the corner from the World Trade Center, across the river from Zamalek (an upper-class neighbourhood), overlooks the Nile, and is very close to many of the facilities that are oriented to foreign tourists. The area then occupied by low-income families became very valuable because Sadat's policies, as he proudly announced, increased the price of the land which was needed to facilitate the operation of capital. The old crowded houses were to be replaced by modern buildings, luxury housing, five-star hotels, offices, multi-storey parking lots, movie theatres, conference rooms, and centres of culture. Officials thus emphasized the urgent need to remove the residents of this old quarter because many international companies were ready to initiate economic and tourist investment in the area. Expected profits from these investments would contribute to national income and assist the state in securing money to build new houses for the displaced groups. The residents' efforts to stop their forced relocation did not materialize and their calls upon the government to include them in the reconstruction of their area were denied. Voices that protested the relocation were quickly silenced and objections raised by the displaced population were considered "selfish". Officials emphasized that the benefit of the "entire nation" should prevail over everything else.

The "local" was also displaced to protect the state orientation to the global. The relocation project took place two years after the famous 1977 riots that protested the increase in the prices of basic daily goods, especially bread. Protesters targeted *infitah*-related facilities such as five-star hotels and nightclubs, and chanted slogans against Sadat's policies. The neighbourhood, with its narrow lanes and crowded streets, made it impossible for the police to chase those who participated in the riots. The relocated group was seen by the state and the state-controlled press as part of "a conspiracy organized by communists" that aimed to distort the achievements of the *infitah* and their housing became an obstacle to the promotion of Sadat's policies and to police attempts to crush protest against these policies.

The rhetorical strategies employed by the state were largely based in the appeal to the global. This appeal was manifested by the emphasis on modernity and its objectification in material forms, rational planning, the importance of visual aspects and the tourists' gaze in representing Cairo, the separation of the home from the workplace, international investment, science, health, hygiene, green areas and clean environment, consumer goods and the importance of the productive agent in the construction of a modern national identity. The global was strategically used to offer the people a "Faustian bargain" (cf. Berman, 1988) which forced the relocated group to pay a high price for Egypt's opportunity to be "modernized". Using force (police) and seduction (by appealing to the global and offering alternative housing), the project removed them from the centre of the city and deprived them of the benefits associated with the modern facilities and the new changes that promised prosperity for everyone. Relocation destroyed most of the group's informal economy, altered their access to many cheap goods and services, and destroyed their social relationships and reordered their personal lives.

As previously mentioned, the group was divided into two parts, each relocated to a different neighbourhood away from the gaze of tourists and upper-class Egyptians. One part, the focus of this study, was moved to public housing *(masaakin)* units constructed for them in al-Zawiya al-Hamra in northern Cairo. The move into these units, which were labelled as "modern", promised to improve the lives of the people and turn them into "healthy modern productive citizens who will contribute in the construction of their mother country". The state's project assumed a transparent relationship between space and identity and totally ignored the role of social actors in transforming and resisting its policies and ideologies. Rather than creating a unified modern city, I argue that these policies created a more fragmented urban fabric and paved the ground for other competing collective identities. Religious identity in particular has successfully presented itself as a powerful alternative that can articulate the various antagonistic identities that are constructed in the relocation site.

Global Discourses and Local Identities

Since Sadat started his open-door policy, Cairo has witnessed the introduction of new forms of communication, more emphasis on international tourism, increasing importance of consumer goods, and a growing flow of ideas related to civil society, democracy and political participation. Theoretical developments in anthropology and cultural studies have demonstrated that these global processes are not producing one dominant culture but present a set of discourses and practices that are juxtaposed in complex ways in local contexts. Thus, contrary to the old conceptualization of the world as becoming a "global village", local differences and identities are not destroyed but are being reinforced in many cases by global forces and processes.

With the growing connectedness between different parts of the globe and with the circulation of global discourses and images facilitated by new systems of communication, the Other is becoming more identified with the self in complex ways. The connectedness and tension between the self and the Other are crucial to understanding how identities are constructed and shift over time and how the Other is simultaneously desired and dreaded. One example can be found in how people in Cairo desire the global (in this case identified as the West) because it is organized, clean, rich and "democratic" and at the same time they distrust it because it is associated with "moral corruption", drugs and violence. The focus on the connectedness and tension with the Other is therefore a necessary step to theorize the different ways that the global is reshaping local identities and redrawing their boundaries. This focus will enable us to conceptualize local identifications not as static but as always in the process of formation and constructed of multiple discourses and as composed "in and through ambivalence and desire" (Hall, 1991:49).

"Globalization", however, should not be reduced to "Americanization" as some authors tend to do. While the "American conception of the world" as Hall, among others, has suggested may be hegemonic in various contexts, people experience the influence of other "globals". People in al-Zawiya al-Hamra not only experience the American culture that is transmitted to them in movies starring Arnold Schwarzenegger but they also experience the global through oil-producing countries where their children and male relatives work as well as through the mixture of people who visit and work in Cairo from different Arab countries. For example, women use oil for their hair that comes from India via their sons who work in Kuwait and collect their wedding trousseau from clothes, sheets and blankets brought from Kuwait; others visit husbands in Saudi Arabia; and many have accumulated electrical appliances from Libya where husbands and sons work. Despite the fact that many of the consumer goods are produced in the West, their meanings are given to them by their users who live in al-Zawiya al-Hamra. For many, consumer goods are investments that can be exchanged for cash when needed. Several families use their refrigerators to cool water during the summer but turn them into closets during the winter to store household appliances. The global is also introducing new forms of identification between the subjects of its processes. People, for example, enjoy watching television, especially some of the global sports events such as the soccer World Cup. Young men and women follow these games very closely; they know the names of the Brazilian, German and Italian players. While watching these games, different identities compete for priority: they shift from supporting African and Arab teams to cheering for third world teams when they play against European teams (Brazil against Germany, for example). People, thus, do not experience the global as a coherent set of discourses and processes that are transmitted from the West to the rest of the world but experience fragments and contradictory pieces that are filtered through other centres and that do not necessarily present a unified "conception of the world". Therefore, "the global", as an analytical concept, should be expanded to include a mixture of images, discourses and goods that are brought to people through various channels such as state-controlled media, commercial video tapes, audio tapes that are distributed by Islamic activists, and consumer goods brought to al-Zawiya al-Hamra by migrants to Arab countries.

People attach multiple meanings to their localities that vary from one context to another. Despite the fact that geographical space is used as a point of reference for several local identities in Cairo, these different contexts share a set of social relationships and identities that include those who are like us (local people) and exclude people who are not like us (outsiders). Thus, when people identify the relocated group as "those from Bulaq", they are trying to exclude them from another collective identity that includes people who have been living in al-Zawiya and identify primarily with it. The relocated people still refer to themselves as "people of Bulaq" despite the fact that they have been living in al-Zawiya for fifteen years. Many also still identify with their old villages and towns that they left more than fifty years ago. In short, there is not one "local" but there are various "locals" that are juxtaposed in complex ways with multiple "globals".

Old Places, New Identities

Here in al-Zawiya, you do not find Pizza Hut and Kentucky Fried Chicken. Such places can never get any profit in areas like this. People are poor and the money they will pay for one meal in one of these restaurants will feed the whole family for a week if not more.
(A male shop-owner who works in al-Zawiya but lives in another middle-class neighbourhood)

To understand the local identities that are in the process of formation in al-Zawiya al-Hamra, it is important to remember that state practices and discourses were based on what Foucault calls "dividing practices" (Rabinow, 1984: 8). The project started by separating and stigmatizing the targeted population as an expedient rationalization of policies that aim to modernize, normalize and reintegrate them within the larger community. Not only were the housing conditions attacked by state officials, but the people themselves were stigmatized and criticized. A "scientific" social study conducted to determine the needs of the relocated group revealed, as stated by the Minister of Construction and New Communities, that the area of Bulaq in general and one of its neighborhoods (al-Torgman) in particular have been shelters for qiradatia (street entertainers who perform with a baboon or monkey), female dancers, pedlars and drug dealers. The "locals" were also represented as passive, unhealthy and isolated people who did not contribute to the construction of the mother-country and who had many social ills. After resettlement, these publicized stereotypes fostered a general feeling of antagonism towards the newcomers. In addition to repeating the same words that were circulated in the media, residents of al-Zawiya added other stereotypes to describe this group such as *labat* (trouble-makers) and *shalaq* (insolent). Women, in particular, were singled out (as they were also singled out by the Minister who described them as dancers or *Ghawazi*); they were described as rude and vulgar, and were used in daily conversation as an analogy for bad manners.

These negative constructions of the relocated group are supported and perpetuated by the physical segregation of their housing (*masaakin*) from the rest of the community. Their public housing is clearly defined and separated from other projects and private houses (*ahali*). Public housing is characterized by a unified architectural design (the shape, the size of the buildings, as well as the colours of walls and windows), whereas private housing has more diversified patterns. This unity in design and shape sharply defines and differentiates public housing from private houses and makes it easier to maintain boundaries that separate the relocated from other groups. In short, neither the discourse of the state nor the shape and location of the housing project enhance the dialogical relationship between the relocated group and other groups in al-Zawiya. After fourteen or fifteen years of resettlement, the relocated group continues to be stigmatized and its interaction with the rest of the neighbourhood is restricted.

With their stigmatization in the state discourse and by the residents of al-Zawiya, and with the hostility that faced them, the relocated population rediscovered their common history and identification with the same geographical area. While people used to live in Bulaq and identify strongly with their villages of origin, after relocation Bulaq became an anchor for the group's sense of belonging and took precedence over other identifications. The attachment to the old place is not single or one-dimensional and Bulaq is remembered and related to differently by gender and age groups. These differences are beyond the scope of this chapter but it is sufficient here to say that Bulaq is of great significance for most of the group in reimagining their communal feelings. Currently, their public housing is called after one of Bulaq's neighbourhoods (*masaakin al-Torgman*) and people express their strong attachment to their old place in songs and daily conversations. Despite the fact that relocation reordered relationships within the group and destroyed a major part of their support system, the old neighbourhood still structures parts of the people's current interaction. They still refer to the people who used to live in Bulaq as *"min 'andina"* (from our place) which not only creates a common ground for identification but also indicates certain expectations and mutual obligations between the people in the current area of residence. At the same time, Bulaq is the point of reference for their identification with those who still live in parts of Bulaq and those who moved to 'Ain Shams.

Through relocation, the group lost, among other things, a major part of its "symbolic capital". This is mainly manifested in two important aspects related to group members' identification with the old location. First, they used to live next to an upper-class neighbourhood, Zamalek. Young men and women, as emphasized by the people themselves and documented in a famous old movie (*A Bride from Bulaq*), could even claim that they were from Zamalek because only "a bridge" separated (or connected) the two neighbourhoods. People also lost the pleasure and satisfaction associated with looking at the beautiful buildings and knowing that people of Zamalek—and much to their shame, as described by one informant—used to see Bulaq with its old and shabby houses.

Second, the group used to live in an "authentic popular" or *baladi* area and perceives its relocation in al-Zawiya as moving down the social ladder. In Bulaq, the "authentic popular" quarter, people used to live next to each other, separated only by narrow lanes that allowed close interaction and strong relationships. They remember the old place in the way people used to cooperate and "eat together". Their rootedness in the same place over a long period of time provided people with a strong support system, open social relationships, and a sense of security and trust. In contrast, al-Zawiya is a relatively new neighbourhood. It was mainly agricultural fields until the 1960s, when the area started to expand rapidly with the state construction of the first public housing project. This project housed families from different parts of Cairo who could not afford to live in more central locations. Immigrants (mostly Muslims) also came to al-Zawiya from different parts of the countryside and many live in private housing. The heterogeneity of its population is used by its residents, especially members of the relocated group, and people around them to indicate that al-Zawiya is not "an authentic popular quarter". Its people are "selfish", "sneaky" and "untrustworthy". It is seen as located between *baladi* and *raqqi* (upper-class areas) which places it, as described by a male informant, in a tedious or annoying (*baaykh*) position. Al-Zawiya, thus, is geographically and socially marginal compared to Bulaq.

A key word in understanding the differences between what is seen as an "authentic" neighbourhood such as Bulaq and "less authentic" newer neighbourhoods such as al-Zawiya is *lama*. This word refers to the growing mixture and gathering of people from different backgrounds who live in the same locality. People from various quarters, villages and religions are coming to live in the same neighbourhood, hang out at the same coffee shop, visit the same market, and ride the same bus. These spaces are defined as *lamin* as compared to a more homogeneous or less *lama* places such as the village and the "authentic popular" quarter based on long established relationships. Being rooted in a certain area, that is, localized in a particular place, allows the development of strong relationships between people. *Lama* is used to classify different localities and points to the difference between a neighbourhood where people know each other by name and face as opposed to more heterogeneous areas where people are strangers and not to be trusted. *Masaakin* is *lama* as opposed to *ahali* housing. Al-Zawiya is *lama* compared to Bulaq and Cairo is *lama* compared to the villages where the inhabitants originally came from.

Relocation and Religious Identity

> Hegemony is not the disappearance or destruction of difference. It is the construction of a collective will through difference. It is the articulation of differences which do not disappear.
>
> (Hall, 1991:58)

Despite the significance of Bulaq in how people reimagine their communal feelings, this identity does not facilitate the group's interaction with the rest of the people who live in al-Zawiya al-Hamra. Relocation rearranged local identities and added to the old identifications: people are now identified with a village (the place of origin), as locals of

Bulaq (where they resided for generations), as occupiers of *masaakin* (which is stigmatized by dwellers in private housing) and as inhabitants of al-Zawiya al-Hamra (not known for its good reputation in Cairo). But above all, they are mainly Muslims. Religion, rather than nationalism, neighbourhood and the village of origin, became a powerful discourse in articulating and socially grounding the various identities of the different groups residing in al-Zawiya al-Hamra. Only the religious identity promises to articulate these identifications without destroying them. Displaced families, *ahali* and *masaakin* inhabitants, people of Bulaq and al-Zawiya, rural immigrants, *Fallahin* (peasants who come from villages in Lower Egypt) and *Sa'idis* (immigrants from Upper Egypt), who are largely pushed from their villages to Cairo in their search for work and a better life, as well as residents who moved from other areas of Cairo, can all find commonality in religion that is expressed in practices such as a dress code and the decoration of houses and shops.

Islam brings people together on the basis of a common religion. Despite the fact that Muslims do not know each other on a personal basis, religion creates a "safe" space (the mosque), a common ground where they are connected to each other, and a sense of trust and rootedness. This is clearly manifested in how the mosque, of all public spaces, is gaining importance in facilitating the interaction of various groups and the formation of a collective identity. To start with, the mosque's growing centrality in daily life is manifested in the many modern services that are provided to the people in it. Through charitable organizations (*jam'iyyat khayriyya*), the mosque provides socially required services such as affordable education, health care and financial support to the poor. It is also the place where discourses circulate that prescribe and/or forbid daily practices. Above all, it is the most acceptable and safest social space where various groups can meet and interact.

To understand the importance of the mosque, we need to go back to the word *lama*. As previously mentioned, people tend to distrust areas and public spaces that are labelled as *lama* such as the market, the coffee shop and the bus. These spaces are seen as "dangerous" and people are very careful when visiting or utilizing them. Compared to such spaces, the mosque, which is a historical space that is legitimated through its naturalized relationship with religion, is currently being actively articulated to frame the interaction between members of different groups as well as to empower emerging meanings, identities and relationships. Those who are labelled as trouble-makers and rude (people who come from Bulaq and live in *masaakin*) as well as the untrustworthy and selfish (people of al-Zawiya as described by people of Bulaq) can all meet in the mosque and collectively identify themselves as Muslims.

Thus, the power of the mosque is being currently reinforced through its promise of an equal and unified community out of a heterogeneous urban population. It is accessible to all Muslims and brings them in on equal terms. The unity of prayers and the importance of communal feelings are manifested in the unifying discourse and the similar movements that are performed simultaneously. The Imam leads the prayer and coordinates the movement of all the attendees through his pronounced signals that indicate when one should bend forward on the knees or stand up straight, and so on. Emphasis is placed upon standing in straight lines, very close to other attendees, in a way that leaves no empty spaces through which the devil could enter among the devout and divide their collectivity.

The feelings that are associated with being part of a collectivity were cited by many, especially by women, as one of the main reasons for going to the mosque. At the same time, the mosque not only brings people together from the same neighbourhood but also encourages people to move from one part of the city to the other. Young men and women, for example, use the city bus to tour the city in their search for the "truth". They cross the boundaries of their localities to go to other neighbourhoods to attend certain mosques where popular sheikhs preach.

The mosque is also becoming more open to women in al-Zawiya al-Hamra. This is perceived by some Islamic activists as essential to counter other spaces that are open to women, such as universities, the workplace, cinemas and nightclubs. Women are identified by men as more vulnerable to the influence of global (defined here as American) discourses and practices. Women's actions, dress and access to public life are seen as threatening the harmony of the Islamic community and as the source of many social ills. Women have internalized these ideas and hold themselves, and not men, responsible for the safety of the morals of the community. As women repeatedly emphasize, men are weak creatures and cannot resist the seduction imposed on them by women who do not adopt Islamic dress. At the same time, women can be very active in the construction of the Islamic community. More voices have emphasized the positive aspects associated with opening the mosque to women who, as mothers, sisters and wives, can be active agents capable of altering their own practices as well as shaping the actions and values of other family members. Thus, to contain the destructive potential of women and promote their constructive power in the formation of the Islamic community, more attempts are made by Islamic activists to incorporate women within the mosque. Currently, women, especially those without jobs and small children, go to the mosque on a regular basis for prayer and to attend weekly lessons, while working women usually attend the Friday prayer. Women are also becoming more active in the mosque through their roles as teachers, students, workers and seekers of social, educational and medical services. In addition, more women help in taking care of the mosque and participate in mosque-related activities such as preparing food and distributing it to the needy.

Globalization and Religious Identities

It is important not to confuse my previous discussion of religious identity with "fundamentalism", "extremism" or "militant Islam", which have been the centre of attention of several studies. Fundamentalism especially has been the focus of studies that aim to examine the relationship between globalization and religion. Such studies limit discussion of the ideology of the leaders of some radical Islamic groups and tend to present these movements as "responses" or "reactions" to the global. The role of ordinary people as active agents in negotiating religious and global discourses in their daily life and the formation of their local identities is largely neglected.

Despite the fact that communal feelings based on religion can be politicized and used as the basis to mobilize the working class (as happened in 1981 in clashes between Muslims and Christians in al-Zawiya al-Hamra), at the daily level religious identity brings people together as connected selves rather than separated and isolated others. It articulates the presence of the group at the neighbourhood level, integrates its members into the mosque and secures a space for them in Cairo. People do not want to relive the past, as some fundamentalists seem to desire, but try to live in the present with its complexity and contradictions. They hence struggle against efforts of some extremist groups who try to impose restrictions on how they appropriate certain aspects of modernity. Nuha, for example, is a twenty-three-year-old woman with a high school diploma who works in a factory outside the neighbourhood. She hears things on the radio, in the mosque and from her friends and then lets her heart and mind judge what she will follow. She expresses her religiosity in adopting the *khimar*. At the same time, she opposes many of the restrictions that extremists try to impose on people, such as forbidding men from wearing trousers and prohibiting eating with a spoon because, as some argue, the Prophet did not do these things. She believes that had these things existed when the Prophet was alive, he would have used them. So it is not a sin (*haram*) to eat with a spoon but, if one chooses to eat with the hands, one will get an extra reward.

The opposition to the "global West", however, is not sufficient to explain the growing importance of the mosque and religious identity in al-Zawiya al-Hamra. There are complex local and national forces juxtaposed with the global to produce religious identity. State oppression, the daily frustrations in dealing with state bureaucracy, alienation, the fragmentation of the urban fabric, and the ability of Islamic groups to utilize various discursive strategies that mobilize people are as important as the economic frustration, the unfulfilled expectations and desires, and the need to have a voice in the global in understanding why religious identity is becoming more hegemonic.

As manifested in the services that are being attached to the mosque in al-Zawiya al-Hamra, certain global discourses and consumer goods are negotiated and appropriated. For example, to avoid state censorship of discourses circulated in the mosque, Islamic activists use cassette tapes to distribute the religious discourse to a large segment of the urban population. Especially for illiterate men and women, tapes provide a powerful means of communication that brings popular preachers (that is, those who are believed to tell the "truth") from the mosque into the home, the workplace, the taxi and the street. These can be replayed until their meanings become clear to the listener. Women can also pass them on to friends and relatives. On several occasions, women gathered to listen to such tapes and expressed strong emotional reactions to the descriptions of death, the horrible torture of the grave and the soothing visions of heaven.

Although the emphasis on the dress code can be seen as a rejection of the influence of the West, I would argue that gender distinctions are the centre of the restrictions applied to women's dress code. Another interesting example could be found in how people negotiate their definition of Islam and modernity. Their rejection of many of the ideas that are circulated by some religious extremists is clearly manifested by the struggle over some consumer goods such as colour televisions, VCRs and tape-recorders which are rapidly becoming signs of distinction. Many families participate in saving associations (*gam'iyyat*) to secure money to buy these goods which are also seen as investments that can be easily exchanged for needed cash.

Television is one of the most popular goods that people incorporate as one of the basic elements of their daily lives. Except for very few people with extreme religious beliefs, there is no housing unit in al-Zawiya al-Hamra without a television set. Each family, regardless of its income, owns a television set that is the centre of attention of all the family members. The television set is a powerful medium that conveys to them many experiences and values that can be described as global and brings the Other closer than ever to the self. The television set and the mosque are competing with each other to connect Muslims in different parts of the world. People of al-Zawiya al-Hamra are connected with other Muslims whom they have never met and who are not assumed to be identical duplicates of the self but are identified as the Other that is closely connected with the self. It is the force that binds people of this neighbourhood with Muslims who fight in Bosnia, Afghanistan and Chechnya. Young men, who are frustrated with the state's restriction on their participation in fighting with the Bosnian Muslims, circulate stories about God's help and support of the Bosnians. People talk about invisible soldiers (angels) and unidentified white planes that bomb the Serbs. Islam, thus, is becoming a force in localizing the global and globalizing the local. The distinction between Muslims who live in al-Zawiya al-Hamra and those who live in the rest of the world (such as the Bosnians) is blurred. On the other hand, television is blamed by Islamic groups for corrupting the people, silencing them, and distracting their attention from God as well as from what happens in their country and the rest of the world. With the total state control of this powerful medium, various Islamic groups do not have any option but to denounce its role in society and try to forbid it.

People are capable of articulating different discourses within their religious identity without seeing contradictions in being oriented to the global and attempting to enjoy what it offers, and being rooted in their religious and local identities. A twenty-year-old factory worker, who was born in Bulaq and was relocated with his family in 1980, dreams of having enough money to buy a villa in Switzerland for skiing during the winter, another villa in India where he will hire singers and dancers to perform for him as he has seen on video tapes, and of a palace in Saudi Arabia to facilitate his performing of pilgrimage every year. As Hall (1991) emphasizes, with identity there are no guarantees. The openness and fluidity of identities and the multiple discourses that are competing to shape them make it hard to guarantee whether an identity is going to be inclusive or exclusive.

Conclusion

> Paradoxically in our world, marginality has become a powerful space. It is a
> space of weak power but it is a space of power, nonetheless.
>
> (Hall, 1991: 34)

I have tried to show in this chapter how the articulation of global discourses and processes is producing contradictory identities at the national and local levels. By destroying old neighbourhood relationships, stigmatizing and physically segregating the relocated population, the project that aimed to construct modern subjects has paradoxically produced antagonistic local identities that empowered the basis of a collective identity which is based on religion. I have also aimed to show the important role of active social agents in mediating the different global practices and selectively articulating certain global discourses in the formation of their local identities. Social agents face the global in collectivities rather than as individuals and the struggle between the local and the global is not simply taking place in human minds. In general, although "new regimes of accumulation" (Hall 1991: 30) are appealing to the individual, alienation, racism and uprootedness are being faced collectively. In fact, being part of a collectivity is necessary to feel at home in the modern world with its rapid global changes. Thus, the local is not passive and local cultural identities are not waiting to be wiped out by globalization as some authors suggest.

Amal's dreams should continue to remind us that people experience the global in structured ways. It should also draw our attention to the fact that many of the writings on globalization are conducted by people who feel at home in the global and tend to celebrate the growing efficiency of transportation, electronic communication and the growing connectedness of the globe (see, for example, Friedland and Boden, 1994). The freedom of travel, however, while experienced by the privileged, is denied for millions of people who find borders of the global (especially, the USA and Europe) closed to them. The relationship between the local and the global cannot be brushed aside by assuming that they are articulated as one. Such statements reduce the complexity of the interaction between the global and the local and ignore the asymmetrical relationship that is still central to this interaction. The analysis presented in this chapter points to the need for more attention and sensitivity to the structured nature of globalization processes. When people experience the global as a violent attack on their cultural identities and self-images, it is not strange that they do not embrace global discourses and its representatives (such as international tourists). In short, more attention should be devoted to those who live on the margin of the marginal: those who are displaced in their own "culture" and the millions who cannot find solutions to the growing number of desires that are brought by the global except through magical means, death and destruction or religion that at least promises them a better life and the glories of eternal existence in Paradise.

References

Berman, M. *All That is Solid Melts into Air: The Experience of Modernity*. (New York: Penguin Books, 1988).

Bourdieu, P. *Algeria 1960*. (Cambridge: Cambridge University Press, 1979).

Friedland, R. and D. Boden (eds.) *Nowhere: Space, Time and Modernity* (California: California University Press, 1994).

Hall, S. 'Old and New Identities, Old and New Ethnicities.' In A.D. King (ed.) *Culture, Globalization and the World-System*. (SUNY: Binghampton, 1991).

Harvey, D. *The Condition of Postmodernity*. (Cambridge: Basil Blackwell, 1990).

Rabinow, P. *The Foucault Reader*. (New York: Pantheon, 1984).

El-Sadat, A.. *In Search of Identity*. (London: Collins, 1978).

This paper originally appeared in A. Öncü amd P. Weyland (eds.) *Space, Culture and Power* (Zed Books,1997): 119–139. It is printed here with the permission of the publisher.

SAMIR KHALAF

The Bourj as a Cosmopolitan Public Sphere

Despite its chequered history, the Bourj, more than its adjoining quarters and eventual outlying suburban districts, has always served as a vibrant and cosmopolitan "melting pot" of diverse groups and socio-cultural transformations. While other neighbourhoods and districts of the expanding city attracted distinct sectarian, ethnic, class and ideological groups and communities and eventually evolved into segregated and bounded urban enclosures—the Bourj always managed to remain a fairly open and homogenizing space.

It is this openness and receptivity to new encounters, particularly foreign cultures, competing educational missions, European trade and an incessant inflow of goods, itinerant groups and borrowed ideologies that account for both its resonant pluralism and assimilating character. These three forces—pluralism, receptivity to change and tolerance to others—became the defining elements of Beirut's centre. It is also those features that accounted for its emergence and survival as a public sphere (I am employing the term here in its conventional sociological usage as propounded by Habermas and reformulated by a score of other contemporary scholars).

Habermas, it must be recalled, traced the emergence of the public sphere back to the eighteenth century when various forums for public debate—clubs, coffee houses, newspapers and periodicals—proliferated. Much like other classical thinkers, he argued that these forms expedited the erosion of feudalism, which was legitimated by religion and custom rather than by agreements and consensus arrived at through public debate, open and unfettered discourse. As such, these emergent forums were of particular relevance and appeal to dislocated groups seeking to forge new identities and consolidate anchorage in the social fabric of the new social order. He went on to argue that such public spheres were given impetus by the extension of market economies and the resulting liberation of the individual from the constraints of feudal and other primordial ties of loyalty.

Newly liberated citizens, particularly the nascent bourgeoisie of property-holders, merchants and traders, among other new sectors in society, could now become active participants in advocacy groups and voluntary associations. At the least, they now had access to vectors through which they could mobilise their concerns about issues of governance and, possibly, participate in dissenting ideological groups to redress the dislocations and injustices in society. But that which enables can also disable. In a perspective that draws heavily on Max Weber's analysis of rationalisation, Habermas argued that the public sphere is threatened by some of the very forces that accounted for its expansion. In other words, as market economies become unstable, the state normally steps in to enforce greater measure of control. With the expansion of the powers of state into virtually all dimensions of social and everyday life, the public sphere is dwarfed. More dishearteningly, and much like other critical theorists, Habermas warns that the state can now seek to redefine problems as technical ones which can hence only be readdressed by technologies and administrative venues rather than by public debate, open discourse and argumentation (Habermas, 1984). Given these resolute and overwhelming constraints, the problem of resurrecting and safeguarding the enabling features of a public sphere becomes all the more vital in the context of post-war Beirut. Such prospects are considerably more compelling since they now involve resisting the impervious risks not only of an inept and unresponsive government bureaucracy but also of the distant forces of globalism and mass-consumerism. Within this context, this chapter explores two related dimensions. First, the genesis and evolution of the Bourj as a public sphere is elucidated. Second, an attempt is made to document and account for how it has managed over the years to reinvent its identity and public image.

Genesis and Emergence as a Public Sphere

The character and role the Bourj came to assume as a vibrant and cosmopolitan public sphere cannot, naturally, Be appreciated without reference to its historic setting as an open and unbounded *maidan, sahl* or *sahat*. It evolved, after all, next to a walled and fortified urban sanctuary. This defining element survived throughout its history. However, it started to embellish and consolidate those features during the first half of the nineteenth century.

Partly because of its compact size and predominantly commercial character, the intermingling and collaboration between the various communities were both inevitable and vital for their coexistence arid survival. Typical of a so-called "merchant republic traders" and entrepreneurs of various communities were partners in private business ventures. They assisted each other in times of austerity and financial need. More importantly, they perceived themselves as members of an urban merchant elite, resisting the hostile elements that threatened their common economic interests.

In the old *souks* and bazaars flanking the Bourj, artisans and traders worked side by side. Spatial segregation and location of shops was occupational and not religious in character. Much like the spatial layout of residential quarters elsewhere in the burgeoning city beyond the Bourj, the bazaars and retail outlets were strikingly uniform in their architectural features. On the whole, social interaction was characterized by sentiments of goodwill and mutual tolerance and personal ties of intimacy, familiarity and trust. Such mutual cooperation was not confined to domestic and commercial relations. It spilled over into other spheres of public life. Christians and Muslims continued to meet together at official functions and served on the same committees, courts and mixed tribunals. For example, during the period of national struggle against Ottoman repression and centralisation of the Young Turks at the turn of the century, between 1880 and 1908, Christians and Muslims transcended their communal differences and participated collectively in underground political movements and secret societies.

Likewise, during the emancipatory struggle for independence and subsequent mass protest movements and demonstrations in support of labour unions, women suffrage, Palestinian mobilisation and other dispossessed groups, the Bourj always served as a vector and rallying ground for giving voice on behalf of neglected and marginalised segments of society. Student demonstrations, often with heightened confrontational strategies, reserved their most virulent expressions to the Bourj.

In the Mandate era, the resort to such public spheres became more pronounced. Elizabeth Thompson advances two plausible structural forces underlying this change (Thompson, 2000). First, the public underwent a massive expansion with the growth of transport and communication, public services such as schooling and health care, new entertainment venues such as cinemas and public parks and the publishing of newspapers and magazines. Second, the public was steadfastly emerging as a public sphere and primary political arena, particularly in the 1930s when the Parliament was shut down by the French for half a decade. Mass demonstrations, market closures, even street battles became the *modus operandi* of the nascent post-colonial political culture. Urban *zua'ma* and other urban notables mobilised their client groups in protest. Dissenting and subaltern movements and other excluded groups took to the street to voice their dissent. Turf battles with the French forces for control of urban space and the virtual public space (freedom of speech and media) became frequent.

The Bourj, largely because the Petit Serail, built in 1883, which served first as headquarters for the Ottoman postal service and later, from 1926 to 1950, became the official "palace" for Lebanese presidents, was the ultimate destination of all public demonstrations. Public protests were legion in the 1940s, particularly demonstrations against poor living standards, inadequate distribution of flour and public-sector workers seeking better pay.

One interesting and unusual feature of the Bourj accounts for the role it played as meeting place for itinerant groups. At a time when transport, telephone, electronic and other virtual forms of communication were nonexistent, the outlets the Bourj devised for such valued access were both inventive and functional. For example, the mushrooming hotels, pensions, *locandas* and residences were used as transit stops and meeting grounds. A nascent hotel industry, as early as the 1830s, was already developed to accommodate the growing stream of foreign travellers. Travellers to the interior always sought to stop in Beirut en route. Travelogues are ecstatic in their praise of the elegance of the hotels they encountered at the time. Some of the graceful hotels, especially the *locandas* and "casinos" (with their terrace-cafes, patisseries and Levantine dragomen) built and managed first by Greeks, Maltese, Italians and then eventually native Lebanese, all came into being during the second half of the nineteenth century. The westward flanks, fronted on the Mediterranean and adjoining the old city (between the Zeitouneh quarter and Minet el Husn Bay) were particularly appealing for such growth. The most legendary were the Grand Hotel d'Orient (Bassoul's), Victoria, Casino Alphonse, Continental (Normandy), Universe and later, in 1930, the Hotel St Georges.

The upsurge in the number of hotels, restaurants and bars is almost similar to the preponderance of these outlets today. In about five years, from 1923 to 1929, the number of hotels nearly doubled and continued to increase in the 1930s. The number of restaurants and bars also increased considerably in the same period: from twenty-one to thirty-two.

Local groups, villagers frequenting the city to attend to their exigent needs, had their own chains of residences and pensions. Interestingly, some of these premises became associated with particular villages. For example, Hotel America became almost the exclusive preserve of visitors from Zahle. To groups in the throes of completing final arrangements or awaiting designated ocean liners for their anguishing departure from Lebanon, these hotels, such as Kawkab, America, Orient Palace, Victoria, Royal, etc, became settings charged with drama and emotional contagion.

Not only hotels but also bus and car terminals, transport agencies, especially coffee houses, served as meeting points for villagers. It was common for Beirut residents to deliver and receive their mail, messages and parcels of personal effects via such venues. To villagers seeking jobs, contacts and other city chores, these places became expedient stopgaps and surrogate homes and offices. Some coffee houses placed makeshift mailboxes for such purposes. Others became intimately associated with particular groups.

This is, doubtlessly, the interlude in Beirut's urban history when displaced and uprooted groups—largely because of the quickening pace of urbanisation—felt the need to reconnect by seeking refuge in urban spaces amenable to such informal and associational contacts. Virtually all such collective public amenities were converted into public spheres. For example, at a time when recognised clubs, galleries, auditoriums and other formal public venues were still rare, coffee houses, restaurants and bars became expedient haunts for intellectuals, artists, poets, journalists and politicians. As early as the 1930s such places acquired notoriety precisely because they became meeting places for particular groups. Regular clients who patronised these places knew exactly what to expect, particularly since the outlets were intimately associated with popular figures and celebrities of the day. Coffee houses like Abou Afif, Republique and Parisienne were frequented by a close circle of poets of the likes of al-Akhtal al-Saghir, Elias Abou Shabakeh, Amin Nakhleh and Said Akl. Singers, performers, songwriters, such as Assad Saba, al-Sibaaly, Zaki Nassif and the Rahbani Brothers, were drawn to the Roxy Bar and Hawi. Journalists and politicians were more likely to be found in Farouq, which later changed its name to Abd al-Nasir. Even when regular public venues, such as the Lebanese Academy of Arts (ALBA), the Lebanese Cenacle and Dar al-Fan, established or relocated their premises close to the centre during the 1940s, these did not detract from the appeal or popularity of the traditional places.

This symbiotic coexistence between traditional outlets and the more specialised, commercial and corporate-like organisations continued throughout the post-independence period and beyond. Indeed, this proclivity to accommodate such "third spaces" was a distinctive attribute of the Bourj. The growth of secular and impersonal associations throughout the 1960s, and until the outbreak of civil hostilities in the mid-1970s, did not displace the conventional shopkeepers, artisans and neighbourhood stores. They merely enriched the plurality and diversity of outlets. Hence, seemingly disparate groups felt equally at home: the villager and regular neighbourhood customer who was seeking familiarity and personal contacts and the itinerant visitor and tourist after novelty and adventure. In other words, both the footloose flaneur and the rooted conformist did not feel any dissonance in the spaces they were sharing.

Because of the protracted civil unrest and the unsettling political circumstances of the past decade, Lebanon lost one of its most coveted venues as an international public sphere. During much of the 1960s and 1970s, as political instability in adjacent regimes was at its height, Lebanon became especially appealing for hosting summits, international gatherings, multinational corporate meetings, academic conferences, symposia and cultural festivals. This has been restored lately. Indeed, its post-war setting, in view of its auspicious process of recovery, has become particularly inviting for such international gatherings.

For example, in preparation for the Francophone and the Arab Summits in October 2002 and much like other such episodes, these became occasions to give Beirut a quick and much-needed face-lift. Gutted buildings that still bore the pockmarks of war were spruced up and festooned with banners and draped with flags and colourful national logos of the twenty-two Arab states. Roads were freshly macadamised and landscaped; sidewalks, doorways, lampposts were spotless and emblazoned with fresh colours.

There was clearly more than banal cosmetics to the spectacles surrounding the eventful summits. Beirut was not just a showcase. Having suffered the deprecating image—often no more than an ugly metaphor for all the brutish "Hobbsian" wars of self-destruction—Lebanon was, of course, eager to display its other, more benevolent image: that of a tolerant and cosmopolitan capital equipped to host, once again, peace conferences and forums for open and reconciliatory dialogue. A few optimistic observers harked back to earlier glories, to remind sceptics of how much the country had done in this respect on behalf of its bickering Arab states. One popular weekly magazine drew an analogy with the last such gathering Lebanon was privileged to host in 1956 in the wake of the Suez crisis. The Arab League summit at the time, presided over by President Camille Chamoun, denounced the joint Israeli, English and French incursions into Egypt. Just as that momentous summit had led to the Israeli withdrawal from Sinai, the magazine expressed the hope that the current summit might well mobilise global pressure to evict the Israeli forces out of the Gaza Strip and the West Bank.

Re-inventing its Identity and Public Image

Throughout its chequered history, and largely because of the multicultural and pluralistic layers of ancient civilizations it sheltered, the Bourj had to reinvent itself repeatedly to accommodate the relentless succession of imperial occupations. The most intractable public label has, of course, been the Bourj—in reference to the imposing tower guarding its seafront ramparts.

Consistent with its ubiquitous and evolving national character, the popular labels and nomenclatures attributed to it have always been in flux and contested. It is rather telling that the first urban form the Bourj assumed was *"al Maidan"*, one which prefigured some of the subsequent striking developments, particularly in its role as a collective common ground, a (public sphere) for itinerant and unanchored social groups. The *maidan* should not be dismissed as merely a fortuitous and insignificant interlude. As it evolved, it incorporated elements which account for the dual role it came to play and, hopefully, will continue to do so in yet another reinvented form: an open space— *"sahat"*—which is not a wilderness, a common ground which is not a home.

From its inception as an open, amorphous *maidan* (and this is how it was first labelled), the Bourj never served as a distinct enclosure or sanctuary. Rather, it acted as an open ground that exacted a measure of collective attachment. This is, after all, what the notion of *maidan*, in its Persian origins, conjures up. It came to be identified with images of plains, meadows, grounds or fields. In its Persian context it was primarily associated with pilgrims, traders and militias. As it found expression in other contexts, such as Cairo, Bombay, Ahmedabad, Calcutta, etc, it embraced many other elements and uses. Throughout, however, the idea of the *maidan* emerged as a result of human intervention directed not toward the addition of identity, events or character but rather towards keeping land free and indeterminate and therefore negotiable. Hence, it should not be confused with enclosed courtyards or cultivated parks. Nor is it a desolate wilderness, a dreary, parched stretch of land. Rather, as A. Mathur (1999) suggested, it is somewhere in- between; it is both nomadic and collective. It is, in fact, close to what Ivan Illich calls "commons", or:

> ... that part of the environment that lay beyond a person's own threshold and outside his own possession, but to which, however, that person had a recognized claim of usage—not to produce commodities but to provide for the subsistence of kin. Neither wilderness nor home is commons, but that part of the environment for which customary law exacts specific forms of community respect.
>
> *Mathur, 1999*

A striking feature of the *maidan*, which is of particular relevance to the Bourj's emergence and metamorphosis, is its predisposition to embrace a diversity of cultures while containing measures of neutrality, anonymity and transcending attributes. As Mathur puts it:

> In cities of increasingly circumscribed social, racial, or economic enclaves, the *maidan* has come to both symbolize and provide neutral territory, a ground where people can gather on a common plane. It is a place that offers freedom without obligation. This ability to accommodate a diverse range of social and political structures makes the *maidan* an extremely significant space in the city. It is a place where people can touch the spirit of commonness.
>
> *Mathur, 1999*

Given the scarcity and inevitable intensification and competition for the use of precious urban space, a realistic re-appropriation of a *maidan* in its original concept or form is naturally a remote likelihood in central Beirut. Its underlying spirit and sentiment are, however, still realisable. Indeed, because of the disappearance of many historical *maidans*, efforts are being made today to appropriate landscapes that lend themselves to both settled and nomadic or ephemeral elements. Hence, open spaces— *"sahls"* and *"sahas"*—made once again available for urban redevelopment are rare and challenging interludes for urban designers. Levelled and open spaces can once again offer rare opportunities to reclaim a measure of freedom and spontaneity within the enclosure of the city. All adjoining areas radiating from Beirut's centre are increasingly commodified, deliberately monitored and exploited in ways that are bound to discourage any spontaneous appropriation or unplanned development. Within such seemingly impervious constraints, where urbanists and landscape architects are seeking efforts to promote qualities of indeterminacy and open-mindedness, the Bourj offers such rare and coveted opportunities.

Naturally, as a reality, *al Maidan's* lifespan was short-lived. Gradually, and with signs of intermittent habitation, it started to acquire the interchanging labels of *sahat* or *sahl*: that is, an open plain. No sooner had itinerant groups started settling within the adjoining remains of the fortified medieval embankments, the Bourj became literally, *"sahat-al-sour"*. For a while—to this day in fact—old-timers, veteran taxi and service car drivers continue to employ the colloquial expression of *"as-Sour"*.

The first definitive change in its public identity occurred in 1772. The imperial Russian fleet, part of the Russian military expedition of 1772, had installed five massive pieces of artillery on its elevated fortifications. According to one source, the cannons were used to destroy much of the fortification of the old medieval walls. Hence the appellation *"Place des Canons"* acquired its notoriety. By 1860, it was the imperial cannons of the French fleet that reinforced that label this time. Prior to that and for a brief interlude after 1850, when Beirut's centre was largely desolate, with only a few nomadic Bedouins from the interior who occupied one of its remaining fortified towers, it bore the designation of *"Sahat Bourj el Kachef"*.

When the French army entered Beirut in the wake of the 1860 civil disturbances, Poujoulat was quite impressed by the sight of this "300 by 150-metre square" with its multicoloured "omnibus" which took passengers to the pine forest at fifteen-minute intervals. He was particularly impressed by the French character of the square with its stylish restaurants, cafés, shops and boutiques *"tenues par des Français"* which made their appearance shortly after the Crimean War. With such preferential hints in favour of the "Frenchness" of the square, its colonial manifestations were deliberately muted by successive Ottoman *walis*. Indeed, by the time Wilhelm II, the German Emperor, made his historic visit to Beirut in 1898, he had labelled it as the "jewel in the crown of the Padishah".

Incidentally, the Emperor's visit, hailed as a milestone in German-Ottoman goodwill, was an occasion to dress up Beirut in its edifying and ceremonial best. Special committees of Ottoman municipal authorities and the city's notables were established to oversee the spectacles and reception prepared for the event. As municipal engineer, Yusuf Aftimos was commissioned to decorate the square and adjacent roadways.

A crowd of 50,000, along with the city's entire student population who enjoyed a special holiday to mark the occasion, had lined the streets along the designated route of the procession. The emperor's guided tour of the spruced-up city ended in *"Sahat al-Bourj"* as it was called then:

> While refreshments were served, His Majesty feasted his eyes on the beautiful view of the city, the harbour, and the deep blue sea. In the other direction, he looked across a densely wooded plain up to the heights of Mount Lebanon ... the return trip resembled a triumphal procession. The route was flanked by countless people, all cheering endlessly. Night had already set in as the procession continued through the brightly illuminated city, across the Canon Square with its decorative public garden, and down to the harbour. Everywhere the streets, the windows, and balconies were lined with people, who were outdoing each other in expressing their joy.
>
> *Hanssen, 2005*

Long before Beirut became capital of the provincial Ottoman *Wilaya* in 1888, *Sahat al-Bourj* was perceived as a potential visual corridor between its port and the traditional city. Imperial Ottoman authorities were adept at exploiting such recurrent rituals of ceremonial commemoration to reinforce the monumentality and visibility of their imposing architecture and public squares. In their initial and subsequent efforts at creating and regulating public spaces, *Sahat al-Bourj* had been a special target of such Ottomanisation. The first such efforts of regularization, shortly after 1860, were predominantly infrastructural in character.

By 1863 the Beirut–Damascus road (originally planned in 1851) was completed, thereby strengthening the link with Damascus and territory beyond Mount Lebanon and the coast. The centrality of the Bourj was reinforced further. A tolled caravan route extended from Bourj in a valley between the Achrafiyeh area and the western regions of Moussaytbeh and Mazraa. Under Dawoud Pasha (1861–8) the streets of Beirut were widened and macadamized to accommodate carriages of the French Damascus Road Company. Greek Orthodox merchants benefited financially from the improving regional economic role of Beirut. In 1873, under Rustum Pasha, a public garden at Hazmieh was constructed on the outskirts of Beirut. Regular festivals and orchestral performances, from which commoners with ordinary native garb were excluded, were held on Sundays.

During the Mutesarrifate, the Municipal Council of Beirut launched a series of magisterial and eye-catching projects in 1879. It is interesting to note in this regard that, unlike other Ottoman provinces, private initiative and foreign capital contributed heavily to changing the urban landscape, particularly in the wake of the economic boom during the last decade or so of the nineteenth century. Initiated at that time, this form of private intervention or concern for the regulation of public space became, off and on, a recurrent feature. For example, as early as 1879, when Fakhry Bek launched his landscaping project of the public garden in the Bourj, about thirty families contributed to the effort. The newspaper *Lisan al-Hal* assumed leadership in supporting the campaign for the beautification of the *sahat*. Special feature-articles appeared, pronouncing and advocating the needs—planting of trees, lanterns, pathways, etc—virtues and appeals of a public garden in such a compelling central space. The paper also launched a subscription campaign and would list, by way of promotion, names, identities and the pledged sums of individual contributors.

The construction of the Petit Serail in 1883 naturally prodded municipal authorities to undertake the first landscape design for the open field or *"al-sahla"* into its front, picturesque courtyard, as it were. An imposing octagonal kiosk with an ostentatious fountain lined with trees and shrubs and decorated with Ottoman-style architectural ornaments became the new landmark of Beirut's centre. It was also then that the nondescript open field or plain (*al-sahla*) was transformed into a fairly modern square (*al-saha*). By then the square had already attracted typical central urban junctions and outlets: transport terminals, banks and government-controlled public enterprises.

This *"Muntazah"*, as it was initially labelled, became the edifying centerpiece of the Bourj. Perhaps because of its novelty and the patrons it drew from a cross-section of the social fabric, the Bourj starred to attract other outdoor cultural outlets for public entertainment. A music kiosk was built. From then on, the Bourj began to evolve into an urban hub or loop which drew in and around it a variety of activities ranging from official state and municipal bureaucracies, travel terminals, hotels, *locandas*, sidewalk cafés to business and retail stores, popular *souks* and other more seamy outlets such as brothels, bars, gambling joints and houses of assignation.

Soon, however, because of its novelty as a public garden, the *Muntazah* started to arouse public concerns about how to shelter it from abuse and neglect. Newspaper accounts of the period ran stories in opposition to the measures taken by the government to fence in the picturesque oval garden or to monitor and restrict public access to it. Others were proposing the destruction of the makeshift shops, stores and shabby, unkempt stalls which mushroomed around the well-tended oval and were, it seems, the source of much disorder and criminality.

Jurji Zeidan, in a poignant autobiographical sketch, tells how for eight years of his sheltered adolescence he was called upon to serve as bellhop in his father's *locanda* located in 1872 in one of the poor, unruly and rundown districts adjoining the Bourj. He recalled how he had to brace himself to cope, at such a tender age, with all the dreadful and aberrant manifestations pervading the area. He bemoaned his surroundings for being the tempting spot for derelicts, deviants and the unemployed, replete with drunkards, gamblers, prostitutes, tempestuous and shady characters.

One might possibly view in this regard the emergence of *Sahat al-Sur* located on the south western flanks of the old city, within this context. It became a natural outlet for the working-class neighbourhoods of Basta and Bashura. Migrant and daily workers would congregate early in the morning in the hopes of being recruited at one of the construction sites within the city. The installation of a new Ottoman telegraph office on the northern end of the *sahat*, next to the public *hammam* (*Zahrat Suriyya*), did not detract from its popular and local character. Unlike the comparatively more orderly and landscaped Bourj Square, *al-Sur* was unbounded and without any marked encircling footpaths or pavements. Hence, perhaps because of its intimate and unstructured character, it continued to be an attractive spot for lower-class coffee houses and other popular haunts. The construction of the tramway, between 1907 and 1909, connected *al-Sur* to other neighbourhoods of the expanding city: the port and Khan Antoun Bey to the north, Nahr Beirut to the east and Ras al-Nabá and beyond to the south.

Naturally, *Sahat al-Sur* was not planned or intended that way. Like other public squares, it acquired a life of its own, unrelated to its original intention. Converting the *sahat* into a public park dated back to 1869 when the newly established municipality appropriated and tore down, not without public outcry, all recently built popular shops and stores. Once again, on the occasion of celebrating Abdulhamid II's jubilee, on 1 September 1900, *Sabil Sahat al-Sur*, with an eight-metre tall white marble fountain, was inaugurated with the pomp and circumstance the Ottomans relished and admired. With the usual contrived crowds waving imperial banners and background military music, the governor turned on the water and ritualistically drank the first cup from the *sabil* pipes. Like the Qantari clock tower, it was designed by Yusif Aftimos. Two prominent local craftsmen contributed to the artistic embellishment of the fountain.

Clearly the Ottomans had special regard for public parks and squares. With an eye for monumentality and spatial visibility, such open spaces were not perceived for their edifying urbanist and aesthetic elements. Rather, their intention was to embody and promote the Hamidian personality cult and inspire a sense of public gratitude and awe to the benevolent sultan. Ironically, the very spaces and monuments intended to reinforce public loyalty and commitment worked to undermine Ottoman and imperial sovereignty. The public spaces became venues for public demonstrations and the mobilization of anti-government protest. Somehow, Ottoman authorities never quite mastered the exacting requirements for managing the control of public spaces. Over the years, al-Bourj, in particular, was highly political and became a paramount political space for public processions and the mobilisation of public dissent on behalf of a variety of national issues and causes. Quite often the demonstrations transcended provincial and local concerns and addressed foreign issues.

For example, as early as 1908, when Austria had annexed Bosnia-Herzegovina, a group of Beiruti notables, intellectuals and public figures organized a street demonstration to protest Austria's violation of the Berlin Treaty.

Another dramatic interlude or threshold in the metamorphosis of tile Bourj was the succession of labels and changes in its identity it had to undergo under the Ottomans. First, it acquired the label of *"Sahat al-Ittihad"* or *"al-Hamidiyyah"* in reference to its Ottoman legacy, the former as an expression of the desired national unity under Ottoman sovereignty and the latter in commemoration of sultan Abdul Hamid. By the time Prince Faysal Ibn al-Husayn made his triumphant visit in May 1919, *Sahat el-Hamidiyyah* became *"Hadiqat al-Hurriyah"* ("freedom or liberation from Turkish oppression").

Freedom and liberation from Ottoman oppression did not, of course, lapse without exacting its heavy toll on a select group of recalcitrant nationalists. Beginning 21 August 1915, Jamal Pasha used the open square of the Bourj to execute, by public hanging, the first group of eleven martyrs. This was followed in 1916 by three other such nationally dreaded executions on 5 April, 6 May and 5 June respectively. Journalistic accounts of the day reveal widespread feelings of collective anguish, trepidation and pride. In 1937, 6 May was declared a national memorial day. The commemoration of martyrs, given the repeated victimization of innocent civilians with which the country has been beleaguered, is naturally a solemn and fitting commemoration.

Commissioning and securing a measure of public consensus on the design and ultimate installation of the memorial was fraught with problems and bitter controversy. The first statue, the work of the prominent Lebanese sculptor Joseph Hoayek in 1930, depicted two grieving women *("Deux Pleureuses")*—a Muslim and a Christian—lamenting the fate of their children. Because of its avowed sectarian motif, the statue became the target of intense and sustained disapproval. So rancorous was the objection that by 1952 the government announced an international competition for all alternate memorial. The winning design by a Lebanese architect, Sami Abdul Baqi, did not fare any better. It depicted a monumental arch enveloping an obelisk and an elliptic arcade of sixteen columns representing the number of martyrs. The project remained a celebrated but unrealized maquette.

Finally it was not until 6 May 1960 that the monument, the work of the Italian sculptor Mazacurati, was at last installed in an official ceremony presided by President Fuad Shihab and Prime Minister Saeb Salam. This too was not uncontested. Although its overall aesthetic and elegant quality was deemed admirable and refined, the monument was criticized for several shortcomings, particularly what was perceived as the "un-Lebanese" features of its four celebrated figures. The theme is one of freedom and liberation, with a woman bearing a torch in one hand and enfolding a young man with the other. Two martyrs enshrine the base of the statue. The artist defended his choice by maintaining that he had wandered through various parts of the country and taken reams of photographs to capture the defining facial and physical features of the archetypal or quintessential Lebanese. He argued that the most pronounced features have much in common with those prevalent in the southern regions of the Mediterranean.

The imposing statue continued to grace the central spot of *Sahat al-Shuhada* (Martyrs' Square), until the outbreak of the civil war. Repeated rounds of heavy street fighting scarred and defaced the statue with deep gaping dents and shrapnel holes. Mercifully, the statue was whisked away to a safe hideout at Kaslik University. Artists commissioned to rehabilitate the statue were successful, in my view, in retaining its war-scarred character: a fitting memorial of Lebanon's belligerent past. Although the statue was ready, it did not reclaim its rightful place in Martyrs' Square without a contentious, often embarrassing, tug-of-war between President Emile Lahhoud and Rafik Hariri, prime minister at the time. As major shareholder in Solidere, Hariri was naturally eager to see such a national icon restored to its historic place. Given Lahhoud's visceral animosity to whatever Hariri stood for, he resorted to his hackneyed and dubious alibis to procrastinate. Incidentally, the Hariri family, through Banque Mediterranée, owns around 8 per cent of Solidere. The remaining shares are divided among more than 6,000 shareholders. No individual or company is allowed to own more than 10 per cent of Solidere. With a market capitalization of more than 1.6 billion dollars, Solidere is considered the largest firm in Lebanon.

A momentous turn of fateful events, propelled by Hariri's brutal murder on 14 February 2005, transformed the Bourj once again into a spectacular public sphere for the mobilization of collective enthusiasm, emancipatory movements and voices of dissent. The solemn funeral procession of Hariri was not just a stunning and hushed outpouring of grief. It turned into a resounding collective protest, transcending all the fractious loyalties and divisions within society. The uprising had all the uplifting elements of a pure and spontaneous, consciousness-raising happening. Unlike other forms of protest, it was an emotionally charged rally, not a riot. After two months of sustained protest often bringing together close to one million agitated individuals from every segment of society, not one episode of disorderly conduct has been reported. It has also generated structural and behavioural changes vital for sustaining the grassroots movements and their auxiliary emancipatory by-products. Again, without access to the Bourj as a pliable and porous public sphere, virtually none of this would have taken place.

Although the labels and collective identities of Beirut's centre were in perpetual change and oscillated, for varying interludes, over a dozen such names, they can be meaningfully regrouped into four general categories. First, as a *maidan, sahl, sahat* or *muntazah* in reference to it as an open space; ranging from an untamed, wild, natural and organic plain or field to a fairly regulated, landscaped and bounded courtyard or public garden. Second, as Place des Canons connoting its colonial legacy; either in view of the brief Russian presence during the Crimean War or of the extended hegemony of the French Mandate. Third, during the Ottoman period it witnessed at least four successive changes in its popular identity in reference to epochal events or political transformations—*sahat al-Itihad, al-Hamidiyyah Hadiqat al-Hurriyah*—and finally as Martyrs' Square to commemorate martyrdom and, hence, the felicitous nationalist sentiment by way of celebrating the country's liberation from Ottoman control. Fourth, as a *bourj*, perhaps its most lasting and enduring label, in reference to the one remaining relic of its ancient medieval walled ramparts.

Regardless of its varying and shifting identities, however, it has displayed throughout its eventful history a proclivity to become a vibrant setting for marshalling inventive and collective voices of dissent. Such prospects, given Lebanon's Janus-like character, are always double-edged. Homogenizing as public spaces may be, particularly when they become such spectacular vectors for the vindication of grievances and collective dissent, they also run the risk, in a fragmented political culture like Lebanon, of becoming sources for reawakening segmental and parochial identities.

This is precisely what transpired in Beirut in the wake of the epochal events sparked by Hariri's assassination. In retrospect, one cannot but marvel at the set of fortuitous circumstances that unleashed and consolidated the quickening and exhilarating turn of events. Had Hariri's family, for example, opted to bury him in Saida rather in the Bourj, the very setting identified with Solidere's formidable restorative venture, it is doubtful whether his stirring martyrdom would have generated such dramatic consequences.

As the Bourj was filled by voices of opposition, demanding not only to unveil the truth shrouding Hariri's murder but also to safeguard Lebanon's freedom, autonomy and independence, the pro-government and pro-Syrian forces took over another public square, Riad el-Solh, to portray and celebrate diametrically polarised views. Although the unfolding events were of much greater magnitude, they were a replay of earlier episodes when the socio-cultural and political identity of the Bourj was starkly different from its adjoining neighbourhoods. By virtue of such differences, most pronounced during the Ottoman period and the French Mandate, the Bourj was largely a meeting place of the upper bourgeoisie and newly affluent social groups eager to display their proclivity for conspicuous consumption and snob appeal. The underclass and itinerant labourers were drawn to quarters like *al-Sour* (present-day Riad el-Solh), which for a while continued to be the favoured meeting ground for the disfranchised and deprived strata of society.

With the public commemoration of the thirtieth day of Hariri's murder, the Bourj was once again destined as a public sphere to play host to a popular uprising with all the formidable and emancipatory manifestations of genuine self-propelled peoples' power movement. If anything, this is another vivid instance of the intimate and reciprocal interplay between social and spatial structures. A particular spatial setting, by virtue of its historic socio-cultural identity, can become a source of collective participation and empowerment. Once transformed, and thereby invested with new meanings and loyalties, the setting itself can become a more persuasive vector for nurturing the civic and cosmopolitan virtues of conviviality, pluralism and tolerance.

References

Habermas, Jurgen. *The Theory of Communicative Action* (Boston: Beacon, 1984).

Hanssen, Jens. *Fin de Siecle Beirut* (Oxford: Oxford University Press, 2005).

Mathur, A. "Neither Wilderness nor Home." In James Corner (ed.) *Recovering Landscape* (Princeton N.J.: Princeton Architecture Press, 1999).

Thompson, Elizabeth. *Colonial Citizen* (N.Y.: Columbia University Press, 2000).

An abridged version adapted from *The Heart of Beirut* (Saqi, 2006): 169–195.

"This Is a Muslim Home":
Signs of Difference in the African-American Row House

Muslims over history have varied widely in their cultural lives. They have, however, generally shared certain practices dependent on space. Muslims' submission of their will to God ideally reappropriates space and reorganizes temporality. *Salat* (formal prayer) requires space both physically and mentally. Fasting makes demands of mental and spiritual space, while altering temporality. The Hajj demands its space and time. In *salat*, for example, boundaries are formed when the prayer space is isolated. The calling of the *adhan* and the *iqamah* signal movement from one reality to another as the Muslim and Muslimah stand before ALLAH. In *salat*, the individual merges with the worldwide (and local) *umma* in a time for God that is distinct and unbounded. Both the practical needs of ritual and the profound juncture of the coterminous nature of the time and space of *salat* with the time and space of the world have a fundamental influence on space.

This essay first briefly describes the main Muslim communities and their congregational spaces in Philadelphia and then turns to a discussion of the city's African-American Muslim homes. Muslims make these homes, built on standard models, into a distinctive "Muslim space" through signage, decoration, and practice.

The Philadelphia Communities and Congregational Space

Philadelphia has been a microcosm of Muslim activity at least since the 1940s. Most Islamic groups in the United States either have members living there or some ties with residents. By the middle of the 1970s, numerous Muslim communities were evident in Philadelphia, among them the Moorish Science Temple of America (1913), the Ahmadiyah movement (1921), three Nation of Islam communities (1930), the American Muslin Mission (1980), the Darul Islam (ca. 1971), and several communities associated with the Muslim Student Association.

"Our divine national movement stands for the specific grand principles of Love, Truth, Peace, Freedom, and Justice," the Moorish Science Temple's statement of belief begins. "It is the great GOD ALLAH alone, that guides the destiny of the divine and national movement". The community expects "the end of tyranny and wickedness" against African-Americans and seek to connect with their Muslim heritage in general and with the descendants of Moroccans in particular. They identify the qur'anic *kufars* (disbelievers, or the ungrateful) as the European-Americans who face imminent destruction as a result of their apparent disbelief and unaccountability while engaging in evil conduct. They understand the nature of reality as spiritual and human existence as co-eternal with the existence of time. They believe that the Christianity taught by European-Americans was designed to enslave Africans, and they regard heaven and hell as conditions of the mind created by individual deeds and misdeeds.

Moorish Science members usually meet in a designated house in a room painted beige or eggshell, with neatly ordered rows of chairs on an uncarpeted floor polished to perfection. In one house I visited, all the chairs faced a small stage with a podium, behind which were seven chairs signaling some persons of importance. On the wall behind the stage were nicely framed portraits and documents: Noble Drew Ali's mother dressed in white, with a long white veil; Noble Drew Ali by himself, looking regal; a charter for the community; arid a set of bylaws. All the other walls were bare, and the only other fixture was a red flag with a green five-pointed star in its center. The sect offers members a space of neatness, cleanliness and order.

The Ahmadiyyians, who originated in the Indian subcontinent in the late nineteenth century, assert that God is active in this world, determining and designing the course of events. They hold that there should be a living relationship with God, from whom revelatory experience is still possible. Because of this belief, other Muslims have accused them of denying the finality of Prophethood, Ahmadis do, however, believe in the Oneness of God, observe the prescribed prayers, fast during the month of Ramadan, pay *zakat*, and perform the pilgrimage to Mecca. They also uphold the Al-Hadith. They are active missionaries, and their journals, *The Review of Religions* and *The Moslem Sunrise*, have been widely used.

In Philadelphia, this community meets in a large house, where there is strict adherence to the code of gender separation, with women having a separate entrance and a separate prayer room. The walls are bare, with the exception of an occasional piece of Arabic calligraphy. Distinct prayer areas are carpeted. Chairs are provided for eating and classes. The Indian subcontinent influences furnishings and other decorations.

The American Muslim Mission (AMM), which has largely replaced the Nation of Islam founded by Elijah Muhammad in the 1930s, is also active. The mission dates from an address delivered in Atlanta in the late 1970s by Elijah Muhammad's son, Warithudeen Muhammad, who disbanded the central authority of the Chicago *masjid,* encouraging decentralization of the community. He "revived true Islam," instituting *salat* at the proper times and encouraging the five pillars. Imams were to be trained in Arabic *tafsir, masjid* administration, and marriage counseling. The AMM continues to emphasize concerns of African-Americans such as self-development, self-accountability, racism, and poverty.

American Muslim Mission communities refurbished their places of congregation to be "orthodox"; they were no longer called "temples" but *"masjids"* or "mosques." Pictures of Elijah Muhammad, Clara Muhammad, and W. D. Fard were removed, along with the characteristic elegant chandeliers, heavy velvet drapes, chairs, and wall lighting. Search areas were turned into cloakrooms to serve as foyers leading into the *masjid.* Women, who had always been present side by side with men, were now separated from men inside the prayer area (the *masala*).

The Darul Islam, finally, used a rehabed house, which in the 1970s was open neither to the general community of Muslims nor to the surrounding community. The members sought seclusion and protection after reports of police mistreatment of their mentors in New York. Guards at the bare entranceway sat behind a counter to scrutinize visitors as to their intent. The community held its prayers upstairs, out of range of observation, with women in a separate room, linked by loudspeakers. Believers lived close to the *masjid* and schooled their children there. The mosque was open twenty-four hours a day.

As these examples illustrate, although the concept of umma is very important to African-American Muslims, it is provincially conceived. Their buildings reflect their many divisions and their perception of American hostility to the Muslim world. For all their sectarian differences, however, African-American Muslims share a great deal, including their use of the home.

"This Is a Muslim Home"

African-American Muslims in large cities have continually attempted to replicate the earliest Muslim communities by locating themselves in physical communities in close proximity to the *masjid*. Some jointly purchase small apartment buildings when available. In a few cases, entire communities have moved to rural areas to be able to live together.

Muslims often mark their homes as a space of difference and separation by a sign on the door. This is especially important for those living outside a Muslim enclave. The sign creates a boundary that signals both a warning and a welcome. To non-Muslims, the sign serves as a polite warning that the visitor is about to enter a different space and time. For other Muslims, it is a sign denoting a refuge. The phrase, "THIS IS A MUSLIM HOME/ PLEASE REMOVE YOUR SHOES" is on the door of hundreds of African-American Muslim homes and apartments in Philadelphia and probably in other major cities as well.

Muslims say that these signs selling for only fifty cents appeared in the late 1960s on the tables of Muslim vendors. Non-Muslim workmen, repairmen, salespersons, and social workers may be annoyed by the sign and resist removing their shoes. Neighbors simply grow used to it.

For the owners of the space the sign symbolizes the success of having created a boundary that defines an area of control. The sign dictates an attitude: in this house, it says, the hostile environment of racism, religious intolerance, and discrimination are locked out; prayer space and hospitality are guaranteed.

African-American Muslims self-consciously and deliberately organize the use of domestic space in the light of teachings found in the Qur'an and Al-Hadith, as well as through the example of immigrant Muslim homes and homes in the Muslim world. These Islamic norms thus inform the basic daily needs characteristic of domestic space—shelter, food storage and use, ritual activities, and social interaction. For African-American Muslims, the home becomes a space for learning and practicing Muslim behavior and for being separate from the larger society.

One of the classical divisions known in Islam, between *Darul Islam* (the House of Islam) and) and *Darul Harb* (the House of War), translates in American usage as the domestic space and the outside community. Domestic space is consciously separated from the space of the House of War, which is viewed as a space of religious intolerance and racism. The use of domestic space creates moreover a sense of shared spirituality with Muslims elsewhere in the Muslim world while fostering a sense of well-being in an environment perceived as hostile.

Juan Campo has recently argued that "the religious meanings of domestic space is an important part of the study of sacred space" that has long been neglected (Campo, 1991:8). In examining the Islamic aspects of Egyptian homes, Campo links a terminology and discourse related to domestic space to a discourse related to God's house (the Ka'ba), sacred history, rules of behavior, and the Hereafter. Campo suggests that the social etiquette and some of the ritual observances defined for the Ka'ba have served as the prototype for all human dwellings. The Qur'an reminds Muslims that the people before them who committed serious errors perished, along with their dwellings. Thus, everyday social life is linked to "ideas about God, right and wrong, purity, and blessings." Many rules relate to women (Campo, 1991: 27). As for Paradise, "In each of these descriptions, the quality of life in Paradise is a idealized rendering of the best aspects of domestic life in this world" (Campo, 1991: 25). Thus the Qur'an's exhortations about the space and time of the Hereafter implicitly remind believers of the importance of the home. The Al-Hadith explicitly makes people's houses and behavior in them regular objects of discourse. Campo argues that because of the moral restrictions on women's movement and seclusion, a great deal of a house's sacrality depends on the reputation of its female occupants.

These issues shape the lives of African-American Muslims living in Philadelphia row houses. There are row homes throughout the city, usually three-bedroom, two-story structures, often with no yard, some with small porches. The interior design is largely uniform. There are few houses with central hallways in the areas where Muslims predominately live. Rooms interconnect, with or without doors, with a small staircase leading upstairs to the small bedrooms and a centrally located bathroom. African-American Muslims have lived in these houses for several decades. Stories of the Prophet Muhammad's life yield a central paradigm for within the house. The house should be austere and near the *masjid*. Prophet Muhammad lived in a one-room dwelling, furnished with the bare necessities for living, with access to prayer space.

Al-Hadith regulate the accumulation of wealth and delineate the responsibilities attached to its use; African-American Muslims furnish their homes within these constraints. Within their homes, Muslims live a distinctive life. Even their concepts of time differ from those of non-Muslims. The Muslim community is seen as a dot on a continuum that began with creation and does not end but shift focus in the afterlife. Ritual practices define Muslim schedules, beginning with the pre-dawn prayer while most non-Muslim neighbors are sleeping. Fasting during the month of Ramadan has led school officials and neighbors to alert social workers to the possibility of child abuse or neglect, causing some Muslim households to become even more insular.

Life in the house is characterized by cleanliness and minimal consumption. There is only one requirement for Muslim space—a place for prayer. The Muslim not only retreats internally for experiencing *taqwá* (piety) for *salat*, but also requires a physical place to face the *Ka'ba* and to perform the prayer undisturbed. This space should above all be free from pollution. Muslims have developed some creative strategies for overcoming the physical structure of their homes. They enter this space by removing their shoes, leaving them in baskets, shoe racks, bookcases, crates, or just a designated space near the front door, since most houses do not have foyers. Women, who typically carry an extra pair of socks to wear inside, are escorted to one portion of the house, while the men are escorted to another. The members of the household also divide themselves along gender lines at this time. The house is usually decorated with Islamic texts and calligraphy, framed as well as unframed, and bronze plates engraved with various Qur'anic *suras*. Qur'anic recitations are the only music generally played in the public rooms of the home. In most living rooms, families have the latest copies of various Muslim newspapers, journals and pamphlets but not issues of *Time, Ebony, Essence,* or *Woman's Day*. Bookcases hold the Qur'an on the top shelf by itself, at least one set of Al-Hadith, and several sets of commentary by Maulana Ali and Yusuf Ali just below them. Other texts, generally originating in Pakistan or Egypt, are also religious. These books are purchased from merchants, the *masjid*, and conventions. The bookcase may hold prayer rugs and veils, and may itself configure the room toward Mecca. The *qiblah,* or direction toward the *Ka'ba* in Mecca, may also be indicated by a wall plaque or by some other piece of furnishing such as a carved screen.

Muslim space is replete with Arabic calligraphy, "oriental" rugs, brassware, latticed screens and so on. Since African-American Muslims are not tied to any particular country, they have drawn on the entire Muslim world for interior design. African-American Muslim adoption of a wide variety of Muslim cultural interior designs has generated probably the only "melting pot" of Muslim culture since the earliest centuries of Islamic history. In some homes, the furnishings for seating remind the visitor of a Moroccan restaurant: fat pillows made from synthetic oriental rugs, tables no more than a foot tall, couches with no legs, or mattresses used as couches. Other homes have traditional American furnishings. Living-room furniture is kept to a minimum in order to be able to turn the living-room space into prayer space without difficulty. Dining rooms are often sparsely furnished so that, along with the living room, they too can become a prayer area. In Philadelphia row homes, the dining room is usually situated between the kitchen and the living room; a *maida* (tablecloth) can be spread on the dining-room floor for meals and a few pillows, usually stacked in a corner, put out for seating.

Window shades, curtains, and drapes are always closed to exclude the view of neighbors in adjoining row houses. When visitors are not present, women are free to unveil and wear any appropriate clothing. When there are visitors, if there is even one adult male in the house, all the women will remain in the kitchen. They only leave to serve food or to pray.

The kitchens may accommodate a small dinette set, which doubles as a space for food preparation, an ongoing event. *Halal* meat (meat raised and then ritually slaughtered according to Islamic law) is purchased at great expense, either shipped in (by United Parcel Service or U.S. mail) or, in some communities, slaughtered by designated men in contractual arrangements with local farmers. Families then buy portions of the slaughtered meat. Breads are often homemade or are purchased from immigrant Muslim bakers or grocery stores. Dietary restrictions are strictly adhered to in all communities, and a great amount of time is thus spent in grocery shopping. Storage of foods is a critical skill. Vegetables are usually bought fresh and cooked daily. Foods regarded as Muslim food include falafel, couscous, humus, curry, lentils, pita bread, and basmati rice. Muslims prefer to cook elaborate dishes with spices, learned from immigrants, and avoid fast foods. Women highly esteem culinary skills.

Muslims do not linger in the bathroom (*hamam*) where jinn are thought to be present. Bathroom doors are kept closed for this reason. Those entering a bathroom wear special shoes or slippers. The bathroom is a space of both pollution and purification. The believer enters with the left foot, acknowledges the dangers of the space with a *du'a,* performs the necessary acts, and leaves on the right foot, reentering prayer space. Some people place pictures or other decorative items in bathrooms that could not be placed in spaces for prayer. There may also be signs with instructions on ablution. In some houses, a curtain or screen is positioned around the toilet to separate it from other facilities in the bathroom, while in others a closed toilet lid suffices.

Full participation in the Muslim community requires certain responses in the domestic space. Homes must reflect Islamic injunctions on prayer space and diet. They must also reflect Muslim prohibitions of certain kinds of art, social entertainment, and mixing of men and women. Muslims recognize some shared values in American life, such as charity, but in general they find non-Muslim values, especially in relation to sex, overwhelming. They seek an ideal Muslim atmosphere inside the house that is wholly separate.

Unlike most of the Muslim world, which welcomes television and radio, African-American Muslims try to shut out Western values and open the door to Muslim values. Fear of compromise of Islamic values prompts many parents to prefer either Islamic education or home schooling, so that in several communities, children have had only brief contact with the larger community.

Dress is also distinctive. Women may wear long-sleeved blouses under short-sleeved dresses or pants under dresses that are above the ankles. Men occasionally wear long shirts reaching the thigh under suit jackets with traditional Muslim headwear. Young girls wear scarves as an early deterrent to assimilation into "Christian" society. To enjoy public entertainments, Muslims may rent an entire roller rink for the evening so that girls or boys can skate, or hold an outdoor picnic in some remote part of a park.

African-American Muslims have taken small portions of various Muslim cultures and wove their own tapestry. Living rooms may contain Berber-patterned rugs, rattan furniture, Victorian lamps, Indian brass vases, and Arabic calligraphy on walls, all together an enthusiastic mixture of worlds. Arabic has mixed with black English. The expression *"Masha'allah,"* which is generally understood to mean "It is what Allah decreed" in happiness over some event or occurrence, is used by most African-American Muslims only as a lament.

African-American Muslims have clearly found that their American nationality is but one small aspect of their identity as prescribed by Islam. They are part of the larger Muslim world and interact with immigrant Muslims, while at times clashing with them and even encountering racism. African-American Muslims are likely in the near future to seek a greater blending of African Islam with African-American Islam and thus to engender an even more distinct African-American Islam. Then, as now, the home will be central to its expression and will be seen, whether explicitly sign-posted or not, as a separate and explicitly Muslim space.

Bibliography

Campo, Juan E. 1991. *The Other Side of Paradise: Explorations into the Religious Meaning of Domestic Space in Islam.* Columbia, S.C.: (University of Southern Carolina Press).

This paper originally appeared in Barbara Metcalf (ed.) *Making Muslim Space in North America and Europe* (University of California Press, 1996): 65-73. It is printed here with the permission of the publisher.

PART TEN

Eroticism, Desire and Sexual Identity

Introduction

Perhaps of all the problems and issues considered in this anthology, the changing nature of sexuality, the role of desire in shaping the dynamics of male-female relationships, the persistence of double-standards, the devaluation and negation of women and the consequent problems of forging meaningful sexual identities in such a changing and ambivalent world are fraught with added uncertainties and tensions. Furthermore, most of these problems, given the cultural sensitivities they are embedded in, continue to be masked from view. They are rarely subjected to the objective and open public debate they deserve. Hence, many of their unsettling consequences compound the magnitude of private anguish. They are seldom transformed into public issues which call for ameliorative attention.

The four essays in this chapter, despite the varied issues they explore—ranging from the interplay between misogyny, mysticism and eroticism in Islam to the sexual everyday lives of Iraqi men and women and the attitudes of Lebanese university students towards sexuality—reveal the centrality but also the contested and problematic character of sexuality in Arab society. At virtually all levels, one encounters markedly inconsistent perceptions and lived realities.

In his intuitive and erudite essay on the "Three Ms" in Islam—namely, misogyny, mysticism and *mujun*—the noted Moroccan socialist, Abdelwahab Bouhdiba, advances an engaging and persuasive thesis. Arab culture, he asserts, abounds with misogynist features which continue to manifest themselves in anxiety and fear over women's omnipresent sexuality. This pervasive fear ultimately finds expression in strategies for devaluing women or in mystical flights which celebrate ecstasy and refuge in the Supreme Being. To Bouhdiba, Mysticism, Sufism and Marabutism do not only become forms of escape, but they are re-invested in a state beyond love. More interesting, and this is where the third "M" becomes visible, it assumes a flight into women, into lechery; in short, *mujun*:

> Make no mistake, misogyny, mysticism and *mujun* are merely variations in three Ms on one and the same thing: sexuality. All these forms of behaviour conceal a veritable obsession, conscious or unconscious, assumed or refused, with woman, whom one devalues only in devaluing oneself. The negation of woman is always a negation of self. Misogyny encloses us in our own empire. Mysticism sublimates us. *Mujun* releases our inhibitions. Three ways of dealing with a single problem.

While tracing the origins of the three Ms in Quranic precepts, *fiqh, sunna* or *hadith*, Bouhdiba is careful to point out how they depart from common perceptions or other derivative forms. For example, he tells us that the negation of women is never total. Indeed for Marabutism, sexuality is exacerbated and not stifled. Both in the Maghreb and the Middle East, it slips very easily into licentiousness and promiscuity. He also reminds us that Sufism borrowed much from Bedouin love, particularly *'Udhrite* love, characterized by the "the rejection of the flesh and the spiritualization of sexuality."

Likewise, he is also keen in indicating how Islamic Sufism differs from its Christian counterpart. At least among the great mystics—e.g. Omar Khayyam and al-Rumi—there is no morbid delight in suffering, "no sense of profound guilt, still less any attempt to achieve union with God through asceticism and renunciation." Indeed, in the popular imagination these celebrated poets stood for the fundamental unity of the flesh and spirit.

> So the paradox is only apparent and one should not be surprised if a "systematic," "strict" Puritanism co-existed in the Arabo-Muslim societies with the art of carrying one's sexual pleasures to their highest summit. Arab eroticism is so refined, so elaborate, so all-inclusive, that, in the eyes of many scholars, it has almost eclipsed all the other aspects of Muslim civilization. There is nothing surprising in this for, if my analysis is correct, we must admit that the value of eroticism comes very largely from the certainty that faith alone can confer.

Repeatedly Bouhdiba affirms that Arab sexuality has its roots in the most authentic Qur'anic traditions. The prophet himself, after all, was very attentive to the needs of sensuality, the art of coupling and sexual pleasures. *Coitus interruptus* and *nikah al-mut'a* were not only tolerated, "they were warmly recommended by the prophet." Also, the sexual act was not confined to procreation. "...Sexual bliss was a way of living in the hereafter by anticipating the co-existence of orgasm and paradise."

It is at the level of the third M (*mujun*) that Arab-Islamic civilization reaches its summit. Unlike Orientalist perceptions which treat *mujun* as worthless and vulgar obscenities, in Islam it is cherished as part of refined *adab*. How else can one account for the profound and long-lasting impact of epics like *The Thousand and One Nights* where eroticism and faith are celebrated? The cities and their suburbs are dense with pleasure taverns and gardens where people can indulge their whims without any sense of shame or guilt:

> These taverns were places where many kinds of pleasure were served up without shame and without exclusion. Singers, dancers, gamblers, but also pleasure-seeking young fellows, homosexuals of both sexes, taught the art of pleasure, without let or hindrance, to a youth whom Islam had freed from any sense of shame or guilt.

The general inference Bouhdiba extrapolates regarding the convergence of the sexual and the sacral in Arab-Islamic culture is worth reflecting upon; particularly since *mujun* reinforces this unity:

> *Mujun* seems to me to be one of the summits of Arabo-Muslim culture and *The Thousand and One Nights* is erected as a monument to the glory of fundamental unity. But we can now see that at the level of everyday life and at every level of social life the sacral and the sexual support each other and are both engaged in the same process: that of the defence of the group. Just as there is a religious ritual, there is an erotic ritual and each parallels the other. Arab eroticism, then, is a refined, learned technique whose mission is to realize God's purpose in us.

To Bouhdiba then, unlike Durkheim's invocation of the sacred and profane as dichotomous entities, he sees no inherent contradiction between eroticization and the glorification of God. "They are welded together as one. So a good orgasm culminates in morning prayers. It is as if prayer is also an expectation of pleasure. Our God, give us this day our daily orgasm!"

In her probing piece, "Narration and Desire: Shahrazâd", Fedwa Malti-Douglas emphasizes the crucial role played by Shahrazâd, an intellectual wonder who has memorized books, poetry and much more. In fact, the most central theme in *The Thousand and One Nights* is Shahrazâd's understanding and mastery of the problematic nature of desire, the proper and improper patterns associated with it alongside the ways of using and fulfilling it. Though at the beginning her extraordinary versatility in the manipulation of desire may appear nothing more than a time-saving device, or merely a determination to liberate the world from Shâhriyâr's tyranny, Shahrazâd's real role is to cleverly shift desire from the realm of sex to the more malleable world of the text and in doing so, create a new kind of desire, one that continues from night to night in the form of storytelling. Thus she wisely and ingeniously breaks the cycle of a short-sighted, immature male pattern of excitement, satisfaction and death as practiced by the king who has each of his brides killed the next morning, replacing it, instead, with a female pattern of extended and enduring pleasurable desire and sophisticated sexuality. Shahrazâd's ultimate success is a long and complex process that lies initially in her ability, through storytelling, to cleverly implement a viable shift, as it were, from sex to text, in order to restore proper sexuality, proper rhythm and proper desire.

Clearly, in order for Shahrazâd to succeed several crucial lessons and intellectual constructs first must be addressed. Chief among them, according to Malti-Douglas, is a longstanding debate entrenched in Medieval Islamic Mentalities, that of the relative value of the senses, primarily the oral as opposed to the visual. Linguistic and philosophical arguments it seems, were in agreement on the superiority of hearing over vision. In the *Nights,* sight and hearing are perceived as two distinct ways of acquiring knowledge; however, the king's attempts at finding truth through the faculty of vision have obviously led him astray. Shahrazâd's ability to brilliantly reverse this disastrous situation is accomplished through the act of hearing. By listening to her storytelling that incorporates "the accumulated wisdom of her civilization," the proper uses of desire are learned by the king. Only when this is achieved can Shahrazâd convince the king to wed her, and in doing so, reinstate, once more, the heterosexual couple as opposed to the homosocial (the king and his brother). She has finally managed to transform the king's previous system of sexual pleasure followed by death and the prevention of heirs to one linked with life and creation. Yet by the end of the story, another reversal occurs when the male homosocial couple is again recreated. At Shahrazâd's request, Shâhzamân's brother and her sister will live with them while the brothers agree to jointly rule the kingdom. The brother-brother and the sister-sister relationships are now made possible because they have been established on firm foundations and are no longer a threat to the heterosexual couple.

With sibling and matrimonial relationships harmonized, the natural outcome of restoring the heterosexual couple is to reinforce patriarchy. Now that Shahrazâd has managed to achieve her ultimate goal, she is able to relinquish her intellect allowing her physical nature to resurface. By reverting back to being an object of desire and allowing the king "to regain his active role and the female her passive one," the traditional binary preference is reinstated. Moreover, Shahrazâd's connection to literature becomes more clearly defined. Although she has been the narrator of the stories, it is the king who takes charge of writing them down and, therefore, to males alone is reserved "the authority and permanence of literature." Finally the story has come full circle, for when Shahrazâd "relinquishes her role as narrator for that of perfect woman: mother and lover," the body has similarly been "transmitted into word and back into body."

"World's Apart," based on the survey Sana al-Khayyat conducted on Iraqi women in the spring and summer of 1982, reveals the inconsistent demands and expectations married women continue to harbor regarding their sexual conduct. Though the 50 interviews she conducted represent three distinct social categories of Iraqi women (illiterate housewives, teachers at two schools in Baghdad and higher professionals), their views converged on a set of overriding concerns which reinforce the traditional patriarchal values of honor and shame. For example, husbands expect to command their wives rather than display any manifestations of love and tenderness. Even husbands who harbor such sentiments feel restrained to express them. This is why, Al-Khayyat argues, wives remain unaware of their husbands' inner-most feelings and inclinations.

Indeed, to Al-Khayyat the survival of such traditional expectations, derived from Bedouin notions of honor and shame, are more salient than education or class in shaping men's attitudes toward women and sexuality.

Such symptoms of ambivalence and anomie are not only salient among women in the traditional communities of Iraq, Damascus, Cairo and elsewhere in the Arab world. They also prevail in the comparatively more liberal and permissive settings of college students at the American University of Beirut (AUB), an institution known for its tolerant and cosmopolitan lifestyles. By extracting narratives and discourse from students in her creative writing courses, Roseanne Khalaf was able to identity and account for their views and perceptions on the nature and place of love, romance and sexuality in their lives. In intimate, often graphic and explicit personal narratives, students in the relatively free and uncensored classroom setting seem similarly plagued by disjunctive cultural expectations.

Khalaf frames her study by depicting the unusual predicament two of her students faced since both—for strikingly different reasons—were unable to participate in spirited class discussions, requesting instead that they do so in the privacy of her office. One, a veiled, reserved student in her late teens or early twenties, a by-product of a traditional Druze family, was adamant about not removing her white veil to uncover her mouth while speaking. Consequently, her muffled speech was inaudible to her colleagues in class. The other, a fashionable "postmodern" student, was unable to remove her tongue and lip rings, the faddish artifice in vogue among her trendy peers that virtually disabled her speech.

Both, in other words, are "damaged" and "deformed" by the very values they subscribe to. Though polarized, they represent extreme but salient reactions to the unsettling transformations affecting the nature of sexuality, intimacy and gender relations. In the words of Khalaf, "the outwardly timid and reserved veiled student, along with her dauntless and liberated cohort, who flaunts the rings on her tongue and other parts of her sparsely dressed body as 'emblems of honor' and daring, represent extreme modes of adaptation which are, no doubt, manifest elsewhere in the Arab World."

Though contrived, the classroom setting, as a contact zone and safety net, was transformed into something akin to a "third space" where students felt free to articulate their most intimate views and anxieties away from the repressive public gaze. Despite the seeming homogeneity of the class, students drawn together in a presumably humanistic setting that promotes a liberal education, views were multiple and wide-ranging. They converged, however, on a set of six themes which epitomize the contested and negotiated character of sexuality in everyday life.

Most striking is the generational (parent/child) differences as an expression of the discrepant sexual ideologies of parents and children. Students are inclined to perceive sexuality in fairly positive terms as forms of self-fulfillment. They also act on their libidinal desires regardless of romantic attachments or marital prospects. Parents, on the other hand, as perceived by their children, are alarmed by the permissive atmosphere of free sexuality unrestrained by love and marriage. They condone physical intimacy only as a prelude to lasting and secure relationships. Indeed, a girl's virginity, as one student put it sinisterly, is treated by her parents as the most effective ploy to trap a worthy spouse!

Khalaf treats the parent/child dualism as symptomatic of the moral divide which differentiates the two views with regard to love, sex and intimacy. In this sense parents are more apt to be regarded as *romantics*, as they are more prone to view sex as a mode of expressing intimate feelings which cannot and should not be divorced from love and affection. Young students, on the other hand, by challenging such archaic orthodoxies, are more *libertarians* in that they are bent on freeing sex from the excessive strictures of custom and tradition.

With noted cynicism, some students are fully aware of the insincerity and duplicity of their parents in that they do not live up to the high moral expectations they preach. Though a few are outraged by their parents' social hypocrisy, they tend to treat this jarring dissonance between overt righteousness and covert misconduct as a microcosm of the deepening malaise they see elsewhere in society.

Another theme emerges from Khalaf's analysis of her student's narrative voices; namely, that the younger generations, perhaps more than other groups, are compelled to grapple more intensely with efforts at negotiating and constructing an identity to accommodate the shifting and inconsistent sexual codes they are facing today. "It is not surprising," she tells us, "that within such a fluid and negotiable setting virtually everything becomes charged with sensual, erotic undertones and, hence, highly contested. Seemingly mundane and prosaic matters—e.g. dress codes, speech styles and the freedom to imagine alternative sexual attributes and practices—begin to assume primacy."

Not unlike the elite Damascene women that Salamandra writes about, AUB students are also keen to make effective use of all the ploys available to eroticize their bodies as part of a competitive game to seduce and attract the male gaze. They are also sending a confounding message: that "men can only look, not touch." Much like the "cockteasers" in Damascus, in other words, their ploys are designed to arouse men but also to keep them at a safe distance. Unlike their Syrian counterparts, however, students in Lebanon seem more permissive, uninhibited and explicit in their language, rhetorical expressions and actual conduct. Indeed, indulging in sexual escapades becomes an unalloyed libidinal drive to be heeded with abandon and for all to see.

Khalaf leaves us with one final compelling inference. Though her data may appear to only represent the cloistered views of students sheltered in the comfort zone of a classroom, we need not belittle or dismiss such voices, for, as sketchy or marginal as they may seem, they have a way of eventually intruding upon mainstream scripts and conventional codes. At the least, they serve to sustain the fluidity of sexual identities and public discourse.

Variations on Eroticism: Misogyny, Mysticism and Mujun

One might be surprised at this variation on Islamic sexuality in the form of three Ms and find paradoxical that misogyny, mysticism and *mujun* may be conceived together. The paradox is only apparent, for these three forms of behaviour are all ways of outwitting the spirit of Islam.

Islamic civilization is essentially feminist. One ought to be able to deduce from this that a Muslim cannot be a misogynist. Islam and hatred of women appear to be incompatible *de jure*. And yet the devaluation of femininity in the Arabo-Muslim countries is such that the mildest of feminism is still widely regarded even today as an anti-Quranic revolution!

This contradiction between law and fact derives fundamentally from the socio-economic status and the socio-cultural situation of Arab women: one really cannot deprive women of their economic and civil rights or frustrate them of what the Quran grants them and at the same time magnify them! Hence that male bad faith that betrays women, sexuality and pleasure in a thousand and one ways.

Hence, too, the flight before woman. Fear of women, anxiety when confronted with the procreative forces that they bear within them, the strange unease that is aroused by that mysterious attraction for an unknown being who is often no more than the unknown of being. In many societies all this frequently turns into a rejection of women.

Arab culture abounds in misogynist features and moral austerity. But mysticism, Sufism and Marabutism also express, in their own ways, this flight from women that is reinvested in a state beyond love. And even sexuality is sometimes regarded as merely a preparatory technique for mystical ecstasy and refuge in the Supreme Being.

But sometimes, too, this flight from woman becomes a flight into woman, into lechery, in short, into *mujun*. Make no mistake, misogyny, mysticism and *mujun* are merely variations in three Ms on one and the same thing: sexuality. All these forms of behaviour conceal a veritable obsession, conscious or unconscious, assumed or refused, with woman, whom one devalues only in devaluing oneself. The negation of woman is always a negation of self. Misogyny encloses us in our own empire. Mysticism sublimates us. *Mujun* releases our inhibitions. Three ways of dealing with a single problem.

In actual fact, many of the texts of the fiqh and sunna, but not a single text of the Quran, can be given a misogynist interpretation. Whatever the authenticity of the hadiths, one has only to remember that an apocryphal one is perhaps even more significant than a true one. It expresses a historical moment, a need felt by the community. Nevertheless tradition is hard on women and on sexuality. It was Muhammad, for example, who declared, on the occasion of his nocturnal ascension, that he had "noticed that hell was populated above all by women." He went on to say, "If it had been given to me to order someone to be submissive to someone other than Allah, I would certainly have ordered women to be submissive to their husbands, so great are a husband's rights over his wife."

If misogyny constantly recurs as a leitmotif in Arab culture it is because it has a meaning. It is evidence for us of a break in the Quranic harmony. Arab societies drew from Islam not the idea of the complementarity of the sexes, but, on the contrary, that of their hierarchy. Misogyny is really no more than a sociological conditioning. The debate about female emancipation thus takes on a striking significance. In any case, it cannot mask the fundamental position of the group that intends to maintain its own economic, patriarchal and male base. Misogyny is something other than an accident along the route of the structuration of Arabo-Muslim societies!

The negation of woman cannot be total. The most misogynist man is forced to recognize the depth of what he is so determined to oppose. Indeed, within Arabo-Muslim society other compensatory attitudes emerge that are a recovery of sexuality in a sublimated form. Mysticism, for example, takes us from the renunciation of woman to her sublimation. Without wishing in the least to reduce it to that, we might say that mystical spirituality was nourished in Islam from the sublimated cult of woman.

I should add that although Marabutism does not necessarily involve a displacement of the object of sexuality, this is certainly not the case with Sufism. Marabutism is a social organization of the religious. And the confraternities constitute collective orders that draw upon the sacred for values that will assist them in realizing their cohesion and upon the social for forces that may be placed at the service of the religious community. Hence the military, committed, militant aspect of Marabutism. If Marabutism can be accused of anything it is that, in a sense, it exacerbates rather than stifles sexuality. It is notorious that Marabutist festivals, the *ziyāra*, both in the Maghreb and in the Middle East, turn very easily into licentiousness.

In concrete terms, we are speaking of a confraternity of men, or of women, who are bound together by the memory of a saint or eponymous ancestor and commune with one another in the course of collective mystical ceremonies. Promiscuity is the rule and it is but a step from ecstatic effusion to amorous effusion.

Sometimes sexuality is exacerbated in the Marabutic ritual, as in extreme cases where the practices include ancient survivals of cults of Cybele, Venus and Bacchus. Nevertheless Marabutism remains a technique of collective exaltation. Hence the importance of the ritual of the confraternity. For Sufism, on the other hand, this can in no sense be the case, since it is essentially a matter of isolating oneself before God. All the affectivity of the Sufi mystic is directed towards God and his Prophet. It involves a significant displacement upwards that implies a sublimation of sexuality.

One remembers the famous hadith, "he who loves, observes chastity and dies of it, dies as a martyr". Some versions add as a condition of martyrdom that the love be kept secret. These two conditions—chastity and secrecy *('iffa* and *kitmān)*—are essential if one is to grasp the very essence of the passage into mysticism. Hence the role of women in the development of mysticism.

Take the Andalusian Mohieddin Ibn 'Arabi. He provides a perfect example of this idealization of woman and sublimation of love: "I bind myself by the religion of love whatever direction its steeds take: love is my religion, love my faith." We know that

Ibn 'Arabi married a pious woman who helped him to discover both profane love and mystical love. It was largely Mariam al-Bajiya who gave him a taste for meditation and contemplation. She certainly nourished his soul, thus enabling him, in experiences that were certainly very rare, to combine orgasm with ecstasy. Ibn 'Arabi remains an example of the man who has lived at its most intense the fundamental unity of poetry and religion, love and faith. From sensuality to spirituality there is a path to be crossed that is the very essence of Sufism and which carries within it the sublimation of sexuality. Profane love is the starting point and spiritual love embraces everything. Sexuality is a mystery of procreation that has meaning only in projection into God. Ibn 'Arabi's *Diwān* would itself require a thorough analysis, for it is from beginning to end a variation on the theme of mystical and profane love.

Sufism borrowed everything from Bedouin love: its ideology, its themes, its motifs, its stereotypes, its images. In fact it is a substitute for it and there is a basic equivalence between the rejection of the flesh and the spiritualization of sexuality. Indeed 'Udhrite love led historically to nothing. It was the gratuitous, chivalric cult of the lady. And, quite naturally, Sufism brought it a finality that it lacked. It is as if the original dissociation of love could not lastingly ignore the carnal aspect of love without having to turn towards the starkest, most ardent faith, that inspired by the love of God. There is a passage from Eros to Agape, the meaning of which appears in each mystic, but, again, in the most admirable way in Ibn 'Arabi and Ibn al-Faridh.

I have purposely taken up here the terms used by the famous Lutheran theologian Anders Nygren. His thesis, which has aroused reservations in Catholic circles, finds a justification in the passage from original Islam to the mystical tendencies. Muhammad unified Eros *qua* genetic force and carnal attraction with Agape, *qua* love of God. Hence for him the profound unity of the love of women and prayer, the work of the flesh and alms. The Sufi mystics "Platonized" the Islamic Agape, just as the 'Udhrites "Platonized" the Muslim Eros.

The relationship with God, then, is Love. But although from the Sufi point of view it is direct and requires annihilation in him, it nevertheless necessitates the mediation of the prophet Muhammad. It is precisely around the personal relationship established with him that Marabutism and Sufism are at one. For Muhammad, the friend of God *(H'abību Allah)* is also the friend of men or quite simply the Friend. His being is at the centre of a network of convergent relations conveying both amorous and mystical forces: those that unite believers and both sexes to his Holy person.

Despite the differences between levels and conceptions, carnal love and spiritual love prolong one another and imply one another. Hence that stress laid on the complementarity of the sexes, on their harmony and understanding. "When husband and wife look at one another, God looks at them both with compassion" *(Madhara rahmatin)*, as a famous hadith, already quoted, puts it. "When the husband takes his wife's hand, their sins fall between their hands," declares the same hadith. One could not express more succinctly the notion of purification through love or the association of God with human love. From the human to the divine there is unity, continuity and ascendance. And it is called Love, of which the various forms (physical, 'Udhrite, mystical) are merely stages of an irreducible totality.

In paradise the vision of God, which is the ultimate in happiness and perfection, is attained only after a series of sexual pleasures. The rain of paradise is a universal sperm. Allah is described in the Quran as *Wadud*, full of love, all-loving. It is God who promises "so remember Me and I will remember you". It is he who promises reciprocity in love: "If you love God ... God will love you". Lastly the soul finds peace in its return to God: "O soul at peace, return unto thy Lord, well-pleased, well-pleasing. Enter thou among My servants. Enter thou My paradise."

Love is reciprocal right up to and including the love that binds man to God. It is this reciprocity that constitutes the mystery and grandeur of the Islamic vision of love. Even in love for God there is an erotic element, which has been especially stressed by Sufi mysticism, just as in Christian mysticism Eros plays a crucial role. Hence the use of carnal images on which the imaginary reference confers an even stronger force than the most sensual earthly love. But unlike Christian mysticism we find, at least among the great mystics, no morbid delight in suffering, no sense of profound guilt, still less any attempt to achieve union with God through asceticism and renunciation.

In private life, many Arab mystics were quite simply pleasure-seekers. In the Persian domain people even came to doubt the mysticism of Omar Khayyan and Jalal Addin al-Rumi. In the specifically Arab domain the ambiguity was scarcely less great. And with good reason! Ibn 'Arabi himself certainly mixed carnal love with mystical love. This is because man's rootedness, even in the case of Muhammad himself, passed through the assumption of sexuality and through physical love. It was through sexuality that the fundamental unity of flesh and spirit was formed. It is sexuality that, realizing personal unity in others, makes possible the quest for God. If the unity of self passes through the two poles of sexuality and the love of God it is because they are ultimately one and the same thing. Moreover in both cases there is reciprocity and reaction. Neither with the human partner, nor with God, does Islam accept one-way love. And reciprocity in one case implies reciprocity in the other.

Contrary to appearances, mystical love cannot really be excluded from *'Udhrite* love. The latter is a renunciation of the flesh, a sublimation turned back upon itself. Mystical love, on the other hand, is a continuity from the carnal to the spiritual. For it, liberation in the flesh and liberation of the flesh are inseparable.

So the paradox is only apparent and one should not be surprised if a "systematic", "strict" puritanism co-existed in the Arabo-Muslim societies with the art of carrying one's sexual pleasures to their highest summit. Arab eroticism is so refined, so elaborate, so all- inclusive, that, in the eyes of many scholars, it has almost eclipsed all the other aspects of Muslim civilization. There is nothing surprising in this for, if my analysis is correct, we must admit that the value of eroticism comes very largely from the certainty that faith alone can confer.

Arab sensuality has its roots in the most authentic or Quranic traditions. I have stressed the importance of legitimated pleasure in the sexual act. The pleasure factor itself may sometimes have eliminated the others: *coitus interruptus* was canonically accepted; a form of *nikah* known as *nikah al-mut'a* was tolerated; the satisfaction of sensuality was warmly recommended by the Prophet.

Coitus interruptus was apparently widespread in the first Islamic community. The Prophet knew this and never regarded it as reprehensible. He even once added: "It certainly does not belong to you, if God has decided to create a soul that will live until the

Last Judgment, to prevent its coming into the world." This *hadith* distinguishes explicitly between the creative acts of God and contraceptive practices. And do not these practices in a sense form part of God's plan?

The Prophet was questioned one day by one of his companions concerning a concubine with whom he liked to sleep on condition that there was no risk of pregnancy. Muhammad then recommended him to practise the "restrictive embrace", adding: "What God has decided for her will happen in any case." In other words there is no incompatibility between coitus reservatus and the mystery of creation. In short, the purpose of the sexual act is not confined to procreation alone.

The *Fatāwā Hindyya*, like so many other treatises, provides valuable information. *Coitus reservatus* is seen there as subject to the agreement of the wife of free condition or the master of the concubine when she is not the property of the man who is practising the coitus. With the fully owned concubine, *coitus reservatus* is subject to no other condition. Abortion, too, may be canonically provoked, on condition that the differentiation of the forms of the foetus have not yet been achieved, which, according to Muslim theologians, occurs only after a hundred and twenty days.

The autonomy of desire assumed such importance that primitive Islam hesitated for a long time. At one moment it even legitimated a very curious type of *nikah, nikah al-mut'a,* temporary marriage, whose purpose therefore was pleasure *(mut'a).* It was, therefore, a temporary, but legal union. Travellers and soldiers could take advantage of it. Pilgrims, too, for whom the ritual of desacralization is a reinsertion in sexual life. The sacralization of *hajj* involved among other things, as we know, total sexual abstinence. The end of the ritual is marked by a return to civil life, by the raising of all taboos, the sacrifice of the hair and a return to sexual life. It certainly derives from a survival of the sacred prostitution that took place in Greco-Roman antiquity. At first Muhammad kept it. Then, at Khaybar, he forbade it. Then he authorized it again on the day of Awtas, then finally forbade it the day he returned to Mecca.

"It is not *nikah* in the ordinary sense of the word, or debauchery, *nikah wa la sifah,* but a sexual pleasure tolerated by God at a particular moment. It is the hiring for money of a woman with a view to sexual pleasure that must last for three days and three nights, after which the two parties separate and their situation is regularized by a deed of *nikah*." In other words, there is a price and a gift, but at the centre there is pleasure, *tamattu', mut'a.*

The Prophet himself was very attentive to the art of coupling, the art of sexual pleasure. For sexual bliss was a way of living in the hereafter by anticipation and I have already demonstrated the extent to which orgasm and paradise were co-extensive. Kissing, the right words, scent, fore-and afterplay are themes on which the Prophet laid particular stress, unhesitatingly setting an example, and thereby inaugurating a whole art of sexual pleasure that is regarded as one of the most complete and most systematic.

It was he who founded in law a veritable erotology, a full, positive science of pleasure in all its physical and psychical forms. If eroticism invades literature, art, everyday life, it is because it is integrated in the Islamic view of the world and is situated at the heart, not at periphery, of ethics.

A typically Arab notion sums up this fundamental feature: *mujūn,* the object both of disapproval in its inevitable excesses and of envious admiration on the part of those who are incapable of abandoning themselves to a happiness that can lead to a permanent, socially recognized commitment. Observe the ambiguous and equivocal richness of the root *ma ja na,* which signifies according to the *Lisan al 'Arab,* the density, the depth, the lack of shame, the frivolity, the gratuity, the art of mixing the serious and the lighthearted pretended austerity true banter. *Mujun* is the art of referring to the most indecent things speaking about them in such a lighthearted way that one approaches them with a sort of loose humour. In principle *mujun* ought not to go beyond words. In fact it is fantasy present through words. It is a collective experience and liberation through speech.

One will understand the import of *mujün* better if one considers the following example taken from two of the greatest *fuqaha* of the period.

This is how a qadi filled a minister's evenings. The vizir Abu Abdallah Al-'Aredh invited the famous faqih Abu Hayan al-Tuahidi to give a series of learned talks on various subjects. We come, in due course, to the eighteenth evening.

> Once the minister said to me: "Let us devote this evening to *mujun.* Let us take a good measure of pleasant things. We are tired of serious matters. They have sapped our strength, made us constipated and weary. Go, deliver what you have to say on that point." I replied: "When the *mujjan* had gathered together at the house of Kufa to describe their earthly pleasures, Kufa's fool, Hassan said: 'I shall describe what I myself have experienced.' 'Go on,' they said to him. 'Here are my pleasures: safety, health; feeling smooth, shiny, round forms; scratching myself when I itch; eating pomegranates in summer; drinking wine once every two months; sleeping with wild women and beardless boys; walking without trousers among people who have no shame; seeking a quarrel with sullen people; finding no resistance on the part of those I love; associating with idiots; frequenting faithful fellows like brothers and not seeking out the company of vile souls.'

Orientalists do not usually translate these texts ... or they do so into Latin. They regard this kind of *mujun* as worthless, vulgar obscenity Yet it forms an essential part of *adab,* the teaching of which must have provided the students of the period with an enjoyable and relaxing break. One may, paraphrasing Mauss, speak of "education through jokes". Indeed Tauhidi himself stressed this, by way of self-justification, at the end of this celebrated eighteenth night—and the vizir did not fail to draw favourable conclusions from so much *mujun.*

> Give priority to the art of *mujun,* he advised him. I would never have thought that it could have furnished a whole session. One may have serious reproaches to make to this kind of discourse. Wrongly, for the soul needs gaiety *(bishr).* I have been told that 'Ibn Abbas was fond of saying, as he sat in the midst of his listeners, after long, thorough commentaries upon the Quran, the *sunna* and the *fiqh*: "Now tell me something spicy" *(ahmidu).* I think all he wanted to do by this was to give balance to the soul so that it might recover enough energy to resume the examination of serious things and to make it receptive and attentive to what would be addressed to it.

The B'uyid minister al-Muhallabi had a salon in which lie would receive the *fuqaha* one day, the *qadi* another and the philosophers *(mutakallimun)* another. In these gatherings, wine, *mujun* and erudition were all partaken of. Yaqut even relates how two nights a week were reserved to *mujun*.

> One then threw off all shame, all restraint. One abandoned oneself to revelry, drunkenness and hubris. These *kadis* were the finest flower of the *fiqh* of the period! Ibn Ma'ruf, Tannukhi Ibn Qāria ... all had fine, white, long beards, like the vizir al-Muhallabi himself. When they were all beginning to enjoy themselves, when the company became pleasant and the ear enchanted, they were all so gay that they generously abandoned the last veils of their shame to the generous workings of wine. Golden goblets filled with glowing red wine were handed round. Everyone wet his beard in the forbidden beverage. When all the liquid had been drunk they sprinkled one another. They then danced, though not before taking off their clothes, though it is true that they kept thick garlands of flowers around their necks.

Of course women were not absent from these "orgies" any more than were pretty boys. "Next day," Yaqut adds, not without a touch of malice, "they returned to their usual puritanism, their self-conscious dignity, their scrupulous respect for the external marks expected of *qadi* and to the shame that befits great sheikhs."

If such was the feeling of men who were reputed to be pious, if that was their attitude, what must have been the behaviour of people less close to religion, of the young, of the ordinary people?

Each social category had its *mujun*! And to judge by the innumerable descriptions in the *Book of Songs*, the *Golden Meadows* or *The Thousand and One Nights*, Arab civilization integrated *mujun* as much as faith. The cities had in their suburbs or in the surrounding countryside highly frequented pleasure gardens, with open-air cabarets and cafés set up on the farms attached to Byzantine, Roman, or Persian castles, or even Christian monasteries. In the best traditions, the monks provided plenty of wine and pretty girls for the "joyous companions of sincerity", the *fityana sidqin* of which Abu Nawas speaks.

These taverns were places where many kinds of pleasure were served up without shame and without exclusion. Singers, dancers, gamblers, but also pleasure-seeking young fellows, homosexuals of both sexes, taught the art of pleasure, without let or hindrance, to a youth whom Islam had freed from any sense of shame or guilt.

> These cabarets, which the poet Ibn al Mu'tazz called the "ephemeral paradises", were generally set up in large gardens where the limpid water supplied by a canal gushed forth in artificial springs and cascades; large benches covered with matting were arranged under the trembling shade of sycamores, poplars, willows that stood beside cypresses, pomegranate trees, orange trees and palm trees.

The pleasure of going out and breathing fresh air and partaking, in the shade, of roast kid and good wine or mead, while listening to music, was increased by a pleasant outing on a gondola and a return journey by the same means to the city; for these regions were marked by endless canals winding through the plains where barley and wheat stretched as far as the eye could see.

Throughout the whole of the Muslim world, from the end of the Ommiads, a set of permanent characteristics appeared that bore the mark of a *mujun* that we still find almost intact in our own time, despite the enormous upheavals to which that society has been subject for centuries. A desperate love of pleasure that spread beyond the courts and wealthier classes of the city, *mujun* was an *ars vitae*, a permanent *carpe diem*. The Andalusian *muwashshah's aghrim zamānak la yafut* had and still has its counterpart throughout every section of the population.

The great monument of *mujūn* and of Arab eroticism remains incontestably *The Thousand and One Nights*. Apart from the Quran there are few books in Arabic that are so widely read, so well-known, so popular and so rich. One has to have attended a popular gathering at which extracts are read to grasp the importance and role played by these tales. The erotic vision that emerges from them is so total and so totalizing that it seems inseparable from the socio-cultural context in which it came to birth and in which life integrated Eros, in which everything sang of faith in God, love of life and absolute pleasure. The lyrical vision of life is mingled in it with the fantastic and the marvellous. It is a festival of the real and the imaginary. Dream becomes act and act is transfigured into overflowing oneirism.

The very project of *The Thousand and One Nights* brings us to the heart of eroticism. Indeed is it not a question of arousing the desire of king Shahryar? What Shahrazād is trying to do is to put off from night to night the execution of the terrible threat that hangs over her. The tales begin with a noble challenge and are presented as a strategic ruse, a response to the inhuman cruelty of a king determined to despise and punish women in general and virgins in particular. Had he not decided once and for all to put to death one virgin each night after satisfying his sexual appetite with her? Indeed the tales begin with a terrible declaration of misogyny. All men are cuckolds, for all women are whores. "Trust not at all in women, smile at their promising, for they lower or they love at the caprice of their parts. Filled to the mouth with deceit ... Only a miracle brings a man safe from among them." The only solution is to marry, without leaving the wife time to become unfaithful. In order not to become cuckolds husbands have only to become cruel: the alternative of death and love. But by the end of the tales Shahrazād will have substituted an alternative of love and life.

For Shahrazād, then, it is not only a question of saving her own head and that of all the threatened virgins, but also of outwitting destiny, restoring the rights of femininity and demonstrating that nothing can conquer women. Shahryar, whose sexual appetite is renewed, after having been very well satisfied, was in no doubt that he was giving in against his will to a militant, frenetic, ardent, but effective feminism and in every point in accordance with Islamic teaching.

The myth of Shahryar and Shahzaman, the two brother kings, takes us to the very heart of conversion through love and eroticism. Here are two apparently happy men. They have everything, power, intelligence, money, pleasure, love. Love? No—and that is the point. They thought they had it. But they know what anguish, what "spleen" drove them towards one another. *Tawah hasha ba'dahuma ba'dan*, as the Arabic text puts it. The brothers want to meet. They both feel a lack of fraternal affection. Here fraternal love prefigures that of the two sisters Shahrazād and Dunyazad. It is as if the brotherly and sisterly relationship was the only pure, full, positive one. Throughout the tales it is this relationship alone that is not affected by crises of one kind or another. On the contrary it always provides a haven in time of danger.

Shahzaman, then, gets ready to go away. But, of course, it is a false departure and he is already cuckolded. He has not yet left when he discovers his misfortune. He takes his revenge there and then by killing the two guilty parties. But the evil is deep-seated: he realizes at last that he lacked love, that is to say, the essential thing, precisely when he thought he was at the peak of happiness.

When he arrives at his brother's, he soon discovers that they both share the same misfortune, which goes some way towards consoling him! The two go off on a journey and then discover that cuckoldom is universal, that what has happened to them is no fortuitous accident. They realize the reason for their anxiety: woman, whom man hopes to be pure, modest and faithful, is essentially a thieving, libidinous creature, devoid of feeling. "They are all whores." There is no such thing as love. When one realizes that, everything collapses. Men are left with only one course: female infidelity must be matched by cruelty. This is because unhappy experiences in love not only make men unhappy; they also make them unjust, bloody and terrifying.

We are here at the peak of misogyny. Then Shahrazād appears to reverse the tendency dialectically. For her, it is a question of curing the king. She sets in train a whole therapeutic process through the spicy tale, eroticism, words, fantasy, dream. Shahrazād is self-revelation through the mediation of woman. Woman, who brought man to perdition, can also save him. "How beautiful and marvellous is your story!" Shahryar constantly repeats. This is because Shahrazād is "educated". She has studied the whole of human history, biographical treatises, poetry, the celebrated *adab*, the *fiqh,* astronomy ... Shahrazād is the Arab Diotima. Still more so perhaps, for she adds eroticism to femininity. To knowledge she adds accomplishments. She reinvents the secret that cures souls: eroticism, which alone soothes crises of conscience and restores trust in life. This conversion to life in a thousand and one sessions is an initiation into knowledge through love. We have to admire the triptych: eroticism, knowledge, imagination. Eroticism directed against misogyny allows us to rediscover the meaning of Allah's work and, in doing so, the vertigos of knowledge. We pass from extreme hallucination to extreme exaltation. Hence the curative virtue of Shahrazād's enterprise.

But nothing is as "moral" as the tales that Shahrazād tells, we must not forget, in order to save her young sister Dunyazad, hidden under the marriage bed, the scarcely embarrassing, or embarrassed witness of the frolics of her elder sister and her royal and choleric husband. Appearances are always saved. The dénouement of the tales is always such as to satisfy the most demanding puritans. Filial piety, justice, honour, fear of God and honesty are exalted. But above all the most carnal love is always allied with the most spiritual faith. For love is the work of God: It is therefore the divine symbol of perfection and of Allah's creation. God is blessed as the giver of pleasure and the arouser of joy. God is perceived as the support of love and as the permanent arousal of Eros. For the orgasm is a marvel that helps us to become aware of God's effectiveness. It helps us to read the book of creation. Love is a personal experience of the miracles that makes us aware of the work of God. Shahrazād exclaims:

> Glory to Allah who did not create
> A more enchanting spectacle than that of two happy lovers.
> Drunk with voluptuous delights
> They lie on their couch

Their arms entwined
Their hands clasped
Their hearts beating in tune.

In these tales everybody evokes the Quran, God and his Prophet to magnify the work of the flesh. Almond is described thus:

> Her slight body has the colour of silver, and stands like a box-tree; her waist is a hair's breadth, her station is the station of the sun, she has the walk of a partridge. Her hair is of hyacinth, her eyes are sabres of Isfahan; her cheeks resemble the verse of Beauty in the Book; the bows of her brows recall the chapter of the Pen. Her mouth, carved from a ruby, is an astonishment; a dimpled apple is her chin, its beauty spot avails against the evil-eye. Her very small ears were lovers' hearts instead of jewels, the ring of her nose is a slave ring about moon. The soles of her little feet are altogether charming. Her heart is a sealed flask of perfume, her soul is wise. Her approach is the tumult, of the Resurrection! She is the daughter of King Akbar, and her name is Princess Almond. Such names are blessed!

The body of a woman, therefore, is a microcosm of the masterly work of God. To lose oneself in it is to find oneself in God. To run over it is to continue the great book of Allah. For it is a reference to the Quran, the Calam and the Resurrection. To take possession of it and to travel with it towards orgasm is to live in anticipation the delights of *janna*. This is how Shahrazād, towards the end of the cycle, on the 998th night, sings this splendid hymn to divine love:

> Love was before the light began,
> When light is over, love shall be;
> O warm hand in the grave, O bridge of truth,
> O ivy's tooth.
> Eating the green heart of the tree
> Of man!

How can one resist Shahrazad, who knows so many good things about love and who knows how to evoke them in such a way as to move the most insensitive hearts. On innumerable occasions she describes the joys of the flesh with consummate art:

> Then the girl suddenly dropped her nonchalant pose, as if driven by some irresistible desire, and took me in her arms, and held me tight against her body, and, turning quite pale, swooned into my arms. And she was soon in movement, panting and bubbling over with so much pleasure that the child was soon in its cradle, with no cries, no pain, like a fish in water. And, no longer having to concern myself with my rivals, I could give full vent to my pleasure. And we spent all day and all night, without speaking, without eating and without drinking, in a contortion of limbs. And the horned ram did not spare this battling ewe, and his thrusts were those of a thick-necked father, and the jam he served was the jam of a big pizzle, and the father of whiteness was not inferior to the prodigious tool and the one-eyed assailant had his fill, and the

stubborn mule was tamed by the dervish's stick, and the silent starling sang in tune with the trilling nightingale, and the earless rabbit marched in step with the voiceless cock, and the capricious muscle set the silent tongue in movement, and, in short, everything that could be ravished was ravished, and what could be repeated was repeated; and we ceased our labours only with the appearance of morning, to recite our prayers and to go to the baths!

One can see how Shahryar was seduced during a thousand and one nights! Who could have complained! In any case Shahrazād was able to interpose between her and her terrible companion the enchantments of love poetry and its poetic loves had an immediate effect since they created in the most admirable way a durable love, a peace of hearts. So much so that at the end of the cycle the king is cured. He emerges convinced that the love in which, when he was jealous and selfish, he did not believe is something marvellous and majestic. It is the king himself who draws these conclusions when he declares to Shahrazād's father: "May God protect thee, since thou hast married to me thy generous daughter, who hath been the cause of my repenting of slaying the daughters of the people, and I have seen her to be ingenuous, pure, chaste, virtuous. Moreover, God hath blessed me by her with three male children; and praise be to God for this abundant favour!" To be converted to love, therefore, is to be converted to God. The more one cultivates the flesh the better one worships the Lord and the worship of God is a continuous, heartrending call to savour again, to savour forever the constantly renewed joys of a pleasure that is divine in essence. The fervour of the flesh is a fervour of God.

What is even more astonishing is that Shahrazad does not invite us to this conversion by travestying sexuality, by concealing women's defects. On the contrary, the realism, the honour, the cruelty that unfortunately exist and that often exasperate love are not killed, but exposed and often elaborated quite crudely. One abandons everything, business, kingdom, wealth, parents, to find the love that is presented, as in the olden days, as total, embracing all its deviations. For *The Thousand and One Nights* is a sort of sexological encyclopedia before its time. And nothing is missed out: prostitution, polygamy, homosexuality, male and female, impotence, frigidity, voyeurism, narcissism—and almost anything one can think of.

If *The Thousand and One Nights* was so popular it is because its tales do not in fact idealize and magnify woman as she was represented in courtly society. They also succeed in showing the back of the decor. They allow the humble to speak for themselves, but they show everything that women are capable of.

Indeed love is universal and everybody has a right to it, the street porter and the vagabond, as well as the prince and the rich merchant. But, alas, not everybody realizes his dream. And, in *The Thousand and One Nights* not every love is satisfied. There is for example the unhappy tailor who is tricked by a woman who promises to give herself to him, but in fact denounces him to her husband. He is forced to work free of charge for the suspicious husband. His fate is often that of the poor and humble. He loses everything. Five things combine to bring him low: love, lack of money, hunger, nakedness, tiredness. Tricked and ridiculed, he is thrown out naked into the street.

The tales also convey the social values of love. They are imbued with sociality. They are like a social protest through the demand for love: brigands, *ayyarun,* are not always antipathetic and there are hunchbacks who know how to make love admirably. And why is it so surprising if a woman who has fallen into the hands of a grumpy or suspicious husband takes revenge on him in her own way by cuckolding him? She avenges her class in avenging her sex. Shahrazād wins our applause for adulteries that are merely good tricks played on old greybeards.

Take the lady who, having collected the rings of a hundred lovers who have slept with her, makes this confession:

> "The givers of these seal-rings have all coupled with me on the unwitting horns of this *Ifrit*. So now, O brothers, give me yours!" Then they gave her their seal-rings, taking them off their hands. Whereon she said: "Know that this *Ifrit* carried me off on the night of my marriage, prisoned me in a coffer and placed that coffer in a box and fastened about the box seven chains, yes, and then laid me at the bottom of the moaning sea that wars and dashes with its waves. But he did not know that whenever any one of us women desires a thing, nothing can prevent her from it."

This is pure *mujun*, but assumed in the lucid mode of radical feminism. From misogyny to intransigent feminism, *The Thousand and One Nights* develops a remarkable logic.

It is the same continuity that I have tried to develop through the variations evoked in this chapter. These variations situate us in relation to eroticism at points and counterpoints that seem to be contradictory, but are in fact subtly connected to one another through the combined dynamics of love and faith. Misogyny is ultimately a homage to physical love in the sense in which hypocrisy is a homage to virtue, or, to put it another way, it is an anti-homage paid to *mujün*.

Mujun seems to me to be one of the summits of Arabo-Muslim culture and *The Thousand and One Nights* is erected as a monument to the glory of fundamental unity. But we can now see that at the level of everyday life and at every level of social life the sacral and the sexual support each other and are both engaged in the same process: that of the defence of the group. This ethics of marital affection based on frenetically lyrical vision of life leads to a veritable technique of Eros that is itself indissociable from its religious base. Just as there is a religious ritual, there is an erotic ritual and each parallels the other. Arab eroticism, then, is a refined, learned technique whose mission is to realize God's purpose in us. It is therefore a pious, highly recommended work. Indeed it is a matter of helping nature, concretizing life in its most beautiful, most noble aspects and realizing the genetic mission of the body.

In this respect eroticism is a technique of the body and of the mind. Perhaps Arab misogyny is an illusion after all! Supposing it were merely a ruse of love? Or the starting point for any conversion? In every Arab man there may be a dormant Shahryar and in every Arab woman an unsuspected Shahrazād. And here the identification of the teller and the told is not a gratuitous device. It is not a tendency to be sublimated, but an example to follow and a fantasy to be realized. Hence, it seems to me, that unity in functionality of both the descriptions of paradise and the techniques of love. It is not a question of opposing the superior and the inferior. They are welded together as one. So a good orgasm culminates in morning prayers. It is as if prayer is also an expectation of pleasure. Our God, give us this day our daily orgasm!

Lyricism and sacralization of life, the art of assuming sexuality and satisfying it, on the one hand, glorification of God and of his works, on the other, combine in a single reaction: wonder. Wonder conceived by the imaginary and realized in orgasm gives, beyond appearances, the unity of the personality in Arabo-Muslim society. Hence, ultimately, that dialectic of the sacral and the sexual of which misogyny or blasphemy are merely negative moments, and therefore herald the full positivity of orgasm and the vision of God.

An abridged version adapted from *Sexuality in Islam* (Saqi Books, 1998): 116–139. Printed here with the permission of the author.

FEDWA MALTI-DOUGLAS

Narration and Desire: Shahrazâd

Shahrazâd, the female spinner of tales in *The Thousand and One Nights,* queen of narrators East and West, has long been the symbol of storytelling. Her power over words and her perceived ability to control discourse have provoked the envy of male writers from Edgar Allan Poe to John Barth.

In his delightful and critically conscious novel, *La Lectrice* (now also a film), Raymond Jean blends sexual and literary desire, feminine seductiveness and narration. Like a modern-day Shahrazâd, his comely heroine narrates texts (actually she reads aloud) to a series of listeners who readily confuse literature and sexuality. What most distinguishes the twentieth-century French heroine from her Arabo-Persian predecessor is her lack of control. Desire swirls around her, while she has little hold on it. All the more striking by contrast is Shahrazâd's mastery. It is she who controls the relation between desire and the text, at least up to a point.

The Shahrazâd we shall examine is also a sexual being, who manipulates discourse (and men) through her body. It is the latter that permits her to speak, as male violence is met with her sexuality, articulated through her body and her words. At the same time, Shahrazâd uses narrative to redirect desire and, hence, sexuality.

The frame story of *The Thousand and One Nights*—that is, the work's prologue and epilogue, as they are usually termed—is without doubt one of the most powerful narratives in world literature. It is not simply from its mixture of sex and violence that the frame of the *Nights* draws its enduring appeal. Rather, this lies in the unique relationship it forges between sexual and narrative desire.

Innumerable critics have written on *Alf Layla wa-Layla.* (A "thousand and one" might not be an exaggeration.) And the frame story is mentioned in much of the criticism. Most of the interpretations divide themselves into two schools: the time-gaining, on the one hand, and the healing, on the other. From Shahrazâd's perspective, the frame becomes a "time-gaining" technique, similar to other time-gaining or lifesaving acts of narration in the body of the Nights themselves. To quote Mia Gerhardt (1963), "Shehrezâd temporizes by making one story follow another, until at last she has gained her victory." Likewise, Bruno Bettelheim (1977) notes that "delivery from death through the telling of fairy tales is a motif which starts the cycle." But Bettelheim is representative, indeed probably the best representative, of the "healing" school. For the psychoanalytic critic, there are two protagonists, Shâhriyâr and Shahrazâd. She is the ego, while her male counterpart is dominated by the id, and the entire text functions as an "integration of the king's personality." Integration of personality, now translated into Jungian terms, is also central to Jerome Clinton's discussion (1985). The interpretive arguments of time-gaining and healing are clearly interrelated.

All these views of Shahrazâd and the frame have one overriding characteristic in common: they are prefeminist and pre-gender conscious, in the intellectual, not the chronological sense. Making Shahrazâd represent beings of desire (or equating her with speech), confining her to the role of healer, draws attention away from both the strength of her personality and her mastery of the situation, while occulting male-female power dynamics.

Striking in this nonfeminism is its articulation, even exaggeration, in the writings of the noted Moroccan feminist, Fatima Mernissi (1988), for whom Shahrazâd is "an innocent young girl whom a fatal destiny led to Shâhriyâr's bed," and her achievement, "the miraculous triumph of the innocent." Such a view belittles Shahrazâd's wisdom and cleverness, on the one hand, and her initiative and mastery, on the other. She is not led by a fatal destiny to the king's bed, nor is her triumph due to miraculous chance.

Ironically, it has been male creative writers themselves who have most clearly perceived, and most forcibly reacted against, the feminist implications of the frame story, with its image of mastery through narration. That is why authors like Poe ("The Thousand-and-Second Tale") and Barth *(Chimera),* for example (aided in this by a slightly misplaced professional jealousy—after all, Shahrazâd is not the work's author, only its principal narrator), feel the need to conjure away either Shahrazâd's literary or her sexual and interpersonal achievements.

The frame, despite the literary interludes of the Shabrazâdian-narrated nights, is a complete literary unit, and its prologue should not be separated and considered a "prétexte" (or fore-text). The epilogue of the frame—usually dismissed cavalierly, when not overlooked completely—is an integral part of the story, redefining through its literary closure the meaning of the prologue itself. Many critics have called attention to what they consider an incongruity between the ostensible purpose of Shahrazâd's storytelling and the contents of many of the stories told, providing as they do examples of evil women. Such a line of argument runs a double danger: either an overreliance on a mechanistic type of psychological explanation or a tendency to judge the significance and impact of individual stories outside the larger corpus of the *Nights* as a whole. In either case, the entire issue is, in a certain sense, irrelevant, since the storytelling frame has, as will become clear, proper ties independent of the content of the stories told.

For analytical purposes, the frame can be divided into six sections:

1. The first section opens with Shâhriyâr's desire to see his younger brother Shâhzamân, from whom he has been separated for twenty years. This desire instigates Shâhzamân's voyage to his brother, which in turn becomes the occasion for the discovery of his own wife's infidelity. It is also while visiting Shâhriyâr that he discovers the perfidy of the older monarch's wife.

2. The second section consists of a voyage as well. This one involves both brothers, who abandon their kingdoms because of their wives' adulterous behavior. On this journey, they encounter the *'ifrît* and the young woman, who forces them under threat of death to copulate with her. At the end of this experience, they decide to return to their kingdom, and to abandon the permanent company of women.

3. The third section, embodying Shâhriyâr's violent reaction to the past events in the

frame, narrates his one-night sexual encounters that culminate in each case with the murder of his female partner.

4. With section four, Shahrazâd enters the scene. Despite her father's protests, she insists on being offered to the monarch and enlists the help of her sister, Dunyâzâd, in her act. Here begins the narration.

5. The frame does not stop at this point; and its fifth section is its continuation during Shahrazâd's thousand and one nights of storytelling. The storytelling must not be equated with the contents of the stories told. If the stories that Shahrazâd tells are outside the frame (or might one better say inside?), the act of telling them is the continuation of the frame. It should be remembered that once she has begun, Shahrazâd does not disappear like some now-obsolescent literary device. She is a most intrusive narrator, who appears at a minimum at the beginning and end of every night. Shâhriyâr and Dunyâzâd, also characters from the frame story, make occasional appearances as well.

6. The last part of the frame is its closure with the happy ending. Shâhriyâr is told that he has meanwhile fathered three sons (fortunate conceptions, indeed) and Shahrazâd is rewarded in a wedding ceremony. In a longer version, Shahrazâd weds Shâhriyâr, Dunyâzâd weds Shâhzamân, and the text of the *Nights* is set down in writing. All live happily till death do them part.

Desire is at the root of the frame of the *Nights*, but desire as a problem. There are proper desires as there are improper ones. Or, to speak more precisely, there are proper and improper patterns of desire, and ways of using and fulfilling desire. Proper and improper, here, are more than moral antinomies: they reach beyond the relatively restricted domain of the just and the unjust to the more worldly regions of the appropriate and the ultimately satisfying.

The importance of desire is clear from the first events of the frame. Shâhriyâr longs for his brother (*ishtâqa ilâ*). This longing, seemingly at the outset quite natural, is, however, problem-generating, since it sets in motion the events that will follow. The fulfillment of this desire, i.e. Shâhzamân's voyage to visit his brother, permits the younger monarch to discover the perfidy of his wife, only the first in a series of such discoveries. More than simply a wish to see the brother, Shâhriyâr's desire can be defined as a need for another, in this case, a male. What we are observing in the opening events of the text is an allusion to the formation of a homosocial desire and coupling that will prove crucial in subsequent events in the *Nights*. *Homosocial* must be distinguished from *homosexual* and by no means implies a sexual relationship, but rather a social relationship between two individuals of the same gender. There is a tendency in the West to interpret examples of homosociality as indexes of latent or overt homosexuality. But this is really a reflection of the obsessional relationship of Western culture with homosexuality, and the culture's homophobia, since the later Middle Ages. In the Arabo-Islamic cultural sphere, true homosexuality, while certainly present, poses less of a psychological problem for the culture. Classical Arabic authors felt no embarrassment in discussing male homoeroticisim, occasionally in the context of heterosexual eroticism. The crisis with which the *Nights* begins is one that is itself initiated by male homosocial desire. The resulting problematic male couple is, in its own way, as important as the pair Shâhriyâr-Shahrazâd. As we shall see, the male couple is a crucial phenomenon in the gender dynamics of classical Arabic literature.

For the frame of the *Nights*, the male couple is a central problem. This relationship, a constant in all versions, seems superficially anomalous and has been effectively ignored by most critics. After all, the story could seem to function without the couple: a king sets off on a journey, comes back suddenly to discover his wife's infidelity, dispatches her, sets out again with a heavy heart, and meets the *'ifrît* and his young woman, after which he turns against all woman kind, deciding to sleep with and kill a new partner each night (this is indeed the way the story is related by Fatima Mernissi). Clearly then, the male couple must be fulfilling some other function.

It is as a homosocial couple that Shâhriyâr and Shâhzamân decide to flee from the world after the older brother has seen his wife copulating with the black slave. The repeated use of the Arabic *dunyâ* is not without significance. Etymologically the basest of places, it represents the world negatively, as the opposite of spirituality, and is often associated, again negatively, with sex and the female. But it is precisely when the homosocial couple of the two brothers goes off together that things turn topsy-turvy in the text.

The homosocial couple is contrasted with the heterosexual one, the latter not merely problematic, but in a state of crisis. It is perhaps the coexistence of the two types of couples that is most explosive and unleashes unnatural events. It is when Shâhzamân goes to bid farewell to his wife—that is, when he is about to fulfill Shâhriyâr's homosocial desire—that he discovers her adulterous act. Her perfidy is all the more vile, not only because of her choice of mate (a cook), but also when set against the king's devotion. And it is when Shâhriyâr and Shâhzamân go off on their homosocial voyage that they encounter the *'ifrît* and the young woman, an encounter which, as we shall see, dramatically alters the rest of the narrative.

Homosocial desire is intricately linked in the frame of the *Nights* with the idea of voyage. Travel is normally a learning and maturing experience, as are, for example, the voyages of Sindibâd. The implications of the term *dunyâ* and Shâhriyâr's statement that they should go forth "in the love of God" even add the flavor of a spiritual quest.

Shahrazâd is an intellectual wonder, who has memorized books, poetry, wisdom, and more. She is knowledgeable, intelligent, wise, and an *adîba* (woman learned in the arts of literature and society). Her desire is initially expressed to her father: she wishes him (*ashtahî minka*) to marry her to the king. She will liberate everyone or die. Her father gets angry and tries to discourage her by explaining the situation to her, going so far as to tell her an "exemplary tale," but to no avail. So her father informs the king of her desire. The latter is happy (*fariha*) and tells the vizier to bring her that night. The vizier then tells Shahrazâd, who is also very pleased (*farihat*). She explains to Dunyâzâd that she will send for her and that she should ask for a story after she has seen that the king has performed the act. Dunyaâzâd patiently waits under the bed for the king to perform his act. This virtual ménage à trois posits Dunyâzâd and Shahrazâd as potential counterweight to the male pair, Shâhriyâr/Shâhzamân. Then the younger sister asks for the story, as she was told, the king approves, and Shahrazâd's role in world literature is launched. Yet it is Dunyâzâd who links sex and narration by first witnessing the act, then requesting the story.

The parallel happiness of Shâhriyâr and Shahrazâd (expressed by the same Arabic verb— *fariha*) puts the two on an equal footing. The relationship has been created. Shahrazâd is unlike all the previous females presented in the text. They embodied physical desire that was purely sexual, expressed in the most direct manner possible. The men are sex objects. Clearly, all women preceding Shahrazâd's entrance in the text are physical, if not overly physical, beings. Their exploitive use of desire is part of the problem that must be corrected by the vizier's daughter.

Earlier females are limited to the vagina, which means that their desire functions on an exclusively physical plane. Shahrazâd adds to this the word, permitting, as we shall see, a transposition and transformation of desire. There is a sense, however, in which Shahrazâd comes close to other members of her gender. The earlier women's behavior was defined in terms of its *kayd:* its guile, its trickery. Shahrazâd also uses a ruse, that of narration, to achieve her ends. Her storytelling, after all, consists of structuring the stories so that the listener will be left in suspense at the break of dawn. Hers could be argued to be the ultimate in female trickery, since it represents a continual game of attraction (the storytelling) followed by denial of satisfaction (the end of the story, which must await yet another night).

This manipulation of narrative desire is far more than merely a means of gaining time, though, of course, in the beginning it is that. It is a key pedagogical tool. Rather than taking on directly the king's fractured pattern of physical lovemaking, Shahrazâd shifts the problem of desire from the area of sex, the realm of Shâhriyâr's trauma, to the superficially more distant and more malleable world of the text. Her storytelling teaches a new type of desire, a desire that continues from night to night, a desire whose interest does not fall and which can, therefore, leap the intervening days. In sexual terms, this is a replacement of an immature male pattern of excitement, satisfaction, and termination with what can be called a more classically female pattern of extended and continuous desire and pleasure. Of course, it is this extension of desire through time that permits the forging of relationships, and with it the nonexploitive approach to sexuality. In effecting this transformation, Shahrazâd functions as a mistress of desire, not unlike the sexually wise women of the erotic manuals, one of whose duties is the initiation of males into a more sophisticated sexuality.

Shahrazâd's mastery of the entire process can be most easily seen when her story is compared with an ancient Egyptian ancestor, best known as *The Eloquent Peasant.* Like the frame of *The Thousand and One Nights,* the Pharaonic tale is concerned with the interrelationship among text creation, justice, and the whim of an all-powerful monarch. The Old Kingdom peasant, however, is manipulated by his sovereign rather than the other way around. Justice is apparently denied him by an aesthetically sophisticated ruler who wishes to stimulate the peasant's eloquent pleas for justice, in order that they may be written down and preserved for posterity. Of course, another difference, often overlooked by those who wish to make Shahrazâd a model of Arabic woman's authorship, is that the vizier's daughter, unlike the peasant from the oasis, has not created her text. She has merely learned it and is transmitting it. Similarly, the parallel writing of the generated text at the end of each tale has a different function. It does not consecrate Shahrazâd's authorship but merely transfers oral to written transmission, a point to whose significance we shall return.

Shahrazâd's desire, couched in her wish to liberate the world from Shâhriyâr's tyranny, is to wed the monarch. This is by no means insignificant. She wishes to set in motion once again the heterosexual couple, which previously has only been contrasted with the homosocial male couple, in various explosive and unnatural situations. It is not coincidental that Shâhzamân, we are told, has been dispatched to his own kingdom. The danger of another male couple forming and threatening the Shahrazâd-Shâhriyâr heterosexual duo has been averted.

But this task is by no means a simple one. Shahrazâd must rectify the situation by restoring proper sexuality, proper rhythm, and proper desire. She, a woman, must undo the lessons that have been instilled by another woman, the *ifrît's* companion. Dunyâzâd and Shahrazâd act as a pair in the transition from sex to text, just as Shâhriyâr and Shâhzamân were jointly possessed by the *ifrît's* female prisoner.

Several lessons and intellectual constructs that have been learned by the monarch will simply have to be unlearned, if not completely dismantled. Male knowledge before Shahrazâd's arrival on the scene was aggressively visual. References to the act of seeing abound. Shâhzamân watches the scene of his sister-in-law's infidelity from beginning to end, and his act is, in effect, a voyeuristic one. As such, it parallels the earlier discovery of his own wife's infidelity. When Shâhzamân reveals to his brother the queen's infidelity, he speaks of "the misfortune he saw." Shâhrayâr does not believe the accusations and insists that he must see the events with his own eyes. Shâhzamân replies that "if you wish to see your misfortune with your own eyes" to believe it, then they should pretend to go out on a hunt, and instead enter the city secretly and go up to the palace, where Shâhriyâr can see the events with his own eyes.

These repeated allusions, when combined with Shâhzamân's voyeuristic activity, call attention to a certain type of male active power, of the subject/looker on the object/looked upon. This is male scopic activity. The males would then be in the active position. Male visual dominance certainly rules. But, at the same time, male power is called into question, subverted. The women, the objects watched, are, in fact, the active members in another relationship, the sexual, since they are the ones whose activity (sexual) is of interest. Even the moral character of this voyeurism is ambiguous. As obsessional activity, it could be seen as "illicit sight" in Phyllis Trible's terms, though the females' adultery is also clearly blameworthy (1985). This visual/scopic emphasis is a commentary on desire as well. Shâhriyâr's insistence that he must "see" shows the force that is driving him. Again it is the fulfillment of this improper desire that sets in motion drastic narrative events.

Shahrazâd's path is clearly the opposite. She narrates a text. Hers is the oral approach, in which the male becomes the auditor, the passive partner. Sight and hearing are cast in the frame of the Nights as alternative ways of acquiring knowledge. We are firmly on the ground of a debate well entrenched in medieval Islamic mentalities, that of the relative value of the senses, specifically the oral versus the visual. Which was the better, hearing or vision? Linguistic and philosophical arguments conclude that hearing is superior to seeing. Shâhriyâr's continued attempts to find the truth through his faculty of vision have only led him astray. It is rather through his faculty of hearing, through listening to Shahrazâd's narratives, that all will be set aright.

Shahrazâd's stories lead to another dichotomy, that between "reality" and fiction. Shâhriyâr's search and desire for reality through what he can plainly see is illusory, since this is shown to be the wrong tactic. Rather, it is through fiction that the proper uses of desire can best be learned. The odyssey he has undertaken with Shâhzamân, his *rihla fî talab al-ʿilm* (the medieval Islamic journey in search of knowledge) is a physical voyage whose consequences must be corrected by Shahrazâd's narrative voyage. Her narrative "nights" become, then, journeys into desire and the unconscious. Again, literature must correct experience. But it is not a modern conception of literature that is at issue here. What the learned Shahrazâd provides in an entertaining form is the accumulated wisdom of her civilization, which, delivered in the right manner, can correct the mislearnings of a far more limited individual experience.

It is perhaps in the closure of the frame story that the consequences of Shahrazâd's lessons on desire come to fruition. The closure of the frame occurs at the end of the *Nights*, in what some have called the epilogue. This may seem much too obvious a point. But when the work is compared with a similar text, *The One Hundred and One Nights*, which also operates around female infidelity and narration, a very important difference emerges. The closure of the story in that text is presented before the narration even begins. In fact, closure in classical Arabic literature poses special critical problems, and *The Thousand and One Nights* from this perspective comes closest to a Western text.

Two versions for the closure of Shahrazâd's *Nights* exist, a shorter one and a longer one. In both versions, Shahrazâd has meanwhile given birth to three sons. She makes this fact known to the monarch and asks him to spare her life for the sake of his sons, who will otherwise have no mother. He replies that he had long ago decided not to kill her, having discovered that she was "virtuous, pure, free, and pious" (*ʿafifa, naqiyya, hurra, taqiyya*). When the monarch extols her virtues to her father, he exchanges her piety for her intelligence (*hurra, naqiyya, ʿafifa, zakiyya*). The king extends his generosity to the entire kingdom, the city is decorated, goods are distributed to the poor: beneficence reigns. Only death brings an end to this idyllic situation.

The longer version distinguishes itself by the presence of an elaborate marriage ceremony. Shâhriyâr declares that he will wed Shahrazâd and then summons Shâhzamân. The older king tells his younger brother all that has befallen him, including Shahrazâd's stories, at which point Shâhzamân reveals that he has also been bedding one woman every night and then killing her the next morning. Now, he wishes to marry Dunyâzâd. Shahrazâd agrees to this only if the couple remains with them. The two women are then paraded in an array of dresses before their respective spouses, for a total of seven dresses. The narrator describes first one woman, and then the other, with Arabic verses. The narrative and verse descriptions make it clear that an elaborate erotic game is being played out. The young women's costumes are associated with different erotic models and roles, some quite traditional and others more daring, even suggesting the erotic appeal of transvestism and gender ambiguity. Shahrazâd smiles and sways seductively; the two sisters leave their royal mates filled with amorous longing. At the end of the fashion show, each male retires with the appropriate female. The vizier is appointed ruler of Samarkand. As for the two brothers, they rule alternately for one day each. Shâhriyâr orders that all that has befallen him with Shahrazâd be inscribed by copyists and the books stored in his treasury. Again, only death disturbs this idyllic arrangement. Another ruler then follows who discovers the books, reads them, and has them copied and widely distributed.

The closure demonstrates, first and foremost, that Shahrazâd's desire, expressed in her wish to wed the king, was indeed the proper one. The sexual act has been transformed from one linked with death to one leading to creation. She has, after all, given birth to three sons. This change is a result of a shift in rhythm. It is the extension of desire into longer relationships that permits the begetting of sons. Shâhriyâr's (and, in the longer version, Shâhzamân's) earlier system, if it provided sexual pleasure, prevented the personally and politically vital creation of heirs. These men would have seen their lines come to an end.

In some respects, this closure stands in contrast with the somewhat feminist implications of the prologue of the frame story. After all, there we saw an independent, courageous Shahrazâd, risking her life to save those of her sisters, and in the process, despite appearances, controlling the situation and educating the monarch. Little wonder that the conclusion of the tale has angered some feminists who consider such an ending the invention of male storytellers. Why would a courageous, well-educated heroine like Shahrazâd marry an obvious lout like Shâhriyâr?

Of course, the original tale is far more traditional in its morality, recuperating, even conjuring away the feminist implications of the prologue in the epilogue. This recuperation is made even clearer in the longer version of the closing section. Shahrazâd is in both versions no longer a storyteller, since an anonymous narrator is talking about her. But she has become in a much more real sense the object, rather than the producer or even the controller, of literary discourse. This is achieved through the poetic selections, given over completely to the physical description of Shahrazâd and Dunyâzâd in their erotic displays. And poetry, it should be remembered, has always had a far greater literary prestige in Arabo-Islamic society than prose. Nor is it a coincidence that the poetry describes, even magnifies, a situation in which Shahrazâd is the object of desire. Further, most of these verses are repeated from an earlier part of the *Nights,* where they were effectively part of Shahrazâd's narration. No longer their narrator, she becomes their object.

But the display is more than literary—it is also preeminently visual; and as admiring audience for this floor show, Shâhriyâr and Shâhzamân regain their scopic relationship to desire, now in a context of sexual mastery. As the women become objects of desire, the male has regained his active role and the female her passive one. In place of her intellect, it is now Shahrazâd's physicality that comes to the fore.

Even the male homosocial couple is recreated, since, at Shahrazâd's request, Shâhzamân and his bride will live with Shâhriyâr and Shahrazâd. The fusion of the royal brothers is also accomplished, since they will jointly rule the kingdom. With a solution like this, of course, one no longer risks dangerous voyages. The brother-brother (and the sister-sister) couples are no longer a threat to the heterosexual one, since this last is now established on solid foundations. Sibling and matrimonial relationships are harmonized. The presence of children shows how restoring the heterosexual couple saves patriarchy.

The longer version also clarifies Shahrazâd's relationship to literature. She may have narrated the stories, but it is Shâhriyâr who has them written down, to be eventually copied and distributed by his male successor. Her world is the evanescent one of oral performance. It is both measured by and linked to time: a thousand and one nights. To the males is reserved the authority and permanence of written literature. Thus, the longer version of the closure makes explicit what was only implicit in its shorter form. Shahrazâd's extraordinary role is also a temporary one: necessitated by a crisis, it comes to an end with the end of that crisis. The frame story is a giant parenthesis whose closing is both the closure and the conclusion of the *Nights* as a whole. The "nights" are like dreams that end with the rise of the literary sun of vision, reality, and male preeminence.

In the process, body has been transmuted into word and back into body. Corporeality is the final word, as Shahrazâd relinquishes her role of narrator for that of perfect woman: mother and lover.

References

Barth, John. *Chimera* (New York: Fawcett Crest, 1972): 9–64.

Bettelheim, Bruno. *The Uses of Enchantment: The Meaning and Importance of Fairy Tales* (New York: Vintage Books, 1977).

Clinton, Jermoe W. "Madness and Cure in *The 1001 Nights.*" Studia Islamica 61 (1985): 107–125.

Gerhardt, Mia I. *The Art of Storytelling: A Literary Study of the Thousand and One Nights.* (Leiden: E.J. Brill, 1963).

Jean, Raymond. *La Lectrice* (Paris: Actes Sud, 1986).

Mernissi, Fatima. *Chahrazad n'est pas marocaine.* (Casablanca: Editions Le fennec, 1988.)

Poe, Edgar Allan. "The Thousand-and-Second Tale of Scheherazade." In *Edgar Allan Poe, Greenwich Unabridged Library Classics* (New York: Chatham River Press, 1981): 491–502.

Trible, Phyllis. *Texts of Terror: Literary-Feminist Readings of Biblical Narratives.* (Philadelphia:Fortress Press, 1985).

An abridged version adapted from *Woman's Body, Woman's Word* (Princeton University Press, 1991): 11–28. Article is printed here with permission of the publisher.

Worlds Apart: Sexual Life for Women and Men in Iraq, Attitudes towards Sex

Q: How well would you say you and your husband get on, in general?

A: The most important things for him are food and sex. When we first married, I had such a rough time living with his sister. I couldn't wear make-up or dress up the way I like, as she gets jealous. He used to say to me, "Stop wearing make-up, don't do this, don't wear that. What are you trying to do? She gets hurt." When she got married, that was one problem out of the way.

Q: Is your husband an affectionate person? Does he express it? In what way?

A: A wife needs sympathy and understanding, but he hardly says a nice word to me. Sometimes I ask him whether he loves me and he says, "If I didn't, I wouldn't buy you and your children all that you need." I say, "But a woman likes to hear a nice word from her husband." He replies, "Women who hear soft talk misbehave." I'm telling you, if he smiled once I'd say, "The sun's come out."

Q: What about his anger? Does he express it? In what way?

A: He has a loud mouth. He always shouts at me and threatens me with divorce. He demands my approval for everything he does.

Q: What about the sexual side of things? Have you had any difficulties or problems with this?

A: Whenever he wants me, I'm ready. If he goes to the bedroom, even if he doesn't call me, I go to him and ask if he wants me. Sometimes he says yes; others no, he's tired. I think I must fear God. I believe that if women don't obey men particularly in such matters, God, the heavens and the holy spirits will never bless them.

Q: What about you? Do you think sex is important for women too?

A: Well, he doesn't really care much whether I do or not. Sometimes I even try to mention it to him indirectly, but he doesn't pay any attention. You know, I'm very good to him. He doesn't like me to go out, so I don't. I obey all his orders. I take good care of him, but he doesn't take care of me. Sometimes I get angry. Once, I decided to say "no" to him. He said, "What about God and the holy spirits? Don't you fear them?"

Q: So it was he who taught you that?

A: No, I already believed it. It was my mother, God bless her soul, who taught me that and I told him about it. (*Majida*)

I have quoted Majida's answers at length because they may be seen as representative of the experience of many Iraqi women. From what she and other women told me, it is obvious that the relationship between husbands and wives in Iraq remains, as it has traditionally been, based on power. Husbands expect to command their wives rather than love them. Even when they care about their wives the social system does not allow them to show it, so the wives are unaware of their husbands' feelings. It is believed that there is a fundamental biological difference between men and women: sexual satisfaction is seen as a "need" for men and as a "service" for women. Thus women's nature is believed to be receptive and frigid, while men have strong sexual desires and are active in the sexual act. Girls are socialized to regard sex as predominantly a male concern; they are brought up to avoid any behavior defined as sexual, such as dressing in a particular way, laughing or even walking freely, because an "honourable" girl ought not to do anything which might lead men to desire her.

Young females are socialized to fear men and sexuality and to protect their virginity at all costs. They are taught to avoid strenuous exercise, jumping from heights, or sitting on sharp edges, in order to keep their hymen intact. Correspondingly, the parents' most important duty is to ensure their daughter remains a virgin until her wedding day. This part of a girl's body is considered to be more important even than her eyes, arms or lower limbs. (El Saadawi, 1980)

The majority of young women enter marriage in a state of almost complete sexual ignorance, which is seen as a sign of honour. (El Saadawi, 1980) Young women are expected to be pure and virginal in mind and body, or to be frigid: this makes their exploitation complete and absolute. The women I interviewed described experiences that derive from this social conditioning:

> I remember that from a very early age I was afraid of men. I used to hear a lot of stories—about this woman whose life was ruined because she was raped, and another girl who got pregnant and her family killed her ... and so on. I was so terrified that when I went to buy material for a dress and the salesman touched my hand, I felt as if I'd committed a crime. (*Jumana*)

> One of my friends told me about how a woman gets pregnant. She told me that this could happen starting at the age of 10, which worried me. I was even more worried when my mother told me at the age of 12 not to sit on the bath seat [a small wooden seat] when taking a bath after my father or my brother unless I washed it very thoroughly with hot water. She also told me not to mix my clothes with theirs on the same washing line on the roof, for fear I might get pregnant. The idea gave me lots of worries and nightmares. (*Fadwa*)

On the other hand many men, particularly in urban areas, have some sexual experience before marriage. This is accepted by society, though it tends to be limited experience and gained mainly with prostitutes. Both sexes consider pre-marital sexual experience for men to be an advantage. The lack of such experience may be seen as a reason for unsuccessful marital relations and even the breakdown of the marriage.

From my observations and from the answers given to me, it seems that social traditions which derive from Bedouin roots are still so strong that education and social class have little bearing on men's attitudes towards women and sexuality. Samar's words support this view:

He got his higher degree from the US; he's quite sophisticated. Of course, he knows all about women and sex, but a degree doesn't always make much difference; it's more important how you're brought up. Don't you agree?

Sexual experience for women, on the other hand, is generally considered to be a disadvantage, even if "legitimately" gained in a previous marriage. In the marriage market, a female who is a virgin is more desirable than one who is not. (Cosar, 1980) Men tend to leave a woman they love if she consents to a sexual relationship of any kind, regarding her as "loose" and dishonourable, and certainly not to be trusted as a wife.

Because females are so thoroughly socialized to fear sexual relations, the honeymoon, while pleasurable for the man, is invariably the worst period of marital life for the woman. Limited and often inaccurate sexual knowledge provides the woman with false ideas of sexuality. She carries this fear to her wedding day, making it a day of dread. In order to counteract this fear and to determine whether their hymen was intact, most of the women I interviewed took medical advice before their marriage, in case they had lost their virginity by accident—if they were no longer virgins, they might not have gone through with the marriage.

Despite these precautions, the fear is easing slightly nowadays. The old custom of showing a blood-stained sheet on the wedding night, to prove the bride's virginity, has now almost vanished among middle-class urban Iraqis. Another fast-disappearing traditional practice is the bridegroom's slaughtering a cat as the bride enters the bridal chamber before they have sexual intercourse. This was done to scare the bride into obedience, based on the belief that if she were to disobey the husband's demand for sex on the first night of marriage, it might make him permanently impotent. Even among the urban poor, this custom is fast disappearing.

For some of the women I spoke to, their first experience of sex can only be described as traumatic:

I started to fear men the first day I was married. He attacked me all of a sudden. I saw him forcing me. He was like a wolf. It was a nightmare. Some men start by talking to the woman, trying to make it easier for her, but he didn't. (*Fawzia*)

He raped me in the train on our wedding day. I was 13 years old. I met him face to face for the first time that day; we were on the way to our honeymoon in Basra. I started screaming as I was so scared, but I stopped when he started hitting me. I remember very well now that all I wanted then was my mother. I felt that I was with a stranger who was harming me badly. After he finished having sex with me he left me alone, but I felt it was the end of the world for me; everything seemed ugly and those children who I used to play with seemed so far away and I was so alienated. (*Zahra*)

Sex and Knowledge

Although women have very limited knowledge of sex before marriage, I was interested in discovering where such knowledge came from. The following comment is fairly typical:

My information about sex began during my adolescence and came through my friends at school. That information was very limited, and wasn't at all applicable to the real situation I came to know after marriage. (*Zainab*).

Ignorance on the part of both women and men can make sex a problem. Even when partners become sexually experienced, as sometimes happens after long years of marriage, they may still feel insecure regarding their own sexuality. Many women are unaware that a female orgasm exists. They try not to admit that they need satisfaction or to mention such needs even to their husbands "to keep their dignity". Thus women experience a conflict at this level, which can develop into considerable unhappiness within marriage.

Iraqi men tend to have minimal knowledge of female anatomy, and they either do not know how to or do not wish to arouse their wives. (Vieille, 1980) Most of the interviewees said that they experienced no physical contact as such during intercourse, apart from genital contact. Despite this lack of physical intimacy several women indicated that their husband had a very strong sex drive:

> Sex is the most important thing to my husband. It may be the only thing in life that's important to him. He always wants me to dress up in my sexiest nightgown and respond happily and willingly to all his desires. But look at me; I come home from work very tired. At home, the children and the housework make me even more tired, so l don't feel like wearing make-up every evening and doing what he wants, because I'm exhausted. I'd like to talk to someone about my problems, but he doesn't listen to me because he thinks it doesn't concern him. When I don't get changed and dress the way he wants me to, I feel as if I'm punishing him for what he's doing to me. I know this is wrong, but to tell you the truth, I don't care much about sex. I don't know why. (*Suha*).

Suha's experience highlights the fundamental paradox. Men's expectations of sex are high, but since women have no experience and their husbands have no interest in making it pleasurable, it is hard for them to achieve sexual satisfaction. It is important to stress that the men themselves do not wish to initiate their wives into sexual fulfillment because they believe it will make them promiscuous. Furthermore, they treat their wives as possessions and take them for granted—this is in strict contrast to the period before marriage, when they try to be seen as considerate and charming.

Fatima was the only woman I spoke to who had married for love and been friends with her husband for three years beforehand. Nevertheless:

> In the engagement period, we used to go out for meals and he used to give me a lot of presents. Then after our marriage, he stopped doing that. Only then did I realized he was mean, he's not romantic, and is very limited in the way he expresses his love to me.

Her husband's attitude changed with marriage: he no longer had to be considerate or say nice words to her, because marriage was the end of the matter. He knew his wife could not afford to leave him because she had become "used" and would not be able to get another man with his "good qualities". For a man, probably the most important reason to marry is sex. (Hijazi, 1981) It is interesting to consider Fatima's reply to my question, "What about the sexual side of things?"

> In this area, he's all right. At school sometimes, I hear other teachers talking about the way their husbands attack them like wolves when they demand sex. I would say mine is not like that at all.

All the women's answers confirmed how paradoxical sexuality is for Iraqi couples. For women the dilemma is particularly acute. Women are brought up to believe that sex is filthy, shameful and sinful; however, sex is their duty in which they should fulfill the husband's needs. Yet if it is sinful, why did God instruct people to practice it? A woman must please her husband, yet remain chaste and demure. This leads us to the issue of sex and duty.

Sex and Duty

Iraqi women are taught to believe that to treat their husband well in bed, that is, to obey demands for sexual intercourse, fulfils their duty to God. Because of this, they put up with their husband's bad behaviour, and try to please him just the same. Khadija's response illustrates this point:

> When he wants it, he gets it and right afterwards, he treats me like a pig. I never cared about sex, and when somebody scares you 24 hours a day and swears about your mother and father, how would you see him? Plus he always gives orders. He doesn't ask for it in a nice way, but, again, I tend to say, "It's my duty. God will not bless me if I don't do it."

Interestingly, while both Khadija and Majida regarded sex as "fulfilling their duty to God", they were otherwise not religious. Majida showed clearly that her husband was using her belief to dominate her.

Girls are also taught from an early age that men in general are unfaithful and not to be trusted. By keeping a watchful eye on her husband, treating him well and trying to please him, particularly in bed, a wife will ensure that he remains faithful to her. (Patai, 1973) Despite being subjected to ill treatment, women cite numerous reasons for complying with their husband's demands for sexual intercourse. But the key factor, which emerged from the interviews, is the deep-rooted belief that women are "naturally" subservient to men. So totally indoctrinated are they with this ideology that they fear that any attempt to overthrow it would result in "justifiable" violence. Here are some of the women's answers to my questions:

> For him, a woman's place is in the home, taking care of her husband and children and doing the housework; she shouldn't complain or object to anything. She should be ready for her husband with her best make-up on before going to bed. She ought to drop everything if he asks her to come to bed.

Q: Do you do what you said; wear make-up and so on for him before going to bed?

A: You know, even if I were very busy, he would demand it of me, and if I refuse, he'd make a scene.

Q: What about you? Do you think sex is important for women too?

A: It isn't important to me I don't care much about it. I almost always allow him to have sex with me but, to tell you the truth, I really wish he wouldn't touch me But I don't let him know that because, once when I did tell him, we had a big fight. He told me even if we'd had a big fight and he'd beat me, I should still say yes to sex with him afterwards if he asked for it, that I am a woman and ought to obey him. "Why have I married you?" he asks. You know, I sometimes think of a solution; I think, what if I pretended I want him and that I enjoyed sex? Then I change my mind. Knowing him, even if I could keep pretending forever, which is difficult enough, it wouldn't solve the problem. He is a very jealous man. He'd accuse me of having affairs then. (*Muna*)

He takes but he never gives sometimes when I don't feel in the mood, he forces me, saying it's his right. I say, "All right, but you shouldn't order me around like that." If someone is upset or has problems, why should they always have to be willing? He will say, "But I work away; when I come home, I demand my rights." Well, what can I do? I usually say it's all right. I know if I don't, he'll be very angry and he might spend the following day screaming at everyone.

Q: What about you? Do you think sex is important to you?

A: Not really. I don't like any of his behavior towards me. And I'm always tired; I work both inside and outside the home. How do you expect me to respond to him? (*Shada*)

Like Muna and Shada, lots of the women saw sex as an exclusively male concern. Thus they tended to see it as a duty:

Well, yes, some women enjoy sex, but they're exceptional. Most women don't. They just don't attach much importance to such matters. (*Zainab*)

Women don't care much for these things. I don't believe any women care about sex. Women are different from men, you know what I mean? (*Zahida*)

I can't speak for others, but myself I don't care about it at all. (*Sahira*)

The following passages clearly indicate that sex is a duty. There was no foreplay during sexual intercourse; the wives were treated purely as vehicles for the sexual act:

He thinks women are created to please men. If he wanted me in bed, he'd just get on with it right away and then turn his back and go to sleep. If he doesn't want me he goes to sleep just the same, without a word. I feel like I've just lost my feelings. (*Iqbal*)

Listen, I've been married for twenty-two years. Since I got married, I've learnt about attitudes towards women. The minute a man finishes having sex with a woman he treats her differently. (*Fatin*)

I believe that companionship is more important. That is what I believe. Sex is just a five-minute thing. If husbands and wives understood each other, sex wouldn't affect the relationship much. It's true that I've read in magazines that sex is an important part of marriage and is sometimes the cause of divorce, but personally I don't agree with that. (*Salwa*)

Given these statements, it is no surprise that almost half the women said sex was an unpleasant duty for them.

It seems that the sex act is usually quick and women are probably left feeling frustrated, even though they do not recognize or admit it. Because the sex act is so brief, men are probably frustrated too.Although men find release in sex, it does not bring real fulfillment and satisfaction to either partner. The use of prostitutes adds to the paradox of sex in Iraqi society. Most men have premarital sex only with prostitutes, who are regarded as cheap, filthy and dishonorable. In many cases the prostitute is forced to practice her trade for economic survival. But the man who seeks her services is regarded as "a real masculine man who can indulge in sex as he pleases"; he continues to hold himself in high esteem.

This paradoxical belief has its origins in the family: although young children are discouraged from discussing sexual matters, adults tend to turn a blind eye when male teenagers show an interest in sex. Indeed, society expects the young male to seek out sexual encounters, and while his mother might inwardly disapprove, she has been conditioned to accept such interests as a necessary part of her son's socialization; it is believed that abstinence could seriously damage the boy. As in the West, men proudly discuss their sexual adventures. In Iraq, however, this is limited to women outside the family circle; to discuss relatives would not be honourable. Any woman discussed is reduced to an object of disgust and is regarded publicly as deviant.

Women tend to put up with the situation—it would be beneath their dignity to beg for love and affection:

He doesn't know much about how women should be treated. I don't think he deliberately mistreats me this way, but I don't know what to say. Sometimes I think he's maybe too busy, or something. Maybe you can beg for other things, but you can't beg for affection and love. (*Ibtihal*)

Sex is clearly a duty, based on limited knowledge, and prostitutes are frequently the only sexual models that males encounter. However, these are not the only reasons for not showing love to the wife. The family hierarchy stresses the importance of a lover never having sexual intercourse with his beloved. Marriage is religiously sanctioned sexuality, not the union of two lovers.

Sex and Love

Classical Arabic literature has many references to a romantic or platonic love known as *Udrite* love. Yet *Udrite* love is forbidden to women, and the *Udrite* lover never has sexual intercourse with his beloved. The famous poet Gamil was not allowed to marry his beloved Bouseaina who was betrothed to a hideous suitor in order to protect her. Qais was prevented from marrying Laila. Afra was eternally separated from her passionate lover, Orwa ibn

Hizam. (Mernissi, 1975; El Saadawi, 1980) Thus it is obvious that even non-sexual love is discouraged, the assumption being that the woman must have deliberately attracted her lover, and that such behavior would bring dishonor on the tribe. In fact girls should not even allow their lovers to mention their names in poems, as this would bring them into disrepute. *Udrite* love is recognized as the only honest love. But the *Udrite* lover cannot marry as marriage involves sex, thus once again, marriage appears to be divorced from love.

Physical love, which involves sexual attraction or sexual feelings, might lead to a sexual act between two lovers. Thus it also tends to result in the separation of the lovers, because men do not trust girls who indulge in such behavior. The belief is that if a girl "does it with them" she will "do it with others". Any girl acting in this way would not be trusted to be a good wife. This partly explains the segregation of the sexes in Arab society. Furthermore Arab sexual mores assume that whenever a man and a woman find themselves alone, they will be driven to have sex. (Patai, 1973)

Women in Arab culture are sexually oppressed and isolated, full freedom being given only to men; there is no balance in relationships between the sexes. As El Saadawi notes, true love is based on an exchange between equal partners, but men and women are not equal in Arab society. Women are oppressed by men; they are passive and self-sacrificing. The structure of society itself makes true love an impossibility. (El Saadawi, 1980) Thus even in present-day Iraq, the connection between sex and love is not strong; indeed, in most cases there is no such connection. The expression "love making" or "make love" has no equivalent in modern Arabic, nor does it exist in classical Arabic, or in the various regional languages throughout the Arab world.

It might seem from the answers the women gave me that there is no love at all between spouses. There may be love, but it is not expressed, certainly not in the ways it is expressed in the West. It is considered to be very private, even for husbands and wives they are not encouraged to show love to each other in front of other people—it would be considered dishonourable on the part of the wife and a weakness if it came from the husband. Even when the couple are on their own, love is not expressed due to reasons connected with upbringing, lack of models, and so on. Husbands assume that for them to show affection might "spoil" the wife, who would take advantage of them and become demanding. This was confirmed by Majida's words at the beginning of this chapter when she quoted her husband: "Women who hear soft talk misbehave."

However, women are now becoming more aware of Western customs, through television and films. They expect their husband to show affection in ways, which are not customary for Arabs:

> I've never felt any love or affection from him. We've been married for sixteen years. Even by mistake, he's never told me how he feels. Sometimes I get very depressed, but he never asks what's wrong, he never suggests we go out, or takes us for a picnic. Sometimes in the spring, when the sun's shining and it's a beautiful day, we all feel like going out. He's got a car, which I'm not allowed to drive. He takes the car and goes out, but he never takes me or the children anywhere. (*Muna*)

The reason for such diversity in emotional reactions between men and women may be found in patterns of child rearing. Men are taught from childhood to be tough and not to express affection, which is seen as a sign of weakness. This does not apply to expressing anger, however, which is linked very strongly with the notion of masculinity.

When I asked the women whether their husbands were affectionate, the majority said that not only were they not affectionate, they hardly ever expressed feelings of love. However, a few of them said that their husbands had expressed some love and affection before marriage while they were engaged. A few women said their husbands expressed love to them, on certain occasions, mainly with gifts and sometimes with sweet words.

Not only do Iraqi husbands show no affection to their wives they are actually aggressive towards them:

> He's very irritable and short-tempered. If he's angry about something he never goes to sleep until he's shouted at us and made a scene, particularly at me and my daughter. He behaves a little better with the boys. When he gets angry, he really gets angry; I mean he loses all control. Sometimes he comes home like that and takes it out on us. I try my best to calm him down by doing everything he wants, his way, but even that doesn't work with him. He gets better, and then he does it again. I really don't know what else I can do. I obey all his orders. If he says don't go to your parents even if I badly want to, I won't. What more can I do to satisfy him? (*Muna*)

Society operates a double standard as far as morals are concerned, recognizing only male sexuality. Moreover, this sexuality is regarded as sacred. The idea that women's sexuality and passionate nature, once aroused, will prove to be too strong to control, and could threaten the whole of the social system, is still a powerful force behind the treatment of women and the behaviour of men. This idea dies hard and is still very prevalent in Iraqi society. If a woman feels any sexual desire it must not be admitted, even to her husband. I only found two exceptional women who cautiously admitted to feelings of sexual desire:

> Frankly, in our society, men play the positive role in sexual relations and women are supposed to play the passive or negative one. I disagree with this, but if I make a positive approach, he backs off. I don't know why. Maybe it's due to his relations with a prostitute before we got married. He doesn't like it coming from me, because he considers his wife should act the opposite of these women. Whenever he wants intercourse with me, I respond in order to please him, even if I don't feel like it. I believe it's my duty. If I don't satisfy him, I might lead him to have affairs with other women, or he might try to harm me by acting against my interests in other daily matters, so I respond to avoid problems. (*Rafida*)

> He doesn't really care much about how I feel. I don't discuss this with him because, for me, it's a matter of keeping some dignity, even though I think it's very important, and I try to drop hints by talking nicely to him when we go to bed, but he acts like he just wants me to shut up. No response at all. I always try to wear my sexiest nightgowns and make-up and perfume, but it doesn't seem to make any difference to him. When he wants sex, he demands it, ignoring my feelings. I get very upset about it sometimes. It really makes me depressed,

but then I get over it. As a matter of fact, I do believe that it's my right too, but I feel shy talking about it with him. (*Ansam*)

Postscript

This chapter is concerned with an explanation of some of the effects of the patriarchal system, in Iraqi society, on female sexuality. It was originally published in *Honor and Shame: Women in Modern Iraq* and was based on my PhD thesis. The thesis was a comparative study between women in Iraq, and women in other cultures but this comparison was mostly lost when the thesis was converted into a book. Male attitude to female sexuality is not unique to Iraqi men. In fact, research shows that 60 per cent of American women, for example, who are supposedly emancipated, are not sexually satisfied. Whether the difference between male and female sexuality can be understood as social or biological, is a continuing debate.

Much has happened since 1982–83, the date of the original research. The key alterations in marital relationships that have taken place since then, relate largely to the effect on Iraqi families. The Gulf War of 1991, followed by economic sanctions lasting twelve years, as well as the invasion of 2003 and the subsequent occupation of Iraq. All have created immense instability and suffering, leaving indelible marks on the family and obviously have affected sexuality as well as other aspects of family life. Women are burdened day and night with the safety of their families. They frequently report fearing their children will be born with birth defects.

Since 1991, obtaining the basic essentials of everyday life from food to medicine is an uphill struggle for Iraqi women. Everyday services, such as rubbish collection, delivery of gas and petrol, which were previously taken for granted, are presently non-existent. There are still shortages of electricity and clean water throughout Iraq. Incidences of divorce, and marital breakdown, have increased considerably since the first Gulf war. The number of widows in Iraq is estimated at two million. Some studies calculate that the number of Iraqis who have lost their lives in the US war and occupation could be near 1,252,595.

I am involved with a charity helping displaced Iraqis in Syria, and have had the opportunity to speak with a large number of women in the Iraqi community there. A common factor emerged through such conversations, which relates to this chapter, namely the loss of sexual appetite among men. This appears to be directly related to the general war situation, but in particular, to the use of Depleted Uranium during the Gulf War in 1991 and 2003. The use of Depleted Uranium by the US forces had devastating consequences that impacted all aspects of life in Iraq, naturally affecting families and marital relationships.

Depleted Uranium affects both fertility and potency. It can cause sterility and sexual dysfunction. Women spoke to me in confidence about the reduced sexual activity on the part of their husbands. Given the scarcity of resources, there is no treatment available. One woman said to me: "My mother-in-law is putting pressure on my husband to divorce me because I have been married for three years and have not become pregnant. But I cannot tell her that my husband (her son) hardly comes near me; I would not be exaggerating if I say he sleeps with me once every four or five months."

Another woman commented, "I have seven female cousins all are married and aged 22–47. They have all mentioned, in one way or another, that their husbands are not interested in them. One said he is married to his computer, another that he preferred being with his mother, and another that he does not find me attractive."

A score of recent studies have documented some of the adverse effects of Depleted Uranium on neurological abnormalities, kidney stones, various forms of skin and organ cancer. Sexual dysfunction, particularly impotency and lack of interest in sexual activity, is very salient.

What compounds these problems is the absence of medical facilities. Doctors, hospitals and dispensaries are scarce. Since the 2003 invasion scientists, university lecturers and professors, and huge numbers of highly qualified medical doctors were assassinated. Others have simply left Iraq for fear of being killed. They left behind a huge vacuum. Hospitals are run down, equipment, services and medication are lacking.

If the US army refused to even treat its own personnel why should they be concerned about making treatment available to the Iraqi people? The above-mentioned facts show that a population living under such conditions suffers greatly. The fear of having babies that suffer from congenital anomalies, coupled with the highly decreased sexual appetite and performance in men, has instigated severe anxieties in marital relationships.

References

Cosar, Fatma Mansur, 'Women in Turkish Society', in Lois Beck and Nikki Keddie (eds), *Women in the Muslim World*, (Cambridge: Mass, Harvard University Press 1980)

Mernissi, Fatima. *Beyond the Veil: Male Female Dynamics in a Modern Muslim Society*, (New York: John Wiley 1975)

El Saadawi, Nawal. *The Hidden Face of Eve* (London:Zed Press 1980)

Hijazi, Azzat. "Does the Arab Woman Play a Valuable Role in Development?" (*Social Science Journal*, 1st part special issue, vol.5 1981)

Patai, R. *The Arab Mind* (New York:Scribner 1973)

Vieille, Paul, 'Iranian Women in Family Alliance and Sexual Politics', in Lois Beck and Nikki Keddie (eds), *Women in the Muslim World*, (Cambridge: Mass, Harvard University Press 1980)

Originally published in *Honor and Shame: Women in Modern Iraq* (Saqi Books, 1990): 79–96.

Breaking the Silence: What AUB Students Really Think About Sex

When I informed my Creative Writing classes that a number of our seminars would focus on the topic of sex, the initial reaction was silence followed by utter disbelief. "Wow!" exclaimed one enthusiastic male student. "Just what every guy dreams of but can't talk about openly." Next a rather amusing incident occurred when two animated young women attempted to speak at the same time but managed only to produce strange, inaudible sounds. Unfortunately the laughter and commotion that ensued made it impossible for me to rescue them from this embarrassing situation. Later that afternoon, in the quiet calm of my office, Layla let drop the white veil that covered her mouth while Samar adjusted her tongue rings. As they engaged in articulate conversation I marveled at how two female students, one traditional, the other post-modern, had eagerly attempted to express their views only to be hindered by contrasting differences in attire and adornment that ultimately rendered them silent.

Ironically, both have been "deformed" and made speechless by the very values they adhere to. In a most visible sense, they also epitomize the dissonant normative expectations and lifestyles that continue to polarize certain segments of Lebanese society. That both are seeking an "American" liberal education and happen to be in the same "creative writing" seminar makes the setting all the more compelling. The outwardly timid and reserved veiled student, along with her dauntless and liberated cohort, who flaunts the rings on her tongue and other parts of her sparsely dressed body, as "emblems of honor" and daring, represent extreme modes of adaptation which are manifest elsewhere in the Arab world.

Contrived as it may seem, a classroom setting devoted to creative writing offers a unique and discerning opportunity to explore sensitive issues related to sexuality, and allows a better understanding of how a group of intelligent students are groping to forge a meaningful and coherent sexual ideology. However, working critically with the writer's personal experience to relocate it to the classroom in a way that allows for a more meaningful engagement with experience can be immensely challenging (Kamler, 2001). In my study, the task became even more daunting because the topic of sex requires venturing into sensitive, often forbidden territory. To craft sexual narratives, students had to enter unmapped terrain as well as stretch language beyond neutral communication in order to express ideas and inhabit spaces not normally explored in the classroom. Delving into highly private realms of experience often required the use of sexually explicit language that ran the risk of exceeding the comfort zone of certain students and testing their threshold of tolerance. At times we even faced a "linguistic void", ostensibly because students have not yet developed a comfortable or adequate way of expressing their views, nor have they found acceptable language to use in a classroom setting. Initially, it was somewhat testy to generate natural rapport since language had to be carefully negotiated. Luckily students were quick to overcome the barriers and, to my delight, out of the closet tumbled amazing stories. Fortunately the rush of tales moved beyond local and segmental allegiances to assume wider significance.

Not surprisingly, the questionnaire I administered in the early stages of this experimental study (see Appendix) revealed the majority of students to be multilingual, multicultural, highly mobile and diverse. Many are border crossers by virtue of having lived, together with their families, in a number of countries to escape the atrocities of the Lebanese civil war that ravaged the country for nearly two decades. Today, students struggle to reconcile the romantic and nostalgic Lebanese narratives told to them by their parents with the realities of a postwar society. What they are witnessing is a country in limbo populated with self-serving politicians and a dysfunctional government that remains, for complicated reasons, incapable of addressing any of the underlying issues and tensions that instigated the war in the first place. Predictably, whatever reserves of optimism and determination students possess are quickly dashed in the wake of the countless daily obstacles they encounter. Unless they have the good fortune of joining a family business, decent jobs remain scarce, salaries low, and the future highly uncertain thanks to local and regional political instability. Given this dire situation, it is little wonder that students are attracted to rampant consumer culture and quick fixes inevitably ushered in by the trappings of globalism. Postwar Lebanese society has instilled an insatiable desire to make up for lost time. This impetuous hankering for the "good life", to enjoy the moment at the expense of not looking back, is a desperate attempt to erase all traces of a violent past. As one perceptive student remarked, "It seems that war and violence are never far away." When peaceful times are perceived as nothing more than brief interludes, it's easy to comprehend why my students behave the way they do.

Creating a space where issues regarding sex can be openly debated, discussed and written about freely offered students the opportunity to give voice to their views on sexuality. By delving into such seemingly private zones of personal autonomy they acquired an expansive sense of control and empowerment. As a result, students began to assume some of the enabling attributes of a diminutive "public sphere" and/or "third spaces" [For an elaboration of these concepts, see Habermas (2001); Hall (1991); Bhabba (1990); Hannerz (1996).]

This was only possible because our *contact zone* remained protected from the threatening outside gaze by the *safety net* of a classroom setting where critical exchanges that deal with difference served primarily to broaden awareness. The transformative power of discourse and personal writing was evident right from the beginning when repeatedly students expressed their desire to be change agents with regard to matters of sex. Yet they were acutely aware that the acceptance of diversity in our created "third space" was a distant cry from their real and lived environment. Here there was no posturing for they were not being judged in any way. Whatever diverse practices and attitudes they revealed were welcome in our shared arena and, perhaps even more important, the information remained entirely within their control. The ability to engage in text creation under a safety net served to increase and heighten awareness, to unsettle and transform fixed, often rigid ways of seeing. In the end, the acceptance of difference gave new shape and meaning to their initial views on sexuality that developed into a sense, real or imagined, of empowerment and control. Despite the shifting uncertainties and complexities of postwar Lebanon, students now felt they exercised power in this particular sphere.

Six Thematic Categories

For the sake of clarity I have divided the recurring and salient ideas in the *sex narratives* and discourse of students into six thematic categories or rubrics, each of which is given an appropriate title: *Breaking Away: Parent/Child Dualism; Writing in the Margins; Sexual Identity in Flux; The Exhibitionist: Indecent Exposure; Male/Female Sex Language;* and *The Freedom to Choose* and *Imagine.* It is essential to keep in mind that none of the themes are mutually exclusive: all inevitably contain overlapping material presumably because notions regarding sex are more often than not interconnected, especially in discourse. The following pages contain a brief analysis of each thematic grouping along with excerpts taken from student narratives in an attempt to capture their voices and reveal, in their own words, intimate thoughts and feelings regarding issues of sexuality.

Parent/Child Dualism

Conflicts over sexuality between AUB students and their parents have to do with divergent views, a struggle between two opposing sexual ideologies. Students, on the one hand, view sex as a positive form of self-fulfillment and an opportunity for open experimentation. As such, sexual expression is given legitimacy in all consensual relations regardless of romantic or enduring bonds. Parents, on the other hand, emphasize the dangers involved in free sex outside the secure confines of love and marriage. Physical intimacies, they argue, must act as a prelude to enduring relationships. Consequently, it comes as no surprise that differences concerning sexuality between the two generations are hugely polarized with each group attributing meaning and purpose to their particular views by drawing on an entirely different set of values. Such strong intractable positionings seem to account for the sharp divisions between the two generations.

Recurring themes of parent/child dualism depict an on-going struggle over the role of sexuality in everyday life. Because the stories are told entirely from the moral perspectives of students, they offer a critique of their established positions as they act and react against the conservative values of their parents, with each strongly rejecting the sexual values of the other.

> My parents are limited. They just think like they have been programmed to think. They have experienced the 60s and 70s without the sexual revolution. So as far as they are concerned, being active sexually is bad. Taking drugs is bad. Bisexuality and gay people don't even exist. (*Fadi*)

An awareness of the attitudes assumed by parents is essential in order for students to negotiate and reinvent their sexual identity inside the parent/child dualism. Only when they have labeled and "othered" the views of their parents can they be free to imagine and forge into existence entirely new visions and approaches. Careful examination and rejection of the ideas embraced by their parents allow for new alternatives that challenge the existing, taken-for-granted values, offering instead limitless possibilities.

> As for myself, I believe in sexual experimentation. Most of the older people I know, including my parents, are disgusted by gays, but I have nothing against them. Actually, I admire their honesty. I believe every individual should have the freedom to choose same sex partners if they so wish. (*Maya*)

Students are not only able to identify and account for these generational differences, they are also surprisingly quick to expose the problematic nature of their parents' traditional approaches to sexuality.

> My parents allow me to have a relationship as long as no sex is involved. No sex at all. No kisses, no hugs, and no nothing. Of course I know that what they are asking is impossible so I can never be open and honest with them on this issue. (*Manal*)

In assuming a more liberal stance as they react to the views of their parents, some students totally disregard or ridicule what their parents have to say about sex, while others attempt to come to terms with feelings of resentment and defiance as they search for a new voice capable of challenging what they perceive to be outdated ideas.

> At a young age I developed a morbid fascination with sex because it was a forbidden word in our household. (*Hiam*)

> My parents are convinced that by returning to Lebanon they will no longer need to worry about their children growing up in a promiscuous society. Now I will be able to catch a decent, rich guy from a good family who comes from a similar background and we will live happily ever after in total boredom. Naturally, I have no intention of living out their fantasies. My career will be the most important thing in my life. I certainly am not going to be bossed around by any guy. If I fall in love, I plan to live with my boyfriend so I can maintain my freedom. (*Nour*)

> A girl's virginity, my parents insist, guarantees the right and the ability to trap a worthy spouse (rich and from a good family). I find the whole thing abhorrent. (*Nadia*)

Though the fortuitous and not-so-random nature of the sample under study does not allow generalization, the men appear to go beyond the disapproving stance of their women colleagues to decry and disavow the cultural predispositions that reinforce parental authority and allow parents to serve as arbiters and gatekeepers of social conduct. They are particularly concerned about those normative expectations associated with their exclusive and dogmatic role of safeguarding and upholding family honor and dignity. Others go even further by searching for strategies that will assist their efforts in forging more pliable images and patterns of conduct.

> Because I am the only boy in our family, my parents consider it my duty to be the guardian of my sister's virtue. If my sister is not allowed to have sex, why

should I be any different, and above all, why should I or anyone else need to guard her virginity? (*Adib*)

Yet one of the major contributions of these narratives is the creation of images that focus on new ways of seeing and living outside the parent/child dualism. The forging of themes not only against but also outside and beyond old attitudes offers fresh incentives and perspectives.

> I believe that sex is a personal choice that one makes and it plays an important role in self-discovery and maturity. Sexual experimentation is good experience and it does not always have to take place with a person of the opposite sex. Having a person of the same sex touch you or going to a gay bar will allow the discovery of something new. (*Bahij*)

Clearly an underlying moral divide exists between the two generations with respect to love, sex and intimacy. Seidman (1992) has attributed this dissonance to opposing schools of thought that he labels as, sexual *romantics* versus *libertarians*. The *romantics* view sex as a way of expressing intimate feelings that have to do with bonds of affection and love: feelings that should never be taken lightly because they involve reciprocal obligations. By contrast, a libertarian sexual ethic defines sex as a mode of bodily sensual pleasures. "Libertarians intend to free individuals of the excessive social controls that inhibit sexual expression and stigmatize transgressive desires and acts" (Seidman, 1992: 188). *Libertarians* play a role in challenging sexual orthodoxies. They aim to free sex from excessive strictures, focusing more on its pleasures and expressive possibilities. Such views remain in sharp contrast to the dominant social groups that impose higher moral purposes such as procreation, love and family on sex.

It is interesting to note that the majority of students agree their parents are definitely *romantics* when it comes to sex. Students themselves, however, do not all fit neatly into the *libertarian* category. Indeed, there are some who harbor serious ambivalence and uncertainty in this regard, for instead of assuming a liberal stance they are inclined instead to favor the views of their parents seeing absolutely no reason to reject the values they grew up with.

> I was brought up by strict parents who do not believe in sex before marriage. However, by the time I entered university, I formed my own ideas that are not very different from those of my parents. I believe that when a girl loses her virginity before marriage, she loses the respect of her future husband as well as the people around her. (*Maha*)

To my surprise, a number of students touched on a highly sensitive and rather embarrassing issue, namely, the double standards, cynicism and social hypocrisy of their parents. Goffman's (1971) metaphors of *front stage* and *backstage* appropriately exemplify the contradictions students observed and criticized in the behavior of their parents. Backstage parents often relinquish their *nice scripts* by acting in ways that contradict the polite, moral front they maintain in public or in *front stage* situations. When parents uphold strict moral values that are not in step with their actual behavior, their children are the first to notice.

The jarring dissonance between the overt righteousness and covert misconduct of their parents is to my students a microcosm of the deepening malaise they see elsewhere in Lebanese society. Such aberrant symptoms, particularly when their parents are presumably their own moral arbiters and role models, are not lightly dismissed.

> My parents lead separate lives. I know they both have lovers. Well to be perfectly honest, my father fools around with many women. At first my mother was angry, but now she does her own thing. Of course, in front of their kids they act like a normal and happy couple. (*Reem*)

> How can my parents pretend to believe in traditional values regarding sex and marriage when their relationship has been dead for years. (*Maher*)

Clearly the insincerity of parents compounds their sense of moral outrage. They are, after all, trapped in a socio-cultural setting that demands they pay deference to parents whose values and conduct are no longer relevant or meaningful to their own situations. Perhaps what is even more telling about these views of parental hypocrisy is that students embrace another set of romantic values, that relationships should be honest and not dead sexually.

Writing in the Margins

Although students are positioned in families and communities, the majority openly reject the sexual values upheld by mainstream groups. The very act of questioning and challenging the status quo moves them to the margins where they speak from silent places in an attempt to register their disapproval and eventually destabilize the center. Here the self/other distinctions raise critical questions because by producing their own narrative subjectivities, student writers are excluding or "othering" those who have "othered" them. In this way, as DeVault (1997) reminds us, their personal accounts make excluded voices "hearable". By writing their sex narratives they are able to articulate and give voice to their own stories. The ability to render the invisible visible is, in and of itself, an enabling act: a bold attempt to gain control of one important aspect of their lives.

> Unfortunately, my parents avoid the topic of sex. My generation is much more comfortable with our sexuality. We talk openly about it and experience it in ways that our parents would never approve of. I discuss sex only with my friends because I think it is entirely my business. (*Kamil*)

> On the surface our society is very conservative when it comes to sex. The reality is that older people have sex in secret with many partners while pretending to be virtuous. When young people talk openly about sexual relationships it makes older people uncomfortable because they feel threatened. I argue a lot with the older generation. I really hate it when they laugh or ignore my ideas. Mostly they shove my views aside as if they are of no importance. (*Rami*)

Such symptoms of recalcitrance notwithstanding, on the whole students' perspectives and views of sexuality remain worlds apart from the mainstream groups they are exposed to. As a result, they felt their ideas are not taken seriously and there was a concerted attempt, at least in their view, to ignore and thus marginalize whatever they had to say about sex. Curiously, students were unable to imagine that their parents may have had other views when they were young.

Sexual Identity in Flux

Students' narratives not only define the essentialism and fixity of their parents' views on sex, they also prod them to examine and redraw the boundaries that categorize them as different. Positions and stories that create established parameters are rejected in much the same way that notions having to do with grounded or fixed ideas are quickly examined and dismissed. The formation of their positionings are not situated within some established public ideal but formed through the diversity derived from competing ideas. Their narrative voices are the outcome of shifting and conflicting tensions brought into play when sexual codes are viewed with apprehension and suspicion. Hence they are clearly inclined to favor more situational and constructed normative standards and actual modes of conduct.

By posing hard questions, new choices and endless possibilities start to take shape and provide more open-ended multiple models. There is an eagerness to move beyond invisible barriers, to resist the pressure of conforming to rigid and absolute forms of sexual identity that translate into established and predetermined positions. By challenging the views of mainstream groups, students create a *fluid space* (Bauman, 2000), in which ongoing experimentation leaves room to construct new views and sets into motion a struggle against definition by others, against the fixity of what is considered normal sexuality as opposed to diversity in sexual patterns. Students consider sex to be shaped by difference, thus the labels given are seen as mere fictions serving primarily as a means of social control because they inevitably block out the many subcultures and sexualities.

> Labels limit people in ways that they aren't even conscious of. Nothing is set in stone and I hate how the sexual complexities of our lives become diluted into one defining category: *The rape victim, the heterosexual, the homo, the lesbian, the pervert,* etc. Ironically, it was only when I stopped feeling the need to be labeled that I was able to be in a healthy relationship. (*Hind*)

Students reject simplistic, fixed labels because, in their eyes, sexual identities exist on uncertain ground and are constantly subjected to displacements. They challenge the idea of sexual normality, substituting instead an ever-shifting terrain. In this sense, they are more inclined to veer in the direction of more situational than absolutist ethical yardsticks. Morality becomes, as it were, how one feels afterwards.

> Although I was also attracted to men my experiences with them were never fulfilling. At one point in my life, I decided to explore my attraction to women. After a year I became completely disillusioned with the lesbian community but I knew if I disclosed my feelings for men I would be shunned and called a traitor. Slowly I drifted away from the gay scene realizing that if there is no place for someone like me there I must create my own place. Now my friends are people like me who have rejected the term *normal* when it comes to sexual identity. (*Fayrouz*)

Like Fayrouz, students reshape and reinvent their sexual identity through experimentation with alternative frameworks, seeking to define themselves against a shifting landscape of possibilities. It is not surprising that within such a fluid and negotiable setting, virtually everything becomes charged with sensual, erotic undertones and, hence, highly contested. Seemingly mundane and prosaic matters—e.g. dress codes, speech styles and the freedom to imagine alternative sexual attributes and practices—begin to assume primacy. Students are often in danger of viewing everyone as "other" and having their individual tastes become so "selved" that they will never match up with the tastes of others. The question that arises here is how many of these individualized alternatives can be enacted in a world of others who are also equally individualized?

The Exhibitionist: Indecent Exposure

The AUB campus is densely populated with women students wearing suggestive clothing that reveals tattooed and pierced bodies among other more lurid and sultry manifestations of eroticization. Why female students conform to a highly fashionable, exaggerated dress code that serves to exhibit the body in provocative ways initiated a lively and rather humorous class debate. To some (and Siham is a typical example), this investment in body image is not only seen as an intrinsic, natural desire to embellish femininity and enhance feelings of self-worth, it is also readily recognized for its extrinsic, instrumental value: a means to seduce and attract men. Furthermore, as Rima candidly admits, the competition for this scarce commodity (men) is so intense that many women on campus are engaged in a competitive game of "outdoing" each other.

> It is a natural and innate desire to wear sexy clothes in order to attract men. I know that my body is appealing and so it feels good to wear short skirts and low cut tops. It's a way of seducing men visually. (*Siham*)

Female students who wear suggestive attire use their sex appeal to tempt men but also to keep them at a safe distance. They exhibit their bodies to feel attractive and desirable while simultaneously sending a clear message that men can look but not touch. It became immediately evident that to many of my women students, playing the role of a seductive temptress is fully exploited and thoroughly enjoyed.

> My friends and I try to out do each other when it comes to wearing sexy clothes. One of my friends comes from a very religious family that think she should dress in a modest and conservative way. Instead of fighting with them, she hides her clothes in my car and changes into tight jeans at my house before going to her classes at AUB. It's worth the inconvenience because we both enjoy looking cool in order to attract men. (*Rima*)

Though male students remain divided on this issue, they have been made readily aware of the games their women friends play. To Wael, the campus becomes an enchanting and great place to watch "sexy females exhibiting themselves all day long." Samir, however, decries the vulgarity and bland uniformity of this obsession with body image.

AUB campus is a great place to watch sexy female students exhibiting themselves all day long. (*Wael*)

Actually to me, most of the girls on campus look alike because they dress in the same vulgar way. (*Samir*)

AUB is a place of extremes. Girls either reveal all or hide all. (*Khatir*)

The abandon with which the young are eroticizing their bodies should not be lightly dismissed as merely a trendy and fashionable craze. It is a reflection of a deeper and more nagging societal conflict; almost a textbook instance of anomie: i.e., a disjunction between normative expectations which condone, indeed cajole, young women to be *sexually attractive* but condemns them if they become *sexually active*. Many young women, even the most adept at reconciling these inconsistent societal expectations, are the ones, as therapists have urged, to bear the psychological toll. They are the surrogate victims of such cognitive dissonance but dissonance, after all, is the price of individuality as is anomie (see Durkheim, 1951). If students want to be "different" or "individual" the price is psychic dislocation and in scripting terms the intrapsychic is more important since it is the place where dissonance is negotiated.

This problem, incidentally, has been recently compounded by a disheartening demographic reality. Because of the disproportionate out-migration of young Lebanese men in pursuit of more promising career options, the sex ratio is visibly skewed. Demographers put the estimate at approximately four to one; i.e., one male for every four females of eligible age. Once again, it is the growing pool of single women who must, in one way or another, deal with the scarcity of eligible men. The eroticization of the female body and other associated ploys to embellish their sex appeal, seem like an appropriate strategy to gain a competitive edge over their cohorts when it comes to soliciting the attention of the scare and coveted male. In the language of Bourdieu (1993) this eroticization becomes a judicious resource in the "social capital" that single women need to cultivate and jealously guard.

Male/Female Sex Language

Linguistic approaches are often used in discourse to provide evidence of gender differentiation. An analysis of men's and women's speech style reveal that they are mostly organized around a series of global oppositions, for example, men's talk is "competitive", whereas women's is "cooperative"; men talk to gain "status", whereas women talk to achieve "intimacy" and "connection" (Cameron, 2002; Coates, 1996; Tannen, 1991). These stereotypical notions or conventional language distinctions proved problematic among my students as the woman did not form a homogeneous group. Many positioned themselves alongside the men by assuming dominant discourses that conjured up a liberal sexual environment. Like their male peers, they adhere to the *opportunity-taking* narrative pattern in which they see themselves as the initiators, the "doers" of sexual activity. In the context of our previous remarks this too becomes part of the "social capital" women need to skillfully cultivate. Here, as well, women can no longer afford to remain passive and resigned victims. Instead, they depict themselves as active agents directly involved in resisting the circumstances that undermine their autonomy and wellbeing. As decision makers, they assume complete control over their sexual activities. Moreover, sex is considered to be autonomous from love or intimacy. Subsequently as modern liberated individuals, they initiate, engage in and enjoy sex outside the confines of love and marriage. In their texts and discourse, they break with and undermine the stereotypical notions and conventions that resort to restrictive language and behavior. Sexual encounters are disclosed in language that is explicit and direct, with a surprising degree of distance and control.

Dalia is so unabashedly explicit in this regard that her sexual encounters are completely divorced from any ethical stance or intimate feelings. Indulging in sex becomes an unalloyed libidinal resource to be fully exploited. If her younger boyfriends fall short (because of premature ejaculation) of fulfilling her expectations, she readily seeks older and more experienced men.

> Lately I have been having sex with older men because I got pissed off with guys my age who come quickly leaving me dissatisfied. Now that I have taken matters into my own hands, sex is pleasurable. I am beginning to enjoy multiple orgasms with mature men who know how to fulfill my sexual needs. (*Dalia*)

These female students differ from their male peers only through the inclusion of resistant or emancipatory discourses that incorporate feminist rhetoric laced with fierce criticism of misogyny and prejudice. There is a strong determination among this group of women students to defend their rights.

> My father lectures me about the dangers of premarital sex because he wants me to be a chaste, ignorant virgin when I get married. My brother, on the other hand, is encouraged to indulge in sex, even with prostitutes. You might think that my father is an illiterate, old man but actually he is an AUB graduate. When I tell my father that I reject his double standards he threatens to cut off financial support. He considers me disobedient and says he is no longer proud of me. The truth is that I am not proud of him either. This is my life and I alone decide when, with whom, and how often to have sex. (*Nayla*)

In sharp contrast, a more conservative group of women students have developed strategies which enable them to approach the topic of sex alternatively, from a more inhibited discourse rooted in polite, acceptable language. They are careful to avoid explicit terminology, adhering instead to expressions of a traditional and patriarchal kind. To be happy, they argue, a woman should seek a long-term heterosexual relationship. Not surprisingly, they invoked the rhetoric of love, intimacy, chastity, romance, marriage and motherhood.

> Sex should be shared only with the person you marry. My virginity and faithfulness is a special gift I will offer to my husband because I want to be perfect and beautiful for him. (*Suha*)

Sexuality, as their texts demonstrated, is accompanied by a discourse of distaste and fear. Premarital sex is not only wrong and dangerous, but transgressive pleasure is closely linked to morality and social punishment.

> I believe it is immoral and unacceptable to have premarital sex. Our society is correct in punishing women who are promiscuous. In the past, Americans were moral and strict when it came to sex. Now it is as simple as eating or drinking. I do not mean to offend Americans, but their values are not acceptable in our culture. I, like most of my friends, cannot take sex lightly. (*Manal*)

> If I have sex before getting married I will live in fear that my family might find out and punish me severely. I really don't think it's worth the risk. (*Youmna*)

In general, this group of women seems comfortable acting in accordance with prescribed essentialist social rules: the sexually attractive woman is the beautiful one who, to please men, must guard her virtue. They favor the passive as opposed to the proactive narrative pattern but in restrictive and tentative ways, being that their options remain closely tied to gaining acceptance through the *male gaze*. Because they long to be the objects of male desire, one overriding concern is the need to remain feminine, to be a *real* woman in the eyes of men. Once the centrality of men is established and confirmed in the narratives and discourse of this group, they immediately focus on the need to achieve and maintain their femininity presumably to remain objects of desire. Yet ironically, the notion of femininity seems to create extreme feelings of anxiety and competition.

> It is very important for a woman to remain attractive especially if she wants to find a suitable husband. Some girls are lucky because they are naturally good looking. I have to work hard at it and I am sometimes afraid men will go after the more beautiful girls. (*Amina*)

The sharp divide between the conservative female discourse of passivity that coexisted with one that assumed a far more liberal stance, constructing sex as autonomous from traditional relationships, assumed striking proportions and initiated lively and heated class debates. However, it remains the liberal stance and terminology towards sex-related issues, so boldly adopted by a considerable number of women students, that blurs the conventional distinctions between male/female sex texts. It is rather strange that none of my women students raised the possibility of being interesting to men or even happy with them in non-sexual ways.

The Freedom to Choose and Imagine

Given the ambivalence, fluidity and inconsistent expectations young students in Lebanon are subjected to, it is little wonder that a prosaic academic elective (a seminar in creative writing) should become an accessible and meaningful vector for the expression and mobilization of pent-up energy. Sheltered in the sanctuary of a classroom, students are released from the constraints of the outside world. The opportunity to write becomes both an outcome of, and direct agency for the articulation of this newfound freedom.

Of course writing itself can be viewed as a practice of freedom. Texts focus on the personal, and as such, they allow the *freedom to imagine* while blocking out the *freedom from interference*. The freedom to imagine is crucial if students are to develop a sexual identity that enables them to envision sexuality in ways that permit alternative possibilities because it identifies and innovatively addresses the gap between what is, as opposed to what is longed for. By creating diverse themes and navigating forbidden territory, students are able to articulate new ways of understanding crucial issues that have to do with their sexuality. Narratives provide the freedom to change existing norms through reinterpretation thus offering fresh perspectives and new ways of seeing. The images that emerged in this study are those of diversity, daring experimentation and, ultimately, growth.

Narrative texts and discourse offered space away from and beyond the outside gaze, a space in which "hidden transcripts" can be created and explored. Eventually these "hidden transcripts" may hold the potential to counteract the cultural givens that might otherwise define the sexual identity of students. Weeks has, I believe, correctly argued that, "The radical oppositional identities which arise against hegemonic ones offer narratives of imagined alternatives which can provide the motivation for inspiration and change" (1995: 99). Pushing beyond normalizing and imposing sexual strictures allows students to map out new sexual possibilities that widen their vision. They think and write boldly about unarticulated expectations, about what could or should be when it comes to sex-related issues and the control of their bodies. Imbedded in their narratives are themes that demand a collective awareness of the need to respect diversity, a call for the celebration of difference, including the right of each and every individual to choose. Most striking is an approach to sex that is at once rational, experimental and expansive, rather than moral and judgmental.

> I do not believe that one should be restricted to a single partner for life because it is possible and important to have sex with many people over time. (*Serene*)

> I like guys, but I'm not sure I don't like girls too. Sometimes I check them out and declare which is sexy, pretty, etc. I examine them like a guy would. Is this normal? If I lived abroad I might have sex with a girl just to see how it feels. Also because virginity is such a big deal here, I'm determined to lose it. (*Ibtihaj*)

> Who we love and have sex with is entirely our own business. No one has the right to decide for anyone else. There are enough rules to define our social lives. How can we allow people to control the sexual aspect of our lives as well? (*Nadim*)

> My parents are divorced and I can't really remember a time when I saw them together in a loving relationship. This is probably why I hold my current view on the uselessness of marriage. I would like to experiment with different kinds of relationships and arrangements with the opposite sex before I decide how best to live my private life. (*Joumana*)

> To me, sex is art and art is freedom. To deny a person sex is the same as denying that person his/her freedom of expression. People say music is the universal language in the world, but I think sex is because its boundaries are limitless. (*Hani*)

> Religion, race, age and social class will never be a hindrance if I am attached to a person. Before I came to AUB I never thought this way. However, I have

to admit that after watching a lot of love making on campus, I have changed my views and become much more liberal. (*Dana*)

Sex is happening and girls are enjoying it too. I wish I could confront this hypocritical Lebanese society we live in and tell them that sex is a fantastic language between people. (*Samir*)

Girls are told that the most precious gift they can offer their husbands is their virginity. But then why should a man not offer the same to his wife? No way! If he does, he'll be called weird names because a Lebanese man must prove his manhood. I think all this stuff is rubbish. (*Ghassan*)

Students do not regard heterosexual couples as the building block of social life presumably because they do not envision any kind of "proper" sexuality for all. The fixity of "normal" sexuality is viewed with scepticism. Instead, they opt for the diversity of sexual patterns. Their scripts and discourse are impatient and defiant when it comes to set social constructions that demand the regulation of sexual behavior. While to Suha fidelity and virginity are a "special gift" she intends to offer her husband on their wedding night, Ibtihaj remains defiant. "Because it is such a big deal," she declares, "I am determined to lose it." She also need not confine herself to heterosexual sex. "If I lived abroad I might have sex with a girl just to see how it feels."

In other words far from being unnatural or deviant, homosexuality is seen as a way of constructing or reconstructing sexual arrangements and relationships to suit real human needs. It is a personal choice one makes and, as such, deserves respect and acceptance.

Although I am a heterosexual male I do not mind bisexuals or homosexuals since sex is about feeling comfortable and having the freedom to choose. (*Ahmad*)

My sister is a lesbian but my parents don't know because she is afraid they will punish her. I don't see anything wrong with her sexual identity. I am still very close to her. In fact, I respect her courage and determination to be who she is. (*Rashid*)

I don't have anything against gays. In fact, I have many gay friends. My dad, however, insists they are abnormal and a threat to society. (*Nina*)

Many people in Lebanon hate homosexuals. They think they are immoral. I think sexuality should be a matter of choice and I think it's fine to have a gay relationship. How else can one discover something new about themselves? (*Zuheir*)

Concluding Inferences

Initially, in undertaking this exploratory case study I was fully aware of the unusual nature of the sample and its rather contrived classroom setting; more so since it focused on textual material and discourse rather than actual sexual behavior. Given, however, the resilient cultural taboos in Lebanon that continue to impose formidable constraints on free and candid discussion of sexuality, the classroom became an expedient and "natural" sanctuary in which to explore such forbidden and censored issues. Judging by the positive reactions of students, the experience was more than just an expressive outlet of repressed desires and hidden fantasies. It proved also cathartic and didactic and, thereby, revealed the importance of providing such neutral settings and diminutive "public spheres" where the young can freely communicate and share common concerns away from the public gaze.

Throughout the study, students persistently and repeatedly argued for a liberalized conception of sex. Collectively they voiced their determination to move sex into an arena where rational and experimental approaches rather than moral thinking and behavior can and indeed should occur. If I am to invoke a common conceptual distinction, one can discern a shift from an essentialist to a constructionist perspective.

Students also recognized the urgent need for a new language. There seems to be no adequate vocabulary to articulate the expanding possibilities in the intimate sphere of their sexual experiences. Their healthy, open attitude towards sex allowed them to explore the vital role it plays in their lives with little or no inhibition, yet they all complained that language remained a constraining factor.

Finally, I would like to extract a few broad and unanticipated inferences from the study; particularly as they prefigure the need for a decentered and more public debate on such sensitive but contested issues. The fact that these voices represent no more than the cloistered views of students sheltered in the comfort zone of a classroom should not belittle or undermine the significance of the results, marginal or sketchy as they may seem. Pinar (1997), among others, has urged that when marginal views are given voice they begin to circulate in the mainstream where they are invariably taken into account and recorded. Although they remain in danger of being controlled or greatly modified by a regulatory regime (Foucault, 1980), they still possess the power to disrupt and discredit those at the center once they form a space capable of being analyzed in articulation with others. Judith Butler (1990) recognizes the need "both to theorize essential spaces from which to speak and simultaneously deconstruct these spaces to keep them from solidifying" (p.118). Keeping sexual identities fluid leaves room for diversity, which will, in turn, open up yet more spaces from which to speak.

The students in my study, judging by subsequent conversations I have had with them outside the classroom, seem determined to continue exploring the changing shape of sexual differences. They also remain acutely aware that crossing boundaries only sets up new boundaries that must be continuously transgressed in order to avoid the strictures that accompany the static nature of rigid, inflexible views. Once again, in other words, the seemingly private emotional narrative engagement had the potential to expand further than the confines of our classroom setting. It provided students with the opportunity to move beyond situated literacy as well as the mere crafting of sex texts and discourse. In telling their stories they ventured out of the margins to negotiate public and private positionings. By externalizing their ideas they formed a realm capable of being analyzed in articulation with others. The autonomous *comfort zone* was transformed into a participatory *contact zone* where diverse ideas could be openly debated against a shifting landscape of possibilities and alternative frameworks: where awareness could be refined and heightened through imaginative text creation, open and critical discourse. At the same time, all of this occurred under a safety net of confidentiality and trust. In our shared space, diverse perceptions concerning sexual identity served to increase and sharpen awareness among students in ways that ultimately unsettled and transformed rigid ways of seeing both in and beyond the classroom.

Appendix

Methodology

The study examines the personal texts and discourse of forty-three students enrolled in three creative writing sections over the course of one academic semester (fall 2003). Students were given a short questionnaire before being asked to craft personal narratives in which they explore their views, feelings and lived experiences with regard to sex. Emotional narrative engagement offered the opportunity to navigate the terrain of sexual identity by reflecting on the issues they themselves deemed to be of immediate significance in their lives.

From the very start, class discussions were informal, interactive and lively. Students proved highly adept in critically engaging with and workshopping their texts. As our class discussions progressed, discourse took a more spontaneous turn when students eagerly and openly began exchanging opinions. Soon it became clear that I was not dealing with a passive group. They were as interested in my views as I was in theirs. Curiosity was quick to surface with questions ranging from why I had chosen to examine the issue of sexuality to what were the goals and scope of my research, and most importantly, what would I do with the findings? In many ways the queries of my students prompted me to face issues I had not, as yet, given much thought to. They knew all too well that the *sex texts* would provide a glimpse into the intimate details of their lives. Consequently, I found it necessary to reassure them that real names would not be used in any published data. Once this sensitive issue was settled, all were disarmingly eager to participate.

The Questionnaire

The structured questionnaire was self-administered during class sessions to forty-three creative writing students (three sections) during the fall semester of 2003. My intention was to better understand the sample that populated my classes before asking students to engage in personal narrative writing and discourse. The findings reveal that the majority of students are between nineteen to twenty-one years of age, nineteen are male and twenty-four female. The sample consisted of four sophomores, twenty-one juniors, seventeen seniors and one graduate student. All came to creative writing, an elective course, from a wide range of disciplines. In fact, only six of the forty-three students were majoring in English. In terms of nationality, 62% of the sample is Lebanese, 11% hold dual citizenships, while the rest are from other countries. High mobility and multilingualism seem to be distinguishing factors common to the majority of respondents.

Table 1: Age

Students	Age	Percent
3	18	7
18	19	41.9
12	20	27.9
5	21	11.6
3	22	7
2	23	4.6

Table 2: Sex

Students	Sex	Percent
19	M	44.1
24	F	55.8

Table 3: Academic Class

Students	Academic Class	Percent
4	Sophomore	9.3
21	Junior	48.8
17	Senior	39.5
1	Prospective Graduate	2.3

Table 4: Major

Students	Major	Percent
1	Computer Engineering	2.3
4	Computer Communication Eng	9.3
5	English Language	11.6
1	English Literature	2.3
1	Computer Science	2.3
5	Business	11.6
1	Education	2.3
2	Psychology	4.7
7	Graphic Design	16.3
3	Biology	7.0
2	Physics	4.7
2	PSPA	4.7

Students	Major	Percent
2	Economics	4.7
1	Mathematics	2.3
1	Civil Engineering	2.3
2	Nutrition 4.7	4.7
3	Mechanical Engineering	7

Table 5: Place of Birth

Students	Place of Birth	Percent
22	Lebanon	62.7
2	Brazil	4.6
4	UAE	9.3
6	KSA	13.9
3	USA	6.9
2	Kuwait	4.6
1	Germany	2.3
1	Jordan	2.3
1	Cyprus	2.3
1	Austria	2.3

Table 6: Countries Lived in

Students	Countries Lived In	Percent
16	1	37.2
8	2	18.6
15	3	34.8
3	4	6.9
1	5	2.3

Table 7: Nationality

Students	Nationality	Percent
27	Lebanese	62.8
3	Palestinian	7
1	Lebanese/Brazilian	2.3
4	Lebanese/American	9.3
1	Saudi Arabian	2.3

1	Kuwaiti	2.3
2	American	4.7
1	Lebanese/German	2.3
2	Jordanian	4.7
1	Palestinian/Jordanian	2.3

Table 8: Native Language

Students	Native Language	Percent
27	Arabic	62.7
2	Portuguese	4.6
5	English	11.6
2	French	4.6
1	Armenian	2.3
4	Arabic/English	9.3
1	Arabic/German	2.3
1	Arabic/French	2.3

Table 9: Languages Spoken

Students	Languages Spoken	Percent
13	2	30.2
21	3	48.8
9	4	20.9

References

Bauman, Z. (2000). *Liquid Modernity*. (Malden: Blackwell).

Bhabba, H.K. (1990). *Nation and Narration* (London: Routledge).

Bourdieu, P. (1993). *The Field of Cultural Production* (New York: Columbia University Press).

Butler, J. (1990). *Gender Trouble: Feminism and Subversion of Identity*. (New York: Routledge).

Cameron, D. (2002). "Beyond Alienation: An Integrated Approach to Women and Language." In M. Toolan (ed.), *Critical Discourse Analysis: Critical Concepts in Linguistics* (London: Routledge): 280–305.

Caotes, J. (1996). "Gossip Revisited: Language In All-Female Groups." In Jennifer Caotes and Deborah Cameron (eds.), *Women in Speech Communities*. (London: Longman): 94–121.

DeVault, M. (1997). "Personal Writing in Social Sciences: Issues of Production and Interpretation." In R. Hertz (ed.), *Reflexivity and Voice* (London: Sage): 216–228.

Durkheim, E. (1951). *Suicide: A Study in Sociology*. (New York: Free Press).

Foucault, M. (1980). *Power/Knowledge: Selected Interviews and Other Writings* C. Gordon, (ed.), (New York: Panthen).

Goffman, E. (1971). *The Presentation of Self in Everyday Life.* (New York: Doubleday).

Habermas, J. (2001). "Civil Society and the Political Public Sphere." In Calhoun et al (eds.), *Contemporary Sociological Theory* (London: Blackwell): 358–376.

Hall, S. (1991). "The Local and the Global: Globalization & Ethnicity." In A.D. King (ed.), *Culture, Globalization and the World System* (Bighamton: SUNY).

Hannerz, U. (1996). *Transactional Connections* (London: Routledge).

Kamler, B. (2001). *Relocating the Personal.* (Albany: State University of New York Press).

Pinar, W. (1997). "Regimes of Reason and the Male Narrative Voice." In W. Tierney and Y. Lincoln (eds.), *Representation and the Text.* (Albany: State University of New York Press):81–113.

Seidman, S. (1992) *Embattled Eros.* (New York: Routledge).

Tannen, D. (1991). *You Just Don't Understand: Women and Men in Conversation.* (London: Virago).

Weeks, J. (1995). *Invented Moralities.* (New York: Columbia University Press).

Originally published in Samir Khalaf & John Gagnon (eds.) *Sexuality in the Arab World* (Saqi Books, 2006): 175–98.

PART ELEVEN

Beyond Expectations:
The New Media in the Arab World

Introduction

The tangible impact of mass media in the Arab World as a transformative agency for profound political and socio-cultural transformations has been over-stated ever since Daniel Lerner heralded its advent in the 1950s. The proliferation of the new media via websites, chat rooms and other gadgets of the digital, electronic and virtual technologies, has also exaggerated the ability of satellite deliveries to transgress cultural borders. Hence the new globalized media spaces are seen as irresistible mass incursions bound to erode all the vestiges of indigenous and local sources of information.

Others go further to suggest that access to such global media could well revolutionize Middle Eastern societies by acting as vectors of liberal change and, hence, wipe out authoritarian and repressive political regimes.

Kai Hafez, in his survey of the "Mass Media in the Middle East", provides a more realistic assessment of the impact of the new media by proposing that the new technologies are not as appealing to consumers and popular culture. Nor are they as socially mobilizing as often assumed by public opinion.

Trans-border flows of communication, since the 1990s, have enabled a considerable number of consumers—particularly those with access to the new technologies—to interact with global discourse and bypass the constraints of authoritarian systems of information and control. As Hafez argues, there is, of course, an intimate relationship between the forms and substance of communication, yet there is no predetermined association between the two. For example, traditional forms of communication in many countries (mosques, souks, informal networks etc.) remain important sources of political information. Conversely, traditional and reactionary political movements (as was the case with Ayatollah Khomeini's spread of his revolutionary message through videotapes before the Iranian Revolution in 1978–9), have begun to use modern print and electronic media as tools for their aims.

Ahmed Abdalla, in his essay on *Al-Jazeera*, arguably one of the most prominent Arabic satellite news networks, provides a compelling and instructive case study on the interplay between local considerations and the exposure to global discourses on sensitive issues such as religion, pluralism, democratization, freedom of expression and populist participation in the dissemination of news and views.

Perhaps its most instructive function is something akin to an "audio-visual Athens." Viewers are exposed to the virtues of public debate where, ideally, they are transformed from passive listeners who uncritically absorb all the official clichés and censored messages to active and engaged participants keen on partaking in the process of airing their views and grievances and creating unprejudiced sources of information. In a striking sense, *Al-Jazeera* has evolved into a modern-day version of the Media style of renaissance enlightenment and modernization. Paradoxically, it is a "free" and independent news channel but also state funded.

In populist terms, since it is both a news medium and entertainment show-place, it provides viewers with an accessible platform to express their most emotive views and impressions. Indeed, their sensational talk shows, where listeners enjoy a format of uncensored airtime, have become one of the most coveted programs. The demand of such access is so intense, that the program faces critical shortages in accommodating the throngs of listeners eager to wire in their messages and appear on global airways.

The channel has become adept at treading gently in its exposition of certain sensitive and testy issues while maintaining its abrasive and confrontational tone in others. Generally it lives up to its proverbial dual course: "Sober language for the news and fiery language for their views." It is the latter though which accounts for its notoriety. Its most sensational talk show (*The Opposite Direction*) is arguably one of the most highly rated programs in the region. Its broadcaster and anchor person, unlike those on one-tracked monolithic channels who merely echo official preset agendas, reflect a mélange of salient ideological groups, particularly Islamists, secularists and nationalists.

Perhaps more interesting than *Al-Jazeera*, is the proliferation of new styles of religiously oriented music video channels on Pan-Arab satellite television. The preponderance and popularity of this new genre of religious music videos, along with "clean" cinema and other Islamic satellite productions, reflect the shifting trend in arts and entertainment within the fold of Islamic Revival. In her essay on "Islamic Pop Culture in Egypt," Patricia Kubala explores the popularity of such novel genres to capture what she terms a "particular cultural moment in the Arab World in which popular culture is increasingly becoming the site of ethical-aesthetic interventions aimed at moral and social reform."

The basic thrust of her essay is to substantiate the shift that this new mode of popular culture represents. It is a clear departure from earlier trends prevalent in the 1970s and 1980s when state television broadcast religious music during major religious holidays. The songs were usually older recordings in classical Arabic without instrumental accompaniment and with montages of stock images of the Quran, Arabic calligraphy and Muslims engaged in ritual acts. In contrast, the video channels of the pop culture of today combine lyrics in colloquial Arabic with the *Shababi* (youthful) style of instrumental music with high-tech, commercially appealing images. The videos were not confined to religious holidays but appeared throughout the year, emphasizing the "dignity and humanity of Islam and its harmonious integration with a comfortable, middle-class modern lifestyle." Many of these clips stress the responsibility of the artist to serve as a model of moral decency and to convey socially constructive messages.

For example, the hit music video *Al-Muʿallim* (The Teacher) by Sami Yusuf, which incidentally is used by Amr Khalid in his programs, illustrates graphically this relationship between the artist, social responsibility and Islamic piety. The video juxtaposes English and Arabic lyrics in praise of the prophet Muhammad with images of a chic young photographer, portrayed by the singer who behaves kindly to his veiled old mother and the people in his community; and teaching religious lessons to children amidst the splendor of Islamic Cairo's medieval architectural heritage. At the end of the video, he drives off in an SUV to undertake a solo photography shoot in the desert, and in the darkness, he captures on film the image of a glowing Kaaba-like structure radiating light, perhaps meant to symbolize *Al-nur al-muhammadi* (the primordial light of Muhammad).

To Kubala, the video highlights the special role that the artist plays in devoting his talents "to express the beauty of God's creation and the truth of the prophet's message. The fact that he leads an exemplary and pious life in the community does not detract him from enjoying all the technical amenities and comforts of a modern life."

KAI HAFEZ

Mass Media in the Middle East:
Patterns of Political & Societal Change

The mass media in the Arab world and the Middle East have undergone profound changes since the beginning of the 1990s. The introduction and spread of new technologies such as satellite television and the Internet have extended media spaces beyond the local, national, and regional realm. Transborder flows of communication have enabled some consumers—those with access to the new technologies—to interact with a global discourse and bypass the limits of authoritarian information control. Since the Gulf war in 1991, when people in the Middle East tuned into CNN to receive fresh (albeit U.S. censored) news from the Gulf, media development in the area has been determined by both indigenous and external factors. An effective closure of national media spaces against the forces of globalization is less likely today than it ever was before.

The question remains however, whether new access to external media and the widening of media horizons is sufficient to generate political and social changes in the Arab world and the Middle East. To suggest that access to foreign media alone could revolutionize Middle Eastern societies, wipe away authoritarian rule, or modernize traditionalist lifestyles would be rather simplistic. Western satellite TV, to take one example, is no substitute for domestically produced television; it is not even particularly competitive in many countries. Technical or financial hurdles and, more importantly, cultural and language barriers mean that extensive exposure to foreign programs has been limited to elites while the vast majority of TV audiences continues to consume indigenous programs. The size and composition of the audiences vary from country to country. Due to the different styles of French and British colonialism, the understanding of French programs in the francophone Maghreb (Algeria, Libya, Morocco, Tunisia) poses less of a problem than the consumption of English programs in the Middle East. Even in the Maghreb, however, French channels like TV 5 or France 2 are primarily consumed by members of the educated and well-off upper and upper-middle classes. The lower-middle or lower classes have less aptitude in French and often feel a greater cultural gap between their own lifestyles and those represented in French programs. Larbi Chouikha has spoken of a "cut" (*coupure*) between the audiences of external satellite programs and those who are more oriented towards the indigenous media (Chouikha 1992: 44). One of the greatest limits to the effect of external TV and radio is the fact that the lower-middle classes (students, teachers, state officials, military, etc.), who through their membership in nationalist and, more recently, Islamist movements have had a considerable influence on the history of the area, are still primarily consumers of the indigenous media.

Another problem is that even if the consumption of foreign (Western) media can be considered a mass phenomenon, the content and quality of the programs leave doubts as to whether they can have any real impact on the development of the Middle East. Western media rarely cover the Middle East, with the exception of, for example, certain crisis periods and special aspects such as Muslim fundamentalism. Although Western and international programs are often welcomed as alternative sources of information, there is also considerable skepticism regarding the quality of Western foreign reports and the image of Asians and of Islam they depict. Muhammad Ayish argues that even the vernacular external media, such as BBC Arabic Service, which deal on an ongoing basis with the affairs of the Arab world and the Middle East and have gained a large audience among Arab populations, cannot substitute for the indigenous media's principal task of creating public opinion and successful communication between state and society. He therefore proposes to look at the external programs primarily in terms of a challenge, but not an alternative to the development of the domestic media of the Middle East:

> From a political perspective, the BBC's "stealing" of national radio listeners is likely to disrupt communications between ruling elites and masses in the Arab World via radio and other media. Turning to BBC en masse, particularly in crisis times, seems to widen the gap between the rulers and the ruled. (...) [A]udiences lost to foreign media may be regained only through development of national good quality programme output capable of surmounting the temptations of outside broadcasters. In the light of the current mass media situation in the Arab World, this challenge does not seem to be seriously considered by Arab broadcasters. (Ayish 1991: 383).

In terms of its direct effects, the media from outside the Middle East are not as appealing to the consumers and societies of the Middle East or as socially mobilizing as one might suppose. There have been a number of indirect effects, however. The new globalized media spaces have begun to change the fabric of the mass media in the Middle East, whether state-owned or in private ownership. Whereas Ayish's doubts as to whether the indigenous media would be able to cope with the global challenges were justified in 1991, analyses in the mid-1990s sound more optimistic. John Sinclair, Elizabeth Jacka, and Stuart Cunningham argued in 1996:

> Although evidence from Europe and elsewhere indicates that satellite services originating outside national borders do not usually attract levels of audience that would really threaten traditional national viewing patterns, the ability of satellite delivery to transgress borders has been enough to encourage generally otherwise reluctant governments to allow greater internal commercialization and competition. (Sinclair et al. 1996:2).

One of the most important questions relating to prospects of political and societal change in the Middle East is whether the old and new mass media of the Middle East will be politically and culturally liberalizing in the age of globalized media spaces. Although some positive aspects of this development are already visible, countertrends are also apparent. It is rather doubtful whether the new indigenous media allow for greater freedom of speech than the state media. The use of the media for participatory development and modernization is less important in current media debates than it was in previous decades.

Instead, there is an inherent danger that the discourse on communication and mass media will become an integral part of new ideological debates about a supposed cultural gap between "the West" and "Islam."

Information Control and Ownership

Comparative analyses of global media development consider the Middle Eastern media system the most closed and controlled in the world. Without doubt, information control and censorship are severe in the Middle East. At the same time Wolfgang Slim Freund has maintained that the diversity of the media often counteracts its negative reputation and that the Arab press, for example, is more critical and open in some countries than in others. To maintain that the Middle Eastern media is the most controlled in the world is to presuppose that there is some definite and ultimate criterion for comparison with China, for example, or large parts of south Asia or the Far East which are not famous for defending freedom of speech. Before resorting to vague generalizations, it seems useful to look at some significant contemporary patterns of media development in the Arab world and the Middle East concerning freedom of speech and media ownership.

Media Freedom and Control

In 1979 William Rugh distinguished between three different types of Arab press: (1) the "mobilized press," which is characterized by the almost total subordination of the media system to the political system and is controlled by revolutionary governments (Algeria, Egypt, Iraq, Libya, Syria, South Yemen, and Sudan); (2) the "loyalist press," which is privately owned and sometimes not even exposed to state censorship, but continues to support the regimes, especially as those regimes can still control their resources and persecute journalists through the legal systems (Bahrain, Jordan, Qatar, Saudi Arabia, Tunisia, United Arab Emirates); and (3) the "diverse press ," where the press is free (Morocco, Lebanon, and Kuwait, although Kuwait and Morocco also revealed loyalist features) (Rugh 1979: XVII).

Rugh's basic typology is, by and large, still in use and can be extended to other media beyond the print media. However, his analysis of freedom of speech and media freedom in individual countries no longer applies in some cases. The categorization of some countries has to be revised, and others bear traits of more than one category. Kuwait has partially restricted its formerly lauded freedom of the press through state censorship since 1986, the year when the national constitution was suspended and the Gulf War of 1991 has favored a trend towards loyalist self-censorship among journalists. Egypt in the era of Sadat and Mubarak has diversified its private press, and even state-owned papers like *Ruz Al-Yussuf* often criticize the government. The result, however, is that journalists are often persecuted and publications that "insult" the state or interfere with national security and public order are banned. Even after the revocation of Law 93 (of 1995) in 1996, journalists remain vulnerable to such charges. The print media in Jordan before 1993 and in Algeria around the early 1990s was quite diverse. However, in the course of the decade both countries reintroduced heavy information control. Insecurity over the political and economic situation and growing opposition led to a reversal of press liberalization. In Jordan, King Hussein was afraid of internal (Palestinian) criticism of the peace process with Israel; in Algeria, the regime became increasingly sensitive about critical voices against its treatment of the Islamists. The same is true of Algeria's neighbors, Morocco and, even more so, Tunisia, which "has become among the most restricted in the Arab world," according to the Committee to Protect Journalists (CPJ). Even in Lebanon, which Rugh classified as an open system allowing press freedom in 1979, the government—under the influence of Syrian and Israeli military occupation—restricts licenses for oppositional sectarian papers like those controlled by Hizbollah, the Phalange, or the Communists. Israel, without doubt the country with the most diverse media system in the Middle East, applies heavy military censorship to its own and to the Palestinian and southern Lebanese press. Somewhat like Turkey, where pro-Kurdish political commentary is effectively banned and journalists are prohibited from freewheeling in the country's southeast, Israel has given up democratic principles for the sake of national goals. Iran is the country with a contradictory media development.

There are some states in the Arab world and the Middle East such as Saudi Arabia and the Arab Gulf states, Iraq, Syria, Libya, Pakistan, or Afghanistan where such fluctuations in press freedom do not occur. Freedom of speech is restricted in almost all Arab and Middle Eastern countries, but except for very strict countries the execution of restrictions, whether legalist or purely arbitrary in nature, fluctuates depending on regime requirements. The limits on freedom of speech are therefore hard to define. The degree of press freedom corresponds to the nature of the respective political system in the sense that systems that are semiauthoritarian and patrimonial (Egypt, Morocco, Jordan, etc.) have allowed for more diversity than totalitarian and technocratic (military) systems (Iraq, Syria, etc.). But because the character of many or most systems has changed gradually with successive regimes—the increase of political liberalism from Nasser to Mubarak in Egypt is one example—and because each regime has varied its policies on freedom of speech, the typology of media systems is always in flux.In 1979, when Rugh analyzed the Middle East press, TV and radio broadcasting were owned and controlled by the state in all countries.

Today this picture has changed. Satellite TV and radio have transgressed country borders from outside the area and have induced a number of states to encourage the domestic private sector to face this foreign competition. The Middle East Broadcasting Center (MBC) and Arab Radio and Television (ART) are owned by wealthy Saudi businessmen. Most private TV networks, like most big private newspapers in the region, are "loyalist" in the sense that, despite their professional, often Westernized news policies, their programs include critical reports and commentary only insofar as they do not concern the national government or the governments of befriended states. For example, MBC has broadcast criticism of the Oslo peace process between Israel and the Palestinians, but no mention of state repression, torture, or similar issues in the Arab world is ever made. The only TV channel that deserves to be called "diverse" is Al-Jazeera (Qatar), a popular channel in the whole Arabic speaking world due to its treatment of "hot issues" like corruption and Islamic polygamy. In the final analysis, Rugh's typology of "mobilized," "loyalist," and "diverse" press systems can be transferred to the broadcasting systems in the area. State-owned national "mobilized" programs coexist with private "loyalist," and, in the case of Al-Jazeera, "diverse" programs.

Rugh's typology, however helpful and correct, seems insufficient for the classification of modern media systems in the area of freedom of speech. With the spread of fax machines, xerox machines, computers, video recorders, and all sorts of hardware necessary for media reproduction, the definition of what "mass media" really is becoming increasingly problematic. If we use the very vague and tentative definition of a mass medium as a means to communicate texts or programs on a regular basis to large audiences, then there is another important sector of the mass media that is often ignored or underestimated: the "alternative-independent" media. Formally, the term describes the low-budget media sector, such as magazines with a print run of only a few thousand. A second criterion for describing media as alternative is their ability to uphold different positions from the official or loyalist media. Using this definition, we become aware that even countries with a "loyalist" press system—Iran, for example—can have a very "diverse" alternative media sector. The Iranian government, to stick with this example, applies censorship to newspapers and to books, but it excludes magazines and allows public opinion greater freedom in this publication segment.

However, in the final analysis the above record of media freedom with regard to the press and TV/radio shows that the growing reception of external, foreign, mostly Western satellite channels in many countries of the Middle East has not been accompanied by a definite and clearly identifiable move by the indigenous mass media towards liberalization. On the contrary, even gradual liberal developments in the print and electronic media are often countered by a rollback in the national policies of information control and the tightening up of media laws. At the same time, the sheer growth in the number of media in many countries will make it increasingly difficult for authoritarian governments to control public opinion.

From the point of view of comparative democratization theory the only way to "erode" authoritarian rule is to establish firm programmatic and institutional alternatives. This can be achieved primarily by those who oppose the authoritarian status quo—which in the case of the mass media is quite naturally the journalists. The resistance of Egyptian journalists to Law 93 finally forced the Mubarak government to make concessions. The Arab Journalism Federation (AJF) has also protested repeatedly against all sorts of repression by Arab governments. Future research must address the question whether Arab journalists consider themselves an avant-garde of democratization or whether they, in fact, collaborate with the rulers and exercise self-censorship.

Media Ownership

Another trend is becoming increasingly obvious: the alteration of the structures of media ownership. Three main factors have motivated some states, such as Egypt, to gradually let go of their TV and radio monopolies. Firstly, as already mentioned, the competition of global, mostly Western satellite programs has made it necessary for Middle Eastern states to fill the professionalization and information gap between the old national state-owned and the foreign programs. To this end, private capital has been allowed into the game, financing satellite TV networks, film production, or advertising activities. Secondly, external competition has spurred the ambitions of some countries in the Middle East to broaden their influence in the region and make their new programs attractive to larger audiences beyond their national confines. This in turn has heightened regional competition. Saudi Arabia has built up a whole media empire for the Arab world with a growing number of satellite programs. Thirdly, pressure from the World Bank and the International Monetary Fund (IMF) has increased the willingness of Middle Eastern governments to include the media sector in their economic adjustment and privatization programs.

Regional competition has contributed greatly to the alteration of ownership and the privatization of indigenous media in the Arab world and the Middle East. The Saudi TV empire adds to the influence already exerted by Saudi Arabia through other media: it owns or partly owns media in many Arab countries as well as a large share of the Arab press published outside the Arab world (especially in London). It is also the most important customer of the Arab and especially Egyptian TV film industry, which is almost entirely dependent on the Saudi-dominated market and therefore often hesitates to touch upon matters sensitive to the Saudi state and its traditional-puritan Islamic value system. In Saudi-financed projects, "drinks" or kisses may not be shown, unless the couple is actually married in real life. Critics have identified an inner-regional brain drain from the media industries of many Arab countries to those of their rich cousins of the Arab peninsula. Nabil Abd al-Fattah of the Centre for Political and Strategic Studies/Al-Ahram Foundation in Cairo even refers to the "beduinization of Arab culture." Although the Saudi state felt threatened by radio broadcasts from Arab socialist Egypt in the 1960s, Saudi Arabia now seems to have found an effective means of turning the tables and exerting a very authoritarian and conservative influence on the media systems of the Middle East, which used to be a lot more diverse.

With the concentration of private capital, especially Saudi capital, there is an inherent danger that the Arab states' broadcasting monopolies will merely be replaced by private oligopolies. If this is the case, even privatization is no guarantee for liberalization and diversity. Moreover, privatization is sometimes a form of continued, but disguised state control, as in the case of Saudi satellite TV where the private owners of the new media are in fact relatives of the ruling Saud family and the Saudi King. In other countries the borderline between state and private capital becomes blurred because private owners are part of a "neopatrimonial" power framework in which private and state interests are inseparably intertwined. In cases like these, the private media are inclined to be loyal to the state and the government and to resist liberalization and the diversification of programs.

In the final analysis, private ownership does not necessarily lead to liberalization in the same way as state ownership is not equivalent to censorship and information control, as the European experience of the BBC, for example, has shown. In the Arab world and the Middle East, however, where most if not all governments and regimes resist the democratization of society, privatization of media ownership seems to be a prerequisite for media freedom.

Mass Media and Development

"Participatory development," a phrase used by Muhammad Ayish, is based on the idea that mass communication is a central means to include the people in political, societal, and cultural developments. In the classical works of modernization theory, mass communication is seen as a precondition for socioeconomic change, as knowledge can be exchanged, reproduced, or enriched by large-scale social interaction. Many theorists have looked at the mass media as a development instrument for the Third World, and according to Ithiel de Sola Pool, mass communication can create a process of global knowledge accumulation whereby the electronic media in particular represent important "flood gates of discourse" (Pool 1983: 251).

The contribution of the Arab and Middle Eastern mass media to participatory development is certainly limited. Many of the media do not, in fact, transfer "knowledge" and information but act as a government-controlled apparatus to create and distribute pseudo-facts and disguise information about the most important political, social, and cultural developments in the country concerned. Such control over information, which means that it cannot be properly exchanged, reproduced, or enriched, is the opposite of participatory development through mass communication, however.

At the same time, development and modernization are not the responsibility of the state alone. The question is how Arab and Middle Eastern societies as a whole articulate themselves through the mass media.

One important segment of the media for knowledge generation is books. In many respects, book publishers are really the "gatekeepers of ideas" and the gatekeepers of the abovementioned "floodgates of discourse." Whereas Middle Eastern book production and consumption is still impressive in terms of quantity, the banning of books is very widespread in the area, as in the case of the book *Muhammad* by the highly renowned French Orientalist Maxime Rodinson. The American University in Cairo (AUC) removed the book from its shelves and library database after a columnist in the *Al-Ahram* newspaper (May 13, 1998) had called the book an insult to Islam. By doing this, the university, which certainly deserves credit for being among the most open and critical institutions in the region, went beyond the Higher Education Ministry's request to remove the book from a teaching course. The incident shows that the banning of books is not limited to state intervention. On the contrary, governments often react to what they perceive to be the dominant public mood. As in the case of Rodinson's work and the American University, neoconservative self-censorship and the restriction of participatory development through mass communication have many social agents.

The Internet is another development issue. The medium has raised high hopes for participatory development. These hopes have not yet been fulfilled, however. In many Arab states the system is used for chat lines or, at best, commercial advertising. However, despite the growth of cyber cafés in cities like Cairo, access to the Internet is almost confined to a Western-oriented, English-trained and commercially successful upper or upper-middle class. The lower and lower-middle classes, who are important for participatory development, are much less involved here than in the abovementioned case of satellite TV. Hopes for a top-to-bottom effect of information diffusion and pessimistic visions of an ever-growing "information gap" between the users and nonusers of the Internet are firmly rooted in the old but still vivid competition between mainstream modernization and dependency approaches.

Like the "new" forms of communication, such as the Internet, some of the very "old" forms—personal communication in markets, in the mosque, and so forth—could also be of importance for development. The Arab world and the Middle East consist of very different societies, some literate and metropolitan, others illiterate and rural. In rural areas especially, people use traditional forms of communication. The idea that traditional communication is affirmative because it transports traditional values confuses the "medium" and the "message." Of course, there is an intimate relationship between the forms and substances of communication, in the sense that the use of traditional communication will more often coincide with traditional conservative views of politics and the world, whereas the use of modern media tends to correspond with modern views. However, there is certainly no predetermined relationship. On the contrary, traditional communication in many countries and regions is the most important source of political information. In many cases, where modern mass media became victims of state censorship, traditional communication took care of the distribution of the banned items of information. At the same time, reactionary Islamist groups have begun to use modern print and electronic media as tools for their aims, as was the case with Ayatollah Khomeini's spread of his revolutionary message through videotapes before the Iranian revolution in 1978–79. If these examples show that there is no fixed relationship between message and medium, then it seems quite natural to look at traditional communication as a source of development, especially when combined with modern mass media.

Media, Communication and Culture

Having dealt with political and socioeconomic patterns of media development it is time to consider what Goodman and Green (1992) call the "cultural circumstances" of information technology. Although the impact of the media on political and economic development in the Third World was debated in previous decades, the discourse in the Arab and Islamic world has shifted towards culture. Many governments, communication theorists, and Islamist groups agree in their critique of the West's "cultural invasion" via mass media and media imperialism either through direct broadcasting or by means of Western texts and programs in the indigenous media. Governments like that of Saudi Arabia, whose rule is based on religious-cultural legitimacy, employ the invasion paradigm as an ideology to justify restrictions against satellite TV, the Internet, or any other mass media. Likewise, their own media empires are designed to counteract the supposedly detrimental influence of foreign media (which is at the same time a political challenge for those governments).

According to Majid Tehranian, Islamic information and communication theory has three characteristics: it is normative, heterogeneous, and it is not unique (Tehranian 1988: 191). Although this typology might in itself be simplistic given the large corps of theoretical Islamic writing published in the nineties, there is still evidence for Tehranian's viewpoint:

1. Islamic communication theory cannot claim uniqueness as the first and only theoretical body to consider social or cultural factors of communication. Although it is surely legitimate and important to reconsider Koranic and other traditional Islamic views to show that Western culture does not have a monopoly

on communication thought, all too often "Islamic communications" and "Islamic communication theory" are not as culturally distinct as their titles suggest.

2. Normative character of communication theory: The wide-spread view among Muslim thinkers that Western media is a tool of Western cultural "invasion" is rejected by Western scholars. Indeed, the invasion paradigm seems rather a normative than an empirically based theory. One of the major arguments against the cultural imperialism approach is that national and regional media production in countries like Egypt or India has not been destroyed through Western competition. India produces more films today than Hollywood, and Egypt is still the most important center for films and books distributed in the Arab world. A second argument against the cultural imperialism view is that it ignores the processes of media usage on the part of the consumer. The mass media are not omnipotent. In fact, the messages are manipulated by audiences and the public. Even seemingly standardized fiction like the soap operas *Dallas* and *Dynasty* are filtered by the consumer through structures of meaning construction on a national, local, or individual level. The example of Algeria in particular shows that the consumption of foreign media does not necessarily destroy indigenous cultures, but can easily bring about cultural mixes and new intercultural media spaces and lifestyles, or can even help to revitalize traditional cultures. In this regard, Western satellite TV or Western programs in the national media do not simply "invade" the Arab world and the Middle East, but provide a stimulus for new discourses on culture.

3. Heterogeneity of Islamic communication theory: The fact that there are opponents as well as advocates of the cultural invasion paradigm in the Middle East indicates that Islamic information theory is heterogeneous in nature.

Given these arguments one gets the impression that a considerable amount of Islamic thought on communication and the media, especially ideas on "cultural invasion" by Western mass media, aims at a normative distancing from the West. The culture and the media of the West are deemed to be pornographic, violent, and unsocial in nature and engaged in an "imperialist" crusade against the Islamic world. The cultural invasion paradigm is a simplistic form of Islamic thought on communication that demonstrates that communication and the media have become an integral part of culturalist ideologies—like Samuel Huntington's *Clash of Civilizations*—that have become fashionable since the end of the Cold War era. Culturally based criticism is possible, but it must be based on sophisticated theories of global and intercultural communication, solid empirical research, and should address concrete problems such as the often very one-sided view of Islam in Western media, the hegemony of Western news agencies in the international information flow, or the growing gap between the information-rich and the information-poor countries.

A second very important aspect is the fact that the cultural discourse on the mass media tends to distract attention from essential problems of the mass media development in North Africa and the Middle East: media freedom and the role of the mass media in political and social development. Insofar as the cultural invasion paradigm is used to justify the banning and censorship of "non-Islamic" thought in Arab and Middle Eastern media, the cultural discourse seems detrimental for political and social development. The reaction of the Arab media to the Salman Rushdie affair was ample evidence for the fact that it is not only governments but sometimes also journalists and intellectuals who adopt censorship and self-censorship in order to protect Islam. Analysis has shown that in most cases journalists in the Middle East did not support Khomeini's death verdict (or religious expert opinion [fatwa], to be more precise), but the argument that Rushdie's book should be banned was very widespread. These traditionalist-culturalist views contradict the abovementioned protests of other Arab journalists against censorship and information control and endanger the future of critical Arab journalism.

References

Ayish, Muhammad. "Foreign Voices as People's Choices. BBC Popularity in the Arab World." *Middle East Studies* 1991, 3:374–389.

Chouikha, Larbi. "Etatisation et pratique journalistique." *Revue Tunisienne de communication* 1992, 22:37–46.

Goodman, S.E., & J.D. Green. 1992. Computing the Middle East and North Africa. http://www.sas. upenn.edu/African_Studies/Comp_Articles/Computing_10174.html (February 28, 1997).

Pool, Ithiel de Sola. *Technologies of Freedom*. (Cambridge: Harvard University Press, 1983).

Rugh, William A. *The Arab Press: News Media and Political Process in the Arab World*. (Syracuse, NY: Syracuse University Press, 1979).

Sinclair, John, Elizabeth Jacka, & Stuart Cunningham. "Peripheral Vision." In *New Patterns in Global Television*, edited by John Sinclair, Elizabeth Jacka, & Stuart Cunningham, (Oxford: Oxford University Press, 1996): 1–32.

Tehranian, Majid. "Communication Theory & Islamic Perspectives." In *Communication Theory: The Asian Perspective*, edited by Wimal Dissanayake, (Singapore: Asian Mass Communication Research and Information Center, 1988): 190–203.

An abridged version of a chapter originally published in Kai Hafez (ed.) *Mass Media, Politics and Society in the Middle East* (Hampton Press, Inc. 2001): 1–15. Printed here with the permission of the publisher.

AHMED ABDALLA

The Arabic Satellite News Network: Al-Jazeera

When a videotape of Osama Bin Laden threatening the U.S. with more terror was delivered to Al-Jazeera's trusted Kabul correspondent Tayfeer Alouni shortly after September 2001, he knew he was sitting on an incendiary world exclusive. He called Al-Jazeera's executives for advice. Without watching the footage, they told Alouni to broadcast it immediately. Al-Jazeera does not bury bad news. The tape was televised, unfiltered, uncensored, from the Middle East to the world, and Al-Jazeera created more news as a result: anti-American riots erupted in Gaza City and the cult of Bin Laden was strengthened; fear and loathing grew in the U.S., together with a certain bitterness that Bin Laden could win the propaganda war with one speech to one camera, and a mainline into the biggest, freest, most popular Arabic news station ever.

Al-Jazeera does not try to filter reality to create a perception of a restrained, diplomatic objectivity that tiptoes on the tightrope between opposing opinions. The Qatar-based station's concept of objectivity is to show "the view and the other view" (a slogan it trumpets with pride), beaming both extremities around the world, and creating a new space of freedom in between.

Al-Jazeera's unflinching coverage of the attack on Afghanistan and the airtime it gave to Bin Laden epitomised the station's comfort with controversy—a price it willingly pays for its pioneering, fiercely independent style. Since Al-Jazeera's creation in 1996, every single country in the Arab League has taken offence at the station's brusque style and made a complaint; the U.S. joined the condemnation when they filed a formal diplomatic complaint with Qatar, criticising the station for being a conduit for al-Qaida, Bin Laden's terrorist network. "At best, Osama Bin Laden's message is propaganda, calling on people to kill Americans," the White House press secretary Ari Fleischer said. "At worst, he could be issuing orders to his followers to initiate attacks." But for Al-Jazeera it is anathema to impose a no-platform policy. The liberal philosophy of their commentary programmes suffuses their news coverage too.

Despite the official complaints and the reservations about Al-Jazeera, the network provides a unique window on the Arab world and its political sensibilities. A subtitle on the channel during the first night of the U.S. bombing of Kabul described the Taliban firing at "the enemy's planes". Interestingly, the U.S. had to depend on Al-Jazeera during the early days of the attack on Afghanistan for its exclusive pictures of the bombing—Al-Jazeera was the only news channel to have working offices in Kabul under the Taliban. The U.S. was forced into the rare position of being reliant on foreign media, even if the pictures it broadcast of civilian casualties were detrimental to the U.S. propaganda war. The U.S.

government was also conscious of the massive popularity of Al-Jazeera in the Middle East and beyond: the station reaches more than 3 million Arabs, including 150,000 in the U.S. (At the height of the war, CNN only broadcast to three million.) Accordingly, cabinet members Colin Powell, Condoleezza Rice, and Donald Rumsfeld all appeared on Al-Jazeera to try to convince the Arab world that this was a war on terrorism, not a war on Islam. Charlotte Beers, the U.S. under secretary of state for public diplomacy, even considered buying advertising space on the channel to get the American message across. But when western stations reopened their Kabul offices after the Taliban left town and the U.S. no longer had to rely on the controversial station for its gritty pictures of the bombing, the Al-Jazeera offices themselves were bombed. Al-Jazeera officials believed it was a deliberate strike, a U.S. conspiracy to win control of the propaganda campaign. The chief editor, Ibrahim Hilal, said: "I still believe the decision to exclude our office from the coverage was taken weeks before the bombing. But I don't think they would do that while we were the only [news broadcasters] in Kabul." The Pentagon dismissed Al-Jazeera's claims as just a conspiracy theory.

Just as the Gulf War made CNN famous in the west and infamous in the east, the attack on Afghanistan gave Al-Jazeera the opposite standing—famous in the east and infamous in the west. A station almost unknown outside the Arab world before 11 September 2001, it has now become the focus of U.S. attention because of its perceived anti-American, pro-al-Qaida bias. The station was approached, together with CNN, by a man claiming to represent al-Qaida, asking them to submit questions to Bin Laden. The cautious reaction of CNN throws into sharp relief the gung-ho attitude of Al-Jazeera, which had already broadcast an interview with Bin Laden in 1998. Wolf Blitzer, the CNN anchorman, said: "We want to stress that CNN has no information about Bin Laden or whether he is dead or alive. We do not know how al-Qaida communicates with Al-Jazeera or how Al-Jazeera plans to get the questions to Bin Laden." The implication is of a dubious connection between Al-Jazeera and al-Qaida—a significant mistrust of Al-Jazeera's professionalism which is entirely misplaced.

Professionalism

The channel may be immature and prone to a "scoop" mentality—a willy-nilly attitude towards fast-breaking news that characterises less seasoned media organisations—but it is not naive. Long before Al-Jazeera aroused the suspicions of the west, its long-standing popularity in the Arab world came about as a result of its precise professionalism as well as its liberal principles. Al-Jazeera's professionalism began with the conscious realisation of this raison d'être. The managing director Mohamed Jasem Al-Ali explained, "Arab viewers used to get their entertainment from local channels but relied on foreign channels for their news and views. Based in the Arab world, we tried to fill that vacuum. We stormed a field from which others escaped. It was a risk, but the popularity of this type of programming by the BBC and CNN was an indication that we too might be successful."

Entry into the unmapped Arab world of independent news media was no guarantee of success, no matter how much courage or calculation was involved. Attracting viewers required a more cohesive philosophy. Al-Ali said, "We began by addressing the problem of objectivity, impartiality and respect for the viewer's discretion. Thus precise information became our bridge to the viewer's trust."

Precise information, however, does not completely account for the prestige attained by such a small channel over a relatively short period of time. Other dimensions of professionalism are no less important: charismatic broadcasters who are masters of classical Arabic, alert correspondents—like Tayfeer Alouni in Kabul—who quickly follow up events, and an impressive list of commentators and guests, including foreign analysts who speak Arabic—something quite fascinating to Arabic viewers. These subjective features are enhanced by the more objective attractions of fast-breaking news, informative programmes, instructive documentaries—translated or tailored— and amusing talk shows.

To Al-Jazeera, talk shows are no less important than the news. Al-Jazeera walks on two legs, or rather flies with two wings - news and views. Illustrating this is a promotion spot with a broadcaster's voice referring to Al-Jazeera's "journey behind events everywhere" while remaining true to its promise to show both sides of every story.

This brings Al-Jazeera more closely into the arena of freedom of expression, but Al-Ali still analysed it as a challenge of professionalism. "There are demarcation lines for a professional operation: in order to present a view we must also present the other view. And if a representative of the other view is not present, the broadcaster himself should present it or let viewers do so by telephone. The channel does not endorse a particular viewpoint or adopt a particular cause. But given enough space, just causes press their point and gain sympathy."

Freedom

An efficient, professional media can be a catalyst for freedom in the political sense. However, freedom is not necessarily a by-product of professionalism, either in society in general or in the media in particular. Freedom is the one just cause that is served by an ardent and endless effort to deliberately realise it. Are Al-Jazeera's men (and, notably, women) unaware of a subconscious drive for freedom? On the contrary, freedom of debate is their totally conscious motivation and the yardstick of their professional performance.

Al-Jazeera has served the cause of freedom in the Arab media by broadcasting political, on-air talk shows, discussing thorny issues, allowing unconventional views, hosting opposition politicians and intellectuals and by airing viewers' opinions received by telephone and fax.

In doing so, Al-Jazeera has become an initiator and an accelerator of competition in the Arab satellite media. This is positive feedback from its professional standards, The lesson here: not only does censorship curtail freedom, it is also responsible for bad journalism. This is an axiom Al-Jazeera has passed on to the bulk of the Arab media—which is free of freedom. Al-Jazeera's very creation was a reaction to censorship. The station replaced a BBC Arabic news channel which collapsed when its Saudi Arabian sponsors deemed it too liberal and pulled the plug. With the munificence of the Emir and the rehired BBC staff, Al-Jazeera was created to broadcast what censored stations would not be inclined to.

By combining a good news service and the free expression of views, Al-Jazeera has brought the Arab viewer to the qualitatively higher level of having informed views, rather than merely ending up with an expression of an impression. The channel's insistence on broadcasting the opposite poles of an emotive issue enhances the process of democratisation in the Arab world by presenting aspects of freedom of expression and acknowledging pluralism. As a result, this format of an audio-visual Athens—albeit by satellite—constitutes a socialisation process which teaches viewers how to debate (and not to listen unthinkingly to official clichés from other Arab channels).

The experience is enhanced by Al-Jazeera's participatory framework, which gives viewers airtime in talk shows. The demand from viewers who wish to have their say is astonishing; scores of them wait on the telephone and send faxes. The need and obvious enjoyment of expressing themselves is a reflection of the many grievances harboured by Arab citizens under stifling political systems in their own countries.

By addressing Arab viewers in the Middle East and North Africa and in the world at large, and by making a point of covering the affairs of all Arab countries, Al-Jazeera has established itself as a pan-Arab channel while other stations remain parochial, tied to a particular region and to a particular government. Al-Jazeera's diverse list of guests on both sides of programming—news and views—has influenced the formation of an Arab political and intellectual elite. Some of Al-Jazeera's guests, a number of whom made their first appearances on the channel, have become well-known figures at home and abroad.

By linking the global with the regional, Al-Jazeera has contributed to the ongoing debate about globalisation. As well as having grievances against the autocracy of their national systems, Arab citizens also have grievances against the imbalances and injustices of the global system—issues which have become even more urgent since 11 September 2001. Some would adopt isolationism, especially in reaction to the west, as a premise for attaining Arab independence and freedom. Al-Jazeera's broadcasting has prompted an alternative means of attaining Arab rights through the interactive process of engagement with the rest of the world—even if its relationship with the U.S. remains turbulent.

The channel takes pride in having replaced CNN and the BBC in providing Arab viewers with a good news service, with management and personnel almost exclusively Arab.

Critique

Al-Jazeera's trajectory to success was not smooth and its current authority and acceptability in the west are still tenuous. Since the beginning it has provoked the animosity of many influential groups: Arab governments (literally all of them), political parties, other competing TV channels, writers and journalists. But the criticism is wide-ranging: there is a considerable distance between the accusations that Al-Jazeera is pro-Iraqi and that it is pro-Israeli. This suggests that complaints arise out of a piqued pride; to Al-Jazeera complaints are therefore proof that they are doing something right.

Al-Jazeera's main weapon of defence is its viewers, millions of them, who appreciate its service and find themselves reflected in its broadcasts. In populist terms, Al-Jazeera is stronger than its adversaries. But this should not prejudice the more serious criticisms levelled against the channel or, even more importantly, the need to acknowledge the limitations and drawbacks of its structure and service.

Al-Jazeera is a "free" news channel, but, paradoxically, it is also state-funded (like the BBC)—a dependent relationship that probably makes it vulnerable to censorship or self-censorship in the interests of national security. There is nothing to guarantee the continuing coincidence of interest between Al-Jazeera and the Qatari state, which has gained tremendous prestige through its hosting of the channel. Al-Jazeera is a contemporary version of the Medici style of renaissance, enlightenment and modernisation: the subsidising family remains in control until the subsidised agent gains full autonomy over a long historical process, with compromise and constraints imposed or self-imposed along the way.

Al-Jazeera's pluralism leaves it in a vulnerable position in the Middle East. Large Arab states such as Egypt, Iraq and Syria have all threatened to ban the channel. After 11 September 2001, the U.S. examined ways of blocking satellite reception of Al-Jazeera for its citizens, but they found the technology too complex and too diffuse to obstruct. Smaller countries too have the means to hit back at the channel: Kuwait mobilised its press and Tunisia its diplomatic apparatus.

What Al-Ali referred to as "difficulties" are more a matter of pressure than actual crises. Al-Jazeera has deftly narrowed the range of items which might alienate certain Arab governments, including Jordan, where the channel's office has been closed. It is an ongoing game which requires, at the very least, mitigating the language of criticism from time to time. More importantly, Al-Jazeera, for all its journalistic objectivity, does not cover the corruption of the ruling elites of Arab states. While criticism of Arab regimes is allowed, the mentioning of leaders by name is avoided.

In particular, sensitivities surrounding religious issues impose a priori calculations of reactions on the part of the channel. This was explained by Maher Abdalla, the presenter of, *Sharia and Life,* Al-Jazeera's only talk show on religious issues, where the one guest taking questions from viewers is an authority on religious matters.

> My conviction is that there are no administrative restrictions on discussing religious issues but there are cultural restrictions. However, I do not hesitate to tread onto some sensitive terrain, like inviting a Shi'ite sheikh in a predominantly Sunni society. To some people this is [dangerous ground]. Nevertheless, I tell my critics it is not wrong to invite a Shi'ite once a year—that is one-fifty-second of the space of our weekly programme. The one aspect I have to take into account—willingly or not—is that this programme needs to be credible to its viewers. You are a journalist and showmaker and you cannot afford to lose your viewers. This is not to be opportunistic. But I must invite guests who have religious credibility to the man in the street. The latter sometimes asks simple questions, while we are discussing sophisticated issues. Also, many protest telephone calls come from the conservative environment of the Gulf. When a guest of the programme adopted the notion of citizenship, some viewers considered this yielding to western pressure. Some even think we have an agenda aiming at the destruction of Islam altogether.

Al-Jazeera lives with the contradiction of its dual discourse: sober language for the news and fiery language for the views. While it goes to lengths to use terminology which is not value-charged in its news bulletins (for example distinguishing between freedom fighters and terrorists), it lets the fires flame in its views programmes—even at the cost of being attacked by the press in certain countries or having its offices closed there.

The channel's sensational talk shows are often criticised for their abrasive language in which the outcome turns into "a mere release of tensions that express themselves in talk rather than action". The bulk of the attacks are directed at Al-Jazeera's most sensational talk show, *The Opposite Direction*. This programme has infuriated every Arab government; some take action while others let it be known where they stand. Al-Ali admitted that, "We have problems with governments. But some of them do not respond to our queries and everyone accuses us of bias. There is also a scarcity of speakers from certain Arab countries."

For the presenter of *The Opposite Direction*, Faisal Al-Kassem, the programme's format and ratings are interconnected:

> The political programme ... requires a theatrical touch. Why not? It must be exciting and there is no harm in some allurement and sensation. Political programmes in the Arab world usually attract only the elite. We aim at attracting a larger constituency that had hitherto no interest in politics. All strata watch our programme, including young people and housewives. This is an achievement in itself. We are criticised for having a show of "cockfighting", and, truly, some episodes have been really hot. But if that were all, Arab governments would not have become that furious about it [twenty volumes of articles written against it in three years]. The programme deals with the most sensitive topics and has hosted persons no one had dared to invite before. In so doing we have been true to Al-Jazeera's slogan of "The View ... and the Other View". The culture of dialogue is absent in the Arab media, where you have one opinion. Instead of settling differences by bullets and warfare, dialogue can be a safety valve for the Arabs.

The Opposite Direction, according to Al-Kassem, has had an impact. "The fruit of our programme is raising awareness and motivating the mind in the long term. Years would prove it was not a mere release of tensions." It remains to be seen whether Al-Jazeera's talk shows represent a flash of lightning that quickly extinguishes, or a radiation of enlightenment that will endure, reach maturity and become a part of culture.

Like any other channel, Al-Jazeera is faced with the subjectivity of its own broadcasters. This difficulty is more acutely felt than at other channels, since Al-Jazeera purports to be freer than most Arab channels where broadcasters are merely parrots echoing official pronouncements. Like its societal milieu, Al-Jazeera has its own Islamists, secularists and nationalists. Elements of in-house ideological disagreements, power struggles and professional jealousies are to be found within Al-Jazeera off-screen.

The style of presentation of each individual broadcaster adds another dimension which amplifies the differences. Al-Jazeera's off-screen mélange is concrete proof of its belief in and practice of pluralism, although it takes considerable executive ability to manage the differences.

Al-Jazeera is also faced with the subjectivity of its viewing constituency. It takes pride in having reached millions of viewers inside and outside the Arab world. Yet, every group of viewers appears to have a stake in the channel, as well as something to hate about it: Islamists vs. secularists, traditionalists vs. modernists, pro-Iraqis vs. anti-Iraqis, pro-reconciliation vs. pro-confrontation over the Middle East conflict, even pro-Kosovans vs. anti-NATO.

Pluralism is the mother of ambivalence. Everyone wishes to make a space for her or his own freedom, be it individually or collectively. To instil a universal belief in freedom on the part of its viewers would be an impossible mission for Al-Jazeera. Instead, the channel tries to promote freedom in a real way.

Conclusion

Within the context of Arab media, it is no small credit to both its news objectivity and its liberty of views that Al-Jazeera has succeeded over a short span of time in attracting such a large audience; in linking, on subjects of common interest, Arabs from the interior and from the outside; in allowing viewers from the silent majority to speak up; in giving visibility to the ignored members of the disenchanted elite; in making a place for professional standards in Middle Eastern news broadcast; in sowing the seeds of uncensored debate and a culture of dialogue; in opening the critical eye of the viewers; in accelerating competition for quality broadcasts from that part of the world (at least in the satellite sphere); in forcing "freedom" as an issue for realisation, thus pushing the enemies of freedom into the defensive (creating space by default); and in sustaining the pressure for broader democratisation in the Arab world.

Al-Jazeera has achieved many of these Ten Commandments in the five years since its creation. Despite its problematic relationship with the west, it has successfully shifted the paradigm of mass communication in the Arab world and is building the dialogic framework that will eventually facilitate increased democratisation. Its integral coverage of the war on terrorism will be crucial in establishing Al-Jazeera as a major media player—a bridge to the west, and a liberator of the Arab nation.

Originally published in E.Van der Plas et al. *Creating Spaces of Freedom* (Saqi Books, 2002): 173–186. It is printed here with the permission of the publisher..

PATRICIA KUBALA

The Music Video and Muslim Piety:
Satellite Television and Islamic Pop Culture
in Egypt

With the proliferation of music video channels on pan-Arab satellite television in the past decade, new styles of religious-themed videos are appearing on these alternative outlets to state television broadcasting. The growth and popularity of this new genre of religious music videos, along with "clean" cinema and Islamic satellite television productions, reflect shifting discourses concerning the arts and entertainment within the Islamic Revival. This essay explores the appearance of these music videos within a particular cultural moment in the Arab world in which popular culture is increasingly the site of ethical-aesthetic interventions aimed at moral and social reform.

Before the advent of the satellite era, state television channels did (and continue to) broadcast religious genres of music during major Islamic religious holidays and during the month of Ramadan. These songs are usually older recordings in classical Arabic, with limited instrumental accompaniment and juxtaposed with montages of low-quality, stock images—primarily of natural phenomena, religious sites, Arabic calligraphy and the Qur'an, and Muslims engaged in ritual acts such as circumambulation of the Kaaba in Mecca. Very rarely are the singer or singers (frequently, but not always, male) depicted alongside the images, and in general, these videos convey a sense of solemn religiosity set apart from the ordinary rhythm of daily life.

In contrast, popular pan-Arab satellite music video channels such as Mazzika, Melody, and Rotana broadcast a new style of religious music video that combines lyrics in colloquial Arabic in praise of God and the prophet Muhammad with *shababi*(youth) style instrumental music and a new set of high-quality, commercially appealing images and storylines in contemporary settings. Although they are broadcast more frequently during the month of Ramadan and religious holidays, the most popular songs appear throughout the year and like other music videos that circulate within the prospering satellite television-mobile phone economy, they are available for downloading as ring tones or videos onto viewers' cell phones.

This new trend of commoditized religious music video emphasizes the dignity and humanity of Islam and its harmonious integration with a comfortable and chic modern lifestyle. The popular Egyptian boy-band WAMA, for example, released in 2005 the popular hit *Kan Nifsi* (I wish that I could)—a slow, lyrical song with no musical features to mark it as "religious" except the faint sounds of the call to prayer, set against the background noise of a busy metropolitan city, that begin the track. Using the simple colloquial language that predominates in *shababi* music, the four university-aged members of the group take turns singing of their desire to meet the prophet Muhammad, to sit with him and his companions in heaven, and to follow his path in Islam.

Dressed in chic, all-white casual clothing, the boys wander among the golden sand dunes of a beautiful remote desert location, the kind that financially comfortable Egyptians, not just foreigners, increasingly frequent as the national tourist industry taps into the disposable incomes of the new moneyed classes created by the neo-liberal economic policies of the past three decades. The video ends with the boys walking into the sunset shoulder to shoulder, conveying a message of brotherly unity in Islam.

Pious performers

Although many of these stylish religious songs, like the WAMA video described above, present male homosocial worlds and bonding experiences in Islam, others prominently feature female performers. One example is the song *Illa Ibn Abdallah* (Except for the Son of Abdallah), which was first aired around the time of the Prophet's birthday celebration (*Mawlid al-Nabi*) in 2006. A response to the Danish cartoon controversy, the video features a large group of pan-Arab singers staging a peaceful protest to express outrage over the derogatory treatment of the Prophet and their love and respect for the son of Abdallah (the name of Muhammad's father) and his religion. The female performers, dressed in fashionable white veils, sing in the chorus and alternate with their male counterparts as soloists; one of the female singers, Sahar Fadil, is a "repentant" artist who used to star in racy music videos of the variety referred to by critics as "*burnu klibhat*" (porno clips). Another example from Ramadan 2006 is the song *Khaliha Ala Allah* (Leave the Matter to God), performed by the respected Syrian singer Assala Nasry. The lyrics in colloquial Egyptian praise God and describe the singer's pious love and devotion, and the images depict her (veiled) in prayer and reading the Quran, and (unveiled) donating food and breaking the Ramadan fast with her children in her well-appointed, upper-class home. While representations of women in these videos as mothers, devout believers, and socially responsible members of their communities and the Muslim *ummah* are more common than depictions of women in sexual relationships as lovers or even wives, a few videos, such as Hossam Hajj's *Ithagabti* (You Put on the Veil), aim to present audiences with religiously appropriate love stories in which the romantic relationship strengthens, rather than compromises, the couple's relationship to God.

The growing number and popularity of songs such as these reflect the broader trend toward public displays of Islamic piety and increased support for Islamist socio-political visions that have marked Arab society as a whole since the 1970s. But it must be stressed that the Islamic Revival has affected the Arab world's entertainment industry, in particular its twentieth-century capital, Egypt, in a number of different ways. In the 1980s and early 1990s, popular Egyptian cassette and television preachers such as Shaykh Abd al-Hamid Kishk, Shaykh Muhammad Mitwalli al-Shaarawi and Shaykh Umar Abd al-Kafi criticized Egypt's national entertainment industry as morally harmful to Muslim audiences and called upon performers to repent and retire from their professional activities. The Egyptian national press sensationalized cases of these "conversions" and attributed them to the spread of extremism and corrupting Gulf influences on Egyptian society. While male stars were also part of this phenomenon, the veiling and repentance of female entertainers by far received the most attention in the popular media. Although most of these "repentant" female artists left the entertainment industry, a few, such as Huda Sultan, donned the veil but continued to work under conditions acceptable to their new sense of religiosity.

Since the late 1990s, many male and female performers and media personalities have embraced the latter alternative. The advent of transnational satellite television broadcasting in the Arab world in the late 1990s has been accompanied by an explosion in private, commercial television productions with Islamic themes. Muslim scholars, popular preachers, and producers are actively encouraging the creation of alternative forms of pious entertainment, and the growth of religious satellite television programming in the last decade has provided numerous opportunities for formally retired male and female media personalities to utilize their talents, but this time appearing in Islamic-appropriate dress as preachers, hosts of talk show programs, or actors in television serials with suitably pious roles. In the Egyptian cinema industry, a growing number of filmmakers, actors, and actresses, veiled and unveiled, refuse to visually portray sexually explicit scenes, appear in immodest clothing, or depict immoral characters. The new regime of morally disciplined representations in the "clean cinema" trend, as Egyptian critics have dubbed it, marks a shift in the Islamic Revival towards regarding the entertainment industry as an arena for refashioning religio-ethical norms, particularly ones surrounding the female body and sexuality. In this new site of social reform, as Karim Tartoussieh notes in a perceptive recent analysis of clean cinema, "The sinfulness of art—a discourse that was prevalent in the 1980s and resulted in many female actors renouncing their artistic careers and veiling—is replaced by a different discourse that is amicable to popular culture as an arena of social purity and morality" (Tartoussieh, 2007:41). This alternative discourse of *al-fann al-hadif* (purposeful art) stresses the responsibility of the artist to serve as a model of moral decency and to convey socially constructive messages in his or her work.

Purposeful art

The increasing presence and popularity of religious videos on satellite music television channels reflects this shift towards *al-fann al-hadif* within the Islamic Revival's discourse regarding entertainment and the arts, a discourse that is often reflected in the images and narrative tropes of the music videos themselves. Sami Yusuf's hit music video *al-Mu'allim* (The Teacher) provides an exemplary illustration of the proper relationship between artists, social responsibility, and Islamic piety articulated within the discourse of *al-fann al-hadif*. A transnationally acclaimed British artist of Azeri origin, Yusuf was introduced to Arab satellite television audiences by the popular preacher Amr Khalid, whose discussions on culture and media on the program *Sunna' al-Hayah* (Lifemakers) encouraged young Muslim artists not to retire but use their God-given talents in the service of strengthening the Muslim community. A trained musician and composer but not a native Arabic speaker, Yusuf's albums blend primarily English lyrics with Arabic, Turkish, and Hindi vocals and refrains, and his compositions employ a range of Middle Eastern and Western instruments, rhythms, and melodic themes. The singer's first album, entitled *al-Mu'allim* (The Teacher)—referring, of course, to the prophet Muhammad—was released in 2003, and a music video of the title track was shot in Egypt using an Egyptian director (Hani Usama) and production team. It debuted on Arab music satellite television stations during Ramadan 2004, and it has remained one of the most popular and frequently aired religious music videos since then.

The video of *al-Mu'allim* juxtaposes English and Arabic lyrics in praise of the prophet Muhammad with images of a chic young photographer, portrayed by the singer, going about his daily life; working in his studio in his large, chicly decorated suburban home; behaving kindly to his veiled old mother and the people in his community; and teaching religious lessons to children amidst the splendor of Islamic Cairo's medieval architectural heritage. At the end of the video, he drives off in an SUV to undertake a solo photography shoot in the desert, and in the darkness, he captures on film the image of a glowing, Kaaba-like structure radiating light, perhaps meant to symbolize *al-nur al-muhammadi* (the primordial light of Muhammad). The video thus emphasizes the special role that the artist, in this case a photographer, plays in devoting his talents to expressing the beauty of God's creation and the truth of the Prophet's message. At the same time, he leads an exemplary and pious life in his community, all the while enjoying the technological amenities and comforts of a modern, cosmopolitan lifestyle. In this way, Yusuf's on-screen music video persona embodies the ideals of *al-fann al-hadif*—chic and tasteful art with an appropriate message of moral respectability and social responsibility—a persona that is reinforced by the singer's interviews and website statements that articulate his dedication to working for the well-being of the Muslim *ummah*.

Importantly, the music video as a genre on the whole stands in sharp contrast to the moral parameters of *al-fann al-hadif* in the minds of many viewers in the Arab world. The same satellite music channels that broadcast the new style of religious videos also broadcast a notorious and controversial style of racy music videos, labelled "*burnu klibhat*" (porno clips) by critics, with which the genre of music videos as a whole has become associated. While the banal love lyrics, hackneyed tunes, and apolitical nature of these videos also draw criticism, what audiences and critics most object to are the revealing clothes and overtly seductive dance moves of the female models and singers. These sexualized representations of female entertainers, as well as the considerable outcry against them, echo the centuries-old debate in the Islamic tradition over the moral character of artists and the potentially dangerous effect of music and entertainment upon the subjectivity of the audience (Al-Faruqi, 1985). As the work of Karin van Nieuwkerk, among others, demonstrates, female entertainers are regarded as particularly threatening because the improper display of their bodies is understood to easily tempt male spectators to commit adultery and other grave sins (van Nieuwkerk, 1985).

By adhering to the chaste conventions of the clean cinema genre, which many television dramas as well as the new style of religious music videos also uphold, male and female entertainers and media personalities distance themselves from the cultural association of art with immorality. In this way, performers of religious pop songs mark out a respectable place for themselves in a media genre (the music video) which has become overwhelmingly associated with immodesty and sexual immorality. The recent appearance and popularity of these religious music videos on pan-Arab satellite television point to the increasing influence of the discourse of *al-fann al-hadif* in the realm of pop culture, as well as the growing importance of mass-mediated entertainment as a site of moral and social reform in the Arab world.

Bibliography

Al-Faruqi, Lois. "Music, Musicians, and Muslim Law," *Asian Music* 17, no. 1 (1985): 3–36.

Tartoussieh, Karim. "Pious Stardom: Cinema and the Islamic Revival in Egypt." *Arab Studies Journal* 15, no. 1 (2007).

van Nieuwkerk, Karin. *"A Trade Like Any Other": Female Singers and Dancers in Egypt* (Cairo: The American University in Cairo Press, 1996).

Originally published in *ISIM Review* (Autumn, 2007): 60–61 as "Satellite TV & Islamic Pop Culture in Egypt." It is printed here with the permission of the International Institute for the Study of Islam in the Modern World.

PART TWELVE

Focus on Transnational Islam

Introduction

The new and escalating presence of transnational Muslims in European societies, because of their recent social visibility, has provoked contradictory reactions within the host countries. It has also sparked a heated academic debate among protagonists of the "clash of civilizations" and "cultural relativists" within the context of the predisposition of local Islamic cultural self-assertion to adapt to the unsettling forces of globalization. Demographically, the relentless inflow of immigrants is understandably a source of concern, often bordering on collective anxiety tinged with Islamophobia. By the end of WWII, there were fewer than one million Muslims in Western Europe, mostly in France and the United Kingdom. Today, the figure has exceeded the fifteen millions in almost all European societies, from Scandinavia to Italy.

The predicament of this "New Islamic Presence," as a diasporic group, is not just a matter of numbers. Foremost, and contrary to popular perception, they are not a monolithic group. Though they might share the same faith and a common set of religious beliefs, culturally and ethnically, they are multi-faced with sharp sectarian divisions. Unlike, for example, the early conventional Muslim residents in the United Kingdom and France who came as migrants, today they are mostly "guest" and itinerant workers. They are also drawn from different ethnic, national and cultural backgrounds. Hence, it is inconsistent to speak of Arabs, African, Indian and the South Asian Islam. Their pattern of settlement in Europe reflects their national origins. Hence, one can easily speak of Muslim Turks and Kurds in Germany, Maghrebis in France and South Asian in the UK.

Despite their differences and their varied reception by the various host societies, all transnational Muslims are struggling today with the same existential predicament; namely how to incorporate the basic ingredients of liberal democracy, human rights and the requirements of civil society into the Muslim transnational identity. Tariq Ramadan and Bassam Tibi are particularly suited to address this compelling issue. Ramadan is a Suiss Muslim academic and theologian. He is the grandson of Hassan al-Banna, founder of the Muslim Brotherhood in Egypt. His father was a prominent figure in the Brotherhood and was exiled from Egypt to Switzerland. Bassam Tibi is also a Muslim scholar but German citizen who descends from a centuries-old Muslim-Damascene notable family. Both reject the binary separation of the world into *dar al-Islam* (the abode of Islam) and *dar al-Harb* (the abode of war), treat migration as a component of globalization and both provide prescriptions for how to deal with the issues of forging Muslim identities in Europe.

As the title of his paper—"To Be a European Muslim"—suggests, Tariq Ramadan is not only advocating the merging of the two identities but his eventful life as a scholar, citizen and activist is an embodiment of such a reality. Like most other strategies proposing a convergence, Ramadan elaborates on his own three-fold typology. At one extreme, he places the *assimilationist* pattern which supposes a total amalgamation between the Muslim and Western cultural way of living. At the other extreme, there is the *isolationist* pattern which is based on the preservation of the Muslim identity through the creation of an organized religious and cultural community which wards off global and Western incursions. Between the two extremes lies the *integrationist* pattern which provides both a protection to the Muslim identity and an individual status for citizenship.

To Ramadan, the polemics and debates surrounding those three alternatives have not been conducive for revealing the actual realities which beset Muslims living in the West. The first involves, in effect, that Muslims should become Muslims without Islam. This is clearly a byproduct of the prevailing view that to be too much of a Muslim means that one cannot be integrated into the Western way of life and its values. At best, the faithful Muslim could observe his religious ordinances within the confines of his intimate and private life. At no point, however, can they spill over into the public sphere.

To avoid melting down into European society, many Muslims find refuge in creating ghetto-like communities by recreating a microcosm with few contacts with the host population. The intention, as Ramadan puts it, is to be in *"Europe but at home."* To displaced migrants who continue to harbor nostalgia and commitment to their mother country, to be in Europe in any other way is understood as a betrayal of Islam and, in effect, to jeopardize the Muslim identity. It is not very unusual, Ramadan tells us, to encounter groups in recent years in France, Belgium and Sweden who try to protect themselves from society by cutting off and shunning all modes of European life. "They are Muslims against the European model and the only way out is to live, although in Europe, out of Europe." Naturally, for some European states such attitudes of confinement are not considered threatening. Indeed, the creation of such insulated communities was often encouraged for they appeared to promise social calm and stability.

As a way out of these two extremes—i.e. being a "Muslim without Islam" or a "Muslim in Europe out of Europe,"—Ramadan opts for a "Middle path" which allows a Muslim to be immersed within a European culture while being committed to four vital sources of an authentic Muslim identity: faith with practice and spirituality, intelligence of text and context, education and transmission and, finally, action and participation. Only in this way, and his essay is an elaboration of these essential prerequisites, can Muslims develop and shape the picture of their present and future European identity.

Within much the same context, Bassam Tibi in "Muslim Migrants in Europe: between Euro-Islam and Ghettoization" is also groping to validate a third way between salient "Islamophobia" and the "demonization of Europe." If one is committed to genuine intercultural dialogue, "one should not simply replace one phobia for another." Just as much as Europeans are called upon to de-ethnicize their identity to allow the newcomers to become Europeans, it makes sense that Muslim migrants should be requested to redefine their identity in diaspora by adding a European component. Only in this way, Tibi asserts, can we avoid falling into "one-way change" and "one-way tolerance."

By embracing typologies advanced by Manuel Castells (1997), Ernest Gellner (1992), Nazar Al-Sayyad (1996) and John Kelsay (1993), he departs from the "artificial categories" of binary distinctions: East/West, tradition/modernity, global/local, First World/Third World, "Jihad/McWorld," "Lexus and the Olive Tree." Instead, he argues that "identities are always under construction and that societies are constructed in relation to one another ... and that each individual belongs to many cultures and people have multiple cultural identities." He provides a sketch of the changing history of Muslim migration and considers prospects for a Euro-Islamic identity. He then advances his central thesis by arguing that within a perspective of cultural pluralism, particularly if claims of Islamic dominance are given up, a Euro-Islamic identity would be compatible with liberal democracy, individual human rights, and the requirements of a civil society.

By employing the metaphor of "bridges" as opposed to "boundaries," he revisits earlier moments of Western-Muslim encounters to demonstrate how they were mutually beneficial in laying the foundation for genuine inter-civilizational dialogue. For example, during Medieval times Muslim thinkers were able to combine Aristotle's method and spirit with their Islamic mind and identities. "Such was the height of Islamic tolerance at the time that the great Islamic philosopher al-Farabi was considered second to Aristotle." He also cites his own personal example. As a Muslim living in the West, he has chosen to become a European citizen by claiming to maintain his Islamic cultural identity, while combining it with political identity of *citoyennite*. Unlike multiculturalism which demands that migrants deny their cultural identity to be assimilated, Tibi opted as a cultural pluralist to maintain a triple identity: "religio-culturally, I am a Euro-Muslim; ethnically, I am a Damascene Arab; and politically, I am a German citizen."

Jan Pieterse, like Tariq Ramadan and Bassam Tibi, is also concerned with the predisposition of Islam to reinvent itself by incorporating some of the secular features Muslims encounter as diasporas in Western cities. Like other diasporas, Islam may also, in his view, be treated as part of an emerging global civil society in that it can merge with the host culture and generate new hybrid forms. To substantiate such prospects, his essay addresses two distinct features about travelling Islam. First he demonstrates how Islam changes in the process of migration, particular as it provides shelter and a sense of community for uprooted and dislocated groups. Second, by focusing on the metaphor of "Mosques without Minarets" he evokes the fractured and distorted image of Islam as a subculture on the margin. Though this is the price Muslims are expected to pay in their adaptation to secular orders, Pieterse advances a cosmopolitan and fluid view of Islam as a venue for globalism. In this regard, he tells us, it should not be treated as an anti-modern or reactionary ideology but as a form of "alternative modernity."

He frames his discussion by reminding us that Islam is not monolithic and that dislocated groups adapt differently to the discrepant demands of their new settings. To delocalized groups, the Qur'an becomes a "portable Islam" and the mosque provides shelter for the poor, offering orientation, basic education and a sense of historical depth. Transnational Islam may also display increasing orthodoxy. Because of the ideological void generated by the waning appeals of nationalism and socialism, political and popular Islam step in by their promises for reinstating a "moral economy that claims to reunite the community of believers ... and offering ideals of social justice, a politics of redistribution that is egalitarian and provides a place for the poor."

By focusing on the different patterns of adaptation Islam observed in the Netherlands and the UK, Pieterse asks a fundamental question: Does Islam travel *in* or *out*? In answering the question he reminds us that throughout history Islam, through *hajj* (annual pilgrimage to Mecca) and *hijra* (the religious obligation to migrate and simultaneously break ties and form new bonds of brotherhood), had institutionalized migration. It becomes a question for knowledge abroad. But as a form of globalism, Islam both "colludes and competes

with world Capitalism." Through the oil trade and recycling of petro-dollars, Islam has
served as an impetus to Western capitalism. But conservative and reactionary Islam have
been staunch opponents to "Western decadence", manifested in mass consumerism and
permissive life styles which are perceived as a threat to traditional virtues of modesty and
honor. Purity and sexual modesty provide a sense of moral superiority to compensate for
the inferior socio-economic standing of Muslim in diaspora.

Within such a context it is understandable how the mosque begins to assume more
prominence in the private and collective lives of Muslims and why the image "from prayer
rugs to minarets is a narrative of achievement of social mobility: from humble origins to
proud attainment." The attachment to and celebration of such religious edifices should
not, however, be taken to mean that Islamic organizations promote isolation rather than
emancipation. Pieterse provides ample manifestations of *syncretism*. In the Netherlands,
for example, Muslims who "respect Ramadan but also buy presents and a Christmas tree
so that their children will not feel left out; mosques that would like to use the Qur'an
class-room to offer computer courses; hybrid figures such as the 'educated believer.'" Such
cultural crossover is the common trend among second and third generation immigrants
in the Netherlands. In France it can be observed among the *beurs*, the audience of *raï* and
rap but who also claim *"Le droit a l'ambiguite."*

The general inference that one can extract from Pieterse's essay is that if there is a
"Muslim mélange," then the various sites of European diaspora are producing their own
novel forms of hybridization and chauvinism.

In the Netherlands the combined tendencies of pillarization, ethnicization and
integration make for a different field than in Britain with its predominant discourse of
racialized cultural difference, while in France secularism and *laïcité* make for yet another
arena of difference.

Smaller countries in the West such as the Netherlands may offer greater opportunities
for crossover culture than the larger countries: when the numbers of immigrants are smaller,
immigrant enclaves are too small to sustain reproduction, either culturally or economically,
and cultural chauvinism is weaker. Hence opportunities and incentives for hybridization
are greater. This offers yet another form of peripheral Islam.

The French government passed a law (early in 2004) prohibiting from public schools
any clothing that clearly indicated a pupil's religious affiliation. Although worded in a
religion-neutral tone, everyone understood the law to be aimed at keeping Muslim girls
from wearing headscarves in school. The law was based on recommendations issued
in late 2003 by two prestigious commissions, one formed by the Parliament, the other
appointed by President Jacques Chirac (The Stasi Commission). Their hearings and the
media coverage of the issue depicted grave dangers to French society and its tradition
of secularism (*laïcité*) presented by Islamic radicalism, a trend toward "communalism,"
and the oppression of women in the poor suburbs. Although some Muslims objected
that the proposed law would violate their right to express religious beliefs and many
observers doubted that a law banning scarves would seriously address the severe problems
of integration in French society, the two commissions voted with near-unanimity for the
law, and the measure passed with large majorities in the National Assembly and in the
Senate. It went into effect in September 2004.

Since its passage, the law has sparked a spirited debate about *Why the French Don't Like Headscarves* (title of a recent book by John Bowen). The French public seems, as a result, sharply divided. There are those who treat the headscarf as an expression of recent problems France has been beset with—especially anti-semitism, Islamic fundamentalism, growing ghettonization in the impoverished suburbs and disorder in the classroom. Others see the headscarf as part of France's intention, as a secular state, to reinforce the principles of liberty, equality and fraternity.

Either way, the "headscarf affair" began to epitomize the public presence of Islam in France and, hence, symbolized all the external and internal threats to France's *laïcité*. This is, precisely, the context within which Joan Scott explores the impact of Muslim perceptions of sexuality, desire and the role of the veil in curbing the dangerous sexuality of women. She begins her chapter, "Sexuality and the Politics of the Veil," by asserting that the law banning headscarves in public schools made a clear distinction between acceptable and unacceptable signs of religious conviction.

The clothing and religious signs prohibited are *conspicuous* [*ostensible*] signs, such as a large cross, a veil, or a skullcap. Not regarded as signs indicating religious affiliation are *discreet* [*discret*] signs, which can be, for example, medallions, small crosses, stars of David, hands of Fatima, or small Korans.

She draws particular attention to the words "conspicuous" and "discreet" because they involve, in her view, the difficulty the Stasi Commission faced in articulating their main concern. She invokes the works of Arab anthologists like Abdellah Hammoudi and Saba Mahmood to support her claim that in Muslim juristic tradition, "ostentation" and "conspicuous" (i.e. *tabarruj*) are to be avoided at all costs. Also women are assumed to be objects of sexual desire and temptation (*fitna*) and, hence, sources of political disorder. The goal of modest dress for women was to prevent such excitement. It is in this fundamental sense, Scott argues, that Muslim modesty is taken to be sexually perverse because the veil represented the subordination, humiliation and inequality of women. As such, it cannot be sanctioned by those who believe in the republican principles of liberty and equality. In conceptual and concrete terms, the veil's disturbing sexual manifestations to the French stemmed from the fact that it represented a system of gender relations diametrically opposed to theirs. For Muslims, the veil represents the need to curb sexual impulses; while for the French, sex is celebrated and is free of social and political risks. No wonder some French observers go further to polarize the distinction between the two cultural systems: Islam is seen as a system which oppresses women, whereas French republicanism as one that liberates them. Hence, the conflict is actually a confrontation between two irreconcilable systems: "emancipatory modernity and oppressive traditionalism".

Scott provides yet another perspective on the "headscarf affair" by arguing that the veil represents a departure from the republican virtues of *mixites*, the mixing of the sexes in schools, hospitals and elsewhere. She is keen here on reminding us that the Stasi Commission was also concerned about the *visual* status of the bodies of women and men. To validate her point, she notes that even if beards are worn for religious reasons, they do not constitute the same alienation for men that veils did for women. It is precisely the covering over of women's sexuality that is so troubling since the veil is a denial of women as objects of desire. By doing so, the veil interferes with what she perceived to be a natural psychological process; namely, the visual appreciation of women's bodies by men. It is this appreciation which brought women's feminity into being.

In this view, girls were lost to their feminine identity if their bodies could not be seen. Identity was conferred by men's being able to see them as sexual objects. Feminine identity depended on male desire; male desire depended on visual stimulation.

Beyond the loss of feminine identity, the veil became intolerable because it undermined the sexual freedom of women. It pitted a "psychology of recognition" against a "psychology of denial." So outraged by its outward visibility, some prominent French philosophers and activists decried it as a form of "psychological, sexual and social mutilation." To André Gluckman it was nothing short of an act of aggression or outright terrorism. A group of feminists who had lived under Islamist regimes established a movement in 2002 to protest physical violence against women, because it was clear to them that women would not choose the veil unless they were compelled to. The Islamic veil, they claimed, "subjects all of us, Muslim and non-Muslim alike, to an intolerable discrimination against women."

To Be a European Muslim

The general and widespread statement that Muslims living in the West must have the right to protect their Faith, their identity and their religious practice seems to rely on evidence which, as such, is not disputed. At least among those Muslims who continuously repeat that this objective has to be achieved. Yet, reflecting on this issue, it appears that the discourse identifying the notion of Muslim identity is very theoretical and imprecise and does not rely on an analysis of the concrete situation of the Muslims in Europe. It is as if the "identity" were a collection of rules sufficient to portray what a Muslim is, and what he is not. Unable to establish distinctions and classify the problems they are facing, Muslims confuse and mix up the different dimensions of the latter. Legal issues are often approached from an emotional angle whereas aspects of one's intimate life and feelings are reduced to a configuration of predetermined rules. We have already discussed some elements of the former but within the notion of identity we are totally engaged in the latter dimension. It is, in fact, a very complex notion since, from an Islamic point of view, the Muslim identity is altogether Faith, rulings, emotions, and feelings which have to be organised, shaped and harmonised within a spiritual and active way of life.

Therefore, we must avoid being deceived and misled by appearances when discussing such a sensitive subject. To be assimilated—that is to lose one's own identity—or to remain alien—that is to live apart from society in order to protect oneself—are not states we can assess simply on the basis of some manifest features. We must be very cautious and tactful when dealing with such notions for they appeal to diverse and sensitive parts of every human personality. What has to be noticed is that, on the scale of possible postures, when living as a minority, these two extreme attitudes are the more natural and normal ones that a human being seeks to adopt. To try, on the one hand, to appear and act as the majority do, in order to become the least visible possible, is indeed a spontaneous tendency whereas, re-acting to and affirming one's difference through a process based on clear separation, up to the point of sectarian disposition, is also an instinctive posture we witness in all human societies. Therefore, young Muslims who, within European societies, act in one of these two ways cannot be criticised or misjudged for, in fact, there is nothing more natural than to re-act as they do.

The problem, in fact, rests precisely on that point: both attitudes, even if it is not apparent in the first ease, are purely a *re-action* to the environment since it is a question of accepting or refusing it. Thus, they are the first natural step in the formation of one's identity in the sense that, at this stage, the identity is defined from outside, through the type of relations the individual has elaborated with his environment. This is the kind of attitude we can witness nowadays in young and not so young Muslims and they can take very subtle forms at the highest level of intellectual development or academic elaboration.

Nevertheless, it is clear that such identity is borrowed insofar as "something is missing" which is indeed the assertive reflection and definition from within in order to determine what the Muslim identity is *per se*, according to Islamic sources. In other words, what is the identity of the one who says the *shahada* once we acknowledge that it is not the simple words we pronounce but, above all, a disposition of the heart which we want to keep alive? This was the teaching of the Prophet when he was told by a Companion that a man, who had seemingly said the *shahada* out of fear, was still had killed. Upset, he answered: "How were you able to know what was in his heart?"

There is a need today to define the Muslim identity in the West so as to avoid the reacting process. This means considering both the Islamic teaching and the European environment in order to bring about a thorough reflection of very sensitive issues (such as Faith, emotion, psychology, education, study, culture, etc.) and at different stages of human growth (i.e. as individuals and in community) in order to elaborate adapted answers and means of transmission and education in Europe. This seems the only way that will, in the future, permit Muslims in the West to avert the reactive posture and instead direct themselves towards a more assertive and confident self-representation.

This step is of the greatest importance. As long as a consistent number of Muslims do not reach an autonomous perception of their own identity in the West it will be very difficult for them, if not impossible, simply to believe that they have something to give to the society they live in. They will hardly consider that they are able to have a positive impact on this society, let alone have their contribution recognised. Yet, this is the second aspect of *shahada*. Muslims are commanded to testify that their message conveys dignity, justice, generosity and brotherhood. How can this possibly be transmitted through a reactive and nervous attitude which expresses either an attempt to disappear or a strong rejection of others? Between these two extremes, the middle path is the more difficult, the more demanding: to be confident and assertive "in-between" requires acting in the name of both one's Faith and a well understood identity and not re-acting with or against others. This is indeed the less natural tendency.

The new presence of Muslims has created problems in European societies. The sudden awareness, because of their recent social visibility, that there are now millions of Muslims residing in the West and that almost half of them are already citizens, has provoked various and contradictory reactions within the indigenous populations. For some, it is the obvious sign of a perilous invasion whereas for others, still a minority, it is considered as a factor of enrichment. Politicians and academics have attempted to tackle the problem by formulating diverse strategies to integrate this new component of Western society. Sociologists, reconsidering the old concepts relating to minority presence, have tried to classify these strategies and propose a typology of possible approaches. The three patterns—which work nowadays as concepts of reference—are well known: at one extreme we find the assimilationist pattern which supposes a total amalgamation between the Muslim and Western cultural way of living which welcomes him. At the other extreme, there is the isolationist pattern which is based on the preservation of the identity through the creation of an organised religious and cultural community within the global society. In the middle, the integrationist pattern should provide both a protection to the Muslim identity and an individual status of citizenship (like indigenous peoples). This theoretical approach, while seeming to clarify the diverse strategies, still reveals several difficulties, not least because the two main concepts, identity and integration, are used outside of their clear and precise definitions. This, in fact, leads to much confusion for a close study shows that neither sociologists nor politicians agree on the exact content of the concepts used and, even less, on the correct appellation fitting such or such society. The French model of integration is considered as assimilationist in the majority of other European countries whereas the British multicultural society is called isolationist in France and, as such, represents the recurrent anti-model. Within the twists and turns of such complicated debates, the reality of the Muslim living in the West seems lost. Yet, it is necessary to draw a more accurate and experimental picture of this reality before trying to propose a definition of the Muslim identity and the modes of a positive integration which signifies, from an Islamic point of view, a genuine "integration of the intimate life of the hearts."

1. A European Muslim without Islam

For the last four hundred years, European societies have gone through a very deep process of secularisation. Faith, Religion, and practise no longer play an important role in social life. It is as if two logics were co-existing without being linked: on the one hand, the social dimension, based on freedom, rights, individualism, work and efficiency and, on the other, the personal dimension within which every single human tries to determine his belief, fix his values and organise his intimate life. The freedom of everyone is guaranteed by the relative neutrality of the public space: Europeans are no longer used to a public manifestation of religious presence in their day-to-day lives and they themselves are, in the great majority, either not practising much or not practising at all. Pope John Paul II, in one of his latest encyclical letters, conveys his fear that secularism, as conceived in industrialised societies, might be a simple appellation, a screen, behind which the reality of atheism and irreligiousness is concealed. Without going to such extremes, we can say that the fact that religion should be a private affair which does not interfere in public affairs leads us to witness, today, contradictory tendencies: on the one hand, an indifference towards religion and, very often, a new and worrying phenomenon called religious illiteracy and, on the other hand, a scattered and sometimes chaotic questioning of values along with an expressed need for spirituality through groups, sects or a very hierarchical community.

The former tendency is of course the stronger today and it is possible to state that our industrialised and modern society is, to a very great extent, *areligious* and that the values associated with its culture, such as freedom, individualism or efficiency, do not echo exactly the religious teachings based on recognition of the Creator, the necessity of Faith and the antithetical notions of good and evil. In the minds of many Europeans, their societies, over the course of history, have positively liberated them of the oppressive yoke of religion. They salute this evolution and perceive it as a process of liberation carried out in the name of the ideal of the individual and his right to freedom. The ascendancy of such a view and its impact on people is considerable, for it is difficult to resist such a strong and vigorous stream, which when backed by the media, films, advertisements, and the way of life itself, sweeps along billions of people not only in the West but in almost all large cities throughout the world. The so-called process of globalisation is, for some scholars, nothing but the fulfillment of the thorough Westernization of the world.

It seems normal and just for some politicians and academics to ask Muslims, in the name of common sense, to join the dominant and, without doubt, positive "train of progress". This means, according to them, that the Muslims have to adopt the same way of dealing with their Faith and the prescriptions of religion. In other words, to become citizens like the indigenous population and to be true proponents of individualism freedom, efficiency, to be involved in social life as citizens, and only as citizens. As for their Faith and their practices, they are of a secondary nature and pertain to their private life which means hidden, invisible, almost nonexistent. No matter what the Muslim identity is or what the Muslims say about it, the fact is that a choice must be made between religion and progress, enslavement and liberation, the old tradition of duties and the modern culture of genuine freedom. Discourses do not convey the terms of these alternatives in such a brutal way and one will hear a great many pleas for recognition of the Muslim identity which are respectful and of incomparable historical value. Yet nothing is said about the content of this theoretical identity which is ceaselessly referred to while, on the other hand, history appears a dimension of little concern.

Whatever concept is used, thereafter, to describe this project of society—*assimilation, integration* or *isolation*—the reality remains the same. In short, the Muslims should be Muslim without Islam, for there exists a widespread suspicion that to be too much a Muslim means not to be really and completely integrated into the Western way of life and its values. Once again these statements are general and vague and rely on both the idea of religious people having their own experience and the image of Islam shaped through the spectacular events which take place on the international scene. Therefore, to speak too much about God and His Revelation, to perform daily Prayers, to refer to Faith, spirituality and morality is to give out signs of non-adaptation and so of suspicious behaviour. If, furthermore, Muslim communities ask for mosques or cemeteries and organise themselves through organisations and specific activities, the picture is perfected: "such Muslims do not wish to live with us ... like us."

This last nuance distinguishing "with" and "like" is less trifling and insignificant than it appears at first glance. If "with us" is to signify "like us", this clearly means that the reference is to "us" and that the pattern of society which is proposed, whatever it is called, rests on the idea *we* have of *ourselves* and *others*. In fact, we would like to integrate the "idea of the other" we have and not his integration as a being who determines his identity by himself in light of both his own references and those of the West. The gap between the integration of a simple representation and one of hearts is great and, in the short as well as long term, only the latter provides for a true and positive coexistence. Still its conditions are demanding for it is not a question of simply *adapting* oneself (inwardly or outwardly) to a specific environment but rather of finding the way to feel that the being genuinely *is* and *exists*, that the Muslim has the opportunity to live and develop the essential dimensions of his identity ... his heart, his Faith and his emotions.

For some Muslims, in Europe and even in the Middle East and Asia, to be part of today's world is to adapt oneself to the Western way of life. According to them, Islam most certainly is a universal message, but to be "modern" its prescriptions have to be rethought and actualized following the dominant model of the West which seems to be the universal expression of modernity. By arguing so, they reduce the message of Islam to theoretical values and manifestations of good and moral intent but which, henceforth, are at the periphery of social life. Therefore, the Muslim identity becomes just general prescriptions shared by all people along with some cultural or artistic features exhibited at times of festival or marriage. Such a concept, in fact, is based on the belief—although the apparent discourse conveys the opposite—that Western values and lifestyles are the sole universal ones and, hence, must be followed. The universality of the Islamic message, recognised in theory, is confined to one's intimate life, exiled from public view, invisible, exactly as other religions have become. There is no alternative; to be progressive, open-minded and modern, to be authentically European, means to rethink and even modify the Islamic teachings in such a way that the Muslim identity fits its environment. In such Muslims' eyes it is the latter which is the real norm and at a time of globalisation the intensity of Faith, prescribed values and recommended behaviour must be reconsidered and adapted. They neglect, and even ignore, both the internal dynamic of Islam through its legal instruments and the nature of the Muslim identity.

The great majority of Muslims living in Europe do not have much concern for these questions and problems. Whether they like it or not they are swept along by the dominant stream and they seemingly live as others do. Nevertheless, the process of acculturation which looks to be irreversible, within second and third generations, is not as efficient as it appears at first glance and the question of identity is arising among young Muslim generations in all Western societies.

2. Living in Europe out of Europe

To avoid being absorbed into Western societies, many Muslims, almost instinctively, have found a refuge within community life. When circumstances allowed them, and even pushed them to as in Britain, to gather together in an area they imported or rebuilt the social fabric which had organised and directed their life in their country of origin. The aim is to be "at home", in *Europe but at home*. This process offers an important guarantee for the protection of identity: Muslims coming from India, Pakistan or anywhere else allowed to reproduce a social microcosm within which they live among themselves with few contacts with the indigenous population or society as a whole. From their point of view, this is the most appropriate means of protecting both their ethnic and Islamic identities.

In fact, what is actually protected, for instance in Britain, is strictly speaking neither the Asian ethnic group nor the Muslim identity but rather the *Asian way of living Islam*. Social relations, family bonds and models of education (with the teaching of Urdu or Punjabi languages) are imported and implemented in the micro-society without much attention being paid to the global environment in the West. There is, however, much confusion in the minds of some Muslims who know nothing else except their country of origin and this imported social fabric: Islam, in their eyes, is nothing but the way they used to live it in their cities or villages in India or Pakistan. Thus, to be faithful to the Islamic teachings means to be faithful to the Asian model of actualizing them: to question or reconsider the model, for we live in Europe, is understood as a betrayal of Islam that may jeopardize the Muslim identity. Paradoxically here, we contemplate the same shortcoming as above: once again, the Message of Islam is reduced to its traditional or cultural dimension but, this time, for exactly the opposite reasons, because of a fear generated by the environment.

It is not rare, within such communities, to meet young people from second or third generations who cannot even speak English properly or do so with an Asian accent despite their being born in Britain. This phenomenon is very common among young girls who are treated as if they are in India or Pakistan and who are frequently denied the opportunity to accomplish and perfect their studies. The Western environment has, of course, an important influence on the values, fashions and behaviour of our Muslim youth but the way of dealing with these and the method of education are still traditional, adapted to another era in another context.

In the majority of European countries we witness this same tendency among the youth. As already stated it is a natural reaction to an environment perceived as foreign, aggressive and oppressive. Their situation is not as it is in Britain or in the United States, for instance, for the Anglo-Saxon model of integration is based on the recognition of the community space within the idea of multiculturalism. Nevertheless, they try to develop, on a small scale, similar structured groups living according to internal rules as if they were out of Europe. In France, Belgium and Sweden some groups in recent years have tried to protect themselves from society by cutting themselves off from European modes. They do not refer to the specific traditions of their countries of origin but, instead, very often to the way of life of the Prophet and his Companions: they change their dress, wear turbans or *jelabjyya,* assiduously frequent the mosques and avoid contact with the external world and non-Muslims. Confusing Islamic teachings with the way of life and customs of the desert inhabitants of the 7th century, they express the same questioning, the same fragility with regard to their identity: they are Muslims against the European model and the only way out is to live, although in Europe, out of Europe.

For some European States such attitudes of confinement are not considered dangerous and indeed the creation of such isolated communities was often encourage for it appeared to promise social calm and stability. Furthermore, such communities and groups living in a kind of ataraxy were manageable for they were still dependent—socially, politically and even more economically—on the wider society and the State. Finally the circumscribed presence of Islam and Muslims within certain traditions, cultures or fashions still permitted Western societies to consider their own references and traditions as undisturbed.

3. The middle path

At a time when the process of globalisation—not only economically but also and above all culturally—is so powerful, it becomes all the more important to determine some milestones in the global landscape. The current is so strong that we cannot be satisfied with some referential concepts which give a very partial idea of the reality of European societies. We can continue to speak about *assimilation, integration* and *isolation,* but they are still empty concepts as long as we do not know who the subject, both literally and philosophically, is that we are speaking about. In other words, who is this Muslim we want to assimilate, integrate or isolate: without a clear definition of this entity *"who"*, these last three concepts could mean exactly the same thing, implicitly conveying different intuitions as to the meaning and content of the Muslim identity.

Furthermore, from an Islamic point of view, the use of the notion of subject is by no means accidental. For Muslims to understand who they are and what they stand for means that they are able to determine their identity *per se*, according to their Islamic references and no longer through the image others develop of them as if they were but objects of some alien elaboration. It is only by acting in this way that European Muslims will feel that they are subjects of their own history, accountable before God, responsible before mankind.

With regard to the five essential fields of Islam *(al-masalih al-khams)* and *shahada,* we can identify four elements or dimensions which, altogether, should provide appropriate content for the concept of Muslim identity. It is, in fact, a question of extracting the esence of this identity out of the accident of its actualization in a specific area or time. In other words, our object and aim is to distinguish Islam from Arab or Asian cultures, traditions or customs so that we can conceive in which manner the image of the European-Muslim is to be portrayed.

1. Faith, Practice and Spirituality:

The first and most important element of Muslim identity is *faith,* which is the intimate sign that one believes in the Creator Who has no associates. This is the meaning of the central concept of *tawhid,* the belief in the Oneness of God, that is confirmed and testified by the *shahada.* In this sense, it is the purest expression of the essence of Muslim identity beyond space and time. It naturally takes concrete form in the practice of worship (prayer, zakat, fasting, etc.). Closely linked to these two realities as their immediate consequence in the life of the Believer is the fundamental dimension of *spirituality.* Spirituality, from the Islamic point of view, is the way in which the Believer keeps alive, intensifies and strengthens his faith. Spirituality is memory, remembrance and the intimate effort to fight against the natural human tendency to forget God, the meaning of life, and the Hereafter. All the prescribed practices of Islam, and above all, of course, prayer, are in fact a way to remember *(dhikr).*

> Verily I—I alone—am God; there is no deity save Me. Hence worship Me alone,
> and perform the prayer; so as to remember Me.(Qur'an, 20: 14)

Excellence, defined as the ideal behaviour for the Muslim, would be to reach a state where one would no longer forget. Excellence *(ihsan),* said the Prophet, is "to worship God as though you were seeing Him, for while you see Him not, yet truly He sees you." That is, to try to be with God in every single circumstance.

In the multiple debates among sociologists and political experts, this dimension is very often neglected as if "faith" or "spirituality" could not be considered as "scientific constitutive elements" of an "objective identity". Yet, the word "Islam" itself means "submission" to God, literally expressing an act of worship along with its spiritual horizon. Therefore, to respect the Muslim identity does mean to recognise this first and fundamental dimension of faith and, by extension, to allow Muslims to perform all the practices which shape their spiritual life.

Muslim identity therefore is, in its first axis, "a faith, a practice and a spirituality". This is basically the dimension of intimacy and of the heart.

2. An Understanding of Texts and Context:

There is no true faith without understanding: for a Muslim, this means to understand both the sources (the Qur'an and the *Sunna*) and the context within which he or she is living. The responsibility of every Muslim is based on this twofold aspect of "understanding": that is to develop, in concomitance, an "intelligence of the texts" and an "intelligence of the context" in order to find the way to remain faithful to the Islamic teachings. This has been the fundamental teaching of Islamic legal practice since the time of the Prophet, unceasingly kept up by the great scholars over the centuries. As such, *Muslim identity is not closed, confined within rigid and fixed principles.* On the contrary, it is based on a permanent dynamic and dialectic movement between the sources and the environment, in order to find a way to live in harmony. This is why the development of intellectual skills is so important in Islam and, as such, partakes of the foundations of Islamic teachings. The Muslim cannot be satisfied with a hypothetical state of nature: to be a Muslim means to strive in order to increase one's capacity, to seek tirelessly to know more, to such an extent that, in light of Islamic sources, we could state that, once the dimension of worship has been mentioned, "to be a Muslim is to learn". The Prophet said: "Seeking knowledge is compulsory for every Muslim, man and woman."

More globally, this knowledge is the condition to understanding not only the meaning of the Islamic sources themselves, but also the Creation and creatures. According to the Qur'an, which ceaselessly appeals to human beings to make use of their intelligence, both knowledge and understanding are means of intensifying one's God-consciousness:

> Of all his servants, only such as are endowed with knowledge stand truly in awe of God. (Qur'an, 35: 28)

This is one of the two aspects of understanding, the other being that the Muslim, having to act according to the Islamic teachings, should use this capacity to make choices between what is right and what is wrong, to find the best way to please God in whatever environment he finds himself. If it is plain that there is no choice without freedom, as we mentioned, we have yet to add that there is no choice either without knowledge and, furthermore, comprehension. Choice and ignorance are antithetical words. Therefore the elements of Muslim identity which come immediately after faith and spirituality are *comprehension based on knowledge and choice relying on freedom.* Together they constitute the dimension of *responsibility.*

Muslim identity, in its second axis, can thus be seen as open, since it is based on an intellectual attitude in which the understanding of the texts is allied to that of the context. It is therefore defined through an active and dynamic intelligence requiring knowledge, freedom and a sense of responsibility.

3. To Educate and Transmit:

Faith (*iman*) is a trust (*amana*) and Muslims are asked to pass on this *amāna* to their children and relatives and, as already explained, to bear witness to it before mankind. To be a Muslim is to educate and to transmit and the Prophet himself was so ordered in the early months of the revelation:

> And warn (whomever thou canst reach, beginning with) thy kinsfolk. (Qur'an, 26:214)

Once again, the Muslim's identity is not closed and confined within his individual and personal sphere as if it only affected himself and his relation with God. To be a Muslim, on the contrary, is to uphold and to convey a conception of life founded on faith, spirituality and a fundamental comprehension of moral prescriptions. Educating one's children in order to give them the opportunity to receive the trust and, afterwards, to choose freely, is part of Muslim identity for a woman, for a mother, for a man, for a father. One of the most important functions of parents, is to offer their children an understanding of what they are and then the children, responsible before God, will choose what they want to be, for, the Qur'an says (6:164), *"No one will bear the burden of another"*.

The third axis of Muslim identity lets it be seen as open and always active since it is based on "being a Muslim" defined through the act of educating and transmitting.

4. To Act and to Participate:

The accomplishment of Muslim identity is to express and manifest one's belief through coherent behaviour. Faith, understanding, education and transmission together represent the substratum of the Islamic ethic and as such they should direct the Believer's acts. To be a Muslim is to act according to the Islamic teachings whatever the environment, and there is nothing in Islam that would command the Muslim to keep away from society so as to be nearer to God. It is quite the opposite and, "to attain to faith" is often, and almost essentially, linked in the Qur'an to the fact of behaving in a good way, of "doing good works". The Prophet, as we have seen, was ceaselessly pointing to this dimension of Muslim identity. The authentic flowering of Muslim identity is linked to the possibilities one has to act according to what one is and *believes in*.

This action, whatever the country or the environment, is based on four major aspects of human life: to develop and protect spiritual life within society, to spread religious as well as secular education among people, to act for more justice within each sphere of social, economic and political life, and finally, to promote solidarity with all types of needy people. In the North or in the South, in the West or in the East, a Muslim is a Muslim when he clearly understands this fundamental dimension of his presence on earth: to be with God is to be with fellow humans, not only Muslims, but as the Prophet said, with "people", that is mankind as a whole:

> "The best one among you is the best one towards people." (Hadith, Bayhaqi)

For the individual, attaining to faith must be expressed through coherent action. He can act by himself before God. Yet this is not enough, and it is his duty to strive towards participation, which clearly expresses the idea of acting with others, in a given society with the fellow citizens that make it up. The fourth axis of Muslim identity associates these two dimensions of the active being and the participating being, in other words of the individual and of the social being, which define being a Muslim through the relationship with society and with the world.

These four elements draw the appropriate picture of what the fundamentals of Muslim individual and social identity are, outside its cultural reading in a specific part of the world: the core of *faith, with practice and spiritually* is the light by which life and the world are perceived; *intelligence of texts and context* makes it possible to structure one's *mind as regards oneself* and one's environment; in a broader sphere, *education and transmission* allow both to pass on the trust of faith and to transmit the message; and finally, more broadly still, *action and participation* are the fulfilled manifestation of this identity through the way one behaves *for oneself* towards others and the Creation (*action*) and with one's fellow citizens and mankind at large (*participation*). It clearly appears that the definition of Muslim identity can not only be seen as open, dynamic, based on principles indeed, but in constant interaction with the environment.

The great responsibility of Muslims in the West is to give an adapted European shape to these four dimensions of their identity in light of their Islamic sources which, as to their conception of life, death arid creation, remain the fundamental reference. This process has been taking place for at least 15 years and is still going on, making it possible to give birth to an original Muslim identity, neither totally diluted within the European environment nor in reaction against it, but rather based on its own foundations according to its Islamic sources. That is the meaning of integration from a Muslim point of view.

On the middle path between being *a Muslim without Islam and a Muslim in Europe out of Europe*, there is the reality of a Muslim aware of his four-fold dimension of identity and who is ready, while respecting those requirements, to be involved in his society and play the role which is his, as Muslim and citizen. There is no contradiction, as we see it, between these two belongings as long as the Muslim fulfils his engagement to act according to the law and that he is not asked to sever himself from a part of his identity. This means that his Faith, his concept of life, his spirituality, his need to learn and understand, to speak and educate, to act for justice and solidarity should be respected by the country of which he is a resident or citizen. Nor should the Muslims be discriminated against, legally or administratively, in their freedom to organise themselves and respond adequately and actively to the call of their Faith and conscience. These kinds of hindrances happen every day in European countries because of both the image of Islam conveyed by the media and the widespread feeling that there exists an Islamic threat which in turn is confirmed by the news media relating the dramatic events of Algeria, Afghanistan and the like. Used to living in a secular society, many Europeans, politicians as well as average people, are prone to thinking that the only safe Muslims are those who neither practise their religion nor manifest their Muslim identity. Out of fear or sometimes bad faith, they interpret the law in a very tendentious and discriminatory way and do not hesitate, at times, to justify their behaviour by resorting to arguments about Muslim fundamentalists and fanatics. One sees such attitudes in the denial of numerous rights to Muslims (the organization of general activities, the building of mosques, Islamic schools' funding support, etc.) which other religions and institutions, in the name of the law and its implementation, have enjoyed for decades.

Nevertheless, it is the law which should be the reference and the parameter and a close study shows that in a majority of European countries the respective constitutions allow Muslims, to a very great extent, to live in accordance with their identity. On the one hand, they must insist upon a just and equitable application of the law towards all citizens and all religious. On the other they have to face and assess their own responsibilities in order, within the wide scale of freedom they enjoy in Europe, to provide Muslim communities with courses, study circles, and all kinds of institutions and organization whose essential objectives are to keep alive the Islamic Faith and spirituality, to diffuse a better understanding of both the Islamic teachings and the environment, to educate as well as transmit the message of Islam and finally to make Muslims truly involved within society. Nothing prevents them from doing this.

This also means developing a new and confident attitude based on a plain awareness of the essential dimensions of the Islamic identity. This feeling should lead Muslims to objectively and equitably assess their environment. Mindful of the prescriptions of their religion, they should not neglect the important scale of adaptation which is the distinctive feature of Islam. It is this that has permitted Muslims to settle in the Middle East, in Africa as well as in Asia and in the name of the same and unique Islam, to give to its implementation a specific shape and dimension. Once again, as for the form of its implementation, it should be a European-Islam just as there is an African-Islam or an Asian-Islam. To adapt themselves, from an Islamic point of view and as far as new Muslim generations are concerned, does not mean conceding but rather building. They should take advantage of the most efficient methods (education, management, etc.) as well as of scientific and technological discoveries (which in themselves do not contradict Islamic teachings) in order to face their environment armed with appropriate means. These breakthroughs pertain to human heritage and they are part of Western societies and Muslims, especially those who live in the West, cannot neglect or simply reject them for they are not Islamic. The Islamic teaching is plain: as far as social affairs are concerned (*mu'amalat*) all the means, traditions, arts, customs that do not, in themselves or by the way they are used, contradict Islamic rulings are not only acceptable but Islamic by definition. Therefore, within the European background and environment, Muslims must make choices in line with their identity. In this way, they can develop and shape the picture of their present and future European identity.

A slightly abridged version of a chapter originally published in *To Be a European Muslim* (The Islamic Foundation, 2005): 179–208. Printed here with the permission of the author.

BASSAM TIBI

Muslim Migrants in Europe:
Between Euro-Islam and Ghettoization

Instead of rooting my discourse in the notion of an inevitable and much-publicized "clash" between Islam and Europe, I choose to underline the potential for intercivilizational dialogue. Such needed dialogue over values presupposes an awareness of difference and of its limits, that is, the limits of pluralism. This, in turn, requires a willingness by those involved to open themselves to one another in pursuit of a cross-cultural consensus over values valid in the political culture. While I respect "difference," and submit that coping with it is an essential element of tolerance and pluralism, I also maintain that it is unacceptable to stop at simply acknowledging difference, as cultural relativists do, without providing prescriptions for how to deal with it.

In his criticism of cultural relativism, Ernest Gellner (1992) has argued that religious fundamentalism is a variety of absolutism. Following this view, it might be expected that cultural relativists and fundamentalists would find themselves in conspicuous conflict with one another. But Gellner has noted that "in practice, this confrontation is not very much in evidence." The reason for this is that cultural relativists generally apply their views only to those who espouse Western values, and they stop short of proceeding in a similar manner with non-Western cultures. Moreover, cultural relativists mostly confuse the critiques of premodern cultures with an often misconceived "cultural racism."

Unfortunately the popularity of the cultural relativist position has become so widespread that it has now been adopted even by people belonging to these non-Western cultures—for example, Islamic reformers and secularists. As a Muslim scholar who descends from a centuries-old, Muslim-Damascene notable family but who lives today as a migrant in Europe, I maintain that the types of positions cultural relativism leads to—victimology accusation, self-accusation, and self-denial—are inappropriate for dealing with "difference" and the issue of Islamic migration to Europe.

There is a need to overcome Western Islamophobia, but the demonization of Europe, as pursued by some, is not the proper way. If one is committed to intercultural dialogue, one should not simply replace one phobia with another.

Identity and Change

Migration to Europe today is a new process, one that involves several actors. In common debate on the issue one often hears the demand that Europe needs to change, which is utterly correct. Indeed, Europe needs to adjust to globalization—to the very process it set in motion through the European expansion. And in the present age, migration is surely one component of this globalization. However, it is not only Europe that needs to change; the migrants need to change as well. Thus, the call for a de-ethnization of European identity must apply equally to the identity of migrants. Otherwise, it would involve only "one-way change" and "one-way tolerance."

In embracing the typology of Manuel Castells (1997) concerning identity-building I want to single out his ideal type of "project identity." By this, Castells means that social actors need to "build a new identity that redefines their position in society ... No identity can be an essence." Thus, as much as Europeans are called upon to de-ethnicize their identity to allow the newcomers to become Europeans, it makes sense that Muslim migrants should be requested to redefine their identity in the diaspora by adding a European component. My position relies on the assumption that no prudent person would choose to be alien forever, and that the will to live in Europe is ultimately irreconcilable with a wholesale rejection of Europe, as those who demonize European civilization commonly do. In my book on Europe in the age of migration, I thus proposed that Europeans overcome their Euro-arrogance, while Muslim migrants engage themselves in the unfolding of a Euro-Islamic identity (Tibi 2008). Muslims living in Europe need to find a commonality between themselves and European civilization. At the same time, the de-ethnization of Europe is a prerequisite for the feasibility of Euro-Islam.

In short, both actors are today challenged to change and redefine their identities. It is as wrong to essentialize Europe as "racist, genocidal, and so on," as it is to essentialize Islam in an Islamophobic manner. Europe and the Islamic world are separate civilizations, with centuries-old records that encompass enmity and cordiality equally. In this regard, dichotomies built on this legacy—such as East versus West and First World versus Third World—are based on "artificial categories," as Nezar Al-Sayyad (1996) has rightly argued. Al-Sayyad has added that "societies are constructed in relation to one another and are... perceived through the ideologies and narratives of situated discourse." When it comes to the construction of identities—as based on the production of meaning—academics need to free themselves from their "preoccupation with globalization" in acknowledging that "each individual belongs to many cultures, and people have multiple cultural identities... Identity is always under construction and in constant evolution." My vision of an Euro-Islamic identity for Muslim migrants has been developed along such lines that question constructed dichotomies—however, without overlooking real value conflicts.

The Underlying Issues

The term New Islamic Presence has been coined to describe the increasing contemporary migration from Muslim countries to Western Europe. By the end of World War II there were fewer than one million Muslim people living in Western Europe, mostly in France and the United Kingdom. This figure has now risen to about twenty-three million, as Muslim migrants now live in almost all European societies, from Scandinavia to Italy.

It is of course wrong to relate the presence of Islam in Europe exclusively to migration. There are about ten to twelve million native European Muslims, who mainly live in southeast Europe. However, since the focus of this chapter is on Western Europe, I shall set aside this native Muslim community and concentrate on Muslim migrants to Europe's west. From an American perspective, it is first important to ask why Muslims born in France, the United Kingdom, or Germany are even considered migrants at all, and not natives. The answer is that in Europe the second and even the third generation of Muslim migrants have still not been accepted as part of the polity. In many cases, being considered a migrant would actually represent an improvement in status—in particular, over the view that Muslims are merely *Gastarbeiter*, or "temporary residents." In considering their present legal and social status, I continue to address Muslims in Western Europe as migrants struggling for citizenship and acceptance.

It may be misleading to talk in general about Muslims in Europe at all. Such a broad grouping overlooks the fact the migrant community is ethnically multifaceted and strongly divided along sectarian lines. For example, Muslims living in France have been, and still are, predominantly migrants from the Maghreb. Meanwhile, those living in the United Kingdom have been, and still are, mostly from South Asia (Pakistan, India, and Bangladesh). Until the early 1960s, the Muslim presence in these countries was almost exclusively related to French colonial rule in North Africa, and to British colonial rule in the Indian subcontinent. In addition, sectarian divisions in Europe are severe. Thus, for example, the Muslim Sunni community in the German state of Hessen has refused in its appeals for recognition to include Shi'is, Alevis, or Ahmadis as Muslims.

Since the 1960s the situation has been changing, as labor migration linked to the booming economies of Europe has boosted Islamic migration's statistical significance. Western European countries today need labor but lack the internal demographic growth to provide it. In this context, Western European countries other than France and the United Kingdom have started to encourage people from the Mediterranean to come there to earn money.

Until the end of the Cold War brought a loosening of Europe's internal boundaries, there was generally no talk about migration in Western Europe. In Germany for instance, the majority of workers (i.e., not simply Turks, but also south and southeast Europeans working in German factories) were perceived both by themselves and by Germans as guest workers—people whose presence in the country would end when their labor was no longer needed. Critically minded Germans have stated with equal prudence and repentance: "we have imported labor and have overlooked the fact that we were importing human beings." Despite the official German slogan "We are not a country for migration," the office of Commissioner for Issues Concerning Aliens of the former Christian Democratic-Liberal government has introduced the very term migration in its documentary entitled "Foreigners Residing in Germany." Among these legal aliens, there exists in Germany a considerable Muslim community of more than four and a half million (more than two million being Turks and Kurds). Yet, although the new earlier Social Democratic/Green German government is more open-minded toward the migrants, it has continued an intrinsic level of duplicity by confusing real integration with simply granting a German passport. In a country with no tradition of citizenship, receiving a passport in line with the new German citizenship law is no more significant than acquiring a piece of paper. A passport does not provide a citizen identity if the cultural underpinning is lacking. Most important, it does not convey membership in "The Club" (Tibi 2007a).

The majority of those who now comprise the new Muslim labor force in Western Europe—in particular Turks who have migrated to Germany—came, and still come, from rural areas and have quite low levels of education and training. It follows that such migrants not only lack in technical skills, but are also considered by some as lacking a fundamental understanding of their own religion and culture. Most important, because there is a lack of spokespersons among this community—who might have been expected to come from an educated elite—such spokespersons are now coming from outside the migrant community without being knowledgeable of its needs. Today such people are mostly imams who do not speak German, English, or French, and who have no clue as to the problems and concerns of young Muslims born in Western Europe. These imams have either been imposed on the migrants by Islamist groups, or they have been appointed by the Muslim governments of countries such as Turkey or Morocco. In Germany, even Saudi Arabia has acquired considerable influence by using its petrodollars to fund such appointments—despite the fact that there are no Saudi migrants there.

History

As stated earlier, in 1945 there were less than one million Muslims living in Western Europe. In the 1960s workers were requested to come, and those Muslims who came were welcomed because they were needed. But by the early 1990s the situation had changed considerably as a rapid increase in the inflow of Muslims to Western Europe coincided with an end to the boom years for the European economies. Among other things, this meant that as unemployment rose, there was no longer as great a need for unskilled migrant labor.

The present wave of Muslim migration has had more to do with the worsening economic conditions in Muslim countries than with the need for labor in Europe. In particular, the populations of the southern and eastern Mediterranean have suffered from poverty and unemployment, and migration to Europe has been seen as a principal source of hope. In this context, the total number of Muslim migrants in Europe climbed at the end of the 1990s to an estimated fifteen million and is still increasing tremendously to reach the figure of 23 millions around 2007. At a time when most European economies have levels of unemployment that average almost 10 percent, illegal migration is thriving. In fact, illegal migration and the abuse of the right to political asylum are now the primary instruments for gaining access to Europe. The common view among migrants is that it is more dignified to live on the benefits of welfare as an asylum-seeker in Western Europe than it is to live in a suburban *gececondu,* or shack, in Ankara or Istanbul, or in the slums of Casablanca or Algiers, with no income at all.

In Germany for instance, the average monthly income of welfare benefit recipients (regardless of whether they are Germans or foreigners) based on the earlier currency is DM 1000 per adult. According to the official figures (published in August 1998), almost three million residents out of a population of eighty-two million (including legal aliens) are receiving welfare payments in Germany (7 percent more than in 1997). This amounts to a total annual expenditure of DM 52 billion. Despite the fact that only 8 percent of those eighty-two million residents are aliens (i.e., do not enjoy German citizenship), 23 percent of the recipients of welfare are aliens.

Such statistics, regularly published in the local press, have only furthered xenophobia in Germany including anti-Islamic sentiments. The irony is that not only does Germany receive more unwanted migrants and asylum-seekers than almost any other European state due to extremely lax laws, but it also provides them with the most generous payments. The increasing inflow of illegal migrants and unprosecuted asylum-seekers attracted by such financial largesse has, however, exposed Muslims living legally in Germany to increased levels of xenophobia and Islamophobia.

The Inquiry: A Challenge and the Responses to It

Unlike the classical Muslim residents of France and the United Kingdom, most other Muslim workers on the continent—for example, the Turks in Germany—initially came not as migrants, but as a temporary labor force. They were looked at as staying in Europe only long enough to earn enough money to return to their countries of origin with the means to start a new existence there. The implication was that these workers would leave Europe when they were no longer needed.

In other words, apart from exceptions and some militant Muslims who relate migration to the religious obligation of *hijra* as discussed later, most first-generation Muslims, like native Europeans, originally did not view the "presence of Muslims in Europe" as a lasting phenomenon. However, the continuing nature of their stays, and the fact that a second (and, by now, a third) generation are not only living in Europe, but have been born there, have contributed to radical changes in perception. In Germany, as in other European states, this has made migration an increasingly complicated issue for both parties. Until the legislation of the new citizenship law in 2000 by the 1998 elected Social Democratic government, German law did not allow double citizenship. Even though most Turks want to acquire German citizenship, they do not want to give up their Turkish one. Therefore, they mostly do not apply for German citizenship. Adding to the problem is that Turks born in Germany are despised in Turkey as *allemanci* (something negative like "Germanized"). But neither are they considered to be Germans, even if they were born there, nor to be Turks in their country of origin.

Such issues concerning the interrelation of identity and migration have been dealt with extensively elsewhere. The focus here is on future strategies for addressing the risks and opportunities of Muslim migration to Western Europe. The most important issue in this regard is clearly that a large majority of the twenty-three million Muslims now in Europe are there to stay and thus can no longer be considered temporary residents. As indicated, this population is comprised of basically three big, comparable subgroups: Muslim Turks and Kurds (three and a half million—more than two million of them in Germany); Maghrebis (more than five million—about four million of them in France); and South Asians, basically in the United Kingdom, but also in all other European countries.

In addition to these large basic groups, there are migrants from all over the Islamic world in Europe. For example, 30 percent of the residents of the city of Frankfurt are foreigners, carrying the passports of 165 different nations. Among this number are representatives of almost all the Muslim countries. The ethnic and sectarian divides among Muslim migrants in Europe are reflected in the structures of their mosques and their related religious associations. These may be Sunni or Shi'i, Turkish, Bosnian, Arab, or Pakistani, again divided into Ahmadi and Sunni sects. Seldom are there comprehensive

Islamic organizations. Such a fragmented structure naturally leads to concerns that the politicization of internal divides within the community of European Muslims could lead to inter-Islamic rift and violence.

Bearing these realities in mind, a central question must be whether these Muslim migrants will be able to integrate politically into Europe as citizens of Muslim faith, or whether they will continue to live in Muslim ghettos, divided along ethnic and sectarian lines (Tibi, 2007b).

Prospects for a Euro-Islam

The Muslim presence in Western Europe is often incorrectly viewed as monolithic, in much the same distorted manner that Western-dominated international media normally presents images of Islam outside Europe. The richness of Islam has long been related to its cultural diversity; it is a misperception to see it as an expression of a monolithic worldwide phenomenon.

Despite a unity of belief Muslim migrants living in Europe have different ethnic, national, and cultural backgrounds. Across these lines they also subscribe to diverse political and social strategies for articulating their views and options concerning their status in society. In this regard, it is not a contradiction to speak in each case of a culturally distinct Arab, African, Indian, or South-Asian Islam. The identity of Muslims is thus the identity of culturally different people who nevertheless share the same faith. If it is therefore possible to talk about Afro-Islam for African Muslims or Indo-Islam for Indian Muslims, why should it not be possible to talk about Euro-Islam in the context of Muslims who have migrated to Western Europe?

In a project at the Institute du Monde Arabe in Paris in 1992 I outlined my concept of Euro-Islam. The concept of Euro-Islam is intended to provide a liberal variety of Islam acceptable both to Muslim migrants and to European societies, one that might accommodate European ideas of secularity and individual citizenship along the lines of modern secular democracy.

In other words, Euro-Islam is the very same religion of Islam, although culturally adjusted to the civic culture of modernity. In European civil societies, an "open Islam" could be as at home as, for instance, Afro-Islam, having been adjusted to domestic African cultures. As I have described them, the major features of Euro-Islam would be *laicité*, cultural modernity, and an understanding of tolerance that goes beyond the Islamic tolerance restricted to Abrahamitic believers (*ahl al-kitab*). In addition, by acknowledging cultural and religious pluralism, Euro-Islam would give up the claim of Islamic dominance. Thus defined, Euro-Islam would be compatible with liberal democracy, individual human rights, and the requirements of a civil society (Tibi 2008, chapter 6). It would also contrast sharply with the communitarian politics that result in ghettoization. To be sure, the politics of Euro-Islam would not allow complete assimilation of Muslims. Yet it could enable the adoption of forms of civil society leading to an enlightened open-minded Islamic identity compatible with European civic culture.

There have, of course, been other responses directed at the challenge. German Orientalists, for example, regard Muslim migrants arrogantly as "protected minorities."

This is originally an Islamic concept describing enemy aliens who have been given temporary safe-conduct. In other words, they are people who would continue to be aliens. For German Orientalists, tolerance lies in keeping the aliens away from Europe.

Unlike this xenophobic position, multiculturalists are usually much more benevolent, arguing from a cultural-relativist angle that presents "differences" from a favorable point of view. Nevertheless, the result is the same: Islamic ghettos—in this case, however, in the name of communitarian multiculturalisim. Despite different positions, the outcomes are comparable.

Although by no means multiculturalists, the Islamists among the migrants to Europe are nevertheless usually more sympathetic to multicultural positions than they are to democratic integration. The reason is that they understand perfectly well how to instrumentalize multicultural views—how to make use of them for fundamentalist ends. Thus, Islamists often willingly confuse assimilation with political integration in order to rebuff the latter in their pursuit of politics of Islamization (Tibi 2006).

This chapter takes the view that Euro-Islamic political integration is the best response to the pending challenge. Muslims need to become members of the European body politic they live in—without, however, giving up their Islamic identity. Citizenship issues ought to be seen within this framework. And toward this end an enlightened Islamic education might serve to maintain Islamic identity without promoting segregationist ends.

Shedding Light on Muslim Migration to Europe: The Global Context

Many varieties of migration have been studied by historians, and there is no doubt that migration patterns today differ from earlier patterns in many respects. The present moment has been described as a "global age." And in the context of a "global village," ever-unfolding structural and institutional networks in economy, politics, transportation and communication have brought an unprecedented degree of interaction among culturally diverse people. A novel pattern of mass migration all over the world has been one of the many by-products of this globalization.

Such a level of migration implies great potential for conflict and it necessitates the development of peaceful solutions that address identity-related issues. Generally the emerging "global village" has been equated with the "McWorld" of consumption. But present fascination with these ideas has obscured the fact that culture refers in more basic terms to norms, values, and worldviews that result from a social production of meaning. Eating hamburgers, watching videos, handling computers, wearing fashionable dress, and the like are only outcomes of more fundamental social processes. Likewise, the development of a global culture has far more profound bases than the simple spread of an American popular culture of consumption. The rampant use of the global village notion as a sweeping critique of McWorld-culture has also led to wrong and misleading assumptions about impending cultural standardization. Despite the structural reality of the global village, there in fact exists no global culture based on outlooks shared by the entire humanity.

On cross-regional and cross-cultural grounds, I believe it is today possible to observe both globalization and local cultural self-assertion. As a Muslim living in the West, I am at pains to be a mediator, seeking to establish bridges between the Islamic world and the West. In this pursuit, I distinguish between economic interaction as bargaining; political interaction among states as negotiation; and cultural interaction on the civilizational level as cultural dialogue. In terms of the latter, it often becomes important to question the notion of "cultural racism," especially when it is implied indiscriminately. The focus of the ensuing analysis will be on the nonstate-related level of cultural interaction.

Muslim migration to Europe has revived the significance of the Euro-Mediterranean region as a classical intercivilizational basin linking the West to the core of the Islamic world. It would be dishonest to avoid the central question of whether Europe and the Mediterranean are one international society. In the understanding of Hedley Bull (1977), an international society exists when states share "common values... [and] conceive of themselves to be bound by a common set of rules in their relations with one another ... An international society in this sense presupposes an international system, but an international system may exist that is not an international society." In applying these insights to today's Mediterranean region one may see a combination of system and society. North of the Mediterranean, the European Union forms a society of states interacting with another one. Another society, of predominantly Islamic states, exists south and east of the Mediterranean. Interaction between the two societies takes place on the grounds of an international system in which both state groupings are sub-systemic parts. However, Islamic migration to Europe has blurred the boundaries between system and society and complicated the issue.

European moralists have suggested that the Mediterranean embodies the basin of a single civilization that combines a northern (European) and a southern (Islamic) component. This view was, for example, presented by several Dutch politicians at an intercultural dialogue held by the European Union at The Hague in March 1997. However, an honest cultural dialogue between Islam and the West would dissociate itself from such disruptive moralistic views and meaningless mutual assurances. It would recognize instead that while both groups of states share formally in certain established international norms and values, they simultaneously belong to different civilizations, with different outlooks and worldviews.

In viewing the Mediterranean as a bridge and not a boundary (let alone a warrior frontier), the need arises to determine common and shared values. My view is that such Euro-Mediterranean relations and the related migration issues are not basically interstate affairs. A prominent American student of Islam, John Kelsay (1993), has emphasized the fact that "the rapidity of Muslim immigration... suggests that we may soon be forced to speak not simply of Islam *and*, but of Islam *in* the West".

The outcome of this situation will ultimately be related to how Muslims and Europeans deal with cultural divergences in the course of the present civilizational interaction, of which migration is a basic part. Politicians on both sides of this issue have attempted to deny and obscure how it involves fundamental differences in worldview. Those involved must go beyond the censorship of political correctness to address impending and real issues. This must involve both an inclination to reconcile, not antagonize, divergent views, and a clear commitment to avoid concealment. Only in this manner will it be possible to realize how foolish it is to deny existing cultural differences.

Unfortunately, the debate on migration has largely been related to the concept of a "clash of civilization" between Islam and the West. Instead, one might reconsider John Kelsay's reference to the shift in Islam's importance for the West from Islam *and* the West (an issue of neighborly relations between states) to Islam *in* the West (an issue of neighborhoods within one's own state). Among the premises of this chapter is a belief that a common discourse about ethics needs to be linked to the migration debate. The outcome could be a civic culture shared by all.

Islam in the West: What Choices?

As a Muslim living in the West, I have chosen to become a European citizen—however, with a clear commitment to the French notion of citoyen, not to the German ethnic concept of *Staatsbürgerschaft*. I claim to maintain my Islamic cultural identity, while combining it with the political identity of *citoyennité*. In so doing I find myself in conflict both with an inherent European racism based on exclusive ethnicity and with an opposed trend of multicultural communitarianism that has been combined with the claims of some Islamist leaders in Europe for a separate Islamic entity within the West. In general, those Islamic migrants who want to become citizens of the West are caught between these views: between rejection, and the pressure to join a cultural ghetto. Such polarization is particularly harmful to Muslim juveniles who have been born in Europe and are seeking to unfold identities and personalities there.

Among Germans, two attitudes exist currently which represent two extremes toward Muslim migrants: the anti-Islamic, and the philo-Islamic. Such a polarization has led on the one hand to those who demonize Islam while glorifying themselves, and on the other to those who have moved from European universalism to cultural relativism, with the result of self-denial. Of course, there exists a third group which combines cultural open-mindedness with a commitment to the enlightened values of European civilization. But it is unfortunate to see that the extreme views (Euro-arrogant exclusiveness, and self-denial presented as self-opening) are now being represented as dominant.

Muslims like me who subscribe to the Ibn Khaldunian notion of *asabiyya*—a kind of *esprit de corps*, or civilization awareness—believe that such pseudo-opening to others in the shape of self-denial actually represents a decline in the West, concealed as open-mindedness. It is very important that Europeans grasp how a low degree of *asabiyya* is not the alternative to Euro-arrogance and racism. Just as philo-Semitism cannot overcome anti-Semitism, so is cultural-relativist self-denial only the other side of Eurocentric exclusivity.

Likewise, the choice that migrants make regarding the variety of "Islam in the West" will be decisive for the future of Europe. The outcome of the cooperation of the parties involved, as well as their ability to dialogue with one another, may lead to common responses to the pending challenges. In arguing that there is no such thing as an essentialist Islam, just as there is no such thing as an essentialist Europe, one must realize there exists no constant pattern of Islamic or European identity. Islam will always be an ever-changing cultural system designed by Muslims themselves. Similarly, Europe can be an open society in which there is a place for Muslims as equal citizens.

Both inclinations among Europeans—the exclusivist and the self-denying—are great obstacles to intercultural dialogue based on reason. But this dialogue is essential to determining what variety of Islam will prevail in Europe in the future. Migrants could have a multiple identity, a position I support in relation to my own multiple identity as both a Middle Eastern Sunni Muslim and a European citizen.

As much as I am concerned with European exclusiveness, I am equally concerned about the maintenance of orthodox Islamic views among parts of the Muslim community in Europe, and in particular their view that migration is related to the *da'wah*, that is, the call to Islam in the understanding of proselytization. According to this view, like missionaries, Muslims in Europe consider themselves an outpost for the spread of Islam. This belief—and, of course, the publicizing of its rhetoric—can only encourage anti-Islamic attitudes among Europeans and bolster existing prejudices. Thus, for example, among the exiled groups of Muslim extremists in London was one led by Sheikh Omar Bakri, called "Movement of the Muhajirun." Bakri has clearly linked the status of migrants to the doctrine of *hijra* in the pursuit of the *da'wah*. And like his late predecessor, the fundamentalist Kalim Siddiqi, who established the Islamic Counter-Parliament in London, Bakri had become prominent through the British media before he left to return to the Middle East after 9/11. Bakri stated in a BBC television interview that Muslims in Europe "are all Osama bin Laden." Slogans like this have proven to be a great disservice not only to Islam, but to all Muslims living in Europe.

A dialogue is imperative to establishing the grounds for a search for commonalties. Though I oppose Euro-arrogant exclusiveness and assimilation, I do not favor cultural-relativist multiculturalism, nor that related cultural communitarianism which has clearly been abused by Islamists. My objection to multiculturalism is related to its inherent support for cultural ghettos and to its negation of the universality of civic identity patterns and the assertion of one law for all.

I favor honest intercultural dialogue in which both sides, with adequate standing, may seek out positive commonalties among themselves in search of foundations for a civic culture.

Honest dialogue of this sort will not overlook areas of disagreement, but address them consciously while developing an ability to deal properly with disagreement. The goal of this combination of realism and humanism is a commitment to live together in peace, mutual respect, and self-respect, without feelings of superiority. For enlightened Muslims, it is therefore imperative to reject all kinds of Western missionarism, as well as reverse missionarism. By this statement, I address the need for Muslims to be committed to reason-based dialogue and not to confuse this with the *da'wah*, as some Muslim fundamentalists in the diaspora do. The Qur'an clearly states "*Lakum dinakum wa liya din* (You have your religion I have mine)." One cannot turn down Western missionarism and dialogue in favor of one's own, and at the same time be honest and committed to true dialogue and mutual tolerance.

Western-Muslim Encounters: Lessons From the Past

Earlier, I referred to a distinction between dialogue and negotiation. While the latter is pursued between states, dialogue is not bound to political constraints that can create gaps between rhetoric and action, word and deed. But true inter-civilizational dialogue needs to be both honest and rational—that is, reason-based. This understanding is in line with both the tradition of medieval Islamic rationalism and with the European Enlightenment. It is also in line with the current political culture of democracy and human rights.

In making the choice in favor of dialogue, it is important to learn from history. For example, Prince Hassan Ibn Talal of Jordan has stated, with crucial insight, that "Muslims and Europeans have been at their worst when they sought to dominate each other, and at their best when they looked to learn from each other." Research on Muslim-Western relations supports this view. For example, in my view the opening of the Islamic mind to Hellenism, and the ensuing Hellenization of Islam in the medieval period, were the factors that led to the height of Islamic civilization. In time, European adoptions from Islamic rationalism at the eve of the Renaissance also led to beneficial new processes within European civilization.

During medieval times Muslim thinkers were able to combine Aristotle's method and spirit with their Islamic mind and identities. They thus accorded Aristotle the status of *mu'alim al-awwal* (the first teacher). Such was the height of Islamic tolerance at the time that the great Islamic philosopher al-Farabi was considered second to Aristotle.

My friend and intellectual mentor at Harvard, the late Iraqi Muslim philosopher Muhsin Mahdi, believed that al-Farabi was the greatest thinker in Islamic political philosophy. In fact, al-Farabi was by origin a Turk; but his cultural language was Arabic, and his commitment was to Islamic civilization, not to any particular ethnicity. The Farabian Islamic *aql*-based philosophy is a lasting indication of a Euro-Islamic encounter in its best terms, and could provide the common secular ground for a new Western-Muslim relationship in the age of migration.

Cultural Pluralism is not Multicultubalism

As a Muslim migrant to Europe, I am opposed to all varieties of monoculture, favoring instead a plurality of cultures. My commitment to civic culture is in clear opposition to that tenet of cultural relativism which denies the importance of common values. Multiculturalism is based on cultural relativism; thus, European multiculturalists look with a sense of romantic-eccentric mystification at other cultures, viewing aliens in the Eurocentric tradition as *bons sauvages*. There are multiculturalists who consider Cordoba an example for multiculturalism, when in fact they lack clear knowledge of the subject. Such mystification is extremely important in understanding the distinction between cultural pluralism and multiculturalism.

To understand the implications of the distinction, one needs to return to the question of choices. Do Muslims living in Europe want to belong to a peripheral minority with respective minority rights? Or would they rather become members of the European polity itself, with all its respective rights and duties? I see no contradiction between being a European and a Muslim. But there are Islamist groups in Europe which have no interest in Muslim migrants serving as a bridge between civilizations. They are instead interested in using the Muslim diaspora to create political confrontation. In arguing from the point of view of an open-minded Islam, one might again refer to the words of Prince Hassan:

Muslims respect the rule of their host states and the applicable laws. For the principles of Islam require a Muslim minority to obey a state in which it is resident, just as a Muslim state expects non-Muslims to respect and to abide by its laws. The Muslims of Europe are therefore not asking for special privileges, and do not demand what is denied to others. They are merely asking for their religion to be recognized within the European context.

It must by now be clear that such an enlightened Muslim position does not accord with those forms of multicultural communitarianism which demand different laws and different treatment for people of different cultural communities. It should be noted that the issue is *intercultural*, not one of "multicultural discourse." The difference is determined by whether one accepts or rejects the paramount importance of a single shared civic culture. I view multiculturalism as a romantic ideology, one that is clearly distinguished from a more realistic cultural pluralism (Tibi 2007b). In refitting the multicultural reference to Spain, I want to state that Islamic Spain was a society characterized by cultural pluralism; it was not a multicultural society in the cultural-relativist sense that is now spreading through Europe. In other words, Islam was the culture of Arab Spain, and Arabic was its language. No such thing as cultural relativism existed there.

Concluding Remarks

In this analysis, I have tried to establish a clear distinction between multiculturalism and cultural pluralism, and between political integration and assimilation. I have recommended the political integration of Muslim migrants into Europe. Granting citizenship rights and duties to migrant Muslims will have the effect both of smoothing the way for their membership in the secular "Club of Europe" and demanding from them loyalty to the democratic polity in which they live. In particular, the acceptance of secular European laws—and, above all, secular constitutions separating religion from politics—will require Islamic migrants to reconsider the concept of the legitimacy of the *imam*. Cultural reforms must enable a Muslim migrant to live under the governance of a non-Muslim *imam*/ruler. But cultural reforms are needed on the European side, as well. In particular, the process of cultural reform must make it feasible for European states to accept Muslims as citizens. Remaking the club by altering the conditions for membership is thus not only an issue that requires Europeans to change. Muslim migrants need to change, too.

Unlike political integration, however, demands that migrants be assimilated involve the effort to deny cultural identity. This assimilation contradicts the notion of cultural pluralism. An Arab Muslim migrant may have a triple identity: religio-culturally, I am a Euro-Muslim; ethnically I am a Damascene Arab; and politically I am a German citizen. I believe that the combination of these identities is feasible within the framework of cultural pluralism and political integration.

The argument I have made in support of cultural pluralism also clearly runs counter to those notions of multicultural communitarianism pursued equally by Muslim segregationists and European cultural relativists. My criticism of these multiculturalist views is based not only on my commitment to a shared civic culture, but on my opposition to rampant universalisms. As a Muslim with a European education, I oppose all varieties of hegemonic Western universalism, and believe that multiculturalism is just another variety of them.

In my rigorous criticism of advancing cultural relativism to a rampant universalism, I also share the view of the late Ernest Gellner (1992).

> Three principle options are available in our intellectual climate: religious fundamentalism, relativism, and Enlightenment rationalism ... Logically the religious fundamentalists are of course also in conflict with the relativists ... In practice, this confrontation is not so very much in evidence.

Gellner states further that both religious fundamentalists and cultural relativists oppose Enlightenment rationalism which earlier succeeded in building bridges between Islam and Europe during two previous encounters. The rationalism of Islamic philosophy was the seed of an Islamic Enlightenment that was prevented from unfolding by the Islamic *fiqh* orthodoxy. It emerged out of the Hellenization of Islam, which I have said was the first positive Euro-Islamic encounter. The second positive encounter was the impact of Islamic rationalism on the European Renaissance. In contrast, the Islamic fundamentalism of our age may succeed only in materializing the wrongful prophecy of a clash of civilizations, not in building bridges between them. The spread of such an Islamism in the European diaspora will cause Muslim migrants great pains, because it will only lead to the rise of anti-Islamism and result in the isolation of Muslim migrants in dreadful ghettos.

Ethnic identities are exclusive identities. If cultivated in the diaspora, they will lead to a kind of neo-absolutism and related social conflicts. The alternative is an all-inclusive civil identity based on cultural pluralism. Thus, while fundamentalism is a modern variety of neo-absolutism, pluralism would encourage people to represent different views while at the same time being strongly committed to shared cross-cultural rules—and, above all, mutual tolerance and respect (Tibi 2007a). Tolerance can never mean that only one party has the right to maintain its views at the expense of the other. For this reason, the exclusivist bias of multi-cultural communitarianism stands in clear contrast to cultural pluralism and tolerance. One-way tolerance is the tolerance of the loser. Muslim migrants cannot deny others what they require for themselves.

The granting of multicultural minority privileges to Muslim migrants in Europe may prove to be a double-edged sword with far-reaching consequences. On the one hand, it may facilitate unwanted interference by mostly undemocratic Islamic-Mediterranean governments in the affairs of Muslim migrants in Europe. But its political effects could also run in the opposite direction. Thus on the other hand, ghettoized minorities in Europe could provide the base from which exiled representatives of political Islam act to topple existing governments in the Islamic world. And these Islamists would by no means be democrats.

In subscribing to the Euro-Islamic view that Muslim migrants should act as a bridge between Islam and Europe, I find myself in opposition to those who would make Europe a refuge for Islamic fundamentalists. Such fundamentalists have no interest in the integration of Muslim migrants. And in siding with the concept of civic culture for all on grounds of cultural pluralism, I also find myself in opposition to multiculturalists and their cultural relativism. I argue that the bottom line for a pluri-cultural (not a multicultural) platform is the unequivocal acceptance of secular democracy, individual human rights for men and women, secular tolerance, and civil society. In my understanding, this is exactly what is involved in Euro-Islam, as opposed to Islamism (Tibi 2008). It is not ghetto Islam or fundamentalist Islam. It is at the turn of the century that Muslim migrants in Europe must choose the destiny they want for themselves and for their children: to continue to be alien; or to join the changed club—without, however, being forced to assimilate.

Due to the great burden of history in Europe and the view of most Europeans that their continent is not designed for migration, the study of Muslim migrants in Europe should not be confused with the same issue in the United States. In Europe these matters are more complicated, have a different scope, and need the type of sensitive insight that only people familiar with both worlds, Islam and Europe, can provide. Europe has its own strong identity and this needs to be taken into consideration in addressing these issues, also by US scholars who make recommendations for Europeans, but fail to understand Europe and Islam as well.

References

Al-Sayyad, N. "Culture, Identity and Urbanism in a Changing World." In M. Cohen, ed. *Preparing for the Urban Future* (Baltimore: Johns Hopkins Press, 1996).

Bull, H. *The Anarchical Society: A Study of Order in World Politics* (N.Y.: Columbia University Press, 1977).

Castells, M. *The Power of Identity* (Oxford, UK: Blackwells, 1997).

Gellner, E. *Postmodernism, Reason and Religion* (London: Routledge, 1992).

Kelsay, J. *Islam and War: A Study in Comparative Ethics* (Louisville, KY: John Knax Press, 1993).

Tibi, B. (2006) Europeanizing Islam or the Islamization of Europe, in: Peter Katzenstein and Timothy Byrnes *Religion in an Expanding Europe* (New York: Cambridge University Press, 2006).

Tibi, B. (2007a) A Migration Story From Muslim Immigrants to European Citizens of the Heart, in: *The Fletcher Forum of World Politics*, vol. 3, 1 (Winter 2007).

Tibi, B. (2007b) Euro-Islamic Religious Pluralism for Europe, in: *The Current* (Cornell University), vol. 11 (Fall 2007), pp. 89–103.

Tibi, B. (2008) *Political Islam, World Politics and Europe* (New York: Routledge, 2008).

A slightly abridged and updated version of a chapter originally published in Nezar Al-Sayyad and Manuel Castells (eds.) *Muslim Europe or Euro-Islam: Politics, Culture and Citizenship in the Age of Globalization* (Lexington Books, 2002): 31–52. Printed here with the permission of the publisher.

JAN NEDERVEEN PIETERSE

Travelling Islam: Mosques without Minarets

Historical and cultural differences within Islam are so considerable that the category "Islam", with its unitary ring and its homogenizing aura, may need to be put in quotes. Like Christianity, Islam is a term that works at a distance; a range, finer distinctions are necessary. There is a common core to the diverse expressions of Islam but what is in the core, its size and halo vary considerably. The collective self-awarenesses that identify and proclaim the existence of Islam are not unproblematical. Further, to what extent is it justified to call migrants from Muslim countries "Muslims"? They may be categorized in that way by administrative and clerical authorities in their countries of origin and residence, thus serving the interests of discursive and administrative neatness, but to what extent is Islam central to their lives? There may be cultural and religious Muslims, nominal and observant Muslims. For some, Islam may be part of what they have moved away from. Besides the mosque communities there is the circuit of coffee-houses and, in addition, there are those who frequent neither. The meaning of Islam, then, is not to be taken for granted; statistics are to be bracketed, their significance is not obvious.

The relationship between the global and the local is one of recurrent tension in Islam. Islam has a universalist vocation but no single organizational structure. Islam is a form of globalism that is organized mainly in local structures. Islam is a holistic religion, an ideology of alignment between religion and politics, society and state, but it survives and is revitalized amidst the process of differentiation which is a feature of complex societies.

For centuries Islam has spread worldwide carrying a universalist vocation, as part of the historical momentum of globalization. Intercontinental Muslim trade and knowledge networks have long been part of the infrastructure of what is now called world capitalism and which is presented as if it were an invading force alien to the world of Islam, rather than one whose momentum the Islamic world has helped to shape. What is the place of Islam in contemporary globalization? According to Hassan al-Turabi, the leading ideologue of the Muslim Brotherhood of Sudan: "If pan-Islam is partly an outcome of the increasing internationalization of human life, it would also give an impetus to that momentum" (Turabi 1993: 18). The Muslim diaspora, like other diasporas, may be viewed as part of an emerging global civil society: yet how does this accord with the integrist claims of Islam? Will Islam in the West be "secularized" as it is exposed to the same influences that have led to the gradual depopulation of Christian churches (in Europe, more than in the Americas), the creeping impact of urbanization, education, the media, as part of the process of acculturation? Will the Muslim diaspora merge with the host cultures and generate new, hybrid forms? In Asia and Africa Islam has generated new forms and articulations: what is the course of Islam in the West?

Migration is induced by global differentiation and at the same time an attempt to cushion and negotiate its impact. The question considered here is migration/refiguration, or how does Islam change in the process of migration? One of the fallacies in thinking about cultural difference is the reification of difference, viewing it in solid and static terms. Both migrants and host cultures tend to be represented with a peculiar emphasis on their allegedly uniform and unchanging cultural characteristics—except for the young of the second and third generations. This is odd if only because migration is a travel experience and in most cultures travel is one of the central metaphors of change. Or, may migration also be viewed as a process of cultural conservation and reconstruction?

The first part of this chapter deals with travelling Islam generally, and the second part deals with Islam travelling in the West and with some of the patterns of intercultural cohabitation: mosques without minarets. "Travelling Islam" deals with internal migration, the changing political economy of overseas migration, and compares the impact of internal and overseas migration. "Islam in the West" considers the patterns of intercultural cohabitation shaped by the historical treatment of cultural differences in societies, as reflected in legislation and ideological orientations: it is within these contexts that immigrant culture is reconstructed. Thus there are distinct differences between multi-culturalism in Britain and pillarization in the Netherlands, but both have in common that they define immigrant groups in terms of "ethnicity" rather than "religion". Finally, the boundaries that mark cultural identities and their degree of fluidity are discussed. The rise and decline of boundaries is one way of looking at the encoding and recoding of identity constructions: do enclave cultures persist or are hybrid identities emerging?

Travelling Islam

Migration/urbanization

Internal migration and urbanization entails leaving village life behind and entering a complex, differentiated social world. In the urban centres one's social world and religious community no longer coincide, as in village Islam. Religion becomes privatized. It becomes optional and no more than a segment of life. Part-time Muslims may become Islamists precisely because of this, to compensate for the effect of segmentation. But not all migrants adhere or turn to Islam nor would it carry the same meaning for those who do. The overall relationship between religion and society changes. If society is primarily defined as secular, as in Turkey, religious communities may become counterforces to secular society and the relationship becomes one not of complementarity but of opposition, and Islam can become a vehicle of protest.

Migration from the countryside is encouraged in the first place by the opening up of rural economies as a consequence of the advance of capitalist relations. When this occurs in conjunction with the retreat of the state from its welfare functions, as now increasingly happens in many countries, Islam in some form may step into the space left by the state. Likewise, Islam steps into the ideological void left by the waning appeal of nationalism and socialism. Where communal relations have been shattered, political Islam reinstates a moral economy that claims to reunite the community of believers. Offering ideals of social justice, a politics of redistribution that is egalitarian and provides a place for the poor, it presents a moral economy in the vernacular of tradition. In the process tradition is being reconstructed. Circumstances have also changed and, under the banner of sameness, Islam has changed. Islam is being politicized in a manner unlike both the official "Islam of the powerful" and the popular Islam of the village.

If the twin processes of integration into world capitalism and the retreat of the state are crucial conditions for the reorientation of political Islam and the emergence of Islamism, in a broad kind of sense the same may hold for religious revival movements such as *Hindutva* in India, and ethnic and separatist movements in other societies: vernaculars of discontent, negotiating the present by reclaiming and reworking the past. In reinvoking and reconstructing moral economies these movements attempt to serve as a buffer against and vantage point amidst the advance of capitalism. They are a socio-cultural expression of the process of informalization induced by the tide of market globalization, part of the cultural politics of informalization, and part of the global politics of post-Cold War emancipation. The question is, can they be more effective than nationalism and socialism which, each in different ways, have sought either to channel or to counter the impact of capitalism? At any rate, power accrues to a wide variety of religious and ethnic entrepreneurs who give their own ideological and political inflection to this process.

What changes does Islam undergo when travelling? Initially it may become more central and prominent in some people's lives than it used to be in the countryside. Delocalized from the village Islam may show increasing orthodoxy. A tendency towards growing "scripturalism" has been in evidence throughout Islam since the nineteenth century as manifested in an increasing emphasis on Qur'anic teaching, Islamic education and mosque-building (Geertz 1968; Gellner 1992). The scripturalist tendency comes at the expense of the folk Islam of saint worship, healing, sufism and local brotherhoods and guilds. The imam rather than the saint, *marabout* or sage becomes the central figure. The tendency of clericalization is reinforced in the migration process. When Islam leaves its original landscape, what travels are not the *marabout* shrines nor the rural folk practices and brotherhoods, but the Qur'an and Qur'anic teachings: the Qur'an is portable Islam. The return to scriptures, while presented as an orientation to unchanging revelation and a holding fast to tradition, is itself a mode of modernization and a major indicator of change, because it makes cultural reproduction independent of local circumstances. It turns on literacy which, according to Bourdieu, is the benchmark of modernity. High Islam is modern Islam, modern precisely because of its scriptural orthodoxy. Because of this translocal orthodoxy, high Islam can travel. In the plural, of course, as Sunni and Shia orthodoxies. How these modern orthodoxies work out depends on the journey and the destination of travel.

Besides providing shelter from the storm of economic uprooting, the mosque serves as the university of the poor: offering orientation, basic education, a sense of historical depth. The imams are the intellectuals of the migrant working class. "The holy text or traditions give certainty in a world of moral void; they are a sure protection against the dehumanizing impact of cynicism" (Parekh 1993: 141). In addition, mosques are platforms of power, arenas of contestation, aligned with the state, with non-state circuits of power or with emerging forces.

In Turkey, Serif Mardin (1977) distinguishes various streams of Islam: the official Islam of the state, the localistic Islam of the *tarikas*, and the craft Islam of the bazaar; but notes that the multi-dimensionality of Islam has been ignored in Turkish research.

These different streams have not been static over time nor have they remained neatly separated. One angle is to interpret the changes that have been taking place in Islam as the expression of tension between different kinds of Islam, as the cultural capital shared and claimed by a variety of social forces, in between the polarities of cosmopolitan Islam and village Islam. Cosmopolitan Islam, extending through caravan and maritime trade, through diasporas and settlements, through knowledge networks and through military expansion, has given shape to the historical dynamics of globalization, of which world capitalism is one manifestation. Village Islam has been part of the tribal underpinnings of this global expansion. The two have both overlapped (when tribal leaders came into, political and economic power, when power followed communitarian imaginaries) and clashed (when village Islam urbanized and contested the power of the official Islam of the powerful).

What forms this takes differs from place to place as each locality brings together a different ensemble of influences. The vortex of rural-urban cohabitation shapes the local play of class and culture, of economic and political forces and ways of experiencing and viewing them through maps of meaning. Local histories of rural-urban relations, patterns of state-society relations and the local mix of regional and global influences make for different alignments in Egypt, Algeria, Turkey, Sudan and northern Nigeria.

There is no firm or stable demarcation between the global and the local because, like different kinds of dough in a marble cake, they mingle and interpenetrate. The global and the local are not merely geographical categories but also ways of seeing, optical devices, discursive frames.

Islam itself is a form of globalism, a global civilizational ethos and, as pan-Islam, an aspiring world order (Beeley 1992). More than in other religions of the book, in Islam religion has been secularized in that spiritual order and temporal power are merged, making religion equivalent to political formation. In some respects this is a particularly modern feature and one reason why Islam, including contemporary political Islam, should not be viewed as an anti-modernity, as is common in contemporary polemics, but rather as an alternative modernity (for example, Al-Azmeh 1993).

Islam in the shadow of the World Trade Center

In colonial times the cities in the colonies were the most internationalized; now another kind of internationalization is occurring in the postimperial metropolitan centres. The skylines of global cities have been changing under the influence of the restructuring of corporate activity over the past decades. In the in-between places of the metropolitan centres, beneath the shadow of the glossy façades of megacapital, with a view of the changing skylines from below, an immigrant workforce instals itself. Saskia Sassen observes the presence of a migrant or immigrant workforce in the United States especially "in major cities, which also have the largest concentration of corporate power".

> We see here an interesting correspondence between great concentrations of corporate power and concentrations of an amalgamated "other" ... The fact that most of the people working in the corporate city during the day are low-paid secretaries, mostly women—many of them immigrant or African-American

women—is not included in the representation of the corporate economy or corporate culture. And the fact that at night a whole other, mostly immigrant workforce installs itself in these spaces .. and inscribes the space with a whole different culture (manual labor, often music, lunch breaks at midnight) is an invisible event. (Sassen 1993: 101).

Internal migration in Muslim countries was largely induced by world capitalism travelling overseas, whereas overseas migration means travelling into the sphere of world capitalism, seeking shelter in the shadow of the World Trade Centers. On the one hand, the internationalization of economies promotes the outflow of labour and, on the other, the casualization of the labour market in global cities makes for an expansion in the supply of low-wage jobs generated by major growth sectors. This twofold process both produces new migrations and facilitates their absorption (Sassen 1991: 316–19).

Islam and capitalism may both be described as "world processes" and as such they intersect in the matrix of migration. In Islam, "the institutions of *hajj* (annual pilgrimage to Mecca) and *hijra* (the religious obligation of Muslims to migrate and simultaneously break ties, distance oneself from evil, and form new bonds of religious brotherhood) have over the centuries institutionalized migration." Migration in the quest for knowledge abroad is also a motif that has been recognized since medieval Islam.

There are different ways, then, of preserving orthodoxy in a changing world. The key issue is that while generally travel is a metaphor for transformation, in Islam, under the image of the *hajj* and the *hijra,* travel serves as a metaphor for reconstitution: both of these are journeys undertaken to preserve the faith. (There are similar notions of migration and diaspora as regrouping in Judaism, where it is combined with endogamy.) This is an intrinsic tension within Islam and part of the paradox of travelling Islam: is travelling out acknowledged in Islam or only travelling in?

In the matrix of migration, local and global processes interpenetrate. The global standing and aspirations of Islam are locally meaningful: they inspire a sense of identity and self-worth among the Muslim diaspora; they maintain the transnational infrastructure of Islamic culture, from the *hajj* to subventions and donations from various quarters of Muslim power. At the same time, global Islam is fragmented along denominational, political and ethnic lines and the awareness of global unity and momentum is simultaneously an awareness of fragmentation, division and conflict. The Muslim diaspora is the counter-image of the hub in Mecca, an outflow as compared to an in-gathering. In the Muslim diaspora the paradox of Islam becomes manifest: a global project organized in local structures. In terms of organizational structure, Islam resembles Protestantism (strong localism, weak overarching structures), not Roman Catholicism.

As a form of globalism, Islam both colludes and competes with world capitalism. As mentioned before, the intercontinental trade networks of the Muslim world are part of the infrastructure of world capitalism. Along the oil trail multi-faceted networks of cooperation with global capitalism have been generated. While investments from oil-rich Muslim countries, through the recycling of petro-dollars since the 1970s, underpin the expansion of world capitalism, there has also been an investment in contesting the cultural and political manifestations of global capitalism in Muslim countries. Capitalism is being nourished on the investment end and being rejected, on the ground, on the consumer end ("Western decadence"). This overlaps with a wider contradiction which can be summed up as: "Western technology, Islamic values". The bombing of the World Trade Center in New York presumably by a militant Islamist group from Egypt, which may have been sponsored by orthodox forces in Saudi Arabia, illustrates the dramatic scope and intensity of contradictions within Islam.

Mosques without minarets in the Netherlands

What is the difference between internal migration and overseas migration, as the deterritorialization of Islam? The long-term tendency towards growing orthodoxy and clericalization may be reinforced in either mode of migration. In other respects the experience of migration is shaped and differentiated by many factors, such as the status of migrants—rural or urban, illiterate or educated; the gender of migrants and their position in the family; the character of migration—as traders or workers, for gain, knowledge or refuge; the direction of travel—East or West. To Asia and sub-Saharan Africa, Muslims came as traders and *ulamā* at times when Islam was in the ascendant. Their settlements often formed separate quarters within towns where they sometimes enjoyed a distinct legal status as trading minorities. The recent migrations of Muslims to the West, however, involve workers and take place at a time when, on the whole, global Islam has been on the defensive.

Does it make sense to generalize about migration experiences? What shapes the migration experience and the formation of local Muslim cultures in global spaces are the patterns of intercultural cohabitation which differ from country to country and the mix of transnational and cross-cultural influences which Muslims encounter. This is best looked at in specific terms. We will consider the case of Muslims in the Netherlands and then turn to Britain for a contrasting case.

The general point of this part of the chapter is to engage the paradox of travelling Islam, the complexity of the Islamic diaspora: on the one hand, the *umma* is being affirmed and realized in the diaspora, and, on the other, Islam while travelling is fractured along multiple lines—through cultural differentiation or "ethnicization", political differentiation among and within nationalities, and generational differentiation.

In the West, mosques and minarets may be controversial markers of cultural presence. If the presence of migrants in the corporate city centres is marginal, little noticed or invisible—such as the cleaners who come in as the white-collar workers leave—in the neighbourhoods the immigrant presence may be highly visible. Reflecting on the reactions to the construction of a minaret in Dalston in the north-east London borough of Hackney, Gilsenan observes:

> Imagine—and it is very difficult for those who have not experienced the world of the colonized—the effect that outside forces, over a relatively short period of time, can have on the transformation of the whole of the relations that make up urban space, including its sacred geography and unquestioned givens of the way things are in cities. Imagine, not only one building being constructed on an alien model, but an entire system of urban life in its economic, political, and

symbolic-cultural forms being imposed upon already existing towns and cities
that have been organized on quite different bases. (Gilsenan 1982: 195)

"Mosques without minarets" evokes a fractured image of Islam on the move. Among
Muslims a preferred image would be "from prayer rugs to minarets", an image that reflects
the gradual process of institutionalization of travelling Islam. In the course of thirty years,
from the first labour migrations in the 1960s to the present, Muslim workers in Europe,
many of them illiterates from the countryside, have brought over their families, set up
enterprises, sent their children to school and have worked themselves up to establish a
cultural presence. "From prayer rugs to minarets" is a narrative of achievement and social
mobility: from humble origins to proud attainment.

Mosques without minarets evokes the image of a subculture on the margins. In the
Netherlands, a number of newly built mosques do in fact feature minarets, although the
large majority does not—being converted school buildings, old churches or synagogues,
old factories, or homes converted for use as prayer halls. What minarets there are do not
tower above other buildings, do not claim prominent public sites, as is most often the
case in Muslim countries, especially for newly built mosques. The minarets are lower than
the high-rise offices of capital, lower than the World Trade Centers, lower even than the
apartment high-rises among which they are nestled, proud and yet modest, substantial and
yet, to outsiders, hardly noticeable. What is the cultural silhouette of a two-storey mosque
with a slightly higher minaret, located next to a twenty-storey apartment high-rise?

In some ways the place of the new mosques matches that of the old churches, as part
of wider shifts in the sacred geographies, the maps of meaning and profiles of power in the
West. The status and function of Christian churches have changed over time: long gone
are the days of *ecclesia triumphans* when churches were the dominant structures in the
land and townscapes. Gone are the days when the church in height and location competed
only with the palace or town hall. Now banks and corporate real estate, towering on the
model of the World Trade Center, dominate the cityscapes spatially and architecturally.
Inner-city churches are being vacated, converted to galleries, shops, offices or apartments,
and new churches are built on the outskirts, in architectures that are usually more abstract,
modest, introverted.

In the Netherlands, the main groups of Muslims are Turks, Moroccans and Surinamese.
These reflect different migration histories: colonial migration for the Surinamese and
labour migration. Colonial migration is multi-class and involves greater familiarity with
and a greater degree of integration in the metropolitan culture, in terms of language,
education and jobs. The Surinamese are more integrated in Dutch society and on the
whole rank higher in the cultural status hierarchy than Turks and Moroccans. Over
time the composition of migration flows has changed. Family reunification brought
greater numbers of women. Recent chain migration is bringing new marriage partners
from the home countries. The shift to the migration of refugees and dissidents reflects
economic and political instability in the countries of origin as well as the closing off of
labour migration in Western Europe. Asylum seekers often break ties with their country
of origin and thus stand in a different relationship to the community centres in which
the culture of origin is reconstructed. Immigrants are further differentiated, of course,

according to their regional origin, time of migration, the generation they belong to, political and religious affiliations, level of education, and employment.

The spatial location of the various mosques differs: Turkish mosques are often centrally located in cities and secondly in neighborhoods; Moroccan mosques are typically found in low-income city neighborhoods; Surinamese/South Asian mosques in low-income suburbs or neighborhoods; while smaller communities congregate in rural towns, such as the Moluccan Muslims with their mosque in Ridderkerk.

There are many different nodes to the Islamic world network and each locality brings together a different ensemble of diverse currents. A brief overview of mosque communities in the Netherlands and their cultural, national, ethnic and political diversities may illustrate the mix of global and local influences and the way the Muslim diaspora is implicated in the vicissitudes of transnational politics and political economy.

Among Turkish Muslims the main organization is the Netherlands Islamic Foundation which comes under the governmental Directorate for Religious Affairs in Ankara. This subsidizes the construction and upkeep of mosques and brings over imams schooled in Turkey. Presently it owns around 150 mosques and rents another ten. The aim of this government involvement is to control the growth of orthodox and extreme Muslim groups in Europe, presumably also because it could affect the political situation in Turkey. The head of the organization in The Hague is seated under a portrait of Kemal Ataturk. For several years the world Muslim organization *Rabita (Rabitat al-Alam al-Islami)* in Mecca sponsored the Turkish imams sent to the Netherlands, but one of the conditions was that they preach in Arabic.

One of the competing organizations among Turkish Muslims in Western Europe is the Teblig movement led by Cemalettin Kaplan in Cologne, also known as the "Khomeini of Cologne". With funding from Iran shrinking, the mosques associated with Kaplan have been decreasing as well; the funds for the upkeep of mosques and imams were simply lacking.

Of the approximately 250 mosques in the Netherlands in 1989, 100 are Moroccan. The Moroccan government also exercises influence over Moroccan mosques but without the tight organization of the Turkish government and without providing funding. UMMON (Union of Moroccan Mosques in the Netherlands) and Amicales are influential government arms, but the mosques are run by local foundations. Moroccans in the Netherlands hail mainly from the Rif mountains and from the south, rural populations who are newcomers to orthodoxy and among whom regional divisions play a large part. Some years ago a few Moroccan mosques turned for funding to the Islamic Call Society in Libya, founded by Gadaffi in 1972, a loose organization which seeks to merge Islam with Gadaffi's Green Book ideas of socialism and women's emancipation. In order to quell Moroccan infighting this organization sent Libyan and Filipino imams to the Netherlands.

Surinamese and South Asian Muslims are organized in the World Islamic Mission which controls some forty-two mosques for Surinamese, Pakistanis and Indians, united by Urdu as a common language. Established in 1976 the Mission is affiliated with the Muslim World Congress headquartered in Karachi. Affiliated with the Mission are the large mosques in the Bijlmer (a suburb of dormitory high-rises constructed in the 1970s in the south-east of Amsterdam which houses many immigrants) and in Utrecht, which were originally established with funding from Saudi Arabia and other Arabic states.

There are many other Muslim organizations active in the Netherlands, such as the Ahmaddya movement, the Suleymanci group and several Sufi orders. Attempts to establish a federation of Muslim organizations, a central Muslim council and umbrella institutions such as Islamic broad casting have failed repeatedly. Instead there is a coming and going of organizations, councils and federations that are unevenly funded from various quarters including Saudi Arabia, Kuwait and Libya. Establishing Muslim institutions is also a form of transnational fundraising and job creation, a way to establish silver links with oil-rich Muslim countries. According to the imam of the London Central Mosque: "In one small area with a population of approximately 3,000 people, I counted no less than six Muslim societies". It shows the dispersed and scattered infrastructure of global Islam: one Mecca, many centres.

Islam in the West

Vortexes of cohabitation

The Netherlands is a relatively open country with a higher degree of international interdependence than neighboring countries: a much higher percentage of Dutch GNP is generated abroad, through trade, services and investments, than in the neighboring countries. This openness goes back a long time in Dutch history. From the twelfth century onwards the Low Countries developed a special niche in the region in which they competed with their neighbors on the basis of openness as a selling point. By deliberate strategy, merchants and nobles combined in imposing no limitations on trade with foreigners and non-Christians, setting low tolls and permitting the right of return of ships and cargo in time of war. I have termed this the political economy of tolerance. For the Dutch "tolerated" minorities have historically been *traits d'union* to the world economy. All of this is now long forgotten but the principle of toleration remains a value in Dutch culture. A brief comparison between English and Dutch ways of relating to cultural difference may illustrate the role of cultural orientations and their political ramifications.

In England, the head of state is the head of the Church of England and other denominations have a less privileged status. English legislation does not take account of Islam: the blasphemy law does not apply to Islam and ritual slaughter, polygamous marriage and female circumcision are not recognized. Muslims are treated as ethnic minorities under statutes derived from human rights conventions. Religious institutions receive no general support from the state but can be recognized as charities and be granted tax exemptions: in 1985, 329 mosques were thus recognized.

In the Netherlands since the early nineteenth century the principle of equality of religions has been anchored in the constitution. Equal rights in terms of state support for education was granted to Catholics only in 1917. State financing of schools founded by religious organizations established the system of "pillarization", also known as the "silver strings" between the state and Christian denominations. In the revised constitution of 1983 the principle of equality also extends to non-religious convictions. Accordingly Muslims are placed in the same position as Jewish, Hindu or Humanist groups. The blasphemy law also applies to Islam and days off for Islamic holidays are also legally recognized. In

1987 the rules applying to the ringing of church bells were extended to calls to prayer from mosques.

While multi-culturalism in Britain has been patterned on the colonial experience as the main way in which cultural difference has been historically recognized, that is as an experience taking place *outside* the nation, pillarization, the Dutch mode of cultural pluralism from the 1910s to the 1970s, refers to the history of religious and political differences *within* the nation, among Catholics, Protestants and the non-church affiliated. Pillarization valorizes cultural difference from the angle of religion; multi-culturalism in Britain "ethnicizes" cultural difference. At the same time, Dutch policies follow a double track in recognizing ethnic difference or national origin over religious difference.

A further dynamic is the relationship between residential patterns, employment and other indices of social participation. It has been argued that in postindustrial welfare states such as the Netherlands this relationship has become quite weak: "In postindustrial societies the labour market no longer appears to be the primary field of interaction determining other spheres of societal interaction. Housing, work and education have become (relative) autonomous circuits." The welfare state and especially municipal councils in which the Labour Party predominates, as in the big cities where immigrants are concentrated, control the allocation of social housing.

Unemployment among Moroccan and Turkish immigrants is high and their level of schooling is low. For immigrants this has led to the adoption of a compulsory reporting system on hiring practices by companies and to policies of fostering integration by making learning Dutch obligatory for newcomers.

The Amsterdam skyline is lower than that of New York, London or Paris, and high-rises are scattered around rather than located within the inner city. There are concentrations of multinational capital around the World Trade Centre, as part of the south axis of corporate real estate extending towards Schiphol airport. Other areas of corporate concentration are in the south-east and the teleport on the north axis of the city. It is in the interstices of the edifices of megacapital that migrant labour finds a place. In sweatshops, particularly in the garment industry, the migrant workforce delivers the goods for just-in-time capitalism. Turkish-owned sweatshops form an important infra-structure of the Amsterdam garment industry.

There may be a different way of looking at migrants and the role they play in economic restructuring: "Rather than being a marginal mass of workers, or a specific category in the segmented market, they become a 'vector' of restructuring" (Pellerin 1994: 14). Specifically, the situation in many industrialized receiving countries allows:

> the coexistence of high levels of unemployment among the indigenous labour force, and economic decline more generally, with significant levels of employment amongst foreign workers, or at least some categories of foreigners. Consequently, rather than regulating economic cycles, migrants seem to participate in the deregulation of the productive process in many industries (Pellerin 1994: 13).

In the context of the prevailing political economic regime, there may well be a limit to minority employment schemes and to expectations for the gradual integration of immigrants in the primary labour market and society at large. With or without diplomas, the second and third generation may not find enough jobs, because they compete with indigenous white- and blue-collar sectors whose unemployment has been growing, in an environment where cultural capital counts. Are immigrants destined then to remain in enclaves, economically and culturally? Two qualifiers may alter this picture. One is that in intercultural society, intercultural capital itself becomes an asset, that is, ethnic entrepreneurship and hybrid entrepreneurship may themselves be generators of growth. The second is the role of cultural cross-over which enhances the ability of immigrants to compete in the labour market.

The rise and decline of boundaries

Common understandings of the way Muslims define their boundaries with Dutch society focus on the areas of purity, sexuality and religion. Purity relates to food and drink (pork, halal meat, alcohol) and habits of cleanliness. Sexuality relates to the position of women. And with respect to religion, Muslims might view Dutch culture as anti-Islamic because of its degree of secularization and separation of church and state. Such boundaries give a sense of self-worth. Purity and sexuality provide a sense of moral superiority which may compensate for class inferiority.

Non-Muslims construct similar boundaries of cultural difference with shifts in emphasis and meaning, focused on the suppression of women; notions of "backwardness"—as in common comparisons, benevolent or otherwise, between immigrants and Dutch people in the past; and religion—as in ideas about Islamic orthodoxy and "fundamentalism".

How firm and stable over time are these boundaries? To each there are elements of stretch and in-built boundary-crossing moments. The purity boundary may be the most permeable. The higher the level of education, the more likely Muslims are to ignore dietary restrictions and integrate with Dutch society; here the same pattern prevails as in internal migration. Another effect is manifested in cities with Muslim concentrations: in the marketplace cultural boundaries are increasingly being crossed. Due to recession and unemployment which reduce immigrant purchasing power, ethnic entrepreneurs turn to native or cross-ethnic customers and adjust their products accordingly. Dutch retailers have long been stocking "ethnic" produce: a fish stall which first imported fish from Spain and Portugal, then from the Caribbean, now stocks Moroccan fish.

The boundary of sexuality and the position of women in some respects clash with Dutch laws and customs as regards the scope of parental authority, obligatory schooling, marriage and life-style. Over the years there have been a series of clashes between municipal or state authorities and Muslim parents on restrictions imposed on women and daughters, reported in the popular press. Without going into details, it is obvious that this is an unstable and conflict-ridden boundary, particularly for youngsters of the second and third generations.

"The first generation of migrants often becomes more religiously active than they were in their homeland". The second generation faces a different situation: "To follow the parental religious model, to adopt an alternative style of Islamic observance or to give up religious identity at all will become a matter of choice for them". In the process, the meaning of religion itself changes. Religious discourse not only structures experience but is also structured and changed by the different circumstances (Sunier 1992).

Ooijen (1992) asks a pertinent question: do Islamic organizations promote emancipation or isolation? The degree of choice experienced by the second generation is also a matter of educational level. Among Moroccans, the general educational level is lower than among other Muslims in the Netherlands. As a consequence also their international connections are not as well developed as are those of other nationalities. For Moroccans Islam remains the most important basis for self-help organizations.

There are ample manifestations of everyday syncretism: Muslims who respect Ramadan but also buy presents and a Christmas tree so that their children will not feel left out; mosques that would like to use the Qur'an-classrooms to offer computer courses, also to have something to empower the jobless second generation; hybrid figures such as the "educated believer".

To Dutch stereotyping of Muslim immigrants there is an in-built time slide: "backwardness" may be overtaken by social climbing or, at least, by the adoption of symbolic markers of integration in dress and life The test of how these boundaries are constructed, deconstructed and redrawn is in the neighborhoods. Here residential familiarity makes it possible for distinctions to become fine, rather than crude generalizations, and to identify where they fade or are redefined. In Amsterdam neighborhoods, Moroccan youths have taken over the spots and streetcorners where previously Surinamese Creole boys gathered. The latter have moved on from the streets to youth centers and thence to coffee shops and other commercial venues, a path that was followed earlier by white working-class youth. Accordingly class tracks and careers may prove to be stronger than patterns based on cultural difference.

In France, the second and third generation of *beurs*, the audience of raï and rap, claim "le droit a l'ambiguité", which is resisted by ethno-nationalists and Islamists (Gross et al). In the Netherlands cultural crossover is the common trend among second and third generation immigrants from Muslim countries and resistance to cultural mixing is weak. What comes across in many reports is that what matters in the neighborhoods is socio-economic prospects—jobs, education, living conditions, moving to a better neighborhood—and municipal and state policies, rather than cultural difference or "ethnicity". That these concerns are shared by immigrants and natives alike shows a common reaction to living in the postindustrial welfare state.

By way of conclusion

This chapter has raised questions about the meaning of travel in Islam: does Islam recognize only travelling in or also travelling out? And it has raised questions about the complexity of the Islamic world mirrored in the Islamic diaspora. Rather than revisiting the rhetorics of unity and homogeneity—upheld by advocates and opponents alike—it has considered some of the fractures and divisions in the world of Islam on the move.

High Islam is modern Islam, which ironically is more orthodox than local Islam. Modern Islam travels well because it does not depend on local circumstances for its cultural reproduction, but what if travel leads outside the ring of Islam? What scope for intercultural mixing does Islam offer? The tension within Islam—a global project organized in local structures—is affirmed in the Muslim diaspora. If Islam is varied enough within the Arab world and in adjacent Iran and Turkey, the new Islams that have developed in the peripheries of this heartland, in Asia, Africa and more recently in Europe and North America, further add to the Muslim *mélange*.

Part of the paradox of the Islamic world is its complex pattern of collusion and contestation with world capitalism. The Islamic presence in the West is both substantial and modest; Europe's second largest religion boasts many mosques but mosques without minarets, in a word, religion without power. To an extent this is made up for by prestige architecture such as the new mosque in New York and the new mosque in Rome: Europe's largest mosque for Europe's second largest religion erected in the spiritual capital of Europe's largest religion.

In the diaspora the *umma* is affirmed and broken up in cultural sub-units, some of which generate novel combinations. The sites of diaspora produce their own opportunity structures. In the Netherlands the combined tendencies of pillarization, ethnicization and integration makes for a different field than in Britain with its predominant discourse of racialized cultural difference, while in France secularism and *laicité* make for yet another arena of difference.

Smaller countries in the West such as the Netherlands may offer greater opportunities for crossover culture than the larger countries: when the numbers of immigrants are smaller, immigrant enclaves are too small to sustain reproduction, either culturally or economically, and cultural chauvinism is weaker. Hence opportunities and incentives for hybridization are greater. This offers yet another form of peripheral Islam. But of course these conditions also exist in different localities within the larger countries.

Acknowledgement

I am indebted to Azza Karam for her comments on an earlier version of this chapter.

References

Ahmed, A. S. and Donnan, H. (eds.), *Islam Globalization and Postmodernity*. (London: Routledge, 1994).

Al-Azmeh, A. *Islams and Modernities*. (London: Verso, 1993).

Amersfoort, H. van "Ethnic Residential Patterns in a Welfare State: Lessons from Amsterdam 1970-1990." *New Community* 18 (3): 439-56 (1992).

Antoun, R. T. "Sojourners Abroad: Migration for Higher Education in a Post-peasant Society." in A. S. Ahmed and H. Donnan (eds.), *Islam, Globalization and Postmodernity*, (1994).

Beeley, B. "Islam as a Global Political Force." In A. G. McGrew, et al. (eds.), *Global Politics*. (Oxford: Polity Press, 1992).

Eickelmann, D. F & Piscatori, J. (eds.), *Muslim Travellers: Pilgrimage, Migration, and the Religious Imagination*. (Berkeley: University of California Press, 1990).

Geertz, C. *Islam Observed: Religious Development in Morocco and Indonesia*. (Chicago: University Press, 1968).

Gellner, E. *Postmodernism, Reason and Religion*. (London: Routledge, 1992).

Gerholm, T & Lithman, Y. G. (eds.), *The New Islamic Presence in Western Europe*. (London: Mansell, 1988).

Gross, J., McMurray, D. & Swedenborg, T. "Rai, Rap and Ramadan Nights: Franco-Maghribi Cultural Identities." *Middle East Report* 22 (5): 11—16.

Gilseman, M. *Recognizing Islam* (N.Y.: Pantheon, 1982).

Landman, N. *Van mat tot minaret* (VU: Amsterdam, 1992).

Lans, J.M. van der and Rooijackers, M. "Types of Religious Belief and Un belief among Second Generation Turkish Migrants." In W.A.R. Shadid and P. S. van Koningsveld (eds.), *Islam in Dutch Society*, (1992).

Lithman, Y. G. "Social Relations and Cultural Continuities: Muslim Immigrants and their Social Networks." In T Gerholm & Y.G.. Lithman (eds.), *The New Islamic Presence*, (1988).

Mardin, S. "Religion in Modern Turkey." *International Social Science Journal* 29 (2): 279-97, (1977).

Massey, D. "Power-geometry and a Progressive Sense of Place." In J. Bird et. al. (eds.), *Mapping the Futures: Local and Global Change* (London: Routledge, 1993).

Ooijen, H. van. "Religion and Emancipation: a Study of the Development of Islamic Organizations in a Dutcu Town." In W. A. R. Shadid & P. S. van Koningsveld (eds.), *Islam in Dutch Society*, (1992).

Parekh, B. "Between Holy Text and Moral Void." In A. Gray & J. McGuigan (eds.), *Studying Culture*. (London: Edward Arnold, 1993).

Pellerin, H. "Global Restructuring and the Transnationalisation of Migration Limits and Promises of the Movement of People in the Emerging World Order".Unpublished paper, (1994).

Pred, A. & Watts, M. J. *Reworking Modernity: Capitalism and Symbolic Discontent.* (New Brunswick, NJ: Rutgers University Press, 1992).

Rath, J., Groenendijk, K. & Penninx, K. "The Recognition and Institutionalization of Islam in Belgium, Great Britain & the Netherlands." *New Community* 18 (1): 101—14. (1991).

Sassen, S. *The Global City*: New York, London, Tokyo (Princeton, NJ: Princeton University Press, 1991).

_____. "Rethinking Immigration." *Lusitania* 5: 97—102 (1993). Sunier, T. "Islam and Ethnicity among Turks: the Changing Role of Islam & Muslim organizations." In W. A. R Shadid & P. S. van Koningsveld (eds.), *Islam in Dutch Society*, (1992).

Al-Turabi, H. "Islam as a Pan-National Movement and Nation States." Unpublished Paper, (1993).

Waardenburg, J. "The Institutionalization of Islam in the Netherlands 1961—86." In T. Gerholm & Y. G. Lithman (eds.), *The New Islamic Presence*, (1988).

Originally published in Ayse Öncü and Petra Weyland (eds.) *Space, Culture and Power* (Zed Books, 1997): 177–200. Printed here with the permission of the publisher.

JOAN SCOTT

Sexuality and the Politics of the Veil

The law banning headscarves in public schools made a clear distinction between acceptable and unacceptable signs of religious conviction.

The clothing and religious signs prohibited are *conspicuous* [*ostensible*] signs, such as a large cross, a veil, or a skullcap. Not regarded as signs indicating religious affiliation are *discreet* [*discret*] signs, which can be, for example, medallions, small crosses, stars of David, hands of Fatima, or small Korans.

I have drawn attention to the words "conspicuous" and "discreet" because they resolved the difficulty the Stasi commission and its advisors had in articulating what they were after. As is usual in political debate of this kind, there was a great deal of disagreement among legislators and others about the exact wording to use in the law. For a long time, the talk was of banning "ostentatious" signs, but that word was dropped because it ascribed motives to the wearer of the sign that might be difficult to prove. Then there was the word "visible"; the head of the National Assembly committee recommended that all "visible signs" of religious affiliation be banned from public schools. His colleagues demurred, largely because they thought the prohibition of all visible emblems was too broad and would conflict with the European Court's rulings that protected religious expression as an individual right. "Conspicuous" seemed a good alternative because it attributed the meaning of the sign to the sign itself; there was something objective about it and yet objectionable. It was more than visible; it was, well, conspicuous. The legislators opted for "discreet" as a way of distinguishing acceptable from unacceptable signs, since visibility could still be an ambiguous notion (things that are conspicuous, after all, are also visible).

One of many commentators pointed to the futility of these academic distinctions: it might be possible abstractly to separate "ostentatious," "conspicuous," and "visible," he said, but in practice it would be very difficult to distinguish among them. Still, I think the effort is worth our attention, not so much because it exemplifies the obsessive concern with language that one thinks of as characteristically French, but because it reveals the hidden preoccupations that directed the discussion. I was struck in particular by the sexual connotations carried by the words the lawmakers chose. When "ostentatious" or "conspicuous" refers to an excessive display on or by a body, especially if it's a woman's body, it conveys a sense of erotic provocation. "Discreet" is the opposite of ostentatious or conspicuous: a discreet object doesn't call attention to itself; it downplays the attractiveness of the body in question; it is somehow neutral—asexual. In the opposition between "conspicuous" and "discreet," the language of the law intensified its philosophical disapproval of the headscarves' violation of *laïcité* with a veiled reference to unacceptable sexuality. There was something sexually amiss about girls in headscarves; it was as if both too little and too much were being revealed.

But in what way "too much"? After all, according to the girls who wore them, headscarves signified modesty and sexual unavailability. In the Muslim juristic tradition, "ostentation" was to be avoided at all costs. The Moroccan-Arabic word invoked by theologians is *tabarruj*. Abdellah Hammoudi (2006, p.42) tells us that it means "ostentatious," and it is "the invariable term for a bearing that is deemed immodest or conspicuous." There is another Arabic word, *fitna*, adds anthropologist, Saba Mahmood (2005, pp.110–117) that means both sexual temptation and the disruption of political order. Women were assumed to be objects of male sexual desire and thus inherently provocative, "an assumption that has come to justify the injunction that women should 'hide their charms' when in public so as not to excite the libidinal energies of men who are not their immediate kin." The goal of modest dress for women was to prevent such excitement. By what standard could girls wearing headscarves be considered immodest or conspicuous? They did stand out in a classroom filled with girls in Western dress, but not because their clothing was more revealing. If anything, it was more discreet; more of the body was covered. How then account for this seemingly strange reversal? Muslim modesty is taken to be sexually aberrant by French observers, who condemn it not only as different but as somehow excessive (ostentatious, conspicuous), even perverse. The reason given by politicians and many feminists was the same: the veil represented the subordination of women, their humiliation, and their inequality. It must not be sanctioned by those who believed in the republican principles of liberty and equality. I don't think that this is a sufficient explanation for the kind of disturbing sexual connotation the veil had for its critics. It was not the absence of sexuality but its presence that was being remarked—a presence underlined by the girls' refusal to engage in what were taken to be the "normal" protocols of interaction with members of the opposite sex.

The veil's disturbing sexual connotation for French observers stemmed from its significance in a system of gender relations they took to be entirely different from their own. For Muslims, the veil is declaration of the need to curb the dangerous sexuality of women (and also of men), a response, as Hammoudi puts it, "to the risks associated with [our] vital impulses." It is a recognition of the threat sex poses for society and politics. In contrast, the French system celebrates sex and sexuality as free of social and political risk. At the same time, sex poses a tremendous difficulty for the abstract individualism that is the basis for French republicanism: if we are all the same, why has sexual difference been such an obstacle to real equality? I will argue in this chapter that the headscarf pointed up this contradiction in the French gender system: Islam's insistence on recognizing the difficulties posed by sexuality revealed more than republicans wanted to see about the limits of their own system.

It is important to note here that it is idealized gender systems I am talking about. These, of course, have some relationship to how people behave and perceive one another, but they are not as fixed or all-encompassing as they seem. Like any categorization, they overstate prescriptive norms and underestimate the diversity of practices individuals actually engage in. It is the work of representation these idealized concepts do that I am interested in; because even for those who do not follow them to the letter, they offer a powerful point of reference around which understandings of difference are organized. Here again we see the objectification of Islam, on the one side, and France, on the other: Islam is seen as a system that oppresses women, French republicanism as one that liberates them.

The French who supported the headscarf ban talked in terms of a conflict between emancipatory modernity and oppressive tradition. Even though the French schoolgirls who chose to wear headscarves did so not as members of traditional societies or communities, they did accept a distinction they attributed to Islam. I would say that they wanted to operate in a discursive system different from the French one in which they found themselves. In the terminology offered by sociologist Farhad Khosrokhavar (1995, p.145) the difference is between an "open" approach to gender relations and a "covered" one, both terms referring to the treatment of the sexed body. In "covered" systems, gender relations are regulated by codes of modesty. "Modesty and honor are defined in direct relation to the bodily and mental covering-over of the woman (the woman as the shield of honor for the community; the woman as manager of private space, closed to public space)." If traditionally, the order of the family and the purity of the entire social body rested on the separation of the sexes, for young Muslim girls in France it was their own bodily integrity, their own honor, that was at stake. In contrast, "open" systems are those which don't see the exposure of the body, its visibility, as detrimental. In these systems, "a certain type of voyeurism and exhibitionism ... is positively valued ... The language of the body is that of its accessibility to the other sex."

As Western feminists have often pointed out, uncovered bodies are no more a guarantee of equality than covered ones. In both societies or systems women have been deemed inferior to men and their legal rights have been restricted, though it is certainly true that many societies with "open" systems have by now granted some measure of formal equality to women. In France, despite the bitter opposition of the same politicians who passed the headscarf ban in the name of women's rights, there is even a law on the books (enacted in 2000) that calls for equal numbers of women and men on the ballots in almost all elections. But the parity law, as it is called, has not stopped the devaluing of women that reduces them to their sex, and that led the Socialist Party colleagues of politician Ségolène Royal to try to check her presidential ambitions by reminding her that the race for the presidency "is not a beauty contest."

Until their ideological confrontation with Islam, many French feminists saw the sexual exhibitionism of their society—particularly as it applied to women—as demeaning to women because it reduced them to a sexed body. But in the heat of the headscarf controversy, those concerns were set aside and equality became synonymous with sexual emancipation, which in turn was equated with the visibility of the female body. As was the case with laïcité and autonomous individualism, the French system of gender was offered as not only the best, but the only acceptable, way to organize relations between the sexes. Those who did not conform to it were by definition inferior and therefore could never be fully French. The issue of covered or uncovered sexuality, I want to argue, gave the headscarf affair both its resonance and its intensity. Here was proof of the irreconcilable difference between the "culture" of Islam and France.

Visibility

In the headscarf controversy, opponents of the veil were consumed with the idea that it denied what they referred to as Mixité, the mixing of the sexes, in schools, hospitals, and elsewhere. (Debré, Vol. 1: 77; 2003) The veil, according to the Stasi commission (and to innumerable witnesses who appeared before it), was an expression of Islam's strict segregation of the sexes. In fact, at least in the case of schools, the opposite was true: wearing a headscarf allowed girls to attend coeducational schools who otherwise would have been unable to. But the real concern of some of the experts who testified to the Stasi commission was less mixité than it was the same *visual* status for the bodies of women and men. Hence, when psychoanalyst Elisabeth Roudinesco was asked if she thought beards should be prohibited in schools, since they could also be a form of Islamist identification, she replied that there could be no legislation about beards. Not only was such legislation impractical, but beards, even if worn for religious reasons, did not constitute the same alienation for men that veils did for women. Of course, beards have a lot to do with sexuality; the difference was that beards were visible, while women's bodies were disguised by veils. "I'm absolutely convinced that the real problem posed by the veil is that it covers over [*il recouvre*] a sexual dimension. It denies the equality between men and women upon which our society rests." (Debré, Vol. 2: 52; 2003) It was precisely the covering over of women's sexuality that so troubled her: the veil was a denial, she said, of women as "objects of desire." (Debré, Vol. 2: 2003) Roudinesco was not bothered only by the veil's association with women's inequality, a contradiction of a specific republican principle. She also thought the veil interfered with what she took to be a natural psychological process: the visual appreciation of women's bodies by men brought women's femininity into being.

In this view, girls were lost to their feminine identity if their bodies could not be seen. Identity was conferred by men's being able to see them as sexual objects. Feminine identity depended on male desire; male desire depended on visual stimulation. Stasi talked of the veil as "objectively" alienating women, not only from the exercise of their fundamental rights, but also from their own sexuality, and Iranian feminist Chahdortt Djavann, one of many refugees from an Islamist theocracy, called the veil a form of "psychological, sexual and social mutilation." It denied a young girl any possibility of "becoming a human being. (*Pro Choix*, 2003) Mutilation was a big preoccupation for many commentators. Some even equated wearing the veil with genital mutilation. (Ibid, 2004) Philosopher in *L'Express*, (November 17, 1994) André Glucksmann described the veil as "stained with blood" (a reference to terrorists and Nazis, but also with inevitable connotations of cutting). The logic of Glucksmann's observation seemed to go like this: terrorism constitutes the breaking of all the rules of political deportment; veiling violates the rules of gendered interaction; the rules of gendered interaction are the basis of social and political order; therefore, veiling is terrorism.

According to this logic, it was difficult to maintain the view that Muslim girls and women were victims; wearing the headscarf itself became an act of aggression. Jacques Chirac said as much in a speech in Tunisia in December 2003. "Wearing the veil, whether it is intended or not, is a kind of aggression." (Deltombe, 2005, p.347) In this comment, Chirac was conflating terrorism and the veil with an oblique reference to the hidden danger of women's repressed sexuality. Out there to see, women's sexuality was manageable; unseen, it might wreak havoc—political as well as social.

But Chirac was also saying something else. The aggression he referred to was twofold: that of the veiled woman but also of the (Western) man trying to look at her. The aggression of the woman consisted in denying (French) men the pleasure—understood as a natural right (a male prerogative)—to see behind the veil. This was taken to be an assault on male sexuality, a kind of castration. Depriving men of an object of desire undermined the sense of their own masculinity. Sexual identity (in the Western or "open" model) works both ways: men confirm their sexuality not only by being able to look at—to openly desire—women but also by receiving a "look" from women in return. The exchange of desirous looks, the availability of faces for reading, is a crucial aspect of gender dynamics in "open" systems.

Headscarves don't actually cover the faces of their wearers; they cover their hair and ears and necks, but the faces are plainly visible. Despite this fact, commentators conflated women in the Gulf States with those in France and insisted on referring to headscarves as if they covered *faces*. For example, when the French media figure Bernard Henri Lévy was interviewed on National Public Radio in the United States about (among other things) the headscarf ban, his clinching point concerned the face. After listing a number of objections to the "veil" and explaining the need for a law banning it in public schools, he ended by talking about how sad it was to cover the beautiful faces of young girls—that in the end was Islam's worst offense. His remark is at first perplexing, for the faces of the girls in question were not actually covered. It becomes clear, though, when we realize that the uncovered face stands for the visibility of the entire body and, more importantly, its sexual availability. In this reasoning a body whose contours cannot be seen becomes a hidden face. So it's understandable that Lévy confuses the headscarf and the veil, not because both are variations on a Muslim style of dress, but because both signify modesty and the sexual unavailability of the woman. That unavailability is profoundly disturbing to the way identity is lived by French women and men.

While Lévy seemed bemused and saddened by being deprived of the sight of female beauty, another common response is aggression. Here is the way the psychiatrist Frantz Fanon, writing in the 1950s, described male colonizers' attitudes to veiled women in Algeria:

> There is also in the European the crystallization of an aggressiveness, the strain of a kind of violence before the Algerian woman. Unveiling this woman is revealing her beauty; it is baring her secret, breaking her resistance, making her available for adventure... In a confused way, the European experiences his relation with the Algerian woman at a highly complex level. There is in it the will to bring this woman within his reach, to make her a possible object of possession. This Woman who sees without being seen frustrates the colonizer. There is no reciprocity. She does not yield herself, does not give herself, does not offer herself.

In the 1950s this "will to bring women within reach" had to do with the sexualized fantasies of colonial domination; white men conquering indigenous women. In the new century, it has to do with a perceived attack on (aggression against) what its French defenders insist is the right way (perhaps the only way) to conduct relations between the sexes. It is no longer the conquest of a new territory that is at stake, but the (aggressive) defense of the homeland, of the republican principles of liberty and equality. A distinctively French form of sexuality was even posited as a trait of national character. It was, in historian Mona Ozouf's (1995) words, "la singularité française (the French singularity)."

In what can only be described as a burst of nationalist fervor, many French feminists took up the cry for the liberation of Muslim women, forgetting their own critique of the visual exploitation they had protested in the past. To be sure, during the "string" affair, objections were voiced to the oversexualized style young girls had adopted. Ségolène Royal, for example, warned that "in the eyes of boys, the string reduces young girls to a behind." (*Le Monde,* October 17, 2003)) She and others cautioned that the tyranny of this fashion was not liberating, but they did not go as far as some American critics—students of Islam—who questioned the superiority of "open" to "covered" ways of dressing: "Can our bras, ties, pants, miniskirts, underwear and bathing suits all be so easily arrayed on one side or another of [the] divide" between freedom and captivity? (Hirschkind and Mahmood, 2002)) Aren't there, instead, two different systems of subjection at play?

Aside from one or two articles equating the veil and the string as two sides of the same oppressive coin, there was not much discussion in France of the limits of Western dress. It was the veil that must be removed in the name of equality. Not, I would argue, the equality of women and men, but that of Muslim *women* and French *women.* Although, of course, there were many types of Muslim women, some veiled and some not, and many types of French women as well, the representation of this issue offered only two contrasting categories. The point was to bring Muslim women up to the standard of their French sisters (a version of the civilizing mission with all of its racist and colonial implications), free to display their bodies and experience the joys of sex—as French society (women and men) understood them. Minister of the interior Nicolas Sarkozy said precisely this in 2005: "We are proud of the values of the Republic, of equality between men and women, of laïcité, and of the French ideal of integration. So let us dare to speak of these to those we welcome here. And let us bring pressure to bear so that the rights of French women apply also to immigrant women."(Sarkozy, 2006).

Sexual Freedom

On the eve of the passage of the headscarf ban, the feminist political scientist Janine Mossuz-Lavau wrote an eloquent appeal against the law. "When I pass a woman with a veil in the street," her article began, "I feel a pang of emotion." Not, she explained, because she was hostile to the woman's religion, but because the veil designated the woman as "a source of sin," and "as a potential whore." As such she was "prohibited from sex with anyone but her husband or future husband." Mossuz-Lavau felt deeply for this woman, deprived as she was of the sexual liberation that was hers by right.

But such liberation, the sociologist went on, could only come from being exposed to modern ideas at school. Indeed, public opinion polls demonstrated that modern liberal attitudes were held by those with high levels of education; the most bigoted members of French society were those with no degrees. Mossuz-Lavau then cited a study she had done in 2000-2001 of sexual practices in French society. Of the Muslim women she interviewed, "the only ones who transgressed [Islamic] norms and who had sexual relations before marriage were students and managers with advanced degrees." "These young women

refused the dictate of virginity until marriage and it was no accident that all of them had...
a higher education." If the test of liberation were sexual freedom, she concluded, then
girls with headscarves must be allowed to stay in school. "I think that school, at whatever
level, can have this function and will aid those who are permitted to remain there to direct
themselves to a freer life." (*Le Monde*, December 16, 2003)

Chahdortt Djavann, whose claim to expertise was her own experience in Iran, offered
sensationalist tales of women's lack of freedom in Muslim countries. That neither she
nor her most attentive followers distinguished among different Islams—Islam as a state
religion in a theocracy run by mullahs is not the same as the minority religion followed
by those living in France—is indicative of the hysteria that informed much of the debate.
Djavann stated not only that women were oppressed in "Islamic societies" but also (in
terms reminiscent of some colonial attitudes) that the separation of the sexes necessarily
gave rise to rape and prostitution. It was as if the veil, by designating women as dangerously
licentious, encouraged the attacks. Pedophilia, too, was common: "if relations sexual,
nonsexual, and nonconjugal between two consenting adults are prohibited and severely
sanctioned by Islamic laws, no law protects the children." (Deltombe, 2005, p. 352) In
her accounts, neither women nor children were spared the attention of predatory males,
an attention stimulated by the sharp segregation of the sexes. All of Islam was organized
on these men's behalf, she maintained. Only a law banning headscarves would prevent
similar developments in France. This law, she believed, might even offer hope to women in
theocratic regimes such as Iran. Absent from Djavann's discussion was any acknowledgment
of the complexity of life in Iran (where, as I have already mentioned, women vote and serve
in parliament even if they wear veils) or of the existence of mistreatment of women in
France. As feminist sociologist Christine Delphy put it, Muslims do not have a monopoly
on the abuse of women.

Although Mossuz-Lavau and Djavann differed on the question of the wisdom of the law,
they shared a belief in the innate desire of women for emancipation in Western terms. It was
clear to them that women would not choose the veil unless they were forced to. This was the
position also taken by *Ni Putes, Ni Soumises* (Neither Whores nor Subjected), a group of
feminists that included many who had lived under Islamist regimes. The group was formed
in 2002 to protest physical violence against women perpetrated in the name of Islam. In a
widely circulated petition they supported the ban on headscarves because "the Islamic veil
subjects all of us, Muslim and non-Muslim alike, to an intolerable discrimination against
women." (Guénif-Souliamas and Macé, 2004, p. 9) This outlook stunned the two Muslim
women who coauthored *One Veiled, the Other Not*. Dounia Bouzar, who did not wear a
veil, nonetheless marveled at the misunderstanding of Islam contained in the standard of
liberation offered by French feminists. "The leitmotif of their messages revolves around the
idea that when Muslim women are free to sleep with as many men as they want to, then
they will be integrated. Liberty is measured by the number of sexual acts they engage in."
Saïda Kada reminded Bouzar of the first images to appear in France of the liberation of
Kabul. "Women putting on make-up. What symbolism: from the burqa to lipstick! They
[the French] were reassured not about the well-being of humanity but about the capacity
of women to live up to Western models." (Bouzar and Kada, 2003, pp. 58-59)

Bouzar's point about integration is telling. She rightly perceives that sexual liberation is
at the heart of objections to the veil and to Islam more generally. It is not simply a question

of individual autonomy being hampered by communal loyalty or religious prescription interfering with the secular construction of the self. The self the legislators and their feminist supporters imagined was not only sexed but sexual; not only sexual but sexually active in familiar ways. Commenting on a particularly scandalous set of events in the Muslim community in 1989 (two brothers had killed themselves after killing their sister, who had dated a French man; honor killings of this kind, though rare, were mistakenly attributed to Islam as such), the television journalist Christine Ockrent drew a moral conclusion: "This sordid story makes clear in an exaggerated fashion the difficulties, the tensions, the obscure innermost recesses of belonging to another culture where sexuality in particular is lived differently." (Deltombe, 2005, p. 70) Jean Daniel, the editor of *Le Nouvel Observateur*, writing in 1986 about whether Islam could be transformed by its contact with "French civilization," noted that "the problem of women, of the woman, the problem of sexuality, counts enormously in this story." (Ibid, p.65) Sexuality was the measure of difference, of the distance Muslims had to traverse if they were to become fully French.

The Clash of Gender Systems

When Elisabeth Roudinesco testified before the Stasi commission, she assured its members that a law banning head-scarves was justified. In order to stress its urgency, she talked about it not as a routine piece of legislation but as a fundamental prohibition, equivalent to the law against incest. (Debré, Vol. 2: 53; 2003) The reference to the incest taboo is revealing. It suggests a deep uneasiness evoked by Islam's different ways of regulating sex and sexuality. It expresses as well the idea that Islam was not regulating sexuality as it should, that something excessive, even perverse, was going on in Muslim communities and households. Incest, after all, is taken to be a deformation of what is universally moral, healthy, and natural. At the beginning of this chapter, I noted that many objections to the headscarf conveyed the feeling that not just too little but also too much was being revealed by it. Now it is time to return to that point.

French supporters of the ban on headscarves insisted that their notion of gender equality was not only French but (like the incest taboo) universally desirable. This was precisely the objection of some of the Muslim women I have cited; they refused the claim that the French system was necessarily more egalitarian, and they resented the caricature of their own beliefs. At issue was not just a conflict between "open" and "covered" cultures but a specifically French theory that addresses the relationship between abstract individualism and sexual difference. As I will explain in what follows, the French theory involves *denial* of the problem of reconciling those two concepts. In contrast, sexual difference is *recognized* as a potential political problem by Muslim theorists; the separation of the sexes is a way of addressing it. Ironically, Islamic theory puts sex out there as a problem for all to see by conspicuously covering the body, while the French call for a conspicuous display of bodies in order to deny the problem that sex poses for republican political theory. I will characterize the difference between Islam and French republicanism by referring to a psychology of recognition and a psychology of denial.

By banning the headscarf, French legislators insisted they were removing *the* sign of women's inequality from the classroom and, in so doing, declaring that the equality of women and men was a *first* principle of the republic. Anyone who would pledge allegiance to the republic must endorse that principle. It was one of the tenets of *laïcité*. "Today, *laïcité* cannot be conceived without a direct link to equality between the sexes." (Stasi, 2004, p. 114) The discussions before the Stasi commission and elsewhere (in the press, on television, in various public forums) emphasized sexual self-expression as the primary test of equality; an expression consisting of what Mona Ozouf (1995, p. 395) referred to as "happy exchanges between the sexes." The visibility of the bodies of women and men, their easy accessibility to one another, the free play of seduction, were taken to be hallmarks of liberty and equality, the expression on the personal level of what it means to live in a politically free society. Sex was not dangerous to political intercourse (as Rousseau and other political theorists had once warned) but, on the contrary, a positive influence on it.

And yet women have long presented a challenge to French republican theorists, one that has become more difficult since they were granted the vote in 1945. Citizenship in France is based on abstract individualism. The individual is the essential human regardless of religion, ethnicity, social position, or occupation. When they are abstracted from these traits, individuals are considered to be the same, that is, equal. Equality in the French system rests on sameness. The one obstacle to sameness for many years was sexual difference: women were "the sex" and so could not be abstracted from their sex; men could be so abstracted. Hence, abstract individuals were synonymous with men. The sexual difference of women was taken to be a natural distinction and therefore not susceptible to abstraction. How then could women be citizens? The history of French feminism demonstrates how difficult it was to grapple with this dilemma: women must strive for abstraction in order to become equal (the same as men), but the difference of their sex (they were not men) disqualified them in advance. Can women be the same and yet different? Well, yes and no. Yes, because according to republican political theory, citizens are abstract individuals indistinguishable from one another. So once women are citizens, they are individuals. No, because by definition, sexual difference means that not all individuals are the same; nature has decreed a lack of sameness (an inequality) that society cannot correct. Men can escape their sex; women cannot. There is then a deep incompatibility between the reasoning of political theory and the dilemma posed by sexual difference; sexual difference does not seem susceptible to republican logic.

When women got the vote, it was as a particular group, not as individuals. In the recent debates about the parity law, the heterosexual couple was offered as a substitute for the singular individual. Men and women could complement each other in their difference, it was suggested, and this complementarity was a kind of equality. But just as the division of labor between husbands and wives in marriages has hardly produced regimes of perfect equality, so that division imported into politics keeps creating difficulties for women who want to run for office. The brutal treatment of Ségolène Royal (which persisted even after her nomination by the Socialists) is not the worst example of its kind. Both notions—citizens who were women, not individuals, and the complementarity of difference—were put forward to correct, but not to alter, the bottom line of French republicanism: equality is still based on sameness. (This idea that sameness is a prerequisite for equality, of course, is what leads to the insistence on assimilation as a passport to Frenchness.)

There is, then, a persistent contradiction in French political theory between political equality and sexual difference. Politicians and republican theorists have dealt with this contradiction by covering it over, by insisting that equality is possible while elevating the differences between the sexes to a distinctive cultural character trait—Ozouf's *"singularité française."* As if to prove that women cannot be abstracted from their sex (men, of course, can be), there is great emphasis on the visibility and openness of seductive play between women and men, and especially on the public display (and sexual desirability for men) of women's bodies. The demonstrable proof of women's difference has to be out there for all to see, at once a confirmation of the need for different treatment of them *and* denial of the problem that sex poses for republican political theory. We might say then that, paradoxically, the objectification of women's sexuality serves to veil a constitutive contradiction of French republicanism. This is what I mean by the psychology of denial.

Islamic jurists deal with sexual difference in a way that avoids the contradiction of French republicanism by acknowledging directly that sex and sexuality pose problems (for society, for politics) that must be addressed and managed. The systems of address and management vary (neither the Taliban nor the ayatollahs of Iran represent all of Islam), and they may not seem acceptable to Western observers, but we do not have to accept them to understand what the dynamic is and why it might be so upsetting to French republicans. Modest dress, represented by the headscarf or veil for women and loose clothing for men, is a way of recognizing the potentially, volatile and disruptive effects of sexual relations between women and men, driven, by impulses, Hammoudi (2006, p. 195) says, "that are a source of continuity; but also of merciless dangers and conflicts." Modest dress declares that sexual relations are off-limits in public place. Some Muslim feminists say this actually liberates them, but whether it does or not, or whether, indeed, every woman who wears a headscarf understands its symbolism in this way, the veil signals the acceptance of sexuality and even its celebration, but only under proper circumstances—that is, in private, within the family. This is a psychology not of denial but of recognition.

I do not mean to say that the system is not patriarchal; it is, of course. But the French system is patriarchal too; women are objectified in both systems, although in different ways. My point is that sex and sexuality are differently represented, differently managed in these two systems. Paradoxically, for Islam it is the veil that makes explicit—available for all to see—the rules of public gendered interaction, which are in no way contradictory and which declare sexual exchanges out of bounds in public space. It is this explicit acknowledgment of the problem of sexuality that, for French observers, makes the veil ostentatious or conspicuous in the sexual sense of those words. Not only is too much being said about sex, but all of its difficulties are being revealed. Woman may be formally equal, but the difference of their sex somehow belies that equality. The pious pronouncements of French politicians about the equality of men and women are at odds with their deep uneasiness about actually sharing power with the opposite sex. These are difficulties that theorists and apologists for French republicanism want to deny.

The power of the psychology of denial is what led so many French feminists to abandon their critique of the status quo in France and rush to support a law that offered *laïcité* as the ground for gender equality. It would take another book to analyze the reasons for the abandonment of the themes of job and wage discrimination, glass ceilings, and domestic violence— what some have referred to as the "exhaustion" of the militant feminism of the 1970s and 80s. Suffice it to say here that—in a kind of racist benevolence reminiscent of some of their predecessors—feminists turned to the salvation of their less fortunate immigrant sisters. (Their insistence on bringing emancipation to these benighted women reminds us of Laura Bush's defense of the war on Afghanistan as an effort to liberate the women there.) Entirely forgotten in the glorification of the freedom of French sexual relations was the critique of these same feminists, who for years have decried the limits of their own patriarchal system, with its objectification of women and overemphasis on their sexual attractiveness. It is the power of their unconscious identification with the republican project—their own acceptance of the psychology of denial—that led many of them to unequivocally condemn the headscarf/veil as a violation of women's rights and to talk as if the status of women in France were not a problem at all. Banning the headscarf became an act of patriotism. "By rising up against 'foreign' signs of sexism," wrote Christine Delphy sarcastically, "doesn't our society prove that it won't tolerate sexism? Therefore, that it isn't sexist?... The difference of others as sexists is confirmed while the absence of sexism among us is proof of the foreignness of the sexists." The conclusive evidence of the inassimilability of Muslims was the difference of their approach to sex and sexuality.

Conclusion

The preservation of a mythical notion of "France" in its many aspects was a driving force in the *affaires des foulards*. The deep psychic investments revealed by the issue were less about fears of terrorism (there were surely better ways to deal with terrorism than banning the headscarf, some of which were suggested by the various commissions) than about defending French national identity—an identity in which the French way of addressing the relations between the sexes was a critical, inviolable component. Indeed, as sociologist Eric Fassin has noted, the new emphasis (only about ten years old) on the foundational nature of sexual equality is a way of insisting on the immutability of the republic in its current incarnation. Sexual equality (like *laïcité*) has become a primordial value. Those who don't share this value (Muslims in this case) are not only different but inferior—less evolved, if capable at all of evolution. The ultimate proof of the inassimilablity of Islam thus comes down, or adds up, to sexual incompatibility. This incompatibility was so profound that it compromised the future of the nation—its literal reproductive future as well as its representation. "One and indivisible" might include men and women, but it couldn't accommodate more than one arrangement of the relations between them because the existing arrangement was said to be rooted not just in culture but in nature. The French gender system was represented, then, as not only superior but "natural." Hence the profound psychological repugnance for a way of being whose difference, from this perspective, could only be perverse.

References

Bouzar, Dounia and Kada, Saïda *L'une voilée, l'autre pas: Le témoinage des deux musulmanes françaises* (Paris: Albin Michel, 2003)

Chafiq, Chahla and Khosrokhavar, Farhad, *Femmes sous le voile face a la loi islamique* (Paris: Editions du Félin, 1995)

Debré, Jean-Louis, La laïcité à l'école, *Rapport* No. 1275 vol. 1 and 2 (Paris: Assemblée Nationale, 2003)

Delphy, Christine, "Une affaire française," in Nordmann, *Le foulard islamique*, pp. 64–71.

Deltombe, Thomas, *L'Islam imaginaire: La construction médiatique de l'islamophobie en France, 1975-2005* (Paris: La Découverte, 2005)

Fanon, Frantz *A Dying Colonialism*, trans. Haakon Chevalier (New York: Grove Press, 1965)

Guénif-Souliamas, Nacira, and Macé, Eric, *Les féministes et le garçon arabe* (Paris: Editions de l'Aube, 2004)

Hammoudi, Abdellah, *A Season in Mecca: Narrative of a Pilgrimage*, trans. Pascale Ghazaleh (New York: Hill and Wang, 2006)

Hirschkind, Charles and Saba, Mahmood, "Feminism, the Taliban, and the Politics of Counter-Insurgency," *Anthropological Quarterly* 75, no. 2 (Spring 2002), pp. 352–353.

Mahmood, Saba *Politics of Piety*, pp. 110–117. Saba Mahmood, *Politics of Piety: The Islamic Revival and the Feminist Subject* (Princeton: Princeton University Press, 2005)

Ozouf, Mona *Les mots des femmes: Essai sur la singularité française* (Paris: Fayard, 1995)

Pro Choix, nos. 26–27 (Autumn 2003), pp. 103–4.

Pro Choix, no. 28 (Spring 2004), p. 57.

Pierre-Brossolette, Sylvie "Laïcité, le jeu de loi," *Figaro Magazine*, December 13, 2003; and "Les religions face à une nouvelle loi," *Le Monde*, December 15, 2003.

See Sarkozy's blog: http://www.sarkozyblog.com/2005/ immigration—une-immigration-choisie/. I am grateful to Eric Fassin for this reference. See his "La démocratic sexuelle et le conflit des civilisations," *Multitudes*, no. 26 (Fall 2006), pp. 123–31.

Stasi, Bernard, *Laïcité et République*, (Paris: La Documentation française, 2004)

Originally published in Joan Scott *Politics of the Veil* (Princeton University Press , 2007):157–174. Printed here with the permission of the author.

Contributors

Abdelwahab Bouhdiba is Professor of Islamic Sociology at the University of Tunis, where he is also Director of the Center d'Etudes et de Recherches Economiques et Sociales. He is an advisor to international organizations such as UNESCO and the UN, and to the Tunisian government on issues dealing with development and human rights.

Ahmed Abdalla is a political scientist. He received his PhD from Cambridge in 1984. His main interests are in the field of human rights, child labour, democracy and freedom of expression. His publications include 'The Egyptian National identity and Pan-Arabism', published in *Cosmopolitanism, Identity and Authenticity* in the Middle East (1999).

Amin Maalouf is an eminent and widely popular novelist. His books include *Leo the African, Samarkand, Ports of Call*, and *The Rock of Tanios*, which won him the 1993 Goncourt Prize, France's most prestigious literary award. He was formerly director of the leading Beirut newspaper *an-Nahar* and editor of *Jeune Afrique*. He resides in Paris.

Aminah Beverly McCloud, an Assistant Professor in religious studies at De-Paul University, specializes in Islamic studies. She is the author of *African-American Islam* (1995).

Asef Bayat is Chair of ISIM. He has taught sociology and Middle East studies at the American University in Cairo. He has held visiting positions at the University of California, Berkeley; Columbia University, New York; and the University of Oxford. His academic interests range from Political Sociology, Social Movements, to Urban Space and Politics, International Development, Contemporary Middle East, and Islam and the Modern World. He has conducted ethnographic research in the areas of popular mobilization in the Iranian Revolution; labor movements; politics of the urban poor; development NGOs; everyday cosmopolitanism; comparative Islamisms; and Muslim youth cultural politics, primarily in Iran and Egypt.

Bassam Tibi is Professor of International Relations at the University of Göttingen, Germany, and the 1998 Robert Bosch fellow at Harvard University. He is the author of several books in English, including *Arab Nationalism, Conflict and War in the Middle East, 1067-1981, The Crisis of Modern Islam*, and *Islam and the Cultural Accomodation of Social Change*.

Bertrand Russell is among the towering intellectuals and humanitarian figures of modern times. He won a Nobel Prize in Literature (1950).

Charles Taylor was Professor Emeritus at McGill University (until his recent death in 2008) where he established himself as one of the most profound philosophers, political theorists and public intellectuals. In his book, *Explanation and Behavior* (1964), he critiqued the psychological theory of behaviorism, arguing that the explanation of human action must include reference to purpose and elements of interaction. In *The Ethics of Authenticity* (1991), he considered ways to reconcile the conflict between individualism and social groups. He was the recent recipient of the Keyto Prize, "Japan's Nobel", for his life-time contributions to the scientific, cultural and spiritual betterment of humankind.

Christa Salamandra is Associate Professor of Anthropology at Lehman College, City University of New York. She received her Ph.D. from the University of Oxford, and has been a Visiting Lecturer in the Department of Anthropology, the School of Oriental and African Studies, University of London, and a Fulbright Scholar at Lebanese American University in Beirut. She is the author of *A New Old Damascus: Authenticity and Distinction in Urban Syria* (Indiana University Press, 2004). Her current fieldwork among Syrian television drama examines the recent expansion of the pan-Arab satellite TV industry.

Clifford Geertz is among the most eminent American anthropologists of the latter half of the twentieth century. Until his death in 2006, he was Professor Emeritus at the Institute for Advanced Study in Princeton. Famous for advocating a Weberian approach to culture, he did fieldwork in Java, Bali, and Morocco. He has explored the interpretive and critical methodologies of anthropology and argued that cultures should be interpreted as texts, much like literature. A prolific and highly gifted writer, his works include *Peddlers and Princes* (1963), *Agricultural Involution* (1963), *Islam Observed* (1968), *The Interpretation of Cultures* (1973), *Myth, Symbol, and Culture* (1974), *Negara: The Theater State in Nineteenth-Century Bali* (1980), *Local Knowledge* (1983), *Works and Lives* (1988), and a memoir, *After the Fact* (1995).

C. Wright Mills is arguably one of the most influential sociologists of the twentieth century. Until his untimely death in 1962, at the age of forty-six, he was Professor of Sociology at Columbia University. He is best known for his trilogy on the changing character of political power in the U.S. His book, *The Sociological Imagination,* is one of the most frequently cited works in the Social Sciences.

Edward Said was the author of more than twenty books, including *Orientalism* (which was nominated for the National Book Critics Circle Award); a regular contributor to newspapers in Europe, Asia, and the Middle East; and music critic for *The Nation.* He was also an accomplished pianist who collaborated with Daniel Barenboim and Yo-Yo Ma. Born in Jerusalem, he lived most of his adult life in New York City. He died in 2003.

Egbert Harmsen is a Ph.D. candidate at the International Institute for the Study of Islam in the Modern World (ISIM).

Fadwa El Guindi is currently Distinguished Professor of Anthropology at the Department of Social Sciences, University of Qatar. She is founding director and research anthropologist at El Nil Research in Los Angeles. In 1981 she retired from the Department of Anthropology at the University of California, Los Angeles (UCLA) where she had been a professor of anthropology from 1972. Her field research ranges from Nubia to Mexico, to Egypt, to Islam, to Arab and Muslim America. She serves on the editorial board of a number of scholarly journals and is the author of *Veil: Modesty, Privacy and Resistance* and, most recently, *Visual Anthropology: Essential Method and Theory.* Guindi has made a number of visual ethnographies (films) on Arab/Muslim culture which have received international awards.

Farha Ghannam is an Assistant Professor with the Social Research Center and the Forced Migration and Refugee Studies Center of the American University in Cairo. She was program associate at the Population Council and is a member of the Reproductive Health Working Group.

Fedwa Malti-Douglas, a native of Lebanon, is the Martha C. Kraft Professor at Indiana University where she is also Professor of Gender Studies, Comparative Literature, and Adjunct

Professor of Law in the Indiana University School of Law. Her honors include the 1997 Kuwait Prize for Arts and Letters and she was inducted into the American Philosophical Society in 2004. She is the author of over 100 articles in Arabic, English and French. Her books include *Blindness and Autobiography: Al-Ayyam of Taha Husayn* (1988); *Medicines of the Soul: Female Bodies and Sacred Geographies in a Transnational Islam* (2001); *Arab Comic Strips: Politics of an Emerging Mass Culture* (with Allen Douglas) (1994); as well as two novels *Hisland* (1998) and *The Bush-Saddam Tapes: From the Secret Iraq War Archives* (2008).

Homa Hoodfar is a Professor of Social Anthropology at the University of Kent in Canterbury. She has conducted field research on development and social change issues in Egypt and Iran, with an emphasis on gender, households, work and international migration in the Middle East. Further key research areas are women and Islam, and codification of Muslim family laws in the Middle East, Muslim dress code in diaspora, and the impact of long-term forced migration on family structure and gender relations on Afghan refugees in Iran and Pakistan. She has authored, edited, and co-edited a series of books: *Between Marriage and the Market: Intimate Politics* and *Survival in Cairo*; *The Muslim Veil in North America: Issues and Debates* (co-edited with Sajida Alvi and Sheila McDonough); *Building Civil Societies: A Guide for Social and Political Participation* (with Nelofer Pazira).

Jan Nederveen Pieterse, Professor of Sociology at University of Illinois Urbana-Champaign, specializes in globalization, development studies and cultural studies. His recent books are: *Is there Hope for Uncle Sam? Beyond the American Bubble* (Zed, 2008), *Ethnicities and Global Multiculture: Pants for an Octopus* (Rowman & Littlefield, 2007), *Globalization or Empire?* (Routledge, 2004), *Globalization and Culture: Global Mélange* (Rowman & Littlefield, 2003) and *Development Theory: Deconstructions/Reconstructions* (Sage, 2001).

Jared McCormick is a Ph.D. candidate at Harvard University studying Social Anthropology. He completed his MA work at the American University of Beirut (AUB) and is interested in issues related to identity, gender, sexuality and more recently tourism. One of his papers was previously published in *Sexuality in the Arab World*.

Joan Wallach Scott is the Harold F. Linder Professor in the School of Social Science at the Institute for Advanced Study. Her books include *Parité!: Sexual Equality and the Crisis of French Universalism* and *Gender and Politics of History*.

Kai Hafez is a Professor of International and Comparative Communication Studies and currently the Director of the Department of Media and Communication Studies at the University of Erfurt, Germany. He was a Senior Research Fellow at the German Institute for Middle East Studies in Hamburg, Germany (1995-2003), a guest professor at the Institute of Sociology, University of Bern, Switzerland, a Senior Associate Fellow at St. Antony's College, Oxford and academic/political advisor to the German government. Hafez is on the editorial boards of several international academic magazines. Among his English publications are: *Islam and the West in the Mass Media* (2000); *The Islamic World and the West* (2000); *Mass Media, Politics, and Society in the Middle East* (2001); *Media Ethics in the Dialogue of Culture*; *Journalistic Self-Regulation in Europe, the Arab World, and Muslim Asia* (2003); *The Myth of Media Globalization* (2007); *Arab Media–Power and Weakness* (2008).

Katherine Zoepf has written about the Arab world for the *New York Times*, *The Chronicle of Higher Education*, *The New York Observer*, and the *New York Times Magazine*, among other publications. Her book about young women in the Arab world will be published by Penguin Press in 2009.

Lara Deeb is Associate Professor in Women's Studies and Anthropology at the University of California, Irvine. She is the author of *An Enchanted Modern: Gender and Public Piety in Shi'i Lebanon* (Princeton, 2006).

Mai Ghoussoub, artist, author and playwright, left Beirut for London in 1979, where she co-founded Saqi. Her art has been exhibited internationally, and her play *Texterminators* was performed in London, Liverpool and Beirut in 2006. Her many publications include *Leaving Beirut, Imagined Masculinities*, with Emma Sinclsir-Webb, and *Artists and Vitrines*, with Shaheen Merali. Her stories have appeared in *Hikayat: Short Stories by Lebanese Women* and *Lebanon, Lebanon*. She was a regular contributor to *al-Hayat* and *Open Democracy* until her untimely death in 2006.

Mai Yamani was appointed lecturer in Social Anthropology and Sociology at the King Abdul Aziz University, Jeddah. Subsequently she has been a Research Fellow at the Center for Cross-Cultural Research on Women at Oxford and Academic Advisor to the Center for Contemporary Arab Studies at Georgetown University. She is a research associate at the Center of Islamic and Middle Eastern Law at the School of Oriental and African Studies (SOAS), University of London, and a Research Fellow with the Middle East Program at the Royal Institute of International Affairs. She has lectured extensively in Britain, the United States and the Middle East on social, economic, cultural and human rights issues in Arab states. In addition to her academic publications, she writes on social affairs for Arabic newspapers.

Miriam Gazzah is a Ph.D. candidate at the International Institute for the Study of Islam in the Modern World (ISIM). Her ethnographic research focuses on the relationship between music and identity construction processes among Moroccan youth in the Netherlands. Her other research interests include the anthropology of music in general and the anthropology of North Africa.

Mohammad Farid Azzi is a researcher and head of the Opinion Polls Section at the Emirates Center for Strategic Studies and Research (ECSSR). For twenty years he served as a lecturer in Political Science at the University of Oran in Algeria. He has authored a score of articles focusing on the state and political system in the Maghreb and has directed and participated in a number of opinion surveys in the Arab region.

Nadia Hashmi, a Ph.D. researcher at the European University Institute, Florence, obtained a degree in Social Psychology from the London School of Economics, and then when on to study law. Her research areas include immigration policies in the EU, the integration of ethnic and religious minorities, and women and young people in Islam.

Najla Hamadeh who holds a PhD in philosophy from Georgetown University has taught philosophy at the Lebanese American University (LAU) since 2000 and was a faculty member at the American University of Beirut (AUB) 1987–99. Hamadeh is a member of the Lebanese Association of Women Researchers and the Advisory Board of *al-Raida*, a journal published by the Institute for Women's Studies in the Arab World. She has published in the following areas: the philosophy of psychoanalysis, citizenship, gender issues and education. Hamadeh edited the *al-Raida* issue on Women in Lebanese Legislation and co-edited several volumes in Arabic.

Nawal El-Saadawi is an internationally-renowned Egyptian writer and feminist. After studying psychiatry in Cairo, she practiced medicine both in Egyptian cities and in the countryside. She became director of health education in Egypt, but her writing made her increasingly the focus of controversy. Her book, *Women and Sex*, published in 1972, dealt openly with subjects considered taboo. Several of her novels have been translated into English: *Two Women in One*, *Memoirs of a Woman Doctor* and *The Fall of the Iman*.

Orhan Pamuk is the author of many books, including *The White Castle*, *The Black Book* and *New Life*. In 2003 he won the International IMPAC Award for *My Name is Red*, and in 2004 Faber published the translation of his novel *Snow* and *Istanbul: Memories of a City* in 2005. Pamuk, who was awarded the Nobel Prize in Literature (2006), lives in Istanbul.

Patricia Kubala has an M.A. in Religious Studies from the University of California, Santa Barbara. She is currently a Ph.D. student in the Department of Anthropology at the University of California, Berkeley. Her research interests include pan-Arab religious satellite television programming and the role of the arts and entertainment in the Islamic Revival.

Roseanne Saad Khalaf is Assistant Professor of English and Creative Writing at the American University of Beirut. She is the author and editor of five books, among them *Transit Beirut*, a 2003 collection of literary snapshots from today's Beirut, and *Hikayat: Short Stories by Lebanese Women* (2006). Her experience spans creative, academic and editorial work in Lebanon as well as in the US and UK.

Salwa Ismail is Director of the Middle East Politics Programmes in the Department of Politics at the University of Exeter.

Samir Khalaf is Professor of Sociology and Director of the Center for Behavioral Research at the American University of Beirut. He has held academic appointments at Princeton, Harvard, MIT and New York University. Among his books are *Sexuality in the Arab World* (with John Gagnon), *The Heart of Beirut, Civil and Uncivil Violence in Lebanon, Cultural Resistance, Beirut Reclaimed* and *Lebanon's Predicament*. He is the recipient of numerous international fellowships and research awards, a trustee of several foundations and serves on the editorial boards of a score of international journals and publications.

Sana al-Khayyat was born in Iraq and is an independent scholar based in London. She graduated in sociology from Baghdad University and gained her PhD from Keele University in 1985. Al-Khayyat has lectured widely on Middle Eastern and Iraqi women's issues on the international circuit and worked as an adviser for The National Associate of Citizens Advice Bureaux (1987–9). She has been a guest speaker on numerous TV and radio talk shows and is a co-founder of the charity International Action for Iraqi Refugees. Her book *Honour and Shame* was published by Saqi (1991), translated to German and Japanese, and used as a textbook in many UK and international universities. Al-Khayyat is co-writer of *Iraq since the Gulf war* (Zed Press 1993).

Suad Joseph is Professor of Anthropology and Women and Gender Studies and Director of the Middle East/South Asia Studies Program at the University of California, Davis. She founded the Association for Middle East Women's Studies; the Arab Families Working Group; and the Middle East Research Group in Anthropology (Middle East Section of the American Anthropological Association). General Editor of the six-volume *Encyclopedia of Women and*

Islamic Cultures (2003–2008, Brill), Joseph has also edited and co-edited seven books and published 100 articles and book chapters.

Susan Schaefer Davis is an independent scholar and consultant. She is an anthropologist with extensive experience as a development practitioner with a focus on gender in North Africa (Morocco, Algeria, Tunisia and Egypt) for agencies including the World Bank, FAO, USAID and the Peace Corps. Her Ph.D. is from the University of Michigan; her post-doctoral work was done at Harvard. She has taught at several universities, focusing on Moroccan women and adolescence. Davis has written numerous articles on these topics and two books, *Patience and Power: Women's Lives in a Moroccan Village*, and *Adolescence in a Moroccan Town*. She considers the website www.marrakeshexpress.org her personal development project. It shares her knowledge of Moroccan textiles, and the non-profit section "Women Weavers OnLine" illustrates the combination of gender and ICT.

Tariq Ramadan teaches philosophy (College of Geneva) and Islamic Studies (Fribourg University). Through his writings and lectures he has contributed substantially to the debate on the issues of Islam in the West and in the contemporary world. He is an expert on Islamic revival and the identity and challenges of Muslims living as a minority. His books include: *Les Musulmans dans la Laïcité: Responsabilités et Droits des Musulmans dans les Sociétes Occidentales* (1994), *Islam, Le face á Face des Civilisations: Quelle Projet pour Quelle Modernité?*(1995), *De la Souffrance: Etudes Nietzscheéne et Islamique* (1998), *Muslems in France: The Way Towards Coexistence* (Islamic Foundation, Leicester, 1999) and *Peut-on Vivre Avec L'Islam*, with Jacques Neirynck (Favre, 1999).

Vernon James Schubel is chair of the Department of Religion at Kenyon College, where he teaches courses on Islam, Hinduism, and the History of Religions. He is the author of *Religious Performance in Contemporary Islam*.

Index